QUMRAN AND JERUSALEM

*Studies in the Dead Sea Scrolls
and the History of Judaism*

Lawrence H. Schiffman

WILLIAM B. EERDMANS PUBLISHING COMPANY
GRAND RAPIDS, MICHIGAN / CAMBRIDGE, U.K.

© 2010 Lawrence H. Schiffman
All rights reserved

Published 2010 by
Wm. B. Eerdmans Publishing Co.
2140 Oak Industrial Drive N.E., Grand Rapids, Michigan 49505 /
P.O. Box 163, Cambridge CB3 9PU U.K.

Printed in the United States of America

16 15 14 13 12 11 10   7 6 5 4 3 2 1

Library of Congress Cataloging-in-Publication Data

Schiffman, Lawrence H.
Qumran and Jerusalem: studies in the Dead Sea scrolls and the history of Judaism /
Lawrence H. Schiffman.
p.   cm.   — (Studies in the Dead Sea scrolls and related literature)
Includes bibliographical references and index.
ISBN 978-0-8028-4976-2 (pbk.: alk. paper)
1. Dead Sea scrolls.   2. Qumran community.
3. Judaism — History — Post-exilic period, 586 B.C.–210 A.D.
I. Title.

BM487.S3127 2010
296.1′55 — dc22

2009040151

www.eerdmans.com

STUDIES IN THE DEAD SEA SCROLLS AND RELATED LITERATURE

Peter W. Flint, Martin G. Abegg Jr., and Florentino García Martínez,
General Editors

The Dead Sea Scrolls have been the object of intense interest in recent years, not least because of the release of previously unpublished texts from Qumran Cave 4 since the fall of 1991. With the wealth of new documents that have come to light, the field of Qumran studies has undergone a renaissance. Scholars have begun to question the established conclusions of the last generation; some widely held beliefs have withstood scrutiny, but others have required revision or even dismissal. New proposals and competing hypotheses, many of them of an uncritical and sensational nature, vie for attention. Idiosyncratic and misleading views of the Scrolls still abound, especially in the popular press, while the results of solid scholarship have yet to make their full impact. At the same time, the scholarly task of establishing reliable critical editions of the texts is nearing completion. The opportunity is ripe, therefore, for directing renewed attention to the task of analysis and interpretation.

STUDIES IN THE DEAD SEA SCROLLS AND RELATED LITERATURE is a series designed to address this need. In particular, the series aims to make the latest and best Dead Sea Scrolls scholarship accessible to scholars, students, and the thinking public. The volumes that are projected — both monographs and collected essays — will seek to clarify how the Scrolls revise and help shape our understanding of the formation of the Bible and the historical development of Judaism and Christianity. Various offerings in the series will explore the reciprocally illuminating relationships of several disciplines related to the Scrolls, including the canon and text of the Hebrew Bible, the richly varied forms of Second Temple Judaism, and the New Testament. While the Dead Sea Scrolls constitute the main focus, several of these studies will also include perspectives on the Old and New Testaments and other ancient writings — hence the title of the series. It is hoped that these volumes will contribute to a deeper appreciation of the world of early Judaism and Christianity and of their continuing legacy today.

PETER W. FLINT
MARTIN G. ABEGG JR.
FLORENTINO GARCÍA MARTÍNEZ

To my colleagues in the
Skirball Department of Hebrew and Judaic Studies
New York University
With thanks and hopes for many more years of fruitful cooperation
and learning from one another.

Contents

Preface	x
Acknowledgments	xiv
Abbreviations	xvii
Introduction: The Qumran Scrolls and Rabbinic Judaism	1

THE SCHOLARLY CONTROVERSY

1. The Many "Battles of the Scrolls"	15
2. Literary Genres and Languages of the Judean Scrolls	44
3. Halakhah and History: The Contribution of the Dead Sea Scrolls to Recent Scholarship	63

HISTORY, POLITICS, AND THE FORMATION OF THE SECT

4. Community without Temple: The Qumran Community's Withdrawal from the Jerusalem Temple	81
5. Political Leadership and Organization in the Dead Sea Scrolls Community	98
6. The New Halakhic Letter (4QMMT) and the Origins of the Dead Sea Sect	112
7. The Place of 4QMMT in the Corpus of Qumran Manuscripts	123

CONTENTS

JEWISH LAW AT QUMRAN

8. Legal Texts in the Dead Sea Scrolls — 143
9. Codification of Jewish Law in the Dead Sea Scrolls — 170
10. Pre-Maccabean Halakhah in the Dead Sea Scrolls and the Biblical Tradition — 184
11. Contemporizing Halakhic Exegesis in the Dead Sea Scrolls — 197
12. Halakhic Elements in 4QInstruction — 204

RELIGIOUS OUTLOOK OF THE QUMRAN SECTARIANS

13. The Early History of Jewish Liturgy and the Dead Sea Scrolls — 219
14. The Concept of Covenant in the Qumran Scrolls and Rabbinic Literature — 235
15. Holiness and Sanctity in the Dead Sea Scrolls — 256
16. Messianic Figures and Ideas in the Qumran Scrolls — 270
17. The Concept of Restoration in the Dead Sea Scrolls — 286
18. Jerusalem in the Dead Sea Scrolls — 303

QUMRAN SECTARIANS AND OTHERS

19. The Pharisees and Their Legal Traditions according to the Dead Sea Scrolls — 321
20. Pharisees and Sadducees in Pesher Nahum — 337
21. Inter- or Intra-Jewish Conflict? The Judaism of the Dead Sea Scrolls Community and Its Opponents — 353
22. Non-Jews in the Dead Sea Scrolls — 365

LANGUAGE AND LITERATURE

23. Pseudepigrapha in the Pseudepigrapha: Mythical Books in Second Temple Literature — 383
24. Second Temple Literature and the Cairo Genizah — 393

Contents

25. Inverting Reality: The Dead Sea Scrolls in the Popular Media   411

    Bibliography   424

    Index of Modern Authors   457

    Index of Subjects   464

    Index of Ancient Sources   471

Preface

The present volume is a cross between a book of collected studies and an independently written volume. Like a volume of collected studies, most of the chapters represent extensive revisions and updating of articles that I have published, primarily after the release of the full corpus of the Dead Sea Scrolls. At the same time, however, much of my research during this period has been involved in exploring the wider relevance of the literature found at Qumran and the nearby Judean Desert sites for the study of Judaism in Late Antiquity. While these articles were written separately, then, they are essentially part of an ongoing research project that is brought together here, properly organized and able to express the overall thesis that serves as the basis of these various studies.

The essays included here have been substantially revised. Although in the acknowledgments, I have provided full documentation of the original place of publication of the articles, readers will often find that the chapters here have been reorganized, and in some cases that material has been omitted to prevent duplication or to remove excessively specialized discussions. The aim was to make this volume understandable to a wider audience.

A word should be said about the relationship of this volume to my full-length study, *Reclaiming the Dead Sea Scrolls.* Some of the chapters here contain research that served as the raw material for several chapters in that volume and, hence, additional detail on those subjects can be found here. Other chapters may represent later expansions on sections of that book. It is expected that many readers of this volume will have read that book and, again, an attempt was made to avoid unnecessary duplication. Whereas *Reclaiming* has a polemical tinge to it, arguing strongly against approaches to scrolls research that I thought were mistaken, I am happy to say that, in sending this book to press so many years later, I felt no need to make such arguments. Fortunately, I think that most scholars now agree about the need for a strong focus on the Jewish context of the scrolls and understand that such an approach also allows the scrolls to play an even more fructifying role in our understanding of early Christianity.

A word should be said about what is not in this volume. First, overly specific or philologically-based studies have been omitted in the hope that this book will be read widely by scholars of early Judaism and Christianity. Second, studies on the *Temple Scroll* have been excluded as they will hopefully appear soon in a separate volume. Most importantly, studies were included in this volume only if they contributed to our overall understanding of the ongoing process of rediscovering the place of the Qumran sectarians within the wider context of Second Temple Judaism and illuminating that process of rediscovery.

The aim of this volume as a whole is to show the close relationship between the Judaism we discover at Qumran and that practiced by the opponents of the sectarians, generally associated with Jerusalem and its temple. At the time that the Qumran sect flourished, another type of Judaism centered in Jerusalem also flourished, and, after the demise of the sect, the Jerusalem-based Pharisaic interpretation of the Torah eventually became the rabbinic tradition. The argument put forward here aims to show that even within the context of the many struggles that went on between the differing groups in Second Temple Judaism, certain basic commonalities characterize that Judaism. Only by understanding the complex dialectic of agreement and disagreement are we able properly to chart the religious landscape of the ancient land of Israel. We aim to show that one cannot study Qumran without Jerusalem nor Jerusalem without Qumran. This remains true despite the fundamentally different orientations and ideologies of the various groups that constituted the Jewish community at that time.

The studies are divided into several groups. After the introduction, opening up the major issues pertaining to the relationship of the Qumran scrolls to rabbinic Judaism, we start out by reviewing, from the perspective of where we stand today, scholarly controversies that raged over the scrolls when they were first discovered. In a general overview of the languages and literary genres of the scrolls from the Judean Desert, we argue the need to consider these several collections of texts as interconnected. We then set the stage for most of what follows in an essay describing the manner in which the Dead Sea Scrolls have influenced the modern study of ancient Jewish law.

From this contemporary point of interest, we take a step back into the

Second Temple period itself, to deal with several issues regarding the sect's withdrawal from the Jerusalem temple, its political organization, and the nature of its community organization. In this respect, we consider the significance of 4QMMT as a historical document and evaluate as well its place within the Qumran collection. Our efforts then turn to certain overall issues regarding Jewish law, what the rabbis called halakhah, in the life of the Qumran community. After all, the centerpiece of our approach to the scrolls is to see the legal teachings as the core descriptor of any form of Judaism. Accordingly, we survey the legal texts in the Qumran corpus and deal with the literary forms in which legal material is presented. Several important Qumran halakhic texts are shown to be based on material reaching back into the pre-Maccabean period. At the same time, we investigate the contemporizing legal interpretation found in the scrolls and the role of halakhic elements even in the sectarian sapiential texts.

We then discuss various aspects of the religious outlook and practice of the Qumran sectarians. While much in the area of Jewish liturgy is similar in the scrolls and rabbinic literature, the Qumran sectarians evince very different points of view regarding the pre-Israelite and Israelite covenants between God and his people. Closely linked together are the concepts of holiness and sanctity, eschatological vision, including the various approaches to restoration, and the sectarian understanding of the centrality of the city of Jerusalem.

As is well known, the Qumran sectarians defined themselves over against their opponents. Much information is available in the scrolls regarding the sectarians' view of the Pharisees and their legal traditions. Further, they also polemicize against the Sadducees from whom they derived so much of their halakhic tradition but from whom they had certainly split over the course of the history of the sect. We investigate the manner in which the sectarians are to be evaluated in the context of the other approaches to Judaism held by their opponents and investigate also the sect's attitudes to non-Jews, both in the present and in their eschatological framework.

We close the volume with several studies that deal with the reception of sectarian texts, real or imagined. We tackle the issue of mythical pseudepigraphic texts and discuss as well the survival of certain Second Temple texts into the Middle Ages where they are found among the Cairo Genizah manuscripts. Finally, we deal briefly with the problem of the strange way in which the scrolls have been received in the contemporary popular media which often completely distorts reality and presents legitimate scholarship as if it were bogus and pseudoscholarship as if it were fact. We can only hope that volumes like this continue to help the public to understand the scrolls based on the collective research of so many excellent scholars.

Preface

I want to thank Professors Florentino García Martínez, Martin Abegg, and Peter Flint for inviting me to include this volume in their prestigious series. I cannot even begin to recount the many colleagues who have contributed indirectly or directly to the research presented in this volume. Work on the scrolls is by nature a collaborative activity, and one learns much from close colleagues and students. I trust that they will all accept a collective vote of thanks as well as the hope that I have tried to reciprocate in kind, in our ongoing academic dialogue. Two of my graduate students, Dr. Alex Jassen, now of the University of Minnesota, and Dr. Joseph Angel of Yeshiva University, were extremely helpful in the preparation of the manuscript and the bibliography. Their comments helped greatly to eliminate duplication and provide updating within the volume. Yisrael Dubitsky undertook the preparation of the indices and helped greatly to improve the accuracy and usefulness of the volume.

As always, my wife Marlene indefatigably helped to edit the volume and to knit the various chapters into a coherent whole. I cannot thank her for the many late nights and weekends that she devoted to this task. She constantly pushed me to revise and update sections. Thanks to her efforts, the book reads more like a volume than a collection of studies written over a long period. She painstakingly unified the style of the various sections, edited, and reedited each chapter. She also extensively revised the footnotes and bibliography, working as only a librarian could to insure consistency between the footnotes and bibliography, a gargantuan task considering the multiple editions of some works used over the years.

This volume is dedicated to my colleagues in the Skirball Department of Hebrew and Judaic Studies at New York University, from whom I have learned so much and with whom I have enjoyed working for so many years. It is an honor to be associated with such a distinguished group of scholars, whose expertise reaches over the full gamut of Hebrew and Judaic Studies, stretching from antiquity to contemporary times. Their work, even when appearing distant from mine in chronology and method, has had a tremendous influence on me and has helped greatly to mold my views on the significance of the scrolls within the context of the history of Judaism.

New York University

Acknowledgments

I am grateful to the publishers and editors of the following who allowed revised versions of the articles listed below to be reprinted in this collection.

Introduction: "The Qumran Scrolls and Rabbinic Judaism." Appeared in *The Dead Sea Scrolls after Fifty Years: A Comprehensive Assessment,* ed. P. W. Flint, J. C. VanderKam, 2:552-71 (Leiden: Brill, 1999).

Chapter 1: "The Many 'Battles of the Scrolls.'" Appeared in *Archaeology and Society in the 21st Century: The Dead Sea Scrolls and Other Case Studies,* ed. N. A. Silberman and E. S. Frerichs, 188-210 (Jerusalem: Israel Exploration Society and the Dorot Foundation, 2001).

Chapter 2: "Literary Genres and Languages of the Judean Scrolls." Appeared under the title "The Contribution of the Dead Sea Scrolls to the Study of Hebrew Language and Literature," in *Turim: Studies in Jewish History and Literature Presented to Dr. Bernard Lander,* ed. M. Shmidman, 1:233-55 (New York: Touro College Press, 2007).

Chapter 3: "Halakhah and History: The Contribution of the Dead Sea Scrolls to Recent Scholarship." Appeared in *Jüdische Geschichte in hellenistisch-römischer Zeit,* ed. A. Oppenheimer and E. Müller-Luckner, 205-19. Schriften des Historischen Kollegs, Kolloquien 44 (Munich: Oldenbourg, 1999).

Chapter 4: "Community without Temple: The Qumran Community's Withdrawal from the Jerusalem Temple." Appeared in *Gemeinde ohne Tempel=Community without Temple: Zur Substituierung und Transformation des Jerusalemer Tempels und seines Kults im Alten Testament, antiken Judentum und frühen Christentum,* ed. B. Ego, A. Lange, and P. Pilhofer, with K. Ehlers, 267-84 (Tübingen: Mohr Siebeck, 1999).

Acknowledgments

Chapter 5: "Political Leadership and Organization in the Dead Sea Scrolls Community." Appeared under the title "Utopia and Reality: Political Leadership and Organization in the Dead Sea Scrolls Community," in *Emanuel: Studies in Hebrew Bible, Septuagint, and Dead Sea Scrolls in Honor of Emanuel Tov*, ed. S. M. Paul, R. A. Kraft, L. H. Schiffman and W. W. Fields, 413-27 (Leiden: Brill, 2003).

Chapter 6: "The New Halakhic Letter (4QMMT) and the Origins of the Dead Sea Sect." Appeared in *BA* 53 (1990) 64-73. Also appeared in *Mogilany 1989: Papers on the Dead Sea Scrolls*, ed. Z. J. Kapera, 1:59-70 (Krakow: Enigma, 1993).

Chapter 7: "The Place of 4QMMT in the Corpus of Qumran Manuscripts." Appeared in *Reading 4QMMT*, ed. M. J. Bernstein and J. Kampen, 81-98. SBLSymS (Atlanta: Scholars, 1996).

Chapter 8: "Legal Texts in the Dead Sea Scrolls." First half of "Legal Texts and Codification in the Dead Sea Scrolls," which appeared in *Discussing Cultural Influences: Text, Context, and Non-text in Rabbinic Judaism*, ed. R. Ulmer, 1-21. Studies in Judaism (Lanham, MD: University Press of America, 2007).

Chapter 9: "Codification of Jewish Law in the Dead Sea Scrolls." Second half of "Legal Texts and Codification in the Dead Sea Scrolls," *Discussing Cultural Influences: Text, Context, and Non-text in Rabbinic Judaism*, ed. R. Ulmer, 21-39. Studies in Judaism (Lanham, MD: University Press of America, 2007).

Chapter 10: "Pre-Maccabean Halakhah in the Dead Sea Scrolls and the Biblical Tradition." Appeared in *DSD* 13 (2006) 348-61.

Chapter 11: "Contemporizing Halakhic Exegesis in the Dead Sea Scrolls." Appeared in *Reading the Present in the Qumran Library: The Perception of the Contemporary by Means of Scriptural Interpretations*, ed. K. de Troyer and A. Lange, 35-41. SBLSymS 30 (Atlanta: SBL, 2005).

Chapter 12: "Halakhic Elements in 4QInstruction." Appeared under the title "Halakhic Elements in the Sapiential Texts from Qumran," in *Sapiential Perspectives: Wisdom Literature in Light of the Dead Sea Scrolls: Proceedings of the Sixth International Symposium of the Orion Center for the Study of the Dead Sea Scrolls and Associated Literature, 20-22 May, 2001*, ed. J. J. Collins, G. E. Sterling, and R. A. Clements, 89-100. STDJ 51 (Leiden: Brill, 2004).

Chapter 13: "The Early History of Jewish Liturgy and the Dead Sea Scrolls." Appeared under the title "The Dead Sea Scrolls and the Early History of Jewish Liturgy," in *The Synagogue in Late Antiquity*, ed. L. I. Levine, 33-48 (Philadelphia: American Schools of Oriental Research and New York: Jewish Theological Seminary of America, 1987).

Chapter 14: "The Concept of Covenant in the Qumran Scrolls and Rabbinic Literature." Appeared in *The Idea of Biblical Interpretation: Essays in Honor of James L. Kugel*, ed. H. Najman and J. H. Newman, 257-78. JSJSup 83 (Leiden: Brill, 2004).

Chapter 15: "Holiness and Sanctity in the Dead Sea Scrolls" Appeared in *A Holy People: Jewish and Christian Perspectives on Religious Communal Identity*, ed. M. Poorthuis and J. Schwartz, 53-67. Jewish and Christian Perspectives (Leiden: Brill, 2006).

Chapter 16: "Messianic Figures and Ideas in the Dead Sea Scrolls." Appeared in *The Messiah: Developments in Earliest Judaism and Christianity*. ed. J. H. Charlesworth, 116-29. The First Princeton Symposium on Judaism and Christian Origins (Minneapolis: Fortress, 1992).

Chapter 17: "The Concept of Restoration in the Dead Sea Scrolls." Appeared in *Restoration: Old Testament, Jewish, and Christian Perspectives*, ed. J. M. Scott, 203-21. JSJSup 72 (Brill: Leiden, 2001).

Chapter 18: "Jerusalem in the Dead Sea Scrolls." Appeared in *The Centrality of Jerusalem*, ed. M. Poorthuis and Ch. Safrai, 73-88 (Kampen: Kok Pharos, 1996).

Chapter 19: "The Pharisees and Their Legal Traditions according to the Dead Sea Scrolls." Appeared in *DSD* 8 (2001) 262-77.

Chapter 20: "Pharisees and Sadducees in Pesher Nahum." Appeared in *Minḥah le-Naḥum: Biblical and Other Studies Presented to Nahum M. Sarna in Honour of His 70th Birthday*, ed. M. Brettler and M. Fishbane, 272-90. JSOTSup 154 (Sheffield: JSOT, 1993).

Chapter 21: "Inter- or Intra-Jewish Conflict? The Judaism of the Dead Sea Scrolls Community and Its Opponents." Unpublished.

Chapter 22: "Non-Jews in the Dead Sea Scrolls." Appeared in *The Quest for Context and Meaning: Studies in Biblical Intertextuality in Honor of James A. Sanders*, ed. C. A. Evans and S. Talmon, 153-71. Biblical Interpretation 28 (Leiden: Brill, 1997).

Chapter 23: "Pseudepigrapha in the Pseudepigrapha: Mythical Books in Second Temple Literature." Appeared in *RevQ* 21 (2004) 429-38.

Chapter 24: "Second Temple Literature and the Cairo Genizah." Appeared in *PAAJR* 63 (1997-2001) 139-61.

Chapter 25: "Inverting Reality: The Dead Sea Scrolls in the Popular Media." Appeared in *DSD* 12 (2005) 24-37.

Abbreviations

AB	*Anchor Bible*
ABD	*Anchor Bible Dictionary,* ed. D. N. Freedman. 6 vols. New York: Doubleday, 1992.
ABRL	Anchor Bible Reference Library
AGJU	Arbeiten zur Geschichte des antiken Judentums und des Urchristentums
ALBO	Analecta lovaniensia biblica et orientalia
ALGHJ	Arbeiten zur Literatur und Geschichte des hellenistischen Judentums
AOS	American Oriental Series
AOT	*The Apocryphal Old Testament,* ed. H. F. D. Sparks. Oxford: Clarendon, 1984.
ASOR	American Schools of Oriental Research
ASTI	*Annual of the Swedish Theological Institute*
BA	*Biblical Archaeologist*
BAR	*Biblical Archaeology Review*
BASOR	*Bulletin of the American Schools of Oriental Research*
Bib	*Biblica*
BibOr	Biblica et orientalia
BJS	Brown Judaic Studies
BRev	*Bible Review*
BRS	Biblical Resource Series
BZAW	Beihefte zur Zeitschrift für die alttestamentliche Wissenschaft
CahRB	Cahiers de la Revue biblique
CBQ	*Catholic Biblical Quarterly*

CBQMS	Catholic Biblical Quarterly Monograph Series
CHJ	*Cambridge History of Judaism,* ed. W. D. Davies and L. Finkelstein. 4 vols. Cambridge: Cambridge University Press, 1984-2006.
CJAS	Christianity and Judaism in Antiquity series
CRINT	Compendia rerum iudaicarum ad Novum Testamentum
CSJH	Chicago Studies in the History of Judaism
DCH	*Dictionary of Classical Hebrew,* ed. D. J. A. Clines. Sheffield: Sheffield Academic, 1993-.
DJD	Discoveries in the Judaean Desert
DJG	*Dictionary of Jesus and the Gospels,* ed. J. B. Green and S. McKnight. Downers Grove: InterVarsity, 1992.
DSD	*Dead Sea Discoveries*
EDSS	*Encyclopedia of the Dead Sea Scrolls,* ed. L. H. Schiffman and J. C. VanderKam. 2 vols. New York: Oxford University Press, 2002.
EM	*'Enṣiqlopedyah Miqra'it.* 9 vols. Jerusalem: Bialik Institute, 1950-1988.
EncJud	*Encyclopedia Judaica,* ed. C. Roth. 16 vols. Jerusalem: Keter, 1971.
ER	*Encyclopedia of Religion,* ed. M. Eliade. 16 vols. New York: Macmillan, 1987.
ErIsr	*Eretz-Israel*
FO	*Folio orientalia*
HAR	*Hebrew Annual Review*
Hen	*Henoch*
HS	*Hebrew Studies*
HSS	Harvard Semitic Studies
HTR	*Harvard Theological Review*
HUCA	*Hebrew Union College Annual*
IDB	*Interpreter's Dictionary of the Bible,* ed. G. A. Buttrick. 4 vols. + sup. Nashville: Abingdon, 1962.
IEJ	*Israel Exploration Journal*
IMJ	*Israel Museum Journal*
JANESCU	*Journal of the Ancient Near Eastern Society of Columbia University*
JAOS	*Journal of the American Oriental Society*
JBL	*Journal of Biblical Literature*
JBLMS	*Journal of Biblical Literature Monograph Series*
JBTh	*Jahrbuch für biblische Theologie*
JD	*Journal of Documentation*

Abbreviations

JJS	*Journal of Jewish Studies*
JNES	*Journal of Near Eastern Studies*
JQR	*Jewish Quarterly Review*
JS	*Jewish Studies*
JSJ	*Journal for the Study of Judaism*
JSJSup	Journal for the Study of Judaism: Supplement Series
JSOT	*Journal for the Study of the Old Testament*
JSOT/ASOR	Journal for the Study of the Old Testament/American Schools of Oriental Research monographs
JSOTSup	Journal for the Study of the Old Testament: Supplement Series
JSPSup	Journal for the Study of the Pseudepigrapha: Supplement Series
JSS	*Journal of Semitic Studies*
LCL	Loeb Classical Library
Leš	*Lešonénnu*
MdB	*Le Monde de la Bible*
MGWJ	*Monatsschrift für Geschichte und Wissenschaft des Judentums*
Mus	*Muséon*
NJPS	New Jewish Publication Society Version
NTOA	Novum Testamentum et Orbis Antiquus
NTOA.SA	Novum Testamentum et Orbis Antiquus, Series Archaeologica
OTP	*The Old Testament Pseudepigrapha*, ed. J. H. Charlesworth. 2 vols. Garden City: Doubleday, 1983-85.
PAAJR	*Proceedings of the American Academy of Jewish Research*
PEQ	*Palestine Exploration Quarterly*
RB	*Revue biblique*
RevQ	*Revue de Qumran*
SAOC	Studies in Ancient Oriental Civilization
SBL	Society of Biblical Literature
SBLBSNA	Society of Biblical Literature Biblical Scholarship in North America
SBLEJL	Society of Biblical Literature Early Judaism and Its Literature
SBLMS	Society of Biblical Literature Monograph Series
SBLRBS	Society of Biblical Literature Resources for Biblical Study
SBLSCS	Society of Biblical Literature Septuagint and Cognate Studies
SBLSP	*Society of Biblical Literature Seminar Papers*
SBLSymS	Society of Biblical Literature Symposium Series
SBT	Studies in Biblical Theology
ScrHier	Scripta Hierosolymitana
SDSSRL	Studies in the Dead Sea Scrolls and Related Literature
Sem	*Semitica*

ABBREVIATIONS

Sifre Deut	*Sifre on Deuteronomy*, ed. L. Finkelstein. New York: Jewish Theological Seminary, 1969.
SJLA	Studies in Judaism in Late Antiquity
SNTSMS	Society for New Testament Studies Monograph Series
SSN	Studia Semitica Neerlandica
SSS	Semitic Study Series
STDJ	Studies on the Texts of the Desert of Judah
SVTP	Studia in Veteris Testamenti pseudepigrapha
TDOT	*Theological Dictionary of the Old Testament*, ed. G. J. Botterweck, H. Ringgren, and H.-J. Fabry; trans. J. T. Willis et al. 17 vols. Grand Rapids: Wm. B. Eerdmans, 1974-.
VT	*Vetus Testamentum*
VTSup	Supplements to Vetus Testamentum
WUNT	Wissenschaftliche Untersuchungen zum Neuen Testament
ZDMG	*Zeitschrift der deutschen morgenländischen Gesellschaft*

INTRODUCTION

The Qumran Scrolls and Rabbinic Judaism

The study of Judaism in Late Antiquity has developed rapidly over the past century, spurred on by more general developments in the field of religious studies, as well as by the rise of the State of Israel, where Judaic studies in all areas play so important a role. Major steps have been taken in the production of textual editions, archaeological research, manuscript studies, philology, and in tracing the history of the primary documents — the Mishnah, Talmuds, and Midrashim. Yet there still are fundamental questions left to be investigated and answered.

Judaism in Late Antiquity and the Dead Sea Scrolls

The basic questions to be asked of Judaism in the Second Temple and talmudic periods relate to the "crossroads," that turn of the eras which is familiar to us but which went virtually unnoticed in contemporary texts. It was in this period that the temple-centered Judaism of the First and Second Commonwealth periods gave way to the Torah-centered rabbinic tradition. It was in this period that Judaism turned so assiduously to the cultivation of the oral law, that vast corpus of traditions later to be redacted into the Mishnah, Midrash, and Talmuds.[1] It was in this period that messianic tendencies and yearn-

---

1. Josephus mentions laws from the tradition of the fathers not written in the laws of Moses in *Ant.* 13.297, and a similar notion is reflected in Mark 7:3 and Matt 15:2. Josephus also states in *Ant.* 18.12 that the traditional interpretation of the law is more binding than the written Torah. See E. Schürer, *The History of the Jewish People in the Age of Jesus Christ (175 B.C.-A.D. 135)*,

ings would lead many Jews into the Great Revolt against Rome in 66-73 C.E., the Diaspora Revolt of ca. 115-117 C.E., and the Bar Kokhba Revolt of 132-135 C.E. It is this set of transitions that must be the primary point of departure for our research. We can ask how the variegated Judaism of the Second Temple period eventually would yield the consensus that developed around rabbinic Judaism by the onset of the Middle Ages. What were the processes and developments that led to this consensus? How did the biblical traditions of the Hebrew Scriptures lead, ultimately, on the one hand, to the rabbinic tradition and, on the other, to the new Christian community with its distinctive religious traditions?

It is no accident that this turning point was neglected for so long by scholars of rabbinic Judaism. The modern, scientific study of Judaism in Late Antiquity began with the *Wissenschaft des Judentums* in the nineteenth century.[2] Scholars at that time, like their counterparts who worked on the history of Christianity, were only slowly uncovering the variegated texture of Second Temple Judaism.[3] Judaic scholars dealing with this period were primarily rabbinic scholars for whom the tasks of the day were otherwise. Rabbinic manuscripts were still to be cataloged and studied, critical editions were to be made, and new texts published, especially from the Cairo Genizah, and the methodologies of the fields of history and religious studies were still to be brought to bear, primarily in the twentieth century.

Among its treasures, the Cairo Genizah yielded up the Zadokite Fragments,[4] later to emerge as well from the Qumran caves.[5] When the Dead Sea Scrolls began to appear from 1947 on, it became clear immediately that this find would enrich the study of Judaism in Late Antiquity. Yet, because of the prevalent definitions of the academic fields involved, and due to a va-

---

rev. ed. by G. Vermes and F. Millar, with P. Vermes and M. Black (Edinburgh: T. & T. Clark, 1979) 2:390-91.

2. I. Schorsch, *From Text to Context: The Turn to History in Modern Judaism* (Waltham, MA: Brandeis University Press and Hanover, NH: University Press of New England, 1994) 151-359.

3. S. Heschel, *Abraham Geiger and the Jewish Jesus.* CSJH (Chicago: University of Chicago Press, 1998) 76-105.

4. S. Schechter, *Documents of Jewish Sectaries,* vol. 1: *Fragments of a Zadokite Work* (Cambridge: Cambridge University Press, 1910; repr. Library of Biblical Studies [New York: Ktav, 1970]). The best edition is E. Qimron, "The Text of CDC," in *The Damascus Document Reconsidered,* ed. M. Broshi, 9-49 (Jerusalem: Israel Exploration Society, Shrine of the Book, Israel Museum, 1992). On the use of the term "Zadokite Fragments," see below, p. 67n.14.

5. J. M. Baumgarten, *Qumran Cave 4, XIII: Damascus Document (4Q266-273).* DJD 18 (Oxford: Clarendon, 1996); M. Baillet, J. T. Milik, R. de Vaux, "Document de Damas," in *Les 'Petites Grottes' de Qumrân,* 128-31, 181. DJD 3 (Oxford: Clarendon, 1962).

riety of other factors,⁶ this impact was minimized. Rabbinic scholars, by and large, continued to limit their corpus — or better, canon — to the traditional rabbinic writings,⁷ while the new scrolls were left to scholars of the Hebrew Bible and students of the New Testament and the rise of Christianity. Presently, however, research has attempted to permeate these barriers and to redefine the chronological and textual limits of the study of Second Temple and rabbinic Judaism⁸ so as to allow these new scrolls to cast their increasingly brighter light on rabbinic Judaism and talmudic literature. This approach illuminates the context from which the talmudic tradition developed.

Halakhah and Sectarianism

From the earliest discussions of the nature of the group that we now term the Dead Sea sect, much attention has been given to issues of Jewish law. The original debates regarding the identity of the sect took place soon after the discovery of the *Zadokite Fragments (Damascus Document)* among the manuscripts of the Cairo Genizah.⁹ These debates only intensified after the discovery of the Qumran scrolls in 1947.¹⁰ The publication of the *Temple Scroll*,¹¹ 4QMMT,¹² the Qumran manuscripts of the *Zadokite Fragments*,¹³ and the re-

---

6. See L. H. Schiffman, "Confessionalism and the Study of the Dead Sea Scrolls," *JS* 31 (1991) 3-14.

7. Exceptional was L. Ginzberg, who had written a lengthy commentary on the *Zadokite Fragments*, first published as *Eine unbekannte jüdische Sekte* (New York: L. Ginzberg, 1922), appearing later in an expanded English translation as *An Unknown Jewish Sect* (New York: Jewish Theological Seminary of America, 1976). In addition, S. Lieberman published two papers, "Light on the Cave Scrolls from Rabbinic Sources," *PAAJR* 20 (1951) 395-404; and "The Discipline in the So-Called Dead Sea Manual of Discipline," *JBL* 71 (1951) 199-206; both repr. in S. Lieberman, *Texts and Studies* (New York: Ktav, 1974) 190-207.

8. For a synthesis of the history of this period, see L. H. Schiffman, *From Text to Tradition: A History of Second Temple and Rabbinic Judaism* (Hoboken: Ktav, 1991).

9. Ginzberg, *An Unknown Jewish Sect*, 304-37; J. A. Fitzmyer, "Prolegomenon," in Schechter, *Documents of Jewish Sectaries*, 1:14-15.

10. H. H. Rowley, *The Zadokite Fragments and the Dead Sea Scrolls* (Oxford: Blackwell, 1952).

11. Y. Yadin, *Megillat ha-Miqdash*. 3 vols. (Jerusalem: Israel Exploration Society and Shrine of the Book, 1977), and its English edition, *The Temple Scroll*. 3 vols. (Jerusalem: Israel Exploration Society and Shrine of the Book, 1983).

12. E. Qimron and J. Strugnell, *Qumran Cave 4.V: Miqṣat Ma'aśe ha-Torah*. DJD 10 (Oxford: Clarendon, 1994).

13. Baumgarten, DJD 18.

INTRODUCTION

maining halakhic fragments from Qumran,[14] has further placed the subject of Jewish law at the center of the debate regarding the Dead Sea Scrolls.

By Jewish law, we refer to what the rabbis would later term "halakhah."[15] Such English words as "law," "legal," etc. imply for Western readers civil and criminal law. For ancient Jews, indeed for Jews throughout the ages until the rise of modernity, the life of Torah, in its various interpretations, was the dominant form of law and religious expression. The commands of the Bible were understood to encompass all areas of human life, including civil, criminal, political, religious, moral, ritual, and familial issues. The determination of proper behavior in all these areas was believed to be accessible through exegesis of the biblical text and, in the case of the Pharisaic-rabbinic teaching, from the traditions enshrined in the oral law. Technically, the term "halakhah" should only be used to describe the legal system developed in rabbinic literature, representing the Pharisaic-rabbinic trend within Judaism in Late Antiquity. However, no English term can possibly describe this system of law and practice as well as the term "halakhah" and so, with due apologies, for lack of a better term, it will be employed here.

An appreciation for the central role of Jewish law in the study of Second Temple Judaism is crucial to the very definition of a sect in this context. Whereas in the sociology of religion, the use of the term "sect" implies a normative "church" to which the sect may be contrasted, it has become customary to use this term for the various competing trends which existed among the Jews in Second Temple times. Among the distinguishing characteristics which separated these groups from one another was their practice of Jewish law.[16]

To some extent, the view that halakhah can be an important key to understanding Jewish sectarianism is best substantiated by taking a long view of the history of the Jews and Judaism. For us, as scholars working in the field of Dead Sea Scrolls, it may already come naturally, since this form of analysis has been utilized since Solomon Schechter first published the *Fragments of a Zadokite Work* in 1910.[17] It can be shown that issues of Jewish law were at the

---

14. J. M. Baumgarten, et al., *Qumran Cave 4.XXV: Halakhic Texts*. DJD 35 (Oxford: Clarendon, 1999).

15. On this term, see M. Elon, *Ha-Mishpaṭ ha-'Ivri* (Jerusalem: Magnes, Hebrew University, 1973) 143-44.

16. For the application of sociological method to Jewish sectarianism, see A. J. Saldarini, *Pharisees, Scribes and Sadducees in Palestinian Society: A Sociological Approach* (Wilmington: Michael Glazier, 1988; repr. BRS [Grand Rapids: Wm. B. Eerdmans and Livonia: Dove, 2001]); and A. I. Baumgarten, *The Flourishing of Jewish Sects in the Maccabean Era: An Interpretation*. JSJSup 55 (Leiden: Brill, 1997).

17. Schechter, *Documents of Jewish Sectaries*, vol. 1.

root of the Karaite-Rabbanite controversy, the rise of the Hasidic movement, the reform movement in Germany in the early nineteenth century[18] and the eventual establishment of Reform and Conservative Judaism in America.[19]

I would contend that all these controversies are based on the nature of Judaism, defined as primarily a halakhic system (at least up to modern times). While controversies in Christianity would primarily swirl about matters of doctrine and belief, those of the Jewish community would both be based upon and express themselves in issues of halakhah.

It is in accord with this essentially phenomenological understanding of Judaism that we see halakhic issues at the center of Jewish sectarianism in the Second Temple period. Halakhah and its theoretical underpinnings separated the various sectarian groups from one another. As the various movements sought to define themselves, they, in turn, intensified their differences in interpretation of Scripture and in the attendant practices that they followed. For this reason, Jewish legal issues must stand at the center of all discussions of sectarianism in Second Temple times.

The Dead Sea Scrolls present us with documents composed over a long period of time. In studying the legal traditions preserved at Qumran, one must be mindful of the fact that some texts are presectarian, representing the heritage that the Dead Sea sectarians brought with them when they established their group. Other texts that include halakhic material were composed by the sectarians themselves. Further, important texts argue implicitly or explicitly with legal rulings of other Jews, thereby providing information about competing systems of halakhah with which those who gathered the scrolls would not have agreed. These various texts allow us to reconstruct much about the state of Jewish law in the Hasmonean period and even earlier in the Hellenistic era. These texts indicate how the various groups manifested their particular character through their approach to an interpretation of Jewish law.

Sectarian Halakhah

The study of the limited corpus of Qumran texts available in the early years after the discovery led to significant conclusions about the halakhah of the

---

18. M. A. Meyer, *Response to Modernity: A History of the Reform Movement in Judaism* (New York: Oxford University Press, 1988) 100-224.

19. Meyer, *Response to Modernity*, 225-384; M. Davis, "Jewish Religious Life and Institutions in America (A Historical Study)," in *The Jews: Their Religion and Culture*, ed. L. Finkelstein, 274-379. 4th ed. (New York: Schocken, 1971).

Qumran group. Among the important conclusions drawn from this material was a general sense of how the sectarians understood the authority of Jewish law. The sectarians saw the extrabiblical law as derived *in toto* from inspired biblical interpretation, thus denying such concepts as the "traditions of the elders" of the Pharisees or the later rabbinic oral law concept.[20]

Further, scholars observed that the legal material in the Qumran corpus (to the extent that it was then known) was entirely dependent on, or at least linked to, biblical interpretation. Such linkage distinguished it from the Pharisaic view. Nevertheless, many sectarian regulations appeared to have no link with the biblical traditions. Yet attempts to trace these regulations to Hellenistic origins must be seen as equally unsuccessful, despite the efforts of some scholars.[21]

The Qumran sectarian texts display a unique combination of halakhic views with the particular sectarian regulations of the Qumran group. While Pharisaic-rabbinic tradition also shows a tendency to combine their sectarian regulations with the halakhic system, this phenomenon is certainly more pronounced in the Dead Sea sectarian corpus.

In the cases we are discussing here, it is not simply that a group follows a particular set of halakhic rulings, as is to be expected. Rather, we are dealing with a use of halakhic rulings, or of an admixture of law and sectarian regulations, which functions to mark off the boundaries of the group. It is not simply that halakhic differences divide groups of Second Temple–period Jews. Legal rulings also function as sociological boundary markers, a role that they have also played in later Jewish history and which they continue to play today. We speak here not of boundaries with non-Jews or with Jews who deny the obligation to live according to any halakhic norms. Rather, we are discussing drawing lines between various groups of Torah-observant Jews.

Several examples from the Qumran corpus will illustrate this phenomenon. We turn first to the rules for entry into the sectarian group. Entry to the sect was a process, as it was also for the *ḥavurah* described in tannaitic texts,[22]

---

20. L. H. Schiffman, *The Halakhah at Qumran*. SJLA 16 (Leiden: Brill, 1975) 75-76.
21. M. Weinfeld, *The Organizational Pattern and the Penal Code of the Qumran Sect*, 10-57. NTOA 2 (Fribourg: Éditions Universitaires and Göttingen: Vandenhoeck & Ruprecht, 1986). Note Appendix E: "The Recent Monograph of Schiffman," 71-76, in which he disputes my derivation of numerous rules from biblical tradition. Cf. É. Puech's "Review of M. Weinfeld, *The Organizational Pattern*," *RevQ* 14 (1989) 147-48.
22. A. Oppenheimer, *The ʿAm ha-Aretz: A Study in the Social History of the Jewish People in the Hellenistic-Roman Period*, trans. I. H. Levine. ALGHJ 8 (Leiden: Brill, 1977) 118-56. Most writers link the *ḥavurah* described in tannaitic sources directly with the Pharisees. However, there is no explicit evidence for such a connection.

of ascending a ladder of increasing ritual purity.[23] Progression through the ranks meant permission to come in contact first with solid foodstuffs and only later with liquids, which were more susceptible to impurity according to sectarian as well as Pharisaic-rabbinic law. Transgression of sectarian norms involved demotion within the purity context as part of the penalty. The punishment of one year meant exclusion from the liquid foods of the sect until status was regained after the designated period. One penalized for two years was demoted also as regards the pure food and had to wait the full two years until reentry to the pure meals.[24] These meals, governed as they were by sectarian purity regulations, were reflections of eschatological banquets and so expressed as well the messianic aspirations of the group for a society of perfect holiness.[25]

This example is one in which the sectarian order of affairs is expressly linked to halakhic norms. The same may be said, for example, of the role of the *mevaqqer*, the sectarian overseer, in the collection of charity from the sectarians of the communities (outside Qumran, apparently) described in the *Zadokite Fragments (Damascus Document)*.[26] In this case, as in the description of the Essenes in Philo,[27] the collection and distribution of charity is done in accord with sectarian halakhic norms that differ to some extent from those of the Pharisaic-rabbinic community. Examples of the interaction of halakhah and aspects of sectarian law extend even to the Sabbath, where the presumption of a communal settlement may explain certain details of the Sabbath laws.[28] In the case of civil law, the role of the *mevaqqer* certainly places these laws in sectarian context. It is most likely that the same courts judged violations of sectarian regulations and offenses against Torah laws.

One of the most distinguishing features of Qumran halakhah, the division of the law into *nigleh* and *nistar*,[29] is intimately related to the sectarian character of the group. *Nigleh*, the "revealed" law, refers to the written Torah

---

23. Comparisons of the tannaitic laws of purity and their relation to entry into the *ḥavurah* with those of the Qumran sect are found in C. Rabin, *Qumran Studies*. Scripta Judaica 2 (London: Oxford University Press, 1957) 1-21; J. Licht, *Megillat ha-Serakhim mi-Megillot Midbar Yehudah* (Jerusalem: Bialik Institute, 1965) 145-48; cf. his discussion of the tannaitic laws of purity, 294-303; Lieberman, *JBL* 71 (1951) 199-206; repr. *Texts and Studies*, 200-7.

24. L. H. Schiffman, *Sectarian Law in the Dead Sea Scrolls: Courts, Testimony and the Penal Code*. BJS 33 (Chico: Scholars, 1983) 165-68.

25. L. H. Schiffman, *The Eschatological Community of the Dead Sea Scrolls: A Study of the Rule of the Congregation*. SBLMS 38 (Atlanta: Scholars, 1989) 53-67.

26. CD 14:12-16; cf. Schiffman, *Sectarian Law*, 37-38.

27. Philo, *Good Person*, 87.

28. Cf. Schiffman, *Halakhah at Qumran*, 115.

29. Schiffman, *Halakhah at Qumran*, 22-32.

or the Bible which contains laws available to all Jews. These laws are contained in what later tradition would refer to as the "plain" sense *(peshaṭ)* of the biblical legal texts. The *nistar* is the "hidden" law, known only to the sectarians to whom it has been revealed in divinely-inspired study sessions as part of the progressive revelation of God's will. Those outside the sect, the texts tell us, are to be punished for their violation of the "hidden" sectarian law, even if its prescriptions are unknown to them. Indeed, the sectarians are commanded to keep this part of their teaching secret.

Accordingly, one of the primary features of the sectarian outlook is that only members of the group possess accurate knowledge of the will of God. To be an insider is to have available this esoteric knowledge. To be an outsider is to be denied, or at least to lack, such knowledge. Halakhic knowledge, then, defines or at least is characteristic of members of the group, and outsiders are characterized by ignorance and violation of the true laws of the Torah.[30]

This feature is intimately linked to the eschatological expectations of the sect. The *War Scroll* and related texts expected that in the end of days the sectarians and their heavenly retinue would emerge victorious from the great war of the Sons of Light against the Sons of Darkness. In this war, the sectarians expected the downfall and death of the nations but also of all Israel except for those who had joined, or who were predestined to join, the Qumran sect. The rest of Israel had been predestined for its lot and, therefore, lacked the teachings of the sectarian law. Hence, they do not merit participation in the eschatological banquet of the Rule of the Congregation. Thus, halakhah, sectarianism, and eschatology are intimately linked for the Qumran sectarians.

Common Halakhah

Despite Pharisee-Sadducee- and Dead Sea sect–disputes, it must be stated that the vast majority of legal rulings regarding the observances of sacrificial law, Sabbath, purity laws, and other halakhic practices were common to Second Temple period Jews.[31] This common Judaism was practiced by the masses (later termed *ʿam ha-areṣ*)[32] who had little to do with the detailed disputes of the various elites who enrolled in the sectarian groups. The debates

---

30. Cf. N. Wieder, *The Judean Scrolls and Karaism* (London: East and West Library, 1962) 53-57.

31. E. P. Sanders, *Judaism: Practice and Belief, 63 BCE–66 CE* (London: SCM and Philadelphia: Trinity Press International, 1992) 45-303.

32. See Oppenheimer, *The ʿAm ha-Aretz*, 67-117, for a survey of rabbinic sources regarding the *ʿam ha-areṣ*.

The Qumran Scrolls and Rabbinic Judaism

and differences of opinion we observe are often blown out of proportion. It must be remembered that our sources tend to emphasize disagreements over commonalities.

In this respect, let me cite one example: the *tefillin* (phylacteries) found at Qumran. While indeed these have been shown to reflect some differences with later rabbinic rules for the making and copying of phylacteries,[33] the basic practice of wearing *tefillin* was not limited to one sect. Numerous *tefillin* were found in the Qumran caves which were in use at the same time as Pharisaic-rabbinic Jews wore them. Two types of phylacteries seem to have existed.[34] One contains the same exact scriptural passages as required by the rabbis, and these may be termed "Pharisaic" *tefillin*. The other type is based on the same selection of basic texts but adds additional material to each passage, something clearly forbidden by the later rabbis.[35] These phylacteries are apparently reflective of the Qumran sectarian approach or that of some other non-Pharisaic groups. Yet these differences in detail pale when taken in context: the practice of wearing *tefillin* transcended sectarian bounds, and the *tefillin* of the competing groups were generally constructed in similar fashion. The law was even observed in Egypt in Hellenistic context, although we cannot be certain how widespread it was. Yet if the Nash Papyrus was intended for *tefillin*,[36] the dissemination of this observance would have extended into the Fayyum as well.[37]

We cite this example only to show how the disagreements were greatly outnumbered by aspects of common halakhic observance. Numerous such common Jewish practices could be cited from the scrolls, Josephus, the New Testament, and Pharisaic-rabbinic sources.

---

33. J. T. Milik, *Qumrân Grotte 4.II, Part 2: Tefillin, Mezuzot et Targums (4Q128-4Q157)*. DJD 6 (Oxford: Clarendon, 1977) 34-79; Y. Yadin, *Tefillin from Qumran (X Q Phyl 1-4)* (Jerusalem: Israel Exploration Society and Shrine of the Book, 1969); A. M. Habermann, "'Al ha-Tefillin bi-Yeme Qedem," *ErIsr* 3 (1953/54) 174-77.

34. Milik, DJD 6:47; E. Tov, "Tefillin of Different Origin from Qumran?" in *A Light for Jacob: Studies in the Bible and Dead Sea Scrolls in Memory of Jacob Shalom Licht*, ed. Y. Hoffman and F. H. Polak, 44*-54* (Jerusalem: Bialik Institute and Tel-Aviv: Chaim Rosenberg School of Jewish Studies, Tel Aviv University, 1997).

35. Note that phylactery texts from Qumran generally exhibit harmonistic tendencies. Cf. E. Tov, "The Nature and Background of Harmonizations in Biblical Manuscripts," *JSOT* 31 (1985) 3-29.

36. For a summary, see M. Greenberg, "Nash Papyrus," *EncJud* 12:833.

37. Cf. L. H. Schiffman, *Reclaiming the Dead Sea Scrolls: The History of Judaism, the Background of Christianity, the Lost Library of Qumran* (Philadelphia: Jewish Publication Society, 1994; repr. ABRL [New York: Doubleday, 1995]) 305-12.

INTRODUCTION

Continuity and Discontinuity

As Qumran materials widen our understanding of rabbinic Judaism in the post-70 C.E. period, the question arises: To what extent was there continuity and to what extent was there discontinuity from pre-70 to post-70 C.E. Judaism? Do we observe a radical break, a cleavage, or even chasm, at the destruction? Was the rabbinic tradition largely the creation of the post-70 Tannaim?

Recent trends in scholarship have tended to adopt a model of extreme discontinuity. Careful study of the Qumran materials would argue against such a viewpoint in a variety of ways. It appears now that all the groups of Second Temple Jews for whom we have evidence already shared certain of the traits that were later dominant in rabbinic Judaism. These are: the centrality of Jewish law, the notion that there must be some form of extrabiblical Jewish law, the substitution of some sort of ritual for the sacrificial ritual (including daily prayer), the development of a nontemple liturgy, the extension of ritual purity from the temple to daily life, and other areas such as messianism and mysticism.

Furthermore, the very same kinds of issues are treated in the Dead Sea texts as are treated in more developed form in tannaitic literature. There is only one possible explanation for these similarities. It is that these same issues debated later already constituted the agenda of Jewish discourse in Second Temple times, apparently in all Jewish religious circles of whom we know.

In this regard, 4QMMT is of especial significance. This text provides us with a number of laws that deal with issues raised in tannaitic literature. Some of these, indeed, are even phrased in terminology strikingly similar to that of later Pharisaic-rabbinic texts, even if the rulings that the texts record do not agree. In *m. Yad.* 4 there are five debates said to have taken place between Pharisees and Sadducees. Four out of five of these appear together in MMT.[38] This leads us to suggest that these debates may have circulated as a collection already in the pre-70 period.

One law in the *Temple Scroll,* pertaining to permissible sexual unions, has been shown to be formulated in a manner similar to that of tannaitic literature.[39] Certain tannaitic formulations indeed must be sought in the Hasmonean period. It is simply impossible to continue to maintain that the entire corpus of the Mishnah and Tosefta is made up of ideas, concepts, and

---

38. L. H. Schiffman, "The Temple Scroll and the Systems of Jewish Law in the Second Temple Period," in *Temple Scroll Studies,* ed. G. J. Brooke, 250-51. JSPSup 7 (Sheffield: JSOT, 1989).

39. Yadin, *The Temple Scroll,* 1:368; D. Weiss Halivni, *Midrash, Mishnah, and Gemara: The Jewish Predilection for Justified Law* (Cambridge, MA: Harvard University Press, 1986) 30-34.

The Qumran Scrolls and Rabbinic Judaism

sayings that were created in the post-70 period. We are slowly discovering that some materials were formulated, perhaps in a few cases even redacted, in the Hasmonean period. The entire matter needs to be reconsidered, and it may be time to reexamine the anonymous portions of the Mishnah and Tosefta and those sayings attributed to early sages. By the careful use of linguistics and philology, as well as comparative study of legal traditions, we may find that a fair amount of tannaitic material was already moving toward its present form before the destruction of the Temple.

The Dead Sea Scrolls have shown us that we must be open to the existence of a greater degree of continuity between pre- and post-70 C.E. Judaism than was hitherto assumed. Nevertheless, rabbinic Judaism is predominantly a continuation of the Pharisaic tradition, although ideas and trends from other groups seem to have entered as well in the last years before the destruction and in the Yavnean period. The bulk of the Qumran corpus cannot be expected to be congruent with Pharisaism in light of its having been collected by a group that was diametrically opposed to many Pharisaic teachings.

The discovery of the Dead Sea Scrolls has presented us with the opportunity to learn a great deal not only about the group that collected the "ancient library," but about the entire constellation of sects of the Second Temple period. Therefore, now that the texts from the Qumran caves have been published, our knowledge of the background against which rabbinic Judaism emerged will become much clearer. We will see that ideas and practices that we could date no earlier than the destruction of the Temple can now be shown to be earlier. The Tannaim will increasingly be seen as inheritors of tradition who expanded, developed, and adapted that tradition to new circumstances, most notably the destruction of the Temple and the cessation of sacrificial worship. Yes, the Second Temple was a period in which different approaches vied with one another for the mantle of history, and the Dead Sea Scrolls negate the assumption of a monolithic Judaism. Yet these very same scrolls are helping us to understand how, after the revolt and the destruction, this period of great variegation gave way to that of standardization and consensus, and the emergence of rabbinic Judaism.

If we are to understand the transition that brought about what we call talmudic or rabbinic Judaism, it will have to be against a much wider backdrop than that previously drawn. For in this way we will be able to see not only the marked changes that took place in this new manifestation of Judaism but also the essential continuity that it evidences with the varieties of Judaism of the Second Temple period.

THE SCHOLARLY CONTROVERSY

CHAPTER 1

The Many "Battles of the Scrolls"

The study of the Dead Sea Scrolls is undergoing a virtual revolution. Scholarly interest has risen sharply in the past few years and has been manifested in a plethora of books, articles, and colloquia. Most importantly, the reorganization of the scrolls publication project has led to the rapid publication of the entire corpus, and, as a result, major changes in our view of this collection of texts and its significance for the study of the history of Judaism and Christianity have also taken place. Yet for the most part, these new ideas have percolated only among a small group of scholars who dedicate themselves to the study of the scrolls. In what follows I hope to introduce readers to some of these new ideas, placing emphasis to some extent on the results of my own research.

In the early days of Dead Sea Scrolls research, in the early 1950s, it was customary to speak of "the battle of the scrolls." This phrase referred to the heated public debates that swarmed over the importance of the scrolls and the identity and dating of their authors. Later on, in the '70s and '80s we again witnessed a battle of the scrolls, this time over the publication of the texts and access to them for scholarly research. Now that the scrolls are published in their entirety, it is time to turn our attention to the important contribution that the scrolls make to our knowledge of Second Temple Judaism.

What is in these scrolls, why are they important, and is anything new likely to come out of the study of the newly published material? Indeed, has anything changed in the last sixty years of research? These questions will turn out to be complex, and the answers reveal much about the fascinating discipline of Dead Sea Scroll or Qumran studies, the field that has now occupied me almost full time for forty years.[1]

History of Research

The field of Qumran studies really began long before the discovery of the Dead Sea Scrolls by Bedouin in 1947. In 1896, Solomon Schechter, then Reader in Rabbinic *(sic)* at Cambridge University in England, a talmudic scholar (later president of the Jewish Theological Seminary of America), traveled to Egypt to locate and purchase the remains of the Cairo Genizah,[2] a vast treasure trove of Hebrew manuscripts from the storehouse of the synagogue in Fustat, Old Cairo. Even before his trip, Schechter had acquired for Cambridge Genizah manuscripts of the apocryphal Ben Sira, previously known only in Greek and Syriac (Eastern Aramaic) translations. Later, Hebrew copies would be found at Qumran and Masada. Manuscripts from the Genizah had already been purchased by various collectors and eventually ended up in libraries in Europe, Russia, the U.S., and Israel. Among the materials Schechter brought back to Cambridge was another text of particular significance for what would become Qumran studies, two medieval manuscripts of part of a hitherto unknown work, entitled by Schechter, *Fragments of a Zadokite Work*.[3] (Many scholars now term this text the *Damascus Document*.)

This work, later found in several manuscripts in the Qumran collection,[4] consisted of two parts, a section termed the "admonition," a sort of his-

---

1. For a survey of the significance of the scrolls, see L. H. Schiffman, *Reclaiming the Dead Sea Scrolls: The History of Judaism, the Background of Christianity, the Lost Library of Qumran* (Philadelphia: Jewish Publication Society, 1994; repr. ABRL [New York: Doubleday, 1995]). Translations of virtually the entire nonbiblical corpus are available in F. García Martínez, *The Dead Sea Scrolls Translated*, trans. W. G. E. Watson. 2nd ed. (Leiden: Brill and Grand Rapids: Wm. B. Eerdmans, 1996); M. O. Wise, M. Abegg, and E. Cook, *The Dead Sea Scrolls: A New Translation* (San Francisco: HarperSanFrancisco, 1996); G. Vermes, *The Complete Dead Sea Scrolls in English* (1997; rev. ed. London: Penguin, 2004); D. W. Parry and E. Tov, eds., *The Dead Sea Scrolls Reader*. 6 vols. (Leiden: Brill, 2004).

2. The word *genizah* in Hebrew refers to a storage room where holy books and other Hebrew writings are "hidden away" *(gnz)* after they are no longer usable, since discarding them otherwise would be an act of disrespect.

3. S. Schechter, *Documents of Jewish Sectaries*, vol. 1: *Fragments of a Zadokite Work* (Cambridge: Cambridge University Press, 1910; repr. Library of Biblical Studies [New York: Ktav, 1970]); S. C. Reif, *A Jewish Archive from Old Cairo: The History of Cambridge University's Genizah Collection* (Richmond, Surrey: Curzon, 2000).

4. J. M. Baumgarten, *Qumran Cave 4.XIII: The Damascus Document (4Q266-273)*. DJD 18 (Oxford: Clarendon, 1996) publishes eight Cave 4 manuscripts. Fragments were also found in

torical and homiletical discourse, and a body of laws. Schechter immediately realized that these overlapping manuscripts represented the texts of an ancient Jewish sect that he identified with the Dosithe021an sect of the Samaritans whom he saw as closely linked with the Sadducees.

It was Louis Ginzberg, an even more important talmudic scholar (who later joined Schechter at JTSA), who in a series of articles[5] on these texts was able to outline the nature of the Qumran sect even before the Dead Sea Scrolls were discovered. He realized that this document represented the remnant of a sect of Jews who had separated from the dominant patterns of Second Temple Judaism, and he described their laws, theology, and even aspects of their history. Only in regard to his emphasis on the closeness of these sectarians to Pharisaism do we now know Ginzberg to have missed the mark.

Besides Ginzberg's analysis, the new text sparked numerous other theories, identifying the sect as early Jewish Christians, medieval Karaites, Sadducees, and practically any other imaginable Jewish group. The only true unanimity was in the rejection of Schechter's claim of Samaritan provenance. All these theories would emerge again when the Qumran scrolls were later discovered. The furious debates about this text had only briefly died down, quieted as they were by the interruption of scholarly discourse that resulted from World War II and the effects of the Holocaust on Judaic scholarship, when the discoveries in the Judean Desert reignited them.

In 1947, Bedouin shepherds wandered into a cave on the cliffs near Wadi Qumran, overlooking the Dead Sea just south of Jericho, and discovered the first scrolls. This cache of seven scrolls was eventually sold, in two lots, to the Hebrew University and the new State of Israel and is housed today in the Shrine of the Book of the Israel Museum in Jerusalem. Yet as the British mandate over Palestine drew to a close and the State of Israel was proclaimed, action shifted to the Kingdom of Jordan, which, as a result of the military action of the Israel War of Independence, now controlled the rocky area from which the scrolls had emerged.

While archaeologists attempted to search for additional scrolls, the Bedouin were quick to uncover enormous numbers of fragments and some complete scrolls, leaving the archaeologists and the Jordanian Department of An-

---

Cave 5 (5Q12; M. Baillet, J. T. Milik, and R. de Vaux, eds., *Les 'Petites Grottes' de Qumrân*. DJD 3 [Oxford: Clarendon, 1962] 181) and Cave 6 (6Q15; DJD 3:129-31).

5. "Eine unbekannte judische Sekte," originally published in *MGWJ* 55 (1911)–58 (1914); then privately published as a book in 1922. Ginzberg expected to publish additional material, but when World War II began, he forswore publishing in German. As a result, only with the appearance of the English edition, *An Unknown Jewish Sect* (New York: Jewish Theological Seminary, 1976), was his full study published.

tiquities to follow in their wake. In the 1950s, vast numbers of fragments, now known to be the remnants of some nine hundred manuscripts, were collected at the Palestine Archaeological Museum (now the Rockefeller Museum) in East Jerusalem, then under Jordanian control. These manuscripts eventually included the Samaria papyri from Wadi Daliyeh dating to the fifth and fourth centuries B.C.E. and some materials from the period of the Bar Kokhba revolt against Rome (132-135 C.E.) as well.

These manuscripts were carefully sorted by an international team of scholars assembled primarily from the American Schools of Oriental Research and the École Biblique, the French Catholic biblical and archaeological school in Jerusalem. The initial achievements of this group, including assembling the fragments into larger columns (stored in "plates"), transcription of the texts, and the preparation of a concordance, were remarkable. It was only later, when funds ran out and other factors, personal and political, intervened, that work came to a virtual standstill for almost twenty years.

In the meantime, in Israel, the work of publishing the complete scrolls that Israel had acquired proceeded fast apace. Three of the scrolls had already been published by the American Schools of Oriental Research before Israeli acquisition.[6] The remainder, with the exception of parts of the Genesis Apocryphon (a retelling of the book of Genesis), were speedily published.[7] The late Israeli archaeologist Yigael Yadin recovered texts from Masada and from the Bar Kokhba caves, and these have now all been published. Three volumes of Masada texts have appeared[8] as well as the Greek, Hebrew, and Aramaic materials from the Bar Kokhba caves at Naḥal Ḥever[9] and the Naḥal Ḥever texts that had been misidentified as originating in Naḥal Ṣe'elim.[10]

---

6. E. L. Sukenik, *'Oṣar ha-Megillot ha-Genuzot* (Jerusalem: Bialik Institute and Hebrew University, 1954/55).

7. M. Burrows, J. C. Trever, and W. H. Brownlee, eds., *The Dead Sea Scrolls of St. Mark's Monastery*, vol. 1 and vol. 2, fasc. 2 (New Haven: ASOR, 1950-51).

8. J. Naveh, *Masada I: The Aramaic and Hebrew Ostraca and Jar Inscriptions* (Jerusalem: Israel Exploration Society, 1989); H. M. Cotton and J. Geiger, *Masada II: The Latin and Greek Documents* (Jerusalem: Israel Exploration Society, 1989); S. Talmon, "Hebrew Fragments from Masada," in *Masada VI: The Yigael Yadin Excavations 1963-1965: Final Reports*, ed. Talmon with C. Newsom and Y. Yadin (Jerusalem: Israel Exploration Society and Hebrew University of Jerusalem, 1999) 31-149.

9. N. Lewis, ed., *The Documents from the Bar Kokhba Period in the Cave of Letters: Greek Papyri* (Jerusalem: Israel Exploration Society, Hebrew University, Shrine of the Book, 1989); Y. Yadin et al., *The Documents from the Bar Kokhba Period in the Cave of Letters: Hebrew, Aramaic, and Nabatean-Aramaic Papyri*. 2 vols. (Jerusalem: Israel Exploration Society, Institute of Archaeology, Hebrew University, Shrine of the Book, Israel Museum, 2002).

10. H. M. Cotton and A. Yardeni, *Aramaic, Hebrew and Greek Documentary Texts from*

The five legible columns of the Genesis Apocryphon, the last of the Israeli scroll acquisitions to be published, appeared in the edition of Yigael Yadin and Nahman Avigad in the fall of 1956.[11] Thus, Israeli scholars had completed their obligation to publish the scrolls in their possession.

Research on the scrolls was sufficiently advanced so that in July of 1957 International Team members Joseph Fitzmyer and later Raymond Brown and Willard G. Oxtoby began to compile a concordance on index cards. This concordance was eventually used by Ben Zion Wacholder and Martin G. Abegg to produce the multivolume computer-reconstructed text, the first volume of which effectively broke the monopoly of the International Team in 1991.[12]

In July of 1958 the last of the Cave 4 texts were purchased from the Bethlehem-based antiquities dealer Khalil Iskander Shahin, known as Kando. He had single-handedly served as the agent for purchase of all materials found by the Bedouin, on behalf of the Palestine Archaeological Museum. This brought to a close an important stage in the history of Qumran research. These fragments, however, would wait years before seeing the light of day and, indeed, were finally published only in 2001.

Throughout this period, Israeli archaeologists had watched with great interest as Bedouin continuously unearthed scrolls in the Jordanian-controlled part of the Judean Desert. In March 1955 the first season of an archaeological survey was carried out at Masada, the Herodian fortress further south on the shore of the Dead Sea. Masada had been the last stand of the rebels in the Jewish revolt against Rome in 66-73 C.E. Some of the same texts found at Qumran were also found at Masada.[13]

In the spring of 1960, the appearance of John M. Allegro's edition of the *Copper Scroll*[14] caused great friction amongst the scholars. Allegro, as a member of the International Team, had gained access to the scroll while it was in Manchester being unrolled. The *Copper Scroll* was assigned to Josef T. Milik for publication, and he, indeed, had published a preliminary edition in *Revue*

Naḥal Ḥever and Other Sites: With an Appendix Containing Alleged Qumran Texts (The Seiyâl Collection II). DJD 27 (Oxford: Clarendon, 1997); A. Yardeni, *Textbook of Aramaic, Hebrew and Nabataean Documentary Texts from the Judaean Desert and Related Material*. 2 vols. (Jerusalem: Hebrew University, Ben-Zion Dinur Center for Research in Jewish History, 2000).

11. N. Avigad and Y. Yadin, eds., *A Genesis Apocryphon: A Scroll from the Wilderness of Judaea* (Jerusalem: Magnes, Hebrew University, and Shrine of the Book, 1956).

12. B. Z. Wacholder and M. G. Abegg, eds., *A Preliminary Edition of the Unpublished Dead Sea Scrolls: The Hebrew and Aramaic Texts from Cave Four*. 4 fasc. (Washington: Biblical Archaeological Society, 1991-96).

13. Talmon, "Hebrew Fragments from Masada."

14. J. M. Allegro, *The Treasure of the Copper Scroll* (Garden City: Doubleday, 1960).

Biblique in 1959.[15] Allegro's book was the first major rival edition of a text to be published by a team member — and he was never forgiven for this, perhaps especially because of his view that the treasure purportedly described in the scroll was real. In the early 1960s, Allegro conducted two expeditions to try to find the treasure. None was ever found, but the quest continues even to the present day.

In June 1960, funding by the Rockefeller family came to an end. The members of the International Team scattered to their various universities. By this time the work of sorting the entire collection had been basically completed, and almost all the texts had been transcribed in preliminary fashion. Had publication ensued quickly, the International Team would have emerged as heroes for their expert and speedy work. But the various delays that took place after they left Jerusalem, coupled with the denial of access to other scholars, eventually led to the controversy of recent years.

When the International Team disbanded, 511 manuscripts of Cave 4 had been identified and arranged on 620 museum plates, with 25 plates of material still unidentified. The final series of photographs was also completed then.

As early as 1955, the Israeli government planned to build a permanent home for the scrolls and to put them on display. With the help of the Gottesman family, who had purchased the four scrolls in 1954, the Shrine of the Book of the Israel Museum was completed and dedicated in 1965 to house those four scrolls amongst more recent purchases.[16] The Shrine of the Book in West Jerusalem remains one of the most distinctive landmarks of the city today, located opposite the Knesset, Israel's parliament.

In November of 1966, the Jordanian government nationalized the Palestine Archaeological Museum. This step became significant when Israel conquered East Jerusalem in the 1967 Six Day War, for the Israel Department of Antiquities would come to control this important collection of unpublished Dead Sea Scrolls in the renamed Rockefeller Museum. A few scrolls that had been on exhibit at Amman during the war, as well as several of the fragmentary Cave 1 manuscripts, still remain in Jordan along with the Copper Scroll, recently conserved by the French Electric Company (EDF).

But the crown of Israeli achievement in this area was the recovery of the *Temple Scroll* in the aftermath of the Six Day War in 1967. This was the end of a story that had begun in 1960. A certain Reverend Joseph Uhrig showed

---

15. J. T. Milik, "Le rouleau de cuivre de Qumrân (3Q15): traduction et commentaire topographique," *RB* 66 (1959) 321-57.

16. See M. Broshi and Z. Sternhell, *The Shrine of the Book* (Jerusalem: Israel Museum, 1991).

The Many "Battles of the Scrolls"

Yadin a small sample of a scroll in return for a deposit of $10,000, but the deal never materialized.[17] By 1967 Yadin was apparently aware that the scroll was in Kando's hands. In the early days of the war, he sent intelligence officers to Kando's house in Bethlehem where they seized the scroll, thereby saving it from rotting under Kando's floorboards. Later Kando was compensated with a payment of $108,000. The subsequent publication of the *Temple Scroll* by Yadin in Hebrew and English editions[18] made this important text available to scholars. Other texts began to appear in the late 1970s from the original Jordanian lot, now in Israeli hands after the war. Along with *Enoch* fragments published by Milik[19] and important liturgical texts published by Maurice Baillet,[20] the *Temple Scroll* sparked renewed interest in the field.

The physical location of the scrolls and the politics of the Middle East affected the publication process as well. One result of these factors was the exclusion of Jews, and certainly of Israelis, from Roland de Vaux's editorial team in the 1950s through the mid-1980s.

So why were the scrolls kept secret for so long? The answers are in reality prosaic. Those who were supposed to publish them failed for a variety of reasons. Funding was insufficient. Some lost interest, some died, and some were stricken with alcoholism. Some lacked sufficient linguistic skills to get the job done in a reasonable amount of time. Some believed that only they could do the job correctly and that they and the students they chose had rights to the material in perpetuity. The Israeli conquest of East Jerusalem would set off a chain of events that ultimately led to the release of the entire corpus and to a wider understanding of the nature of the ancient library. But this was a delayed reaction lasting well into the 1990s.

Immediately after the war, Israeli officials agreed to let the existing International Team continue their work, expecting that it would soon be completed. In retrospect, the allotments of texts to each editor were simply too large for publication within a reasonable time.

---

17. H. Shanks, "Intrigue and the Scroll," in *Understanding the Dead Sea Scrolls* (New York: Random House, 1992) 116-25; N. A. Silberman, *The Hidden Scrolls: Christianity, Judaism, & the War for the Dead Sea Scrolls* (New York: Putnam's, 1994) 162-64.

18. *Megillat ha-Miqdash*. 3 vols. (Jerusalem: Israel Exploration Society and Shrine of the Book, 1977); *The Temple Scroll*. 3 vols. (Jerusalem: Israel Exploration Society and Shrine of the Book, 1983); and the more popularly written *The Temple Scroll: The Hidden Law of the Dead Sea Sect* (New York: Random House, 1985).

19. J. T. Milik, *The Books of Enoch: Aramaic Fragments from Qumrân Cave 4* (Oxford: Clarendon, 1976).

20. M. Baillet, "Textes liturgiques," in *Qumrân Grotte 4.III (4Q482-4Q520)*. DJD 7 (Oxford: Clarendon, 1982) 105-214.

Yadin's revelation of the *Temple Scroll*, first in a series of public lectures and then in his edition of 1977, capped a process already observable earlier of seeing Qumran materials in a Jewish context. Now a scroll entirely of Jewish law, the same size as the book of Isaiah, was on the reader's table.

Furthermore, Yadin had identified the authors of the *Temple Scroll* with the Qumran sectarians. Therefore, his new scroll led to full recognition of the halakhic character of that group, that is, their grounding in Jewish law.

In September 1971, Pierre Benoit succeeded de Vaux as editor-in-chief of the International Team and the Discoveries in the Judaean Desert (DJD) series. Although several publications did appear, much of the work, especially on the Cave 4 texts, was not really proceeding at all. These problems were already clear in September 1984 when Benoit retired and the Israeli Department of Antiquities confirmed John Strugnell of Harvard as editor-in-chief of the scrolls publication project. Strugnell expanded the team to include some twenty members, amongst whom were a number of Israelis — Devorah Dimant, Elisha Qimron, and Emanuel Tov. He also furnished a timetable to the Israeli Department of Antiquities (that in the meantime had become the Israel Antiquities Authority), but the deadlines he specified there were not kept and could not be enforced.

The revelation of a few lines of the *Halakhic Letter*, also known as 4QMMT, by Qimron at the 1984 International Conference on Biblical Archaeology naturally greatly stimulated curiosity as to what other such "bombshells" might still lay hidden in the unpublished corpus of Qumran texts. Scarcely a year later, at the New York University Conference on the Dead Sea Scrolls, Morton Smith delivered an impassioned plea for the immediate publication of photographs of the entire corpus. Hershel Shanks, editor of the *Biblical Archaeology Review (BAR)*, took up the struggle in his popular magazine. He editorialized extensively on this problem and began in earnest his campaign to "liberate" the scrolls. The call for release and publication of all the documents grew progressively louder, surfacing regularly at scholarly conferences and in the press. Amir Drori, Director of the Israel Antiquities Authority, was beginning to feel the pressure for change. However, the "monopoly" was soon to be broken by the efforts of scholars themselves.

The clamor for open access was greatly increased when Robert Eisenman and Philip Davies formally requested to read the unpublished *Zadokite Fragments* in the Rockefeller Museum and were rebuffed by Strugnell. The exchange of letters was published in *BAR*.[21]

21. H. Shanks, "Dead Sea Scrolls Scandal — Israel's Department of Antiquities Joins

The Many "Battles of the Scrolls"

In 1990, Stephen A. Reed of the Ancient Biblical Manuscripts Center in Claremont, California, came to Jerusalem to prepare the first complete catalog of scrolls materials and negatives, making use of an earlier private catalog of Qimron's. Reed's catalog clarified the extent of the still unpublished material and focused attention on its proper conservation and restoration.[22]

The official editorial team, while significantly widened by 1990 to include some thirty scholars, Jewish and non-Jewish of many nationalities, still was holding exclusive access to texts and producing text editions much too slowly for use by other researchers. Many disenfranchised scholars proposed that access be granted to any and all on the basis of research or university affiliation. Shanks stressed this point in his journal and proposed that photographs of the texts be distributed.

Then in November 1990, Strugnell's health deteriorated, and after inappropriate remarks in an interview in an Israeli newspaper,[23] the Israel Antiquities Authority stepped in to appoint Emanuel Tov of the Hebrew University in his stead as editor-in-chief of the International Team and head of the Discoveries in the Judaean Desert series. Émile Puech of the École Biblique, Eugene Ulrich of the University of Notre Dame, and Tov were designated general editors by the members of the team. They expanded the International Team to some fifty-five editors.

As the new team began to edit their assignments, events leading to the eventual release of the scrolls swiftly followed one another. In 1991, the newspapers carried the reports of the computer-aided reconstruction of the still-hidden texts by Ben Zion Wacholder and Martin Abegg of Hebrew Union College in Cincinnati. This edition was produced from a privately-distributed concordance prepared by the original editorial team in a limited edition of about thirty copies. The Wacholder-Abegg reconstruction was published by the Biblical Archaeology Society with a foreword by *BAR* editor Shanks.[24] The date of release of the reconstructed edition was chosen to precede a Nova television documentary that had been in the works for over a year. On September 22, also before the airing of the Nova documentary, the Huntington Library in San Marino, California, announced that it would release its full set

---

Conspiracy to Keep Scrolls Secret," *BAR* 15/4 (1989) 18-21, 55; "Dead Sea Scrolls: Dead Sea Scroll Variation on 'Show and Tell' — It's Called 'Tell, But No Show,'" *BAR* 16/2 (1990) 18-21.

22. S. A. Reed, comp., with M. J. Lundberg and M. B. Phelps, *The Dead Sea Scrolls Catalogue: Documents, Photographs and Museum Inventory Numbers*. SBLRBS 32 (Atlanta: Scholars, 1994).

23. A. Katzman, *Ha'aretz* (9 Nov 1990) [Hebrew]; appeared in English as "Chief Dead Sea Scrolls Editor Denounces Judaism, Israel," *BAR* 17/1 (1991) 64-65, 70, 72.

24. Wacholder and Abegg, *Preliminary Edition*, fasc. 1:vii-viii.

of photographic negatives of the scrolls. On October 15, 1991, the Nova documentary, "Secrets of the Dead Sea Scrolls," appeared on nationwide television in the U.S. It had been hastily updated to include the latest events in the scrolls publication controversy. An audience of more than 13 million viewed the Nova special, and it amply demonstrated the role of the media in the release of the scrolls by making people aware of the controversy and stimulating further press reports.

It had to be expected that in a world growing increasingly democratic, the concept of freedom of information would triumph over all other considerations, even legitimate scientific concerns. Beginning in 1990 new technological advances and aids to scholarship were produced that not only opened up the scrolls to all scholars but allowed better readings of the manuscripts. In that year carbon 14 tests of a selection of manuscripts were run, and these generally supported the palaeographic and archaeological dating that had been previously proposed.[25] Several editions of photographs were released of varying degrees of usefulness. The microfilms of the Huntington Library, while they struck a blow for the "liberation" of the scrolls, were not of sufficient quality for serious research.

At about the same time, copies of photographs of the unpublished fragments were reaching Robert Eisenman, Chairman of the Department of Religious Studies at California State University at Long Beach, from an undisclosed source. Eisenman was a natural conduit for such photographs because of the outspoken position he had taken demanding the release of the scrolls. Together with James Robinson of the Institute for Antiquity and Christianity at Claremont, he organized these for publication in a two-volume set, eventually preceded by a foreword by Shanks discussing the publication controversy and relating his role in it.[26] These publications led the Israel Antiquities Authority to reformulate its own policies on access to photographs of the scrolls. In October of 1991, it allowed open access to all photos, but asked scholars to refrain from publishing editions of texts assigned to others for editing. Since then, all scholars were able to view any photographs of the manuscripts in either Jerusalem, Claremont, or Oxford.

Along with the photographs, Shanks published a transcription of the *Halakhic Letter,* then being prepared for publication by Qimron and

---

25. G. Bonani et al., "Radiocarbon Dating of the Dead Sea Scrolls," ʿAtiqot 20 (1991) 27-32. Cf. A. J. T. Jull et al., "Radiocarbon Dating of Scrolls and Linen Fragments from the Judean Desert," ʿAtiqot 28 (1996) 85-61.

26. R. H. Eisenman and J. M. Robinson, *A Facsimile of the Dead Sea Scrolls: Prepared with an Introduction and Index.* 2 vols. (Washington: Biblical Archaeological Society, 1991), Publisher's Foreword by H. Shanks, 1:xii-xlv.

Strugnell. Qimron sued Shanks in Israeli court for copyright violation of his reconstruction of the text and won, and he even won an appeal before the Supreme Court of Israel.[27]

With the release of the Huntington microfilms and the Eisenman-Robinson-Shanks facsimiles, it was clear that high quality, properly indexed photographs of the entire Judean Desert corpus would have to be issued. The Dutch publishing house Brill, with the cooperation of the Israel Antiquities Authority, issued a set of positive microfiches in 1993. This project, of high quality, is the most complete set of photos ever issued and has recently been supplemented with the Allegro collection of 1,600 images and a CD-ROM edition. Today, anyone who can read Second Temple Hebrew and Aramaic texts in their original scripts can study the entire corpus. Finally, this important part of humanity's heritage is available to all.

With the opening of the entire corpus to scholars, the speed of publication progressed, and all the texts have been published in official editions. More texts had been published between 1990 and 2000 than in the preceding forty years! The greatest benefit of open access is that it is now possible to gain an accurate sense of the nature and significance of the entire collection. A new era of intense, in-depth research is now well under way.

The publication controversy encouraged increased publication efforts, and the team of scholars was widened in order to speed up the publication process. Those of us now doing research in Qumran studies constitute to a great extent a new generation, neither part of the original publication process nor veterans of the "battles of the scrolls." We come to the field with new approaches and theories. Indeed, much progress has already taken place. Before discussing these new developments, we shall first have to assess the old theories.

Initial Theories

Already in the early years after the discovery of the *Zadokite Fragments* and their publication by Schechter, a fierce battle raged over the identity of the sect. The Qumran scrolls simply raised all the same issues anew. One group of scholars, following Solomon Zeitlin, argued for medieval Karaite origins,

---

27. A full discussion and analysis of this case is found in T. H. Lim, H. L. MacQueen, and C. M. Carmichael, eds., *On Scrolls, Artefacts, and Intellectual Property*. JSPSup 38 (Sheffield: Sheffield Academic, 2001); D. Nimmer, "Copyright in the Dead Sea Scrolls: Authorship and Originality," *Houston Law Review* 38/1 (2001) 5-217.

constantly misinterpreting the documents to suit their theories, while at the same time pointing out many valid parallels with Karaite halakhic and exegetical literature.

Another group argued for a dating in the late first century C.E., seeing the scrolls as connected with the Zealots or early Christians. These theories did not succeed because they flew in the face of the archaeological dating of the ruins of Qumran, the dating of the scrolls by palaeography (the study of the forms of the letters), and the carbon 14 dating of the cloths in which the scrolls were wrapped in ancient times. The end result was a virtual consensus that the scrolls are to be dated primarily to the Hasmonean and Herodian periods, with some earlier material.

This dating was strengthened by the constant excavation in the early 1950s of the Qumran ruins and caves by the archaeologists who followed in the wake of the Bedouin. Unfortunately, the leader of the dig at Qumran, Roland de Vaux of the École Biblique, never succeeded in publishing his excavation reports, although preliminary reports and a survey volume appeared.[28] Nonetheless, the evidence was enough to convince virtually everyone that the ruins of Qumran were connected with the scrolls found in the area, and that Qumran was inhabited in the Hasmonean and Herodian periods and up to the destruction of Judea by the Roman armies in the Great Revolt of 66-73 C.E.

But there was still the issue of who the sectarians were. It was not long before there developed the Essene hypothesis, first put forth by E. L. Sukenik.[29] This theory states that the sectarians are to be identified with the Essenes described by Josephus, Philo, Pliny, and other ancient sources.[30] This view was fully elaborated in the works of Frank M. Cross,[31] Millar Bur-

---

28. The site was excavated in 1953-56. Reports appeared in *RB* 60 (1953)–63 (1956). The survey volume was first published in French in 1961 and then revised as R. de Vaux, *Archaeology and the Dead Sea Scrolls*. Schweich Lectures 1959 (London: Oxford University Press, 1973). Two volumes of his material have been published as *Fouilles de Khirbet Qumrân et de Ain Feshka: Album de photographies, répertoire du fonds photographique, synthèse des notes de chantier du Père Roland de Vaux*, presented by J.-B. Humbert et A. Chambon. NTOA.SA 1 (Fribourg: Éditions universitaires and Göttingen: Vandenhoek & Ruprecht, 1994); and *Die Ausgrabungen von Qumran und En Feschcha: Deutsche Übersetzung und Informationsaufbereitung durch F. Rohrhirsch und B. Hofmeir*. NTOA.SA 1A (Freiburg: Universitätsverlag and Göttingen: Vandenhoeck & Ruprecht, 1996). See now also J. Magness, *The Archaeology of Qumran and the Dead Sea Scrolls*. SDSSRL (Grand Rapids: Wm. B. Eerdmans, 2002).

29. E. L. Sukenik, *Megillot Genuzot mi-tokh Genizah Qedumah she-Nimṣe'ah be-Midbar Yehudah*. 2 vols. (Jerusalem: Bialik Institute, 1948-1950) 1:16.

30. L. H. Schiffman, *Texts and Traditions: A Source Reader for the Study of Second Temple and Rabbinic Judaism* (Hoboken: Ktav, 1998) 275-91.

31. *The Ancient Library of Qumran and Modern Biblical Studies* (Garden City: Doubleday,

rows,[32] and others, and quickly became and still remains the reigning theory. But who were the Essenes, and why do scholars connect the Qumran sect with them?

The evidence of Josephus, Philo, and Pliny the Elder, when taken together, describes a sect of Jews who had a center at the shore of the Dead Sea and members spread throughout the cities of Judea as well. This group was said, in the view of these scholars, to have lived a communal life and to have practiced the same initiation rites and organizational patterns as the sect that had left behind the library at Qumran. This Essene group was assumed, therefore, to be the authors of virtually all the scrolls except those of the Bible and some previously known apocrypha.

There was another dimension to this theory too. It followed well on some views already expressed before the discovery of the Qumran scrolls, namely, that there were certain parallels between the doctrines of the Essenes, now taken to be synonymous with the Qumran sect, and early Christianity.

The identification of the sect with the Essenes was quickly supplemented with a circular set of arguments: If the sectarian materials could be identified with the Essenes, then all information in the Greek sources (Philo, Josephus, and Pliny) could be read into and harmonized with the evidence of the scrolls. And if the scrolls were Essene, then they could in turn be used to interpret the material in Philo, Josephus, and Pliny. But this was not enough. By this time the scrolls and the Essenes were re-created as a precursor to Christianity, perhaps even a harbinger, so that material from the New Testament regarding the early church was read back into the scrolls and vice versa. This approach, the dominant hypothesis for some forty years, yielded the "monks," "monastery," "bishop," celibacy, and numerous other terminological exaggerations used to describe Qumran texts, behind which lay a set of distinct preconceptions.

Somehow this theory escaped the scrutiny of most scholars. For some forty years, however, I scrupulously abstained from terming the sectarians of Qumran "Essenes." Indeed, it was the late Louis Ginzberg, in the days when the only available text was the *Zadokite Fragments,* who correctly termed this group "an unknown Jewish sect." It was a methodological absurdity definitively to identify a sect when only a small part of its so-called library had been published.

We shall see that a variety of factors came together to call aspects of this

---

1958; repr. Grand Rapids: Baker, 1980). This work appears now in a third revised and extended edition, *The Ancient Library of Qumran* (Sheffield: Sheffield Academic, 1995).

32. *The Dead Sea Scrolls* (New York: Viking, 1955); and *More Light on the Dead Sea Scrolls* (New York: Viking, 1958).

hypothesis into question. More importantly, in the last twenty years there has been a turn more and more to see the Qumran materials as part of the complex history of Judaism that leads from the Hebrew Bible to the rabbinic tradition. Indeed, it is only when such an approach is followed that the true significance of the scrolls for evaluating the background of Christianity can be understood.

The Second Generation

In about 1960, most publication and interest on the part of the original International Team of scholars in the field of Qumran studies came to an end.[33] This was certainly the case for those on the publication team who, for the most part, ceased to be active in this area in the early 1960s. Among the causes of this loss of interest may be two: First, the specialties of this generation of scholars had been primarily in the Hebrew Bible and New Testament. It soon became clear that the biblical texts among the scrolls testified to the state of the text of the Hebrew Bible in the first two centuries B.C.E. and would not help in restoring an *Urtext* (original text) of the Hebrew Scriptures. Second, it soon became apparent that the texts still to be published contained primarily material relative to the Judaism of the period and not to Christianity and the issues surrounding its origins.

Among the second generation were some younger scholars, Christian and Jewish, including this author, who were not bound by these theories. These scholars of the second (and even third) generation undertook the study of the particularly Jewish issues in the scrolls — Jewish history, law, theology, and messianism — and gradually began to cast very different light on the materials. Regardless of their own religious convictions, these scholars realized that recognizing the Jewishness of the scrolls was the only scientific method by which to utilize this gold mine of material for the reconstruction of Second Temple Judaism as well as for the study of the prehistory of Christianity.

Finally, the publication of the *Temple Scroll* by Yadin and many of the *Enoch* fragments by Milik caused scholars to look more and more at the uniquely Jewish aspects of the material. Perhaps more importantly, the public interest that Yadin's new *Temple Scroll* generated led to greater attention to the scrolls, and his monumental edition and commentary opened anew all kinds of questions.

---

33. T. M. Heisey, "Paradigm Agreement and Literature Obsolescence: A Comparative Study in the Literature of the Dead Sea Scrolls," *JD* 44 (1988) 285-301.

The Many "Battles of the Scrolls"

All along, minor contradictions with the "official" Essene hypothesis were being observed. Many of these questions were being raised at a series of conferences. The first of these was the one I had the honor to organize in 1985 under the sponsorship of the Hagop Kevorkian Center for Near Eastern Studies at New York University.[34] Others were soon held at many other cities around the world, producing conference volumes that added much to the progress of current research. This interaction was symptomatic of the desire of scholars to ask new questions and advance their field of learning. New groups of younger researchers gradually became the major carriers of this field as the first generation did not appear at these conferences and refrained from exchanging ideas on the scrolls. (John Strugnell was a notable exception to this rule.)

Gradually a new nonconsensus was emerging. It held that many issues regarded as settled were not settled, and that these required thorough study and, of course, the full publication of the still hidden scrolls. It also called for postponing definite conclusions on the identity of the sect until the publication of the entire corpus. Accordingly, an entire series of issues was opened up. We shall survey here some of the ramifications of these questions.

The Nature of the Library

It is now clear that the character of the ancient library must be reevaluated. Let us recapitulate what is actually in this library. There are books of the Bible, copies of previously known apocrypha and pseudepigrapha (i.e., Second Temple–period Jewish literature), sectarian texts belonging to the Qumran sect itself, and a variety of other types of compositions as well, including sapiential (wisdom) and liturgical material.[35] Further, there are *tefillin* (phylacteries) and *mezuzot*.[36] The sectarian (i.e., Qumranian) material in this collection of manuscripts is certainly at the core, leading to the conclusion

---

34. L. H. Schiffman, ed., *Archaeology and History in the Dead Sea Scrolls: The New York University Conference in Memory of Yigael Yadin*. JSOTSup 8. JSOT/ASOR Monographs 2 (Sheffield: Sheffield Academic, 1990).

35. D. Dimant, "The Qumran Manuscripts: Contents and Significance," in *Time to Prepare the Way in the Wilderness: Papers on the Qumran Scrolls by Fellows of the Institute for Advanced Studies of the Hebrew University, Jerusalem, 1989-90*, ed. Dimant and L. H. Schiffman, 23-58. STDJ 16 (Leiden: Brill, 1995).

36. Y. Yadin, *Tefillin from Qumran (X Q Phyl 1-4)* (Jerusalem: Israel Exploration Society and Shrine of the Book, 1969); J. T. Milik, *Qumrân Grotte 4.II, Part 2: Tefillin, Mezuzot et Targums (4Q128-4Q157)*. DJD 6 (Oxford: Clarendon, 1977) 33-85.

that the Qumran sect, whoever they were, collected these books. But how and why?

Although the scrolls may have originally constituted the library of this group, only Cave 4 could have served this function in antiquity. Archaeological evidence indicates that it must have been outfitted with shelves to hold scrolls, and it was located close to the Qumran buildings. The other caves, scattered along the marl terrace above Qumran and to the north of it, were too inconvenient for use on a regular basis by those who inhabited the ruins. We must conclude that the scrolls were stashed there to avoid their destruction or desecration just before the Roman invasion. It might have been the inhabitants of Qumran, or perhaps some other Jews who may have fled there, who saved the scrolls.

One theory held that the scrolls in Cave 4 were ripped up by Roman soldiers after the conquest of Qumran in 68 C.E. This theory was called into question by the extremely technical research of Hartmut Stegemann[37] regarding the patterns of deterioration in the preserved fragments. His studies provide us sufficient information almost assuredly to conclude that the deterioration of the manuscripts took place over time as a result of natural causes, and that the texts were by and large placed whole into the caves in antiquity.

The notion that every book in the library was somehow canonical, i.e., holy and authoritative, in the life of the Qumran sect has been increasingly called into question as well. Instead, we have to see these treasures as a corpus of books of which there is a central collection of certain biblical manuscripts plus sectarian materials generally written according to the linguistic peculiarities of the sect.[38] In addition, there are a variety of texts collected by those who lived there, the official status of which was at best undefined and perhaps nonexistent. Other texts that Qumranites apparently possessed, many of which doubtless were brought to Qumran from elsewhere, were held because they had affinities with the beliefs of the sectarians. These texts would have emerged from earlier circles or from contemporary groups close in their ideology to the Qumran sect.

This conclusion is greatly strengthened by the publication of the nonbiblical fragments from Masada by Shemaryahu Talmon.[39] These fragments,

---

37. H. Stegemann, "Methods for the Reconstruction of Scrolls from Scattered Fragments," in Schiffman, *Archaeology and History*, 189-220.

38. E. Tov, "The Orthography and Language of the Hebrew Scrolls Found at Qumran and the Origin of These Scrolls," *Textus* 13 (1986) 32-57.

39. "*Qiṭʻe Ketavim Ketuvim ʻIvrit mi-Meṣadah*," ErIsr 20 (Yadin Volume, 1989) 278-86; "*Qetʻa mi-Megillah Ḥiṣṣonit le-Sefer Yehoshuaʻ mi-Meṣadah*," in *Shai le-Ḥayim Rabin: ʼAsuppat Meḥqere Lashon li-Khevodo bi-Melʼot Lo Shivʻim ve-Ḥamesh*, ed. M. Goshen-Gottstein,

together with the fragments of the Qumran *Sabbath Songs (Angelic Liturgy)* also found there,[40] show that the defenders of Masada possessed books that, like those found in the Qumran collection, were the common heritage of Second Temple Judaism. In other words, many of these works did not originate in — and were not confined to — Qumran sectarian circles.

The Origins of the Sect

The Essene hypothesis is in serious need of reevaluation in light of the text known as *Miqṣat Ma'aśe ha-Torah* (lit., "Some Rulings Pertaining to the Torah," abbreviated 4QMMT, 4Q referring to Cave 4 from Qumran), sometimes called the *Halakhic Letter*. The existence of this text, essentially a foundation document of the sect, was revealed only in 1984.[41] This "letter" contains a series of approximately twenty-two laws that the authors assert constitute the reasons for their having broken away from the Jerusalem establishment. They assert that they will return if their opponents, who are pictured as knowing that the sectarians are right all along, will recant and accept the sectarian interpretation of the Torah.

Investigation of the laws in the document in light of talmudic sources from somewhat later proves beyond doubt that the origins of the sect are to be located in a Saducean group that broke away from their fellows when the Hasmonean high priests took control of temple worship after the Maccabean revolt (168-164 B.C.E.). At that time, the Hasmoneans made common cause with the Pharisees, a situation that lasted for much of the Hasmonean period. These Sadducees, the ones who purportedly sent the *Halakhic Letter*, were not willing to adjust to the new reality and compromise their deeply held legal and exegetical principles, as did so many of their fellow Sadducees. The let-

---

S. Morag, and S. Kogut, 147-57 (Jerusalem: Akademon, 1990); "Fragments of a Psalms Scroll from Masada, MPs[b] (Masada 1103-1742)," in *Minḥah le-Naḥum: Biblical and Other Studies Presented to Nahum M. Sarna in Honour of His 70th Birthday*, ed. M. Brettler and M. Fishbane, 318-27. JSOTSup 154 (Sheffield: JSOT, 1993). All these texts have appeared in final publication as Talmon, "Hebrew Fragments from Masada."

40. C. Newsom, "Shirot 'Olat ha-Shabbat," in *Qumran Cave 4.VI: Poetical and Liturgical Texts, Part 1*, ed. E. Eshel et al. DJD 11 (Oxford: Clarendon, 1998) 173-401.

41. E. Qimron and J. Strugnell, "An Unpublished Halakhic Letter from Qumran," in *Biblical Archaeology Today: Proceedings of the International Congress on Biblical Archaeology, Jerusalem, April 1984*, ed. J. Amitai, 400-7 (Jerusalem: Israel Exploration Society, Israel Academy of Sciences and Humanities, in cooperation with ASOR, 1985); and (a different article by the same name) *IMJ* 4 (1985) 9-12. For full publication, see Qimron and Strugnell, *Qumran Cave 4.V: Miqṣat Ma'aśe ha-Torah*. DJD 10 (Oxford: Clarendon, 1994).

ter argues with these compromising Sadducees in its halakhic section, but at the end turns to the Hasmonean ruler and attempts to sway him to their views by warning him that God blessed only those rulers who followed His ways.[42]

The revelations contained in the *Halakhic Letter* demand that we reevaluate some of the older theories identifying the sect with known Second Temple groups. The theories tying the emergence of the sect to some subgroup of the Pharisees are certainly no longer tenable. The dominant Essene hypothesis, if it is to be maintained, requires radical reorientation. Those holding this theory might now argue that the term "Essene" came to designate the originally Sadducean sectarians who had gone through a process of radicalization until they became a distinct sect. Alternatively, they might broaden their understanding of the term to include a wide variety of similar groups, of which the Dead Sea sect might be one.

The Scrolls and the Jewish Sects

Now that all the texts have been published, and as our understanding of the nature of the collection has been widening, it has become increasingly clear that it is possible to learn much more from the scrolls than simply the nature of the sect that collected them. The scrolls are emerging as the primary source for the study of Judaism in the Second Temple period in all its varieties. Almost no other primary Hebrew and Aramaic sources exist for the reconstruction of the Judaism of this period, and this hoard of manuscripts includes material representing a variety of Jewish groups and polemics against others. In this way, the documents from the Judean Desert are providing the background for the study of the later emergence of rabbinic Judaism and the early Christian church.

Specifically, it used to be believed that we had no contemporary sources for Pharisaism (the Jewish group that bequeathed its approach to rabbinic Judaism) in the Hasmonean period and that our only sources were the later ac-

---

42. See "The New Halakhic Letter (4QMMT) and the Origins of the Dead Sea Sect," Chapter 6 below; L. H. Schiffman, "The Temple Scroll and the Systems of Jewish Law in the Second Temple Period," in *Temple Scroll Studies*, ed. G. J. Brooke, 246-50. JSPSup 7 (Sheffield: JSOT, 1989); "*Miqṣat Maʿaseh Ha-Torah* and the *Temple Scroll*," *RevQ* 14 (The Texts of Qumran and the History of the Community: Proceedings of the Groningen Congress on the Dead Sea Scrolls 3, 1990) 435-57; "The Prohibition of the Skins of Animals in the Temple Scroll and *Miqṣat Maʿaseh ha-Torah*," in *Proceedings of the Tenth World Congress of Jewish Studies, Division A* (Jerusalem: World Union of Jewish Studies, 1990) 191-98.

The Many "Battles of the Scrolls"

counts in Josephus, the polemics of the New Testament, and the scattered references in talmudic literature to the precursors of the mishnaic rabbis.[43] About the Sadducees much the same thing was said, and there was little evidence of the various apocalyptic groups the existence of which could only barely be assumed.

Only in the last few years have we succeeded in showing that this evaluation was incorrect. Certainly, the scrolls inform us about the sect that inhabited the ruins of Qumran. But so much can be learned about the other groups as well.

Let us begin with the Pharisees. This elusive group of lay teachers and expounders of the Torah is now coming to life before our eyes. The scrolls include material on the Pharisees only in polemical context. The polemics are of two kinds. In the better known sectarian texts the Pharisees (called by various code words like the similar sounding "Ephraim") are said to be the "builders of the wall," indicating that they built fences around the Torah by making regulations designed to ensure its observance. These fences were no more acceptable to the Qumran sect than the *halakhot* ("laws") of the Pharisees, whom the sect called derisively, in a play on the word *halakhot*, "*doreshe ḥalaqot*," best translated "those who expound false laws." The same text refers to the *talmud* of "Ephraim" as falsehood. The reference is certainly to the Pharisaic method of deriving laws from Scripture similar to that found in some early midrashic texts. Clearly, in these texts we see that the accounts of Josephus describing the Pharisees and their traditions of the fathers, the precursor of the rabbinic oral law concept, are in fact confirmed for the Pharisees in the Hasmonean period by the Dead Sea Scrolls.[44]

Miqṣat Maʿaśe ha-Torah provides a series of polemics in which the authors of the text castigate the Jerusalem establishment. In each of these cases the writers speak of their own view and then specify the violation of the law as practiced by their opponents. In a number of these cases the laws of the authors represent views directly opposed to those of the Pharisees, yet matching those of the Sadducees, according to later rabbinic texts. As such, we have good reason to believe now that we have here twenty or so laws, *halakhot* as they were already called in the Hasmonean period, that were held by the Pharisees and their opposing rulings as practiced by the Sadducees.

These laws also contribute to our evaluation of the reliability of tal-

---

43. J. Neusner, *The Rabbinic Traditions about the Pharisees before 70*. 3 vols. (Leiden: Brill, 1971).

44. See Chapter 19 below, "The Pharisees and Their Legal Traditions according to the Dead Sea Scrolls."

mudic reports. The letter corroborates two historical issues in rabbinic sources, disproving the theory of prominent modern scholars who doubted the reliability of the rabbis.

First, the Pharisaic view did indeed dominate for much of the Hasmonean era, even in matters of temple practice. This historical circumstance is not a later talmudic anachronistic invention. Second, the terminology and even some of the very same laws that are recorded in rabbinic sources, some in the name of the Pharisees, others in the names of anonymous Tannaitic sources, were those that the Pharisees espoused. Put otherwise, rabbinic Judaism is not a postdestruction invention, as some scholars had maintained. Its roots reach back even further than the Hasmonean period, as can be proven from the Dead Sea Scrolls.

We can also learn something about the Sadducees from the Qumran texts. In Pesher Nahum they are termed the "House of Manasseh," the opponents of Ephraim — as we already noted, a code word for the Pharisees.[45] The description of the Sadducees as aristocratic members of the ruling class fits that period in which the Sadducees had come close to the Hasmoneans and the Pharisees had fallen out with them, just before the Roman conquest of Palestine in 63 B.C.E. All this accords perfectly well with the descriptions of Josephus and shows that in regard to the Sadducees he is generally accurate. In addition, we learn from MMT that the sectarians, originating amongst pious Sadducees, broke away from the Jerusalem establishment when the Hasmoneans took over the priesthood.

Does this mean that the sect was Sadducean? Not quite. It seems that there was a process of growing sectarianism and separatist mentality. As a result, a group of originally Sadducean priests, under the leadership of the Teacher of Righteousness, who in my view came to lead the sect only after the *Halakhic Letter* was written, developed into the group that left us the sectarian texts.

Yet it may be that even more can be learned about the Sadducees. There are a variety of parallels between the laws of MMT and the *Temple Scroll*.[46] In some cases the *Temple Scroll* provides a scriptural basis when MMT cites only the law. This legal formulation suggests that some of the sources of the *Temple Scroll* (not its final redaction, which is Hasmonean) must date to the presectarian period, when these were indeed Sadducean teachings. The author/redactor of the complete scroll, whether a member of the Qumran sect or of

---

45. S. L. Berrin, *The Pesher Nahum Scroll from Qumran: An Exegetical Study of 4Q169.* STDJ 53 (Leiden: Brill, 2004).

46. Schiffman, *RevQ* 14 (1990) 435-57.

some related or similar group or a lone author, used these Sadducean sources.[47] As such, as we continue to recover the sources of the *Temple Scroll,* the views of the Sadducees are starting to come to light. Indeed, we are finally understanding their brand of literalism, which allowed for exegesis but required that all laws emerge from Scripture, and their rejection of laws unrelated to the Bible.

We are also able to learn from the scrolls about various apocalyptic groups whose teachings were important for the later development of aspects of Jewish mysticism and Christian apocalypticism. But in the case of these groups, we lack all social and historical context. We do not know for sure if there even were groups or just single authors who read each others' treatises and passed them on to their students. I am referring here to the authors of the many Danielic and Enochic materials and such compositions as the *Book of Noah,* all works in which heavenly secrets of the present and of the end of days are revealed to the hero. These books often involved heavenly ascents and other such journeys reminiscent of later Jewish mysticism. Yet their notions of immediate messianic fulfillment, shared as they are with the Qumran sect, must have greatly influenced both Christian messianism and the pressures for Jewish resistance against Rome that were in evidence in the two revolts of 66-73 and 132-135 C.E., both of which had messianic overtones.

The Scrolls and Early Christianity

Extremely important is the light the scrolls throw on the rise of Christianity. In the early years of Qumran studies there was indeed an attempt to use the scrolls as a source for discovering "Christian origins," a matter we have already explained. Yet now that we have progressed so far beyond this simplistic way of looking at the scrolls, what is their true value for the study of early Christianity?

There can be no question that in regard to many expressions, motifs, and concepts found in the New Testament the scrolls have shown that the background of these ideas is to be found in the sectarian Judaism of the Second Temple period. Further, the attempt to use rabbinic literature as the primary source for establishing and interpreting the background of Christian

---

47. L. H. Schiffman, "The *Temple Scroll* and the Nature of Its Law: The Status of the Question," in *The Community of the Renewed Covenant: The Notre Dame Symposium on the Dead Sea Scrolls,* ed. E. Ulrich and J. VanderKam, 37-55. CJAS 10 (Notre Dame: University of Notre Dame Press, 1994).

ideas turns out to be somewhat misguided in light of our current knowledge of the variegated character of Judaism in the Greco-Roman period. Such ideas as the dualism of light and darkness, the presentation of the figure of the Messiah as combining a variety of leadership roles known from earlier Hebrew sources, the immediate messianism — all these are ideas that we can trace in the scrolls.

Yet the quest for parallels and antecedents must remain secondary. The proper way to use the scrolls for understanding Christianity is to recognize them as documents illuminating the full spectrum of Jewish groups in the Hellenistic period in Judea. When we compensate for the sectarian emphasis of the collection, it turns out that the contribution to the prehistory of Christianity is even greater.[48]

Exaggerated reports have led the public to believe that the scrolls included New Testament manuscripts[49] and references to the life and death of Jesus or to a "pierced Messiah."[50] In fact, nothing could be further from the truth. The supposed New Testament fragments, claimed to derive from the gospel of Mark, are in actuality fragments of the Greek version of the book of *Enoch* found in Aramaic fragments at Qumran.[51] The "Pierced Messiah" text, in fact, describes not the killing of the Messiah but rather the killing of the Romans and their general at the hands of the messianic leader of the sect in the final eschatological battle.[52] Reference in one text to a "Son of God" is best taken not as an allusion to Jesus, since the text probably dates to the third or early second century B.C.E., but instead as indicating that for some Second Temple–period Jews, "Son of God" could indeed be a designation for the Messiah, a notion that helps to provide the background for incipient Christianity.[53]

It is now clear that Second Temple Judaism was a transitional period in which the sectarianism and apocalypticism of this era gradually gave way to

---

48. Cf. F. García Martínez, "Significado de los Manuscritos de Qumran para el Conocimiento de Jesucristo y del Cristianismo," *Communio* 22 (1989) 338-42.

49. C. P. Thiede, *The Earliest Gospel Manuscripts? The Qumran Papyrus 7Q5 and Its Significance for New Testament Studies* (Exeter: Paternoster, 1992).

50. Schiffman, *Reclaiming the Dead Sea Scrolls*, 344-47.

51. E. Muro, "The Greek Fragments of Enoch from Qumran Cave 7 (7Q4, 7Q8, & 7Q12= 7QEn gr= Enoch 103: 3-4, 7-8)," *RevQ* 70 (1998) 307-12.

52. S. J. Pfann, P. S. Alexander et al., *Qumran Cave 4.XXVI: Cryptic Texts and Miscellanea, Part 1*. DJD 36 (Oxford: Clarendon, 2000) 228-46; M. G. Abegg, "Messianic Hope in 4Q285: A Reassessment," *JBL* 113 (1994) 81-91; G. Vermes, "The Oxford Forum for Qumran Research: Seminar on the Rule of War from Cave 4 (4Q285)," *JJS* 43 (1992) 85-90; "The 'Pierced Messiah' Text — An Interpretation Evaporates," *BAR* 18/4 (1992) 80-82.

53. Schiffman, *Reclaiming the Dead Sea Scrolls*, 341-44.

the development of rabbinic Judaism, while at the same time early Christianity was coming to the fore. Indeed, it is now clear that the Second Temple period was one of a sorting-out process.

Up until the Maccabean revolt (168-164 B.C.E.), the Jewish communities in Palestine and in the Diaspora faced the issue of the extent to which they would partake of the Hellenistic culture around them. This issue led to a fierce debate and was only resolved as a result of the successful revolt. The outcome was the overwhelming rejection of extreme Hellenism in Palestinian Judaism. Yet the challenge of Hellenism brought about the splitting of the Jewish community into various groups, each seeking to dominate the religious scene. The writings of some of these groups and information about others, as we have noted, are preserved in the Dead Sea Scrolls.

The competing approaches vied with one another, indeed, debated one another, throughout the Hasmonean period. This debate was to be resolved only in the Roman period. Apocalyptic messianic tendencies, now much better understood from the sectarian texts of the Qumran group and from some of the other writings preserved in the caves of Qumran, continued in some circles to become more and more pronounced and led eventually to the Jewish revolts against Rome in 66-73 C.E. and 132-135 C.E. Some of these very same trends led a small group of Jews to conclude that their leader, Jesus of Nazareth, was indeed the "Son of God," a term known from an Aramaic apocalypse preserved at Qumran.[54]

It emerges, therefore, that rabbinic Judaism based itself on Pharisaism in the main, with the inclusion of certain aspects of the traditions of the sectarian and apocalyptic groups, while Christianity primarily inherited the immediate apocalypticism of these groups, certain dualistic tendencies, and a wide variety of motifs. In other words, Christianity is to a great extent the continuation of trends within Second Temple Judaism that were rejected by the emerging Pharisaic-rabbinic mainstream.

The History of the Biblical Text

Among the most significant of the Qumran scrolls are certainly the biblical manuscripts. These documents will shed important new light on the history of the biblical text in Second Temple times.

This last statement is itself much more important than meets the eye. In

---

54. G. J. Brooke et al., eds., *Qumran Cave 4.XVII: Parabiblical Texts, Part 3*. DJD 22 (Oxford: Clarendon, 1996) 165-84.

the early years of Qumran studies, it was thought that the biblical texts from Qumran would somehow illuminate the "original" text that emerged from ancient Israel. This entire notion has been proven wrong. It is now clear that the biblical text has a history of transmission, and that major parts of this history, which indeed testify to the place of Scripture in the Judaism of the post-biblical period, are to be understood from the scrolls. Indeed, we now know that many textual variants result not only from transmission, but from interpretation and linguistic updating, phenomena that, before the discovery of the scrolls, could not have been understood.[55]

Very early in the study of the biblical manuscripts, a theory was put forward, first by W. F. Albright[56] and then more fully by F. M. Cross,[57] that spoke of three text types. These were the Hebrew texts that stood behind the Masoretic Text (the traditional Jewish Hebrew text adopted by rabbinic Judaism as authoritative), the Samaritan (before the introduction of Samaritan polemical changes), and the Hebrew that stood behind the Greek translation in the Septuagint Bibles. These three textual families were shown to coexist at Qumran, and it was widely assumed that they were represented in roughly equivalent numbers of texts, although the theory was, in fact, based on consideration of a limited sampling.

Recent studies require a modification of this approach. It is now clear that the proportions of the three text types are grossly unequal. Proto-Septuagintal and proto-Samaritan texts are available only in small numbers. In fact, most of the biblical manuscripts at Qumran indicate that the proto-Masoretic text type was predominant. Thus, the process of standardization, whereby this text became authoritative in rabbinic Judaism, may have taken place much earlier than was presumed, so that by the Hasmonean period the proto-Masoretic was in ascendance. More likely, it may simply be that this text type was the more ancient and, hence, most common. It would therefore emerge that the process of standardization was in reality one of eliminating variant texts. This, indeed, is the picture that is presented by rabbinic literature.

A second modification is emerging from the study of this material. Most biblical texts at Qumran represent to some extent mixtures of the various text types. They share readings found in one or another text and cannot

---

55. See S. Talmon, *The World of Qumran from Within* (Jerusalem: Magnes and Leiden: Brill, 1989) 71-141.

56. "New Light on Early Recensions of the Hebrew Bible," *BASOR* 140 (1955) 27-33.

57. "The Contribution of the Qumran Discoveries to the Study of the Biblical Text," *IEJ* 16 (1966) 81-95; "The Evolution of a Theory of Local Texts," in *Qumran and the History of the Biblical Text*, ed. Cross and S. Talmon, 306-20 (Cambridge, MA: Harvard University Press, 1975); *The Ancient Library of Qumran*, 121-42.

be understood as purely representing one family.[58] This indicates that the notion of text types is somewhat a retrojection of the textual witnesses that were known to us before the Qumran finds.[59] Had we not had the Septuagint and the Samaritan Bibles, we never would have concluded from the Qumran material that three families existed. Rather, a more accurate picture would call for trends that seem to be evident in varying degrees in different texts. This would explain much better the predominance of mixed texts of the Hebrew Bible.

The texts in the Qumran corpus reveal many methods of biblical interpretation that were practiced by the Qumran sect as well as by other contemporary Jewish groups. In the scrolls collection, we find the earliest examples of Bible translation, including fragments of the Greek Septuagint and Aramaic Targum. These translations share certain formal elements and literary techniques. The scrolls also reveal early attempts to explain the plain sense of Scripture (termed *peshaṭ* by the later rabbis). We also find books like the *Genesis Apocryphon* and *Jubilees*, that retell, or rather, reinterpret, the biblical stories and that reflect the specific hermeneutics of each author.

The sect inherited a method of legal interpretation we find represented in the *Temple Scroll* and underpinning some of the laws in the *Halakhic Letter*. We also see aspects of such an interpretive approach in the harmonizing tendencies found in the expanded Torah scrolls known as *Rewritten Pentateuch*. This interpretive technique was most probably based on that of the Sadducees, as far as can be gathered from Josephus's short description and later rabbinic evidence. In addition, the sect had its own method of halakhic exegesis that gave rise to much of its legal teachings. Alongside these other methods was a form of contemporizing biblical interpretation called *pesher* that interpreted prophetic texts as referring to present events and the history of the sect itself.[60]

We have already shared something of the sensational effects that the publication of so many texts has had on the study of the history of Judaism in

---

58. See E. Tov, "A Modern Textual Outlook Based on the Qumran Scrolls," *HUCA* 53 (1982) 11-27; "Hebrew Biblical Manuscripts from the Judaean Desert: Their Contribution to Textual Criticism," *JJS* (1988) 5-37; "Groups of Biblical Texts Found at Qumran," in *Time to Prepare the Way in the Wilderness: Papers on the Qumran Scrolls by Fellows of the Institute for Advanced Studies of the Hebrew University, Jerusalem, 1989-1990*, ed. D. Dimant and L. H. Schiffman, 85-102. STDJ 16 (Leiden: Brill, 1995).

59. "Textual witnesses" is a term scholars use to designate the Masoretic Hebrew, Samaritan, and Septuagint Greek versions that are seen as evidence for the state of the biblical text in Late Antiquity.

60. Schiffman, *Reclaiming the Dead Sea Scrolls*, 211-41.

general, and Qumran studies in particular. The new documents have changed the focus of the entire field, continuing a process already started by the discovery and publication of the *Temple Scroll* by Yigael Yadin.

Yet much more is still to come. We have already alluded to changes in scholarly views resulting from the full publication of the biblical material that is now available in its entirety. Some idea of the scope of these manuscripts can be gleaned from the fact that copies or fragments of more than 250 biblical manuscripts have been preserved at Qumran.[61]

Extremely important are a series of biblical "paraphrases." These expanded pentateuchal texts have some five long additions that include material that Yadin thought was from fragments of the *Temple Scroll* and that Strugnell saw as a source for the *Temple Scroll*. These "parabiblical" texts are composed of scriptural texts with exegetical expansions and harmonizations with parallel passages.[62] In addition, the *Genesis Commentary* has provided interesting information on sectarian biblical interpretation and has given rise to a long series of articles on its exegetical character.[63]

A number of halakhic texts (manuscripts dealing with Jewish law) are now available to scholars. These include the texts of the *Zadokite Fragments* (also known as the *Damascus Document*) from Cave 4 edited by J. M. Baumgarten (eight manuscripts),[64] that include about twice as much as the text previously known from the Cairo Genizah manuscripts published by Schechter. In addition, other "halakhic" texts include 4QHalakhah and 4QTohorot, laws related to purity (six manuscripts).[65] Extremely important is 4Q625 (designated SD or *Miscellaneous Rules*), which represents a combination of material from the *Manual of Discipline* and the *Zadokite Fragments*. This material demonstrates how both of these documents served as codes governing the life of the sect. The publication of the ten manuscripts of the *Manual of Discipline*,[66]

---

61. The only book so far not identified is the book of Esther.

62. E. Tov and S. White, "Reworked Pentateuch," in *Qumran Cave 4.VIII: Parabiblical Texts, Part I*, ed. H. Attridge et al., 187-351. DJD 13 (Oxford: Clarendon, 1994).

63. M. J. Bernstein, "4Q252: From Re-Written Bible to Biblical Commentary," *JJS* 45 (1994) 1-27; "4Q252: Method and Context, Genre and Sources," *JQR* 85 (1994-95) 61-79; G. J. Brooke, "The Thematic Content of 4Q252," *JQR* 85 (1994-95) 33-59; "The Genre of 4Q252: From Poetry to Pesher," *DSD* 1 (1994) 160-79; "4Q252 as Early Jewish Commentary," *RevQ* 17 (1996) 385-401.

64. Baumgarten, DJD 18.

65. E. Larson, M. R. Lehmann, and L. H. Schiffman, "Halakhot: 4QHalakha A," in *Qumran Cave 4.XXV: Halakhic Texts*, ed. J. M. Baumgarten et al., 25-51. DJD 35 (Oxford: Clarendon, 1999); J. M. Baumgarten, "Halakhot: 4QHalakha B," DJD 35:53-56; "Tohorot," DJD 35:79-122.

66. P. Alexander and G. Vermes, "4QSerekh ha-Yaḥad," in *Qumran Cave 4.XIX: Serekh*

for which Milik previously published a list of textual variants, has been most helpful in clarifying the textual history of this document.[67]

Numerous Aramaic texts have come to light, and most of these are fully published. These texts have already contributed much to the study of early Jewish Aramaic. The manuscripts of the book of *Jubilees* and *Pseudo-Jubilees* have aided greatly in the efforts to recover the Hebrew text of this important book.[68] Other apocryphal texts include Tobit in Aramaic and in Hebrew,[69] the *Aramaic Levi Document*,[70] *Testament of Naphtali*,[71] and *Testament of Qahat*.[72]

The calendar of the sectarians,[73] based on solar years and solar months, differed from that of Pharisaic-rabbinic Judaism, which followed lunar months and lunar years synchronized approximately every three years with the solar cycle. The sectarian calendar, also followed in *Jubilees* and *Enoch*, was prefixed to the text of *Miqṣat Maʿaśe ha-Torah*. This calendar has been clarified significantly with the publication of the *Mishmarot (Priestly Courses)*, dealing with the division of the year according to the priestly families who would serve in the temple.[74]

The Qumran *Hodayot (Thanksgiving) Scroll*, originally pieced together and edited by E. L. Sukenik (the father of Yigael Yadin),[75] has now been completely reordered as a result of the careful, reconstructive research of Hartmut Stegemann and Émile Puech.[76] This research, as well as the publication of 4QHodayot,[77] will revolutionize our view of this significant text from Cave 1 that many scholars have attributed to the Teacher of Righteousness.

---

ha-Yaḥad and Two Related Texts, ed. Alexander and G. Vermes, 1-206. DJD 26 (Oxford: Clarendon, 1998).

67. S. Metso, *The Textual Development of the Qumran Community Rule*. STDJ 21 (Leiden: Brill, 1997).

68. J. VanderKam and J. T. Milik, "Jubilees," in Attridge et al., DJD 13:1-185.

69. J. Fitzmyer, "Tobit," in M. Broshi et al., *Qumran Cave 4.XIV: Parabiblical Texts, Part 2*. DJD 19 (Oxford: Clarendon, 1995) 1-76.

70. M. E. Stone and J. C. Greenfield in Brooke et al., DJD 22:1-72.

71. M. E. Stone, "Testament of Naphtali," in Brooke et al., DJD 22:73-82.

72. É. Puech, *Qumrân Grotte 4.XXII: Textes araméens, première partie, 4Q529-549*, 257-82. DJD 31 (Oxford: Clarendon, 2001).

73. S. Talmon, J. Ben-Dov, U. Glessmer, *Qumran Cave 4.XVI: Calendrical Texts*. DJD 21 (Oxford: Clarendon, 2001).

74. According to the Qumran *Mishmarot* texts, there were twenty-six courses to equal half of a solar year. Each group of priests would serve twice a year for a one-week period.

75. Sukenik, *'Oṣar ha-Megillot ha-Genuzot*, pls. 35-58.

76. See E. Schuller, "Hodayot," in *Qumran Cave 4.XX: Poetical and Liturgical Texts, Part 2*, ed. E. G. Chazon et al., 70-71. DJD 29 (Oxford: Clarendon, 1999).

77. Schuller, DJD 29:69-232.

A large number of biblical pseudepigrapha are in the Qumran collection, including texts concerning Joshua,[78] Ezekiel,[79] and Jeremiah.[80] The Pseudo-Daniel material has direct bearing on the dating and history of the book of Daniel and the history of Jewish apocalypticism.[81] The best known of these texts is the *Prayer of Nabonidus*.[82] The *Visions of Amram*,[83] extant in seven manuscripts, is also of great interest.

The sapiential texts of Qumran are evidence of an entire corpus that continued the biblical wisdom tradition into Second Temple times.[84] These manuscripts show us a glimpse of the daily life of the times as well as the tribulations and, along with the related Mysteries texts,[85] provide evidence of the rich religious teachings of the time.

This list is nowhere near exhaustive. However, it serves to give us a relative idea of the number of works and the scope of the material beginning to have a major impact on the study of ancient Judaism. Students of Second Temple Judaism and its relevance to talmudic Judaism and early Christianity have a veritable feast awaiting them now that the full corpus is available in excellent editions published in the last few years.

Other material from the Judean Desert, specifically Masada and the Bar Kokhba caves, is of extreme importance. These texts, which have recently appeared in print, will help us to reconstruct aspects of the political, social, and economic history of the land of Israel and the Jewish people in the first and early second centuries C.E. They cast important light on the history of the Hebrew and Aramaic languages and the state of the biblical text. Further, the Greek and Nabatean Aramaic texts illuminate the legal usages and formularies of these languages as well.

Finally, of the Samaria papyri from Wadi Daliyeh found in 1962, half the texts have appeared of a total of some thirty,[86] and it is hoped that the re-

---

78. C. Newsom, "Apocryphon of Joshua," in Brooke et al., DJD 22:237-62.

79. M. Smith, "Pseudo-Ezekiel," in Broshi et al., DJD 19:153-93; D. Dimant, "Pseudo-Ezekiel," in *Qumran Cave 4.XXI: Parabiblical Texts, Part 4: Pseudo-prophetic Texts*, 7-88. DJD 30 (Oxford: Clarendon, 2001).

80. M. Smith, "Apocryphon of Jeremiah," in Broshi et al., DJD 19:137-52; D. Dimant, "Apocryphon of Jeremiah," DJD 30:91-260.

81. J. Collins and P. Flint, "Pseudo-Daniel," in Brooke et al., DJD 22:95-184.

82. J. Collins, "Prayer of Nabonidus," in Brooke et al., DJD 22:83-93.

83. Puech, DJD 31:283-405.

84. J. Strugnell, D. J. Harrington, and T. Elgvin, *Qumran Cave 4.XXIV: Sapiential Texts, Part 2*. DJD 34 (Oxford: Clarendon, 1999).

85. L. H. Schiffman, "Mysteries," in *Qumran Cave 4.XV: Sapiential Texts, Part 1*, ed. T. Elgvin et al., 31-123. DJD 20 (Oxford: Clarendon, 1997).

86. See D. M. Gropp in *Wadi Daliyeh II: The Samaria Papyri from Wadi Daliyeh*, ed. Gropp

mainder, fragmentary as it is, will be speedily published. The significance of this material for the reconstruction of Jewish and Samaritan history in the Persian period is immeasurable, since these documents fit precisely into the dark age between the accounts of the Hebrew Bible and the conquest of the Near East by Alexander the Great.[87]

Now that the publication of all these documents is complete, scholars have an entirely new set of sources for the history of the Jews and Judaism in the Persian, Hellenistic, and Roman periods. Together with the new advances in method and research that we have described here, the scrolls from the Judean Desert have brought to life a period of immense significance for the history of the Western world.

The Bottom Line

Qumran studies have come a long way since the days in the early 1950s when seven scrolls were under discussion. However, because of the many difficulties that have beset the field, some of which are described above, the impact of this material has remained confined to a small circle of scholars. The true battle of the scrolls is yet to be fought. This is the battle to make the results of scientific scholarship on the Dead Sea Scrolls, based on the availability of the entire corpus, part and parcel of the history of Western Civilization. There can be no question that when the dust clears and the Qumran discoveries have made their mark we shall not only have a better perception of the history of Judaism and Christianity in Late Antiquity, but we shall also have a firm scientific basis on which to hope for greater understanding of our common origins.

---

et al.; M. Bernstein et al., with J. VanderKam and M. Brady, *Qumran Cave 4.XXVIII: Miscellanea, Part 2*, 3-116. DJD 28 (Oxford: Clarendon, 2001).

87. F. M. Cross, "The Early History of the Qumran Community," in *New Directions in Biblical Archaeology*, ed. D. N. Freedman and J. C. Greenfield, 70-89 (Garden City: Doubleday, 1971).

CHAPTER 2

Literary Genres and Languages of the Judean Scrolls

Rather difficult challenges face scholars in using the evidence from the various Judean Desert texts for the reconstruction of the history of Judaism in the Second Temple period. All the fragmentary pieces of evidence — whether Jewish or not, textual or archaeological, Hebrew, Aramaic, Greek, or Latin — are pieces of a giant jigsaw puzzle. Here we will concentrate on a small part of this problem, the integration of the various corpora of Judean Desert manuscripts that provide us with much information about the literary genres and compositions of the period. For the most part, these collections have usually been dealt with as if they have no relationship to one another. It will be demonstrated that an integrative approach presents opportunities for clarifying various important aspects of the trends and evolution in the history of Judaism in the Persian and Greco-Roman periods. In addition, we can begin to formulate some theories about the state of Hebrew language and literature during Second Temple times.

The Corpus

A steady stream of documents has been discovered in the Judean Desert from the legendary entrance of the Bedouin boy into Qumran Cave 1 in 1947 up through Operation Scroll conducted by the Israel Antiquities Authority on the eve of the Israeli withdrawal from Jericho in 1994. These finds have provided an altogether new corpus of documents for research into Hebrew language and literature and other languages used by Jews. In our lifetimes, this corpus has revolutionized our understanding of the linguistic situation in the land of Israel in the Hasmonean, Herodian, and Roman periods[1] and has given us a totally new sense of the scope and variety of the compositions produced in the Jewish community during this period.[2] We shall attempt here to survey the new materials and their relevance, paying special attention to the wider historical value of these new linguistic and literary discoveries and to their significance as well for the history of Judaism. While the term "Dead Sea Scrolls" is usually used to describe the Qumran scrolls exclusively, we will deal here also with the finds from Masada and the Bar Kokhba caves. These three collections together provide a sense of the period as a whole and bridge the linguistic and literary gap that stretches from the Bible to the Mishnah.

The Qumran Texts

The corpus of documents that emerged from the Qumran caves is extensive and varied. Archaeological investigation of the buildings and caves of Qumran[3] and palaeographical examination[4] as well as carbon 14 tests[5] have established that the Qumran manuscripts were copied in a few cases in the third century B.C.E., for the most part in the second and first centuries B.C.E., and in a few cases in the first century C.E. The composition of the texts dates anywhere from the date of the composition of the Torah in Israel's early history to about the turn of the era when the last of the Qumran texts were composed. The documents were gathered at Qumran, preponderantly in Cave 4, sometime after 134 B.C.E., when the sect established a center at Qumran, and before 68 C.E., when the Romans destroyed Qumran during the Great Revolt of 66-73 C.E.[6]

---

1. On the history of Judaism in these periods, see L. H. Schiffman, *From Text to Tradition: A History of Second Temple and Rabbinic Judaism* (Hoboken: Ktav, 1991) 60-176.

2. D. Dimant, "The Qumran Manuscripts: Contents and Significance," in *Time to Prepare the Way in the Wilderness: Papers on the Qumran Scrolls by Fellows of the Institute for Advanced Studies of the Hebrew University, Jerusalem, 1989-90*, ed. Dimant and L. H. Schiffman, 23-58. STDJ 16 (Leiden: Brill, 1995).

3. R. de Vaux, *Archaeology and the Dead Sea Scrolls*. Schweich Lectures 1959 (London: Oxford University Press, 1973) 1-48, 95-102; J. Magness, *The Archaeology of Qumran and the Dead Sea Scrolls*. SDSSRL (Grand Rapids: Wm. B. Eerdmans, 2002).

4. F. M. Cross, "The Development of the Jewish Scripts," in *The Bible and the Ancient Near East: Essays in Honor of W. F. Albright*, ed. G. E. Wright (Garden City: Doubleday, 1961) 170-264.

5. G. Bonani et al., "Radiocarbon Dating of the Dead Sea Scrolls," ʿ*Atiqot* 20 (1991) 27-32; A. J. T. Jull et al., "Radiocarbon Dating of Scrolls and Linen Fragments from the Judean Desert," ʿ*Atiqot* 28 (1996) 85-61.

6. De Vaux, *Archaeology and the Dead Sea Scrolls*, 106-9.

Most of the texts are in Hebrew, with some 20 percent in Aramaic, and a few in Greek. This picture already indicates that Hellenism affected the community who collected and used these manuscripts in only a limited way, but that it used both Hebrew and Aramaic as was common among Jews in the land of Israel at this time.

Cave 4 shows clear evidence that it served as a library for those who inhabited the Qumran buildings. It is an artificially hewn-out cave with holes in its walls that held wooden supports for shelves in antiquity. This cave must have been used regularly for storage of the documents that the members of the Qumran sect utilized. In addition, its location is just a few minutes' walk from the building complex.

Some of the other caves, however, give an entirely different impression. Caves such as 1 and 11 look like refuges into which scrolls might have been thrown as the Romans were coming to destroy Qumran. Yet a profile of the contents of those caves is almost identical to that of Cave 4.[7] Curiously, however, Cave 7 contained only Greek manuscripts, a phenomenon that has no satisfactory explanation. Copies of some manuscripts are found in several caves, indicating that the various caves were all part of what had been one unified library in antiquity.

Throughout this study we will distinguish between texts brought to the Qumran community and those that were composed by its members.[8] Essentially, there are three classes of texts in this corpus. Each of these constitutes roughly one-third of the collection, if we exclude unidentified materials.

The first are biblical texts, covering some part of every book except Esther, which is probably missing only by chance.[9] Many of these manuscripts were certainly copied outside the domain of the sect.

Second are apocryphal compositions and other texts, part of the literary heritage of those who formed the sect or works that were composed by similar groups. These texts originated outside the sectarian center and were brought there, although some of the manuscripts may have been copied there.

The third group of texts we may describe as sectarian. These manuscripts outline the teachings and way of life of a specific group of Jews, some of whom apparently lived at the sectarian center excavated at Qumran. They in-

---

7. Dimant, "Qumran Manuscripts," 30-32.

8. E. Tov, "The Orthography and Language of the Hebrew Scrolls Found at Qumran and the Origin of These Scrolls," *Textus* 13 (1986) 32-57; Dimant, "Qumran Manuscripts," 27-30.

9. Cf. S. Talmon, "Was the Book of Esther Known at Qumran?" *DSD* 2 (1995) 249-67; S. White Crawford, "Has *Esther* Been Found at Qumran? 4QProto-Esther and the *Esther* Corpus," *RevQ* 17 (Hommage à Józef T. Milik; 1996) 307-25.

clude rules for entry into the sect, legal codes, and liturgical compositions. We cannot be sure that all of them, or even most of them, were copied at Qumran.

Although the threefold division of the materials had been recognized early on, until the opening up of the entire corpus we did not truly appreciate the extent to which the collection contained general Jewish literature of the period, not specific to the Dead Sea sect. This appreciation has helped greatly to provide a more accurate sense of the meaning of these documents for the general history of Judaism.

The biblical manuscripts, as mentioned, include parts of the entire corpus of Scripture, except for Esther. The Qumran biblical texts represent a number of different text types.[10] A large number resemble the later, Masoretic (received) biblical text (MT), carefully preserved by the Jewish community throughout the ages. A fair number represent biblical texts written in a specific dialect of Hebrew used by the Qumran sect, and these must have been used within the community. A few texts represent the Hebrew text type from which the Greek translation of the Bible (Septuagint) was made, and a few represent forerunners of the Samaritan text of the Bible.

The nonbiblical documents of the Qumran community are a substantial part of the collection. These constitute some 191 manuscripts and about 115 works. (Some works are represented in multiple manuscripts.) These works are distinguished by a number of characteristics: They generally reflect the practices and organization of the Qumran community, the history of the community and its own self-image, the theological views of the community, and the specific biblical interpretations of the community. Many of these ideas do have parallels outside this community. However, it is the agglomeration of these aspects in a text as well as the specific linguistic character of Qumran sectarian compositions that makes clear that these are distinctively Dead Sea sectarian documents.[11]

As already mentioned, there are many texts that reflect the general literature of the period. These texts have a similar profile to those found in the Masada excavations and certainly cannot be identified with the Qumran sect.[12] Rather, it is simply that Qumran and Masada present samples of the literature that was shared by most Jews in the Second Temple period. These are apocryphal and pseudepigraphal documents, some of which were known be-

---

10. E. Tov, "Groups of Biblical Texts Found at Qumran," in Dimant and Schiffman, *Time to Prepare the Way in the Wilderness*, 85-102.

11. Dimant, "The Qumran Manuscripts," 27-30.

12. Yigael Yadin, however, was of the opinion that these texts had been brought to Masada by those who fled Qumran after its destruction in 68 C.E. See Y. Yadin, *Masada: Herod's Fortress and the Zealots' Last Stand* (New York: Random House, 1966) 172-74.

fore the discovery of the scrolls in other languages and are now known in the original Hebrew or Aramaic.[13] This class of texts has great significance for us in that we seek not only to describe the language and literature of the Qumran sect, but also to use their writings and the writings they collected as a means of uncovering information about a variety of Jewish groups of this period.

The Masada Texts

A much smaller collection of texts was preserved at Masada, the last fortress to fall in the Great Revolt of the Jews against the Romans in 66-73 C.E. According to the dramatic account of Josephus,[14] which, we should mention, is doubted by many historians,[15] those who inhabited this fortress in its last stages of occupation were Sicarii.[16] These members of one of the Jewish revolutionary groups had first attacked fellow Jews who cooperated with the Romans. Ultimately they turned their efforts to full-scale military operations against the powers of Roman occupation. Although Masada had been previously in use in the Hasmonean and Herodian periods,[17] the manuscripts found at the site were clearly brought there by the rebels.

In contrast to the vast majority of Qumran documents, the Masada materials were found during controlled archaeological excavations led by Yigael Yadin between 1963 and 1965. They date for the most part to the first half of the first century C.E., and, of course, cannot be dated after 73 C.E. At Masada one collection of manuscripts was discovered in a room in the casemate defense wall, including part of the biblical book of Psalms. A few other fragmentary "apocryphal"-type items were found in the same place as well as part of the book of Leviticus.[18] These biblical texts were of the Masoretic variety, i.e., es-

---

13. Cf. L. H. Schiffman, *Reclaiming the Dead Sea Scrolls: The History of Judaism, the Background of Christianity, the Lost Library of Qumran* (Philadelphia: Jewish Publication Society, 1994; repr. ABRL [New York: Doubleday, 1995]) 181-210.

14. *J.W.* 7.252-406.

15. A sense of the current debate regarding Masada can be gleaned from a series of articles by N. Ben-Yehuda, J. Zias, and Z. Meshel, appearing under the title "Questioning Masada," *BAR* 24/6 (1998) 30-53, 64-68.

16. Cf. M. Stern, "Zealots," in *Encyclopaedia Judaica Yearbook* (Jerusalem: Keter, 1973) 135-40; D. M. Rhoads, *Israel in Revolution 6-74 CE: A Political History Based on the Writings of Josephus* (Philadelphia: Fortress, 1976) 78-80.

17. E. Netzer, in *Masada III: The Yigael Yadin Excavations 1963-1965: Final Reports, the Buildings, Stratigraphy and Architecture* (Jerusalem: Israel Exploration Society, Hebrew University, 1991) 615-55.

18. S. Talmon, in *Masada VI: Yigael Yadin Excavations 1963-1965: Final Reports*, ed. Tal-

sentially the same as our biblical texts except for some minor textual variations. An extremely important find from that same cache of scrolls was a manuscript of the *Songs of the Sabbath Sacrifice*,[19] a text also found at Qumran. The presence of similar material at Qumran and Masada indicates that these texts were part of the common literature of late Second Temple Judaism.

A second casemate chamber[20] yielded a Psalms scroll including part of Psalm 150 and also the scroll containing the end of the apocryphal book of Ben Sira in its original Hebrew.[21] Previously, only the Greek translation done by the author's grandson and some medieval fragments from the Cairo Genizah were known. Since the discovery at Masada, a large part of the original text has been recovered.[22]

In one of the wall towers, one small fragment was found from a work closely related to *Jubilees*, similar to the *Pseudo-Jubilees* texts of Qumran.[23] Fragments of a Leviticus scroll were also located near the northern palace villa.

In the outer wall of Masada, the rebels had adapted a building for use as a synagogue. It contained two scroll fragments. One was part of Ezekiel and the other of Deuteronomy.[24] These two scrolls are virtually identical to the traditional text used by Jews up to today, except that in Ezekiel there are some variants.

Bar Kokhba Texts

This last corpus of texts emerged from the caves in which Jews took refuge during the Bar Kokhba revolt of 132-135 C.E. and where most met their deaths at the hands of the Romans. This group of texts is actually mislabeled. Most of

---

mon, with C. Newsom and Y. Yadin, 98-137 (Jerusalem: Israel Exploration Society, Hebrew University, 1999).

19. C. Newsom and Y. Yadin, in Talmon, *Masada VI,* 120-32. Cf. C. Newsom, "4QShirot 'Olat Hashabbat," in *Qumran Cave 4.VI: Poetical and Liturgical Texts, Part 1,* ed. E. Eshel et al., 239-52 and pl. XIX. DJD 11 (Oxford: Clarendon, 1998).

20. Yadin, in Talmon, *Masada VI,* 174-79.

21. Yadin, in Talmon, *Masada VI,* 151-252; originally published as Y. Yadin, *The Ben Sira Scroll from Masada* (Jerusalem: Israel Exploration Society and Shrine of the Book, 1965).

22. All the known Hebrew fragments, ancient and medieval, are gathered together in *The Book of Ben Sira: Text, Concordance and an Analysis of the Vocabulary* (Jerusalem: Academy of the Hebrew Language and Shrine of the Book, 1973) 3-67.

23. J. C. VanderKam, "4QJubilees[a-c]" and "Text with a Citation of Jubilees (4Q228)," in *Qumran Cave 4.VIII: Parabiblical Texts, Part I,* ed. H. Attridge et al., 141-85. DJD 13 (Oxford: Clarendon, 1994).

24. Yadin, in Talmon, *Masada VI,* 187-89.

these texts have nothing at all to do with the messianic rebel leader Simeon bar Kokhba, although a few are actual military dispatches from him. The bulk of this collection is made up of legal documents, in Greek, Aramaic, and Hebrew.

These documents were discovered at a number of sites that are located along the western shore of the Dead Sea. We will treat here only the major collections, those of Wadi Murabbaʿat and Naḥal Ḥever, and the so-called Naḥal Ṣeʾelim texts.

The first to be discovered were from the caves at Wadi Murabbaʿat in 1951. By the time the site was excavated, Bedouin had already removed most of the manuscripts; nevertheless, archaeologists recovered important fragments as well. The Murabbaʿat documents, fully published already in 1960,[25] included three biblical fragments, as well as a *tefillin* capsule and *mezuzah*, and documentary texts, many in Aramaic. Exceedingly important is the Hebrew scroll of the *Twelve Prophets,* a manuscript virtually identical with the MT. Also among the Hebrew materials were an unknown literary text, lists of names, abecedaries, letters, military dispatches from Bar Kosiba (the real name of Bar Kokhba), and contracts of various kinds.

The second of these collections stems from Naḥal Ḥever. Israeli excavators discovered these materials *in situ* in 1960-61, again under Yadin. This area yielded what are actually three collections of documents. One is the personal archives of the colorful lady Babatha consisting of Aramaic, Greek, and Nabatean legal documents.[26] A second group of texts are Hebrew contracts written at Ein Gedi.[27] Finally, this trove includes some personal letters from Bar Kosiba,[28] mainly to his agents at Ein Gedi, in Hebrew and Aramaic. Other caves in the area also yielded the Greek *Twelve Prophets Scroll*[29] and other Greek texts.

A third collection is generally designated as Naḥal Ṣeʾelim. Yet these texts, which the Bedouin offered for sale in Jordan and claimed to have come from Naḥal Ṣeʾelim, have been proven to have been discovered at Naḥal

---

25. P. Benoit, J. T. Milik, and R. de Vaux, *Les Grottes de Murabbaʿat.* DJD 2 (Oxford: Clarendon, 1960).

26. Y. Yadin, *Bar Kokhba: The Rediscovery of the Legendary Hero of the Second Jewish Revolt against Rome* (New York: Random House, 1971) 222-53. This material is now published in its entirety in Yadin et al., *The Documents from the Bar Kokhba Period in the Cave of Letters: Hebrew, Aramaic, and Nabatean-Aramaic Papyri.* 2 vols. (Jerusalem: Israel Exploration Society, Institute of Archaeology, Hebrew University, Shrine of the Book, Israel Museum, 2002).

27. Yadin, *Bar Kokhba,* 172-83.

28. Yadin, *Bar Kokhba,* 124-39.

29. E. Tov, *The Greek Minor Prophets Scroll from Naḥal Ḥever (8ḤevXIIgr) (The Seiyâl Collection I).* DJD 8 (Oxford: Clarendon, 1990).

Hever, across what was then the border with Israel. These materials include numerous documents in Hebrew, Aramaic, and Greek. A number of Hebrew letters to and from Bar Kosiba have been found.[30] In addition, it has been shown that some texts alleged to be from Qumran Cave 4 are, in fact, documents from Naḥal Ḥever.[31] Furthermore, texts have been published from several sites in the Judean Desert besides Qumran: Ketef Jericho, Naḥal Sdeir, Naḥal Ḥever/Seiyal, Naḥal Mishmar, and Naḥal Ṣe'elim.[32]

The Linguistic Situation

The discovery of such a large corpus of materials — Hebrew, Greek, and Aramaic — certainly has stimulated discussion about the linguistic situation in the land of Israel in Late Antiquity.[33] Previous to the discovery of the scrolls, to a great extent this discussion had proceeded on the agenda set by New Testament studies that sought to establish the original spoken language of Jesus and the language in which early Christian traditions were initially passed down. Jewish scholars dealing with this field were for their part influenced by nationalistic criteria, especially evident in the works of those writing during the revival of Hebrew. Much of this discussion is rendered meaningless by the collection of Judean Desert texts that allows us to sketch a much more accurate picture.

Earlier scholars had established that the spread of Aramaic throughout the Near East was greatly accelerated by the fall of the Neo-Babylonian Empire and the subsequent rise of the Achaemenid Persian Empire. The Achaemenid chancellery used the Aramaic language as a lingua franca to tie the disparate and far-flung empire together.[34] Then, it is maintained, the result of this development was the gradual replacement of Hebrew by Aramaic in the land of Israel, a process that happened first in the northern part of the

---

30. H. M. Cotton and A. Yardeni, *Aramaic, Hebrew and Greek Documentary Texts from Naḥal Ḥever and Other Sites: With an Appendix Containing Alleged Qumran Texts (The Seiyâl Collection II)*. DJD 27 (Oxford: Clarendon, 1997). The Hebrew letter is found on p. 104. Also, Yadin et al., *Documents from the Bar Kokhba Period*, 279-86, 293-99, 333-40.

31. Cotton and Yardeni, DJD 27:283-4. The texts are published in DJD 27:285-317.

32. J. Charlesworth et al., *Miscellaneous Texts from the Judaean Desert*. DJD 38 (Oxford: Clarendon, 2000).

33. Cf. J. C. Greenfield, "The Languages of Palestine, 200 BCE-200 CE," in *Jewish Languages: Theme and Variations*, ed. H. H. Paper, 143-54 (Cambridge, MA: Association for Jewish Studies, 1978); C. Rabin, "Hebrew and Aramaic in the First Century," in *The Jewish People in the First Century*, ed. S. Safrai and M. Stern, 2:1007-39. CRINT 1 (Philadelphia: Fortress, 1976); G. Mussies, "Greek in Palestine and the Diaspora," in Safrai and Stern, 2:1040-64.

34. E. Y. Kutscher, "Aramaic," *EncJud* 3:266.

country and later in the southern part. It is assumed that the native language of Josephus and of Jesus and his disciples was Aramaic and, therefore, that Hebrew had gone out of use. Both Hebrew and Aramaic were understood to be on the run before the overpowering Hellenistic influence of *koine* Greek, among pagans and even among Jews. The material we have surveyed shows these last statements to be a great oversimplification of the situation.

The Wadi Daliyeh Papyri show that Imperial Aramaic was certainly in use in the land of Israel in the 4th century B.C.E., right up to the onset of the Hellenistic period. These papyri, dating from this era, are slave- and real estate–conveyance documents giving evidence of the nature of Samarian society on the eve of Alexander's conquest.[35] Yet the rise of Hellenism did not lead to a decline in the use of Aramaic. The Qumran scrolls reveal that in the fourth through early second centuries there was a great flowering of Aramaic literature.[36] From a religious and cultural point of view, the richness of this literature is much greater than would ever have been guessed based on the texts known before the discovery of the Qumran scrolls. These texts include occasional Persian loanwords (as is the case also in Second Temple Hebrew material)[37] and clearly stem from the Achaemenid and early Hellenistic eras in which Persian influence in the land of Israel was still strong.[38]

By the time we reach the second century B.C.E., we again encounter a rich Hebrew literature. The earliest material from this period, such as Ben Sira and *Jubilees*,[39] as well as other pre-Qumranian texts found among the

---

35. D. M. Gropp, *Wadi Daliyeh II: The Samaria Papyri from Wadi Daliyeh;* M. Bernstein et al., with J. VanderKam and M. Brady, *Qumran Cave 4.XXVIII: Miscellanea, Part 2*. DJD 28 (Oxford: Clarendon, 2001) 3-116.

36. B. Z. Wacholder, "The Ancient Judeo-Aramaic Literature (500-165 BCE): A Classification of Pre-Qumranic Texts," in *Archaeology and History in the Dead Sea Scrolls: The New York University Conference in Memory of Yigael Yadin*, ed. L. H. Schiffman, 257-81. JSPSup 8. JSOT/ ASOR Monographs 2 (Sheffield: JSOT, 1990); F. García Martínez, *Qumran and Apocalyptic: Studies on the Aramaic Texts from Qumran*. STDJ 9 (Leiden: Brill, 1992); D. Dimant, "Apocalyptic Texts at Qumran," in *The Community of the Renewed Covenant: The Notre Dame Symposium on the Dead Sea Scrolls*, ed. E. Ulrich and J. C. VanderKam, 175-91. CJAS 10 (Notre Dame: University of Notre Dame Press, 1994).

37. On loanwords in Hebrew, see E. Qimron, *The Hebrew of the Dead Sea Scrolls*, 116. HSS 29 (Atlanta: Scholars, 1986); Y. Yadin, *The Scroll of the War of the Sons of Light against the Sons of Darkness* [hereafter *War Scroll*], trans. B. and C. Rabin (Oxford: Oxford University Press, 1962) 260. On Aramaic, cf. also J. C. Greenfield and S. Shaked, "Three Iranian Words in the Targum of Job from Qumran," *ZDMG* 122 (1972) 37-45.

38. E. Stern, "The Persian Empire and the Political and Social History of Palestine in the Persian Period," in *CHJ*, vol. 1: *Introduction: The Persian Period* (1984) 70-87.

39. J. C. VanderKam and J. T. Milik, "Jubilees," in *Qumran Cave 4, VIII: Parabiblical Texts, Part 1*, ed. H. Attridge et al., 1-185. DJD 13 (Oxford: Clarendon, 1994).

scrolls, are all preserved in a form of late Masoretic Hebrew. These works come from circles for whom Biblical Hebrew was very much a living literary language, even if we cannot be sure what languages they spoke in daily life.

When we reach the Hasmonean and Herodian periods during which the Qumran sectarian literature was composed, Hebrew writing occurs in at least two observable dialects. One is the same dialect as that of Ben Sira and *Jubilees,* a sort of late Biblical Hebrew that is found in texts composed outside the Qumran sect but preserved in their collection. The other is what we may term Qumran Hebrew with the strange endings and grammatical forms that typify this dialect.[40] This system of writing — indeed, it is more than just orthography, as it also affects morphology — is found only in the sectarian writings.[41] This particular Hebrew, along with certain specific use of terminology, typifies sectarian composition, primarily between 150 B.C.E. and the turn of the era. This dialect is largely judged to be an archaizing remnant of pre-Masoretic Hebrew. It seems more likely, however, that we are dealing here with a dialect invented by a group of hypersectarians, who chose to separate themselves even further by developing their own linguistic system, at least for written material.[42] In light of the complete absence of this dialect from earlier texts, or from inscriptions or other Second Temple period texts, we cannot accept the notion that this dialect is actually ancient or that it represents a language pattern spread throughout the Judean populace.

Two texts, the MMT document[43] and the *Copper Scroll,*[44] have often been said to represent Mishnaic Hebrew.[45] Thorough study of these texts shows this not to be the case.[46] Although these texts, like the *Temple Scroll,* include features of what we later encounter in Mishnaic vocabulary as well as

---

40. The fullest description of this dialect is Qimron, *The Hebrew of the Dead Sea Scrolls.*

41. E. Tov, "The Orthography and Language of the Hebrew Scrolls Found at Qumran and the Origin of These Scrolls," *Textus* 13 (1986) 32-57.

42. L. H. Schiffman, "*The Temple Scroll* in Literary and Philological Perspective," in *Approaches to Ancient Judaism,* ed. W. S. Green, 2:143-58. BJS 9 (Chico: Scholars, 1980). This same point has been more effectively and thoroughly argued by W. M. Schniedewind, "Qumran Hebrew as an Antilanguage," *JBL* 118 (1999) 235-52. Cf. also S. Weitzman, "Why Did the Qumran Community Write in Hebrew?" *JAOS* 119 (1999) 35-45.

43. E. Qimron and J. Strugnell, *Qumran Cave 4.V: Miqṣat Maʿaśe ha-Torah.* DJD 10 (Oxford: Clarendon, 1994) 44-56. Cf. "The New Halakhic Letter (4QMMT) and the Origins of the Dead Sea Sect," Chapter 6 below.

44. M. Baillet, J. T. Milik, and R. de Vaux, eds., *Les 'Petites Grottes' de Qumrân.* DJD 3 (Oxford: Clarendon, 1962) 210-302; J. K. Lefkovits, *The Copper Scroll (3Q15): A Reevaluation, a New Reading, Translation, and Commentary.* STDJ 25 (Leiden: Brill, 2000).

45. See E. Y. Kutscher, "Hebrew Language, Mishnaic," *EncJud* 16:1590-1607.

46. Qimron and Strugnell, DJD 10:65, 107-8.

some common grammatical elements, these texts nevertheless evidence many of the usual features of Qumran dialectology.[47]

In any case, we need to remember that the two Hebrew dialects we are discussing represent written dialects of Jews whose spoken language we cannot pin down. It is possible that those texts tending toward Mishnaic Hebrew are indeed evidence for spoken dialects, as has been suggested by some.[48] It may even be that many spoke Aramaic, as is indicated by the New Testament.[49] That some Jews, even in the land of Israel, were more at home in Greek than in Hebrew or Aramaic is clear from the presence of some manuscripts of Greek translations of the Bible at Qumran[50] and in the Bar Kokhba corpus.[51] Certainly Hebrew was being spoken, and its use cannot be explained simply as a revival in the Maccabean period under nationalistic aegis. If so, the so-called revival was already in full force in the first half of the second century at what is supposed to be the height of the Hellenistic cultural onslaught.[52]

The Masada documents show the nature of the Hebrew used outside the confines of the Qumran sectarians (or others who may have followed them). Masada brought to light biblical texts in Masoretic Hebrew[53] and apocryphal-

---

47. Qimron, DJD 10:65-108, concludes that the grammar of MMT is closer to Biblical Hebrew than to Mishnaic Hebrew, although the vocabulary is closer to that of Mishnaic Hebrew. Cf. L. H. Schiffman, "The Architectural Vocabulary of the Copper Scroll and the Temple Scroll," in *Copper Scroll Studies,* ed. G. J. Brooke and P. R. Davies, 180-95. JSPSup 40 (London: Sheffield Academic, 2002).

48. Cf. G. Rendsburg, *Diglossia in Ancient Hebrew.* AOS 72 (New Haven: American Oriental Society, 1990) 151-76. See also E. Qimron, "Observations on the History of Early Hebrew (1000 BCE-200 CE) in the Light of the Dead Sea Documents," in *The Dead Sea Scrolls: Forty Years of Research,* ed. D. Dimant and U. Rappaport, 349-61 (Leiden: Brill and Jerusalem: Magnes, Hebrew University, and Yad Izhak Ben-Zvi, 1992).

49. J. A. Fitzmyer, *A Wandering Aramean: Collected Aramaic Essays.* SBLMS 25 (Missoula: Scholars, 1979; repr. *The Semitic Background of the New Testament.* BRS [Grand Rapids: Wm. B. Eerdmans and Livonia: Dove, 1997]) 1-27.

50. Baillet, DJD 3:142-43; P. W. Skehan, E. Ulrich, and J. E. Sanderson, *Qumran Cave 4.IV: Palaeo-Hebrew and Greek Biblical Manuscripts.* DJD 9 (Oxford: Clarendon, 1992) 161-97.

51. E. Tov, *The Greek Minor Prophets Scroll from Naḥal Ḥever (8ḤevXIIgr) (The Seiyâl Collection I).* DJD 8 (Oxford: Clarendon, 1990).

52. On the Hellenization of Palestine, see V. Tcherikover, *Hellenistic Civilization and the Jews,* trans. S. Applebaum (Philadelphia: Jewish Publication Society of America, 1966) 139-74.

53. S. Talmon, "Hebrew Fragments from Masada," in *Masada VI,* 31-97; S. Talmon, "Fragments of a Psalms Scroll from Masada, MPs^b (Masada 1103-1742)," in *Minḥah Le-Naḥum: Biblical and Other Studies Presented to Nahum M. Sarna in Honour of His 70th Birthday,* ed. M. Brettler and M. Fishbane, 318-27. JSOTSup 154 (Sheffield: JSOT, 1993); "Fragments of Two Scrolls of the Book of Leviticus from Masada," ErIsr 24 (1993) 99-110.

type texts in a similar language.⁵⁴ The Ben Sira scroll from Masada is the most substantial text, and it also is written in the Masoretic Hebrew dialect as are the fragmentary materials, such as the *Joshua Apocryphon*.⁵⁵

By the time the Bar Kokhba collection was composed,⁵⁶ Hebrew dialectology had taken a decided turn. Only the Masoretic type now represented Hebrew biblical texts. The collection does not preserve extrabiblical literary materials, but the free and easy use of Hebrew for letters indicates that for some Jews it was very much still a living language, although others must have felt much more at home in Aramaic (perhaps especially in the north) and in Greek. Comparison with talmudic literature, inscriptions, and Targumim indicates that this was a period in which Aramaic was on the rise and was most probably the spoken language of the Jews of the Galilee, outside the Hellenistic cities. Nevertheless, our texts indicate the continued survival of Hebrew as a spoken language.

These documents, stemming from a number of sites in the Judean Desert, represent the archives of some Jews who perished in hiding during the Bar Kokhba revolt.⁵⁷ A small number are actually related to the rebel leader Shimon bar Kosiba himself. While Aramaic is represented in letters, contracts, and other documents, it is no longer used for literary texts. Surprisingly, there remain many lines of contact between the Aramaic legal formulary of the Elephantine Jewish materials of the 5th century B.C.E., Wadi Daliyeh (4th century B.C.E.), and the legal documents in the Bar Kokhba caves. This is so because the Aramaic legal tradition was a continuous one, and it remained in force even during the increasing hegemony of the tannaitic legal system, especially in marriage and divorce documents. Some of these patterns are even observable in later Arabic legal papyri from the Islamic period that also draw on the common Semitic legal tradition.⁵⁸

At the same time, Greek was used extensively for legal documents.⁵⁹ Di-

---

54. S. Talmon, "Hebrew Written Fragments from Masada," *DSD* 3 (1996) 168-77.

55. S. Talmon, "*Qetʿa mi-Megillah Ḥiṣṣonit le-Sefer Yehoshuaʿ mi-Meṣadah*," in *Shai le-Ḥayim Rabin: Asuppat Mehqere Lashon li-Khevodo bi-Melot Lo Shivʿim ve-Ḥamesh*, ed. M. Goshen-Gottstein, S. Morag, and S. Kogut, 147-57 (Jerusalem: Akademon, 1990).

56. Cf. the Hebrew texts in DJD 2; Cotton and Yardeni, DJD 27.

57. Cf. H. Eshel and D. Amit, *Meʿarot ha-Miflaṭ mi-Tekufat Mered Bar-Kokhva.* "Eretz," Geographic Research and Publications Project for the Advancement of Knowledge of Eretz Israel, Tel-Aviv University (Tel-Aviv: Israel Exploration Society, College of Judea and Samaria, and C. G. Foundation Jerusalem, 1998).

58. Cf. G. Khan, "The Pre-Islamic Background of Muslim Legal Formularies," *Aram* 6 (1994) 193-224.

59. DJD 27:133-279; and N. Lewis, ed., *The Documents from the Bar Kokhba Period in the Cave of Letters: Greek Papyri* (Jerusalem: Israel Exploration Society, Hebrew University, Shrine of the Book, 1989) 35-133.

rect Roman rule had brought the use of Greek into prominence, especially among those Jews who resided in the Roman province of Arabia, founded in 106 C.E.[60] In the context of religious history, these documents indicate that Greek and Roman legal principles and practices, even in matters of personal status, were in use side by side with those known from tannaitic halakhah.[61] Hebrew biblical texts were by this time represented only by the Masoretic type. The so-called Bar Kokhba collections do not, for the most part, preserve Postbiblical Hebrew literary materials, only documents.

The Hebrew they employ, however, is much closer to Mishnaic Hebrew, a situation that extends even beyond the legal formulary and technical language that is to be expected in some of these documents.[62] It is certain, though, that Hebrew continued to be developed and to function as one of the languages of the land of Israel as talmudic evidence confirms.[63]

The Khirbet Mird materials testify to profound linguistic changes that came over the country much later, but that no doubt affected its Jewish population as well. These documents date from the fifth through ninth centuries C.E. and are in Greek,[64] Christian Palestinian Syriac,[65] and

---

60. Cf. F. Millar, *The Roman Near East, 31 BC-AD 337* (Cambridge, MA: Harvard University Press, 1993) 414-36; and G. W. Bowersock, *Roman Arabia* (Cambridge, MA: Harvard University Press, 1983).

61. L. H. Schiffman, "Reflections on the Deeds of Sale from the Judean Desert in Light of Rabbinic Literature," in *Law in the Documents of the Judaean Desert*, ed. R. Katzoff and D. Schaps, 185-203. JSJSup 96 (Leiden: Brill, 2005).

62. Cf. E. Y. Kutscher, "Leshonan shel ha-'Iggerot ha-'Ivriyot veha-'Aramiyot shel Bar Kosiba u-Vene Doro: Ma'amar Sheni: Ha-'Iggerot ha-'Ivriyot," *Leshonenu* 26 (1961/62) 7-21; G. W. Nebe, "Die hebräische Sprache der Naḥal Ḥever Dokumente 5/6Hev 44-46," in *The Hebrew of the Dead Sea Scrolls and Ben Sira: Proceedings of a Symposium Held at Leiden University, 11-14 December 1995*, ed. T. Muraoka and J. F. Elwolde, 150-57. STDJ 26 (Leiden: Brill, 1997).

63. See J. Barr, "Hebrew, Aramaic and Greek in the Hellenistic Age," in *CHJ*, vol. 2: *The Hellenistic Age* (1989) 79-114.

64. None of these texts has been published. For a listing, see S. Reed, comp., with M. J. Lundberg and M. B. Phelps, *The Dead Sea Scrolls Catalogue: Documents, Photographs, and Museum Inventory Numbers*, SBLRBS 32 (Atlanta: Scholars, 1994) 223-24; E. Tov with S. J. Pfann in *The Texts from the Judaean Desert: Indices and an Introduction to the Discoveries in the Judaean Desert Series*, ed. Tov, 96-97. DJD 39 (Oxford: Clarendon, 2002).

65. J. T. Milik, "Une inscription et une lettre en araméen christo-palestinien," *RB* 60 (1953) 526-39, pl. XIX; update with photo in G. R. H. Wright, "Archaeological Remains at el Mird in the Wilderness of Judea, with an appendix by J. T. Milik," *Bib* 42 (1961) 21-27; C. Perrot, "Un fragment christo-palestinien découverte à Khirbet Mird (Actes des apôtres, X, 28-29; 32-41)," *RB* 70 (1963) 506-55 (+ pls. XVIII, XIX); M. Baillet, "Un livret magique en christo-palestinen à l'Université de Louvain," *Mus* 76 (1963) 375-401; C. Müller-Kessler and M. Sokoloff, eds., *A Corpus of Christian Palestinian Aramaic*, vol. 1: *The Christian Palestinian Aramaic Old Testament and Apocrypha Version from the Early Period* (Groningen: Styx, 1997); vols. 2A and 2B:

Literary Genres and Languages of the Judean Scrolls

Arabic.⁶⁶ Even with the onset of Arab rule in the seventh century, Jews were still living in a multilingual society. It is no wonder that while Hellenistic Judaism had died out by this point, rabbinic Jews continued to write in Hebrew, Jewish Aramaic, both Palestinian and Babylonian, and in the new vernacular, Arabic, as evidenced in the manuscripts from the Cairo Genizah.⁶⁷

Genres of Ancient Jewish Literature

Open virtually any book dealing with the literature of the Jews in Second Temple times and you will encounter such designations as "Apocrypha," "Pseudepigrapha," and "Dead Sea Scrolls." Behind these designations are indications not of the nature of the literature itself, but rather of the provenance, or of the manner in which the material was transmitted from ancient times to the present. The Apocrypha (with a capital A) are those books from the Second Temple period handed down in Greek, first by the collector(s) of the canon of the Septuagint Greek Bibles and later by the Catholic Church.⁶⁸ The Pseudepigrapha is an uncanonized collection of writings of varied provenance, for the most part passed down to us by Eastern Christian churches that regarded these books as canonical.⁶⁹ The term "Dead Sea Scrolls," whether defined narrowly as the Qumran documents or more widely as the entire corpus of Judean Desert texts, designates the place of discovery of the collection. None of these designations says anything about the period in which the documents were authored, copied, and read. At that time, readers would have been aware of the nature of the texts, perhaps of their noncanonical status and their relationship to what we call biblical literature, their literary structure, perhaps their real provenance (in the land of Israel or the Diaspora), and hopefully of the con-

---

The Christian Palestinian Aramaic New Testament Version from the Early Period (Groningen: Styx, 1998). For additional texts, see Reed, *The Dead Sea Scrolls Catalogue*, 225; and Tov, DJD 39:95-96. Tov's list indicates that some texts have been published since the Reed catalogue.

66. A. Grohmann, *Arabic Papyri from Ḥirbet el-Mird*. Bibliothèque du Muséon 52 (Louvain: Publications universitaires, 1963).

67. S. C. Reif, *A Jewish Archive from Old Cairo: The History of Cambridge University's Genizah Collection* (Richmond, Surrey: Curzon, 2000) 214-24.

68. R. H. Charles, ed., *The Apocrypha and Pseudepigrapha of the Old Testament in English*, vol. 1: *Apocrypha* (1913; repr. Oxford: Oxford University Press, 1968).

69. R. H. Charles, ed., *The Apocrypha and Pseudepigrapha of the Old Testament in English*, vol. 2: *Pseudepigrapha* (1913; repr. Oxford: Oxford University Press, 1968); J. H. Charlesworth, ed., *The Old Testament Pseudepigrapha*. 2 vols. (Garden City: Doubleday, 1983-85).

tent of their messages. None of the "corporeal" designations that we use would have had any meaning to the ancient Jewish reader.

The discovery of the Qumran texts should have finally put an end to the use of these categories for the academic study of the literature of Jews in the Greco-Roman period. We have before us a vast panoply of texts, of many different kinds, that allow us to gain a much more realistic picture of the literature being read by Jews in this period. Future scholarship will have to categorize these texts by genre, language, and date, not by mode of transmission to modern scholars.

The Judean Desert corpus has presented us with a variety of Hebrew texts that, from a literary point of view, present new genres or marked differences from previously known exemplars of the same genres. For example, in their legal materials, the scrolls contain the first postbiblical codes of Jewish law known to us. The *Temple Scroll* creates its code by rewriting the canonical law texts from the Torah into a new document.[70] Interestingly, the author/redactor of this text, finishing his work in about 120 B.C.E., had the benefit of previously existing sources that were arranged topically.[71] These texts proceeded in the manner of the Torah itself, using its language for the most part. Another trend is visible in the sectarian codes of the *serakhim* that are collections of laws on individual topics, such as the list of Sabbath laws found in the *Zadokite Fragments*.[72] Here the language of the Bible can be detected behind the legal formulary of the new texts, but there are virtually no direct quotations of the Bible or reworkings of its actual wording.

Most of the legal documents in the Bar Kokhba texts are written in Aramaic, the language used for such purposes by Jews from time immemorial. The few extant Hebrew legal documents from that corpus show us that mishnaic legal terms, some of which are already in evidence in some sectarian texts as well, were in use in the legal practice of Jews from Judea. These contracts are often the earliest preserved examples of these legal usages, predating parallel mishnaic legal formulations.[73]

---

70. Y. Yadin, *The Temple Scroll* (Jerusalem: Israel Exploration Society and Shrine of the Book, 1983) 1:71-88; cf. L. H. Schiffman, "The Deuteronomic Paraphrase of the *Temple Scroll*," *RevQ* 15 (1992) 543-68; "Codification of Jewish Law in the Dead Sea Scrolls," Chapter 9 below.

71. A. M. Wilson and L. Wills, "Literary Sources of the Temple Scroll," *HTR* 75 (1982) 275-88; M. O. Wise, *A Critical Study of the Temple Scroll from Qumran Cave 11*. SAOC 49 (Chicago: Oriental Institute, University of Chicago, 1990).

72. L. H. Schiffman, *The Halakhah at Qumran*. SJLA 16 (Leiden: Brill, 1975) 84-133.

73. A. Gulak, *Ha-Sheṭarot ba-Talmud: Le-'Or ha-Papirusim ha-Yevaniyim mi-Miṣrayim ule-'Or ha-Mishpaṭ ha-Yevani veha-Romi*, ed. and suppl. R. Katzoff (Jerusalem: Magnes, Hebrew University, 1994) 11-45.

In the area of biblical interpretation, the pesher literature presents us with a new genre from several points of view. Its contemporizing exegesis of parts of the Minor Prophets, Isaiah, and some Psalms features line-by-line commentary arranged in the form of lemma and comment, running primarily in scriptural order.[74] Specific terms are used, like "its interpretation is concerning . . ." and "the interpretation of the matter is . . ." that clearly separate the biblical from the nonbiblical, interpretive material. These are, from the literary point of view, the earliest commentaries we know.[75]

In the area of poetry the scrolls texts offer a rich selection. Some of these texts are actually prayers or hymns, meant for liturgical use. The scrolls provide us with the earliest Postbiblical Hebrew and Aramaic poetry,[76] and this material clearly constitutes a bridge between the poetry of the Bible and that of the early *payṭanim*, the Jewish liturgical poets of the Byzantine period. The poems in the scrolls are of varied character. The *Hodayot*[77] offer introspective religious poetry that expresses the deepest longings of a sectarian author, thought by many (at least for some of the poems) to be the Teacher of Righteousness, the leader of the sect, and at the same time articulates the theological beliefs of the Qumran sect.[78] *The Songs of the Sabbath Sacrifice* describe the beauty of the innermost sancta of the heavens and have intimate links to the later hekhalot mystical poetry.[79] Morning and afternoon benedic-

---

74. The pesher texts are collected in M. P. Horgan, *Pesharim: Qumran Interpretations of Biblical Books*. CBQMS 8 (Washington: Catholic Biblical Association of America, 1979).

75. D. Dimant, "Pesharim, Qumran," *ABD* 5:244-51; G. J. Brooke, "Qumran Pesher: Toward the Redefinition of a Genre," *RevQ* 10 (1979-1980) 483-503; M. J. Bernstein, "Introductory Formulas for Citation and Re-citation of Biblical Verses in the Qumran Pesharim," *DSD* 1 (1994) 30-70.

76. For a detailed study of the Hebrew poetry from Qumran, see B. Nitzan, *Qumran Prayer and Religious Poetry*. STDJ 12 (Leiden: Brill, 1994). For Aramaic, see J. C. VanderKam, "The Poetry of 1QApGen XX, 2-8a," *RevQ* 10 (1979) 57-66; A. S. Rodrigues Pereira, *Studies in Aramaic Poetry (c. 100 B.C.E.-c. 600 C.E.): Selected Jewish, Christian and Samaritan*. SSN 34 (Assen: Van Gorcum, 1997) 10-26; E. G. Chazon, "Hymns and Prayers in the Dead Sea Scrolls," in *The Dead Sea Scrolls after Fifty Years*, ed. P. Flint and J. C. VanderKam, 244-70 (Leiden: Brill, 1998); E. Schuller, "Prayer, Hymnic, and Liturgical Texts from Qumran," in Ulrich and VanderKam, *The Community of the Renewed Covenant*, 153-71.

77. J. Licht, *Megillat ha-Hodayot mi-Megillot Midbar Yehudah* (Jerusalem: Bialik Institute, 1957); E. Schuller, in *Qumran Cave 4.XX: Poetical and Liturgical Texts, Part 2*, ed. E. G. Chazon et al. DJD 29 (Oxford: Clarendon, 1999) 69-254.

78. J. Licht, "The Doctrine of the Thanksgiving Scroll," *IEJ* 6 (1956) 1-13, 89-101.

79. C. Newsom, DJD 11:173-401; cf. L. H. Schiffman, "*Merkavah* Speculation at Qumran: The 4Q *Serekh Shirot 'Olat ha-Shabbat*," in *Mystics, Philosophers and Politicians: Essays in Jewish Intellectual History in Honor of Alexander Altmann*, ed. J. Reinharz, D. Swetschinski, with K. Bland, 15-47. Duke Monographs in Medieval and Renaissance Studies 5 (Durham: Duke Uni-

tions of the daily prayers,[80] and the festival liturgy[81] for the various Jewish holidays testify to a general loosening up of the rigid rules of biblical parallelism and show the burst of creativity that Hebrew poetry experienced in the Second Temple period.

Closely linked to the poetry is the wisdom literature, since some of the wisdom texts (for example, Ben Sira found at Masada and Qumran[82]) are poetic in character. The previously unknown Sapiential texts[83] are in reality an entirely new genre.[84] They seem by their linguistic character and content not to be specifically sectarian texts. Rather, like the biblical wisdom texts, they give good advice to the typical agrarian family of the period and also speak of probing hidden wisdom. These texts have various parallels with the Mysteries texts[85] that, in reality, are also wisdom literature. The Qumran corpus shows that wisdom literature was a major genre in Jewish circles and helps to explain the strong wisdom trends evident in both the New Testament and rabbinic literature.[86]

The scrolls are also replete with apocalyptic literature — descriptions of revealed secrets and depictions of the end of days.[87] We also hear descriptions

---

versity Press, 1982); J. M. Baumgarten, "The Qumran Sabbath Shirot and Rabbinic Merkabah Traditions," *RevQ* 13 (1988) 199-214; B. Nitzan, "Harmonic and Mystical Characteristics in Poetic and Liturgical Writings from Qumran," *JQR* 85 (1994) 163-83; E. R. Wolfson, "Mysticism and the Poetic-Liturgical Compositions from Qumran," *JQR* 85 (1994) 185-202.

80. M. Baillet, *Qumrân Grotte 4.III (4Q482-4Q520)*. DJD 7 (Oxford: Clarendon, 1982) 105-36; D. K. Falk, *Daily, Sabbath, and Festival Prayers in the Dead Sea Scrolls*. STDJ 27 (Leiden: Brill, 1998) 21-57.

81. Baillet, DJD 7:175-215; Falk, *Daily, Sabbath, and Festival Prayers*, 155-215.

82. J. A. Sanders, *The Psalms Scroll of Qumrân Cave 11 (11QPs^a)*. DJD 4 (Oxford: Clarendon, 1965) 79-85, discusses an excerpt from *Ben Sira* included in the *Psalms Scroll*.

83. J. Strugnell, D. J. Harrington, and T. Elgvin, *Qumran Cave 4.XXIV: Sapiential Texts, Part 2*. DJD 34 (Oxford: Clarendon, 1999). Cf. E. J. C. Tigchelaar, *To Increase Learning for the Understanding Ones: Reading and Reconstructing the Fragmentary Early Jewish Sapiential Text 4Qinstruction*. STDJ 44 (Leiden: Brill, 2001).

84. D. J. Harrington, *Wisdom Texts from Qumran* (London: Routledge, 1996).

85. D. Barthélemy and J. T. Milik, *Qumran Cave I*. DJD 1 (Oxford: Clarendon, 1955) 102-7; L. H. Schiffman, in *Qumran Cave 4.XV: Sapiential Texts, Part 1*, ed. T. Elgvin et al. DJD 20 (Oxford: Clarendon, 1997) 31-123; A. Lange, *Weisheit und Prädestination: Weisheitliche Urordnung und Prädestination in den Textfunden von Qumran*. STDJ 18 (Leiden: Brill, 1995) 93-109.

86. Cf. Schiffman, *Reclaiming the Dead Sea Scrolls*, 197-210.

87. On apocalypticism at Qumran, see J. J. Collins, "Apocalyptic and the Discourse of the Qumran Community," *JNES* 49 (1990) 135-44; "Was the Dead Sea Sect an Apocalyptic Movement?" in Schiffman, *Archaeology and History in the Dead Sea Scrolls*, 25-51; *The Scepter and the Star: The Messiahs of the Dead Sea Scrolls and Other Ancient Literature*. ABRL (New York: Doubleday, 1995); *Apocalypticism in the Dead Sea Scrolls* (London: Routledge, 1997); *The Apocalyptic Imagination*, 2nd ed. BRS (Grand Rapids: Wm. B. Eerdmans and Livonia: Dove, 1998) 145-76.

Literary Genres and Languages of the Judean Scrolls

of the eschatological war and of the works of the Messiah[88] in the various versions of the *War Scroll*[89] and associated texts.[90] From a literary point of view, the *War Scroll* points to the existence in this period of religious poetry from which the author derived the liturgical sections, as well as of military manuals that he used to pattern the military sections. This text, a marriage of these very different kinds of material, is therefore also testimony to texts which lie behind those preserved in the scrolls corpus.[91]

Additionally, parts of fifteen biblical and apocryphal scrolls were found in the Masada excavations. The general character of these biblical materials testifies to the ascendancy of the MT by the period of the revolt.[92] Yet the same community, whose biblical texts were by this time standardized, made use of apocryphal compositions as well.[93] Very substantial portions of the book of Ben Sira were found at Masada,[94] the only apocryphal composition actually quoted by the talmudic rabbis.[95]

These texts show that in Second Temple times, apocryphal literature was the widespread heritage of the Jewish people. The attempt to root out these nonbiblical texts, undertaken by the rabbis somewhat later, had not yet occurred, and such books were widely read. Indeed, they are present at Masada and at Qumran, where they constitute approximately one-third of the collection.[96] It is probable that the apocalyptic tradition, represented in some of these texts, with its sense of immediate messianism, helped to drive the Great Revolt against Rome of 66-73 C.E.

Extremely interesting is the presence of the quasimystical "angelic liturgy," termed *Songs of the Sabbath Sacrifice*, at Masada[97] and at Qumran in nine

---

88. 4Q521 has been labeled by its editor "4QApocalypse messianique." See É. Puech, *Qumrân Grotte 4.XVIII: Textes hébreux (4Q521-5Q528, 4Q576-4Q579)*. DJD 25 (Oxford: Clarendon, 1998) 1-38.

89. Yadin, *The War Scroll*; Baillet, DJD 7:12-72.

90. J. Duhaime, *The War Texts: 1QM and Related Manuscripts* (London: T & T Clark, 2004), esp. 23-44.

91. P. R. Davies, *1QM, the War Scroll from Qumran: Its Structure and History*. BibOr 32 (Rome: Biblical Institute, 1977); Duhaime, *The War Texts*, 45-63.

92. Yadin, in *Masada VI*, 31-97.

93. Yadin, in *Masada VI*, 98-147.

94. Yadin, in *Masada VI*, 170-231.

95. M. Z. Segal, *Sefer Ben Sira ha-Shalem*, 2nd ed. (Jerusalem: Bialik Institute, 1971/72) 37-46.

96. D. Dimant, "Qumran Manuscripts."

97. C. A. Newsom and Y. Yadin, "The Masada Fragment of the Qumran *Songs of the Sabbath Sacrifice*," *IEJ* 34 (1984) 77-88 and pl. 9.

manuscripts.[98] Hence, it may be that this angelic liturgy and the mystical approach that it presupposes were not limited to the Qumran sectarians in the last years of the Second Temple, but had spread much further among the Jewish community of the land of Israel. Perhaps it was the precursor of the Merkavah mysticism of the third through eighth centuries C.E.[99] In any case, we have to view the common heritage of Qumran and Masada as typical of the literature that was read by the intellectual and religious elites of Second Temple Judaism.

In general, then, the scrolls provide us with an entire collection of texts of varied genres, showing us how the major types of literature found within the biblical collection continued to develop in the Hasmonean period. Even so, this corpus, when analyzed as a whole, is no doubt only a fraction of the material that was being read by Jews in Late Antiquity, even in the land of Israel. The one major element missing from the scrolls, presaging the situation in rabbinic literature, is historical writing. One of the greatest disappointments about this collection is the absence of 1 Maccabees, a Hebrew text composed in this period but preserved only in Greek, which is probably absent because of the strong anti-Hasmonean stance of the Qumran sectarians.

Conclusion

We have surveyed here only the smallest part of the tremendous contribution that the Dead Sea Scrolls make to the corpus of material in the Hebrew language from the period of Late Antiquity. This treasure trove of material, stretching from the pre-Hasmonean period through the eve of the redaction of the Mishnah, provides new evidence for grammar, lexicography, literary structure, and for an understanding of the interplay of languages in the Jewish communities of the ancient land of Israel. Needless to say, the scrolls are bringing about a reevaluation of many aspects of the history of Judaism, and this, in turn, is providing a new backdrop for the evaluation of the linguistic and literary phenomena we have been studying here. Whatever the outcome of the many academic debates currently raging regarding the scrolls, their discovery certainly has reclaimed for us a new layer in the history of Hebrew language and literature. Like those before and after, this layer testifies eloquently to the linguistic and literary creativity of the Jewish people in their native language throughout their history.

98. Newsom, DJD 11:173-401; cf. Nitzan, *Qumran Prayer and Religious Poetry*, 273-318. Contrast Yadin, *Masada: Herod's Fortress*, 172-74, who argues that members of the Qumran sect fled to Masada after Qumran was destroyed by the Romans in 68 C.E.

99. Baumgarten, *RevQ* 13 (1988) 199-214.

CHAPTER 3

Halakhah and History: The Contribution of the Dead Sea Scrolls to Recent Scholarship

From the beginning of modern Jewish scholarship, the nexus between halakhah and history was realized. Throughout Jewish history, Jewish law has played a decisive role in shaping the character of the Jewish community and has had profound effects on the political, social, and religious history of the Jews. At the same time, Jewish law has itself been affected in many ways throughout history by the historical circumstances in which it developed. Hence, it is virtually impossible to separate Jewish law and Jewish history from one another.

Approaches to the History of Halakhah

It is perhaps a curiosity that despite these virtually self-evident facts, neither one of these disciplines in the premodern period recognized the role of the other. Virtually all of those few medieval Jewish scholars who took up the study of history — those whom we somewhat disdainfully term historiographers — wrote their works as if placing the sages of Jewish law in chronological order was sufficient to claim the title "history."[1] No attention was paid to the evaluation of the contents of Jewish law except as regards the few cases in which the legal materials themselves testify directly to their own history.

---

1. See G. D. Cohen, *Sefer Ha-Qabbalah: The Book of Tradition by Abraham ibn Daud* (Philadelphia: Jewish Publication Society, 1967) l-lvi, for a survey of medieval Jewish historiography and its relation to the Muslim *isnad*, the chain of authorities on which the validity of a tradition is based.

Even the most cursory examination of halakhic literature will show that, even though this material constitutes one of the modern scholar's prime sources for the study of political, economic, and social history, Jewish legal literature barely recognized the role that such factors had in the shaping of its content and character.

Modern conceptions of social and political evolution were quickly grafted onto traditional Jewish legal learning in the nineteenth century, and so the field of the history of halakhah as we know it, indeed as we take it for granted, came into being. In fact, this field of inquiry was greatly encouraged by two interrelated nonacademic factors.

First, the study of the history of halakhah was to a great extent born in the feeling that the scientific investigation of the history of Jewish practice would help in dealing with the challenges posed to traditional Judaism by modernization. Such figures as Abraham Geiger and Zacharias Frankel sought to base the reform and/or preservation of Judaism on such scholarly inquiry.[2]

Second, individual Jewish scholars, many of them pulpit rabbis, saw the academic study of the talmudic texts in which they had been trained for the rabbinate as an effective bridge between the tradition and the modern world in which they now found themselves. One has only to peruse the *Monatsschrift für die Geschichte und Wissenschaft des Judentums* or the *Jahrsberichten* of the various modern European rabbinical seminaries to see how attractive such topics were in the nineteenth century.[3]

With the emergence of Jewish Studies as we know it, which, in fact, should be traced to the opening of the Hebrew University in 1925, the self-conscious vision of the study of the nexus of halakhah and history gave way to what proposed to be dispassionate scholarly inquiry. A new page was turned in the study of the history of Jewish law that would primarily be carried on in universities in Israel and the United States and, to some extent, in American rabbinical seminaries. Although even here ideological considerations were still present, nevertheless a much greater degree of objectivity was certainly achieved. But by the time this transition occurred, fundamental changes in what we may define as the canon of texts in Jewish law would take place. Further, interaction between the study of ancient Judaism and the disciplines of ancient history and classics would bring about such fundamental

---

2. I. Schorsch, *From Text to Context: The Turn to History in Modern Judaism* (Waltham: Brandeis University Press and Hanover: University Press of New England, 1994) 177-204, 255-65, 303-33; M. A. Meyer, *Response to Modernity: A History of the Reform Movement in Judaism* (New York: Oxford University Press, 1988) 62-99.

3. On the rise of the modern rabbinate, see Schorsch, *From Text to Context*, 9-50.

recasting of the political, social, and economic history of the Jews in Late Antiquity as to prepare the way for a totally new vision of the links between halakhah and history.

When scholars of the *Wissenschaft des Judentums* first turned to the study of the history of halakhah and began mining halakhic sources for more conventional historical data, they immediately found themselves working with a much wider set of evidence than had been available to premodern students of this topic. For, in the meantime, important developments had taken place in Jewish and Christian intellectual history. Beginning in the Renaissance, Jews, albeit a small minority, once again became conversant with Hellenistic Jewish literature that had been preserved by Christians.[4] The works of Josephus, Philo, the Septuagint, and the Apocrypha provided numerous examples of halakhic material that appeared to be at variance with rabbinic halakhah and that historically-minded scholars realized predated the collections of rabbinic material as they had been preserved. In Christian circles a series of expeditions and discoveries in the seventeenth, eighteenth, and nineteenth centuries brought to the attention of European scholars Jewish documents of the Second Temple period, which we today imprecisely term Pseudepigrapha. These texts, most notably *Jubilees* and the *Aramaic Levi Document,* contain much halakhic material that sometimes differs from that preserved in rabbinic tradition. More generally, the emerging picture of Second Temple Judaism was greatly advanced by the theologically-colored research of those seeking to establish the background of Christianity. The research of these scholars, for the most part, either ignored or misunderstood the role of halakhah in Jewish history due to their theological prejudices. Nonetheless, they laid the basis for the historical study of the Second Temple period, the work of Emil Schürer, of course, being the prime example.[5]

The availability of this expanded documentary evidence meant that the study of halakhah and its history in Second Temple times had now gone way beyond the mining of rabbinic references to the pre-70 C.E. period. The attempt of Abraham Geiger to reconstruct Sadducean or other forms of non-Pharisaic law,[6] the path-breaking study of *Jubilees* by Chanokh Al-

---

4. See L. A. Segal, *Historical Consciousness and Religious Tradition in Azariah de' Rossi's Me'or 'Einayim* (Philadelphia: Jewish Publication Society, 1989) 27-86.

5. The renewed Jewish interest in the politics, society, and economy of the Jews in Late Antiquity stemmed in Israel from the renewal of Jewish life in the ancient land, whereas in the Diaspora it was, in fact, the opposite consideration, the existence of a Hellenistic Diaspora and religious pluralism, that fueled this interest.

6. A. Geiger, *Urschrift und Übersetzungen der Bibel in ihrer Abhängigkeit von der innern Entwicklung des Judentums* (Breslau: Hainauer, 1857); Hebrew trans. by Y. L. Baruch, *Ha-Miqra'*

beck,[7] the work of Zacharias Frankel on the Septuagint,[8] and the somewhat later work of Bernhard Ritter[9] and Samuel Belkin[10] on Philo had opened up new issues and, in fact, laid a firm basis for the study of Second Temple Jewish law as a field of study truly unthinkable without the newly expanded documentary canon with which these scholars now worked.

The Dead Sea Scrolls and the Study of Jewish Law

It was against this background that we must see the discovery of the first Dead Sea Scrolls, not by a Bedouin boy in 1947 but rather in the medieval manuscripts of the *Zadokite Fragments (Damascus Document)* by Solomon Schechter in 1896.[11] It is now a commonplace that the Cairo Genizah, found more than one hundred years ago, transformed many areas of Jewish Studies, including, of course, the history of halakhah.[12] But in the form of the *Zadokite Fragments,* one document preserved in two partial manuscripts, the Genizah began a revolution in the history of Second Temple Jewish law. We should pause to note that the Genizah yielded up not only the *Zadokite Fragments* but other Second Temple texts as well: partial manuscripts of Ben Sira, and parts of medieval copies of the *Aramaic Levi Document* (formerly called the *Testament of Levi*) and the *Testament of Naphtali,* and the book of Tobit.[13] The *Aramaic Levi Document* should be singled out as a work of halakhic content that, together with its Qumran fragments, has great potential for contributing to the history of halakhah. The publication of the *Zadokite Fragments* was accompanied by the pioneering commentary of Sol-

---

ve-Targumav be-Ziqatam le-Hitpathutah ha-Penimit shel ha-Yahadut (Jerusalem: Bialik Foundation, 1948/49).

7. C. Albeck, *Das Buch der Jubiläen und die Halacha.* Siebenundvierzigster Bericht der Hochschule für die Wissenschaft des Judentums in Berlin (1930).

8. Z. Frankel, *Vorstudien zu der Septuaginta* (Leipzig: Vogel, 1841); *Ueber den Einfluss der palaestinischen Exegese auf die alexandrinische Hermeneutik* (Leipzig: Barth, 1851).

9. B. Ritter, *Philo und die Halacha* (Leipzig: Hinrichs, 1879).

10. S. Belkin, *Philo and the Oral Law: The Philonic Interpretation of Biblical Law in Relation to the Palestinian Halaka* (Cambridge, MA: Harvard University Press, 1940).

11. S. Schechter, *Documents of Jewish Sectaries,* vol. 1: *Fragments of a Zadokite Work* (1910; repr. Library of Biblical Studies. New York: Ktav, 1970). Cf. Y. Sussmann, "Ḥeqer Toldot ha-Halakhah u-Megillot Midbar Yehudah: Hirhurim Talmudiyim Rishonim le-'Or Megillat Miqṣat Ma'aśe ha-Torah," *Tarbiz* 59 (1989/1990) 11-22.

12. Cf. S. C. Reif, *A Jewish Archive from Old Cairo: The History of Cambridge University's Genizah Collection* (Richmond, Surrey: Curzon, 2000) 121-48.

13. "Second Temple Literature and the Cairo Genizah," Chapter 24 below.

omon Schechter, who came to his work with a solid training in traditional Jewish learning but with little of the ideological baggage of his *Wissenschaft* predecessors or their Christian "colleagues." Schechter's choice of a title for this document correctly emphasized its Zadokite/Saducean links,[14] but he incorrectly attributed the document to a group of Saducean-type Samaritans.[15] It was ironic that Louis Ginzberg, who believed incorrectly that the document was proto-Pharisaic in origin, provided in his commentary on this work the keys to understanding virtually every line of its difficult halakhic section.[16]

While the work of Ginzberg, Schechter, and numerous other scholars[17] made possible a fairly thorough understanding of the halakhic content of this text, they were not able to settle the debate about either the historical ramifications of this document, that is to say, the identity of the sect described in it, or its significance for the study of the history of Jewish law. Suffice it to say that between the wars, in what we might call the pre-Qumran era, every possible theory was put forth about the provenance of the *Zadokite Fragments*.[18] And in regard to the importance of this material for the study of Jewish law, a great methodological error was made that must be explained at some length.

Already in the works of Abraham Geiger, it was implicit that Second Temple halakhic sources could not be arranged in some kind of linear, chronological fashion. Geiger's work should have shown that competing halakhic trends vied with one another in Second Temple times and that differences in halakhah could not be ascribed simply to differences of date. But perhaps under the influence of the theory of evolution, as it had been transported to the social and historical world from its original place in the natural sciences,

---

14. The text is now known mostly as the *Damascus Document* because of the few references to Damascus, which in our view is a code word for Qumran. See L. H. Schiffman, *Reclaiming the Dead Sea Scrolls: The History of Judaism, the Background of Christianity, the Lost Library of Qumran* (Philadelphia: Jewish Publication Society, 1994; repr. ABRL. New York: Doubleday, 1995) 92-94. The designation *Zadokite Fragments* should have been retained, however, since it correctly indicates the character of the legal traditions in the text.

15. Schechter, *Documents of Jewish Sectaries,* xxi-xxvi.

16. L. Ginzberg, *Eine unbekannte jüdische Sekte* (New York: Ginzberg, 1922); English translation with additional chapters, *An Unknown Jewish Sect* (New York: Jewish Theological Seminary of America, 1976).

17. For a bibliography of studies of the Zadokite Fragments written before the discovery of the Dead Sea Scrolls, see J. A. Fitzmyer, "Prolegomenon," in Schechter, *Documents of Jewish Sectaries,* 1:29-31.

18. For a short survey, see L. H. Schiffman, *The Halakhah at Qumran.* SJLA 16 (Leiden: Brill, 1975) 1-2.

most early students of the history of Jewish law, even Geiger himself, had fallen into the trap of what we might call "halakhic Darwinism."[19] Hence, the notion that the sources could be placed into a chronological sequence of development incorrectly took hold of the scholars of the history of Jewish law. Further, we can again see here tendencies towards religious reform playing a role in this process as well. Scholars simply assumed that the law had progressed from the stricter to the more lenient, clearly a reflection of their desire to see more lenient approaches applied in their own time, a trend common even amongst traditional Jewish scholars. So there was born the הלכה ישנה, the "old law," a peculiar construct of Jewish scholarship that assumed that the old law was reflected in such texts as *Jubilees* and the *Zadokite Fragments,* as well as in some references in rabbinic literature to earlier practice — משנה ראשונה — and that this old law had been gradually replaced through an evolutionary process with what we may call a "new law" — that of the Pharisaic-rabbinic tradition.

This entire notion, however, as we now know, was entirely false. Both the canon of documentary evidence and the perspective with which the material was approached were radically altered as the result of the discovery of the Dead Sea Scrolls. The first to realize the connection between the *Zadokite Fragments* and the scrolls after the discovery of Qumran Cave 1 in 1947 was Eleazar L. Sukenik[20] who was effectively the founder of Israeli/Jewish archaeology.[21] Even though by 1954 the seven major scrolls from Cave 1 were in the hands of Israel,[22] a series of circumstances, historical, political, and religious, joined together to create an environment in which the study of the scrolls would be dominated by a group of Christian scholars with little interest in Jewish law. This group, because of its unique position in the editorial process and its exclusive access to much of the evidence, especially the Cave 4 collection, was essentially able to shape the history of research until quite recently.[23]

---

19. In fact, a Darwinian approach to the history of Jewish law may well account for the "survival of the fittest" that many scholars identify in the hegemony of rabbinic Judaism in the aftermath of the destruction of the temple.

20. E. L. Sukenik, *Megillot Genuzot mi-tokh Genizah Qedumah she-Nimṣe'ah be-Midbar Yehudah* (Jerusalem: Bialik Institute, 1948-50) 1:21-24.

21. See N. A. Silberman, *A Prophet from Amongst You: The Life of Yigael Yadin, Soldier, Scholar, and Mythmaker of Modern Israel* (Reading, MA: Addison-Wesley, 1993) 7-35.

22. The story of their acquisition is told in Y. Yadin, *The Message of the Scrolls* (New York: Simon & Schuster, 1957) 15-52.

23. Cf. Schiffman, *Reclaiming the Dead Sea Scrolls,* 3-35; "Confessionalism and the Study of the Dead Sea Scrolls," *JS* 31 (1991) 3-14.

The first generation of Qumran scholars, because of both training and *Tendenz*, did not effectively continue the work of Schechter, Ginzberg, or even of Schürer, but sought to find in the sectarians — identified as Essenes — monastic proto-Christians. Accordingly, for these scholars, Qumran research was carried on with little or no attention to the entire second half of the preserved Genizah manuscripts of the *Zadokite Fragments* or to the halakhic materials in the remainder of the Qumran corpus, most of which were left unpublished.[24] The notable exception was the publication by J. T. Milik of the Jewish legal contracts from Wadi Murabba'at.[25]

Despite the virtual ignoring of halakhah by the mainstream of Dead Sea Scrolls researchers in the years between 1948 and 1967, a number of important contributions were made by isolated Jewish scholars. Most notable are the early papers by the great talmudist Saul Lieberman,[26] the work of Chaim Rabin,[27] whose edition of the Genizah manuscripts of the *Zadokite Fragments* became standard, and the work of Joseph M. Baumgarten.[28] We should note, however, that perhaps the most popular of all these works, the Rabin edition of the *Zadokite Fragments*, was effectively a summary of the work of his predecessors, providing for the wider scholarly world a watered-down although improved version of the halakhic researches of Schechter and Ginzberg. In fact, in its efforts to attain usefulness, this book accidentally obscured from its readers the complexity of the halakhic material and its analysis, a lack partly remedied in Rabin's important later book, *Qumran Studies*.[29] It is remarkable that during this period, works of excellent and fair-minded Christian scholars continued to give little attention to the halakhic aspects of the scrolls.

To be sure, the political situation in the Middle East was a factor here. Israeli scholars limited their research primarily to the scrolls bought by Israel, now housed in the Shrine of the Book, since they did not have access to the other material. The excellent commentaries of Yigael Yadin on the *War*

---

24. The halakhic section of the text was ignored in the otherwise incisive study of Philip R. Davies, *The Damascus Covenant: An Interpretation of the "Damascus Document."* JSOTSup 25 (Sheffield: JSOT, 1983), although he discusses the legal aspects of the Admonition, the text's sectarian ideological introduction (105-42).

25. J. T. Milik, in *Les grottes de Murabba'at*, ed. P. Benoit, Milik, and R. de Vaux. DJD 2 (Oxford: Clarendon, 1960) 93-154.

26. S. Lieberman, "The Discipline in the So-Called Dead Sea Manual of Discipline," *JBL* 71 (1951) 199-206; repr. in *Texts and Studies* (New York: Ktav, 1974) 200-7; "Light on the Cave Scrolls from Rabbinic Sources," *PAAJR* 20 (1951) 395-404; repr. in *Texts and Studies*, 190-99.

27. C. Rabin, *The Zadokite Documents* (Oxford: Clarendon, 1954).

28. J. M. Baumgarten, *Studies in Qumran Law*. SJLA 24 (Leiden: Brill, 1977).

29. C. Rabin, *Qumran Studies*. Scripta Judaica 2 (Oxford: Oxford University Press, 1957).

Scroll[30] and Jacob Licht on the *Rule Scroll*[31] certainly dealt with halakhic issues. Yadin's commentary was more influential due to its translation into English[32] and to his renowned expertise in military matters. But Israeli scholars did little to investigate the halakhic aspects of those texts published by the International Team[33] operating on the other side of the Mandelbaum Gate,[34] and they were denied access to the unpublished manuscripts.

Accordingly, in the pre-1967 period, little headway was made in the study of the topic that we are addressing here. Neither the internal history of Jewish law nor its interaction with aspects of political, social, and economic history of the Jews was given any serious treatment in synthetic works published at this time, and the Qumran scrolls were largely treated as a kind of curiosity. Ironically, with all the Christian exegesis of the sectarian corpus, synthetic works on the New Testament and early Christianity likewise demonstrated little impact of the Dead Sea Scrolls corpus, despite the raucous public debate about the relevance of the scrolls to early Christianity that went on after the publication of the work of Edmund Wilson.[35]

By contrast, this very same period, essentially from 1947-1967, saw major advances regarding the similar issues raised in the study of Jewish law in the biblical, medieval, and modern periods. One has only to peruse Jewish studies journals and synthetic works on Jewish history to see the tremendous progress made in these areas. A few examples will be helpful for comparative purposes.

It was during this period that biblical scholars mined the newly available Nuzi documents,[36] sometimes even too enthusiastically, for parallels to biblical law. Indeed, the history of biblical law and its place within the ancient Near Eastern context advanced substantially. The Cairo Genizah materials continued to yield documentary evidence for the geonic period and the development of posttalmudic legal institutions. For the modern period, these

---

30. Y. Yadin, *Megillat Milḥemet Bene 'Or bi-Vene Ḥoshekh mi-Megillot Midbar Yehudah* (Jerusalem: Bialik Institute, 1955).

31. J. Licht, *Megillat ha-Serakhim mi-Megillot Midbar Yehudah* (Jerusalem: Bialik Institute, 1965).

32. Y. Yadin, *The Scroll of the War of the Sons of Light against the Sons of Darkness*, trans. B. Rabin and C. Rabin (Oxford: Oxford University Press, 1962).

33. A team appointed by the Jordan Department of Antiquities consisting of representatives of the Christian biblical schools in the Middle East.

34. The access point to East Jerusalem, held by Jordan between 1948 and 1967.

35. E. Wilson, *The Scrolls from the Dead Sea* (New York: Oxford University Press, 1955).

36. A private archive from the second half of the 15th century B.C.E., these several thousand tablets were found in northeastern Iraq. They proved to be a rich source of information on Hurrian customs and shed light on early biblical history.

same years saw the rise of modern Jewish history as we know it. It was the great accomplishment of Israeli scholarship, especially in the work of Jacob Katz, which understood that halakhah both responded to the massive societal changes that passed over the Jewish people at this time and at the same time helped to shape the manner in which they responded to those changes.[37]

That the study of the halakhah of the Dead Sea Scrolls — indeed of the Second Temple period as a whole — escaped this golden age is only to be understood as resulting from the unique — even bizarre — circumstances that led to the continued suppression of much of the required evidence of the scrolls as well as the absence of cross-fertilization of ideas between Jewish and Christian scholars. This situation would soon change, however, as the result, not of academic trends, but of political affairs.

From the beginning, the study of the Dead Sea Scrolls had a strange interconnection with political affairs in the turbulent Middle East. Sukenik purchased the first lot of scrolls in November 1947 on the very eve of the division of the city of Jerusalem by barbed wire. By the time the dust of the War of Independence had settled, Qumran had passed from British Mandatory Palestine to Jordanian rule. The remaining large scrolls were purchased by Israel from the Syrian Metropolitan under cover of secrecy, while the newly discovered lots from Caves 4 and 11 as well as the Wadi Murabba'at documents were being sold by the Bedouin to Jordanian authorities. Of course, the oddest of all the results of the political situation was the creation of a *judenrein* Dead Sea Scrolls publication team in Jordanian East Jerusalem. Like the Holy City, the scrolls were divided, east and west, only to be reunited in 1967.

The 1967 War was indeed a turning point for Dead Sea Scrolls studies. In the course of the war, Israel recovered the *Temple Scroll* and took nominal control of the unpublished materials still in the Rockefeller Museum. Yadin's preliminary lectures that accompanied the announcement of the recovery of the *Temple Scroll*[38] as well as its publication first in Hebrew[39] and then in English[40] set before the scholarly world, not simply a full-length halakhic work, but perhaps even more importantly for much of the scroll, Yadin's in-depth halakhic

---

37. See J. Katz, *Halakhah ve-Qabbalah: Mehqarim be-Toldot Dat Yiśra'el 'al Medurehah ve-Ziqatah ha-Hevratit* (Jerusalem: Magnes, Hebrew University, 1984) 1-6.

38. Cf. Y. Yadin, "The Temple Scroll," *BA* 30 (1967) 135-39; "The Temple Scroll," in *New Directions in Biblical Archaeology*, ed. D. N. Freedman and J. C. Greenfield (Garden City: Doubleday, 1971) 156-66.

39. Y. Yadin, *Megillat ha-Miqdash*. 3 vols. (Jerusalem: Israel Exploration Society and Shrine of the Book, 1977).

40. Y. Yadin, *The Temple Scroll*. 3 vols. (Jerusalem: Israel Exploration Society and Shrine of the Book, 1983).

commentary that demonstrated the complexity and significance of this material both for the history of halakhah and for Dead Sea Scrolls research.

The Impact of the Temple Scroll and MMT

We have elsewhere discussed the impact of this particular discovery and its publication on the reconceptualization of the Dead Sea Scrolls as Second Temple Jewish documents, a process in which we are proud to have shared along with a fairly large group of Jewish and Christian colleagues. But in the present context, we need to explain that the *Temple Scroll* effectively reenergized the study of the history of Second Temple Jewish law, setting forth what would become an agenda for years to come. Further, the beautiful Hebrew edition of the scroll, replete with rabbinic quotations and citations, drew the attention of talmudic scholars and historians of Second Temple Judaism to this fascinating work.

Throughout the analysis of this document, in Yadin's commentary and in the works of other scholars who dealt with the scroll, the Darwinian theory that had spawned the "old" and "new" halakhah never reared its head. By this time, students of the history of halakhah in other periods, whether in the rabbinic corpus, in the medieval Rabbanite-Karaite debate, or the scientific study of the rise of new movements in modern Judaism, had all made clear the need to recognize that varying opinions coexisted at the same time and that debate and dispute often characterized the history of Jewish law. Further, by this time, new studies of the law of *Jubilees* and other Second Temple documents had greatly enhanced the sense that alongside the law of the Pharisees, later enshrined and developed into the rabbinic tradition, other ideas competed in the halakhic marketplace.

Further, the historical context of this situation was now easily understood since the previous half-century had brought with it tremendous strides in the study of the history of the Jews in Late Antiquity.[41] In the interim, however, the history of rabbinic halakhah had itself entered into a period of furious debate as a result of challenges to the methods for reconstructing the history of both rabbinic literature and Judaism in Late Antiquity. Methods and questions derived from recent progress in New Testament studies were being applied to rabbinic sources. Jacob Neusner challenged the assumption that

---

41. These are, for the most part, summarized in E. Schürer, *The History of the Jewish People in the Age of Jesus Christ*, (175 B.C.-A.D. 135), rev. ed. by G. Vermes and F. Millar, with P. Vermes and M. Black. 3 vols. in 4 (Edinburgh: T. & T. Clark, 1973-1987).

later sources could be used to testify to periods far removed chronologically. He argued that a general approach of credulity and lack of critical sense had led to the construction of a historically skewed picture of rabbinic tradition.[42] Further, and perhaps most important for the present context, Neusner saw rabbinic Judaism as primarily the creation of the post-70 C.E. rabbis. In this respect, he had essentially appropriated a now discredited, originally anti-Semitic idea.

Nineteenth-century Protestant scholars had seen "rabbinism" as a post-30 C.E. development echoing the Christian notion that with the rejection of the messiahship of Jesus — indeed with his crucifixion — Judaism had strayed from its prophetic origins and had entered into a period of legalistic decline. Neusner's theory simply moved the date of this supposed transition forty years later, seeing a profound discontinuity — an almost unbreachable chasm — between pre-70 and post-70 C.E. Judaism. It was not far from this assumption to the provocative claim that ancient Judaism was really "ancient Judaisms," for it was implicit in Neusner's terminology that what separated different approaches to Judaism in this period was greater than what united them. Now these claims had to be evaluated in light of the evidence of the Dead Sea Scrolls.

Throughout Yadin's commentary on the *Temple Scroll*, he alluded to the polemical nature of the text. A casual reader of the scroll, however, would have been impressed by the irenic tone of the author or compiler who chose to build his polemics into positive statements of his own views. But this text is correctly seen as a reformist document, calling for changes in the temple structure, sacrificial practice, even government and military practices in the Hasmonean state in which the author lived. So Yadin was correct in observing that numerous statements of the author constituted polemics against what he termed the הלכה מגובשת (lit., "the solidified law") of the sages. Over and over Yadin pointed to such ideas, but most scholars outside the State of Israel had been sufficiently convinced by the work of Neusner regarding the late date of rabbinic traditions, including those dealing with the pre-70 period, that they implicitly ignored these claims of Yadin. After all, how could a sectarian author writing in the year 120 B.C.E., using sources that went back to the pre-Maccabean period (as we now know), polemicize against views supposedly formulated in the later first century C.E.?[43]

---

42. The fullest statement of this view is in J. Neusner, *The Rabbinic Traditions about the Pharisees before 70*. 3 vols. (Leiden: Brill, 1971).

43. On the sources of the *Temple Scroll*, see L. H. Schiffman, "The *Temple Scroll* and the Nature of Its Law: The Status of the Question," in *The Community of the Renewed Covenant: The*

THE SCHOLARLY CONTROVERSY

The nature of these polemics would not be understood until the announcement of MMT in 1984. However, we must first discuss the substantial progress that occurred in the study of other aspects of Qumran halakhic material and the history of Jewish law between the publication of the *Temple Scroll* in 1973 and the revelation of the existence of MMT in 1984. This was a period in scrolls research that can now be seen in retrospect to have been one of widening the circle of scrolls scholars. During this period, the number of scrolls scholars was swelled substantially by a group of mostly younger scholars who dedicated themselves largely to research on the published scroll corpus since they were not part of the International Team and hence had no access to the unpublished material. A number of these scholars, including the present writer, dealt with Second Temple halakhah.[44] What typified this group of scholars, already inherent in the work of Baumgarten, was the bridging of the gaps in their training that had resulted from their respective religious backgrounds. Jewish scholars began to understand the value of the New Testament and other early Christian materials for the study of ancient Judaism even as regards the study of Jewish law. Christians, initially drawn to the study of Jewish sources in this period because of their value for the background of Christianity, now entered fully into the evaluation of Second Temple Jewish legal sources and were drawn even into rabbinic literature in a first-hand manner through their study of the Dead Sea Scrolls.

There is no question that these tendencies, along with recent ecumenical progress in Israel, America, and Europe, have substantial roots in the quest for a new interreligious understanding that followed from the awareness of the Holocaust as a major event in human history. Nonetheless, this research was for the most part pursued according to the highest standards of academic research and would soon have profound significance for the study of the scrolls. Specifically, the work of these scholars opened the scrolls to a wider public and gradually replaced the Christianizing approach with one that investigated the Judaism of the Second Temple period in a balanced manner, only then using the results of such studies to understand the later history of Judaism and the background and history of early Christianity.

More importantly, it was the collective work of a new generation of scholars that caused the successful movement for the release of the scrolls and then catapulted this new generation of scholars to the center of Qumran re-

---

Notre Dame Symposium on the Dead Sea Scrolls, ed. E. Ulrich and J. VanderKam, 46-51. CJAS 10 (Notre Dame: University of Notre Dame Press, 1994).

44. Most of the works of these contemporary scrolls scholars are listed in F. García Martínez and D. W. Parry, *A Bibliography of the Finds in the Desert of Judah, 1970-1995.* STDJ 19 (Leiden: Brill, 1996).

search. This process, along with, and to some extent as a result of, the publication and discussion of the *Temple Scroll*, placed the study of halakhah and its relevance to Second Temple Jewish history squarely in the center of the debate where it properly belonged.

The polemics against views inherent in later rabbinic literature that Yadin had noticed were soon to be understood by scholars in light of the MMT document.[45] Based on a short allusion to this document and a brief quotation that had been earlier published under the title of 4QMishnique,[46] it had already been proposed that this document as well as the *Temple Scroll* included some Sadducean laws.[47] Indeed, at the very beginning of modern Jewish research, Geiger had sought to reconstruct the influence of the Sadducean tradition on Jewish law. Further, early reformers were, for a variety of reasons, fascinated with the Karaite movement that they saw as a predecessor in revolting against rabbinic authority.[48] As a result, the Sadducees, as the supposed spiritual — even physical — ancestors of the Karaites, had received considerable attention in the early days of the *Wissenschaft des Judentums*. But the only real information on the halakhic differences between the Pharisees and the Sadducees then available was that contained in tannaitic sources. Josephus had reported only theological differences between the Pharisees and Sadducees, not mentioning any specific halakhic disputes. Now, for the first time, in MMT a Second Temple text was available that, as its editors showed,[49] discussed numerous halakhic disputes, some of which were directly parallel to the Pharisee-Sadducee disputes of tannaitic texts. Further, other disputes in this document easily lent themselves to interpretation along the same lines, for they clearly involved differences of opinion that could be

---

45. E. Qimron and J. Strugnell, "An Unpublished Halakhic Letter from Qumran," in *Biblical Archaeology Today: Proceedings of the International Conference on Biblical Archaeology, Jerusalem, April 1984*, ed. J. Amitai, 400-7 (Jerusalem: Israel Exploration Society, Israel Academy of Sciences and Humanities, in cooperation with ASOR, 1985).

46. J. T. Milik, in *Les 'Petites Grottes' de Qumrân*, ed. M. Baillet, Milik, and R. de Vaux. DJD 3 (Oxford: Clarendon, 1962) 225. Milik described the text as "écrit pseudépigraphique mishnique."

47. J. M. Baumgarten, "The Pharisaic-Sadducean Controversies about Purity and the Qumran Texts," *JJS* 31 (1980) 157-70. Cf. M. R. Lehmann, "The *Temple Scroll* as a Source of Sectarian Halakhah," *RevQ* 9 (1978) 579-88.

48. Schorsch, *From Text to Context*, 324, 349.

49. See the halakhic analysis of E. Qimron in *Qumran Cave 4.V: Miqṣat Ma'aśe ha-Torah*, ed. Qimron and J. Strugnell. DJD 10 (Oxford: Clarendon, 1994) 123-77; and the appendix by Y. Sussmann, "The History of the Halakha and the Dead Sea Scrolls: Preliminary Talmudic Observations on *Miqṣat Ma'aśe ha-Torah* (4QMMT)," 179-200. The full version of that appendix is available in Hebrew in Sussman, *Tarbiz* 59 (1989/1990) 11-76.

understood as arising from the hermeneutical assumptions of the Sadducees or as a result of their priestly and temple-centered piety. Clearly, in this document and in the tannaitic material, we were dealing not with Sadducees bent on hellenization, but rather with highly committed Jews whose homiletical and legal tradition differed from those of the Pharisees.

It now became clear that the polemics of the *Temple Scroll* and other halakhic documents from Qumran represented the views of this group whose traditions and interpretations were already to some extent crystallized before the Maccabean revolt. But perhaps, more surprisingly, the aggregate of all such polemics in the halakhic material in the scrolls, whether direct or indirect, pointed toward the existence, certainly by about 150 B.C.E., of a considerably developed Pharisaic system of laws against which these particular priestly sectarian circles were arguing. These conclusions have important relevance to the question of the identity of the Dead Sea sect. Apparently, Sadducean-type law lies at the root of both the schism between the Dead Sea sectarians and the Jerusalem establishment and the laws of the sectarian documents, a conclusion widely accepted even by many of those who still maintain the traditional "Essene" theory regarding the identity of the sect.

This indeed constitutes a major conclusion for the history of Jewish law. For not only was direct evidence for the Sadducean approach recovered but, more importantly, it was established conclusively that the Pharisaic-rabbinic tradition was deeply rooted in the Hasmonean period. In fact, these conclusions are in marked contrast to the claim of radical discontinuity between the pre- and post-70 period that had been put forward by some scholars.

The increase in our knowledge regarding the Pharisees went hand in hand with some previous conclusions drawn by scholars from the *Zadokite Fragments* and the pesher literature. These documents had polemicized against a group known as the דורשי חלקות[50] who preached supposedly false teachings under the leadership of the איש הכזב, the "man of lies."[51] Among the designations of the דורשי חלקות was that they were said to be "builders of the wall," בוני החיץ.[52] Previously, scholars had suggested that the term דורשי חלקות was a pun on the word הלכות (loosely translated as "laws"), and that this derogatory sobriquet, best translated "false interpreters," referred to the Pharisees.[53] Further, the term "builders of the wall" was understood in view of the rabbinic adage עשו סיג לתורה, "make a fence around

---

50. 1QH 10:15, 32; 4QpNah 3-4 i 2, 7; CD 1:18.
51. 1QpHab 2:2; 5:11; CD 20:15.
52. CD 4:19; 8:12, 18; 19:25, 31.
53. Rabin, *Qumran Studies*, 53-70.

Halakhah and History

the Torah,"⁵⁴ to refer as well to the Pharisees. In one passage it was said about this same group אשר בתלמוד שקרם, "that their teaching *(talmud)* is their dishonesty."⁵⁵ It had been suggested that the term תלמוד referred here to an early variety of legal methodology practiced by the Pharisees already in the Hasmonean period.⁵⁶ Taken together, the evidence of the *Temple Scroll*, MMT, the *Zadokite Fragments*, and the pesher literature had in fact provided substantial reflection of Pharisaic teaching and law. Along with what we seem now to be learning about Sadducean halakhah, the scrolls have radically altered our picture of Jewish law of the Second Temple period.

Conclusion

The discovery of the manuscripts from Qumran, as well as those from the other Judean Desert sites, has come at a time in the history of the study of Second Temple Jewish law that is most fortunate. They have provided extremely important information and, indeed, a needed corrective that hopefully will help to dispel some false notions and bring proper balance to the field.

Specifically, the Qumran materials have provided us with what we now know to be an entirely alternative system of Jewish law from Second Temple times, dating at least from the Hasmonean period, and in the case of some laws and even texts, to the pre-Maccabean period.⁵⁷ These documents point to the Sadducean priestly heritage as the locus from which these traditions originate and have allowed us to understand an entirely different system of biblical interpretation that was previously not available.

These documents push back the date of some of the various halakhic debates known from tannaitic sources into the Hasmonean period and also show us that the Pharisaic-rabbinic tradition, at least in certain areas of law and specific halakhot, was well developed and distinct already in the Hasmonean period. In this respect certain false notions recently put forth need to be abandoned.

Perhaps most importantly, the new scrolls allow us to clarify that the linear or evolutionary approach to the history of halakhah will not satisfacto-

---

54. M. 'Abot 1:1.

55. 4QpNah 3-4 ii 8. Cf. S. L. Berrin, *The Pesher Nahum Scroll from Qumran: An Exegetical Study of 4Q169*. STDJ 53 (Leiden: Brill, 2004) 201-5.

56. B. Z. Wacholder, "A Qumran Attack on Oral Exegesis? The Phrase אשר בתלמוד שקרם in 4Q Pesher Nahum," *RevQ* 5 (1966) 351-69.

57. See "Pre-Maccabean Halakhah in the Dead Sea Scrolls and the Biblical Tradition," Chapter 10 below.

rily explain the various halakhic traditions available to us in Second Temple materials. Rather, we must reckon with the notion that competing trends, what we might call priestly/Sadducean and Pharisaic/proto-rabbinic, were operative throughout this period. In this respect some of the earlier studies were correct in emphasizing Sadducean approaches in some of the so-called schismatic or sectarian traditions, and some supposedly "credulous" scholars were correct in assuming that certain Pharisaic traditions were to be dated much earlier than the tannaitic texts in which they were embedded.

We are now set for tremendous advances in this field of study, as is evident from articles and books that have appeared since the full publication of the scrolls and the renewed interest that the release of the scrolls has sparked in this area of research.[58] Several other aspects of Second Temple and early rabbinic research will also intersect so as to stimulate even greater success in the near future.

First, the importance of the other collections of Judean Scrolls for the study of Jewish law is becoming clearer now that they have been fully published and analyzed. The Wadi Daliyeh texts as well as the Hebrew, Aramaic, and Greek documents from the so-called Bar Kokhba caves have yet to have the impact they should have, since they have been widely ignored by scholars of the history of Jewish law. The importance of their testimony about the symbiosis of Jewish and other systems of law, whether Mesopotamian in the first instance or Hellenistic/Roman in the second, means that these texts have important historical implications. Those working on them are sure to continue to illumine these aspects through their work.

Second, archaeological studies have opened up other areas of inquiry regarding ritual objects such as *tefillin* (phylacteries), *miqva'ot*, burial customs, and other issues. Now that we can approach these questions with more sophisticated methods for studying the history of Jewish law as a religious and cultural phenomenon, we will better be able to assimilate the important information that these researchers are providing. Such a synthesis of archaeological data — evidence of material culture — is essential to the history of halakhah.

Finally, we have argued that halakhah and history have a symbiotic relationship. Jewish law had an effect on the history of the Jews in every generation, yet the historical circumstances helped to shape and form the development of the law. It is this dynamic symbiosis that makes this area so fruitful and yet so challenging.

---

58. See the review of L. H. Schiffman, "Milḥemet ha-Megillot: Hitpatḥuyot be-Ḥeqer ha-Megillot ha-Genuzot," *Cathedra* 61 (1991) 3-23; and the later survey of E. Tov, "Megillot Qumran le-'or ha-Meḥqar he-Ḥadash," *JS* 34 (1994) 37-67.

HISTORY, POLITICS, AND
THE FORMATION OF THE SECT

CHAPTER 4

Community without Temple: The Qumran Community's Withdrawal from the Jerusalem Temple

Recent years have seen phenomenal progress in the study of the Dead Sea Scrolls. The availability of the entire corpus, the constant stream of new editions in the series Discoveries in the Judean Desert, and important monographs and conference volumes have stimulated a virtual revolution in the study of the Dead Sea Scrolls.[1] Many areas that had previously been investigated are now being subjected to reinvestigation and reevaluation in light of the tremendous progress in the field. Such is the case with the questions surrounding the attitude of the Qumran community to the temple and the sacrificial system. In this study, we will discuss the purpose and effects of the withdrawal of the Qumran community from participation in the worship conducted in the Jerusalem temple. This issue will be studied from a number of points of view. We will survey the role that the temple plays in the conceptual universe of the sectarians, in their halakhic system, in the organization of the sectarian community, and in their dreams for the eschatological future.

It is best to begin by sketching the historical developments that led up to the separation of the Qumran sectarians from participation in Jerusalem temple worship. During the Maccabean revolt, the Jerusalem temple was defiled by pagan worship.[2] It makes little difference whether this was a case of out-

---

1. For surveys on recent research on the Dead Sea Scrolls, see L. H. Schiffman, "Milḥemet ha-Megillot: Hitpatḥuyot be-Ḥeqer ha-Megillot ha-Genuzot," *Cathedra* 61 (1991) 3-23; E. Tov, "'Al Maṣav ha-Mehqar bi-Megillot Qumran le-'or ha-Mehqar he-Ḥadash," *Mada'e ha-Yahadut* 34 (1994) 37-67.

2. V. Tcherikover, *Hellenistic Civilization and the Jews,* trans. S. Applebaum (Philadelphia: Jewish Publication Society of America, 1966) 195-96; E. Bickerman, *The God of the Maccabees* (Leiden: Brill, 1979) 53-54.

and-out idolatrous practice or whether those who offered pagan offerings considered their god to be identical with the God of Israel. From the point of view of both the Hasmoneans and of those Zadokite priests who would eventually become the sect of the Dead Sea Scrolls, this worship was truly illegitimate and represented an affront to the religion of Israel. Indeed, the Hebrew Bible made clear, especially in Deuteronomy and the works of the Prophets, that only the exclusive worship of Israel's God was acceptable. It is no wonder, then, that the entry of such illegitimate worship even into the holy of holies helped greatly to spark popular support for the incipient Maccabean revolt.

After their victory in 164 B.C.E., the Maccabees purified the temple, restoring monotheistic worship to its precincts. But this effort was short-lived since moderate Hellenists among the Jewish people soon regained a foothold and control of temple worship. It was not until 152 B.C.E., under Jonathan the Hasmonean, that the lengthy process of the establishment of the Hasmonean Empire came to fruition. It was then that, after making an agreement with the Seleucid pretender Alexander Balas (150-146 B.C.E.), Jonathan returned to Jerusalem with his army to again take control of the temple.[3] By this time, Jonathan was apparently fed up with the willingness of many Zadokite, Sadducean priests to participate either in the defilement of the temple that occurred as a result of the Hellenistic reform or in the compromises that had taken place under the moderate Hellenistic high priest Alcimus. For this reason, it seems most likely that the Hasmoneans chose to control the high priesthood and conduct of the temple themselves, together with the increasingly powerful party of the Pharisees. In our view, it was due to these circumstances that the Dead Sea sect came into being.[4] Remnants of the pious Sadducean priests — those who had completely eschewed illegitimate worship at all costs — found it necessary finally to withdraw from participation in the Jerusalem temple because of the changeover from Sadducean practices to those in accord with the Pharisaic point of view. In this environment, the so-called *Halakhic Letter*, 4QMMT, registered the disagreements of these Zadokite priests with the new order of affairs in the Jerusalem temple. It is our view, therefore, that the initial schism that caused the creation of what we know of as the Qumran sect resulted from specific disagreements about details of Jewish law, themselves based for the most part on details of biblical exegesis.[5]

---

3. Tcherikover, *Hellenistic Civilization and the Jews*, 232-34.

4. Cf. F. M. Cross, *The Ancient Library of Qumran*, 3rd ed. (Sheffield: Sheffield Academic, 1995) 103-10, who dates the founding of the sect to immediately after the Maccabean revolt and sees its origins in a group of leaderless "priestly and lay elements of strict faith" (p. 103) after the decay of the Zadokite priesthood.

5. Cf. "The New Halakhic Letter (4QMMT) and the Origins of the Dead Sea Sect," Chap-

This disagreement was of course, only the start of the history of this sectarian group. Throughout the Hasmonean and Herodian periods, the sectarians remained in opposition to the dominant authorities operating the temple. For the most part, the temple leadership continued to be drawn from Sadducean priests who were willing to accommodate to Pharisaic legal norms. This pattern must have changed after a rift developed between the Pharisees and Hasmonean rulers. This rift is well-documented in Josephus, *Pesher Nahum*, and talmudic literature.[6] The end of Hasmonean rule and the return of Sadducean control of the temple, at least for a short time, must have brought brief changes, but by this time the rift was permanent and the Zadokites of Qumran refused to rejoin those who worshiped at the temple.

It seems most likely that we should be able to document in the scrolls the history of the sectarian reaction to the conduct of the temple. Indeed, within the scrolls corpus, we can observe the following sequence or development of ideas: (1) Initially, we can observe a series of disagreements between the sectarians and the temple authorities regarding particular ritual issues. (2) We then find that these disagreements generated the decision on the part of the sectarians to separate from the temple. (3) Next we see that the sectarians sought substitutes for temple worship within the life of the sect and its rituals. At the same time, we observe, and here later rabbinic parallels are instructive, (4) that the sectarians continue to study the laws of temple worship even while being unwilling to participate in it. (5) We are not surprised, then, to find that the eschatological visions of the sectarians included their taking control of the temple, (6) modifying its architecture, and (7) bringing its holy offerings into accord with their legal views. (8) Finally, we should not be surprised that in the end of days the sectarians expected a new, divinely-built temple to substitute for that of the present era. Indeed, we shall find that each one of these phases of the sectarian ideology can be documented in the scrolls.

---

ter 6 below; Schiffman, *Reclaiming the Dead Sea Scrolls: The History of Judaism, the Background of Christianity, the Lost Library of Qumran* (Philadelphia: Jewish Publication Society, 1994; repr. ABRL. New York: Doubleday, 1995) 83-95.

6. Josephus, *Ant.* 13.238-96; 4QpNah 3-4 i 2-8. See "Pharisees and Sadducees in Pesher Nahum," Chapter 20 below; *b. Qidd.* 66a, trans. L. H. Schiffman, *Texts and Traditions: A Source Reader for the Study of Second Temple and Rabbinic Judaism* (Hoboken: Ktav, 1998) 274.

Disagreements Regarding Particular Rituals

The disagreements of the sectarians with the temple authorities are best illustrated from the MMT document. This text lists some twenty-two examples of such disagreements regarding matters pertaining to ritual impurity and sacrifice. The text was probably composed soon after 152 B.C.E. While some scholars initially thought that this text should be seen as an epistle,[7] others have argued that it may have been a sectarian document intended for internal consumption.[8] From our vantage point, however, what is important is that MMT yields some sense of what issues the Qumran sect believed lay at the heart of its conflict with the Jerusalem establishment.

One area of controversy deals with grain offerings and sacrifices donated by non-Jews. The sectarians did not accept the validity of such offerings that, if we can judge from later halakhic texts, were accepted by the Pharisees.[9] This controversy had later ramifications when it served as a boiling point that helped to touch off the Great Revolt in 66 C.E., according to the account of Josephus.[10] Another controversy concerned the eating of the cereal offerings. Whereas the Pharisees apparently assumed that these offerings could be eaten on the same day as the accompanying sacrifice as well as on the following night, the sectarians, apparently following Saducean law, ruled that they had to be eaten before sunset.[11]

An exceedingly important controversy revolved around the ashes of the red heifer that were used to purify those who had contracted impurity of the dead.[12] The Sadducees, followed by those who founded the Qumran sect, believed that this offering had to be made only by those who were themselves totally pure. This meant that only those whose purification periods had

---

7. E. Qimron and J. Strugnell, "An Unpublished Halakhic Letter from Qumran," in *Biblical Archaeology Today: Proceedings of the International Congress on Biblical Archaeology, Jerusalem, April 1984*, ed. J. Amitai, 400-7 (Jerusalem: Israel Exploration Society, Israel Academy of Sciences and Humanities, in cooperation with ASOR, 1985).

8. Strugnell himself expresses hesitation about considering this an epistle in an appendix to *Qumran Cave 4.V: Miqṣat Ma'aśe ha-Torah*, ed. E. Qimron and Strugnell. DJD 10 (Oxford: Clarendon, 1994) 205; and "MMT: Second Thoughts on a Forthcoming Edition," in *The Community of the Renewed Covenant: The Notre Dame Symposium on the Dead Sea Scrolls*, ed. E. Ulrich and J. C. VanderKam, 70-73. CJAS 10 (Notre Dame: University of Notre Dame Press, 1994). He suggests, nonetheless, that this was a document that was sent to a leader, so that his argument regarding the term "epistle" pertains to its use in describing a specific literary genre.

9. Qimron and Strugnell, DJD 10:149-50.

10. *J.W.* 2.409-17.

11. Qimron and Strugnell, DJD 10:150-52.

12. Qimron and Strugnell, DJD 10:152-54.

ended with sunset on the last day of their purification periods might perform these rituals. However, the practice of the temple accorded with the Pharisaic view that purification sufficient for the preparation of such offerings was attained even before sunset on the last purificatory day.[13]

These controversies provide some sense of the issues that separated those who formed the early Qumran sect, who in our view followed Saducean halakhah, from those who ran the Jerusalem temple in early Hasmonean times. The latter generally followed the Pharisaic approach. The numerous controversies detailed in this text can be augmented by examining the sources of the *Temple Scroll* that must pre-date the founding of the Qumran sect and that are most probably pre-Maccabean.[14] Some of the very same controversies found in MMT are found there, although only the view of the Sadducees is reflected in the text.[15] Because of the sheer length of that document, a long list of such controversies could easily be assembled from it.

One of the copyists of the MMT document placed before it a solar calendar of the type known from other sectarian calendrical fragments as well as from compositions such as *Jubilees* and *Enoch*.[16] This calendar consisted of four quarters, each of three months of the lengths thirty, thirty, and thirty-one days. Furthermore, the expanded festival calendar known from the *Temple Scroll*, with the additional firstfruits festivals and other nonbiblical holidays, is represented here.[17] Clearly, it was the view of this copyist that the founding of the sect was at least in part based on the controversy surrounding the calendar. If this is correct, then the sectarian separation from the Jerusalem temple would have been encouraged, if not caused by, disagreement regarding the dates of the festivals. This same claim is made, after all, in the *Zadokite Fragments (Damascus Document)* and can be supported by *Pesher Habakkuk*.[18]

---

13. Cf. L. H. Schiffman, "Pharisaic and Sadducean Halakhah in Light of the Dead Sea Scrolls: The Case of Ṭevul Yom," *DSD* 1 (1994) 285-99.

14. L. H. Schiffman, "The *Temple Scroll* and the Nature of Its Law: The Status of the Question," in Ulrich and VanderKam, *Community of the Renewed Covenant*, 46-48.

15. L. H. Schiffman, "*Miqṣat Ma'aśeh ha-Torah* and the *Temple Scroll*," *RevQ* 14 (The Texts of Qumran and the History of the Community: Proceedings of the Groningen Congress on the Dead Sea Scrolls 3, 1990) 435-57; "The Place of 4QMMT in the Corpus of Qumran Manuscripts," in *Reading 4QMMT: New Perspectives on Qumran Law and History*, ed. J. Kampen and M. J. Bernstein, 86-90. SBLSymS 2 (Atlanta: Scholars, 1966).

16. Cf. S. Talmon, "The Calendar Reckoning of the Sect from the Judean Desert," in *Aspects of the Dead Sea Scrolls*, ed. C. Rabin and Y. Yadin, 164-67. ScrHier 4 (Jerusalem: Magnes, 1958).

17. Y. Yadin, *The Temple Scroll* (Jerusalem: Israel Exploration Society and Shrine of the Book, 1983) 1:89-142; L. H. Schiffman, "The Sacrificial System of the *Temple Scroll* and the *Book of Jubilees*," *SBLSP 1985*, ed. K. H. Richards, 217-33 (Atlanta: Scholars, 1985).

18. Talmon, "Calendar Reckoning," 164-67.

Separation from the Temple

That such ritual debates did indeed cause the sectarians to separate from worship in the Jerusalem temple is claimed by the *Zadokite Fragments*. This text, originally known only in the two partial copies preserved in the Cairo Genizah,[19] can now be examined in the Qumran copies published by J. M. Baumgarten.[20] It is most probable that the *Zadokite Fragments* are to be dated to ca. 120 B.C.E., soon after the separation of the sectarians, both spiritually and physically, from the Jerusalem establishment. This document sets off three cardinal areas of transgression in which the opponents of the sect are said to have engaged.[21] These opponents are termed "builders of the wall," clearly a sobriquet for the Pharisees.[22] In particular, we encounter there the transgression of rendering the temple impure (CD 4:17-18). This, in turn, is explained as not making the proper distinctions according to the Torah, violating laws pertaining to impurity of women as a result of blood flows, and also marrying one's niece (5:6-8). The latter practice is known to have been accepted among the Pharisees and the Tannaim. Later on, in a list of transgressions of which the opponents of the sect are presumably guilty, we again find reference to failure to make proper distinctions between that which is impure and that which is pure (6:17). There as well, we find reference to improper observance of the Sabbath and festivals (6:18). The latter may be a reference to failure to observe the holidays according to the sectarian calendar. All these transgressions of proper temple practice are blamed on the sect's opponents, the Hasmonean high priests, those Sadducees who continue to cooperate with them, and the Pharisees whose views dominated the temple.

Thus, the *Zadokite Fragments* prohibit members of the sect from entering the Jerusalem temple to offer sacrifice there (6:11-12). Temple sacrifice according to the prevailing norms was considered explicitly by this text to be null and void. This strong judgment was, no doubt, based on the many halakhic disagreements between the sectarians and the priestly establishment.

There can be no question, therefore, that the sectarians decided in the

---

19. The best edition of the Genizah texts is E. Qimron, "The Text of CDC," in *The Damascus Document Reconsidered*, ed. M. Broshi, 9-49 (Jerusalem: Israel Exploration Society and Shrine of the Book, Israel Museum, 1992).

20. J. M. Baumgarten, *Qumran Cave 4.XIII: The Damascus Document (4Q266-273)*. DJD 18 (Oxford: Clarendon, 1996).

21. CD 4:12-19; cf. H. Kosmala, "The Three Nets of Belial (A Study in the Terminology of Qumran and the New Testament)," *ASTI* 4 (1965) 91-113.

22. L. H. Schiffman, "New Light on the Pharisees," in *Understanding the Dead Sea Scrolls*, ed. H. Shanks, 219-20 (New York: Random House, 1992).

aftermath of their initial conflicts with the Jerusalem establishment to remove themselves from participation in the Jerusalem temple. It should be noted that the Essenes, as described by Josephus, had special arrangements in the temple whereby they were able to send votive offerings without entering the temple, thus maintaining their own standards of purity.[23] In this respect, their practice contrasts with that described in the *Zadokite Fragments,* which expects absolute abstention from temple sacrifice.

The Sect and Its Rituals as a Substitute for the Temple

Numerous passages in sectarian literature indicate that once the sectarians had decided to refrain from temple rituals, two basic strategies were adopted: seeing the sect as a substitute for the temple and using prayer as a substitute for sacrifice. It must be emphasized that the sectarians did not offer sacrifices at Qumran, despite claims to the contrary by some scholars.[24] There is absolutely no archaeological evidence that would indicate the presence of a cult site or temple at Qumran.[25] Further, the animal bones that were buried around some of the buildings at Qumran cannot be taken as indicative of the performance of sacrificial rituals since no requirement to bury bones is known from any system of Jewish sacrificial practice.[26]

A number of passages speak of the sect itself as a "holy house" (בית קודש), clearly a metaphorical designation for the temple. Whereas Israelite religion assumed that God could best be approached through the sacrificial system in the temple, it was the view of the sectarians that, in light of the impure state of temple worship, life in the sect, following its principles and its laws, would best bring humans into close contact with God. This notion is of sufficient importance that an entire section of the *Rule of the Community* is based on this motif.[27] There we find that the council of the community is de-

---

23. Josephus, *Ant.* 18:19. For a full study of this issue, see J. M. Baumgarten, *Studies in Qumran Law.* SJLA 24 (Leiden: Brill, 1977) 57-74.

24. Baumgarten, *Studies in Qumran Law,* 43, n. 14. Baumgarten correctly follows the opinion of Ginzberg to the effect that sacrifices were not offered by the sectarians.

25. R. de Vaux, *Archaeology and the Dead Sea Scrolls.* Schweich Lectures 1959 (London: Oxford University Press, 1973) 14; contrast the view of J.-B. Humbert, "L'espace sacré à Qumrân," *RB* 101-2 (1994) 199-201; J. Magness, *The Archaeology of Qumran and the Dead Sea Scrolls.* SDSSRL (Grand Rapids: Wm. B. Eerdmans, 2002) 118-19.

26. De Vaux, *Archaeology and the Dead Sea Scrolls,* 14-16, n. 3; L. H. Schiffman, *The Eschatological Community of the Dead Sea Scrolls.* SBLMS 38 (Atlanta: Scholars, 1989) 64-67.

27. 1QS 8:1-16; J. Licht, *Megillat ha-Serakhim mi-Megillot Midbar Yehudah* (Jerusalem: Bialik Institute, 1965) 167-75.

scribed as " an Everlasting Plantation, a House of Holiness for Israel,[28] and an Assembly of Supreme Holiness for Aaron" (1QS 8:5-6).[29] The text continues in a similar vein, speaking of

> a most holy dwelling[30] for Aaron with everlasting knowledge of the covenant of justice, and they shall offer up sweet fragrance. It shall be a house of perfection and truth in Israel that they may establish a covenant according to the everlasting precepts. And they shall be an agreeable offering, atoning for the Land and determining the judgment of wickedness, and there shall be no more iniquity. (8:8-10)

Here we see the sect itself serving as a substitute for the temple in which the sons of Aaron would normally serve. This "holy house" is a place through which to gain atonement. Still further on we find similar motifs in which the sectarian group is described as atoning for guilt and transgression. The text specifically describes gaining acceptance through sacrifice of animals and prayer in terms of "the gift of the lips" and "like a sweet-smelling offering for righteousness" (9:4-5). These expressions describe the perfect way of life that is like "a voluntary meal offering for acceptance" (9:3-5). In these passages and others the sacrifices appear only figuratively. Rather, it is the life of the sectarian within the context of the group that provides the opportunity for atonement, just as would have been the function of the various sacrifices had the sectarians participated in temple rituals in Jerusalem.[31]

In order to create the appropriate atmosphere within the sect to accomplish these goals, temple purity laws were transferred to the lives of the sectarians, a phenomenon especially apparent in the *Rule of the Congregation*. Here, in describing the community of the end of days, the text basically creates a mirror image for the messianic era of present-day, nonmessianic practice. For this reason, practices that were part of the everyday life of the sect appear in this document in the form in which they would be observed in the messianic era. Those laws that, according to the book of Leviticus, disqualified priests from service in the temple (Lev 21:16-24) and those that disqualified sacrificial animals (Lev 22:17-25) were all brought to bear on participants in the eschatological community (1QSa 2:3-11). Those who were not fit for the roles of

---

28. That is, Holy Temple.

29. G. Vermes, *The Complete Dead Sea Scrolls in English* (New York: Allen Lane, Penguin, 1997) 109.

30. Lit., "holy of holies."

31. For a thorough study of this issue, see B. Gärtner, *The Temple and the Community in Qumran and the New Testament* (Cambridge: Cambridge University Press, 1965).

priest and/or sacrifice were disqualified from participation in the community.[32] We should assume, therefore, in light of the *Zadokite Fragments* as well,[33] that such laws were observed by the sectarians in their present, premessianic environment. Accordingly, the life of the sect was conducted as if the community were a virtual temple.

Other elements of this same approach may be observed in the purity laws that served as the basis for entry into the sect.[34] Those who went through the novitiate and sought full status in the sectarian group became increasingly eligible to come in contact with pure food as they rose through the ranks. Initially, after passing two examinations, they were permitted to come in contact only with solid food that had a lesser susceptibility to impurity than drinks. After a third examination a year later, they were permitted to come in contact with liquid food that was of much greater susceptibility.[35] One who violated sectarian regulations could be temporarily demoted, being permitted to come in contact with solid food but forbidden to come in contact with liquid food. For a more serious transgression, one could be demoted even to the level of losing the privilege of touching the pure solid food of the sect.[36] This system can only be understood if the sect itself was regarded as a temple and, therefore, it was obligatory to maintain temple purity laws within the context of the life of the group.

Like the rabbinic Jews later on, the Qumran sectarians and other similar groups were in the process of shifting from temple worship to prayer even before the destruction of the temple in 70 C.E. The destruction simply hastened a long, ongoing process taking place in Judean society throughout the Second Temple period. The significance of prayer as a mode of experiencing God was on the increase.[37] It is no surprise, then, that the Qumran sectarians included in their library prayer texts which they or others recited.[38] These texts were no doubt intended to substitute for participation in the temple that was made impossible either for reasons of distance or, as was the case with the Qumran

---

32. Schiffman, *Eschatological Community*, 37-52.

33. 4Q266 5 ii 1-14; 4Q267 5 iii; and the comments of Baumgarten, DJD 18:51.

34. L. H. Schiffman, *Sectarian Law in the Dead Sea Scrolls: Courts, Testimony and the Penal Code*. BJS 33 (Chico: Scholars, 1983) 161-65.

35. C. Rabin, *Qumran Studies*. Scripta Judaica 2 (Oxford: Oxford University Press, 1957) 3.

36. Schiffman, *Sectarian Law*, 159-68.

37. L. H. Schiffman, *From Text to Tradition: A History of Second Temple and Rabbinic Judaism* (Hoboken: Ktav, 1991) 164-66.

38. Schiffman, *Reclaiming the Dead Sea Scrolls*, 289-301; E. G. Chazon, "Prayers from Qumran and their Historical Implications," *DSD* 1 (1994) 265-84; L. H. Schiffman, "The Dead Sea Scrolls and the Early History of Jewish Liturgy," in *The Synagogue in Late Antiquity*, ed. L. I. Levine, 33-48 (Philadelphia: ASOR and New York: Jewish Theological Seminary of America, 1987); B. Nitzan, *Qumran Prayer and Religious Poetry*. STDJ 12 (Leiden: Brill, 1994) 47-116.

sect, because of ideology. In many ways, it can be said that the Qumran sect, deprived of participation in temple worship by its separatism, traveled the same road that the Pharisees would eventually travel, only much earlier. Long before the Pharisaic-rabbinic Jews were forcibly separated from their temple, the Qumran sectarians had eschewed sacrifice in Jerusalem.

Study of the Laws of Sacrifice

The Dead Sea sectarians, according to the *Rule of the Community*, devoted one-third of each night to studying the Torah. We have little specific information about what this study entailed, except insofar as the results of study sessions of the sect were assembled into collections of laws that became the building blocks of the various communal rules.[39] It does seem, however, that laws pertaining to temple sacrifices were studied and discussed by members of the sect.[40] Evidence for this may be cited from the *Zadokite Fragments* that include various laws pertaining to qualifications of the priesthood and purity and impurity. But it might be argued that, because this text does not contain specific laws regarding the nature of the temple or the sacrificial system, these subjects were not part of the regular study program of the Qumran sect.

Several works of substantial size, however, indicate that some sectarians studied texts that discuss the temple and sacrifices. These texts seem for the most part to stem from groups that existed even before the Qumran sect was formed. This is certainly the case regarding the book of *Jubilees* that contains in it numerous references to sacrifices for various occasions as well as to specific procedures required for sacrificial offerings.[41] The same kind of expertise seems to have been in evidence in the composition of the *Aramaic Levi Document*.[42]

---

39. Schiffman, *Sectarian Law*, 9. Cf. "Codification of Jewish Law in the Dead Sea Scrolls," Chapter 9 below.

40. Cf. R. A. Kugler, "Rewriting Rubrics: Sacrifice and the Religion of Qumran," in *Religion in the Dead Sea Scrolls*, ed. J. J. Collins and Kugler, 90-112. SDSSRL (Grand Rapids: Wm. B. Eerdmans, 2000).

41. See C. Albeck, *Das Buch der Jubiläen und die Halacha*. Siebenundvierzigster Bericht der Hochschule für die Wissenschaft des Judentums in Berlin (1930); and Schiffman, "Sacrificial System."

42. M. E. Stone and J. C. Greenfield, "Aramaic Levi Document," in *Qumran Cave 4.XVII: Parabiblical Texts, Part 3*, ed. G. J. Brooke et al. DJD 22 (Oxford: Clarendon, 1996) 1-72; R. A. Kugler, *From Patriarch to Priest: The Levi-Priestly Tradition from* Aramaic Levi *to* Testament of Levi. SBLEJL 9 (Atlanta: Scholars, 1996) 93-111; L. H. Schiffman, "Sacrificial Halakhah in the Fragments of the *Aramaic Levi Document* from Qumran, the Cairo Genizah, and Mt. Athos

The most extensive collection of sacrificial laws available to the sectarians, in addition to the biblical codes of Leviticus, Deuteronomy, and Ezekiel,[43] are the no-longer-extant sources used by the author/redactor of the *Temple Scroll* writing early in the Hasmonean period.[44] While the *Temple Scroll* was no doubt put into its complete form at a period close to that in which the *Zadokite Fragments* were assembled, the sources are certainly pre-Maccabean and may reach back even into the third century. Laws in these no-longer-preserved sources concerned sacrificial procedure, ritual purity and impurity, and the ritual calendar. In addition, similar texts apparently served as sources for related documents such as 4Q365a, part of an expanded Torah scroll with additional material parallel to certain passages in the *Temple Scroll*.[45] Documents like this, as well as the final or redacted *Temple Scroll*, must have been studied extensively by the sectarians since teachings found in them are also enshrined in the *Zadokite Fragments*.

We shall call attention here to one particular law that exemplifies the existence of sources of sacrificial law that predate the extant Qumran documents. The Pharisaic-rabbinic tradition ruled that the fourth-year produce, about which the Bible said that it was to be given "to the Lord" (Lev 19:24), was to be brought by the owners to Jerusalem where they would eat it. Already in 4QMMT, the point was made that in the sectarian interpretation of this law, no doubt representing the Sadducean trend, the fourth-year produce, like the so-called second tithe, was to be presented at the Jerusalem temple and given to the priests.[46] This law was to find its way as well into the *Tem-*

Monastery" in *Reworking the Bible: Apocryphal and Related Texts at Qumran: Proceedings of a Joint Symposium by the Orion Center for the Study of the Dead Sea Scrolls and Associated Literature and the Hebrew University Institute for Advanced Studies Research Group on Qumran, 15-17 January, 2002*, ed. E. G. Chazon, D. Dimant, and R. A. Clements, 177-202. STDJ 58 (Leiden: Brill, 2005). See also the more recently published commentaries: J. C. Greenfield, M. E. Stone, and E. Eshel, eds., *The Aramaic Levi Documents: Edition, Translation, Commentary*. SVTP 19 (Leiden: Brill, 2004); and H. Drawnel, *An Aramaic Wisdom Text from Qumran: A New Interpretation of the Levi Document*. JSJSup 86 (Leiden: Brill, 2004).

43. Thirteen manuscripts of Leviticus, 30 of Deuteronomy, and 6 of Ezekiel have been identified in the Qumran corpus.

44. A. M. Wilson and L. Wills, "Literary Sources of the Temple Scroll," *HTR* 75 (1982) 275-88; M. O. Wise, *A Critical Study of the Temple Scroll from Qumran Cave 11*. SAOC 49 (Chicago: Oriental Institute, University of Chicago, 1990) 195-98; F. García Martínez, "Sources et rédaction du *Rouleau du Temple*," *Hen* 13 (1991) 219-32.

45. S. White Crawford, "4QTemple?" in *Qumran Cave 4.VIII: Parabiblical Texts, Part 1*, ed. H. Attridge et al. DJD 13 (Oxford: Clarendon, 1994) 319-33; letter from J. Strugnell, in B. Z. Wacholder, *The Dawn of Qumran: The Sectarian Torah and the Teacher of Righteousness* (Cincinnati: Hebrew Union College Press, 1983) 205-6.

46. Qimron and Strugnell, DJD 10:164-65.

ple Scroll and *Zadokite Fragments*.[47] Certainly, both of these texts derive this law and its scriptural basis from sources such as those that served the redactor of the *Temple Scroll*. Such interpretations and the laws that emerge from them must have been part of traditions of Torah study that took place among members of the sect and related groups. Thus, as expected, we find that, even while remaining separated from the temple ritual, members of the Qumran sect continued to study and cherish laws and interpretations of the Torah that pertained to the correct procedures for temple worship and related regulations of purity and impurity.

Control of the Temple

It seems clear that the sectarians expected that at some point in the future they would come to control the Jerusalem temple and to be able to operate it according to their legal rulings and sacrificial procedures. Most likely, they believed that this would take place as part of the unfolding of the divine plan that would lead to the eschaton. The *War Scroll* describes a series of battles in which the sectarians would emerge victorious after destroying all the forces of evil within the Jewish people and in the nations surrounding the land of Israel.[48] While the end of this text is not preserved, it is probable that the final sheet would have dealt with prayers and songs recited by the sectarians upon their return from the battlefield to Jerusalem, most probably prayers of thanksgiving, and sacrifices would have been offered in the Jerusalem temple.[49]

The notion that the sectarians would at some point come to control the temple is implicit in a number of Qumran texts, among them 4QFlorilegium, which makes clear that the future temple will be conducted only for those of appropriate Israelite lineage.[50] Clearly the assumption of these passages is that the illegitimate priesthood currently in control of the temple will be replaced in the end of days by the Zadokite priests of the sect who will maintain the proper standards.

---

47. See Schiffman, *RevQ* 14 (1990): 452-56.
48. See Y. Yadin, *The Scroll of the War of the Sons of Light against the Sons of Darkness* [hereafter: *War Scroll*], trans. B. and C. Rabin (Oxford: Oxford University Press, 1962) 18-37 for the plan of the eschatological war.
49. Yadin, *War Scroll*, 223-28.
50. Cf. G. J. Brooke, *Exegesis at Qumran: 4QFlorilegium in Its Jewish Context*. JSOTSup 29 (Sheffield: JSOT, 1985) 178-84.

The Architecture of the Temple

During the Babylonian exile, the author of the last chapters of Ezekiel dreamt of an expanded temple precinct that would take its place as part of a utopian plan for the city of Jerusalem and the land of Israel. Apparently, such utopian plans were not unique to this author alone. Writing sometime most probably in the third century B.C.E., the author of an Aramaic text entitled *New Jerusalem* wrote of a city of gargantuan proportions that would include an enlarged temple complex.[51] Unfortunately, the details of this temple plan are not extant in the preserved portions of the text. These examples demonstrate the tendency in this period for a variety of Jewish groups to plan larger and improved temple complexes. These very same tendencies would eventually lead Herod the Great to execute the building of his temple structure from 18 B.C.E. on.

It is apparent from the existence of several copies of the *New Jerusalem* text in various caves at Qumran that this composition was widely read by members of the sectarian group.[52] To be sure, they would have derived from it, among other things, the dream of an enlarged and refurbished temple that would accord with their specific ritual requirements. But much more information on the very same subject was contained in the prose temple plan that was included in the *Temple Scroll* by its author/redactor.[53] This temple plan has been found to share certain architectural details with that of the *New Jerusalem,* no doubt because both of these visionary temples were designed in the Hellenistic period.[54]

This plan set forth the architect's greatly enlarged temple that would be

---

51. See F. García Martínez, *Qumran and Apocalyptic: Studies on the Aramaic Texts from Qumran.* STDJ 9 (Leiden: Brill, 1992) 180-213; M. Chyutin, *The New Jerusalem Scroll from Qumran: A Comprehensive Reconstruction.* JSPSup 25 (Sheffield: Sheffield Academic, 1997) 33-69.

52. For a list of manuscripts found in the various caves, see García Martínez, *Qumran and Apocalyptic,* 180-81, n. 1.

53. See the detailed discussion of the architecture of this temple in Yadin, *Temple Scroll,* 1:177-276; J. Maier, *The Temple Scroll: An Introduction, Translation & Commentary.* JSOTSup 34 (Sheffield: JSOT, 1985) 90-115; J. Maier, "The Architectural History of the Temple in Jerusalem in Light of the Temple Scroll," in *Temple Scroll Studies,* ed. G. J. Brooke, 23-62. JSPSup 7 (Sheffield: JSOT, 1989).

54. M. Broshi, "Visionary Architecture and Town Planning in the Dead Sea Scrolls," in *Time to Prepare the Way in the Wilderness: Papers on the Qumran Scrolls by Fellows of the Institute for Advanced Studies of the Hebrew University, Jerusalem, 1989-1990,* ed. D. Dimant and L. H. Schiffman, 9-22. STDJ 16 (Leiden: Brill, 1995); and Wise, *A Critical Study of the Temple Scroll,* 64-86.

built according to architectural principles embodying very different religious ideas from those attributed to King Solomon or evident in the temple of Herod the Great. Specifically, this temple was to include an additional courtyard, approximately 1500 cubits square, that would serve to distance the temple from ritual impurity. The middle court occupied essentially the same function as that of the outer court — the women's court — of the other temple plans. In the middle, of course, was the temple surrounded by the inner court.[55]

This temple plan was based on the assumption that the courtyards would be arranged concentrically, with the temple building itself in the middle.[56] By contrast, in Solomon's temple as well as that of Herod, the courtyards were arranged sequentially such that the worshipper entered further and further into the temple precincts. Each area was of ascending holiness, each essentially behind the other.[57]

These two architectural approaches bespeak different theological approaches. The Solomonic and Herodian approaches indicate that the temple was regarded as a sanctum into which people might penetrate to differing extents depending on their state of ritual purity or impurity and their status as priests, Levites, or Israelites. The concentric approach of the *Temple Scroll*, however, is based on the similar plan of the Israelite camp in the wilderness according to Numbers 10. Here the concept was rather of an inner sanctum from which holiness radiated to all areas of the temple, the city of Jerusalem, and the surrounding land of Israel.[58] Those who read the *Temple Scroll*, and certainly its author/redactor, would have prayed for and expected a temple of this kind. The ultimate purpose of this new temple structure, which, of course, was never actually built, was to insure the greater sanctity of the temple and its sacrificial worship.

What interests us here is that apparently this alternative, utopian temple plan was studied by members of the Qumran sect both before its redaction into the *Temple Scroll* and after. But it is important to emphasize that accord-

---

55. Cf. L. H. Schiffman, "Architecture and Law: The Temple and Its Courtyards in the *Temple Scroll*," in *From Ancient Israel to Modern Judaism: Intellect in Quest of Understanding: Essays in Honor of Marvin Fox*, ed. J. Neusner, E. S. Frerichs, and N. M. Sarna, 1:267-84. BJS 159 (Atlanta: Scholars, 1989).

56. Cf. L. H. Schiffman, "The Construction of the Temple according to the *Temple Scroll*," RevQ 17 (Hommage à Józef T. Milik; 1996) 555-71.

57. B. A. Levine, "Biblical Temple," ER 2:213.

58. L. H. Schiffman, "Sacred Space: The Land of Israel in the *Temple Scroll*," in *Biblical Archaeology Today 1990: Proceedings of the Second International Congress on Biblical Archaeology*, ed. A. Biran and J. Aviram, 398-410 (Jerusalem: Israel Exploration Society, 1993).

ing to the *Temple Scroll* itself the plan put forward was expected to be built in the present age, before the messianic era; it was not a messianic temple.[59] It would allow the fulfillment of the specific halakhic views of the group even before the coming of the messianic era. Even if in the present they had withdrawn from temple worship, they continued to study its laws in preparation for the day when they would return to worship once again at the mountain of the Lord.

Sectarian Law and the Sacrificial System

The sectarians clearly expected that the temple that they would control at the end of days would function according to law as they understood it. In order to facilitate this development, it was expected that an eschatological high priest would be designated. According to one particular scheme, rather widely distributed in the sectarian scrolls, one of two messiahs would be of Aaronide descent. This messiah would be superior to the temporal messiah who would be known as the messiah of Israel. An alternative view expected only one messiah who would be Davidic. In this case, a separate high priestly figure would be appointed.[60] The role of the messianic high priest in the end of days was one of great prominence, as it was expected that sacrificial worship would occupy a major role in the life of the nation. It is possible that this eschatological priest is to be identified with the interpreter of the law who is expected to reappear in the end of days according to sectarian ideology (CD 6:7-8). This interpreter of the law was expected to provide accurate legal rulings on all subjects, no doubt including matters of sacrifice and temple.

Clearly, the halakhic basis for the conduct of temple worship, in the view of the sectarians, was that of Sadducean law.[61] Rulings such as those contained in 4QMMT, the *Temple Scroll*, the *Zadokite Fragments,* and the various minor halakhic tracts found among the scrolls were expected to be put into effect in the future temple. The sectarians' calendar with its expanded list of festivals would be adhered to. The *omer* count (Lev 23:9-22) would com-

---

59. 11QTemple 29:8-10; contra B. Z. Wacholder, *The Dawn of Qumran,* 21-24; M. O. Wise, "The Eschatological Vision of the *Temple Scroll*," *JNES* 49 (1990) 155-72.

60. "Messianic Figures and Ideas in the Qumran Scrolls," Chapter 16 below; cf. Schiffman, *Reclaiming the Dead Sea Scrolls,* 317-50; J. J. Collins, *The Scepter and the Star: The Messiahs of the Dead Sea Scrolls and Other Ancient Literature.* ABRL (New York: Doubleday, 1995).

61. Y. Sussmann, "The History of the Halakha and the Dead Sea Scrolls," in Qimron and Strugnell, DJD 10:179-200.

mence on the first Sunday after the last day of Passover such that the festival of Shavuot would always be celebrated on Sunday.[62] Other important principles would include the observance of the Sadducean view that sunset was required at the end of purification periods[63] and that in cases in which the Torah required seven-day purification periods, ablutions would also be required on the first day.[64] Many other examples of such principles of sectarian law could be cited as laws expected by the sectarians to be observed in the temple of the future.

The Final Temple

Several texts from Qumran, paralleled also by some rabbinic texts, testify to the notion that in the messianic era a new temple, actually constructed by God, would descend from the heavens to replace the temple that had previously been built by humans.[65] In the *Temple Scroll* it is stated that its laws and temple plan would be in effect until such time as there would come a day of blessing[66] — or the day of creation, according to another reading of the text.[67] At that time God would cause his temple to dwell among his people. Such ideas are also found in some apocryphal works of the Second Temple period.

This concept is much more prominent, however, in 4QFlorilegium (also known as 4QMidrash on Eschatology) in which there is a direct allusion to a temple that God will build in the end of days in accord with Exod 15:17. In the interim, God had allowed a temple to be built by humans.[68] This temple probably refers not to the temple of the present day that the sectarians regarded as impure but rather to the sect that could be said to be a virtual temple in which sanctity and holiness were attained by living a life according to

---

62. For a summary of the calendar controversy, see Schiffman, *Reclaiming the Dead Sea Scrolls*, 301-5 (and bibliog. on 433). See also Yadin, *Temple Scroll*, 1:103-5, 116-19.

63. Cf. Schiffman, *DSD* 1 (1994) 285-99, n. 13.

64. J. Milgrom, "Studies in the Temple Scroll," *JBL* 97 (1978) 512-18.

65. Yadin, *Temple Scroll*, 1:181-87; 2:129.

66. 11QTemple[a] 29:9, reading *hbrkh* with Yadin, *Temple Scroll*, 2:129.

67. E. Qimron, *The Temple Scroll: A Critical Edition with Extensive Reconstructions* (Beersheva: Ben-Gurion University of the Negev and Jerusalem: Israel Exploration Society, 1996) 44. Qimron's reading of *hbdyh* is already alluded to by Yadin based on Qimron, "Le-Nushah shel Megillat ha-Miqdash," *Leš* 42 (1978) 141-42.

68. Brooke, *Exegesis at Qumran*, 178-93; D. R. Schwartz, "The Three Temples of 4QFlorilegium," *RevQ* 10 (1979) 83-92; M. O. Wise, "4QFlorilegium and the Temple of Man," *RevQ* 15 (1991) 103-32.

sectarian principles. But the text makes clear that in the end of days a true temple will be built by God for his people. So the sectarians expected that the present-day temple from which they abstained because of ritual disagreements would eventually be replaced by a perfect structure of divine creation.

Conclusion

The Qumran sect played out in advance an important aspect of Second Temple–period Jewish history. Whereas it was the destruction of the temple in 70 C.E. that forced most of the Jewish community to adapt itself and emphasize alternative modes of piety to sacrifice, namely prayer and study of Torah, the Qumran sectarians, like the Jews of the Diaspora, had to face the absence of a temple much earlier. Diaspora Jews were separated from the temple by physical distance, but the Jews of the Qumran sect were separated because of their disapproval of the manner in which the Jerusalem priesthood conducted temple worship. Further, if the sectarian calendar was indeed practiced, it would have served as an additional factor distancing the Dead Sea sectarians from the Jerusalem temple.

Despite some claims to the contrary, the sectarians did not practice sacrificial rites at Qumran. They believed, on the one hand, that sacrifice was only permitted in Jerusalem, the place that God had chosen, and on the other hand, that the rituals and priesthood of the Jerusalem temple of their own day were illegitimate. The sectarians saw their group as a virtual temple in which, through purity regulations, prayer, and, apparently, through study of God's law it was possible to achieve the spiritual connection with the divine that had been vouchsafed to Israel in God's central sanctuary according to the Bible.

At the same time, numerous works discovered at Qumran indicate that the sectarians continued to treasure and study pre-Hasmonean texts that featured sacrificial laws and regulations, like *Jubilees*, the *Aramaic Levi Document*, and the sources of the *Temple Scroll*. Sectarian documents, like 4QMMT, the *Zadokite Fragments*, the redacted *Temple Scroll*, and the *War Scroll*, testify to the continued devotion of the Qumran sectarians to the ideal of sacrificial worship and to their belief that in the end of days they would once again be restored to leadership of Israel's sacrificial worship in the Jerusalem temple.

CHAPTER 5

Political Leadership and Organization in the Dead Sea Scrolls Community

The corpus of some eight hundred scrolls or, mainly, fragments of scrolls that emerged from the Qumran caves can generally be classified into three groups: (1) Hebrew Bible, (2) apocryphal compositions, including many previously unknown texts, and (3) the literature of the Qumran sect, considered by many scholars to be identical with the Essenes described by Philo, Josephus, and a number of Greek authors. This study will concentrate primarily on the last group of texts, those that tell us of the teachings, beliefs, and way of life of the Qumran sect.[1]

In a variety of ways, these texts exhibit a sense of the separation of powers that the sectarians believed was required by biblical law. We will examine the manner in which the separation of powers affected a number of areas of sectarian thought: the division of king and priest, the division of executive and legislative functions, and the interrelationship of religious and temporal power (what we term "church and state") in the ideal Jewish polity. During the period in which the Qumran sect flourished, we can also discern a shift in political power and leadership from an elite group of Zadokite priests to a broader-based constituency.

---

1. See the detailed study of the Qumran library in D. Dimant, "The Qumran Manuscripts: Contents and Significance," in *Time to Prepare the Way in the Wilderness: Papers on the Qumran Scrolls by Fellows of the Institute for Advanced Studies of the Hebrew University, Jerusalem, 1989-90*, ed. Dimant and L. H. Schiffman, 23-58. STDJ 16 (Leiden: Brill, 1995).

Political Leadership and Organization in the Dead Sea Scrolls Community

Kings and Priests

We will begin with a text that lies somewhere on the borderline between the sectarian corpus and the literature that preexisted it. Among the most enigmatic of the Qumran documents is the well-preserved *Temple Scroll,* a kind of rewritten and reedited Torah. Its author/redactor rewrote the sacrificial and legal sections of the Pentateuch in order to express his own particular views on the nature of the temple and its sacrifices, the political system of Hasmonean times, and Jewish law on a variety of topics. The text was compiled some time in the latter half of the reign of the Hasmonean king John Hyrcanus (134-104 B.C.E.) or early in the reign of Alexander Janneus (103-76 B.C.E.).[2]

This document was initially thought to reflect the teachings of the Qumran sect. Nevertheless, numerous differences between the approach of this document and those of the Qumran sectarian texts were immediately recognized after it was published.[3] When the existence of 4QMMT, also known as the *Halakhic Letter,* a foundation document of the Qumran sect, became known in 1984,[4] the true nature of the *Temple Scroll* became clear. It turned out that, despite the date of its completion sometime in the Hasmonean period, this scroll was actually composed of a variety of sources that were earlier than the complete scroll.[5] These sources were most probably Sadducean in nature and provenance.[6] Among the latest of the sources of the *Temple Scroll,* reflecting Hasmonean times in a variety of its polemics, is that known as the "Law of the King."[7]

---

2. See L. H. Schiffman, "The *Temple Scroll* and the Nature of Its Law: The Status of the Question," in *The Community of the Renewed Covenant: The Notre Dame Symposium on the Dead Sea Scrolls,* ed. E. Ulrich and J. VanderKam, 37-55. CJAS 10 (Notre Dame: University of Notre Dame Press, 1994).

3. First noted by B. A. Levine, "The Temple Scroll: Aspects of Its Historical Provenance and Literary Character," *BASOR* 232 (1978) 5-23; cf. H. Stegemann, "The Origins of the Temple Scroll," VTSup 40 (*Congress Volume: Jerusalem 1986,* ed. J. A. Emerton; 1988) 235-56. We cannot accept the dating for the sources of the scroll proposed by Stegemann.

4. Cf. L. H. Schiffman, *Reclaiming the Dead Sea Scrolls: The History of Judaism, the Background of Christianity, the Lost Library of Qumran* (Philadelphia: Jewish Publication Society, 1994; repr. ABRL. New York: Doubleday, 1995) xvii-xviii.

5. A. M. Wilson and L. Wills, "Literary Sources of the Temple Scroll," *HTR* 75 (1982) 275-88; M. O. Wise, *A Critical Study of the Temple Scroll from Qumran Cave 11.* SAOC 49 (Chicago: Oriental Institute, University of Chicago, 1990) 35-194.

6. See Schiffman, "The *Temple Scroll,*" 46-48.

7. Y. Yadin, *The Temple Scroll* (Jerusalem: Israel Exploration Society and Shrine of the Book, 1983) 1:344-62. A full discussion of this text is found in L. H. Schiffman, "The King, His

This section of the scroll, actually a rewriting and expansion of the Law of the King of Deuteronomy (Deut 17:14-20), puts forward a demand for a thoroughgoing reform of the existing political order in the Hasmonean period. Following Deuteronomy, the text requires that, upon assuming office, the monarch must have a Torah scroll written for him that he is to have with him at all times. Here the text is calling for restoration of a constitution based on the Torah that the author sees as violated by the Hasmoneans. We must remember that by this time, the descendants of the Maccabees who had fought so valiantly against Hellenism and foreign influence were already conducting themselves in a Hellenistic manner.

Among the clearest demands of this scroll is that the position of king be separated from that of high priest. Indeed, this text demands that there be a royal council, the supreme legislative and judicial body, to consist of twelve priests, twelve Levites, and twelve Israelites. All decisions of the king are to be subject to ratification by this body. In this way, the power of the king is severely limited by the proposed "constitutional monarchy." Further, the document makes clear that the king is forbidden to conduct an offensive war without the approval of the high priest and consultation of the Urim and Thummim, the oracle that the high priest wore on his breastplate.

All this is clearly a reflection of the severe objection of the circles that produced this document to the system of Hasmonean kingship in which those actually of priestly lineage were for all intents and purposes functioning as kings. In fact, in later Hasmonean times, the priestly rulers even styled themselves kings on their coins. The authors of the Law of the King of the *Temple Scroll,* no doubt followed by the members of the Qumran sect, saw this usurpation as a violation of biblical constitutional law. What was at stake here was the separation of temporal and religious powers, and the authors objected to their confluence in the hands of the Maccabean priest-kings. At the same time, according to this scroll, the king, who was forbidden to be a priest, had to answer to a mostly Levitical council, and the high priest was in some matters the king's superior. Even this separation of powers bordered to some extent on a kind of constitutional theocracy, if we may coin such a phrase.

Those who produced this text, and the Qumran sectarians who read and preserved it, were not the only ones to object to the Hasmonean arrogation of

---

Guard and the Royal Council in the Temple Scroll," *PAAJR* 54 (1987) 237-59. Cf. M. Weinfeld, "'Megillat Miqdash' 'o 'Torah la-Melekh,'" *Shnaton* 3 (1978/79) 214-37 [English trans. "The Temple Scroll or 'The Law of the King,'" in *Normative and Sectarian Judaism in the Second Temple Period* (London T. & T. Clark, 2005) 158-85].

both priestly and royal powers. The MMT document itself, in our view, testifies to unhappiness on the part of Sadducean priests with the Hasmoneans having taken control of the high priesthood.[8] The Hasmoneans had originally been rural members of the lower clergy, not descended from the Zadokite high-priestly family. But for the most part, this document indicates specific objections to the legal rulings that guided the Hasmonean temple.[9]

Yet the strongest opposition to the Hasmoneans came from the Pharisees, the forerunners of the talmudic sages, as described in a baraita preserved in the Babylonian Talmud.[10] This source informs us that the Pharisees were willing to tolerate Hasmonean kingship, even though this Aaronide priestly family was not of the house of David, as required for a true Jewish king. However, they disputed the rights of this family to serve as high priests, asserting that the mother (or grandmother) of Alexander Janneus (John Hyrcanus in the account preserved in Josephus[11]) had been a captive and, hence, that her descendants were disqualified from the high priesthood. The Pharisaic objection to the Hasmoneans as high priests eventually led to civil strife and later to war and devastation in Judea, but that is a story beyond the scope of this study.[12]

The opposition of the *Temple Scroll* and other such documents to the Hasmonean house resulted from the fact that the Hasmoneans served as kings. They were regarded as having violated the age-old separation of royal and priestly powers that the Bible had required. A similar separation was carried over into the complex organizational structure of the Dead Sea sectarians as well.

Priests and Laymen

The Qumran sect came into being as a discrete group in the aftermath of the Maccabean revolt when the Hasmonean high priests decided to ally themselves with the Pharisees against the hellenizing priests, many of whom had

---

8. "The New Halakhic Letter (4QMMT) and the Origins of the Dead Sea Sect," Chapter 6 below.
9. A full discussion of the laws in this document is found in E. Qimron and J. Strugnell, *Qumran Cave 4.V: Miqṣat Ma'aśe Ha-Torah*. DJD 10 (Oxford: Clarendon, 1994) 123-77.
10. *b. Qidd.* 66a.
11. *Ant.* 18.288-96.
12. See Schiffman, *Reclaiming the Dead Sea Scrolls*, 236-38. See also D. R. Schwartz, "On Pharisaic Opposition to the Hasmonean Monarchy," in *Studies in the Jewish Background of Christianity* (Tübingen: Mohr [Siebeck], 1992) 44-56.

been Sadducees.¹³ A group of pious Sadducees left the temple and protested to no avail the abandonment of Saducean priestly practice for the halakhic rulings of the Pharisees. This group, after failing to sway their colleagues and the Hasmonean leaders by means of the *Halakhic Letter* (4QMMT), eventually relocated to Qumran, where they lived lives of piety and holiness, preparing for the end of days.

The sectarian group that eventually came into being, certainly by the sect's heyday after ca. 134 B.C.E., saw itself as a corporate group. This is clear from the various names of the sect. It is often called יחד *(yaḥad)*, "community," a nominal use of an adverb usually meaning "together," and this term may occur in a construct together with other terms.¹⁴ This is the case with עצת היחד, "council of the community," probably identical with the assembly to be discussed below, and ברית היחד, "covenant of the community," a term indicating that the sectarians saw themselves as banding together to observe the "renewed covenant" of God with his chosen ones, the members of the sect.¹⁵ Further, we should note that the term עדה, "congregation," designates the community of the end of days, to which we will return below.

The corporate nature of the group is further indicated by the archaeological remains of Qumran, which apparently functioned as a sectarian center for those who left their scrolls in the nearby caves. Here we can observe facilities for the meals that the sectarians sometimes ate communally as well as for the various occupations such as pottery making, husbandry, and small farming pursued by members. While the actual sleeping quarters cannot be identified, it seems that the members of the group lived either in the nearby caves or tent shelters.¹⁶

The initial leadership of the sect was made up of Sadducean priests, termed the Sons of Zadok over and over in the scrolls.¹⁷ This family descended from Zadok, high priest at the time of Solomon, whose descendants had virtually uninterruptedly held the high priesthood in First and Second

---

13. Cf. F. M. Cross, "The Early History of the Qumran Community," in *New Directions in Biblical Archaeology*, ed. D. N. Freedman and J. C. Greenfield, 70-89 (Garden City: Doubleday, 1971). See also Chapter 6 below.

14. S. Talmon, "The Sectarian *yḥd* — a Biblical Noun," *VT* 3 (1953) 133-40.

15. This phrase is taken from S. Talmon, "The Community of the Renewed Covenant: Between Judaism and Christianity," in Ulrich and VanderKam, *Community of the Renewed Covenant*, 3-24. Talmon's essay also provided the title for the volume.

16. R. de Vaux, *Archaeology and the Dead Sea Scrolls*. Schweich Lectures 1959 (London: Oxford University Press, 1973) 1-48; Schiffman, *Reclaiming the Dead Sea Scrolls*, 37-57.

17. J. Liver, "Bene Ṣadoq shebe-Khat Midbar Yehudah," *ErIsr* 8 (1966/67) 71-81; L. H. Schiffman, *Halakhah at Qumran*. SJLA 16 (Leiden: Brill, 1975) 72-75.

Temple times. For this reason they felt that they were entitled to continue in office, even after the Maccabean victory and the appointment of Jonathan, the brother of Judah the Maccabee, as ruler in 152 B.C.E.

The Zadokite priests who started the sect were apparently soon sharing power with laymen as part of the general tendency toward lay power and democratization in Judaism during the Second Temple period. This general trend abetted the transfer of leadership from the priesthood to lay sages also in Pharisaic-rabbinic Judaism, laying the groundwork for the institution of the rabbinate. Evidence for this transition in the scrolls is found in the requirement of the *Rule of the Community* that decisions be made according to the rulings of the Sons of Zadok[18] and the majority of the men of their covenant.[19] Apparently, at a later stage in the history of this group, this formula and the political reality behind it were replaced by the *rabbim*, the "many," an assembly of members of the sect.[20] All those who had completed the stages of the initiation process into the sect, attaining ascending levels of ritual purity and knowledge of the sect's teachings, could participate in the assembly.[21] Besides its legislative functions, which were linked to its ability to properly interpret Scripture under divine inspiration, the *rabbim* also served as the supreme judicial body, and it appears to have been predominantly lay.

We cannot see this assembly as truly a democratic institution because it did not grant rights beyond a small circle. Only full-fledged members of the sect were permitted to join and, of course, women could take no role in this body. This form of "democracy for the minority" was typical of the so-called democracies of ancient Greece and the Hellenistic cities, in which voting rights were extended only to a minority who had attained the required status.

We have some indication of how this assembly functioned. Each person who wanted to speak had to get the permission of the presiding *mevaqqer* ("examiner"), and it was forbidden to speak out of turn. Generally, members spoke in order from highest to lowest status. Anyone who fell asleep during sessions was penalized with a reduction of his food ration. According to most interpretations, decisions were made by voting, following majority rule, a principle thought by the rabbis to have been enshrined in the Bible (Exod 23:2).[22]

---

18. 1QS 5:2-3, 9-10.
19. 1QS 6:19.
20. Schiffman, *Halakhah at Qumran*, 68-70.
21. For the initiation rites, see Schiffman, *Reclaiming the Dead Sea Scrolls*, 97-103; C. Rabin, *Qumran Studies*. Scripta Judaica 2 (Oxford: Oxford University Press, 1957), 1-21; S. Lieberman, "The Discipline in the So-Called Dead Sea Manual of Discipline," *JBL* 71 (1951) 199-206.
22. Cf. Rabin, *Qumran Studies*, 102-7.

While it is not possible to trace the exact historical development of the increase in lay power, it seems that the Zadokite priestly leadership was increasingly eclipsed as the sect developed, even if to some extent they retained formalistic symbols of their earlier oligarchic — or better hieroarchic — prerogatives. By some time in the Roman period (after 63 B.C.E.), what we might term legislative power had shifted almost entirely from priestly hands to those of the lay members of the sect. Even so, it seems that a priest continued to preside over the meetings of the assembly.

When it came to the everyday functioning of the group, however, members were not all equal. There was a roster that listed members from those of highest to lowest status, and those lower on the list had to follow the directives of those above in regard to matters of sectarian law or the conduct of the sect's affairs.[23]

The courts of the sect are described in the *Zadokite Fragments,* also known as the *Damascus Document.* This text was first discovered in two manuscripts in the Cairo Genizah, and later ten manuscripts emerged from the caves of Qumran.[24] The composition of the sectarian courts as prescribed here provides for a balanced grouping.[25] The basic sectarian courts were of ten judges, probably patterned on the court of ten that appears in the book of Ruth (4:2). The ten were to consist of four of the tribe of Aaron and six from Israel. It has been rightly concluded that the four Levitical members represented the Aaronide priests and the three families of Levites — Gershon, Kohath, and Merari.[26] Accordingly, the basic court consisted of one priest, three Levites and six Israelites, not an unfair distribution of clerical and lay power for an ancient Jewish court. Indeed, the rabbis required the presence of all three classes — priests, Levites, and Israelites — in the Great Sanhedrin, the high court.[27]

These various elements indicate that the Qumran sect sought to create a balance between the power of the priesthood with its God-given prerogatives and aristocratic connections and the common Israelites who, after all, were the vast majority of Jews. Even in this biblicizing, conservative group, the forces of democratization were at work long before the destruction of the temple.

---

23. Schiffman, *Halakhah at Qumran,* 66-67.

24. J. M. Baumgarten, *Qumran Cave 4.XIII: The Damascus Document (4Q266-273).* DJD 18 (Oxford: Clarendon, 1996).

25. See L. H. Schiffman, *Sectarian Law in the Dead Sea Scrolls: Courts, Testimony and the Penal Code.* BJS 33 (Chico: Scholars, 1983) 23-30.

26. J. T. Milik, "*Megillat milḥemet bene 'or bivene ḥoshek* by Y. Yadin (review)," *RB* 64 (1957) 585-93.

27. *Sifre Deut* 153 (ed. L. Finkelstein, 206).

Courts and the Rights of the Accused

Although we have concentrated so far on the issue of separation of powers in Qumran sectarian literature, some remarks about the rights of members of the sect before the courts will also be of interest. Just as in the Pharisaic-rabbinic system enshrined in talmudic literature, in the legal system of the Dead Sea Scrolls there were specific requirements for witnesses to ensure that only reliable individuals could testify.[28] While some have suggested that women were permitted to testify, this view is based on a corrupt passage,[29] and it must be admitted that the Qumran sect disqualified the testimony of women. To be sure, women could not serve as judges or sectarian leaders either, although the texts flatly contradict the suggestion of some scholars that the sect was celibate.[30] Witnesses had to be at least twenty-year-old males and full members of the group, thus guaranteeing that they were truly observant Jews who would testify honestly. Age requirements also existed to guarantee that judges would be experienced enough for the job yet at the same time to exclude those who had become senile.[31]

Ancient Jewish law was concerned to guarantee that the accused had been fully cognizant that his actions violated the law and that he knew of the punishment for his crime before committing the forbidden action. Otherwise, he could not be considered a purposeful violator and could not be punished. To deal with this problem, the sectarians required that the offender be reproved for a previous commission of the same offense before he or she could be punished for the infraction. For the same reason, the rabbis instituted the requirement of *hatra'ah*, "warning," by which the witnesses had to warn the offender and apprise him of the punishment for his act before the commission of the crime.[32]

As in all Jewish legal systems, circumstantial evidence, hearsay, and evidence not based on testimony (forensic evidence) were excluded. All these regulations tipped the scales way in favor of the accused and guaranteed a fair trial to the greatest extent possible. The *Temple Scroll* (11QTemple 51:11-18) prohibits judicial corruption and commands the death penalty for corrupt judges who take bribes.[33] Further, it prohibits the king from taking the prop-

---

28. Schiffman, *Sectarian Law*, 55-63.
29. J. M. Baumgarten, *Studies in Qumran Law*. SJLA 24 (Leiden: Brill, 1977) 183-86.
30. Schiffman, *Reclaiming the Dead Sea Scrolls*, 127-43.
31. Schiffman, *Sectarian Law*, 63-65.
32. Schiffman, *Sectarian Law*, 97-98; "Reproof as a Requisite for Punishment in the Law of the Dead Sea Scrolls," *Jewish Law Studies II: The Jerusalem Conference Volume*, ed. B. S. Jackson, 59-74 (Atlanta: Scholars, 1986).
33. L. H. Schiffman, "The Prohibition of Judicial Corruption in the Dead Sea Scrolls,

erty of his subjects by the use of trumped-up legal procedures (11QTemple 57:19-21).

While human rights as we know them were not a subject of discussion in ancient Israel, it is clear that in continuing the system of biblical jurisprudence and expanding on it the sectarians continued to guarantee a fair trial and an equitable system of justice. Accordingly, some form of due process was provided by sectarian law.

Sectarian Leadership

In discussing the issue of separation and balance of powers, it is important to note the nature of the sectarian leadership. The Teacher of Righteousness was the leader who led the group from its initial opposition to the manner in which temple worship was being conducted in the early Hasmonean period to the sect's full-fledged incorporation as a sectarian body with distinct ideology and organization.[34] The Teacher must have functioned in the early years of the Hasmonean dynasty, in the days of Jonathan (152-143 B.C.E.) or Simon (142-134), one of whom was regarded by the sect as the Wicked Priest, the sworn opponent of the Teacher. The Teacher of Righteousness was clearly a priest as we know from direct evidence in *Pesher Habakkuk*.[35] Part of his duties included that of legislator. He showed his followers how to put the Torah into effect by revealing to them the divinely-inspired *nistar*, the hidden or secret interpretation that was known only to the sect and revealed to them by the Teacher. Therefore, his teachings had as much validity as the Torah itself. The sect always believed that it would be rewarded for its steadfast adherence to the Teacher's authority.

Though it is difficult to be specific on this matter, it seems that the sect suffered a crisis with the death of its first leader. It had expected that the messianic era was soon to dawn and that no successor to the Teacher of Righteousness would be needed. Nonetheless, the sect weathered this crisis and was able to replace its leader with various officers who later managed its affairs.

Philo, Josephus and Talmudic Law," in *Hesed ve-Emet: Studies in Honor of Ernest S. Frerichs*, ed. J. Magness and S. Gitin, 155-78. BJS 320 (Atlanta: Scholars, 1998).

34. Schiffman, *Reclaiming the Dead Sea Scrolls*, 117-21; G. Jeremias, *Der Lehrer der Gerechtigkeit* (Göttingen: Vandenhoeck & Ruprecht, 1963); G. Lambert, *Le Maître de justice et la communauté de l'alliance*. ALBO 2/28 (Louvain: Publications universitaires, 1952); F. F. Bruce, *Second Thoughts on the Dead Sea Scrolls* (Grand Rapids: Wm. B. Eerdmans, 1977) 92-97; G. W. Buchanan, "The Office of Teacher of Righteousness," *RevQ* 9 (1977) 237-40.

35. 1QpHab 2:8.

The duties of the Teacher of Righteousness were apparently carried out after his passing by two officials of the sect, the *mevaqqer* and the *paqid*.³⁶ The *mevaqqer*, "examiner," may very well have been a priest, although there is no direct evidence of his status. The *mevaqqer* was a teacher and guide to his followers, responsible for their spiritual and physical welfare. He tested new members and had to approve their entrance into the community. He supervised all members' business transactions, was responsible for approving marriages and divorces, and he was required to treat his people with love and kindness. The examiner had to be between thirty and fifty years of age. He organized the members in the order of their ranks, from the senior to the most junior, that determined the order in which they spoke at the sectarian assembly and their mustering for the annual covenant renewal ceremony.

The *paqid* (lit., "appointed one") was a priest as well. He is known from the *Rule of the Community* as the official who administered the initial test of those wishing to join the sect. The *Zadokite Fragments* call him "the priest who musters at the head of the community" and say that he must be between thirty and sixty years old.³⁷ This detail confirms that he must be a different person from the *mevaqqer*, although scant information is available about him.

The sect also had various lay leaders known as *maskilim*, who are described in the *Rule of the Community*.³⁸ This name derives from the verb meaning "to enlighten or instruct." The *maskil* was to enlighten the sectarians about the nature of the Sons of Light, those who follow the sectarian ways, and the Sons of Darkness, the rest of the peoples of the world, both Jewish and non-Jewish. Presumably, the *maskil* was responsible for conveying the ideology and theology of the Qumran community to other members of the group. The *maskil* was also expected to be a master of the sectarian legal tradition. He also led the recitation of blessings found in the *Rule of Benedictions* that apply to those who fear the Lord,³⁹ the Zadokite priests,⁴⁰ and the Prince of the Congregation.⁴¹ The *maskilim* were a class of scholars but not priests, and although they shared their knowledge with their fellow sectarians and were per-

---

36. Cf. J. Priest, "*Mebaqqer, Paqqid* and the Messiah," *JBL* 81 (1962) 55-61; R. Marcus, "*Mebaqqer* and *Rabbim* in the *Manual of Discipline* VI, 11-13," *JBL* 75 (1956) 398-402; R. C. Steiner, "The *MBQR* at Qumran, the *Episkopos* in the Athenian Empire, and the Meaning of *LBQR'* in Ezra 7:14: On the Relation of Ezra's Mission to the Persian Legal Project," *JBL* 120 (2001) 623-30, 643-46.

37. CD 14:6-8=D^b 11 ii 10-13.

38. 1QS 9:12-26; cf. 3:13 and CD 12:20-22 and 13:22. Cf. H. Kosmala, "Maskil," *JANESCU* 5 (1973) 235-41.

39. 1QSb 1:1.

40. 1QSb 3:22-28.

41. 1QSb 5:20-29.

haps role models for them, they do not seem to have been assigned any specific administrative functions; the *mevaqqer* and *paqid* filled this role.[42]

All in all, in regard to the conduct of the affairs of the group and its decisions concerning Jewish law, a process of laicization and, hence, democratization was going on throughout the sect's history — from Hasmonean times through the destruction of the temple in 70 C.E. — similar to that in evidence in the Pharisaic-rabbinic context as well. Further, it is interesting that the sect seemed to tend toward a division of executive, judicial, and legislative powers. Yet this division was limited in that the assembly, which was primarily legislative in function, served also as the highest court. Indeed, the same was the situation in the rabbinic legal system described in the Mishnah and Talmud.

Royal and Priestly Messiahs

An entirely different arena in which to look at these questions is that of the sect's dreams for the messianic future.[43] This is especially the case since we know that the sect modeled its life in the present premessianic age on its eschatological aspirations. It sought to create in the present the experience of purity and holiness that it expected would finally commence with the dawn of the end of days.[44]

Equally important to the sectarians was the immediacy of the end of days. They anticipated that the old order would soon die and the messianic era would be established in their lifetimes. The sect lived on the verge of the end of days, with one foot, as it were, in the present age and one foot in the future.[45]

Two separate messianic ideologies coexisted in the sectarian documents. One, like that of rabbinic Judaism, speaks of an individual messiah who is to be a "branch of David," that is, a Davidic scion. A totally different approach speaks of an Aaronide priestly messiah, who is effectively an eschatological high priest, and a temporal messiah of Israel, who is to rule over political matters.[46] Both messiahs would preside over the eschatological ban-

---

42. Schiffman, *Reclaiming the Dead Sea Scrolls*, 121-25.

43. For messianic ideas in the Qumran scrolls, see S. Talmon, *The World of Qumran from Within* (Jerusalem: Magnes and Leiden: Brill, 1989) 273-300; F. García Martínez, "Messianische Erwartungen in den Qumranschriften," *JBTh* 8 (1993) 171-208; J. J. Collins, *The Scepter and the Star: The Messiahs of the Dead Sea Scrolls and Other Ancient Literature*. ABRL (New York: Doubleday, 1995).

44. L. H. Schiffman, *The Eschatological Community of the Dead Sea Scrolls*. SBLMS 38 (Atlanta: Scholars, 1989) 68-71.

45. Schiffman, *Reclaiming the Dead Sea Scrolls*, 321-22.

46. "Messianic Figures and Ideas in the Qumran Scrolls," Chapter 16 below; W. S. LaSor,

quet.⁴⁷ Described in the *Rule of the Congregation,* it would usher in the new age that would include worship at the eschatological temple. Sacrificial worship would be conducted according to sectarian law.

This messianic paradigm of two leaders, based on the Moses/Aaron and Joshua/Zerubbabel model, would later be applied to Bar Kokhba and the high priest Eleazar in the Bar Kokhba revolt (132-135 C.E.).⁴⁸ To the sect, the coming of the messiahs of Israel and Aaron and the eschatological prophet augured the restoration of the old order.

These restorative tendencies are based on biblical prophetic visions, but the Qumran sect went much further. Reflecting the apocalyptic trend,⁴⁹ it anticipated that the advent of the messianic age would be heralded by the great cataclysmic battle described in the *War Scroll* and radical changes in the world order resulting in the victory of the forces of good over those of evil, in heaven above and on earth below. After forty years the period of wickedness would come to an end; then the elect would attain glory. In essence, Jews in the messianic age would surpass their current level of purity and perfection in observing Jewish law. Here in the sphere of Jewish law we again find the utopian trend. Only in the future age will it be possible properly to observe the Torah as interpreted by the sect.

"The Messiah of Aaron and Israel," *VT* 6 (1956) 425-29; J. Liver, "The Doctrine of the Two Messiahs in Sectarian Literature in the Time of the Second Commonwealth," *HTR* 52 (1959) 149-85; K. G. Kuhn, "The Two Messiahs of Aaron and Israel," in *The Scrolls and the New Testament,* ed. K. Stendahl and J. H. Charlesworth, 54-64 (1957; repr. New York: Crossroad, 1992); L. Silberman, "Two Messiahs of the Manual of Discipline," *VT* 5 (1955) 77-82; R. B. Laurin, "The Problem of the Two Messiahs in the Qumran Scrolls," *RevQ* 4 (1963) 39-52; G. J. Brooke, "Messiah of Aaron in the Damascus Document," *RevQ* 15 (1991) 215-31.

47. Schiffman, *Eschatological Community,* 53-67.

48. Cf. E. Schürer, *The History of the Jewish People in the Age of Jesus Christ (175 B.C.-A.D. 135),* rev. ed. by G. Vermes and F. Millar, with P. Vermes and M. Black (Edinburgh: T. & T. Clark, 1973) 1:544.

49. On apocalypticism at Qumran, see C. A. Newsom, "Apocalyptic and the Discourse of the Qumran Community," *JNES* 49 (1990) 135-44; H. Stegemann, "Die Bedeutung der Qumranfunde für die Erforschung der Apokalyptik," in *Apocalypticism in the Mediterranean World and the Near East: Proceedings of the International Colloquium on Apocalypticism,* ed. D. Hellholm (Tübingen: Mohr [Siebeck], 1983) 495-530; J. J. Collins, *The Apocalyptic Imagination,* 2nd ed. BRS (Grand Rapids: Wm. B. Eerdmans, 1998) 145-76; "Was the Dead Sea Sect an Apocalyptic Movement?" in *Archaeology and History in the Dead Sea Scrolls: The New York University Conference in Memory of Yigael Yadin,* ed. L. H. Schiffman, 25-51. JSOTSup 8. JSOT/ASOR Monographs 2 (Sheffield: Sheffield Academic, 1990); *Apocalypticism in the Dead Sea Scrolls* (London: Routledge, 1997); P. R. Davies, "Qumran and Apocalyptic or Obscurum per Obscurius," *JNES* 49 (1990) 127-34; J. Starcky, "Les quatre étapes du messianisme à Qumran," *RB* 70 (1963) 481-505.

In addition to the dual messiahs of Aaron and Israel and the single messiah of the House of David, the Qumran texts also mention other eschatological figures who will appear in the end of days.[50] The Teacher of Righteousness is expected to arise to interpret the law, and the Prince of the Congregation (נשיא העדה) will serve as the sect's military leader in the eschatological battle described in the *War Scroll*. It is also possible that "prince" simply is an alternate name for the king who will rule in the messianic era. Some texts also speak about an eschatological prophet who will announce the coming of the messiah, a figure similar to Elijah in the rabbinic tradition.

The concept of the dual messiahs certainly envisages a division of powers between the religious and temporal, but, as we noticed before in our discussion of the *Temple Scroll*, the priest holds the superior status of the pair. This is reflected when he is commanded to enter first in the description of the messianic communal meal in the *Rule of the Congregation*,[51] an eschatological appendix to the *Rule of the Community*.[52] So again we have the expectation of constitutional theocracy.

Even when a Davidic messiah is indicated in Qumran texts, it is expected that there will also be a messianic high priest. But in these texts there is no sense of the superiority of the priest as there is in those Qumran sectarian texts that expect two messiahs. Just as the sectarians demanded a balance of power in the present between priestly and temporal power, they looked forward to the same in the end of days.

The Messianic Assembly

According to the *Rule of the Congregation* (1QSa 1:25-27), in the end of days there will also be an assembly, which will have specifically-defined powers. This group will also serve as the highest court; it will also be the legislative assembly, but in addition, it will have the power to declare war.[53]

In this regulation, we again see that the king is limited in his powers, so that he may not commit the nation to war without the approval of the assembly. This may very well be a further polemic against, or better, reaction to, the Hasmonean rulers who attacked neighboring territory simply to expand their empire. A similar regulation in the *Zadokite Fragments*, for the present age,

---

50. "Messianic Figures and Ideas in the Dead Sea Scrolls," Chapter 16 below.
51. 1QSa 2:11-22.
52. Schiffman, *Eschatological Community*, 53-67.
53. Schiffman, *Eschatological Community*, 29-32.

requires that offensive war only be undertaken with the approval of a council or *gerousia*, the חבר ישראל.[54]

The community of the end of days would reflect all the sect's aspirations and dreams. The assembly, therefore, would govern the sect under the leadership of the messianic leaders, expanding the functions and procedures of the assembly of the present and allowing all sectarians to participate in the shaping of the society of the end of days.

Conclusion

The authors of the Qumran sectarian documents and related texts dealt with a variety of issues pertaining to the organization of the Jewish people as a whole as well as of their own sectarian community in the present age and the future. They saw their community as the ideal Israel, structured and organized politically and religiously in a way that mirrored their utopian views of the ideal world of the end of days.

The sectarians knew all too well from their own understanding of the Hasmonean dynasty that the concentration of temporal and religious power in the hands of the same people was unjust. Accordingly, they hoped for the day when the two powers would be separated as they understood the Torah to require. They further distinguished the powers of the executive from the legislative, expecting different individuals to be involved in each.

Over time, greater democratization of the sect can be observed, such that lay members attained greater power while that of the priests was reduced. The sectarians balanced priestly and lay members in the courts and in the king's council, protected the rights of the accused to a trial before honest and competent judges, and called for the death penalty for judicial corruption. Only the most reliable witnesses could be employed to convict an offender. In the end of days they expected similar regulations to be in force and, therefore, expected a division of power between priestly and lay messiahs.

In enacting all these various regulations, the Dead Sea sectarians were following their interpretation of the Hebrew biblical tradition, which to them constituted a guide for life in the present age and in the utopian era of the end of days. They earnestly sought a society following the biblical ideal in which powers would be balanced and separated, as a means to the attainment of the perfect holiness of the end of days.

54. L. H. Schiffman, "Legislation Concerning Relations with Non-Jews in the *Zadokite Fragments* and in Tannaitic Literature," *RevQ* 11 (1983) 382-85.

CHAPTER 6

The New Halakhic Letter (4QMMT) and the Origins of the Dead Sea Sect

In the years since the initial announcement of the Qumran text entitled 4QMiqṣat Ma'aśe ha-Torah (4QMMT),[1] it has become clear that this text is very significant for our understanding of the history of Jewish law and, in particular, for unraveling the difficult question of the provenance of the *Temple Scroll* and its relationship to the Qumran sectarian corpus.[2]

Yet the text is important for another issue, namely, the origins of the sect and the early history of the community. This document purports to be a letter from the leaders of the nascent sect to the leaders of the (probably priestly) establishment in Jerusalem. The text sets out some twenty laws on which the writers disagree with the Jerusalem authorities regarding matters of sacrificial law, priestly gifts, ritual purity, and other matters. Stated in polemical manner, these laws clearly represent the views of the founders of the sect, as opposed to those of their opponents, whom they call upon to accept their view. The laws are set within a framework that may allow us to learn much about the ideology of those who authored the text. Such conclusions, together with those that are being gathered from the study of the main body of the document dealing with matters of Jewish law, allow us to draw impor-

---

1. E. Qimron and J. Strugnell, "An Unpublished Halakhic Letter from Qumran," in *Biblical Archaeology Today: Proceedings of the International Congress on Biblical Archaeology, Jerusalem, April 1984*, ed. J. Amitai (Jerusalem: Israel Exploration Society, Israel Academy of Sciences and Humanities, in cooperation with ASOR, 1985) 400-7.

2. L. H. Schiffman, "The Temple Scroll and the Systems of Jewish Law in the Second Temple Period," in *Temple Scroll Studies*, ed. G. J. Brooke, 245-53 (Sheffield: JSOT, 1989); "*Miqṣat Ma'aśeh ha-Torah* and the *Temple Scroll*," *RevQ* 14 (The Texts of Qumran and the History of the Community: Proceedings of the Groningen Congress on the Dead Sea Scrolls 3, 1990) 435-57.

tant conclusions regarding the significance of this text for the question of the origins of the Qumran group.

Above, we were careful to note that this document, preserved in six manuscripts, purports to be a letter. It still remains to be determined if it is an actual letter, dating to the earliest days of the Qumran group, or if it is an "apocryphal" text, written some years, or even decades, later to express the fundamental reasons for the break or schism with the Jerusalem establishment.[3] In any case, as indicated by the number of copies that have survived, this letter was undoubtedly significant in the life of the sect.[4]

This study will discuss the substance of the introductory sentence and the concluding paragraphs of the document in order to analyze its stated ideology. Taking into consideration the halakhic content of the text, some general observations on the historical significance of 4QMMT will be offered.

Structure and Content of the Text

To best understand the matters we will discuss, some sense of the overall structure of the text is necessary. The text can be divided into three sections: an introductory sentence setting out the nature of the letter (B 1-3); a section listing the halakhic disagreements that the founders of the group claim to have had with the Jerusalem authorities (B 3-82); and a concluding section that raises several issues related to the group's separation (C 1-32).

In at least one of the manuscripts in which this section is extant (4Q394), the text proper is copied immediately after a 364-day soli-solar calendar of the type known from some of the Qumran scrolls, *Enoch,* and *Jubilees.*[5] Immedi-

---

3. Cf. J. Strugnell, "MMT: Second Thoughts on a Forthcoming Edition," in *The Community of the Renewed Covenant: The Notre Dame Symposium on the Dead Sea Scrolls,* ed. E. Ulrich and J. C. VanderKam, 57-73. CJAS 10 (Notre Dame: University of Notre Dame Press, 1994).

4. See F. M. Cross, "The Development of the Jewish Scripts," in *The Bible and the Ancient Near East: Essays in Honor of W. F. Albright,* ed. G. E. Wright, 149 (Garden City: Doubleday, 1961), where Cross dates one of the manuscripts of this work to around 50 to 25 B.C.E. He studies this manuscript, then numbered 4QS135^b, on pp. 186-88, and, in the summary (p. 188), he states that this and the other manuscripts of this semi-cursive type "belong to the late Hasmonean period, or, at latest, to the beginning of the early Herodian era." Full publication of the manuscripts and a paleographic study by A. Yardeni are found in *Qumran Cave 4.V: Miqṣat Ma'aśe ha-Torah,* ed. E. Qimron and J. Strugnell. DJD 10 (Oxford: Clarendon, 1994) 3-42. Yardeni dates the manuscripts as follows: 4Q394, no later than the early Herodian period; 4Q395, early Herodian; 4Q396, early or mid-Herodian; 4Q397, first half of the Herodian period; 4Q398, early Herodian; 4Q399, mid-Herodian.

5. See S. Talmon, "The Calendar Reckoning of the Sect from the Judaean Desert," in *As-

ately after this calendar, the MMT text proper begins. Before it lists the halakhic disagreements that the founders of the group claim to have had with the Jerusalem authorities, it has an opening sentence that sets out the nature of the "letter." This initial introductory sentence states that what follows are some of "our words" (note the plural usage by the senders), which are legal rulings (מעשים, as in its use in later Palestinian Hebrew).[6] These are rulings "we hold to" (restored: אנחנו חושבים). Further, the text tells us that these rulings concern only two topics, one in the lacuna and laws of purity (better: rituals of purification). The lacuna must have contained a term like מתנות (gifts to the temple and priests) or קרבנות (sacrifices). Such a term would fit the list of laws which then follows.

From this sentence alone, one can grasp the fundamental point of the text. Yet the more significant aspects for our study come at the end of the "letter," when the authors have completed the accounting of the twenty or so matters of Jewish law that in their view resulted in the schism and the formation of the sect. Presently, we will examine the concluding passage in detail. Yet we must first emphasize the importance of the halakhic disagreements.

The key point made in this section is that the fundamental disagreements that led the group of dissatisfied priests to withdraw from participation in the ritual of the Jerusalem temple pertained to matters of Jewish law. Indeed, the major conflicts of Second Temple Judaism resulted not from the many disagreements about messianism and other such theological matters, but rather from issues of Jewish law.

This does not mean that there may not have been mixed motives. Rather, we speak now of the self-image of the founders of the Qumran sect who saw Jewish legal matters and interpretation of the Torah's prescriptions as the cause of the schism. Indeed, the entire sectarian corpus testifies to such reasons for the split, and this text is in perfect accord with the picture presented by the *Zadokite Fragments,* for example.[7]

The opening of the "letter" contains no designation for the document. The authors use the expression כתבנו, "we have written" (twice, once re-

---

pects of the Dead Sea Scrolls, ed. C. Rabin and Y. Yadin, 162-99. ScrHier 4 (Jerusalem: Magnes, 1958; repr. in Talmon, *The World of Qumran from Within* [Jerusalem: Magnes and Leiden: Brill, 1989] 157-85). Note that this was not the only calendar known at Qumran. The daily prayer texts were tied to a luni-solar calendar such as that known from tannaitic sources. See "The Early History of Jewish Liturgy and the Dead Sea Scrolls," Chapter 13 below; J. M. Baumgarten, "4Q503 (Daily Prayers) and the Lunar Calendar," *RevQ* 12 (1986) 399-407.

6. See Qimron and Strugnell, "An Unpublished Halakhic Letter," 401 and 406, n. 5; DJD 10:139.

7. CD 4:12–5:14.

stored), which does indicate a written text. Normally this text uses כתוב as a rubric for quotation of the Hebrew Bible. Alongside the word תורה for the Pentateuch, the Torah is referred to as ספר מושה, "the Book of Moses," or ספר(ה), "the Book" (i.e., Bible in the literal sense — Greek *to biblion*). But there is actually no formal term used to characterize MMT as a whole. The name of the text, *Miqṣat Ma'aśe ha-Torah,* was given by the editors of MMT based on the description of its contents at the end of the text, but is not intended by the authors as a title.

The Concluding Section

After the final law, the text turns to the concluding section that raises a number of general issues. We first provide a detailed outline of this section of the text.[8]

1. The authors state that they have separated (פרשנו) from the mainstream of the people (רב העם)[9] in accepting the rulings listed above and that, accordingly, they had to withdraw from participation in these rituals as performed by the majority of the people. This assertion is backed up by a general statement that the addressees (plural, ואתם) know that the members of this dissident group are reliable and honest, meaning that the list of laws is indeed being strictly observed as stated by the authors.

2. At this point the letter explains its purpose: the sectarians have written to the addressee (now in the singular) in order that "you" (singular) will investigate the words of the Torah (termed the book of Moses), the Prophets, and David and the history of the generations. This passage, we should note, assumes the threefold canon of Scripture: Torah, Prophets, and Writings. The Writings here are still not closed, yet the text may specifically be referring to the book of Chronicles, the main subject of which is David.[10]

3. Now the text turns to what is to be found in those documents. The addressee is told, again in the singular (after a lacuna), that it was foretold that he would turn aside from the path (of righteousness) and, as a result, suffer misfortune.

4. This leads MMT to an adaptation of Deuteronomic material (the

---

8. A photograph of one of the manuscripts of the conclusion of the text appeared in E. Qimron and J. Strugnell, "An Unpublished Halakhic Letter from Qumran," *IMJ* 4 (1985) 10.

9. Cf. Prov 14:28: ברב־עם הדרת־מלך, "among a large number of people is the glory of the king."

10. But see E. Ulrich, "The Non-attestation of a Tripartite Canon in 4QMMT," *CBQ* 65 (2003) 202-14.

passage is to a great extent fragmentary). The following texts are quoted: Deut 31:29;[11] 30:1-2. The text of MMT foretells that in the end of days you (singular) will return to God (in the first person as is common in the *Temple Scroll*)[12] and that all this is in accord with what is written in the Torah (again called the book of Moses) and in the Prophets. This time the Writings are not mentioned, probably since the blessings and curses referred to in this section of MMT do not occur in the Writings at all, whereas the earlier reference concerned the period of the monarchy that does appear in those texts. (Then follows another lacuna of several lines.)

5. The text now returns to the discussion of the kings, recalling the blessings that were fulfilled during the time of Solomon, son of David, and the curses visited on Israel from the days of Jeroboam, son of Nebat, through the time of Zedekiah (the last king of Judah).

6. The writers (plural) now state that in their view some of the blessings and curses have come to pass and that this (their own day) is the period of the end of days. Israel is called upon to repent rather than to backslide.

7. Accordingly, the addressee (singular) is exhorted to recall the events surrounding the reigns of the kings of Israel and to examine their deeds (*ma'aśehemah*) and to note that those who observed the laws of the Torah were spared misfortune, and their transgressions were forgiven (partly restored). The text brings as an example King David whom the addressee is asked to remember.[13]

8. The authors (plural) sum up why they sent this text to the addressee (singular). Here the phrase מקצת מעשי התורה appears, meaning "some of the legal rulings of (i.e., pertaining to) the Torah." They state that the letter was intended for the benefit of the addressee (singular) and the nation. The addressee is said to be wise and to have sufficient knowledge of the Torah to understand the halakhic matters presented in the letter.

9. The writers call on the addressee (singular) to mend his ways and to remove all incorrect thought, i.e., incorrect views on matters of Jewish law.

---

11. Cf. Deut 9:12, 16; 11:28.

12. ברכה here refers to the blessings promised for the end of days, and קללה denotes the catastrophic period that is to precede the onset of the eschaton. Cf. 11QTemple[a] 29:9 in which, according to the reading of Y. Yadin, *The Temple Scroll* (Jerusalem: Israel Exploration Society and Shrine of the Book, 1983) 2:129, *yom ha-berakhah* refers to the "End of Days." E. Qimron, "Le-Nushaḥ shel Megillat ha-Miqdash," *Leš* 42 (1978) 142, however, reads *yom ha-beri'ah*, written *bryh* (cf. Yadin, *Temple Scroll*, 1:412). We, however, note the lower part of the *kaf* in pl. 14* 2 (infrared photograph) in vol. 3: *Supplementary Plates*.

13. David appears as well in CD 5:1-6. On this passage, cf. L. H. Schiffman, *The Halakhah at Qumran*. SJLA 16 (Leiden: Brill, 1975) 30-31.

This, he is told, will lead him to rejoice at the end of this period (of the end of days, אחרית העת), when he comes to realize that their views are indeed correct. His repentance will be considered as a righteous deed, beneficial both for him and for all Israel, presumably in the eschatological sense.

Nature of the Addressee

One of the interesting features of MMT is the manner in which the number (in the grammatical sense) of the addressee shifts. In the hortatory section, the letter is addressed to an individual (אליך), but in the list of laws, the dispute of the authors is with a group (ואתם, "you," plural). When the list of laws is concluded, and the text returns to its main argument, the singular is used.

The addressee is admonished to take care lest he go the way of the kings of First Temple times. Here, the text is clearly addressing a figure who would find it possible, because of his own station in life, to identify with the ancient kings of biblical Israel.

It appears that this letter was written to the head of the Jerusalem establishment, known to us as the high priest.[14] The comparisons with the kings of Judah and Israel must have been particularly appropriate to one who saw himself as an almost royal figure. True royal trappings were only later to be taken on by the members of the Hasmonean house who already styled themselves kings on their coins. Yet the transition must have been a gradual one.[15] What we must have here is a letter either actually written or purporting to have been written to a Hasmonean high priest.

There is a significant parallel between this text and the *Temple Scroll*.[16] Both texts include sections in which Pentateuchal materials referring to the people of Israel are taken to refer to the king himself. In MMT, Deut 31:29 and 30:1-2 appear referring exclusively to the king (as can be seen from the text that follows). Deut 31:29 is in the plural and seems (if the restorations are correct) to have been adapted to the singular. In this way it was brought into

---

14. Strugnell and Qimron, "An Unpublished Halakhic Letter," 400, suggest that it is from "a leader of the Qumran sect (possibly the Teacher of Righteousness himself) to the leader of its opponents (possibly Jonathan or Simon)." Cf. also their article of similar title in *IMJ* 4 (1985) and DJD 10:117-19. Below we will explain why, in our view, the letter must predate the Teacher.

15. Josephus said of Aristobulus I (104-103 B.C.E.) in *Ant.* 13.301 that he transformed the government into a kingdom. See L. H. Schiffman, "The King, His Guard, and the Royal Council in the *Temple Scroll*," *PAAJR* 54 (1987) 258.

16. The halakhic agreements are the subject of Schiffman, *RevQ* 14 (1990) 435-57.

agreement with Deut 30:1-2, which are in the singular but which in their original context clearly refer to the people of Israel.[17] It may be that the authors of this document actually understood the singular use of Deuteronomy to refer to the king, but the context makes this unlikely. Most probably, we are dealing with the adaptation of passages dealing with the people of Israel to their ruler. The same phenomenon is observable in 11QTemple 59:16-21, in which the biblical rebuke passages directed in Scripture against the people as a whole are modified so as to make them refer to the king.[18] In any case, this usage strengthens our assertion that MMT in its concluding paragraphs is addressing the ruler of the nation.

There is no mention in MMT of the Teacher of Righteousness or any other leader known from the sectarian documents. The official history of the sect presented in the *Zadokite Fragments* claims that the sectarians' initial separation from the main body of Israel took place some twenty years before the coming of the Teacher (CD 1:9-10). It seems most likely, therefore, that the halakhic letter, MMT, was written by the collective leadership of the sect in those initial years. Hence the Teacher does not appear.

Possible Qumran Allusions

Two tantalizing allusions in Qumran scrolls might be understood as referring to this letter. Most important is a passage in *Pesher on Psalms*[a], to Ps 37:32-33.[19] As restored by Yigael Yadin, this passage refers to a "Torah" that the Teacher of Righteousness sent to the Wicked Priest. Yadin suggested that this might be a reference to the *Temple Scroll*.[20] It has been suggested that this Torah was instead the text of MMT.[21]

The latter suggestion seems to us most unlikely. This text of MMT explicitly uses the term Torah and various synonyms several times, and yet never refers to itself by that name. Unlike the author of the *Temple Scroll*, who sees his text as a complete Torah scroll, these authors are fully aware of the

---

17. Targums Pseudo-Jonathan and Neophyti translated the entire passage (Deut 30:1-10) in the plural, whereas Onqelos preserved the singular of the MT.

18. Cf. Yadin, *Temple Scroll*, 1:269-70; and Schiffman, *PAAJR* 54 (1987) 255-57.

19. J. M. Allegro, *Qumran Cave 4.1 (4Q158–4Q186)*. DJD 5 (Oxford: Clarendon, 1968) 42-50. Cf. J. Strugnell, "Notes en marge du volume V des 'Discoveries in the Judaean Desert of Jordan,'" *RevQ* 7 (1970) 216, whose corrections must be used.

20. Yadin, *Temple Scroll*, 1:396.

21. This suggestion is raised by Qimron and Strugnell, *IMJ* 4 (1985), who say that "the mss of MMT may well be exemplars of that letter."

distinction between the "canonical" text of the Mosaic Torah and the letter they are writing. Second, if indeed this halakhic letter is a foundation document, or if it purports to be such, it would refer to a time before the Teacher of Righteousness began to take a leading role in the affairs of the sect. The reference in *Pesher on Psalms* and all other accounts that seem to point to events in the life and career of this sectarian leader would have to have taken place after MMT purports to have been penned.

In view of these strictures, any attempt to relate the "second book of the Torah" of 4QCatena,[22] also mentioned by Yadin,[23] must be discounted. We have to reckon with the possibility that MMT is not alluded to in other sectarian compositions, just as the major Qumran documents do not quote one another. MMT cannot be identified with a previously known text.

Nonetheless, the reference to the "Torah" sent by the Teacher does indicate that such epistles were not out of the question within the chronological and cultural context in which the sectarian scrolls were authored. That a letter such as MMT might have been sent is not beyond the realm of possibility.

Historical Ramifications

4Q*Miqṣat Maʿaśe ha-Torah* has wide ramifications for the history of Judaism in the Hasmonean period. In the twenty or so disputes listed in this text, the opponents of the emerging sect usually agree with the Pharisees or the Tannaim as their views are related in rabbinic literature. In those cases where tannaitic texts preserve the corresponding Pharisee-Sadducee conflicts regarding the same matters discussed in MMT, the view the writers of this document espouse is that of the Sadducees.[24] Only one possible explanation can be offered for this phenomenon. The earliest members of the sect must have been Sadducees who were unwilling to accept the situation that developed in the aftermath of the Maccabean revolt. The Maccabees replaced the Zadokite

---

22. Allegro, DJD 5:67-74; Strugnell, "Notes en marge," *RevQ* 7 (1970) 236-48.
23. Yadin, *Temple Scroll*, 1:396-7; see his restoration there.
24. Some comment on our use of the term "Sadducee" is necessary. Despite the differing pictures of the Sadducees found in the works of Josephus and in rabbinic literature, we take the view that we are dealing here with one group that, as happens so often, is perceived and portrayed differently in various ancient sources. These differing perceptions, as always, result either from differences of opinion on the part of authors or from historical development regarding the group in question. Nonetheless, we see Josephus's Sadducees as the *ṣedoqim* of rabbinic literature, and these, it is now turning out, are closely related to the *bene ṣadoq* ("sons of Zadok") who apparently founded the Dead Sea sect.

high priesthood with their own, and the Zadokites were reduced to a subsidiary position for as long as Hasmonean rule lasted. It had long been theorized that some disaffected Zadokites separated themselves from their brethren in Jerusalem and formed the Qumran sect.[25] This origin would explain why the sect so often refers to itself or its leaders as "the Sons of Zadok."[26] If this is true, our text makes clear that Sons of Zadok is to be taken at face value. The founders of the Qumran sect were Sadducees who protested the following of Pharisaic views in the temple under the Hasmonean priests.

This theory would also explain why the writers of MMT constantly assert that their views are known to be correct by the addressees. Their halakhic polemics (addressed to a plural opponent) were aimed at their Sadducean brethren who stayed in the temple and accepted the new reality. It was they who now followed views known to us from Pharisaic-rabbinic sources and who, in the view of the authors of the letter, knew very well that the old Sadducean practices were otherwise.

This theory has been challenged to explain the more sectarian or radical tendencies, including the animated polemic and the hatred for outsiders, so often found in the later sectarian texts. The radicalism of these later texts is a result of the schism. After attempts like the *Halakhic Letter* (MMT) to reconcile and win over the Hasmoneans and the remaining Jerusalem Sadducees to their system of temple practice, the Qumran Zadokites developed over time the sectarian mentality of the despised, rejected, and abandoned. Subsequently, they began to look upon themselves as the true Israel and to condemn and despise all others. All history, ancient and contemporary, now came to be interpreted as figuring and prefiguring this history.[27]

Put another way, the MMT text is a sectarian document from the earliest stage in the development of the sect, when its members still looked for a return to participation in temple worship. It is not even certain that this text postdates the physical self-imposed exile of the sect. MMT represents the halakhic disagreements that led to the formation of the sect. It was later that the Teacher of Righteousness and other leaders, most probably priestly, developed the sect into what we encounter in the corpus of sectarian texts as a whole.

25. On the priestly origins of the sect, see F. M. Cross, "The Early History of the Qumran Community," in *New Directions in Biblical Archaeology,* ed. D. N. Freedman and J. C. Greenfield, 63-79 (Garden City: Doubleday, 1969); and D. R. Schwartz, "On Two Aspects of a Priestly View of Descent at Qumran," in *Archaeology and History in the Dead Sea Scrolls: The New York University Conference in Memory of Yigael Yadin,* ed. L. H. Schiffman, 157-79. JSOTSup 8. JSOT/ASOR Monographs 2 (Sheffield: Sheffield Academic, 1990).

26. See esp. CD 3:20-4:4.

27. Cf. CD 2:16-3:14.

The New Halakhic Letter (4QMMT) and the Origins of the Dead Sea Sect

It is for this reason that many of the agreements between MMT and the *Temple Scroll* exist.[28] We must bear in mind that disagreements, certainly in detail, do exist. These two texts cannot be regarded as linearly related in any way. Yet at the same time, the similarities do point to the notion that the sources of the *Temple Scroll* also lie in the Sadducean tradition.[29] If so, Qumran is now providing us with insight into this tradition never before available.

Furthermore, MMT leads to a reevaluation of some of the older theories regarding the scrolls. A few of these ramifications will be sketched out here.

It is apparent that the theories which seek to link the sect and its origins with the Hasidim must be abandoned. This designation, which actually described not a sect but a loose agglomeration of people,[30] must be discounted as a solution to the problem of sectarian origins. The attempt of some to see the sect as emerging from some subgroup of the Pharisees is certainly to be rejected now. The dominant Essene hypothesis, if it is to be maintained, would require radical reorientation. It would be necessary to assume that the term Essene came to designate the originally Sadducean sectarians who had gone through a process of radicalization and were now a distinct sect. The notion that the collection of scrolls at Qumran in no way is representative of a sect but must be seen as fairly representing the Judaism of the time must also be rejected.[31] There is no question that the community that collected these scrolls originated in sectarian conflict, and that this conflict sustained it throughout its existence.[32] MMT preserves evidence that this conflict was with those in control of the temple in Hasmonean Jerusalem. Further, the na-

---

28. Schiffman, *RevQ* 14 (1990) 435-57.

29. H. Burgmann, "11QT: The Sadducean 'Torah,'" in *Temple Scroll Studies*, ed. G. J. Brooke, 257-63. JSPSup 7 (Sheffield: JSOT, 1989), asserts this thesis in his title but fails to argue for it in a sustained manner, dealing only with Levitical favoritism in the *Temple Scroll*.

30. For a complete examination of the sources, see J. Kampen, *The Hasideans and the Origin of Pharisaism: A Study in 1 and 2 Maccabees*. SBLSCS 24 (Atlanta: Scholars, 1988). However, our conclusion differs from his.

31. This is the view of N. Golb, "The Dead Sea Scrolls: A New Perspective," *American Scholar* 58 (1989) 177-207. A polemical treatment in book-length form is Golb's *Who Wrote the Dead Sea Scrolls? The Search for the Secret of Qumran* (New York: Scribner, 1995). This theory has been shown to be impossible in a detailed examination of its underpinnings by F. García Martínez and A. S. van der Woude, "A 'Groningen' Hypothesis of Qumran Origins and Early History," *RevQ* 14 (The Texts of Qumran and the History of the Community: Proceedings of the Groningen Congress on the Dead Sea Scrolls 3, 1990) 521-41.

32. Golb is certainly correct in reminding us that the scrolls preserve many compositions authored outside of the group. We see these, however, as assembled by the sectarians because of their affinity for or adherence to the teachings of these texts. The scrolls also preserve much information about other groups of Jews in this period: the Pharisees, the Sadducees, the Hasmoneans, and others known only from their literary compositions.

ture of the collection, even if it contains many texts not explicitly sectarian that might have been acceptable to all Jews in Second Temple times, is still that of a subgroup of society with definite opposition to the political and religious authorities of the times.

There can be little question that the publication of 4Q*Miqṣat Ma'aśe ha-Torah* has necessitated the reevaluation of many aspects of Qumran studies. Among these is certainly the question of Qumran origins and early history. Henceforth, any theory of sectarian origins must place the earliest, pre-Teacher stage in the offshoots of intrapriestly contention and must reckon with the Sadducean halakhic views of those who formed the sect.

CHAPTER 7

The Place of 4QMMT in the Corpus of Qumran Manuscripts

4Q*Miqṣat Ma'aśe ha-Torah* (MMT, or the *Halakhic Letter*) is a composite of six fragmentary manuscripts that have been arranged into one text by Elisha Qimron, based on the work he and John Strugnell did together on this text.[1] The reconstruction of this text is, as Qimron asserts, a matter of scholarly judgment. Nevertheless, the overall structure of the document, as suggested by their research, seems to be clear and will be taken as the starting point for this discussion.

The composite text may be divided into three parts: (A) the calendar at the beginning, (B) the list of laws, and (C) the homiletical conclusion.[2] The suggestion that MMT is originally two documents rather than one[3] we find unacceptable, since two manuscripts (MS d and e) definitely contain elements of both the legal and homiletical sections of the text.[4] Each of the three

---

1. E. Qimron and J. Strugnell, *Qumran Cave 4.V: Miqṣat Ma'ase ha-Torah.* DJD 10 (Oxford: Clarendon, 1994) 44-57. See the earlier articles, Qimron and Strugnell, "An Unpublished Halakhic Letter from Qumran," in *Biblical Archaeology Today: Proceedings of the International Congress on Biblical Archaeology, Jerusalem, April 1984*, ed. J. Amitai, 400-7 (Jerusalem: Israel Exploration Society, Israel Academy of Sciences and Humanities, in cooperation with ASOR, 1985); and (a different article by the same name) *IMJ* 4 (1985) 9-12.

2. Cf. Qimron and Strugnell, DJD 10:109-11.

3. R. H. Eisenman and M. Wise, eds., *The Dead Sea Scrolls Uncovered* (Shaftesbury, Dorset: Element, 1992) 182, 196. For the controversy regarding this book, see the section entitled "Ethics of Publication of the Dead Sea Scrolls: Panel Discussion," in *Methods of Investigation of the Dead Sea Scrolls and the Khirbet Qumran Site: Present Realities and Future Prospects*, ed. M. O. Wise et al., 455-97. Annals of the New York Academy of Sciences 722 (New York: New York Academy of Sciences, 1994); and F. García Martínez, "Notas al margen de *The Dead Sea Scrolls Uncovered*," *RevQ* 16 (1993) 123-50.

4. Qimron and Strugnell, DJD 10:25-28, 34-37.

sections that make up MMT can be studied with regard to its links with other elements of the Qumran corpus. This analysis will better enable us to understand the document as a whole and its evidence for the history of the Qumran sect and the Judaism of the time.

The Calendar

From the earliest discussions of 4QMMT, after its announcement (or better: debut) at the 1984 conference on biblical archaeology in Jerusalem,[5] it was already clear that the relationship of the calendar to the text that followed was a matter of question from a literary point of view. The calendar's conclusion is found in MS a (4Q394 3-7 i), which is immediately followed, on the same fragment, by the introductory sentence to the list of laws and then by the laws themselves.[6] The editors, in the series *Discoveries in the Judaean Desert,* placed another fragment (4Q394 1-2 i-v) above it and restored much of the calendar from parallel Qumran calendrical texts, on which we will have more to say below. This fragment, however, seems out of place since it sets out the calendar in five columns, while the concluding section, that found in the fragment containing the beginning of the legal section, is written in the normal way across the entire column. For this and other reasons, it has recently been suggested that this five-columned fragment should be detached from MMT and that the text be restored in such a way that it would be written across the page. In any case, we would have to reckon with the presence of the very same calendar text.[7]

That the calendar is indeed to be restored above the legal section, and that the calendar to be restored is indeed the so-called sectarian calendar, can be shown from the final words of this section:

---

5. See the description of that event in L. H. Schiffman, *Reclaiming the Dead Sea Scrolls: The History of Judaism, the Background of Christianity, the Lost Library of Qumran* (Philadelphia: Jewish Publication Society, 1994; repr. ABRL. New York: Doubleday, 1995) xvii-xviii.

6. See Qimron and Strugnell, DJD 10:7-8, 109-10. See the photograph on pl. II.

7. The hesitations about the present join and reconstruction are engendered by the unlikely scribal technique involved in having five columns of calendrical material on the top of a column (a page) followed by full-width columns below. Such an approach is not impossible, but certainly is very unlikely in light of what we know of the Qumran corpus. For such irregularly shaped columns, see the Jonathan Prayer (4Q448) in E. Eshel, H. Eshel, and A. Yardeni, "A Qumran Composition Containing Part of Ps. 154 and a Prayer for the Welfare of King Jonathan and His Kingdom," *IEJ* 42 (1992) 200; E. Eshel et al., *Qumran Cave 4.VI: Poetical and Liturgical Texts, Part 1.* DJD 11 (Oxford: Clarendon, 1998) 403-25.

The Place of 4QMMT in the Corpus of Qumran Manuscripts

[... The twenty-eighth day of it (i.e., the twelfth month)] is a Sabbath. To it (the twelfth month), after [the] Sab[bath, Sunday, and Monday, a day is to be ad]ded. And the year is complete[8] — three hundred and si[xty-four] days.[9]

The 364-day calendar is, of course, the calendar known from various Qumran texts, such as the so-called *Mishmarot* detailing the priestly courses and the *Temple Scroll*, as well as previously known pseudepigrapha also found at Qumran — *Jubilees* and *Enoch*.[10] Regardless of whether 4Q394 1-2 i-v is to be joined to the beginning of MMT or which restorations are to be accepted, such a calendar certainly was copied at the beginning of MMT.

In the Qimron-Strugnell reconstruction,[11] the calendar mentions, in addition to the solar months, the specific extra day added after three months of thirty days at the equinoxes and solstices, as well as the ninety-one-day quarter that is the basic division of the year.[12] Further, it also mentions the wine festival on the third day of the fifth month and the oil festival on the twenty-second of the sixth month, as well as the festival of the wood offering starting on the twenty-third of the same month. All these are among the extra festivals associated with the solar calendar in the *Temple Scroll*.[13]

From the beginning there has been a question as to whether this calendar is to be considered integral to the text of MMT or not. It ends in MS a (4Q394 3-7 i line 3 = composite text A 21) after the first word of the line, and the rest of the line is blank. The text begins the halakhic section on the next line with the incipit, "These are some of our rulings" (... אלה מקצת דברינו. [line 4 = composite text B 1]), and the laws follow. Since the substance of this incipit returns towards the end of the homiletical section (C 26-27) that con-

---

8. Cf. *Jub.* 6:30 for a similar expression.
9. Adapted from Qimron and Strugnell, DJD 10:45.
10. For a brief survey of the calendar issue, see Schiffman, *Reclaiming the Dead Sea Scrolls*, 301-5 and bibliog. on 443. See also S. Talmon, *The World of Qumran from Within* (Jerusalem: Magnes and Leiden: Brill, 1989) 147-85.
11. DJD 10:44.
12. The mention of a Day of Remembrance on the first day of the fourth month indicates that the ritual sequence of this calendar differed from that of the *Temple Scroll*, which celebrated only the first days of the first and seventh months. The Days of Remembrance are a regular feature of 4QMishmarot^a and 4QMishmarot^b as well as of the calendar text known as 4QS^e. In addition, they are known from *Jub.* 6:23-29; see L. H. Schiffman, "The Sacrificial System of the Temple Scroll and the Book of Jubilees," *SBLSP 1985*, ed. K. H. Richards, 228-29 (Atlanta: Scholars, 1985).
13. See Y. Yadin, *The Temple Scroll* (Jerusalem: Israel Exploration Society and Shrine of the Book, 1983) 1:116-9.

tains similar wording (ואף אנחנו כתבנו אליך מקצת מעשי התורה), it seems certain that the legal and homiletical section are to be considered as one unit. But it appears to us most likely that the calendar at the beginning of MMT was placed there by a scribe who copied (as far as can be known only in one MS) the sectarian calendar immediately before the so-called halakhic letter or treatise.[14]

This assumption is strengthened by the fact that this calendar is clearly a separate literary unit that, even if it were part of the MMT text, must have been imported whole cloth into the text. The very same calendar lies behind a text termed 4Q*Calendrical Document/Mishmarot A* (4Q320).[15] Since this calendar existed separately, and since a calendar was also attached to one of the manuscripts of the *Rule of the Community* from Cave 4 (4QSe),[16] it is apparent that this calendrical list was not composed by the author of the MMT text. This calendar must therefore be considered extraneous to the original composition.

This view is supported by an examination of the legal and homiletical sections (B and C) of MMT. Surprisingly, calendar issues are never referred to in either of these sections, and none of the additional festivals or characteristics of the Qumran calendrical system are mentioned at all in the preserved text of MMT proper. One would certainly have expected these to be mentioned in a document giving the legal reasons for the foundation of the sect, and that, in our view, is the purpose of MMT.[17] Indeed, it may very well be that the scribe copied the calendar before MMT precisely because calendrical issues were to him determinative and he could not imagine that they were not a factor in the initial schism. But in so doing, he actually added an issue to the document that had never been discussed in the original treatise.[18]

---

14. This same position is taken by Strugnell in an appendix to Qimron and Strugnell, DJD 10:203; also published in J. Strugnell, "MMT: Second Thoughts on a Forthcoming Edition," in *The Community of the Renewed Covenant: The Notre Dame Symposium on the Dead Sea Scrolls,* ed. E. Ulrich and J. C. VanderKam, 61-62. CJAS 10 (Notre Dame: University of Notre Dame Press, 1994). Strugnell further argues that it is most likely that this calendar was not part of MS b (4Q395) because "enough uninscribed leather is preserved before Section B to make it highly probable that no text ever stood before it." This comment is difficult to understand from the photo reproduced as pl. III, at the bottom, unless he is referring to the blank space to the right of the text as being too wide for a columnar margin.

15. S. Talmon and J. Ben-Dov, in *Qumran Cave 4.XVI: Calendrical Texts,* ed. Talmon, Ben-Dov, U. Glessmer. DJD 21 (Oxford: Clarendon, 2001) 37-63.

16. Ben-Dov in DJD 21:195-244.

17. See "The New Halakhic Letter (4QMMT) and the Origins of the Dead Sea Sect," Chapter 6 above; Schiffman, *Reclaiming the Dead Sea Scrolls,* 83-89.

18. Strugnell, DJD 10:203, and "MMT: Second Thoughts," 62, prefers to see it as prefixed for noncontroversialist or nonpolemical reasons.

The Place of 4QMMT in the Corpus of Qumran Manuscripts

The decision of this scribe to integrate the calendar into MMT was not all that unreasonable in light of the situation in the *Temple Scroll*. Like MMT, this scroll reflects the Sadducean trend in Jewish law.[19] In our view the *Temple Scroll* was constructed from Sadducean sources, yet redacted by someone who was either a member of, or close to, the Qumran sect.[20] In rewriting the Torah so as to include his opinions on Jewish law, the author/redactor incorporated a preexistent source known to scholars as the *Festival Calendar*.[21] This source recapitulated the festival calendar of Numbers 28–29 while at the same time integrating material from Leviticus 23 and other sources. In the process, the author of this source wove in elements of the calendar known to us as the sectarian calendar, including the special festivals outlined in that text in detail — the same as those mentioned in MMT. While it was possible to deny that this was indeed the sectarian calendar previous to the availability of all the calendrical scrolls,[22] such a claim is no longer likely, and we must view the calendar of the *Temple Scroll* as identical to that prefaced to MMT by the scribe of MS a or some previous compiler.

Since the legal regulations of MMT are similar in some cases to those of the *Temple Scroll*, there is little reason to be surprised that a scribe would sim-

---

19. See the important article of Y. Sussmann, "Ḥeqer Toldot ha-Halakhah u-Megillot Midbar Yehudah: Hirhurim Talmudiyim Rishonim le-'Or Megillat Miqṣat Ma'aśe ha-Torah," *Tarbiz* 59 (1990) 11-76. An English version of the body of this article and some of the notes, entitled "The History of *Halakha* and the Dead Sea Scrolls: Preliminary Observations on *Miqṣat Ma'ase Ha-Torah* (4QMMT)," appears in Qimron and Strugnell, DJD 10:179-202. The first to realize the Sadducean halakhic tendencies of 4QMMT, when only a short passage from it was known, was J. M. Baumgarten, "The Pharisaic-Sadducean Controversies about Purity and the Qumran Texts," *JJS* 31 (1980) 157-70. Attention was called to Sadducean elements in the *Temple Scroll* by M. R. Lehmann, "The *Temple Scroll* as a Source for Sectarian Halakhah," *RevQ* 9 (1978) 579-87. See also E. Regev, *Ha-Ṣeduqim ve-Hilkhatam: 'Al Dat ve-Ḥevrah bi-Yeme Bayit Sheni* (Jerusalem: Yad Ben Zvi, 2005) 209-14, 417-18.

20. See L. H. Schiffman, "The *Temple Scroll* and the Nature of Its Law: The Status of the Question," in Ulrich and VanderKam, *Community of the Renewed Covenant*, 46-48.

21. On the sources of the *Temple Scroll*, see A. M. Wilson and L. Wills, "Literary Sources of the Temple Scroll," *HTR* 75 (1982) 275-88. On the *Festival Calendar*, see Yadin, *Temple Scroll*, 1:89-142, who did not, however, deal with this as a separate source, only as a literary unit. This source was described in detail in M. O. Wise, *A Critical Study of the Temple Scroll from Qumran Cave 11*. SAOC 49 (Chicago: Oriental Institute, University of Chicago, 1990) 129-54. See also Schiffman, "Sacrificial System," 217-33.

22. As maintained by B. A. Levine, "The *Temple Scroll*: Aspects of Its Historical Provenance and Literary Character," *BASOR* 232 (1978) 7-11; "A Further Look at the *Mo'adim* of the Temple Scroll," in *Archaeology and History in the Dead Sea Scrolls: The New York University Conference in Memory of Yigael Yadin*, ed. L. H. Schiffman, 53-66. JSPSup 8. JSOT/ASOR Monographs 2 (Sheffield: JSOT, 1990).

ilarly assume that the calendar of the sectarians was to be associated with MMT as it was with the *Temple Scroll*. Hence, he copied it above his copy of MMT.

The Legal Section

Temple Scroll

In a previous paper we investigated in detail those laws in MMT that were paralleled in the *Temple Scroll*.[23] In order to clarify this important aspect of the relationship of MMT to the Qumran corpus, we summarize these parallels here.

The *Temple Scroll* (11QTemple 20:11-13) requires that *shelamim* sacrifices (gift-offerings) be eaten by sunset on the very same day that they are offered. This law is paralleled by MMT B 9-13, where it is stated that the meal offering of the *shelamim* is to be offered on the very same day. The opponents of the group are said to have left it over to the next day. We can assume that the meal offerings and the actual meat of the sacrifices had the very same time restrictions. This MMT passage is clearly a reference to the same view as that of the *Temple Scroll*, that the offering be eaten by sunset, as opposed to the Pharisaic-rabbinic view that allowed it to be eaten until dawn, with the proviso of the Tannaim that it be eaten if possible by midnight.[24] In any case, these two texts share the requirement that it be eaten before sunset.[25]

Both texts, in a variety of laws, reject the policy of the Pharisees and later Tannaim[26] to allow the *ṭevul yom*, one who has immersed but not yet completed the sunset of his last day of purification, to eat pure food.[27] The Sadducees, as known from elsewhere, followed by MMT and the *Temple Scroll* in a variety of passages, rejected this possibility, insisting on waiting for sun-

---

23. L. H. Schiffman, "*Miqṣat Ma'aseh ha-Torah* and the *Temple Scroll*," *RevQ* 14 (The Texts of Qumran and the History of the Community: Proceedings of the Groningen Congress on the Dead Sea Scrolls 3, 1990): 435-57. To this material, cf. now the analysis of Qimron in DJD 10:148-77 that Strugnell and he had been kind enough to make available to me already in 1984, and that of Sussmann, DJD 10:187-91.

24. *m. Ber.* 1:1; cf. *m. Zebaḥ.* 6:1.

25. Qimron and Strugnell, DJD 10:150-52; Schiffman, *RevQ* 14 (1990) 436-38.

26. Cf. *m. Neg.* 14:3; *Sifra* 'Emor ch. 4:8.

27. See Qimron and Strugnell, DJD 10:153-54; Schiffman, *RevQ* 14 (1990) 438-42; Baumgarten, *JJS* 31 (1980) 157-61; and L. H. Schiffman, "Pharisaic and Sadducean Halakhah in Light of the Dead Sea Scrolls: The Case of Ṭevul Yom," *DSD* 1 (1994) 285-99, where I deal with the full range of applications of this Sadducean principle in Qumran texts.

The Place of 4QMMT in the Corpus of Qumran Manuscripts

set. The *Temple Scroll* expresses this view in 11QTemple 45:9-10 regarding immersion of one impure from seminal emission who must complete the entire third day through sunset before being permitted to eat of pure food.[28] Regarding purification from the impurity of the dead, 11QTemple 49:19-29 insists on completion of the last day of the seven-day purification period.[29] In 11QTemple 51:2-5 those who come into contact with the impure creeping things (שרצים) are also impure until after sunset.

The same view is expressed in MMT B 13-17 in regard to those who are involved in the offering of the red heifer who must be entirely pure after completing their period of purification at the setting of the sun.[30] As hinted in the polemic of MMT, the Pharisaic-rabbinic tradition disagreed radically. The "elders of Israel" supposedly went so far as to purposely render the priest who would burn the offering impure so as to make him a *ṭevul yom*. The view of MMT is identified explicitly in the Mishnah as Sadducean.[31] We will see below that the *Zadokite Fragments* also agree with MMT and the *Temple Scroll* in this regard.

11QTemple 47:7-15 prohibits bringing hides of animals slaughtered outside the temple precincts into the temenos.[32] Only the skins of animals slaughtered in temple rituals may be used to store food in the temple. This law is paralleled by MMT B 18-23, which prohibits bringing into the temple containers made of hides of animals slaughtered outside. The *Temple Scroll* includes in this prohibition also bones (and hooves as well), and this is made explicit in MMT B 21-23 (according to an almost certain restoration), which also prohibits bringing bone vessels into the sanctuary.[33]

11QTemple 52:5-7 prohibits the slaughter of pregnant animals, making use of the language of Deut 22:6-7 to make clear that it is considered like taking the mother and its young at the same time. MMT B 36-38 shares the same prohibition, but instead derives the law from Lev 22:28. The polemical language shows that this was contrary to the Pharisaic-rabbinic view, which, as we know

---

28. Cf. Yadin, *Temple Scroll*, 1:288-89.

29. Cf. L. H. Schiffman, "The Impurity of the Dead in the *Temple Scroll*," in *Archaeology and History*, 146-48.

30. This same requirement may be referred to in 4Q276–4Q277 (*Ṭohorot* B[a] and B[b]), which requires that the sprinkling be done by a priest who is pure of all impurities. See J. M. Baumgarten, in *Qumran Cave 4.XXV: Halakhic Texts*, ed. Baumgarten et al. DJD 35 (Oxford: Clarendon, 1999) 111-19.

31. *M. Parah* 3:7.

32. Cf. Yadin, *Temple Scroll*, 1:308-11; Schiffman, *RevQ* 14 (1990) 442-8.

33. Cf. Qimron and Strugnell, DJD 10:154-56; Schiffman, *RevQ* 14 (1990) 442-48; Yadin, *Temple Scroll*, 1:308-11.

from later sources, permitted the slaughter of pregnant animals.[34] It took the prohibition on slaughtering an animal and its child, stated in the masculine in Lev 22:28, as referring only to the slaughter of a mother and its young on the same day, not to the prohibition on slaughtering pregnant animals.[35]

The *Temple Scroll* (11QTemple 60:2-4) indicates that various offerings are to be allotted to the priests. These include wave offerings, firstborn, tithe animals, all sacred donations, and "fruit offerings of praise," that is, fourth-year produce. Some of these elements, namely the fourth-year produce and the cattle and sheep tithes, are also assigned to the priests by MMT B 57-59.[36] In this case the *Temple Scroll* and MMT are in agreement. But we must remember that there are more elements in the *Temple Scroll* list than in that of MMT, indicating that these passages are not literarily dependent on one another, but rather are related only in terms of representing the same halakhic tradition.

The final area we will mention is the use of the term "camps" to denote the various levels of sanctity of Jerusalem and the temple complex. The Torah contains various regulations regarding the "camp" of the Israelites in the wilderness. The *Temple Scroll* made use of these passages to derive the levels of sanctity of the three courts of the temple city — the inner court, containing the temple, the middle, and outer courts. In this respect the scroll followed the same scheme as is found in tannaitic sources that interpreted the biblical passages as referring to the camp of the divine presence, containing the tabernacle; the camp of the Levites, including the residence of Moses and the priests; and the camp of Israel in which the rest of the people dwelled.[37] For the *Temple Scroll*, this set of camps, concentrically arranged, constituted the temple complex, which a visionary architect designed in imitation of the tabernacle and desert camp that it represented.[38]

---

34. See *m. Ḥul.* 4:5, where the opinion of Rabbi Meir that "he is obligated for (violation of) the prohibition against slaughtering an animal and its young" refers only to his view that one must slaughter a fully mature embryo that survives its mother's ritual slaughter. In such a case, in the view of Rabbi Meir, it is forbidden to slaughter the embryo on the same day as its mother. The anonymous Mishnah does not require slaughter of the mature fetus, and so the issue is not raised by the other sages. L. H. Schiffman, "Some Laws Pertaining to Animals in *Temple Scroll*, Column 52," in *Legal Texts and Legal Issues: Proceedings of the Second Meeting of the International Organization for Qumran Studies, Cambridge, 1995*, ed. M. Bernstein, F. García Martínez, and J. Kampen, 167-78. STDJ 23 (Leiden: Brill, 1997).

35. Qimron and Strugnell, DJD 10:157-58; Schiffman, *RevQ* 14 (1990) 448-51; Yadin, *Temple Scroll*, 1:312-14.

36. Qimron and Strugnell, DJD 10:164-66; Schiffman, *RevQ* 14 (1990) 452-56.

37. *T. Kelim B.Q.* 1:12; *Sifre Num.* Naso 1.

38. See L. H. Schiffman, "Exclusion from the Sanctuary and the City of the Sanctuary in

MMT seems to take a somewhat different attitude, although some interpreters have sought to harmonize the two texts.[39] MMT alludes to the camps twice. As restored by Strugnell and Qimron, MMT B 29-31 states polemically that the authors think that the sanctuary is equivalent to the tabernacle of the desert period, and that the camp is Jerusalem, and outside that camp is the camp of the cities. This means that the text accepts a three camp notion, with the entire temple as the inner camp, the city of Jerusalem as the middle camp, and the entire settled area of the cities as the camp of Israel.[40] Such a pattern is indeed similar to the three camps of the wilderness, but differs in some respects from the view of the *Temple Scroll.* In B 60-62 we hear that Jerusalem is the most important of the camps of Israel and it is termed the camp of holiness. This clearly refers to the same concept, describing the middle camp that the text of MMT already asserted was Jerusalem.

Here again we see commonality between MMT and the *Temple Scroll,* but the same basic concept is found in tannaitic thought. At the same time, MMT and the *Temple Scroll* differ in significant respects in the way this concept is applied. Indeed, this difference may result from the utopian character of the *Temple Scroll* as opposed to MMT, which deals with the halakhic system of the author's own day, expressing the views of the Sadducean-Zadokite priests.

Zadokite Fragments

The links between MMT and the *Zadokite Fragments* are also close. The *Zadokite Fragments,* initially discovered by Solomon Schechter in the Cairo Genizah,[41] were found subsequently in ten Qumran manuscripts.[42] It is cer-

---

the *Temple Scroll,*" *HAR* 9 (1985) 308-9; "Architecture and Law: The Temple and Its Courtyards in the *Temple Scroll,*" in *From Ancient Israel to Modern Judaism: Intellect in Quest of Understanding: Essays in Honor of Marvin Fox,* ed. J. Neusner, E. S. Frerichs, and N. M. Sarna, 1:267-84. BJS 159 (Atlanta: Scholars, 1989).

39. Qimron and Strugnell, DJD 10:144-45; and the remark of Y. Yadin, "Discussion," in Amitai, *Biblical Archaeology Today,* 429.

40. Cf. Qimron and Strugnell, DJD 10:142-46.

41. His initial publication is *Documents of Jewish Sectaries,* vol. 1: *Fragments of a Zadokite Work* (Cambridge: Cambridge University Press, 1910; repr. Library of Biblical Studies [New York: Ktav, 1970]).

42. The transcriptions of the Cave 4 fragments by J. T. Milik for the Preliminary Concordance were published in reconstructed form in B. Z. Wacholder and M. G. Abegg, eds., *A Preliminary Edition of the Unpublished Dead Sea Scrolls: The Hebrew and Aramaic Texts from Cave Four* (Washington: Biblical Archaeology Society, 1991-1996) 1:1-59. We have provided

tainly the case that the halakhic tradition behind the *Zadokite Fragments* is the same as that of the Qumran sect, even if they represent the members of the sect living in scattered groups ("camps") throughout the country. Here also we see some examples of agreement with MMT.

4Q266 (4QD^a) 9 ii 1-4 provides that a woman who is impure from a nonmenstrual flow of blood must wait "until sunset on the eighth day" to be considered pure. This law, based on Lev 15:25-30, presumes the rejection of the concept of *ṭevul yom*, which we consider to be a "smoking gun" indication of the Sadducean approach to Jewish law.[43]

It is most probable that the fragmentary reference in 4Q266 (4QD^a) 13 4-5, mentioning planting in the third year and sanctification in some other year,[44] originally paralleled the requirement of MMT B 62-63 that the fruit of the fourth year be given to the priests like *terumah*, as opposed to the Pharisaic-rabbinic view that it should be eaten by the owner in the precincts of Jerusalem.[45] This same prescription, as already mentioned, is found also in the *Temple Scroll*.

As part of a list of those forbidden from entering "into the midst of the congregation," CD 15:15-17 = 4Q266 (4QD^a) 17 i 6-9 = 4Q270 (4QD^e) 10 ii 7-9 (restored) includes "one who is weak of the eyes so that he cannot see" as well as one who is deaf.[46] This passage may be compared with the prohibition in MMT of the blind and deaf from contact with the "the sacred food" or from entering the temple precincts, depending on how the passage is interpreted.[47] We should also note that the *Temple Scroll* (11QTemple 45:12-14) prohibits the

---

manuscript numbers (e.g., 4Q266) for these texts as well as letters (e.g., 4QDa), since the letter sigla have been changed over the years. The letters used to designate the manuscripts in Wacholder and Abegg are superseded by those in E. Tov, with S. J. Pfann, *The Dead Sea Scrolls on Microfiche: Companion Volume* (Leiden: Brill, 1993) 38. A full edition is J. M. Baumgarten, *Qumran Cave 4.XIII: The Damascus Document (4Q266-273)*. DJD 18 (Oxford: Clarendon, 1996). For the other Qumran manuscripts, see Schiffman, *Reclaiming the Dead Sea Scrolls*, 469. On the legal material in these texts, see J. M. Baumgarten, "The Laws of the *Damascus Document* in Current Research," in *The Damascus Document Reconsidered*, ed. M. Broshi (Jerusalem: Israel Exploration Society, 1992) 51-62; and L. H. Schiffman, "New Halakhic Texts from Qumran," *HS* 34 (1993) 21-33.

43. Schiffman, *DSD* 1 (1994) 285-99.

44. The text most likely referred to planting in the third year of the Sabbatical cycle that would result in sanctification of the fruits (the fourth-year produce) in year six.

45. *Sifre Num.* 6; *Sifra* Qedoshim parashah 3:8.

46. Cf. L. H. Schiffman, *The Eschatological Community of the Dead Sea Scrolls: A Study of the Rule of the Congregation*. SBLMS 38 (Atlanta: Scholars, 1989) 44-49. This passage, then not known in its original Hebrew, is discussed on pp. 47-48.

47. See Qimron and Strugnell, DJD 10:160-61.

The Place of 4QMMT in the Corpus of Qumran Manuscripts

blind from entering the temple city, in our view equivalent to the temenos, the temple precincts.[48]

While MMT and the *Zadokite Fragments* do have in common the inclusion of these two categories, the blind and deaf, we need to recognize that each occurs in a long list of disqualified individuals of which the other categories are not equivalent. If these laws were truly identical, we would expect the lists to be the same in their entirety. When we bear in mind that the *Temple Scroll* excludes only the blind and the *Rule of the Congregation* excludes an entirely different, though overlapping list from the community of the end of days (1QSa 2:3-11),[49] we recognize that these texts share a trend of interpretation, but that they are not identical in their approach.

It appears that MMT and the *Zadokite Fragments* include the identical prescription regarding the comparison of some kind of illegal marriage with the laws of forbidden mixtures (כלאים). 4Q271 (4QD^f) 1 i 9-11 = 4Q270 (4QD^e) 5:15-16 = 4Q269 (4QD^d) 9:2-3 prohibits giving a girl in marriage to one who is inappropriate (לאשר לא הוכן לה). Such a match is then compared to forbidden mixtures of either plowing animals or threads, in a passage making use of the language of Scripture (Deut 22:10-11). But here there is no specific information on the nature of the inappropriateness of the match. In MMT B 75-82 (the end of the preserved portion of the legal section), we find what must be the exact same law, although it remains difficult to understand. This passage begins by referring to "זונות (sexual immorality) that is performed among the people" and is compared to violation of the laws of forbidden mixtures (all varieties are listed here). From the continuation it seems clear that this is an offense of the priests about whom it is said that "you know that some of the priests and the people are mixing and they mingle and defile the holy seed. . . ." The editors take this statement to refer to priests marrying Israelites, which they claim this document prohibits.[50] Another view that they cite suggests that it refers to marriage with non-Jews.[51] Whatever the correct interpretation of this law, it is most probably the same prescription as that of the *Zadokite Fragments*, and the restoration of that passage will have to be attempted in light of this law in MMT.

---

48. See Schiffman, *HAR* 9 (1985) 309-11; and Yadin, *Temple Scroll*, 1:289-91. Yadin, however, interprets the Temple City to encompass the entire city of Jerusalem. A table comparing exclusion of various classes from the Temple according to MMT and the *Temple Scroll* is provided in Qimron and Strugnell, DJD 10:146.

49. See the detailed discussion in Schiffman, *Eschatological Community*, 37-52. The exclusion of various classes from the army and military camp is taken up there as well.

50. Qimron and Strugnell, DJD 10:171-75.

51. The view of J. M. Baumgarten as reported in Qimron and Strugnell, DJD 10:171, n. 178a.

4Q271 (4QD^f) 1 ii 8 = 4Q269 (4QD^d) 10:3-4 = 4Q270 (4QD^e) 7:20 clearly refers to a prohibition on accepting sacrifices from non-Jews. The continuation also prohibits the reuse by Jews of metals from which non-Jews have made idols. The prohibition on acceptance of sacrifices from non-Jews is paralleled in MMT B 8-9, which castigates the sect's opponents for accepting such sacrifices.[52] Indeed, it is well known that Pharisaic-rabbinic law does permit the acceptance of such offerings.[53] This is certainly another example of a law common to MMT and the *Zadokite Fragments*.

The continuation of this same passage (4Q271 [4QD^f] 1 ii 8-11 = 4Q269 [4QD^d] 10 4-6 = 4Q270 [4QD^e] 7 20-21) refers to the prohibition of bringing to the temple hide, cloth, or any vessel that is susceptible to impurity, unless it has been purified appropriately. This passage may relate to issues raised as well in MMT, although we cannot be certain. MMT B 18-20 refers to the prohibition of bringing certain skins of animals or vessels made of them into the temple precincts. This law has been related to that of the *Temple Scroll* prohibiting skins slaughtered outside from being brought into the temple, as discussed above. If these passages relate to the same issues, then the *Zadokite Fragments* recognize the possibility of purification where MMT and the *Temple Scroll* do not, since for these latter texts the issue is the need for sacral slaughter, not ritual impurity. On the other hand, it is possible that the two laws are unrelated, one dealing with problems of impurity and the other dealing with problems of slaughtering and hides not slaughtered sacrificially.

4Q270 (4QD^e) 9 ii 7-9 lists a variety of offerings that are to go to the priests. These include, among others, the tithe from the herd (cattle) and flock (sheep and goats). The tithe animals are specifically mentioned in a parallel law in MMT B 63-64 that states that they are to go to the priests, as is clear from line 6, despite the disconnected and fragmentary nature of the passage.[54] The longer list of gifts is paralleled in the *Temple Scroll* (11QTemple 60:2-5), where numerous items are listed. But the Pharisaic-rabbinic tradition rules that these animals are to be offered in the temple, the blood sprinkled,

---

52. See Qimron and Strugnell, DJD 10:149-50. This issue was a matter of controversy at the beginning of the Jewish revolt against Rome in 66-73 B.C.E. The prorevolt forces argued that such sacrifices were forbidden, while the antirevolt group argued that it was permitted. See Josephus, *J.W.* 2.409-21, and the echoes of this event in *b. Giṭ.* 56a. See also I. Knohl, "Qabbalat Qorbanot min Ha-Nokhrim," *Tarbiz* 48 (1969/1970) 341-45, for later echoes of the controversy over whether to accept sacrifices from non-Jews.

53. See *b. Ḥul.* 5a; and L. H. Schiffman, *Who Was a Jew? Rabbinic and Halakhic Perspectives on the Jewish Christian Schism* (Hoboken: Ktav, 1985) 49.

54. Qimron and Strugnell, DJD 10:165-6.

and the meat eaten by the owners.⁵⁵ The view of the *Zadokite Fragments* and MMT is also followed in some apocryphal texts as well.⁵⁶ But we should note again that the various lists — the *Zadokite Fragments*, MMT, and the *Temple Scroll*— are sufficiently different in formulation that we cannot assert literary dependence, only that they belong to the same school of legal thought.

The final example was also already encountered in our discussion of the *Temple Scroll*. 4Q270 (4QDᵉ) 9 ii 14-15 refers to the prohibition of slaughtering a pregnant animal, whether a domestic animal (בהמה) or beast (חיה). MMT B 36 contains the same prohibition, explained as a violation of the Torah's requirement that a mother and child not be slaughtered on the same day.

The large number of parallels between MMT and the *Zadokite Fragments* leads one to conclude that there would have been a much larger number of parallels if the entire text of both documents had survived. In any case, the extant parallels can only be attributed to the common halakhic substratum of the Sadducean tradition, which was opposed in the cases we cited to the Pharisaic-rabbinic approach.

Florilegium

Also to be compared to MMT is 4QFlorilegium 1:3-4. This text, a series of eschatological explanations of biblical verses, alludes to the prohibition on entrance into the temple in the end of days by an Ammonite, Moabite, *mamzer*,⁵⁷ foreigner, or proselyte or their descendants forever.⁵⁸ Here the phrase "to enter the congregation" in Deut 23:2-9 is taken as referring to entrance into the temple, whereas these prohibitions were understood as referring to marriage in the Pharisaic-rabbinic tradition.⁵⁹ The *Temple Scroll* also takes this expression as referring to entrance into the temple, as noted above. In any case, MMT B 39-49 takes this as referring to both the entrance into the temple and marriage.⁶⁰ Further, while the lists share the Ammonite, Moabite, and *mamzer*, the

---

55. *m. Zebaḥ.* 5:8; cf. *t. Zebaḥ.* 6:18; baraita in *b. Pesaḥ.* 64b, *b. Pesaḥ.* 37a and 56a; *Sifre Num.* 118; *Sifre Deut.* 78.

56. *Jub.* 13:25-26; Tob 1:6; cf. Schiffman, *RevQ* 14 (1990) 453 and nn. 87-90.

57. Defined by the halakhic tradition as the Jewish offspring of a forbidden marriage whose ancestry disqualified him or her from marriage with free, hereditary Jews of the classes priest, Levite, or Israelite.

58. Cf. G. J. Brooke, *Exegesis at Qumran: 4QFlorilegium in Its Jewish Context.* JSOTSup 29 (Sheffield: JSOT, 1985) 100-2.

59. *Sifre* Deut. 246-49.

60. Qimron and Strugnell, DJD 10:158-60. But cf. M. J. Bernstein, "The Employment and

proselyte and foreigner are not mentioned in the MMT passage, and the two forms of genital injuries mentioned in Deuteronomy are not mentioned in the Florilegium, even though they appear in MMT. This indicates again that although we deal with a common halakhic trend, there is no literary dependence in the legal traditions we are evaluating.

The Homiletical Section

In the final section, the authors of MMT attempt to sway their opponents with arguments of a homiletical nature. This is the section that I have argued is addressed primarily to the ruler, the Hasmonean high priest.[61] My view is conditioned by the shift in this section from the plural form for the addressee found in the halakhic section (although the text is usually restored), to the singular. My argument was that the plural addressee referred to the authors' erstwhile Sadducean colleagues who had remained in the temple, while the singular section at the end referred to the ruler who is compared with the kings of Israel in the First Temple period.

This section, beginning with C 10, "And we have written to you (singular)," is essentially a Deuteronomic rebuke passage, aimed not at the people (a collective you plural), but at an individual. This section is introduced by the explicit reference to the tripartite canon (C 10-11).[62] There follows a passage woven together out of Deut 31:29 and 30:1-3. There then follows the statement that some of these blessings and curses came true in First Temple times and that others are now coming to be in the time of the authors. The example of the First Temple kings is invoked to influence the ruler to follow the ways of the Torah, as understood by the writers, presumably referring to the twenty-two legal rulings they have presented above in the legal section.

What we have, then, is a kind of royal תוכחה (reproach), to which there is only one parallel I know of, at the end of the Law of the King of the *Temple Scroll* (11QTemple 59). The Law of the King is a separate document, one of the sources that make up the scroll.[63] Its veiled allusion to the kidnap and murder

---

Interpretation of Scripture in 4QMMT: Preliminary Observations," in *Reading 4QMMT: New Perspectives on Qumran Law and History*, ed. J. Kampen and Bernstein, 29-51. SBLSymS 2 (Atlanta: Scholars, 1996).

61. See Chapter 6 above; Schiffman, *Reclaiming the Dead Sea Scrolls*, 83-89.

62. See Schiffman, *Reclaiming the Dead Sea Scrolls*, 165-67; N. M. Sarna, *Songs of the Heart: An Introduction to the Book of Psalms* (New York: Schocken, 1993) 11. Contrast E. Ulrich, "The Non-attestation of a Tripartite Canon in 4QMMT," *CBQ* 65 (2003) 202-14.

63. Cf. Schiffman, *"Temple Scroll,"* 46-48.

of Jonathan the Hasmonean (11QTemple 57:9-11),[64] as well as its sustained polemic against the order of the day in Hasmonean times, make it certain that this source was composed no earlier than the reign of John Hyrcanus (134-104 B.C.E.).[65]

After presenting various laws regarding the king and his conduct of the affairs of state and the military, 11QTemple 58:21 concludes with an allusion to the king's succeeding in all his ways if he will "go forth (to battle) according to the regulation which . . ." (and here the text breaks off). There then follows a lacuna of six lines. Some excerpts from Deuteronomy 28, the underlying passage for what follows, must have stood in the text.[66] It is most probable that the singular usage of the Deuteronomic chapter as a whole for the addressee led to the interpretation that it was directed at the ruler.

The body of the preserved text of this passage is 11QTemple 59:2-21. The text picks up by describing the scattering of the people (presumably as a result of the king's transgressions) and their being disgraced, as well as their worship in exile of other gods, based primarily (and not in scriptural order) on Deut 28:36-37, 48, and 64. The text then describes the destruction of the cities based on Lev 26:31-32 and Jer 25:9. Thereafter, the text returns to Lev 26:32 to describe the astonishment of the enemies of Israel. The passage is also based on the content of Deut 31:17-18, but with language based on the Prophets.[67]

The notion of God's hiding his face from Israel is then introduced (also found in Deut 31:17-18). The violation of the covenant by the people — presumably under the leadership of the king — is then described based on Deut 31:16 and Lev 26:15. Following the Deuteronomic schema, the people then repent and God saves them and redeems them from among their enemies, so that he will be their God and they will be his people.

At this point the text returns to the motif of the king. If the king turns away from following the law, he will not have a successor and his dynasty will come to an end. But if he follows the law, then his dynasty will be passed down to his descendants. Further, God will be with him and save him from his enemies and from those who seek to kill him, and he will rule over all his enemies.

These themes are strikingly reminiscent of MMT. It is only by observing

---

64. Yadin, *Temple Scroll*, 1:386-90; L. H. Schiffman, "The King, His Guard and the Royal Council in the *Temple Scroll*," *PAAJR* 54 (1987) 247-49; M. Hengel, J. H. Charlesworth, and D. Mendels, "The Polemical Character of 'On Kingship' in the Temple Scroll: An Attempt at Dating 11QTemple," *JJS* 37 (1986) 28-38, date the scroll to between 103/2 and 88 B.C.E.

65. Schiffman, "*Temple Scroll*," 48-51.

66. Cf. Yadin, *Temple Scroll*, 2:265.

67. Cf. Yadin, *Temple Scroll*, 2:266-67.

the laws of the Torah, as set forth in the Deuteronomic covenant, that the king will be saved from misfortune. The king can guarantee the welfare of the people by following these laws. Indeed, in MMT, at the very end, we find that the observance of the laws of the Torah is considered beneficial both for the king and the people of Israel. It is clearly implied in C 23-26 that obeying the group's interpretation of the law will lead to the ruler's being saved from trouble and misfortune.

It thus emerges that the homiletical section of MMT is also parallel to a section of the *Temple Scroll*. Both the law and the theology of the scroll have much in common with MMT, because the two texts stem from the common legal and theological tradition of the Sadducees. Yet here also, while we find this commonality, there is no evidence of literary dependence.

Conclusions

Our study has shown that the text of MMT has much in common with various documents of the Qumran corpus. As it now stands in one of the manuscripts, it has been combined with the sectarian calendar that its authors probably favored. One of the scribes who prepared the copies of MMT that have come down to us clearly wanted to emphasize that the authors of MMT accepted the 364-day sectarian calendar of solar months and solar years.

With the *Temple Scroll* it shares a variety of sacrificial laws. These parallels are no doubt to be traced to the common Sadducean legal substratum that they share. Yet no literary dependence of either text on the other can be shown.

Regarding the *Zadokite Fragments,* this is also the case for the legal section of MMT. In this context we should call attention to our view that the Admonition of the *Zadokite Fragments* actually refers to the early pre–Teacher of Righteousness days of the sect when the group came into existence in protest over the conduct of the Jerusalem temple and also because of disagreements regarding other matters of Jewish law and interpretation. This is the very same time when the MMT document would have been composed and sent to the Jerusalem establishment according to our understanding of the early history of the Qumran sect.[68]

68. Cf. Schiffman, *Reclaiming the Dead Sea Scrolls,* 92; Strugnell, "MMT: Second Thoughts," 70-73, a section not included in his appendix to DJD 10. In the oral presentation of this material at the Notre Dame Symposium on the Dead Sea Scrolls (April 1993), Strugnell explicitly said that he now agreed with my view that MMT predates the career of the Teacher of Righteousness.

4QFlorilegium, most of which does not concern legal matters, included a similar law to that of MMT, but the extraneous details in each list of excluded persons led to the conclusion that again there was no literary dependence, only common legal rulings. We should recall that MMT exhibits no parallels with the *Rule of the Community* or other such documents that represent the teachings of the sect after it reached maturity.

These conclusions are consistent with the view that MMT reflects the formative period of the Qumran sect. It therefore shares legal rulings with the sources of the *Temple Scroll* and the early laws of the *Zadokite Fragments*. At the same time, it reflects the ideology of parts of the *Temple Scroll*. Yet while the earlier MMT and *Temple Scroll* (and its sources) lack the language of sectarian antagonism, this tone is found in the *Zadokite Fragments*, which was completed after the split was final and which reflects the sectarian animus that would characterize the later documents of the Qumran group.

With MMT we have clearly returned to the early days of sectarian law. The parallels with other legal texts from the Qumran corpus and with Sadducean views known from the later rabbinic corpus open before us the Sadducean heritage of the founders of the sect. These early Hasmonean-period Sadducees, from whom the founders of the sect emerged, were pious priests — as distinct from their hellenized brethren described by Josephus. This pious group is the Sadducees with whom the Pharisees and sages argue according to talmudic sources. They strove to fulfill the words of the Torah as they understood them, seeking to find God in the meticulous performance of the sacrificial worship in his holy temple in Jerusalem and in the constant maintenance of the highest standards of ritual purity. It is this legal system that underlies the law of the Dead Sea Scrolls.

JEWISH LAW AT QUMRAN

CHAPTER 8

Legal Texts in the Dead Sea Scrolls

The field of Dead Sea Scrolls studies actually began with the discovery of one of the core legal texts in the sectarian library, the *Damascus Document (Zadokite Fragments).*[1] This text, discovered in the Cairo Genizah in 1896[2] and later in the Qumran caves,[3] opened the debate over Qumran law in the early twentieth century.[4] Additional Qumran legal texts were published much later, a result of both lack of interest and experience on the part of the Cave 4 publication team. The acquisition of the *Temple Scroll* during the 1967 Six-Day War led to a revival of interest in Qumran halakhah (to borrow the later rabbinic term), which has been greatly encouraged and enhanced by the full publication of the Cave 4 legal texts,[5] including much previously unknown legal material,[6] and the important scholarly research that followed.

Whereas earlier Qumran research, especially in the hands of Christian

---

1. For the discovery of this text, see S. C. Reif, *A Jewish Archive from Old Cairo: The History of Cambridge University's Genizah Collection* (Richmond, Surrey: Curzon, 2000) 113-15.

2. S. Schechter, *Documents of Jewish Sectaries*, Vol. 1: *Fragments of a Zadokite Work* (Cambridge: Cambridge University Press, 1910; repr. Library of Biblical Studies [New York: Ktav, 1970]); M. Broshi, ed., *The Damascus Document Reconsidered* (Jerusalem: Israel Exploration Society, Shrine of the Book, Israel Museum, 1992).

3. 4Q266-73; 5Q12; 6Q15.

4. Cf. L. Ginzberg, *Eine unbekannte jüdische Sekte* (New York: L. Ginzberg, 1922); repr. from *MGWJ* 55 (1911)–58 (1914); additional material in the English edition, *An Unknown Jewish Sect* (New York: Jewish Theological Seminary, 1976).

5. J. M. Baumgarten, *Qumran Cave 4.XIII: The Damascus Document (4Q266-273)*. DJD 18 (Oxford: Clarendon, 1996); J. M. Baumgarten et al., *Qumran Cave 4.XXV: Halakhic Texts*. DJD 35 (Oxford: Clarendon, 1999).

6. Cf. L. H. Schiffman, "New Halakhic Texts from Qumran," *HS* 34 (1993) 21-33.

scholars, tended to emphasize aspects of the scrolls most relevant to early Christianity, renewed interest in legal texts, as well as in a variety of parabiblical texts, has shifted attention back to the Jewishness of the Qumran sect. Identified by most scholars as the Essenes,[7] their legal materials, which we will survey here, have again become central to the debate over the significance of the scrolls and the Qumran sect in the wider context of the history of Judaism.[8]

Because the legal corpus of the scrolls is to a great extent poorly known, we will first survey the various texts, their structure and contents. Then in the next chapter, we will discuss these texts from the point of view of the history of codes and codification in Jewish law, paying attention to issues of literary history and the relationship of the texts.

The legal materials in the Dead Sea Scrolls can be divided into major and minor works.

Description of the Major Legal Texts

CD — Damascus Document (Zadokite Fragments)

First discovered in two medieval Cambridge University manuscripts from the Cairo Genizah by Solomon Schechter in 1896, the *Zadokite Fragments* was later found in several manuscripts at Qumran, mostly in Cave 4. It is now considered to be part of the sectarian literature of the Dead Sea Scrolls.

Schechter's two medieval manuscripts are MS A (T-S. 10 K 6), dating to the tenth century C.E., preserved in sixteen pages (1-16), and MS B (T-S. 16 32), from the twelfth century, consisting of two long pages (numbered 19-20, skipping 17-18). Much of MS B is a somewhat expanded version of pages 7-8 of MS A,[9] indicating that the work survived even into the Middle Ages in varying recensions. In addition, Qumran Caves 4, 5, and 6 have yielded a number of copies.[10] Without question, these fragments confirm the intimate link between the *Zadokite Fragments* and the sectarian texts from Qumran,

---

7. The first to propose this point of view was E. L. Sukenik, *Megillot Genuzot mi-tokh Genizah Qedumah she-Nimṣe'ah be-Midbar Yehudah* (Jerusalem: Bialik Institute, 1948-50) 2:16.

8. L. H. Schiffman, "Confessionalism and the Study of the Dead Sea Scrolls," *JS* 31 (1991) 3-14; "Halakhah and History: The Contribution of the Dead Sea Scrolls to Recent Scholarship," Chapter 3 above.

9. S. A. White Crawford, "A Comparison of the 'A' and 'B' Manuscripts of the Damascus Document," *RevQ* 12 (1987) 537-53.

10. 5Q12 and 6Q15 in M. Baillet, J. T. Milik, and R. de Vaux, *Les 'Petites Grottes' de Qumrân*. DJD 3 (Oxford: Clarendon, 1962) 128-31, 181; 4Q266-273 in Baumgarten, DJD 18.

most notably the *Rule of the Community* (1QS). In general, the Qumran fragments agree with the recension in MS A.[11] The Cave 4 material indicates that the text circulated in various recensions reflecting stages in the history of the Qumran community.[12]

The text as a whole, somewhat like the book of Deuteronomy, consists of two primary units: the Admonition (Exhortation) and the Laws.[13] The Admonition, now believed to constitute some 25 percent of the original complete text, set forth the sectarians' self-image, tracing their history to biblical times and asserting their claim to be the authentic continuators of ancient Israel. The document further set out their fundamental disagreement with the main body of the Jewish people and, in particular, argued against their Pharisaic opponents. This admonition has been compared to the speeches of Moses at the beginning of Deuteronomy in which he lays down a basic conceptual and ideological framework before presenting the Deuteronomic legal and religious codes. Yet such hortatory introductions are not known from later Jewish texts, though we should note parallels in tone to some of the "Testaments" literature.

The sect was constituted by those who perceived the iniquity of their generation, but lacked direction and leadership. The rise soon afterward of the Teacher of Righteousness (or "Correct Teacher") filled this gap. "Damascus"[14] serves as a code word for the sectarian settlement at Qumran (CD 7:19),[15] hence the designation "Damascus Covenant" or "Damascus Document." The Admonition argues for predestination toward the paths of good and evil and condemns the evils of the rest of the Jewish community,[16] alluding to the various groups of Jews existing in the Hasmonean period. The sins of the rest of Jewry are cataloged, and the sectarians are pictured as being the only ones who know the correct interpretation of the Torah, the "hidden" laws, and who properly observe them.[17] Scholars are divided as to whether the text expected one "Messiah of Aaron and Israel" or two separate messi-

---

11. Baumgarten, DJD 18:6-7.

12. J. T. Milik, *Ten Years of Discovery in the Wilderness of Judaea*, trans. J. Strugnell, 38-39. SBT 26 (London: SCM, 1959). Cf. C. Hempel, *The Laws of the Damascus Document: Sources, Tradition and Redaction.* STDJ 29 (Leiden: Brill, 1998) 15-23.

13. These titles were initially employed by C. Rabin in his edition of *The Zadokite Documents* (Oxford: Clarendon, 1954).

14. Cf. Amos 5:27.

15. R. North, "The Damascus of Qumran Geography," *PEQ* 87 (1955) 34-38.

16. C. Rabin, *Qumran Studies.* Scripta Judaica 2 (London: Oxford University Press, 1957) 53-70.

17. L. H. Schiffman, *The Halakhah at Qumran.* SJLA 16 (Leiden: Brill, 1975) 22-32.

anic figures.¹⁸ Parts of the Admonition must have originated as arguments to join the sect, while other sections must have been designed to maintain the loyalty of members of the group in the face of political, religious, and eschatological disappointments.¹⁹

The Admonition quotes *Jubilees* (CD 16:3) and the *Testament of Levi* (CD 4:15) and alludes to older traditions of biblical exegesis and to various legends that were part of early Second Temple Judaism. Much of the text consists of pesherlike interpretations of various biblical texts that the members of the sect and their leaders saw as crucial to their self-definition.

The second section is a compilation of laws arranged topically. These laws are composed of biblical phrases that indicate to modern scholars the exegesis that lay behind each legal ruling. Following Joseph A. Fitzmyer's outline,²⁰ the following topics are covered: rules for entering the sect, laws pertaining to oaths, witnesses and judges, ritual purification, Sabbath laws, miscellaneous laws, relations with non-Jews, additional purity rules, communal organization, and the sectarian penal code. There is a reference in a broken context to what seems to be public scriptural reading on the Sabbath.²¹

The earliest manuscripts of the *Damascus Document* date to ca. 75-50 B.C.E.²² This date puts to rest earlier theories that, before the discovery of the Dead Sea Scrolls, sought to identify this text as medieval Karaite or early Christian. Since the earliest possible date for Qumran settlement in the Hellenistic period is the reign of John Hyrcanus (135-104 B.C.E.),²³ and since this text represents within it several stages of historical development,²⁴ we would have to date its final composition to the latter years of John Hyrcanus or the reign of Alexander Jannaeus (103-76 B.C.E.).²⁵

---

18. Cf. "Messianic Figures and Ideas in the Qumran Scrolls," Chapter 16 below.

19. P. R. Davies, *The Damascus Covenant: An Interpretation of the "Damascus Document"* (JSOTSup 25; Sheffield: JSOT, 1983) 48-104, 143-204.

20. J. A. Fitzmyer, "Prolegomenon," in Schechter, *Documents of Jewish Sectaries*, 18-19; cf. Baumgarten, DJD 18:4-5; Hempel, *Laws of the Damascus Document*, 30-35.

21. 4Q266 5 ii 1-3 = 4Q267 5 iii 3-5 = 4Q273 2 1. See L. H. Schiffman, "The Early History of the Public Reading of the Torah," in *Jews, Christians, and Polytheists in the Ancient Synagogue: Cultural Interaction during the Greco-Roman Period*, ed. S. Fine, 45-46 (London: Routledge, 1999).

22. Milik, *Ten Years of Discovery*, 38.

23. Period Ib has recently been redated to the early first century B.C.E. by J. Magness, *The Archaeology of Qumran and the Dead Sea Scrolls*. SDSSRL (Grand Rapids: Wm. B. Eerdmans, 2002) 65.

24. L. H. Schiffman, *Sectarian Law in the Dead Sea Scrolls: Courts, Testimony and the Penal Code*. BJS 33 (Chico: Scholars, 1983) 7-11.

25. Scholars who see the text as emerging from a pre-Qumranic milieu date the composition of this text somewhat earlier (Davies, *Damascus Covenant*, 202-4).

Legal Texts in the Dead Sea Scrolls

Both the Admonition and the Laws present a consistent view of Jewish law, the source of its authority, and the method of its derivation. The laws are of two types. Those laws clearly mentioned in Scripture are termed *nigleh*, "revealed." These prescriptions are known to all of Israel, who nonetheless violate them. Known only to the members of the sect are the *nistar*, the "hidden" laws, those that are not explicit in Scripture, and that the sect saw as derived through inspired biblical exegesis. All Israel is guilty of violating these prescriptions that pertain to virtually every area of Jewish law.[26] In this way the sect accomplished the expansion of Jewish law beyond its biblical origins.[27] For the sectarians, there had been a onetime revelation at Sinai, and all further laws, for each and every epoch of history, would be derived through their form of legal exegesis.[28]

Immediately after the publication of the *Rule of the Community* from Qumran, the close affinity of the new material from the caves with the *Damascus Document* was clear. Indeed, the new scrolls confirmed the broad outlines of what Louis Ginzberg had described already by 1911 as "an unknown Jewish sect."[29] Yet early studies tended to rely on circular methodology. It was assumed that the *Damascus Document* and the *Rule of the Community* described the very same community and that this was the Essene community also described by Philo and Josephus. Only with the advent of more scientific methodologies did scholars come to see these texts as describing a group of related and similar sects (or subsects) within the broad range of groups and approaches that constituted Second Temple Judaism.[30]

With these advances, the relationship of the *Damascus Document* to the *Rule of the Community* is now much clearer. The *Rule* prescribes the rules and regulations for those living and studying at the sectarian center at Qumran, whereas the *Damascus Document* legislates for those who join the sect but choose to remain in "camps," sectarian communities spread throughout the land of Israel.[31] The *Damascus Document* provides only for the initial stages of the novitiate, but full entry into the sect, possible only at the Qumran settlement, is described in the *Rule*.

---

26. Schiffman, *Halakhah at Qumran*, 22-76.

27. Jewish law was expanded beyond the Bible in several different ways, for example by the Pharisaic "traditions of the fathers," the redaction of the *Temple Scroll* in the form of a direct divine revelation, and the later rabbinic oral law concept.

28. Schiffman, *Sectarian Law*, 14-17.

29. Ginzberg, see above, n. 4.

30. See "The Many 'Battles of the Scrolls,'" Chapter 1 above.

31. A. Rubinstein, "Urban Halakhah and Camp Rules in the 'Cairo Fragments of a Damascus Covenant,'" *Sefarad* 12 (1952) 283-96.

The *Damascus Document* has also been found to have affinities with a variety of other Qumran documents, especially as regards use of the characteristic terminology of the sect, as well as the sharp animus toward outsiders. The relationship of the *Damascus Document* to the *Temple Scroll* (11QTemple) is a more difficult question. Yigael Yadin, the editor of the *Temple Scroll*,[32] saw this text as being in substantial agreement with the *Damascus Document* whenever it dealt with similar issues. In fact, while this is sometimes the case, there are other points at which the two texts diverge or where there is substantial incongruity between them. This is because the provenance of the sources of the *Temple Scroll* is to be found in related and probably earlier circles, but not in the Dead Sea sect itself.[33]

The *Damascus Document* occupies a unique place in the history of modern scholarship. Its publication a half century earlier than the Qumran finds opened the eyes of scholars to the existence of what we now know as the Qumran or Dead Sea sect. In this way it was possible for students of rabbinic Judaism and early Christianity to begin to take this sect into account in the early twentieth century. As a repository of written Jewish legal materials organized by subject, the *Damascus Document* quickly became a source for the study of the history of Jewish law and tradition. With the discovery of the Dead Sea Scrolls, this text has illuminated various groups in the Second Temple period and has provided a firm basis for understanding the sect's image of itself and of its fellow Jews, as well as its relation to the heritage of Scripture that preceded it and to the Judaism that followed it.

4QMMT — Miqṣat Ma'aśe ha-Torah (Halakhic Letter)

Miqṣat Ma'aśe ha-Torah (also known as the *Halakhic Letter* and by its abbreviation, 4QMMT or simply MMT) purports to be a document sent by the leaders of the Qumran sect to the leaders of the priestly establishment in Jerusalem. The title of this text, which may be translated as "Some Precepts of the Torah" or "Some Rulings Pertaining to the Torah," was given to it by its editors as a description of its contents, based on phrases found at the beginning and the end of the text. As is the case with almost all the Qumran manuscripts, the text itself bears no title. This text, found in Cave 4 in six fragmen-

---

32. Y. Yadin, *The Temple Scroll*. 3 vols. (Jerusalem: Israel Exploration Society and Shrine of the Book, 1983).

33. Cf. B. A. Levine, "The Temple Scroll: Aspects of Its Historical Provenance and Literary Character," *BASOR* 232 (1978) 5-23; H. Stegemann, "The Origins of the Temple Scroll," in *Congress Volume: Jerusalem 1986*, ed. J. A. Emerton, 235-56. VTSup 40 (Leiden: Brill, 1988).

tary manuscripts (4Q394-4Q399),³⁴ sets out some twenty laws regarding sacrificial laws, priestly gifts, ritual purity, and other matters about which the writers disagree with the Jerusalem authorities.³⁵ Stated in a polemical manner, these laws clearly represent the views of the founders of the sect as opposed to those of their opponents whom the sect calls upon to accept their views. The laws are set within a framework that may allow us to learn much about the ideology of those who authored the text and about the very origins of the Qumran sect itself.³⁶

4QMMT may be an actual document dating to the earliest days of the Qumran group, or it may have been written later to justify the sectarian schism with the Jerusalem establishment.³⁷ The existence of six manuscripts of this composition testifies to the importance of this text to the sectarians. The earliest manuscripts are late Hasmonean to early Herodian, that is, from the second half of the first century B.C.E.

The structure of the document can be divided into four parts: a 364-day solar calendar found in one manuscript, an introductory sentence setting out the nature of the letter, a section listing the halakhic disagreements between the sect and the Jerusalem authorities, and a hortatory conclusion.³⁸

Calendar. It is questionable if the calendar is really integral to the text of MMT or not, an issue that is connected with the physical reconstruction of the manuscript. It is apparent that this calendrical list was not composed by the authors of the MMT text but was imported as a unit into the manuscript. The calendar mentions, in addition to the solar months, the specific extra day added, after three months of thirty days, at the equinoxes and solstices, and is organized in 91-day quarters that constitute the basic division of the 364-day

---

34. E. Qimron and J. Strugnell, *Qumran Cave 4. V: Miqsat Ma'aśe ha-Torah.* DJD 10 (Oxford: Clarendon, 1994) 3-42.

35. L. H. Schiffman, "The Temple Scroll and the Systems of Jewish Law in the Second Temple Period," in *Temple Scroll Studies,* ed. G. J. Brooke, 239-55. JSPSup 7 (Sheffield: JSOT, 1989).

36. See "The New *Halakhic Letter* (4QMMT) and the Origins of the Dead Sea Sect," Chapter 6 above.

37. E. Qimron and J. Strugnell, "An Unpublished Halakhic Letter from Qumran," in *Biblical Archaeology Today: Proceedings of the International Congress on Biblical Archaeology, Jerusalem, April 1984,* ed. J. Amitai, 400-407). Jerusalem: Israel Exploration Society, Israel Academy of Sciences and Humanities, in cooperation with ASOR, 1985); "An Unpublished Halakhic Letter from Qumran," *IMJ* 4 (1985) 9-12.

38. Qimron and Strugnell, DJD 10:109-10; cf. Strugnell, DJD 10:203-6; and "MMT: Second Thoughts on a Forthcoming Edition," in *The Community of the Renewed Covenant: The Notre Dame Symposium on the Dead Sea Scrolls,* ed. E. Ulrich and J. VanderKam, 57-73. CJAS 10 (Notre Dame: University of Notre Dame Press, 1994).

year.[39] It also mentions some extra festivals such as the wine festival on the third day of the fifth month, the oil festival on the twenty-second of the sixth month, and the festival of the wood offering on the twenty-third of the same month. All these are among the festivals associated with the solar calendar in the *Temple Scroll*.[40]

Introduction. The initial introductory sentence states that what follows are some of "our words" that are legal rulings "we hold to." These rulings concern only two topics, only one of which is preserved, that is, the laws of ritual purity. The other topic, judging from the list of laws, appears to concern sacrificial offerings in the temple.

List of Laws. In this section, the authors list about twenty matters of Jewish law that, they insist, are being violated by the Jerusalem establishment and have caused them to withdraw from the Jerusalem temple and form their sect. This letter is a proof that the major conflicts of Second Temple Judaism did not arise from theological disagreements such as messianism, but from conflicts about the proper way to carry out Jewish law.

The following halakhot or halakhic topics are mentioned in the extant fragments of MMT: the prohibition of Gentile offerings in the temple, purity regulations, slaughter of animals, forbidden sexual unions, the fruit of the fourth year and the cattle tithe to be given to the priests, purification rituals for the leper, and the prohibition of marriages between priests and Israelites.

The views of the authors of MMT are representative of Sadducean halakhah. Some of the same laws are reported in the Mishnah (Tractate *Yadayim*) and the views of our text are there attributed to the Sadducees.[41] These halakhot are usually stricter than those of the Pharisees and later rabbis, and the authors excoriate those who do not accept the sectarians' view.

Hortatory Conclusion. Here the authors state that because of their strict observance of the previous laws according to their own opinion, they have separated themselves from the majority of the Jewish people and from their observances. The sectarians write the addressee in the singular form, asking

---

39. Cf. S. Talmon, "The Calendar Reckoning of the Sect from the Judean Desert," in *Aspects of the Dead Sea Scrolls*, ed. C. Rabin and Y. Yadin, 162-99. ScrHier 4 (Jerusalem: Magnes, 1958); J. C. VanderKam, *Calendars in the Dead Sea Scrolls: Measuring Time* (London: Routledge, 1998) 43-90.

40. Cf. Yadin, *Temple Scroll*, 1:89-136.

41. Y. Sussmann, "Ḥeqer Toldedot ha-Halakhah u-Megillot Midbar Yehudah: Hirhurim Talmudiyim Rishonim le-'Or Megillat Miqṣat Ma'aśe ha-Torah," *Tarbiz* 59 (1989/1990) 11-77; "The History of the Halakha and the Dead Sea Scrolls: Preliminary Talmudic Observations on *Miqṣat Ma'aśe ha-Torah* (4QMMT)," in Qimron and Strugnell, DJD 10:179-200.

him to investigate the words of the Torah and to realize that they must be observed according to the sectarian interpretation, for the biblical kings were blessed when they followed the word of God and cursed when they transgressed. The addressee is urged to repent and spare his nation misfortune.

To whom is this letter addressed? The text alternates between the singular and the plural. When in the singular, the manuscript assumes that it is addressing a leader who can, by virtue of his position, identify with the kings of Israel. It appears that the head of the Jerusalem establishment with such status must be the high priest during Hasmonean times.

Miqṣat Ma'aśe ha-Torah has wide ramifications for the history of Judaism in the Hasmonean period. In the disputes mentioned in the letter, the opinions of the opponents of the sect are those attributed in rabbinic literature to the Pharisees or the Tannaim (mishnaic rabbis). When tannaitic texts preserve a Pharisee-Sadducee conflict mentioned in MMT, the view of the sectarians coincides with that of the Sadducees. For example, the specifics of the required state of purity of the one who prepared the ashes of the red cow according to our text (B 13-17) are mentioned in rabbinic sources as being the custom of the Saducean priests in the temple (*m. Parah* 3:7; cf. *t. Parah* 3:7-8).[42] This phenomenon can be explained by seeing the earliest members of the sect as Sadducees who were unwilling to accept the suppression of the Zadokite high priests in the aftermath of the Maccabean revolt (168-164 B.C.E.). Some of the disaffected Zadokites separated from the high priests in Jerusalem and formed the sect. The sect often refers to itself as "Sons of Zadok." The polemics of the *Halakhic Letter* are addressed to their Saducean brethren who stayed in the Jerusalem temple and accepted the new order, following the Pharisaic rulings, and no longer practiced the old Saducean teachings. This document dates from the earliest stage of the development of the Qumran sect when the sectarians still hoped to reconcile with the Jerusalem priesthood. Later on, sectarian writings, having abandoned that hope, are filled with radical tendencies, animated polemics, and hatred for outsiders.

There is no question that the origin of the community that collected the scrolls was in a sectarian conflict that sustained the community throughout its existence. From MMT we learn the reasons for the schism. Up to now we had no explicit evidence on this subject. Josephus gives the impression that the sects were primarily divided over theological questions,[43] but his explanation was designed to appeal to Greek and Roman readers. Only matters of

---

42. Qimron and Strugnell, DJD 10:152-54.
43. Josephus, *J.W.* 2.119-66; *Ant.* 12.171-73; 18.11-17.

practice are mentioned in MMT. This list of halakhot proves how important were matters of Jewish law, particularly purity regulations, as sources of schism within Judaism of the period.

The contribution of MMT to our knowledge of the history and character of the halakhah of the various groups in the Hasmonean period is of the highest importance. The text polemicizes strongly against a group that is the predecessor of the rabbis, probably the Pharisees. It helps to prove that some Pharisaic laws are older than once thought. This text allows us to date to the Second Temple period a number of practices known only from later rabbinic literature.

The text of MMT has much in common with various documents of the Qumran corpus.[44] Its appearance along with the 364-day sectarian calendar of solar months and solar years gives the impression that the authors of MMT accepted this calendar. MMT shares a variety of sacrificial laws and the same ritual calendar with the *Temple Scroll*. These parallels are no doubt to be traced to the common Sadducean legal substratum that they share, although these texts are not literarily interdependent. The *Damascus Document* also shares many common principles with the legal section of MMT. Here again, no literary relationship can be shown, only a relationship of content.

4QFlorilegium[45] also preserves some common legal rulings with MMT although they are not literarily dependent on one another. MMT exhibits no parallels with the sectarian regulations of the *Rule of the Community* or other such documents that represent the teachings of the sect after it reached maturity.[46]

---

44. See "The Place of 4QMMT in the Corpus of Qumran Manuscripts," Chapter 7 above.

45. J. M. Allegro, *Qumrân Cave 4.I (4Q158-4Q186)*. DJD 5 (Oxford: Clarendon, 1968) 53-57, which must be supplemented by the corrections of J. Strugnell, "Notes en marge du volume V des 'Discoveries in the Judaean Desert of Jordan,'" *RevQ* 7 (1970) 220-25; G. J. Brooke, *Exegesis at Qumran: 4QFlorilegium in Its Jewish Context*. JSOTSup 29 (Sheffield: JSOT, 1985) 80-129.

46. These conclusions are consistent with the view that MMT reflects the formative period of the Qumran sect. It therefore shares legal rulings with the sources of the *Temple Scroll* and the early laws of the *Damascus Document*. At the same time, it reflects the ideology of parts of the *Temple Scroll*. While the earlier MMT and the *Temple Scroll* lack the language of sectarian antagonism, this tone is found in the *Damascus Document*, which was completed after the split was final. Linguistically, 4QMMT, representing the early history of the Qumran sect, demonstrates that much of the halakhic vocabulary known from later tannaitic texts was already known in this period, even to those who used Qumran linguistic forms.

Legal Texts in the Dead Sea Scrolls

1QS — Rule of the Community (Manual of Discipline, Serekh ha-Yaḥad)

The *Rule of the Community*,[47] named for its opening line in Hebrew, *Serekh ha-Yaḥad*, was discovered in 1947 in Cave 1 and was originally entitled by scholars the *Manual of Discipline* because of its ordinances governing sectarian life.[48] Some have suggested that it had to be memorized as part of the entry ritual for candidates of the sect.[49] The importance of this text is further emphasized by the identification of parts of ten more copies of it in Cave 4 (4Q255-264),[50] two fragments in Cave 5 (5Q11),[51] and a reference to it in the *Rule* (5Q13).[52] Of these, 1QRule of the Community is the best preserved copy, dating to between 100 and 75 B.C.E.[53]

The manuscript of 1QS also contains 1Q28a (*Rule of the Congregation* = 1QSa)[54] and 1Q28b (*Rule of Benedictions* = 1QSb)[55] that are independent compositions. Textual analysis and paleographical inspection have been applied in order to determine the possible components of the *Rule of the Community*, to date the sections to various stages in the history of the sect, and to arrange the various manuscripts and fragments in chronological order.[56] Since the text of 1QRule of the Community is presumed to have been in existence by the early part of the first century B.C.E., it must have originated in the previous century. It is tempting to posit that it was composed by the Teacher of

---

47. E. Qimron and J. H. Charlesworth, "Rule of the Community," in *The Dead Sea Scrolls: Hebrew, Aramaic, and Greek Texts with English Translations*, ed. Charlesworth, 1:1-5 (Tübingen: Mohr [Siebeck] and Louisville: Westminster John Knox, 1994).

48. M. A. Knibb, "Rule of the Community," *EDSS* 2:793-97; S. Metso, "Rule of the Community/Manual of Discipline (1QS)," in *Dictionary of New Testament Background*, ed. C. A. Evans and S. E. Porter, 1018-22 (Downers Grove: InterVarsity, 2000).

49. Qimron and Charlesworth, "Rule of the Community," 1:1, 3.

50. P. S. Alexander and G. Vermes, *Qumran Cave 4. XIX: Serekh ha-Yaḥad and Two Related Texts*. DJD 26 (Oxford: Clarendon, 1998) 27-206.

51. Baillet, Milik, and de Vaux, DJD 3:180-81.

52. Milik, DJD 3:181-83; L. H. Schiffman, "Sectarian Rule (5Q13)," in Charlesworth, *Dead Sea Scrolls*, 1:132-43.

53. P. S. Alexander dates the manuscripts on paleographical grounds to 100 B.C.E. for 1QRule of the Community, and the other manuscripts between 50 and 25 B.C.E. See Alexander, "The Redaction-History of Serekh ha-Yaḥad: A Proposal," *RevQ* 17 (Hommage à Józef T. Milik, 1996) 437-47. For differing redactional proposals and the internal history of 1QS, see Metso, "Rule of the Community/Manual of Discipline (1QS)," 1020-21.

54. Charlesworth, *Dead Sea Scrolls*, 1:108-17.

55. Charlesworth, *Dead Sea Scrolls*, 1:119-31.

56. S. Metso posits that there was an original version of the *Rule of the Community* which served as the basis for two versions that are in evidence in the manuscripts. See S. Metso, *The Textual Development of the Qumran Community Rule*. STDJ 21 (Leiden: Brill, 1997) 152-53.

Righteousness because of its ideology about withdrawal to the desert (1QS 8:12-16), but the scroll nowhere gives any definitive support for that supposition and shows strong evidence of being of composite origin.[57]

The *Rule of the Community* evidences some similarities with the *Damascus Document*. Both have regulations that apply to the members of a specific group, but the *Rule of the Community* refers to the sect as the *yaḥad*, whereas the *Damascus Document* calls them the *'edah*. Some say that the *Rule of the Community*, with its emphasis on wilderness ideology, is intended for Essenes who lived at Qumran, while the *Damascus Document* is directed at Essenes who lived scattered throughout the land of Israel. It is certain, however, that these are related communities with closely regulated lives. Like the *Damascus Document*, the *Rule of the Community* contains regulations for sectarian life in the present premessianic age, but the *Rule of the Community* emphasizes the ideology of the wilderness much more.[58]

There are six main divisions in the *Rule of the Community* as preserved in 1QS: (1) introduction, (2) rituals for entering the sect and other covenant ceremonies, (3) a statement of the belief in dualism of good and evil, (4) rules pertaining to the organizational administration of the sect, (5) a description of the council of the community, and (6) a concluding hymn of praise.

Introduction: The Sons of Light and the Sons of Darkness. This first section (1:1-15) emphasizes that the law of Moses is central, and those who observe it strictly, the sectarians, are the Sons of Light while those who pervert it, those outside the sect, are the Sons of Darkness. The introduction reminds the sectarians that they must observe all the festivals mandated by the Torah according to the sectarian calendar and share their property communally upon entry into the sect.

Rituals: Entering the Sect and Other Covenant Ceremonies. The ceremony for entering the sect (1:16-3:12) includes a blessing for the Sons of Light to which all the sectarians respond, "Amen, amen." The annual covenant renewal ceremony, which may have occurred on the Day of Atonement or on the Festival of Shavuot, blesses the Sons of Light with eternal knowledge and eternal peace. The Levites then curse the Sons of Darkness with anger, revenge and destruction, inability to repent or to be forgiven, and all reply, "Amen, amen." Then follows a warning to those who would not complete

---

57. Knibb, "Rule of the Community," 2:796.

58. Cf. S. Talmon, "The 'Desert Motif' in the Bible and in Qumran Literature," in *Biblical Motifs: Origins and Transformations*, ed. A. Altmann, 55-63 (Cambridge, MA: Harvard University Press, 1966); repr. in Talmon, *Literary Studies in the Hebrew Bible: Form and Content: Collected Studies* (Leiden: Brill, 1993) 216-54.

their entrance into the sect and accept all God's statutes. They will be unable to atone and remain unpurified.

The Doctrine of the Two Spirits. This section (3:13–4:26), often termed the Treatise of the Two Spirits, describes the spirit of light and the spirit of darkness that work in the world along with divine predestination. These two spirits battle over each individual. On the face of it, the text appears to argue that each individual is totally dominated by one or the other spirit. Yet some interpreters see the anthropology of this text as much more complex, so that each person is a composite of both tendencies. Among the Sons of Light, the spirit of light prevails, although occasionally, when they do wrong, it is under the influence of the Angel of Darkness. The Sons of Righteousness will attain peace, long life, and many children while the Sons of Darkness will be forever damned. These two forces will hate one another and fight for control of the world until, at the end of time, God will destroy the spirit of darkness forever.

Rules for Entrance into the Community and the Penal Code. This section (5:1–7:25) outlines the rules for entrance into the Community: each member will turn away from deceit, follow the Zadokite priests who expound the law of Moses, separate himself from those who have not accepted the covenant, take an oath to observe the law of Moses, give due respect to those who outrank him, eat the communal meal where the priest blesses the food and partakes of the first portion, and advance to the status of complete purity when he becomes a full member with all rights. These rights include permission to touch the pure solid food of the sect, then the pure liquid food that is even more susceptible to ritual impurity.

The rules also set out the penalties a sectarian would incur for backsliding. Infractions include lying, insulting a fellow sectarian, taking the law into one's own hand, exposing oneself, sleeping in the assembly, and leaving the assembly without permission. Minor penalties resulted in the reduction of food rations for a specified amount of time. More severe infractions resulted in removal from the pure food. The most severe punishment was permanent expulsion from the sect. Such a person may be reinstated by going through the ranks again in the same manner as a novice.

The Council of the Community. Twelve laymen and three priests constitute the council of the community (8:1–9:26a). They must be blameless and uphold truth, righteousness, and justice. Any one of them who inadvertently commits a sin may be punished by removal from the pure food, but if he deliberately transgresses, he is removed from the council. The council itself is considered a holy body that serves as a substitute for the temple sacrifices, in which the sectarians did not participate, and an atonement for the land.

Hymn of Praise. God is praised in this part (9:26b–11:22) as the creator and controller of the movements of the sun and moon, the determiner of seasons and festivals, the righteous and merciful judge of mankind, the One who rewards the righteous and punishes the wicked. The petitioner prays that God judge him with righteousness and cleanse his soul of sin. For humans remain in awe of God and cannot comprehend his glory or his mysteries, wonders, and power. One passage (1QS 10:9-17) alludes to the daily prayers and the recitation of the Shema morning and evening.

1QSa — Rule of the Congregation (Serekh ha-ʿEdah)

The *Rule of the Congregation* (1QSa = 1Q28a), also known as the *Messianic Rule* or by its Hebrew name *Serekh ha-ʿEdah*, is preserved only as an appendix copied on the same 1QS scroll after the *Rule of the Community (Manual of Discipline, Serekh ha-Yaḥad)*, and followed by the *Rule of Benedictions*. The script is Hasmonean, dating to about 100-75 B.C.E. Despite appearing on the same scroll and being related in many ways, the *Rule of the Community* and the *Rule of the Congregation* are clearly two separate documents that need to be studied individually. The *Rule of the Community* and the *Rule of the Congregation* describe, respectively, the ideal world of the present and the ideal world of the messianic age. For this reason, the copyist decided to place them on the same scroll. There are also many parallels between the *Rule of the Congregation* and the *War Scroll* (1QM), involving some of the purity laws, ages of military service, and the concept that angels are among the sectarians, requiring the highest standards of ritual purity.[59]

The *Rule of the Congregation* was clearly considered to be a central text by the sectarians, or it would not have been copied immediately after the *Rule of the Community*. Its content is a description of the nature of the eschatological community as understood by the sectarians. This community would presumably come into being in the aftermath of the great war described in the *War Scroll*. Accordingly, this text was an essential part of the messianic worldview of the Qumran sectarians. When read in comparison with the *Rule of the Community*, it becomes clear that the *Rule of the Congregation* presents a messianic mirror image of the life of the sectarians in the present, premessianic age. One can conclude that life in the present sectarian community is seen as an enactment of what will be the order of the day at the end of

---

59. L. H. Schiffman, *The Eschatological Community of the Dead Sea Scrolls*. SBLMS 3 (Atlanta: Scholars, 1989) 11-52; Charlesworth, *Dead Sea Scrolls*, 1:109.

days. At the same time, the life of the eschatological community reflects a transformation of the present order into the life of the end of days.

The text is composed of several sections, each of which might have originally stood alone before redaction into the complete document as it is now preserved. The title of the text is derived from the opening sentence that specifically alludes to the eschatological character of what follows. The leadership of the sect, even in the end of days, is retained by the Sons of Zadok, the Zadokite priests. They and their followers have kept God's covenant when all others went astray.[60] At the onset of the end of days, the priestly Sons of Zadok assemble with their wives and children and celebrate a covenant renewal ceremony, reading the law aloud. This text most certainly expects normal family life in the eschatological community.

The text then outlines the stages of life of the sectarian, beginning with the earliest education and extending to old age. Twenty is the age of majority for men when marriage and sexual relations are to ensue. The text details various ages for different military roles. At twenty-five the male sectarian enters into full service, and at thirty he may take on a leadership role. At old age, the sectarian would be reassigned according to his abilities. Apparently age was seen as a disqualifying blemish. Mental incompetence disqualifies a man from any but the most subsidiary military duties.

The scroll next specifies that the sect is to be led by members of the tribe of Levi, specifically by the Zadokite priesthood, together with the heads of the clans. The scroll attempts to mirror the ideal period of desert wandering, which is also reflected in the organization of tens, hundreds, and thousands mentioned below.

The duties of the eschatological council of the community are specified as judgment, that is, serving as the highest court of the community and deciding matters of law such as formulating legislation and declaring war. The text assumes that all these activities will continue in the end of days.

There follows a list of those excluded from the council because of ritual impurity or physical deformity, seen by the sectarians as a sign of some kind of moral deformity. They are forbidden to enter the assembly because of the presence of angels, a motif also employed to explain the need for purity in the military camp in the *War Scroll*.

The high point of the text is the description of the expected messianic convocation. The eschatological high priest is to enter, followed by the rest of the members of the priesthood, all sitting before him in order of status. The messiah of Israel will enter followed by the chiefs of clans, according to their

---

60. Cf. Schiffman, *Halakhah at Qumran*, 73-75.

position in the march, patterned on the desert camp of biblical Israel. All the wise men of Israel are to sit before the two messiahs. Some scholars have seen this passage as alluding to the "begetting" of the messiah (2:11-12), alluding to a Christian parallel.[61] This reading should now be rejected, however, in light of new photographs and computer enhancement. While the birth of the messiah may be foretold in the Hebrew Bible (cf. Isa 7:14; 9:5), Jewish sources were unanimous in seeing the messiah (or messiahs) as normal mortals, even if in some views the messiah was expected to experience a miraculous birth.

Finally, the text describes the messianic banquet in which, as in the communal meals of the sect (1QS 6:3-5) in the present, premessianic era, the priest is to recite the blessing over the bread and then the wine and receive the first portion of bread. Then the messiah of Israel is to receive his portion, and then all those in attendance in the order of their status in the community. The text of the *Rule of the Congregation* (1QSa 2:22-23) concludes by stating that this pattern shall be maintained whenever there are at least ten males participating together in a communal meal.

This text has been discussed extensively in an effort to find an early parallel to the Last Supper and the Christian Eucharist that commemorates it. The discussion has centered on the fact that here, as in the early Christian community, the focus of the meal is on bread and wine, and that it is clearly an eschatological experience. Such a parallel is natural, for bread and wine were the normal staples of life in ancient Palestine. Further, the ritual blessing of the food in the Qumran communal meal — in the present and in the end of days — was the required blessing that Jews practiced already in Second Temple times, praising God both before and after eating.

Some scholars have claimed that the practice of blessing the food indicates the sacral character of the meal described here and have suggested, therefore, a similarity to the Eucharist. Yet a sacred meal is one eaten in imitation of a sacrifice or as a replacement for it, in which the eater is somehow transformed by the experience. None of this is present here. The benedictions result only from the normal ritual obligations of the Jew, and the role of the priests here is only an honorary one, paralleled also in rabbinic requirements that priests be served their food first and be given the honor of reciting the grace. This meal should therefore be seen as eschatological rather than sacral.[62]

The text also has significance for the history of Jewish ideology and practice. The *Rule of the Community* describes a messianic banquet, a notion quite widespread in Second Temple Judaism and continued into rabbinic

---

61. For bibliography, see Schiffman, *Eschatological Community*, 53 n. 1.
62. Schiffman, *Eschatological Community*, 56-64.

aggadic tradition. Further, the text attests to the practice of benedictions before food and to the honor given to the priest in non-Pharisaic context earlier than the rabbinic evidence previously known. The minimum of ten males, also found elsewhere in the scrolls (1QS 6:3, 6), indicates that the concept of the *minyan,* a quorum of ten for Jewish religious activity, was already common at this early date.

11QTemple — Temple Scroll (Megillat ha-Miqdash)

The *Temple Scroll* (11Q19 = 11QTemple) was purchased for the Shrine of the Book in Jerusalem in 1967.[63] Although it was originally 8.75 meters long, it is missing part of its beginning and damaged from dampness in the upper edge. The scribal techniques and script are typical of the other Qumran manuscripts. While the language of the scroll has much in common with the dialect in which the sectarian compositions from Qumran are written, in certain linguistic features and in its legal terminology it exhibits more affinities to rabbinic Hebrew than do the other scrolls.[64]

The *Temple Scroll* is also known from two more manuscripts from Cave 11, 11Q20[65] and 11Q21,[66] as well as a related text from Cave 4, 4Q365a.[67] The latter two are very fragmentary and, although they share some similarity in contents with the *Temple Scroll,* they cannot be certainly identified as copies of this text. They may represent closely related compositions or remnants of the sources of the *Temple Scroll.* Another manuscript from Cave 4 (4Q524)[68] is also fragmentary and might also be one of the sources that the *Temple Scroll* utilized, although it is more likely a recension of the scroll. Yadin[69] identified the script of the two scribes of 11Q19 as Herodian, dating to around the turn of the Christian era, but the date of 4Q524 has been established as Hasmonean, making likely a Hasmonean date for the composition.

---

63. Yadin, *Temple Scroll,* 1:1-5.
64. L. H. Schiffman, "The *Temple Scroll* in Literary and Philological Perspective," in *Approaches to Ancient Judaism,* ed. W. S. Green, 2:143-58. BJS 9 (Chico: Scholars, 1980).
65. F. García Martínez, E. J. C. Tigchelaar, and A. S. van der Woude, *Qumran Cave 11.II (11Q2-18, 11Q20-31).* DJD 23 (Oxford: Clarendon, 1998) 35-409.
66. DJD 23:411-14.
67. S. White (Crawford) in *Qumran Cave 4.VIII: Parabiblical Texts, Part 1,* ed. H. Attridge et al. DJD 13 (Oxford: Clarendon, 1994) 319-33.
68. É. Puech, *Qumrân Grotte 4.XVIII: Textes hébreux (4Q521-4Q528, 4Q576-4Q579).* DJD 25 (Oxford: Clarendon, 1998) 85-114.
69. Yadin, *Temple Scroll,* 1:17.

The scroll presents itself as a rewritten Torah that begins with the renewal of the Sinaitic covenant in Exodus 34 and then turns to the building of the tabernacle in Exodus 35. From this point, the scroll continues in the order of the canonical Torah, covering the basic structures of the sanctuary and its courts, the sacrificial system, the various other temple rituals, laws of ritual purity and impurity, and finally a long series of Deuteronomic prescriptions, including a distinct section on the king, the government, and the army. The scroll concludes with the laws of consanguineous marriages.

11QTemple 29:2-10 indicates clearly that the purpose of the *Temple Scroll* was to provide a system of law for the premessianic temple. This temple, it was expected, would be replaced in the end of days with a divinely created sanctuary. Until then, the author/redactor saw his scroll as representing the correct interpretation of the Torah.

The scroll does not simply recapitulate the prescriptions of Exodus, Leviticus, Numbers, and Deuteronomy. Rather it collects the various pentateuchal (and sometimes prophetic) material relevant to the issue at hand and weaves together a unified, consistent text. In this respect it can be said that the text redacts the Torah, combining all materials on a single topic together. In many cases, statements in the canonical Torah referring to God in the third person are shifted into first person divine direct address. In this way the intermediacy of Moses is eliminated and the contents of the scroll are presented as the direct revelation of God to Israel at Mount Sinai.

Yet the scroll goes further. It uses a distinct form of exegesis, in some ways similar to the midrash of the later rabbis, to reconcile the differences between the various pentateuchal texts, so as to create a unified and consistent whole. At times, it makes minor additions to clarify its legal stance. In a few places, extensive passages appear that are not based on our canonical Scriptures. In this way the scroll propounds its own views on the major issues of Jewish law relating to temple, cult, government, and sanctity. It is this exegetical and legal approach that makes the *Temple Scroll* so central for the history of Jewish law and midrashic exegesis, and for understanding the sects of the Second Temple period.

The laws of the scroll include a number of provisions of great interest. The architecture of the temple proposed here differs from biblical accounts, on which the author claims to base himself, as well as from descriptions of the Second Temple in Josephus and the Mishnah. Most interesting is the extension of the *temenos* (the "Temple City") by the addition of a third courtyard, so large that it would have encompassed most of what was then Jerusalem. The courtyards and their gates represent the Israelite encampment in the wilderness. Unique approaches appear here for the construction of the temple furnishings. The sacrificial festival calendar includes a number of festivals not part of the biblical or rabbinic cycle. A second New Year festival is to be celebrated on the first of Nisan, in the spring, followed by annual celebration of the eight days of ordination. Besides the Omer festival for the barley harvest and the firstfruits of wheat (Shavuot), the scroll adds two more firstfruits festivals, each at fifty-day intervals, for oil and wine. The wood offering is also celebrated as an annual festival in the summer. Extensive laws deal with sacrificial procedures and ritual purity and impurity. Here we see a general tendency to provide additional ways to protect the sanctuary from impurity. This brief survey does not even begin to indicate the rich nature of the scroll's exegesis and the many details of Jewish law in which the text diverges from the views of other sectarian documents or rabbinic literature.

Even in its present form, it is not difficult to discern that the *Temple Scroll* has been redacted from a number of sources by an author/redactor. His sources most certainly included the sacrificial festival calendar (11QTemple 13:9–29:1) and the law of the king and army (56:12–59:21). It has also been suggested that the description of the temple precincts and furnishings (2:1–47:18, *passim*) and the laws of purity (48:1–51:10) constituted separate sources.[70] It was the author/redactor who added the Deuteronomic paraphrase at the end (51:11–56:21, 60:1–66:17).[71]

When we turn to the dating of the composition of the scroll, we can reason from several clues. First, all sources now included in the scroll presuppose the existence of a canonical Torah differing from MT only in minor details.[72] Only a few legal rulings can be shown to derive from variant biblical texts. For this reason the scroll had to have been completed after the period of the return (ca. late 6th to mid-5th centuries B.C.E.). Second, the earliest of the manuscripts has been dated to the Hasmonean period.

Therefore, it is logical to seek a *Sitz im Leben* for the *Temple Scroll* in the Hasmonean period. Indeed, the law of the king, the largest sustained nonpentateuchal section, provides clear indications of the historical context of the scroll. For example, it emphasizes the separation of roles of the high priest and king and the need to constitute the *gerousia* so that it would consist

---

70. On the sources of the *Temple Scroll*, see A. M. Wilson and L. Wills, "Literary Sources of the Temple Scroll," *HTR* 75 (1982) 275-88; and M. O. Wise, *A Critical Study of the Temple Scroll from Qumran Cave 11*. SAOC 49 (Chicago: Oriental Institute, University of Chicago, 1990) 1-154.

71. L. H. Schiffman, "The Deuteronomic Paraphrase of the *Temple Scroll*," *RevQ* 15 (1992) 543-68.

72. Contrast Stegemann, VTSup 40 (1988) 246-56, whose proposal that the scroll includes remnants of precanonical Torah materials must be rejected.

of twelve each of priests, Levites, and Israelites. It argues against the use of mercenaries, employed extensively by John Hyrcanus. The *Temple Scroll* requires that the king have a special palace guard to protect him against being kidnapped. Here we have an allusion to the perfidious kidnapping and murder of Jonathan the Hasmonean in 143 B.C.E.[73] The text further polemicizes against campaigns such as those of John Hyrcanus and Alexander Jannaeus when it prohibits wars with Egypt for the sake of accumulating wealth.

Since the law of the king is incorporated into the fully redacted scroll, it is therefore appropriate to date the scroll as a whole to no later than the second half of the reign of John Hyrcanus.[74] At this time, the author/redactor called for a thoroughgoing revision of the existing Hasmonean order, desiring to replace it with a temple, sacrificial system, and government that were in his view the embodiment of the legislation of the Torah. This dating is fully consistent with the paleographic data.

In his initial study of the *Temple Scroll,* Yadin assumed that it, like the rest of the Qumran corpus, represented a text of Essene provenance. Accordingly, he interpreted the scroll to agree with the previously known Dead Sea sectarian texts and Philo and Josephus's descriptions of the Essenes. Many scholars have followed this lead. Others have pointed to the absence of the usual Qumran polemical language and distinctive terminology and the lack of some characteristic linguistic features in these texts.[75] Further, this text has a different view of the origins, authority, and derivation of Jewish law. Whereas the sectarian texts from Qumran generally expect the law to be derived by inspired biblical exegesis from the canonical Torah, the *Temple Scroll* sees extrabiblical laws as stemming from the Sinaitic revelation as an actual Torah. Some recent scholarship now sees the *Temple Scroll* as emerging from a related group that was either contemporary with or earlier than the previously known Qumran sect.

There is an even closer link between the *Temple Scroll* and the *Miqṣat*

---

73. Cf. 1 Macc 13:24.

74. L. H. Schiffman, "The King, His Guard, and the Royal Council in the *Temple Scroll,*" *PAAJR* 54 (1987) 237-59; Yadin, *Temple Scroll,* 1:386-90, dates the scroll to the reign of Hyrcanus or slightly earlier; M. Hengel, J. H. Charlesworth, and D. Mendels, "The Polemical Character of 'On Kingship' in the Temple Scroll: An Attempt at Dating 11QTemple," *JJS* 37 (1986) 28-38, date the scroll to 103-88 B.C.E.

75. Levine, "The Temple Scroll," 5-23; and the responses of J. Milgrom, "'Sabbath' and 'Temple City' in the Temple Scroll," *BASOR* 232 (1978) 25-27, and Y. Yadin, "Is the Temple Scroll a Sectarian Document?" in *Humanizing America's Iconic Book,* ed. G. M. Tucker and G. A. Knight, 153-69. SBLBSNA (Chico: Scholars, 1980); Stegemann, "The Origins of the Temple Scroll," 237-46; Schiffman, *Sectarian Law,* 13-17.

Ma'aśe ha-Torah (4QMMT). 4QMMT takes some positions equivalent to those of the Sadducees in rabbinic literature and ascribes to the Jerusalem priests views identified as Pharisaic. In many cases, this text's rulings agree with those of the *Temple Scroll*. This evidence suggests that the *Temple Scroll* stems from forerunners of the sect who shared Sadducean rulings on many matters.

This scroll is the largest of the Dead Sea Scrolls and for this reason alone it vastly enriches the textual remains of Second Temple Judaism. This text shows that the exegesis of Scripture for the derivation of Jewish law, the activity that the later rabbis called midrash, was already a central part of the Judaism of some groups in the Hasmonean period. This exegesis served as the basis for highly developed legal teachings that are evidence that, among some groups of Second Temple Jews, strict adherence to a living and developing tradition of Jewish law was the norm. Further, some of these Jews objected strenuously to the conduct of the Hasmoneans in both the religious and political/military spheres. These opponents were at the forefront of the movement represented by the Qumran sect. Among the texts they brought with them to Qumran were the sources of the *Temple Scroll*.

4Q265 — *Miscellaneous Rules (Serekh Damascus)*

Miscellaneous Rules, formerly *Serekh Damascus* (4Q265 = SD),[76] was named by the initial editors on the assumption that it represents a combination of the *Serekh ha-Yaḥad (Rule of the Community)* and *Damascus Document*. In truth, *Miscellaneous Rules* does include material that parallels some of these two well-known Qumran texts. Is it a composite or an independent redaction of the same building blocks *(serakhim)* as those of the *Rule of the Community* and *Damascus Document*? Whatever the case, *Miscellaneous Rules* can be considered in light of other Qumran texts that appear to be anthologies[77] such as 4QOrdinances.[78] This problem points to the complex literary history of the larger Dead Sea Scrolls. The manuscript is in Late Herodian script and should be dated to the first half of the first century C.E.

The text, as it now survives, may be divided into the following sections: (1) frg. 3, lines 3-6, quotation of Isa 54:1-2, probably followed by pesher inter-

---

76. J. M. Baumgarten, "Miscellaneous Rules," in DJD 35:57-78. Cf. L. H. Schiffman, "Serekh-Damascus," *EDSS* 2:868-9.

77. Cf. E. Tov, "Excerpted and Abbreviated Biblical Texts from Qumran," *RevQ* 16 (1995) 581-600.

78. L. H. Schiffman, "Ordinances and Rules," in Charlesworth, *Dead Sea Scrolls*, 1:145-75.

pretation and other quotations and interpretations; (2) frg. 3, line 3: prohibition of youths and women from eating the paschal sacrifice; (3) frg. 4 i-ii, line 2: Penal Code; (4) frg. 4 ii, lines 3-9: joining the sect; (5) frg. 5: regarding agriculture; (6) frg. 6-7, line 5: Sabbath Code; (7) frg. 7, lines 6-10: on the sect; (8) frg. 7, lines 11-17: purification rules. We will survey each of these sections.

(1) If the order proposed by the editor is correct, then the text may have had some hortatory beginning, such as in the *Zadokite Fragments (Damascus Document)*. It may have included, as does that section, the quotation of various biblical verses with pesher exegesis provided, all of which would serve to introduce the laws that follow. 4QpIsa^d quotes Isa 54:11-12 in referring to the council of the community, which is alluded to below in frg. 7, lines 7-10.

(2) The text prohibits women and young men from eating of the paschal sacrifice. Such a law is also found in *Jub.* 49:17 and in the *Temple Scroll* (11QTemple 17:8-9) but is contrary to the actual practice of Second Temple Judaism (Josephus, *J.W.* 6.426; *m. Pesaḥ.* 8:1). Exod 12:3-4 seems to require everyone to eat of this offering. But for certain Jewish circles, perhaps the wider Sadducean trend in halakhah, biblical exegesis (איש, Exod 12:4) and purity considerations led to the exclusion of women and young males from this rite.

(3) This section contains parts of a Penal Code which parallels one found in the medieval genizah manuscript of the *Damascus Document* (CD 14:18-22), and much more extensively in the Qumran manuscripts of this same document (4Q266 10 i 11-ii 15; 4Q270 7 i 1-14), and in the *Rule of the Community* (1QS 6:24-7:27).[79] These three recensions of the Penal Code of the sect share a variety of aspects, especially the means of punishment by banishment from pure liquid or solid food of the community, which is tantamount to exclusion from the communal meals, reduction of the food ration for specified periods, and even expulsion from the sect.[80] Yet the various recensions have different punishments, and variant readings indicate such variation even within the same text. Apparently this was an ongoing issue in sectarian life, and the codes developed and were modified constantly in light of decisions and practices of the sect's assembly and its officials.

(4) The text describes the process for joining the sect. It closely parallels the version in the *Rule of the Community* (1QS 6:14-23). First, the novice is to be examined by a sectarian official. If he passes this aptitude test, he studies for one year and is then examined by the council. If he passes this test, he is then taught the sectarian legal provisions. He then may touch the solid food

---

79. J. M. Baumgarten, "The Cave 4 Versions of the Qumran Penal Code," *JJS* 43 (1992) 268-76; Metso, *Textual Development*, 124-29; Hempel, *Laws of the Damascus Document*, 141-48.
80. Cf. Schiffman, *Sectarian Law*, 155-90.

of the sectarians, but may not touch the liquid food, which is more easily susceptible to impurity and which may help to communicate it, for an additional year. After two years he surrenders his property for communal use and becomes a full member of the sect. This procedure appears to be the same one described in the *Rule of the Community*,[81] and the two texts are most likely related to one another from the point of view of their literary history.

(5) The mention of "all that is sown in the earth" and "makes bloom" is all that can be read here. It may be that this section dealt with laws of agriculture, such as are dealt with in the *Zadokite Fragments*. It is also possible that this is a metaphoric reference to the Dead Sea sect.

(6) Several Sabbath prohibitions are mentioned here that for the most part parallel those in the Sabbath Code as preserved in both the medieval genizah version of the *Damascus Document* and the Qumran manuscripts. Included here are prohibitions on wearing dirty clothing, carrying out of the private domain (the tent) on the Sabbath, removing animals from a pit (contra Matt 12:11), allowing animals to walk beyond the Sabbath limit of two thousand cubits (three thousand feet), and a prohibition against Aaronide priests sprinkling waters of purification on the Sabbath. Extremely important is the law of saving a life on the Sabbath as it is formulated here. Based on the Sabbath Code of the *Damascus Document* (CD 11:16-17) there was room to argue whether the sectarians agreed with the Pharisaic-rabbinic tradition in setting aside all Sabbath prohibitions in cases of danger to life. Some scholars argued that the sectarians rejected this notion, but the view that the sectarians also agreed to save life on the Sabbath but sought to minimize Sabbath violation in the process[82] was proven correct by this text's explicit instruction to use a garment, an item not otherwise prohibited for use on the Sabbath, to lift a person out of water.

Appended to this section is a prohibition on eating nonsacral meat in the vicinity of the temple. This regulation is paralleled also in the *Temple Scroll* (11QTemple 52:18-19).

(7) The sixth section parallels the *Rule of the Community* in requiring that there be a learned priest wherever there are ten sectarians (1QS 6:3-4; CD 13:2-3) and setting a minimum of fifteen for setting up a council of the community (1QS 8:1-2). Also parallel is the understanding of the sect itself as a pleasant aroma (1QS 8:9), that is, a substitute for the sacrificial ritual from

---

81. For a full discussion of initiation into the sect, see Rabin, *Qumran Studies*, 1-21; J. Licht, *Megillat ha-Serakhim mi-Megillot Midbar Yehudah* (Jerusalem: Bialik Institute, 1965) 107-20; Schiffman, *Sectarian Law*, 161-65.

82. Schiffman, *Halakhah at Qumran*, 125-28.

which the sect abstained. *Miscellaneous Rules* sees the sect itself as serving as a sacrifice on behalf of the people of Israel in the period of wickedness, in which the sacrifices are not being conducted, in the view of the sect, according to the correct regulations.

(8) The final section is a statement of the laws of the parturient, the woman who has just given birth, following Lev 12:1-6 and *Jub.* 3:9-14. The text of *Miscellaneous Rules* tells us that Adam was brought into the garden of Eden after seven days, presumably so that he could be purified, and then Eve entered seven days later, making a total of fourteen days of purification. This notion is based on the concept of the garden of Eden as a sanctuary, allowing entry to it only by the ritually pure.

While little of this document has been preserved, it certainly shows, along with the minor legal texts from Qumran, that legal literature among the sectarians was much richer than what is preserved. Further, the ongoing process of editing and compiling that resulted in the larger works as we have them is illustrated by this important text.

Description of the Minor Legal Works

4Q251 — 4Q Halakha A[83]

This document contains a series of laws, some of which overlap with laws known from the *Damascus Document, Temple Scroll,* and 4QMMT, and includes some prescriptions that are typical of the Sadducean-type legal system encountered in the sectarian materials. In general, the literary form of this text is much closer to that of rewritten Bible than to abstractly formulated law.

Some Sabbath laws (frgs. 1-2) overlap with prescriptions found in the Sabbath Code of the *Damascus Document* as well as in the *Miscellaneous Rules*. Most of the preserved text is a rewriting of various laws in Exodus 21–22. Also discussed here are laws of firstfruits and new grain, following a scheme similar to that in the Festival Calendar of the *Temple Scroll* (11QTemple 18-23). Other laws discuss the selling of ancestral lands (based on Lev 25:14-17), the giving of fourth-year produce to priests (as opposed to eating it in Jerusalem as the Pharisees ruled), a practice also mandated in the *Temple Scroll* (60:3-4) and 4QMMT (B 62-3). The text also prohibits eating an animal that did not live for seven days (Lev 22:27) and the slaughter of pregnant animals, again shared with the *Temple Scroll* (11QTemple 52:5) and 4QMMT (B 36) but permitted by

---

83. E. Larson, M. R. Lehmann, and L. H. Schiffman, in DJD 35:25-51.

Pharisaic-rabbinic halakhah. The text also includes a list of forbidden consanguineous marriages similar to that in the *Temple Scroll* (66:11-17). Among the laws here is the prohibition of intermarriage with non-Jews and of a priest's arranging for his daughter to marry a nonpriest.

4Q274 — Purification Rules (Tohorot) A

This fragmentary text[84] deals with the laws of impurity resulting, most probably, from the disease צרעת, usually mistranslated as "leprosy."[85] As in the *Temple Scroll* (11QTemple 48:14-15), this text provides for special places for the quarantine of those with this disease. A difficult passage provides that they must remain at least twelve cubits from the pure food, to the northwest of each dwelling, probably meaning to the northwest of each town or village. Such people are forbidden to come in contact even with those already impure, as those with צרעת would require ritual cleansing after contact with other impurities. This indicates that impurity can be contracted in successively stronger layers, so that those with other impurities may not come in contact with those with this skin disease. The requirement of separation, even for the impure, indicates a consciousness also of the contagious nature of such diseases. In the same way, a woman with a nonmenstrual discharge of blood may not touch a gonorrheic or anything upon which he may have sat or with which he may have come in contact. If she does, she must undergo purification, even if she remains in her own original state of impurity. The text goes into several examples to make this general point.

Another issue discussed in this text, also found in the *Temple Scroll* (e.g., 11QTemple 45:7-10), is the requirement that one who is to undergo a seven-day purification period, with sprinkling on the third and seventh days, must undergo ablutions as well on the first day to peel off the initial level of impurity and to allow him or her to begin the normal purification required by the Torah.[86] Until this first-day ablution, he may not eat anything. Further, all sprinkling for purification is forbidden on the Sabbath. Also discussed here are the impurity of semen and reptiles.

---

84. Baumgarten, DJD 35:99-109.
85. J. Milgrom, "4QTohora^a: An Unpublished Qumran Text on Purities," in *Time to Prepare the Way in the Wilderness: Papers on the Qumran Scrolls by Fellows of the Institute for Advanced Studies of the Hebrew University, Jerusalem, 1989-1990*, ed. D. Dimant and L. H. Schiffman, 64-68. STDJ 16 (Leiden: Brill, 1995). Baumgarten, DJD 35:1-2, maintains that it refers to a *zav* (gonorrheic).
86. J. Milgrom, "Studies in the Temple Scroll," *JBL* 97 (1978) 512-18.

JEWISH LAW AT QUMRAN

4Q276 — 4QTohorot B[a] and 4Q277 — 4QTohorot B[b][87]

These two texts, Tohorot B[a][88] and B[b],[89] deal with the ritual of the Red Cow as the means of purification from impurity of the dead as prescribed in Numbers 19. 4Q276 seems to refer at the beginning to the high priest who ministers at this ritual. The text describes the slaughter of the animal and the sprinkling of its blood, as well as other aspects of the ritual as prescribed in the Torah.

4Q277 also mentions the fact that the one who performs this ritual is rendered impure as a result, a paradox mentioned already in the Bible. As in 4QMMT (B 13-17), all participants in the ritual are explicitly mentioned, indicating that they are all rendered impure by their participation. Also hinted at here is the requirement, specified also in MMT, that the priest who officiates must be totally pure himself. In case he has just completed a purification ritual, the sun must have set on his last day of purification.[90] The Pharisaic-rabbinic tradition would have allowed one still awaiting sunset on his last day of purification to perform the ritual. The Sadducees and those who followed their halakhic tradition disagreed. Further, the text lists a number of ways in which the impurity of the dead can be passed from one person to another, expanded to include categories that the Bible specifies for the gonorrheic (Lev 15:4-15).[91]

4Q284a — Harvesting (Leqet)[92]

This text is extremely fragmentary and deals with the requirements for gleaning. According to Lev 19:9-10 and 23:22, grain left in the field may not be collected after the harvest is completed, but must be left for the poor. The Bible

---

87. Baumgarten, DJD 19:111-19.
88. Baumgarten, DJD 35:111-13.
89. Baumgarten, DJD 35:116-19.
90. L. H. Schiffman, "Sadducean Halakhah in the Dead Sea Scrolls: The Case of the *Tevul Yom*," *DSD* 1 (1994) 285-99.
91. 4Q275 (Tohorot B), now called 4QCommunal Liturgy (Alexander and Vermes, DJD 26:209-16), as presently preserved, has no specific legal content, but does refer to the inspector *(mevaqqer)* and to the cursing of someone, perhaps one who is being expelled from the community. Expulsion as a punishment is mentioned in the *Rule of the Community* (1QS 7:1-2, 18-19, 22-25; 8:21-9:2) and *Damascus Document* (CD 20:1-8), and a ritual for expulsion is found in the Qumran fragments of the *Damascus Document* (4Q266 7 i-ii 5-15). 4QTohorot C (4Q278) is extremely fragmentary and relates to impurity which can be transferred by contact, referring to the bed that can be rendered impure if one who contracted impurity has sat on it.
92. Baumgarten, DJD 35:123-29.

supplies no specific requirements for the gleaners, but this text requires that they be ritually pure. Little more can be derived from this text but it no doubt included specifics of this requirement and may have included other agricultural laws.

4Q477 — Rebukes by the Overseer[93]

This document clearly stems from the Qumran sectarian community, recording actual dockets of sectarian legal proceedings against those in violation of sectarian prescriptions. According to sectarian law, it was required that one reprove a fellow member of the sect in front of the overseer *(mevaqqer)* and in front of witnesses after he committed a transgression. Only if this procedure had taken place could a sectarian be punished for a later infraction of the same law. This fragmentary text lists by name specific individuals who had been rebuked as well as their transgressions.[94]

Conclusion

This review of the major and minor legal texts in the Qumran collection serves to point out that there is much legal material here to be analyzed. Although the texts are written by a unique group of people living in a particular time and place, they are grounded, like biblical and rabbinic literature, in issues of Jewish law. The sectarian legal texts give us a window on the way that they read the Bible and determined their laws. They had their own way of deriving authority, their own legal system, their own calendar, ceremonies, and rituals and expressed their opposition to the Jerusalem establishment through the use of polemics. Nevertheless, their legal documents shed much light on Jewish law in Second Temple times amongst the groups that competed with the Qumran sectarians: the Sadducees, Pharisees, and later rabbinic law. Analysis of the Qumran method of codification of Jewish law will demonstrate the similarities and disparities between the sectarian concepts and those of the other groups. This analysis will be taken up in the next chapter.

---

93. E. Eshel in S. J. Pfann and P. S. Alexander et al., *Qumran Cave 4.XXVI: Cryptic Texts and Miscellanea, Part 1.* DJD 36 (Oxford: Clarendon, 2000) 474-83.

94. E. Eshel, "4Q477: The Rebukes by the Overseer," *JJS* 45 (1994) 111-22; C. Hempel, "Who Rebukes in 4Q477?" *RevQ* 16 (1995) 655-56. Cf. Schiffman, *Sectarian Law,* 89-98.

CHAPTER 9

Codification of Jewish Law in the Dead Sea Scrolls

The rich contents of the Qumran materials related to Jewish law are preserved in texts of very different literary character. The literary structure of a number of documents of sectarian regulations or matters of Jewish law lends itself to comparison with biblical texts and later rabbinic literature. Here we will see a mixture of elements common with other Jewish texts and some unique to the various documents found at Qumran.

Literary Structure of the Rules

In order to analyze the Qumran materials, we will have to consider three basic questions: (1) the overall literary character of the collection of laws, (2) the manner of collection or redaction, and (3) the form of individual laws or regulations. These characteristics can then be evaluated as to adherence to biblical forms and compared with the language of rabbinic legal materials.

It is well known that biblical law included both casuistic (if . . . then . . .) statements and apodictic laws (thou shalt . . .).[1] Postbiblical law, however, is usually expressed in different forms. Fundamental to discussion of later Jewish legal documents is a basic distinction between independently formulated laws written in the language of their author (mishnah) and those presented as derived from biblical interpretation (midrash).[2] This second type in the rab-

---

1. A. Alt, "The Origins of Israelite Law," in *Essays on Old Testament History and Religion*, trans. R. A. Wilson, 103-71 (Garden City: Doubleday, 1968).

2. J. Z. Lauterbach, "Midrash and Mishnah," *JQR* N.S. 5 (1914/15) 503-27; 6 (1915/16) 23-95,

binic corpus appears in the form of lemma followed by a commentary. Rabbinic beliefs regarding the sanctity of the written law required that the text and its interpretation be kept thoroughly separate. Among the Qumran documents we find evidence of a similar dichotomy, although differing approaches to the Bible and its text may have been the source for the particular features we find.

Mishnaic laws are generally stated as participial clauses, with the negative indicated by the Hebrew 'en, but the Dead Sea laws are generally stated in biblical style similar to casuistic laws. Negatives are constructed with 'al followed by a verb in the imperfect. Laws of the penal code generally begin with 'im followed by a verb in the imperfect and then go on to specify the punishments in terms of demotion within the sectarian hierarchy or deprivation from a portion of one's food ration. We may generalize and state that Qumran legal materials and rules are composed in a style that is closer to that of biblical law than to the mishnaic legal corpus.

Biblical and Rabbinic Models

Whereas the biblical codes, like their ancient Near Eastern counterparts, intend to assemble a group of laws to be followed by all, Mishnaic literature[3] and the later Jewish codes that flow from it, even up to the Shulḥan 'Arukh,[4] are rather codes of legal curricula. They do not intend to provide simple legal guidance, but rather record a set of opinions of varying authority. They may be used as the raw material for a codification in the normal sense, but as they stand, they provide the curriculum for either abstract study or for the rendering of decisions. For the most part, they do not record decisions. The only possible exception is the code of Maimonides, and even he often veers from this goal to mention variant views or customs.[5]

Certainly, therefore, the term "code" will play out differently when applied to the Dead Sea Scrolls, depending on whether the model is biblical or rabbinic. But things are even more complicated. As the Pentateuch was passed

---

303-23; D. Weiss Halivni, *Midrash, Mishnah, and Gemara: The Jewish Predilection for Justified Law* (Cambridge, MA: Harvard University Press, 1986) 18-104.

3. Cf. L. H. Schiffman, *From Text to Tradition: A History of Second Temple and Rabbinic Judaism* (Hoboken: Ktav, 1991) 188-95.

4. Cf. I. Twersky, "The *Shulḥan 'Aruk*: Enduring Code of Jewish Law," in *The Jewish Expression*, ed. J. Goldin, 322-43 (New York: Bantam, 1970).

5. I. Twersky, *Introduction to the Code of Maimonides (Mishneh Torah)*. Yale Judaica Series 22 (New Haven: Yale University Press, 1980) 97-102.

down to postbiblical Jews — indeed already in the Persian period — it was canonized Scripture. As such, what were, at least from a literary point of view, discrete, and one would assume self-consistent, codes now appeared in a collection — a "supercode," as it were. The supercode now contained varying and even contradicting treatments of the same subjects, now scattered within the literary domicile we recognize as the Torah. The interpretation, reconciliation, and homogenization of these passages is a necessary process before any postbiblical code can be produced. Needless to say, evidence of this process will be visible everywhere in the legal materials of the Dead Sea Scrolls.

In the tannaitic corpus, much of this effort went on in a class of texts called tannaitic or halakhic midrashim (both terms are to some extent misnomers) that are generally not considered to be codes in the normal sense of the word. These texts compare, contrast, and interpret the Torah's codes. The results may be closely related to the Mishnah and the Tosefta, but the midrashim are literarily so different that they are not considered codes.

If we attempt to compare the form of Jewish legal literature in the Dead Sea Scrolls with that of the rabbis, the midrashic materials will also be significant. A long-standing issue in rabbinic studies that also applies to the Qumran material is the classification of texts (or better the building blocks of texts) into midrash and mishnah. While rabbinic literature includes midrashic texts that probe the biblical legal codes in their canonical context, the corresponding approach in the scrolls is the genre of rewritten Bible.[6] The scrolls also contain abstract legal rulings of the mishnaic type, organized by subject, although these tend to be more biblically based in formulation than their tannaitic counterparts. Whereas in the tannaitic corpus we deal with midrash, in the scrolls we deal with the Torah's codes at a much closer distance. This phenomenon is easy to understand in the wider context of the religious approaches of both corpora. The scrolls' authors, and the groups they represented, allowed biblical interpretation and adaptation, not to mention reconciliation and harmonization, to be displayed by invading the text itself and rewriting and even re-redacting it to express postbiblical teachings. To the rabbis, such an approach violated the sanctity of Scripture and the distinction between the written and oral laws, between what they saw as God's word and what they perceived as the product of a divine-human partnership. So often the same ideas can be expressed in the Qumran corpus as rewritten Bible, but in the rabbinic corpus as midrash, which clearly maintains the distinction between Bible and interpretation.

It is therefore fair to say that Qumran documents bear witness already

---

6. G. J. Brooke, "Rewritten Bible," *EDSS* 2:777-81.

in the second century B.C.E. to the existence of what later were termed the mishnaic and midrashic modes for formulating postbiblical law. But partly for chronological and partly for ideological reasons, the Qumran documents hew much more closely to their biblical forerunners. Indeed, it has been correctly observed that the Qumran sectarians saw themselves as living in the biblical age itself,[7] and compilation and editing of biblical materials continued to some extent in Qumran and related sectarian circles up to the turn of the era. It is therefore to be expected that the Qumran versions of these two genres of postbiblical law will be somewhat closer to the biblical forms than to those in rabbinic literature.

Authority of the Codes

This brings us to another contrast between the Qumran materials and those of the rabbis — the question of source of authority. Any code will automatically have to make some claim to authority if it is to be followed. In the Qumran case, we see two approaches coexisting: (1) Qumran sectarian works, such as the legal sections of the *Rule of the Community* (*Serekh ha-Yaḥad*, 1QS), assume that God revealed the written Torah — the *nigleh*, "revealed" — at Sinai. Authoritative sectarian interpretation and the laws that derive from it constitute the *nistar*, "hidden."[8] The latter was revealed in divinely-inspired, continuous revelation at sectarian sessions and was redacted into *serakhim*, lists of laws.[9] This means that the sectarians accepted a onetime divine revelation at Sinai mediated by the process of authoritative, in their view inspired, biblical exegesis. (2) A onetime revelation is also espoused by the author/redactor of the *Temple Scroll*, but he has rewritten the Torah to include his own interpretations, rulings, and even extrabiblical laws. His view is of a onetime revelation that includes what we would regard as canonical and extracanonical laws. Essentially, he believes in a onetime revelation in which God agrees with him![10]

---

7. S. Talmon, "The 'Desert Motif' in the Bible and in Qumran Literature," in *Biblical Motifs: Origins and Transformations*, ed. A. Altmann, 55-63 (Cambridge, MA: Harvard University Press, 1966); repr. in Talmon, *Literary Studies in the Hebrew Bible: Form and Content: Collected Studies* (Leiden: Brill, 1993) 216-54.

8. L. H. Schiffman, *The Halakhah at Qumran*. SJLA 16 (Leiden: Brill, 1975) 20-32.

9. Schiffman, *Halakhah at Qumran*, 60-68.

10. L. H. Schiffman, *Reclaiming the Dead Sea Scrolls: The History of Judaism, the Background of Christianity, the Lost Library of Qumran* (Philadelphia: Jewish Publication Society, 1994; repr. ABRL [New York: Doubleday, 1995]) 245-55; "The *Temple Scroll* and the Nature of Its

These views contrast with the Pharisaic assumption of extrabiblical legal "traditions of the fathers."[11] Nor do they agree with the later rabbinic view that these laws and explanations had been given at Sinai in addition to the canonical Torah.[12]

There is one further issue to be clarified regarding codification. Normally, when we talk about Jewish legal codes, we deal with codes bringing together the usual topics of Jewish law, taking their cue from the Torah's laws as spun out by exegesis and/or tradition, depending on the particular system of Judaism under discussion. In addition, there is a closely related category that is especially prominent in the scrolls corpus because of its sectarian, that is, "in-group," character, namely, regulations for the conduct of the life of the sect that have no direct basis in the Torah. I say "direct" since these organizational laws are often rooted in Torah prescriptions or halakhic categories, but they seek to create a group setting of holiness and sanctity, not to fulfill some specific commandment, positive or negative. These organizational, sectarian regulations have been compared by some to those of Hellenistic schools or guilds.[13] However, these similarities concern only aspects typical of all such groups and especially those existing in a similar environment. In fact, the sectarian organizational regulations are better compared with Pharisaic/rabbinic regulations for the guild of sages, or with those preserved in tannaitic literature for the ḥavurah of Second Temple times.[14] It is well known that these sectarian regulations can be compared profitably with the descriptions of the Essenes and Therapeutae in Philo and Josephus.[15] These regulations

---

Law: The Status of the Question," in *The Community of the Renewed Covenant: The Notre Dame Symposium on the Dead Sea Scrolls*, ed. E. Ulrich and J. VanderKam, 37-55. CJAS 10 (Notre Dame: University of Notre Dame Press, 1994).

11. Cf. L. H. Schiffman, *Texts and Traditions: A Source Reader for the Study of Second Temple and Rabbinic Judaism* (Hoboken: Ktav, 1998) 517-20.

12. Schiffman, *Texts and Traditions*, 520-22.

13. M. Weinfeld, *The Organizational Pattern and the Penal Code of the Qumran Sect*. NTOA 2 (Fribourg: Éditions Universitaires and Göttingen: Vandenhoeck & Ruprecht, 1986); E. W. Larson, "Greco-Roman Guilds," *EDSS* 1:321-23.

14. C. Rabin, *Qumran Studies*. Scripta Judaica 2 (Oxford: Oxford University Press, 1957) 1-21; S. Lieberman, "The Discipline in the So-Called Dead Sea Manual of Discipline," *JBL* 71 (1951) 199-206; repr. in *Texts and Studies* (New York: Ktav, 1974) 200-207; A. Oppenheimer, *The ʿAm ha-Aretz: A Study in the Social History of the Jewish People in the Hellenistic-Roman Period*, trans. I. H. Levine, 118-56. ALGHJ 8 (Leiden: Brill, 1977).

15. See T. S. Beal, *Josephus' Description of the Essenes Illustrated by the Dead Sea Scrolls*. SNTSMS 58 (New York: Cambridge University Press, 1988); R. Bergmeier, *Die Essener-Berichte des Flavius Josephus: Quellenstudien zu den Essenertexten im Werk des jüdischen Historiographen* (Kampen: Kok Pharos, 1993).

are compiled in the scrolls in lists *(serakhim)* similar to those used for the more usual halakhic subjects.[16]

Scripturally Based Codes

We now turn to an analysis of the specific materials in the scrolls corpus that can be seen as legal codes. We will begin with those most scripturally based, or those that imitate biblical legal codes.

The most significant material of this type is found in the *Temple Scroll*, which itself is a compilation of preexistent sources to which has been added a composition by the author/redactor, known as the Deuteronomic paraphrase.[17] The author sought to create a Torahlike text that would contain collections of "biblical" laws stated in accord with his own interpretations and rulings, themselves derived from exegesis. He began his work with a number of distinct documents, each a sort of code on a given topic. He had a temple plan that one might perhaps exclude from this discussion despite its prescriptive character and its biblical basis.[18] After all, it is essentially an architectural plan expressed in prose form. More codelike are the purity source (11QTemple 48:10–51:10), outlining the stringent Zadokite/Sadducee views on ritual purity, and the festival calendar, laying out the specifics of how to harmonize Leviticus 23 and Numbers 28–29 (11QTemple 13:9–30:2).[19] These sections appear in the guise of rewritten Torah. Boldest of all is the Law of the King (11QTemple 57-59), a distinct literary unit that set out the laws of king, government, and army, and it is in this "code" that we encounter the greatest amount of free composition, yet in imitation of biblical style.[20] The

---

16. Schiffman, *Halakhah at Qumran*, 67-68.

17. On the sources of the *Temple Scroll*, see A. M. Wilson and L. Wills, "Literary Sources of the Temple Scroll," *HTR* 75 (1982) 275-88; and M. O. Wise, *A Critical Study of the Temple Scroll from Qumran Cave 11*. SAOC 49 (Chicago: Oriental Institute, University of Chicago, 1990) 1-154.

18. See L. H. Schiffman, "Architecture and Law: The Temple and Its Courtyards in the Temple Scroll," in *From Ancient Israel to Modern Judaism: Intellect in Quest of Understanding: Essays in Honor of Marvin Fox*, ed. J. Neusner, E. S. Frerichs, and N. M. Sarna, 1:267-84. BJS 159 (Atlanta: Scholars, 1989).

19. Cf. L. H. Schiffman, "The Sacrificial System of the *Temple Scroll* and the *Book of Jubilees*," in *SBLSP 1985*, ed. K. H. Richards, 217-33 (Atlanta: Scholars, 1985); Y. Yadin, *The Temple Scroll* (Jerusalem: Israel Exploration Society and Shrine of the Book, 1983) 1:89-176.

20. Cf. L. H. Schiffman, "The King, His Guard, and the Royal Council in the *Temple Scroll*," *PAAJR* 54 (1987) 237-59; Yadin, *Temple Scroll*, 1:344-62; M. Weinfeld, "'Megillat Miqdash' 'o 'Torah la-Melekh,'" *Shnaton* 3 (1978/79) 214-37 [English trans. "The Temple Scroll or 'The Law of the King,'" in *Normative and Sectarian Judaism in the Second Temple Period* (London T. & T. Clark,

final piece is a Deuteronomic paraphrase (11QTemple 51:11–56:21; 60:12–66:12) that compiles laws from Deuteronomy, organizes them by subject to some extent, and interprets them in light of other sources in the Torah.[21] This part was composed by the author/redactor when he gathered the mini-codes — the sources — into the entire scroll, an act analogous to recanonizing the Torah and, in effect, to creating a supercode. In the process of the author's putting forward his own views on matters of the structure of the temple, sacrifices, ritual purity, political organization, and family life, nothing is said of a sectarian group or its conduct.

In terms of its method of codification, the *Temple Scroll* demonstrates several interesting features. The author of each source gives one view and claims divine authority. An editorial process utilizing harmonization, exegesis, and excision creates a straightforward set of laws with no duplication.[22] Since the units represented subjects, the final text is a code arranged by subject, thus solving by re-redaction the overlaps and duplications in the codes of the Torah.[23] So we might be more accurate in describing the *Temple Scroll*, as a whole, as a recodified Torah, rewritten not only to express the views of the author/redactor and his Zadokite circle, but also to turn the Torah into a code on those topics covered. Due to the inherently polemical nature of this text, it did not need to bother with such laws as the Ten Commandments, and, therefore, it cannot have been intended as a stand-alone, all-inclusive, full-service Torah.[24]

If one makes a comparison to the categories of rabbinic literature, the legal collections in the *Temple Scroll* are closest in character to the halakhic midrashim, since they continue the organization of the curriculum of legal study in the order of the Bible. Yet a major difference is the fact that the *Tem-*

2005) 158-85]. See the recent full-scale study of C. D. Elledge, *The Statutes of the King: The Temple Scroll's Legislation on Kingship (11Q19 LVI 12–LIX 21)* (Paris: Gabalda, 2004).

21. L. H. Schiffman, "The Deuteronomic Paraphrase of the *Temple Scroll*," *RevQ* 15 (1992) 543-68.

22. Yadin, *Temple Scroll*, 1:71-88; D. D. Swanson, *The Temple Scroll and the Bible: The Methodology of 11QT.* STDJ 14 (Leiden: Brill, 1995) 8-14, 227-35; J. Milgrom, "The Scriptural Foundations and Deviations in the Laws of Purity of the Temple Scroll," in *Archaeology and History in the Dead Sea Scrolls: The New York University Conference in Memory of Yigael Yadin*, ed. L. H. Schiffman, 83-99. JSOTSup 8. JSOT/ASOR Monographs 2 (Sheffield: JSOT, 1990); "The Qumran Cult: Its Exegetical Principles," in *Temple Scroll Studies*, ed. G. J. Brooke, 165-80. JSPSup 7 (Sheffield: JSOT, 1989).

23. Cf. S. A. Kaufman, "The Temple Scroll and Higher Criticism," *HUCA* 53 (1982) 29-43; G. Brin, "Ha-Miqra bi-Megillat ha-Miqdash," *Shnaton* 4 (1979/1980) 182-225.

24. H. Najman, *Seconding Sinai: The Development of Mosaic Discourse in Second Temple Judaism.* JSJSup 77 (Leiden: Brill, 2003) 43-50.

ple Scroll exhibits a further move toward subject organization — what I term re-redaction — of the preexisting biblical codes.[25]

Some sections of the *Zadokite Fragments* also exhibit the character of rewritten Bible even though, as we will see, this is not the overall form of this text. 4Q251, Halakha A, containing a series of laws based on the Covenant Code of Exodus, adheres closely in wording to the biblical text.[26] This small piece of evidence probably indicates that the *Temple Scroll* — or, to be more precise, that the building blocks of the *Temple Scroll* — was not the only such work representing what must have been more widespread steps toward codification by rewriting and re-redacting Scripture in Zadokite/Sadducean circles.

Abstract Codes

A completely different type of codification is found in the *Damascus Document (Zadokite Fragments)* and MMT. Already with the discovery of the first Dead Sea Scroll, the *Damascus Document,* it was noted that the text presented a combination of elements involving the ideology of a sectarian group closely interwoven with its rules and material drawn from its version of Jewish law.

In general terms we may observe that the laws of these documents are composed with only a few direct citations of scriptural proof texts. Rather, they consist of independently formulated language constructed by their authors. Whereas in the mishnaic material there is little remnant of biblical language, even for laws of clear biblical derivation, the laws of the *Damascus Document* and MMT, while formulated as if independent of biblical derivation, often betray the language of the biblical verses from which they have been constructed. Further, analysis of these laws and their biblical forebears allows us to reconstruct the hermeneutics and interpretations that underlie the legal rules presented by these texts. Thus, the legal material in the scrolls

---

25. This is why the so-called 4QRewritten Pentateuch (4Q364-4Q367) has not been included in our discussion. Its legal material, with the exception of a few extrabiblical passages, is essentially still in pentateuchal order. Further, the entire Torah, "aggadah" and halakhah, is in those texts. Unfortunately, we are still not sure how to deal with the nonbiblical sections of 4QRP (4Q365a) that some scholars think are just versions of laws found in the *Temple Scroll* or closely related to it. Cf. S. A. White [Crawford], in H. Attridge et al., *Qumran Cave 4.VIII: Parabiblical Texts, Part 1.* DJD 13 (Oxford: Clarendon, 1994) 319-33.

26. E. Larson, M. R. Lehmann, and L. H. Schiffman in J. M. Baumgarten et al., *Qumran Cave 4.XXV: Halakhic Texts.* DJD 35 (Oxford: Clarendon, 1999) 25-51; cf. L. H. Schiffman, "Legal Works," *EDSS* 1:479.

never fully sheds its scriptural garb in the manner in which mishnaic prescriptions do. To avoid confusion, we should emphasize that this observation does not apply to the sectarian procedural regulations since these laws do not depend on biblical authority for their formulation and validity. Further, even in those cases in which a sectarian regulation may be saturated with language borrowed from Scripture, the borrowing may often be literary and not relate to the derivation of the content.

The sectarian law, *nistar,* was derived by the sectarians in study sessions that they saw as divinely inspired.[27] These sessions produced legal rulings that in their formulation, as mentioned above, often betray the language of the biblical texts that underlie them. These laws are actually pastiches of biblical phrases drawn from the sources that were midrashically interpreted to produce the laws in question. Therein lies part of the explanation for the archaizing terminology of these texts.[28] From the scroll texts we learn that the laws created in study sessions were redacted into *serakhim,* lists of laws, and these lists were, in turn, redacted into larger texts, along with other nonlegal materials. This literary history explains the short codes (minicodes = *serakhim*) that appear in the *Damascus Document*,[29] as well as those of organizational character redacted into the *Rule of the Community* and its appendices, *Rule of the Congregation* and *Rule of Benedictions,* and some of the minor halakhic texts.[30] Further, this model of redaction explains the varying recensions found in the manuscripts of these texts, as well as the existence of overlapping texts in various compositions and, finally, the existence of *Miscellaneous Rules* (4Q265), a text that redacts parts of the *Damascus Document* and *Rule of the Community* together into one composite document.

Also to be considered here is MMT. In certain ways this text can be considered under the heading of rules and halakhic texts since the main body of

---

27. Schiffman, *Halakhah at Qumran,* 67-68.

28. Rabin, *Qumran Studies,* 108-11.

29. L. H. Schiffman, *Sectarian Law in the Dead Sea Scrolls: Courts, Testimony and the Penal Code.* BJS 33 (Chico: Scholars, 1983) 7-11; J. Murphy-O'Connor, "A Literary Analysis of Damascus Document XIX, 33-XX, 34," *RB* 79 (1972) 544-64; J. M. Baumgarten, "The Cave 4 Versions of the Qumran Penal Code," *JJS* 43 (1992) 268-76; C. Hempel, *The Laws of the Damascus Document: Sources, Tradition and Redaction.* STDJ 29 (Leiden: Brill, 1998) 15-151.

30. Schiffman, *Sectarian Law,* 3-7; J. Murphy-O'Connor, "La genèse littéraire de la Règle de la Communauté," *RB* 76 (1969) 528-49; J. Pouilly, *La Règle de la Communauté de Qumrân: son évolution littéraire.* CahRB 17 (Paris: Gabalda, 1976) 15-63; S. Metso, "The Redaction of the Community Rule," in *The Dead Sea Scrolls: Fifty Years after Their Discovery: Proceedings of the Jerusalem Congress, July 20-25, 1997,* ed. L. H. Schiffman, E. Tov, and J. C. VanderKam, 377-84 (Jerusalem: Israel Exploration Society, Shrine of the Book, Israel Museum, 2000); *The Textual Development of the Qumran Community Rule.* STDJ 21 (Leiden: Brill, 1997) 69-155.

the document consists of a list of rules of ritual purity and impurity and sacrificial laws pertaining to the temple in Jerusalem. Yet this text does not contain any laws pertaining to sectarian organization since MMT represents an early stage in the schism before the sectarian movement had congealed and established its own regulations. At the same time, this list of laws is almost entirely parallel in its concerns to its biblical antecedents and to later rabbinic rulings, although for the most part the Pharisaic-rabbinic texts disagree with the Sadducee-like laws found in MMT. Like the *Damascus Document* and the *Rule of the Community*, this text contains a theological section where the ideological underpinnings of legal observance are set forth.[31] This time, however, the hortatory section comes not at the beginning of the text but at its conclusion. The authors argue that only observance in accord with their particular view of the law will yield continued rule of the high priest to whom it is addressed and that theirs is the true approach of Jewish tradition. Here again, since the schism has not reached its full proportions we do not encounter the specific ideas or terminology of the Qumran sect.

Sectarian Regulations

Two of the documents copied together by a scribe in the so-called *Rules Scroll* are the *Rule of the Community* (1QS) and the eschatological *Rule of the Congregation* (1QSa). The *Rule of the Community* contains a theological introduction in which the sectarian concepts of good, evil, and predestination are set forth. Then follows a compilation of sets of rules for sectarian behavior. Here, as is the case in the *Damascus Document*, we have good reason to suspect that the conceptual texts in question originated as separate compositions that were inserted here as part of a process of redaction or of literary development. The process of combination of legal and procedural materials with conceptual treatises is highlighted by the presence in the text of the Treatise of the Two Spirits (1QS 3:13–4:1)[32] and, at the end of the text, of a long poem, similar in style to the *Hodayot*, bringing the text to a formal close. The theological introduction and final poem constituted a framework for the sectar-

---

31. J. Strugnell, "Appendix 3: Additional Observations on 4QMMT," in E. Qimron and Strugnell. *Qumran Cave 4. V: Miqṣat Maʿaśe ha-Torah*. DJD 10 (Oxford: Clarendon, 1994) 203-6; "MMT: Second Thoughts on a Forthcoming Edition," in Ulrich and VanderKam, *Community of the Renewed Covenant*, 57-73.

32. Cf. J. Licht, "An Analysis of the Treatise of the Two Spirits in DSD," in *Aspects of the Dead Sea Scrolls*, ed. C. Rabin and Y. Yadin, 88-100. ScrHier 4 (Jerusalem: Magnes, Hebrew University, 1958).

ian regulations and fundamental principles that were intended to foster specific beliefs and a special worldview.

The *Rule of the Congregation* differs substantially in the character of its specific content from the *Damascus Document*. The largest part of the nonhortatory section of the *Damascus Document*, often known as the "Laws," covers the normal topics known to us from biblical and postbiblical Jewish law. Prominent among these are Sabbath laws, laws of purity and impurity, and civil law. Interspersed among these are a smaller number of regulations pertaining to the role of the sectarian officials, entrance into the community, and other such matters. It is most likely that the sectarian regulations of the *Damascus Document* concern the members of the sect living in scattered communities in the land of Israel. Yet in the *Rule of the Community* virtually the entire set of rules, apparently compiled from several previously existing collections, concerns matters of sectarian organization for the conduct of the sectarian center at Qumran. While it was the case that some of these regulations have at their root principles of Jewish law, especially regarding ritual purity and impurity, these regulations for the most part almost entirely concern sectarian procedures and do not mention the religious and legal issues that concern the Bible and rabbinic literature.

Both the *Damascus Document* and the *Rule of the Community* share in presenting the sectarian penal code that is extant in several versions.[33] This penal code deals with violations of a variety of sectarian procedural regulations. Punishments are meted out by demotion within the sectarian community, a penalty of one-fourth of the food ration, and in the worst case, expulsion from the group.[34] Such punishments have absolutely no parallel in the earlier or later literature of Jewish law.

Another text combines the sectarian ideology regarding the end of days with what can best be termed messianic halakhah. This is the *Rule of the Congregation*, which sets forth a variety of regulations for the eschatological council of the community and the messianic banquet. Expectations of halakhic perfection in that era stem not simply from the principles of Jewish law but rather from the sect's concept that the end of days would reflect an era of perfection in which the goals and aspirations of the sectarians, embodied in their life in the present age, would all be fulfilled.[35]

---

33. Baumgarten, "Cave 4 Versions of the Qumran Penal Code"; Hempel, *Laws of the Damascus Covenant*, 163-70.

34. Cf. Schiffman, *Sectarian Law*, 168-73; Hempel, *Laws of the Damascus Covenant*, 175-85.

35. L. H. Schiffman, *The Eschatological Community of the Dead Sea Scrolls*. SBLMS 38 (Atlanta: Scholars, 1989) 68-71.

Subject Organization

Aside from the process of their codification, the most stellar feature of these *serakhim*, the minicodes, especially as found in the *Damascus Document* from both the genizah and Qumran manuscripts, is the regularity of subject divisions. A cursory investigation of this material will show that these texts are the result of a redactional process whereby individual laws that were developed in sessions of the sectarian assembly were later collected into *serakhim*, lists of sectarian laws. These lists were later gathered together into legal collections. The redactors intended to organize them by subject, an approach familiar to us from the Mishnah. A similar phenomenon can be found in the book of *Jubilees*, in which laws on one subject were collected together as in the Sabbath laws (*Jub.* 2:17-33, 50:6-13) and the laws of Passover (*Jubilees* 49). But the Qumran collections differ in one important respect. Here we find not only laws pertaining to the usual subjects of Jewish law but also additional sectarian regulations.

In fact, amazingly perhaps, these sections of laws, which can be likened to short tannaitic *massekhtot* (tractates), even have titles embedded in the text. For example, we find על השבועה, "regarding the oath" (CD 9:8), or על השבת לשמרה כמשפטה, "regarding the Sabbath, to observe it according to its (sectarian) regulations" (CD 10:14), in the *Damascus Document* or על העריות, "regarding forbidden consanguineous/adulterous marriages," in the fragmentary 4QHalakha A (4Q251 12 1).[36] What this means, *mirabile dictu*, is that long before the time when traditional historiography claims that Rabbi Akiva invented subject divisions for the Mishnah[37] it was fully established as the norm in presenting Qumran laws that were unquestionably derived from halakhic midrash.

Conclusions

Qumran codes are, of course, based on their biblical predecessors. They seek not only to reorganize biblical materials by subject, in pseudobiblical form, as in the *Temple Scroll*, but also to present them in abstract form, as in the *Damascus Document*. Nevertheless, in both forms they adhere to biblical language, directly in the *Temple Scroll* and related rewritten Torah texts and indi-

---

36. Larson, Lehmann, and Schiffman, DJD 35:45.
37. C. Albeck, *Mavo' la-Mishnah* (Jerusalem: Bialik Institute and Tel Aviv: Dvir, 1959) 76, 99-100.

rectly in laws such as are found in the *Zadokite Fragments*. However, this is not simply a process of codification, even if only one view is being preserved. The authors/redactors of these materials seek to formulate the laws so as to express their rulings or those of the school of law to which they belong. The same basic system of law and exegesis is common to both the biblically based type of law and the abstract, apodictic laws, just as it is in tannaitic literature for both midrash and mishnah. Yet in the Qumran scrolls, even the Mishnah-like statements are in biblical parlance that betrays the sources and even the process of exegesis. The entire system resembles the tannaitic approach in the existence of a more biblically-based type, on the one hand, and a more abstract type, on the other hand. But whereas in Mishnah and Talmud there are whole sections that are "like mountains suspended by a hair" (*m. Ḥag.* 1:8), such laws do not occur in Qumran texts, except in regard to sectarian organizational rules, since the Sadducee/Zadokite approach is tied more closely to the biblical text.[38]

Considering the function of the codes, the Qumran material reflects the biblical model more than do the rabbinic texts that reflect a curriculum of study more than a set of unidimensional rulings that one would expect in a code. Yet when the canonized Torah as a whole is looked at, and this is how all Second Temple period Jews looked at it, it is the rabbinic corpus that most reflects the multivocal character of the *Torah ḥatumah*,[39] the complete Torah. In this respect, the Qumran codes resemble more the well-organized minicodes of the Torah, and the rabbinic texts resemble the Torah more with its apparently disorganized and duplicating legal material and its still unresolved or unharmonized contradictions. For the scrolls sect, as for the minicodes of the Torah, only one view is correct, but for the rabbis, like the multitextured Torah, the various voices are to be debated and harmonized. For the scrolls sect the competing and disagreeing voices are to be silenced, but for the rabbis they are to be celebrated.

If so, the purpose of the Qumran codes — whether of the scriptural or abstract type — is to put forward the authoritative ruling of the authors regarding Torah laws and sectarian regulations, organized by subject and reflecting the Zadokite/Sadducean rulings and interpretations of the authors and redactors. In this respect, the legal texts preserved in the Dead Sea Scrolls are in many ways an example of pure codification, rather than organization

---

38. Cf. *Ant.* 13.297, 18.17; *Megillat Ta'anit*, in H. Lichtenstein, "Die Fastenrolle: Eine Untersuchung zur jüdisch-hellenistischen Gerichte," *HUCA* 8-9 (1931-32) 331; V. Noam, *Megillat Ta'anit: ha-Nusaḥim, Pishram, Toledotehem, be-Ṣeruf Mahadurah Biqqortit* (Jerusalem: Yad Ben-Zvi, 2003) 77-79, 206-16; G. G. Porton, "Sadducees," *ABD* 5:892-95.

39. For the expression, cf. *b. Giṭ.* 60a.

of study curricula of traditional materials. Yet even when looked at in this way, the dual-genre approach of Qumran legal codes — biblical and abstract — and the use of subject organization clearly point forward in time to the later compositional and redactional activity of the Tannaim. Can it be merely coincidence? It seems not. Commonality of style and method can be detected even when there remain deep differences in legal rulings and in conceptions of authority.

CHAPTER 10

Pre-Maccabean Halakhah in the Dead Sea Scrolls and the Biblical Tradition

This study will investigate evidence from the Dead Sea Scrolls for pre-Maccabean Jewish law and its relationship with the Hebrew Bible and the legal materials preserved there. To be discussed are issues of both content and form, showing how both midrashic and apodictic forms of law appear in both collections[1] and how, in particular, the priestly tradition was continued beyond the last books of the Hebrew Bible. Along the way observations will be made about the state of Jewish legal materials in the early Second Temple period.

Any attempt to investigate the nature of pre-Maccabean halakhah must, by definition, be a complex, triangulated extrapolation. The extrapolation proceeds on two axes. One axis is that of chronology, in that certain differences that we observe between corpora written at different times can result from historical development. But other differences between corpora result from the existence of varying approaches to Jewish life and law in different, often competing, groups within the Jewish community. Because these two factors — the issues of chronology and competing approaches, often termed sectarianism — are operative simultaneously in the entire period we will be discussing, we are presented with one of the fundamental methodological challenges for our study. How do we determine if a specific difference between sources results from historical development or from differing halakhic trends, evidence for which happens to be sporadically represented? Closely related to this methodological problem is a paucity of sources. For this study,

---

1. For these terms, see D. Weiss Halivni, *Midrash, Mishnah, and Gemara: The Jewish Predilection for Justified Law* (Cambridge, MA: Harvard University Press, 1986) 6.

in particular, we are confronted immediately by the need for extrapolation in order to reach any conclusions at all.

First, however, we need to clarify the periodization of our study. "Pre-Maccabean" designates the period between the end of the biblical story line, ca. 450 B.C.E., and the Maccabean revolt of 168-164 B.C.E. We speak, then, about the end of the Persian period, the famous dark age of Jewish history for which we have only archaeological evidence, and the Hellenistic age of Alexander's conquest of the land of Israel through the Seleucid conquest in 198 B.C.E., up through the Hellenistic reform and the Maccabean revolt.[2] If we propose to talk about the state of halakhah in this period with such limited source material, we have no choice but to extrapolate.

To be precise, we face the problem of extrapolating forward from the early Second Temple–period biblical texts, through a variety of Persian period or early Hellenistic period Aramaic sources, mostly preserved in the Dead Sea Scrolls. We must also extrapolate back from the later Second Temple texts and early tannaitic traditions into the earlier period, but also factoring in some pre-Qumranian Hebrew texts from the second century B.C.E., most prominently *Jubilees*.[3]

When this chronological, diachronic extrapolation is merged with the synchronic problem of the contemporaneous, competing approaches of Judaism, we arrive at what I have termed triangulation. Only in this way can we possibly construct, or better reconstruct, a halakhic history, or at least the outlines thereof, from the materials at hand. Accordingly, our first task will be to survey the nature of the materials at our disposal, and only then to overlay a framework for providing a general reconstruction.

Biblical Materials

The primary biblical sources for our study are various elements embodied in the books of Ezra and Nehemiah. These books, thought by many to be au-

---

2. For a summary of this period, see L. H. Schiffman, *From Text to Tradition: A History of Second Temple and Rabbinic Judaism* (Hoboken: Ktav, 1991) 33-72; V. Tcherikover, *Hellenistic Civilization and the Jews*, trans. S. Applebaum (Philadelphia: Jewish Publication Society, 1966) 1-234; E. Schürer, *The History of the Jewish People in the Age of Jesus Christ (175 B.C.-A.D. 135)*, rev. ed. by G. Vermes, F. Millar, with P. Vermes and M. Black (Edinburgh: T. & T. Clark, 1973-1987) 1:137-73.

3. On the date of *Jubilees*, see J. C. VanderKam, "Jubilees, Book of," *EDSS* 1:434-38, who dates it to 150-140 B.C.E. Cf. Schürer, 3/1:312-13, who dates *Jubilees* to soon after the death of Judah the Maccabee in 160 B.C.E.

thored by the Chronicler, contain material pertaining to numerous halakhic matters.[4] I shall survey some of these in list format.

1. Intermarriage. A complex adaptation of Exod 34:15-16 and Deut 7:3 (cf. Josh 23:7, 12-13) underlies the narrative of Ezra 9:1-2 and presents us with the law forbidding intermarriage of Israelites with non-Israelites that is also found in the covenant of Neh 10:31(30). This prohibition has become a norm in all trends of Jewish law. In this context we hear about the forcible separation of intermarried Israelite males from their non-Jewish spouses (Ezra 10:3). Here it is assumed, as in later halakhah, that Jewish identity is determined through the mother (Ezra 9:1-2),[5] although some scholars disagree with my view on this.[6]

2. Sukkah. Nehemiah 8:13-18 contains a reference to building sukkot in which the plants constituting the lulav in later Pharisaic-rabbinic tradition[7] are used to build the sukkah. Further, we find in the *Temple Scroll* (11QTemple[a] 42:3-17, 44:6-10) that sukkot were constructed in the temple court.[8] In this way, the pilgrimage aspect of Sukkot, as described in Deut 16:13-17, was harmonized with the obligation to dwell in sukkot discussed in Lev 23:39-42.

3. Temple organization. Several rulings derived by halakhic midrash are connected with temple procedure. These include: donation of one-third shekel annually to the temple, firstfruits, redemption of the firstborn, eating of first-year male animals by priests, ḥallah offerings, *terumah*, the festival tithe, and tithes for temple servitors. Also documented is the attempt to provide for a regular supply of wood for the altar. Here lots were cast to determine who would supply the wood. But we know from reflections in tannaitic literature and the *Temple Scroll*[9] that later traditions understood the word "offering" in different ways.

4. Doing business on the Sabbath. The effort to stop the doing of business on the Sabbath is recorded at the end of the book of Nehemiah. This assumes

---

4. Y. Kaufman, *History of the Religion of Israel*, Vol. 4: *From the Babylonian Captivity to the End of Prophecy* (New York: Ktav, 1977) 324-430. Cf. L. H. Schiffman, "The Halakhah at Qumran" (Ph.D. diss., Brandeis, 1974) 159-80.

5. L. H. Schiffman, *Who Was a Jew? Rabbinic and Halakhic Perspectives on the Jewish Christian Schism* (Hoboken: Ktav, 1985) 14-17.

6. S. J. D. Cohen, *The Beginnings of Jewishness: Boundaries, Varieties, Uncertainties* (Berkeley: University of California Press, 1999) 267-68, also admits that our approach "may be correct."

7. M. Sukkah 3:1-8. Cf. J. L. Rubenstein, *The History of Sukkot in the Second Temple and Rabbinic Periods*. BJS 302 (Atlanta: Scholars, 1995) 31-45.

8. Y. Yadin, *The Temple Scroll* (Jerusalem: Israel Exploration Society and Shrine of the Book, 1983) 1:135-36; Rubenstein, *History of Sukkot*, 64-68.

9. Yadin, *Temple Scroll*, 1:122-31.

exegesis of Isa 58:13 and Jer 17:21-22, 24, 27 grafted onto the overall Sabbath regulations of the Torah. The resulting prohibition is reflected in Nehemiah as a Torah law, in the *Zadokite Fragments (Damascus Document),* and in tannaitic law where it appears as a rabbinic (nonbiblical) injunction.[10]

5. Centrality of Torah study and reading. From the public Torah reading and covenant renewal ceremony described in Nehemiah 8–10, a pattern was set for later Torah study and ritual that seems to have had major impact on all Jewish groups, although not necessarily in the same way.[11]

6. Role of midrash halakhah. Clearly related to Torah reading and study is the phenomenon of halakhic midrash, a very specific methodology of exegesis that is intended to provide harmonizations of disparate biblical sources on a given topic and to allow the derivation of further legal rulings or the retroactive justification of preexistent laws and customs.[12] This methodology overarches many of the issues discussed in late Second Temple works and also is found in Pharisaic-rabbinic and Sadducean/Zadokite trends later on.

Aramaic Texts

We generally date the pre-Qumranian texts preserved in Aramaic to the fourth-second centuries. Various areas of Jewish law are found in these texts. The *Aramaic Levi Document* (ALD), and to a lesser extent the *New Jerusalem* text, preserve sacrificial laws and regulations. The *Aramaic Levi Document* shows an interesting mix of Pharisaic-rabbinic rulings with Sadducean/Zadokite views.[13] We cannot explain historically why this text appears to

---

10. Cf. also L. H. Schiffman, *The Halakhah at Qumran.* SJLA 16 (Leiden: Brill, 1975) 87-90.

11. See L. H. Schiffman, "The Early History of the Public Reading of the Torah," in *Jews, Christians, and Polytheists in the Ancient Synagogue: Cultural Interaction during the Greco-Roman Period,* ed. S. Fine, 44-56 (London: Routledge, 1999).

12. Cf. Schiffman, *Halakhah at Qumran,* 54-60.

13. Cf. L. H. Schiffman, "Sacrificial Halakhah in the Fragments of the *Aramaic Levi Document* from Qumran, the Cairo Genizah, and Mt. Athos Monastery," in *Reworking the Bible: Apocryphal and Related Texts at Qumran, Proceedings of a Joint Symposium by the Orion Center for the Study of the Dead Sea Scrolls and Associated Literature and the Hebrew University Institute for Advanced Studies Research Group on Qumran, 15-17 January, 2002,* ed. E. G. Chazon, D. Dimant, and R. A. Clements, 177-202. STDJ 58 (Leiden: Brill, 2005); R. A. Kugler, *From Patriarch to Priest: The Levi-Priestly Tradition from* Aramaic Levi *to* Testament of Levi. SBLEJL 9 (Atlanta: Scholars, 1996) 93-111; J. C. Greenfield, M. E. Stone, and E. Eshel, *The Aramaic Levi Document: Edition, Translation, Commentary.* SVTP 19 (Leiden: Brill, 2004) 41-44, 171-79; H. Drawnel, *An Aramaic Wisdom Text from Qumran: A New Interpretation of the Levi Document.* JSJSup 86 (Leiden: Brill, 2004) 262-302.

combine both trends, but it may indicate a wider tendency in Second Temple Jewish law.

A variety of topics of halakhah are treated in the sacrificial section of this text. Specifically, the text is oriented towards the priesthood and its obligations. Priests are expected to remain pure of sexual immorality, to avoid impurity of the dead, and to marry Jews only. Before performing the rituals in the temple, they are required to undertake certain ablutions, which are specified here in detail. The text details the types of wood to be used in the sacrificial offerings and discusses various procedures for the sprinkling and covering of blood, offering the limbs of an animal and their salting. Great attention is given to the exact amounts of wood, salt, flour, oil, wine, and frankincense for various offerings.

From the point of view of its sacrificial halakhah, the *Aramaic Levi Document* does not fit well into the usual mold of legal materials known from Qumran. This is the case, notwithstanding the various points of agreement of this literature with the *Aramaic Levi Document*. The issues presented in those texts, usually in polemical contexts, are not the themes taken up here. Rather, as in rabbinic literature, the issues here are more oriented toward sacrificial procedure, toward filling the gaps in the biblical text in describing the manner in which rites are to be performed. Further, the details of the laws discussed here are as close to rabbinic laws as they are to sectarian ones, and this is true even despite the various parallels to the book of *Jubilees* that have been observed by scholars. Thus, this text helps to situate the debates over issues of sacrificial halakhah much earlier in the Second Temple period than previously realized. This text shows us the richness of the debate over sacrificial law even before the sectarian schism, and even before the Maccabean revolt.

Clearly related is also the *New Jerusalem* material, especially that preserved in Caves 2[14] and 11.[15] These fragments include a description of the temple, apparently from outside in, including the discussion of various utensils, the table for the showbread, sieves for sifting the flour of the Omer offering, cups, and cauldrons, as well as descriptions of the high priest's garments. There are also descriptions of the altar, the slaughtering of sacrificial animals, distribution of certain offerings, and festivals such as Passover. Indeed, certain ritual acts, including the distribution of the showbread, are described as if the narrator were present.[16]

---

14. 2Q24, M. Baillet, J. T. Milik, and R. de Vaux, eds., *Les 'Petites Grottes' de Qumrân*. DJD 3 (Oxford: Clarendon, 1962) 84-89.

15. 11Q18, F. García Martínez et al., *Qumran Cave 11.II (11Q2-18, 11Q20-31)*. DJD 23 (Oxford: Clarendon, 1998) 305-55.

16. F. García Martínez, "New Jerusalem," *EDSS* 2:606-10, esp. 608.

These passages, in their present state of preservation, hardly disclose sufficient details as to indicate the rulings on matters of ritual law followed by the author or authors of the *New Jerusalem*. What is clear, however, is that the original text must have contained numerous such halakhic details indicating the well-developed nature of Jewish legal discourse by the date of its authorship. Although the manuscripts are Herodian, the text was most probably composed in the first half of the second century or, perhaps, as early as the late third century B.C.E.[17]

Second-Century Pre-Qumranian Hebrew Texts

Overall, the rulings of the book of *Jubilees* reflect, as we now know from comparison with the scrolls, the Sadducean/Zadokite approach. Nevertheless, we should expect some differences with rulings resulting either from variety within this trend or from the particular stance of *Jubilees* regarding patriarchal observance of the commandments in their entirety, a claim made much later in rabbinic tradition as well.[18] We will survey here just a few aspects of the halakhah of *Jubilees*.[19]

1. Calendar. *Jubilees* follows the solar calendar known also from *1 Enoch*, the *Temple Scroll* and Qumran calendar texts.[20] It is intimately linked with the requirement that Shavuot fall on Sunday, a view attributed by the rabbis to the Boethusians and rejected roundly by tannaitic tradition (*m. Menaḥ.* 10:3).

2. Festival Calendar. *Jubilees*, like the *Temple Scroll*, has an expanded list of festivals including extra new year and tithing festivals besides the festivals mentioned in the Torah and maintained by the Pharisaic-rabbinic tradition. This expanded set of festivals is shared with the *Temple Scroll* and some of the other Qumran sources and calendars.[21]

3. Intermarriage. Clearly the Hellenistic ambience led to the strong polemic here against intermarriage that concurred with the rulings of Ezra and

---

17. García Martínez, "New Jerusalem," 2:610.
18. *M. Qidd.* 4:4, a later addition to the Mishnah. Cf. *b. Yoma* 28b.
19. C. Albeck, *Das Buch der Jubiläen und die Halacha*. Siebenundvierzigster Bericht der Hochschule für die Wissenschaft des Judentums in Berlin, 1930.
20. Cf. S. Talmon, J. Ben-Dov, and U. Glessmer, *Qumran Cave 4: XVI: Calendrical Texts*. DJD 21 (Oxford: Clarendon, 2001) 1-166; J. C. VanderKam, *Calendars in the Dead Sea Scrolls: Measuring Time* (London: Routledge, 1998).
21. Cf. L. H. Schiffman, "The Sacrificial System of the *Temple Scroll* and the *Book of Jubilees*," in *SBLSP 1985*, ed. K. H. Richards, 217-33 (Atlanta: Scholars, 1985); Yadin, *Temple Scroll*, 1:89-137.

Nehemiah. These books cited the Torah as their authority for the prohibition of all marriage between Jews and non-Jews.

4. Concept of Revelation. Here revelation occurs with an angelic intermediary but as a onetime experience.[22] The revealed book is essentially a rewritten Torah, itself showing the literary and, hence, theological approach of rewritten Torah common at Qumran and, apparently, in wider sectarian circles. This literary feature also seems to group *Jubilees* with the Saducean/Zadokite halakhic trend even if a fragment of this text was found among the otherwise Pharisaic-type remains of Masada.[23]

Sources of MMT and the Temple Scroll

The final group of materials to be considered here are the sources of MMT and the *Temple Scroll*. We begin with the issue of the *Temple Scroll* because here the discussion revolves largely around literary sources.

The author of the *Temple Scroll* was actually a redactor, who had at his disposal a variety of sources. These included the purity source, the architectural plan of the temple, the Law of the King, and the Deuteronomic paraphrase at the end of the scroll, which he himself seems to have authored.[24] Evidence greatly favors dating the completed scroll to ca. 120 B.C.E. at the latest.[25] Because of many agreements between this scroll and MMT, it seems that the sources of the *Temple Scroll*, which in no way reflect the sectarian posture of the full-fledged sect of the Hasmonean period, represent the pre-Maccabean heritage of the Sadducean/Zadokite trend, or of some subgroup within it. If so, we can mention a variety of topics which are part of this legal tradition and must be roughly contemporaneous with *Jubilees*.

---

22. Cf. J. C. VanderKam, "The Putative Author of the Book of Jubilees," *JSS* 26 (1981) 209-17; and in H. Attridge et al., *Qumran Cave 4.VIII, Parabiblical Texts, Part I.* DJD 13 (Oxford: Clarendon, 1994) 12.

23. S. Talmon, "Hebrew Fragments from Masada," in *Masada VI: Yigael Yadin Excavations 1963-1965: Final Reports*, ed. Talmon, with C. Newsom and Y. Yadin (Jerusalem: Israel Exploration Society, Hebrew University of Jerusalem, 1999) 117-19.

24. A. M. Wilson and L. Wills, "Literary Sources of the Temple Scroll," *HTR* 75 (1982) 275-88; M. O. Wise, *A Critical Study of the Temple Scroll from Qumran Cave 11*. SAOC 49 (Chicago: Oriental Institute, University of Chicago, 1990) 155-203.

25. Yadin, *Temple Scroll*, 1:386-90; cf. M. Hengel, J. H. Charlesworth, and D. Mendels, "The Polemical Character of 'On Kingship' in the Temple Scroll: An Attempt at Dating 11QTemple," *JJS* 37 (1986) 28-38; L. H. Schiffman, "The King, His Guard, and the Royal Council in the *Temple Scroll*," *PAAJR* 54 (1987) 237-59.

Pre-Maccabean Halakhah in the Dead Sea Scrolls and the Biblical Tradition

1. Calendar. These sources follow the expanded solar calendar as mentioned above.

2. Purity. These sources, like MMT, follow the Sadducean view regarding the *ṭevul yom,* considering one on the last day of his or her purification ritual as absolutely impure until sundown.[26] This view is identified with Sadducees and appears in the Mishnah[27] and in dispute form in MMT.[28]

3. The *Temple Scroll* seeks, like the book of Ezekiel, to propose an expanded temple plan with an added, gargantuan third courtyard.[29] This priestly-type approach seems to be sectarian in its use of the third courtyard to raise the level of all the purity regulations of the temple and distance impurity from the sancta.[30]

4. Theological basis. The various sources of the scroll share the theological notion of a onetime revelation of a rewritten Torah. This means that the author/redactor did not have an oral law concept. Further, these sources share the Deuteronomic name theology, according to which God's presence is termed his "name" and it imparts sanctity to the land, the city of Jerusalem, and the temple.[31]

5. Midrashic method. These texts show an exegetical system of halakhic midrash that hews close to the literal meaning, or at least, for the most part, closer to it than in the Pharisaic-rabbinic materials. While we cannot describe this approach in detail here, it has certain parallels to that used in the books of Ezra and Nehemiah for halakhic midrash, and also in the *Zadokite Fragments (Damascus Document)* and other apodictic Qumran texts. Much of this exegesis is based on analogy to parallel passages or language (like rabbinic *heqesh*) or harmonization of material on one subject which is scattered in the Torah.[32]

---

26. L. H. Schiffman, "Pharisaic and Sadducean Halakhah in Light of the Dead Sea Scrolls: The Case of Ṭevul Yom," *DSD* 1 (1994) 285-99.

27. M. Parah 3:1.

28. E. Qimron and J. Strugnell, *Qumran Cave 4. V: Miqṣat Ma'aśe ha-Torah*. DJD 10 (Oxford: Clarendon, 1994) 152-54.

29. M. Broshi, "The Gigantic Dimensions of the Visionary Temple in the Temple Scroll," *BAR* 13/6 (1987) 36-37; L. H. Schiffman, "Architecture and Law: The Temple and Its Courtyards in the *Temple Scroll,*" in *From Ancient Israel to Modern Judaism: Intellect in Quest of Understanding: Essays in Honor of Marvin Fox,* ed. J. Neusner, E. S. Frerichs, and N. M. Sarna, 1:267-84. BJS 159 (Atlanta: Scholars, 1989); Yadin, *Temple Scroll,* 1:260-76; J. Maier, *The Temple Scroll: An Introduction, Translation & Commentary.* JSOTSup 34 (Sheffield: JSOT, 1985) 91-115.

30. L. H. Schiffman, "Exclusion from the Sanctuary and the City of the Sanctuary in the *Temple Scroll,*" *HAR* 9 (1985) 301-20.

31. L. H. Schiffman, "The Theology of the Temple Scroll," *JQR* 85 (Qumran Studies, 1994) 109-23.

32. J. Milgrom, "The Scriptural Foundations and Derivations in the Laws of Purity of the

Yet freer and more complex exegesis is also present. In our view this is the Sadducean/Zadokite method that we have effectively recovered in the pre-Maccabean sources of the *Temple Scroll*.

Closely related is the tradition (or perhaps literary sources such as those we have just discussed) that lies behind the rulings of MMT. But we are also able to learn here about the Pharisaic approach in this period as well.

1. Calendar. MMT assumes a sectarian calendar. For this reason, a scribe affixed a calendar to the beginning of the text in one manuscript (4Q394).[33] Although the polemic does not indicate the Pharisaic view on this matter, we know it from rabbinic literature.

2. Purity. Here we encounter the prohibition of the *tevul yom* and some other laws known from rabbinic literature to be Sadducean points of view. The dispute form of MMT indicates the opposing view, known to us to be Pharisaic.[34]

3. Dispute form. Here we have dispute statements that are essentially apodictic, as in some later, tannaitic forms. We do not know for certain if the dispute form was also part of the pre-Maccabean heritage of the text, which was composed by 152 B.C.E. in our view.[35] In any case, we would assume that the apodictic formulation did predate the Hasmonean period.

4. Sacrificial laws. Several sacrificial laws of this text appear to be Sadducean based on opposite views expressed in rabbinic literature.[36] It seems, therefore, that a number of previously unknown Pharisee-Sadducee disputes have been uncovered here, and these enrich our knowledge of disputes that existed in pre-Hasmonean times.[37]

Temple Scroll," in *Archaeology and History in the Dead Sea Scrolls: The New York University Conference in Memory of Yigael Yadin*, ed. L. H. Schiffman, 83-99. JSOTSup 8. JSOT/ASOR Monographs 2 (Sheffield: JSOT, 1990).

33. Qimron and Strugnell, DJD 10:44-45, 109-10.

34. Y. Sussmann, "The History of the Halakha and the Dead Sea Scrolls: Preliminary Talmudic Observations on *Miqṣat Ma'aśe ha-Torah* (4QMMT)," in DJD 10:179-200.

35. L. H. Schiffman, "The New *Halakhic Letter* (4QMMT) and the Origins of the Dead Sea Sect," *BA* 53 (1990) 64-73.

36. Cf. L. H. Schiffman, "*Miqṣat Ma'aśeh ha-Torah* and the *Temple Scroll*," *RevQ* 14 (The Texts of Qumran and the History of the Community: Proceedings of the Groningen Congress on the Dead Sea Scrolls 3, 1990) 435-57.

37. We cannot argue for a pre-Hasmonean dating of the text's ideology contained in the hortatory section at the end (Qimron and Strugnell, DJD 10:111-12). It appears to address the issues presented by the circumstances of the Hasmonean takeover of the high priesthood in early Hasmonean times.

Historical Extrapolation

The Persian period was one in which we can speak of several fundamental issues in the history of Jewish law. We will consider a few of the wider historical issues related to our topic.

1. The Samaritan schism and the internal history of Samaritanism must remain beyond the scope of this presentation. It is enough to observe that, in contrast to many scholars, we see Samaritanism as beginning in the biblical period, before the canonization of the Prophets and the Writings. This group developed an early stance on Torah law that is for the most part not researchable. In light of later parallels with Sadducean (and Karaite) law, it appears that besides the basic dispute over who is the real Israel (*Verus Israel*) there must also have been disputes based on interpretation of the Torah, with the Samaritans taking a more literalist view than the Judeans. Further, we can expect that some rules derived in Ezra and Nehemiah from earlier Prophetic writings, for example, those pertaining to Sabbath observance, may not have been accepted by the Samaritans for whom the Prophets were not part of the canon.

2. The need for Ezra to remove foreign wives and Nehemiah to stop marketplaces from operating on the outskirts of Jerusalem on the Sabbath indicates that many Judeans followed a less restrictive interpretation of their Jewish obligations than those of the religious and political leadership. These differences may be the result partly of not having accepted post-Torah laws, as in the case of some Sabbath restrictions, but may also be the result of some laws, especially those proclaimed in Nehemiah's covenant renewal ceremony, having been newly created.

3. By this time, the fundamental notion that biblical exegesis was at the root of legal decision-making had become the norm, as it would remain among all Jewish groups until today. This role is also observable in 2 Chr 35:13 in the exegesis of passages from Exodus and Deuteronomy regarding how to prepare the Paschal Lamb (Exod 12:8, Deut 16:7). Such interpretations are at the root of all forms of postbiblical Jewish law, and the differences in method, form, and theory of exegesis constitute one of the main separators between the various Jewish groups.

4. Later talmudic sources attribute various laws to a group called the Men of the Great Assembly. They are identified in rabbinic literature[38] as the

---

38. L. Finkelstein, *Ha-Perushim ve-Anshe Keneset ha-Gedolah (The Pharisees and the Men of the Great Synagogue).* Texts and Studies of the Jewish Theological Seminary of America 15 (New York: Jewish Theological Seminary of America, 1950) 45-50.

associates of Ezra and Nehemiah, although some nineteenth- to twentieth-century Judaic scholars extended them into an ongoing group meant to bridge the gap between, we might say, the Hebrew Bible and the Hellenistic period.[39] There simply is no evidence for this proposal, one way or another. All these statements show that the laws attributed to the Men of the Great Assembly were assumed by the rabbis to be pretannaitic and quite ancient. Effectively, these claims simply assert the antiquity of the particular regulations.

As the Persian period gave way to the Hellenistic, and the Jews faced issues of Hellenization, it seems that the major issues that characterized the Pharisaic and Sadducean trends of Jewish law came to the fore. It is most likely that the Sadducean priesthood followed many of the rulings proposed in MMT and in the sources of the *Temple Scroll*. This explains the abrupt change that apparently took place in 152 B.C.E. when affairs were settled in favor of the Pharisees upon Jonathan the Hasmonean's ascension as high priest.

The polemics of MMT and the *Temple Scroll* and related documents, and even the *Aramaic Levi Document*, show without question that many Pharisaic laws must have already been in practice in the pre-Maccabean period. This squares with a reading of the chain of tradition in *m. Abot* 1; *m. Ḥag.* 2:2; and *t. Ḥag.* 2:2 as bearing some historical truth. What we are essentially arguing is that certain fundamentals of Pharisaic views on temple and purity issues, as well as a host of other halakhic topics, already existed not only in the Hasmonean period but even before.

Congruent with this theory is the presentation of the Sadducean/Zadokite approach in both abstract, Mishnah-like Qumran works and in a midrash-like rewritten Bible form in others, and even in dispute form in MMT. We have to assume (I admit this is unprovable) that the Pharisaic approach was already being transmitted in several forms in the pre-Maccabean period. This assumption had been the norm in Judaic studies before the mid-twentieth century, but was then discarded as unproven. It seems to me, in light of the Qumran scrolls, when compared with the Persian-period biblical materials, that we must return to the older position that the two forms, midrash and Mishnah, exegetical and abstract, existed in pre-Maccabean times.[40]

Closely related is the observation that in both competing trends of halakhah in this period, the foundation of all legal rulings was clearly the biblical exegetical process. This is common to both the Sadducean/Zadokite and

---

39. Finkelstein, *Ha-Perushim ve-Anshe Keneset ha-Gedolah*, 51-77.

40. J. Z. Lauterbach, "Midrash and Mishnah," *JQR* N.S. 5 (1914/15) 503-27; 6 (1915/16) 23-95, 303-23; E. E. Urbach, "Ha-Derashah ke-Yesod ha-Halakhah u-Ve'ayat ha-Soferim," *Tarbiz* 27 (1957/58) 166-82.

Pharisaic-rabbinic approaches and is obvious to us, but today it needs to be said anyhow in light of some views of earlier scholars to the effect that the biblical derivations constitute post hoc justifications for existing laws. While such processes no doubt occurred to some extent, we should realize that this does not obviate the fact that the root of the fundamental issues that divide the trends of law is based on specific issues of interpretation, and these, in turn, are influenced by the exegetical methodologies that must have developed extensively between the end of the Persian period and the Maccabean period.

In our view there is no question that during the pre-Maccabean period two trends were certainly in existence. They were first documented directly in Josephus's explanation of the sects in the Hasmonean period and then in MMT and in the inherent polemic of the sources of the *Temple Scroll*, well before the sectarian protest against Hasmonean policies and the removal of some Jews to Qumran.

It needs to be emphasized that much of what some scholars see as later developments, in both "sectarian" and Pharisaic-rabbinic materials, are actually pre-Maccabean. If so, we can see the Hasmonean period, and the political-historical background of this period, as providing a fertile ground for gathering and developing traditions and competing approaches that had been created earlier.

Conclusion

We have attempted to trace the extant sources regarding Jewish law in the pre-Maccabean period from the Persian period through the years leading up to the Maccabean revolt. We have also tried to reconstruct the outlines of a history of Jewish law in the same period. Several conclusions result from this reconstruction:

1. Issues of biblical interpretation underlie halakhic derivations and disputes from the early Second Temple period through the Maccabean revolt.

2. The origins of the Pharisee/Sadducee halakhic disagreement go back into the early Hellenistic period, even if we cannot be more specific.

3. The abstract and biblically based systems for studying and codifying Jewish law were both widespread throughout this period, apparently in both major trends of Jewish law.

4. At least for the Hellenistic part of our period, we can identify two competing trends, the Pharisaic-protorabbinic and the Sadducee/Zadokite. These trends entered into various disputes, apparently sometimes preserved

in dispute form, at least in the case of MMT and, for theological issues, in Josephus's three-way comparison of the sects.

5. By extrapolation from some polemics and disputes in the scrolls, and by triangulation with earlier materials in the Hebrew Bible, it can be shown that there is a much earlier history to the Pharisaic approach to Jewish law than is documented in tannaitic literature. In fact, this material, when considered in light of later rabbinic accounts, calls on us to reconsider the possible historicity of the early dating of some Pharisaic-rabbinic laws in talmudic sources, some of which, by the way, are also mentioned in the New Testament.

6. As a result of the discovery of the Dead Sea Scrolls, the study of biblical law can now be widened to include detailed study of its development beyond the era of the composition of the biblical legal materials and their codification. We are now able to trace the continued development of the heritage of these texts, even beyond their time of composition. In doing so, we may get help from the later transmission and exegesis of these texts in understanding their original meaning in their original literary setting. But there is no question that tracing the history of their subsequent exegesis is allowing us to fill in our picture of Jewish law and tradition in the pre-Maccabean period.

CHAPTER 11

Contemporizing Halakhic Exegesis in the Dead Sea Scrolls

Scholars of the Dead Sea Scrolls and related literature have become accustomed to the notion that the Qumran sectarians practiced a form of contemporizing exegesis for prophetic books and the Psalms known as pesher.[1] This form of exegesis involves the understanding of ancient — First Temple–period — texts of prophecy as if they related to the present-day times of the authors of the pesher texts. Further, the pesher literature makes the claim that the inspired interpreter — the pesharist, in our case the priestly Teacher of Righteousness[2] — was the only one to know the true meaning of the passage in question. The pesher form of exegesis, and the texts that flowed from it, were understood to provide an accurate interpretation of an ancient prophet, claiming that his words actually applied, not to the long-ancient past in which he lived, but to the present Greco-Roman period. This approach was in turn founded on certain specific methods of hermeneutical manipulation, yielding a newly relevant prophetic message.

From the early days of Qumran research, scholars have observed the relationship of this kind of interpretation to certain New Testament passages in which the main point is to show that Jesus' life, career, and death had been foretold by the Israelite prophets.[3] Despite the tendentiousness of this herme-

---

1. M. P. Horgan, *Pesharim: Qumran Interpretations of Biblical Books*. CBQMS 8 (Washington: Catholic Biblical Association of America, 1979) 229-59; W. H. Brownlee, *The Midrash Pesher of Habakkuk*. SBLMS 24 (Missoula: Scholars, 1979) 23-36; L. H. Schiffman, *Reclaiming the Dead Sea Scrolls: The History of Judaism, the Background of Christianity, the Lost Library of Qumran* (Philadelphia: Jewish Publication Society, 1994; repr. ABRL [New York: Doubleday, 1995]) 223-41.

2. 1QpHab 2:5-10; 7:1-5.

3. Cf. E. E. Ellis, "Biblical Interpretation in the New Testament Church," in *Mikra: Text,*

neutic, it shared with the equally tendentious and presentist pesher literature the claim that the words of the Hebrew biblical prophets were of direct relevance to the period of the exegete.

The present study seeks to call attention to some examples in the Dead Sea Scrolls of a similar phenomenon in legal, halakhic exegesis. We have in mind the transference of material from its original scriptural relevance to a new, present Second Temple–period context. In these cases, the original historical context of the legislation gives way to a reality that is thrust upon it by the historical circumstances and the reigning interpretation. These passages now assume a meaning perhaps not originally intended but now dominant in sectarian halakhic textual tradition.

The Temple Scroll

We begin with what may be seen as a macro version of this phenomenon, the composition and redaction of the *Temple Scroll*.[4] In the finished scroll, we effectively see a translation of law from the desert period — that of the Levitical code for the most part — from tabernacle to temple setting. This process has numerous ramifications, but the clearest is the temple plan itself. The author of the temple source — the architectural plan of the expanded temple — sought to take the tabernacle and desert camp (on which more below) and use it as a scriptural model to create a "modern" (i.e., Hellenistic-period) ideal plan for a Jewish temple. He therefore had to translate, with the help of material from Kings, Ezekiel, and Chronicles, the details of the tabernacle into specific architectural requirements. He based his plan on a combination of biblical interpretations of the relevant passages and the architectural norms of his day. But the final product of his temple plan created an up-to-date way of realizing the halakhic requirements of the Bible in his own age.[5]

Because this was an ideological plan, the author expected that he could

---

Translation, Reading and Interpretation of the Hebrew Bible in Ancient Judaism and Early Christianity, ed. M. J. Mulder, 691-725. CRINT 1 (Minneapolis: Fortress, 1990).

4. See the editions of Y. Yadin, *The Temple Scroll*. 3 vols. (Jerusalem: Israel Exploration Society and Shrine of the Book, 1983); and E. Qimron, *The Temple Scroll: A Critical Edition with Extensive Reconstructions* (Beersheva: Ben-Gurion University of the Negev and Jerusalem: Israel Exploration Society, 1996).

5. L. H. Schiffman, "Architecture and Law: The Temple and Its Courtyards in the *Temple Scroll*," in *From Ancient Israel to Modern Judaism: Intellect in Quest of Understanding: Essays in Honor of Marvin Fox*, ed. J. Neusner, E. S. Frerichs, and N. M. Sarna, 1:267-84. BJS 159 (Atlanta: Scholars, 1989).

establish the contours of the demographics of the country, even to the point of expecting people to dwell in cities in houses of stones (11QTemple 50:12).[6] This requirement represented his derivation from the Torah's laws of stone homes that had contracted mildew *(sara'at)* of a chronic type (Lev 14:33-57) and other such material in the Bible.

Another good example of this overall hermeneutic of transformation to the author's own time is that of the bringing up to date of the Torah's law of the king that takes place in the so-called Law of the King in the *Temple Scroll*.[7] Here an entire section of Deuteronomy dealing with the appointment of a king, his duties, obligations, the laws of war, and other such matters has been transmogrified by this form of contemporizing exegesis into a proposed ideal political order for Hasmonean-period Judea. This is essentially a call for governmental reform, which was actually never heard, but the author intended this as a full-fledged "interpretation" of the commands of the Torah on this matter.

These examples will suffice for us to remark on how this phenomenon encompassed for the author/redactor the entirety of the Torah. Often gathering together various sections on one topic, based as they are on versions of what biblical criticism considers to be the sources of the Torah, the scroll fuses them together into a sort of companion Torah to the original, canonical text.[8] The very shape of this final product, starting at the end of Leviticus with the tabernacle description and summarizing the law on all kinds of matters relating to temple, sacrifice, political affairs, marital law, etc., points to the whole document as a statement on how God's original Torah calls on a Jew to live in the troubled times in which the author/redactor lived.[9] He uses halakhic

---

6. L. H. Schiffman, "Sacred Space: The Land of Israel in the *Temple Scroll*," in *Biblical Archaeology Today 1990: Proceedings of the Second International Congress on Biblical Archaeology*, ed. A. Biran and J. Aviram, 398-410 (Jerusalem: Israel Exploration Society, 1993).

7. Yadin, *Temple Scroll*, 1:344-62; L. H. Schiffman, "The King, His Guard, and the Royal Council in the *Temple Scroll*," *PAAJR* 54 (1987) 237-59; M. Weinfeld, "'Megillat Miqdash' 'o 'Torah la-Melekh,'" *Shnaton* 3 (1978/79) 214-37 [Eng. trans. "The Temple Scroll or 'The Law of the King,'" in *Normative and Sectarian Judaism in the Second Temple Period* (London: T. & T. Clark, 2005) 158-85].

8. Yadin, *The Temple Scroll*, 1:73-77; J. Milgrom, "The Scriptural Foundations and Deviations in the Laws of Purity of the Temple Scroll," in *Archaeology and History in the Dead Sea Scrolls: The New York University Conference in Memory of Yigael Yadin*, ed. L. H. Schiffman, 83-99. JSOTSup 8. JSOT/ASOR Monographs 2 (Sheffield: JSOT, 1990); "The Qumran Cult: Its Exegetical Principles," in *Temple Scroll Studies*, ed. G. J. Brooke, 165-80. JSPSup 7 (Sheffield: Sheffield Academic, 1989).

9. H. Najman, *Seconding Sinai: The Development of Mosaic Discourse in Second Temple Judaism*. JSJSup 77 (Leiden: Brill, 2003), 43-53, notes that the author did not intend to replace the original Torah, only to supplement it.

pseudepigraphy — placing his own ideas and those of the sources effectively in the mouth of God — in order to present his own views for the present — an update for contemporary times of God's own words.[10]

The Sadducean/Zadokite halakhic trend, like the Pharisaic-rabbinic,[11] faced a major challenge because of the transfer of Jewish life from the desert to the land of Israel. Both trends had to explain how the Torah's laws for the desert camp and tabernacle could be observed in an environment in which Jews now lived in the city of Jerusalem and the surrounding hinterland of the land of Israel. Yet the Torah contained legislation primarily assuming the desert camp. Much of this legislation seemed to contradict itself regarding the sanctity of the camp, and it seems that both trends found a similar, if not actually common solution. This solution, expressed in similar terms in the *Temple Scroll*, 4QMMT and tannaitic sources, essentially explains the Bible's laws in a contemporizing fashion. This interpretation has two steps: differentiation followed by contemporization.

The first stage, that of differentiation, was accomplished by dividing the "camp" references into three types. These included, if we may use the admittedly anachronistic tannaitic terminology, the camp of the divine presence, the camp of the Levites, and the camp of Israel.[12] These, in turn, refer to the tabernacle itself, the area surrounding it that was inhabited by the Levites in the desert, and the camp of Israel, that is, of the rest of the tribes that surrounded the tabernacle and tribe of Levi. This complex exegesis, of which I have given here the briefest of sketches, is what I have termed differentiation, that is, differentiating the various usages of "camp" one from the other. Whether this exegesis accords with the plain meaning of the text is not our concern here.

The next stage was that of contemporization. Here the map of camps

---

10. L. H. Schiffman, "The Temple Scroll and the Halakhic Pseudepigrapha of the Second Temple Period," in *Pseudepigraphic Perspectives: The Apocrypha and Pseudepigrapha in Light of the Dead Sea Scrolls: Proceedings of the International Symposium of the Orion Center for the Study of the Dead Sea Scrolls and Associated Literature, 12-14 January, 1997,* ed. E. G. Chazon, M. Stone, and A. Pinnick, 121-31. STDJ 31 (Leiden: Brill, 1999). Cf. M. J. Bernstein, "Pseudepigraphy in the Qumran Scrolls: Categories and Functions," in *Pseudepigraphic Perspectives,* 1-26.

11. Cf. Y. Sussmann, "Ḥeqer Toldedot ha-Halakhah u-Megillot Midbar Yehudah: Hirhurim Talmudiyim Rishonim le-'Or Megillat Miqṣat Ma'aśe ha-Torah," *Tarbiz* 59 (1989/1990) 11-77. A shortened English version is available as "The History of the Halakha and the Dead Sea Scrolls: Preliminary Talmudic Observations on Miqṣat Ma'aśe ha-Torah (4QMMT)," in E. Qimron and J. Strugnell, *Qumran Cave 4.V: Miqṣat Ma'aśe ha-Torah.* DJD 10 (Oxford: Clarendon, 1994) 179-200.

12. T. *Kelim B. Qam.* 1:12; *Sifre* Num Naso 1; *Num. Rab.* 7:8; b. *Zebaḥ.* 116b; cf. Maimonides, *Hilkhot Bet ha-Beḥirah* 7:14.

was transferred from the Sinai Desert to the city of Jerusalem and the surrounding land of Israel. In this case, it was decided that the temple, whatever its architectural plan, was equivalent in sanctity to the tabernacle, the camp of God's presence; the *temenos* (or Temple Mount) was equivalent to the camp of the Levites; and the city of Jerusalem was equivalent to the camp of Israel. At least so it was for the Tannaim and the authors of MMT. But the *Temple Scroll* went further, with its plan of a three-court temple instead of the two-court tabernacle and Solomonic structures. It placed the camp of Israel inside its outer court, so that the *temenos* became a model of the desert camp, and created named gates for the various tribes in accord with the patterns of the original (or imagined) desert camp.[13]

In either case, after the first process of differentiating the camps, these exegetes updated and so contemporized the Scriptures by means of interpretation, applying in this way biblical law to the circumstances of their own day.

The Admonition of the Zadokite Fragments

A somewhat different form of contemporizing halakhic exegesis occurs in polemical context, as exemplified by the Admonition of the *Zadokite Fragments (Damascus Document)*.[14] In this text, several halakhic rulings are delivered in the context of an attack on others, most notably the Pharisees, who are seen as going astray from the true path of the Torah (CD 4:17–5:11). What is interesting here is that these legal interpretations come in close proximity to pesher interpretations that are similarly polemical (4:12-17). In this case, the contemporizing aspect consists not in any outright allusions to the author's own period. Rather, it is in the selection of the halakhic points of dispute and the claim by the Qumran text that the author's interpretation of the law is necessarily correct. These subjects are clearly sectarian markers — better, hot button issues — that set the sectarians off from their opponents.

---

13. L. H. Schiffman, "Exclusion from the Sanctuary and the City of the Sanctuary in the Temple Scroll," *HAR* 9 (1985) 301-20. Cf. S. Talmon, "The 'Desert Motif' in the Bible and in Qumran Literature," in *Biblical Motifs: Origins and Transformations*, ed. A. Altmann, 55-63. Studies and Texts 3 (Cambridge, MA: Harvard University Press, 1966); repr. in Talmon, *Literary Studies in the Hebrew Bible: Form and Content: Collected Studies* (Leiden: Brill, 1993) 216-54.

14. E. Qimron, "The Text of CDC," in *The Damascus Document Reconsidered*, ed. M. Broshi, 9-49 (Jerusalem: Israel Exploration Society, Shrine of the Book, Israel Museum, 1992); J. M. Baumgarten, *Qumran Cave 4.XIII: The Damascus Document (4Q266-273)*. DJD 18 (Oxford: Clarendon, 1996). See Baumgarten, DJD 18:3 for a table of correspondences of the Qumran manuscripts of the Admonition to the genizah text.

Therefore they fulfill a polemical purpose. The halakhic exegesis is therefore employed to support a ruling that itself is of highly contemporary importance, especially to the community that assembled the Qumran scrolls.

Two examples of this phenomenon, quite well known as they are, will suffice. The sectarians cite the biblical accounts of creation and the flood to justify the claim that polygamy is forbidden (CD 5:1). We all know that there is a dispute about the meaning of the word בחייהם, "in their (masc.) lifetimes." I take it to mean that divorce is permitted but remarriage forbidden unless the spouse dies. Once marriage takes place, the spouses are connected until death (as the Protestants say at weddings, "until death do us part"). Whether one agrees with this view of בחייהם or not, there is no question that the simultaneous marriage of one man to more than one woman is seen as forbidden. This view is, of course, totally at variance with the explicit statement of the Torah and its narratives. This prohibition was later accepted by early Christianity, but was actually really new in Second Temple–period Judaism. The exegesis put forward here is intended to justify a new, i.e., contemporary halakhic ruling.

The second example I wish to put forward is also in the area of marriage law. The sectarians, again like Christians after them,[15] forbade marriage to one's niece (CD 5:8; 11QTemple 66:16-17 = 4Q524 15-22 4;[16] 4Q251 17 2-3[17]), a practice that one later rabbi particularly praised.[18] This prohibition was said to have been derived from a biblical law, namely that a woman may not marry her nephew (= a man to his aunt). We are told by the *Zadokite Fragments* (CD 5:9-10) that the biblical laws of consanguineous marriage are stated from the point of view of the male, with the reverse prohibition assumed. This statement is in fact false, as can be seen from the examination of the two lists of prohibited consanguineous marriages in Leviticus 18 and 20 and their Qumran versions and adaptations. In other words, this again is an exegesis designed to support a new, sectarian prohibition. This is true of this and our previous example, even if other sects, e.g., Christianity, accepted the same views.

These examples need to be seen in light of what we know of the overall theory of "revealed" and "hidden" law, *nigleh* and *nistar*, in Qumran sectarian

---

15. C. Rabin, *Qumran Studies*. Scripta Judaica 2 (London: Oxford University Press, 1957) 91-93.

16. É. Puech, *Qumrân Grotte 4.XVIII: Textes hébreux (4Q521-4Q528, 4Q576-4Q579)*. DJD 25 (Oxford: Clarendon, 1998) 103-7.

17. E. Larson, M. R. Lehmann, and L. H. Schiffman in J. M. Baumgarten et al., *Qumran Cave 4.XXV: Halakhic Texts*. DJD 35 (Oxford: Clarendon, 1999) 45-46.

18. B. *Yebam.* 62b; y. *Giṭ.* 83a; b. *Sanh.* 76b; y. *Yebam.* 13:2 (13c). Such a marriage is recorded in *Ant.* 12.186.

documents. The sect divided the law into two categories — the *nigleh*, "revealed," and the *nistar*, "hidden." The revealed laws were known to all Israel, for they were manifest in Scripture, but the hidden laws were known only to the sect and were revealed solely through sectarian exegesis. The notion of revealed and hidden laws discloses to us a system of sectarian legal theology. The revealed law — that is, the Torah and the words of the Prophets — was known by all of Israel, who, nonetheless, violated it. The hidden, on the other hand, was known only to the sect. These hidden laws constituted the very points of disagreement around which the sect coalesced. The written Torah, originally revealed by God, had been modified later by his prophets through their divine visions. The hidden law, the *nistar*, had also developed over time and would continue to change, but it did not originate at the same time as the revealed Torah. Rather, it represented God's constant, ongoing revelation of Torah interpretation disclosed to the sectarians during and through their study sessions. These two types of law complemented each other and together made up the system of Jewish law as understood and practiced by the sect.[19] This system of supplementing the written Torah allowed for derivation of divinely-inspired biblical legal interpretations. A few passages in the scrolls indicate that these legal interpretations were considered to be עת ועת or עת בעת, "for each time" (CD 12:21, 1QS 9:13), or לפי העתים, "for the (specific) times" (1QS 9:13). This indicates a realization that the law develops and changes through this interpretive technique. Apparently, the sectarians were aware that they practiced contemporizing biblical exegesis, even as part of their polemical program against their opponents.

Conclusion

I have tried to illustrate here a number of examples of how the Qumran documents make use of a variety of techniques to effectively update the traditions of the Bible. Techniques of this kind could be illustrated from inner biblical exegesis as well as from later Jewish legal traditions. Exegesis, in every phase of the history of Judaism, was harnessed both to preserve and to develop the heritage of the past. Along with the well-known phenomenon of contemporizing interpretation of the Prophets and Psalms in Qumran pesher texts, we need to recognize that such exegesis also exists in halakhic texts, sometimes even in cases in which the texts claim the opposite. Law, exegesis, and history can never be separated.

---

19. L. H. Schiffman, *The Halakhah at Qumran*. SJLA 16 (Leiden: Brill, 1975) 22-32.

CHAPTER 12

Halakhic Elements in 4QInstruction

Biblical scholars have long observed that wisdom literature includes substantially less particularistic Israelite teaching than does the rest of biblical literature.[1] In line with this observation, which itself needs to be reevaluated more carefully, we should not be surprised to see that the same is the case with most of the sapiential literature that has been found at Qumran.[2] The more universal or pan-ancient Near Eastern aspects of these teachings are to be expected. Nonetheless, we still need to pay attention to the particularly Jewish aspects of this literature, as well as to aspects that can help us to determine whether Qumran wisdom literature is sectarian in character or not.

One of the elements that can contribute to such an inquiry is the small amount of halakhic material found in these texts, particularly in 4QInstruction (4Q415-418a, 418c(?), 423) in its various manuscripts.[3] At the outset it will be only fair to say that there is very little to consider. We will concentrate here on the mention of woman's oaths and vows, the rules of mixed species *(kil'ayim),* and the law of firstborn animals, and we may note here that there is some discussion of weights and measures, but not in a halakhic con-

---

1. R. E. Murphy, "Wisdom in the Old Testament," *ABD* 6:922.

2. See J. I. Kampen, "The Diverse Aspects of Wisdom in the Qumran Texts," in *The Dead Sea Scrolls after Fifty Years,* ed. P. W. Flint and J. C. VanderKam, 1:211-43 (Leiden: Brill, 1998); L. H. Schiffman, *Reclaiming the Dead Sea Scrolls: The History of Judaism, the Background of Christianity, the Lost Library of Qumran* (Philadelphia: Jewish Publication Society, 1994; repr. ABRL [New York: Doubleday, 1995]) 197-210; D. J. Harrington, *Wisdom Texts from Qumran* (London: Routledge, 1996).

3. J. Strugnell, D. J. Harrington, and T. Elgvin, *Qumran Cave 4.XXIV: Sapiential Texts, Part 2.* DJD 34 (Oxford: Clarendon, 1999) 1-495, 501-39.

text.[4] We should note also that Torleif Elgvin has analyzed a fragmentary passage (4Q421 12 1-5) regarding the requirements for entrance into the temple that for some reason found its way into a sapiential text, 4QWays of Righteousness[b].[5]

The Vows of a Married Woman

Our text contains explicit reference to the annulment by a husband of the vows of his wife, a topic taken up in Num 30:7-9. The text tells us, according to a composite of 4Q416 2 iv 8-10 and 4Q 418 10 8-10:

> And every binding oath of hers to vow a vo[w], (you must) annul with an utterance of your mouth. According to your free will cancel [it so tha]t [she not do (it). With the utterance] of your mouth excuse her [. . .] in order that she not make man[y vows.[6]

This passage comes in the context of discussion of marriage and how a man should treat his wife. The passage is written from the male perspective, as is to be expected of a text from this period. Yet it must be stressed that this text is written from the point of view of a community in which marriage and family are the norm, a matter to which we will return below. The passage immediately preceding, quoting Gen 2:24, speaks of a man's leaving his parents to cleave to his wife and of the husband's dominant role in the family. Also, the text notes that one has to expect that his own daughter will go through the same process and cleave to her husband. Further, anyone else who took this dominant role regarding another's wife has "moved his boundaries" (cf. Deut 27:17; 19:14), trespassing the other man's property. A person is expected to be totally at one with his wife. He is expected to "rule over" or "control" (משל) his wife to make sure that she does not increase (or make a large number of) vows and votive pledges.

The Bible includes laws of oaths and vows in Num 30:3-16 and Deut 23:22-24. We have elsewhere analyzed in detail the realization of these laws and their interpretation in CD 16:6-13, the laws of the שבועת אסר ("binding

---

4. See Strugnell, Harrington, and Elgvin, DJD 34:59, following the interpretation of E. Qimron.

5. T. Elgvin et al., *Qumran Cave 4.XV: Sapiential Texts, Part 1*. DJD 20 (Oxford: Clarendon, 1997) 197-200. Elgvin, DJD 20:173, sees the text as composite in origin and suggests that the section dealing with the temple probably had its origins in a "pre-sectarian priestly milieu."

6. Strugnell, Harrington, and Elgvin, DJD 34:124-30, 236-37.

oath"), and also in 11QTemple 53:9-54:7.⁷ Each of these passages includes discussion of the oath of a married woman, and we will review those prescriptions here in order to be able to place our text in context.

The *Zadokite Fragments* (*Damascus Document*, CD 16:10-12 = 4Q271 4 ii 10-12)⁸ sets out the law regarding oaths of a married woman:

> [Regar]ding a (married) woman's oath: As to that which he (God) sa[id to the effect that] her husband may annul her oath, the husband may not annul an oath about [which] he does not know whether it ought to be carried out or annulled. If it (the oath) is to violate the covenant, he should annul it and not confirm it.

This section states that the law of annulment of oaths by the husband, found in Num 30:7-9, is to be taken as applying only in cases where the husband is certain that the oath should not be carried out. Otherwise, if he does not know, he should not annul it. This, at least, is the usual explanation. Whereas the biblical material discusses both the נדר and אסר, our text from the *Zadokite Fragments* refers explicitly to the שבועה oath. Our text must have taken this biblical passage as referring to a kind of oath, rather than to ordinary vows.

If the above interpretation is accepted, it is necessary to define what types of oaths are to be annulled and which oaths are to be observed. Apparently, some distinctions similar to those of the Tannaim regarding vows are in operation. Tannaitic law limits the right of annulment by the husband to vows of abstinence or self-affliction as well as vows that limit the married woman's ability to discharge her obligations to her husband.⁹ However, we have no right to assume that the sect would have had the same restrictions. The sect may have had some other restrictions of similar nature that specified the types of vows for which the husband had the right to countermand his wife's promises.

A completely different interpretation of this passage is also possible. One of the problems considered in tannaitic sources is the question of what happens if a husband annuls a vow without informing his wife.¹⁰ If she vio-

---

7. L. H. Schiffman, "The Law of Vows and Oaths (Num. 30,3-16) in the *Zadokite Fragments* and the *Temple Scroll*," *RevQ* 15 (Mémorial Jean Starcky, 1991) 199-214.

8. J. M. Baumgarten, *Qumran Cave 4.XIII: The Damascus Document (4Q266-273)*. DJD 18 (Oxford: Clarendon, 1996) 178-80.

9. *M. Ned.*11:1; *Sifre Num* 155 (*Sifre Be-Midbar*, ed. H. S. Horovitz [Jerusalem: Wahrmann, 1966] 206-8); cf. *baraita'* in *b. Ned.* 79b.

10. Cf. *Sifre Zuṭa'* to Num 30:6 (ed. H. S. Horovitz [Jerusalem: Wahrmann, 1966] 327) and *Sifre Num* 153 (ed. Horovitz, 202).

lates the vow, is she to be held culpable or not? It is possible to vocalize *yodi'ennah* in this passage and to translate as follows: "the husband may not annul an oath about which he does not inform her whether it is to be carried out or annulled." The law would then require him to let her know if he annuls an oath. At the same time it would prohibit his telling her that the oath had been annulled when it had not.

According to the view of the Tannaim, oaths to observe or violate the commandments have no validity, since they cannot in any way either annul or supplement the commandments by which all Israel is obligated to observe the laws of the Torah.[11] Our text from the *Zadokite Fragments*, however, seems to take a different view. If, indeed, this passage does refer to **שבועות**, it provides that the husband should not annul any oaths to violate commandments. Apparently our sect, unlike the Tannaim, believed that the husband should annul such an oath. In other words, they took the view that even though one who swore an oath to violate a law of the Torah may not go through with the oath, there still is a valid oath that should be canceled by the process of annulment. Therefore, the sectarians expected the husband to annul the oath. To the Tannaim, such an oath had no validity at all; it neither had to be observed nor annulled. The alternative of suggesting that this passage agrees with the tannaitic view but that it refers to vows (**נדרים**) is extremely unlikely since this entire list of regulations seems to apply exclusively to **שבועות**.

The same issue is treated in a very different way in the *Temple Scroll* (11QTemple 53:16-19):[12]

> If a woman vows a vow to me or swears an oath to impose an obligation on herself while in her father's house, by an oath (taken) during her youth (i.e., while a minor), and her father hears her vow or the obligation that she imposes upon herself, and says nothing to her, then all her vows shall be valid, and any obligation that she has imposed upon herself shall be valid.

The text continues further, after discussing annulment of vows by the father and after a lacuna (11QTemple 54:2-3):[13]

> (As to) [any vow] or any binding o[ath to afflict oneself], her husband may con[firm it], or her husband may annul it on the day when he hears it, in which case I will forgive [he]r.

---

11. M. Ned. 2:2; cf. L. Ginzberg, *An Unknown Jewish Sect* (New York: Jewish Theological Seminary, 1976) 97.

12. Y. Yadin, *The Temple Scroll* (Jerusalem: Israel Exploration Society, 1983) 2:240-41.

13. Yadin, *Temple Scroll*, 2:242.

In the complete scroll, this section contained the scroll's adaptation of Num 30:7-15. Verse 10 was omitted here and moved below to remove ambiguity in the following verses. Lines 1-2 contained the adaptation of Num 30:13b. The missing material dealt with the husband's right to annul the vows and oaths of his wife, the requirement that he annul it on the same day, and the (presumably first person) statement that God forgives the wife for her inability to fulfill the oath that the husband has annulled. Lines 1-2, concluding the lacuna, have been restored to adapt Num 30:16, which serves as a fitting conclusion to the section on the married woman.[14] This verse states that if the husband annuls it on a subsequent day, he bears the guilt for her transgression.[15]

The *Temple Scroll* continues after the lacuna with its adaptation of Num 30:14-15. The passage leaves out the repetitive verse 15, including only the words "on the day when he hears it," a phrase that, in fact, tells the entire story of the omitted material. The scroll here repeats the pronouncement that "I (God) will forgive her," based on Num 30:13. The entire section is a fitting continuation to the section on the oaths of married women since it takes up the special case of the married woman's vows or oath of self-affliction and the husband's right to countermand them.

The content of this law contains nothing not already found in Scripture. It therefore raises the same exegetical difficulty as the biblical text itself: why single out vows and oaths of self-abnegation? The Tannaim derived from this verse that the husband could annul only vows that involve self-affliction.[16] In other words, the Tannaim understood this command to cast light on the rest of the material in Numbers 30. This interpretation founders on the question of why the entire prescription requiring annulment on the same day must then be repeated here. This repetition seems to argue that the original text singled out the case of vows and oaths of self-abnegation for some reason. Our text of the *Temple Scroll* gives no inkling as to how this problem was dealt with by the author, except that if he had understood the biblical passage as did the Tannaim, he would certainly have folded this passage into the general law of annulment of the wife's vows, which originally stood in the lacuna. This is the method with which the *Temple Scroll* regularly deals with passages it regards as duplicating one another.[17]

---

14. Yadin, *Temple Scroll*, 2:242.

15. 1 Sam 1:23 in LXX and 4QSam^a pictures Elkanah as confirming the vow of his wife Hannah. See A. Rofé, "The Nomistic Correction in Biblical Manuscripts and Its Occurrence in 4QSam^a," *RevQ* 14 (1989) 247-54.

16. *Sifre Num* 155 (ed. Horovitz, 296).

17. Yadin, *Temple Scroll*, 1:73-77; and L. H. Schiffman, "The Deuteronomic Paraphrase of the *Temple Scroll*," *RevQ* 15 (1992) 543-68.

All in all, the material we have looked at shows that the sapiential text does not reflect the sectarian approaches to oaths and vows either of the *Zadokite Fragments* or the *Temple Scroll*. According to these texts, it is up to the husband to decide if he wishes to annul his wife's vow. We have instead in the sapiential material a requirement that all vows be annulled by the husband.

The Law of Mixed Species (כלאים)

The second law we will consider here is that regarding mixed species (כלאים). These laws are found in Leviticus 19 and Deuteronomy 22. The passage in our text is in the context of advice, apparently regarding commercial transactions (4Q418 103 ii 6-9):[18]

> Do not mix your merchandise with that of [your neighbor.] Why should it be mixed species like a mule? Then you would be like one who wear[s linsey-woolsey] made of linen and flax, and your work like that of one who plow[s] with an ox and a do[nk]ey [to]gethe[r]. And also your crop will [be for you like that of] one who sows mixed species together, for whom the seeds and the full growth and the crop [of] the [vineyard] will be sanctified together.[19]

Before beginning to analyze this passage, an additional word must be said about its context, at least as can be observed from the preserved fragments. Frg. 103 speaks beforehand of what appears to be another agricultural offering, probably that of firstfruits (on which see below). Below, the motif of property seems to be continuing, although it is impossible to tell for sure what is being discussed. What the text seems to be requiring is the scrupulous separation of one's crops (or other merchandise) from that of one's neighbor, presumably to avoid later conflicts over ownership or payments delivered upon sale. Contrary to the editors' short comment,[20] the presence of agricultural material in a sapiential text is most natural. Just as we noted above that

---

18. Strugnell and Harrington, DJD 34:329-33.

19. Despite the long note (pp. 333-34), the editors' translation, "to be set apa[rt (for the sanctuary)]" (p. 331), misses the point. The root *qdš* in this context means to render the entire vineyard unfit as a result of the mixing of species. Cf. Onkelos and Rashi to Deut 22:9 followed by J. H. Tigay, *Deuteronomy*. Jewish Publication Society Torah Commentary (Philadelphia: Jewish Publication Society, 1996) 202.

20. Strugnell and Harrington, DJD 34:330.

these texts envisage a society in which marriage and the family are the norm, so they also envisage a society of small farmers, what we so often label with the somewhat pejorative term "peasants."[21] Indeed, such people are mentioned explicitly in line 2 of this fragment.

The laws pertaining to mixed species, as we noted, appear in two different places in the Torah. Leviticus 19:19 commands three aspects of this set of laws. It prohibits the breeding of mixed species of animals, the planting of mixed species of seeds, and the wearing of garments made of a mixture of wool and linen. Deuteronomy 22:9-11 prohibits the sowing of a vineyard with mixed species of seeds, quite a similar prohibition to that of Leviticus, the plowing of fields with a mixed team of animals and the wearing of garments of mixed species (שעטנז). This analysis shows that in actuality there is only one common prohibition in both commands, that of mixed species in clothes. Similar, and understood by the rabbis as virtually identical, are the prohibitions of sowing a field and a vineyard of mixed seeds, but there is a fundamental difference. The Torah informs us that in the case of the vineyard, the crops are all prohibited as a result (Deut 22:9). This is not the case in the field. Further, only Leviticus prohibits crossbreeding of species, and only Deuteronomy prohibits plowing with mixed teams of animals.

The issue of mixed species comes up in several passages in the scrolls. In 4QText Mentioning Mixed Kinds (4Q481 1 2), which we cannot really explain since it is so fragmentary, there is reference to דייני כלאים, "judges of mixed species."[22] Much more important are two passages that deal with marriage, one in 4QMMT and one in the *Zadokite Fragments*.

The first passage we will consider is that of 4QMMT B 75-82:[23]

> Regarding the sexual immorality that is being done among the people, although they are the so[ns] of the holy [seed], as is written, "Israel is holy" (Jer 2:3); and concerning his (Israel's[24]) pur[e (domesticated) ani]mals, it is written that he may not breed it with mixed species; and regarding [his] garment, [it is written] that it [may not] be mixed species; and not to sow his field and [his] vi[neyard with mixed species; be]cause they (Israel) are

---

21. On small farming, cf. Z. Safrai, *The Economy of Roman Palestine* (London: Routledge, 1994) 352-70.

22. L. H. Schiffman and E. Larson, in G. Brooke et al., *Qumran Cave 4.XVII: Parabiblical Texts, Part 3*. DJD 22 (Oxford: Clarendon, 1996) 303-4.

23. E. Qimron and J. Strugnell, *Qumran Cave 4.V: Miqṣat Ma'aśe ha-Torah*. DJD 10 (Oxford: Clarendon, 1994) 54-57. For a detailed study of this passage, see A. Shemesh, "4Q271.3: A Key to Sectarian Matrimonial Law," *JJS* 49 (1998) 244-63.

24. That is, of any Jew.

holy. But the sons of Aaron are the ho[liest of the holy ones. And yo]u know that sons of the priests and [the people are intermingling, and they are] uniting (in marriage) and rendering impur[e] the seed of [holiness, and even] their (own) [see]d with sexual immorality. F[or it is incumbent on the sons of Aaron . . .

This passage has been discussed extensively in terms of the question of the nature of the forbidden marriages involved.[25] Elisha Qimron takes the view that this passage describes a prohibition that the authors believed was in force against priests marrying out of priestly families. Joseph M. Baumgarten, on the other hand, suggested that this refers to intermarriage, that is, marriage of priests with non-Jewish women. Whatever the exact meaning of the passage, it clearly refers to priests' violating marriage restrictions, and this action is compared to violation of the law of mixed species.

We must emphasize an aspect of the inner logic of this passage. The passage starts off by criticizing the action of the priests and calling it sexual immorality. It then offers in comparison the obligations of the entire people of Israel to observe the laws of mixed species as stemming from the sanctity of the Jewish people. It is then stated that if this requirement applies to the people of Israel, then how much more so should the priests, who are of a higher level of sanctity, be obligated to avoid the particular forbidden unions that the passage concerns.

The only detail in which the law of mixed species in this text differs in any way from that of the Bible is that it states that the prohibition of mating diverse species applies only to pure, that is, kosher animals. According to tannaitic halakhah, this prohibition applied also to impure animals.[26] For purposes of this study, we have to note that the sapiential text we are talking about gives as an example of mixed species the פרד, "mule," a result of breeding two impure animals, the horse and the donkey. If so, there can be no question that these two Qumran texts are following different approaches. The sapiential text apparently follows a view similar to that found later in the rabbinic tradition,[27] probably the Pharisaic approach, whereas the MMT text accords with the sectarian, that is, the Sadducean view.

There is an additional passage in which the law of mixed species serves a didactic purpose in connection with the teaching of another aspect of Jewish

---

25. Qimron and Strugnell, DJD 10:171-72.

26. *Sifra Qedoshim* (*Sifra*, ed. I. H. Weiss [Vienna: Schlossberg, 1861/62; repr. New York: Om, 1946]) *Pereq* 4:15, 89b.

27. J. Babad, *Minḥat Ḥinukh*, in *Sefer ha-Ḥinukh* (Jerusalem: Mekhon Yerushalayim, 1989/1990) 2:237 (commenting on the beginning of sec. 244).

law. This passage is in the *Zadokite Fragments* in several manuscripts from Cave 4. There the text is discussing the appropriate wife that a man should marry as well as the requirement of virginity or, in the case of a widow, chastity before remarriage. The text addresses the question of what a person should do if his daughter has certain blemishes in connection with arranging her marriage. The text requires that the husband-to-be be informed of them in advance. It then addresses the requirement that a father give his daughter in marriage only to one who is appropriate for her. One who is not appropriate is described as follows:

> for [it is mixed species, an o]x and a donkey, and a garment of wool and linen together (4Q271 3 9-10).[28]

We must note at the outset that this passage refers to only two of the forms of mixed species mentioned in the Torah. In fact, checking the passages will clearly indicate that our passage in the *Zadokite Fragments* is dependent on Deut 22:9-11, in which both the prohibitions of not plowing with a mixed team and not wearing a garment of mixed linen and wool occur. At the same time it is apparent that the language of Lev 19:19 has also influenced our passage.

The very same requirement that a father disclose the physical characteristics of his daughter to one about to betroth her is found in 4QInstruction (4Q415 11 6-7=4Q418 167a+b 6-7):[29]

> Describe [a]ll her blemishes to him . . . and make known [to him] (about) her bodily parts . . .[30] for when in the dark his foot stumbles, it will be a stumbling block before him.

The text here says that the father of a prospective bride must disclose any defects in advance lest, upon perceiving them later on, they become a stumbling block to the groom. The intention here is to avoid later disappointment upon discovery of these defects. The entire fragment has one common theme, namely that the prospective groom should choose his mate according to her spirit, not according to her looks.[31]

---

28. Baumgarten, DJD 18:175-77. Also preserved in 4Q269 9 2-3 (DJD 18:132) and 270 5 15-17 (DJD 18:154-55).

29. Strugnell and Harrington, DJD 34:57-61, 389-90.

30. The note of the editors, DJD 34:60, stating that the meaning "her bodily defects" is found in M. Jastrow, *Dictionary of the Targumim, Talmud Babli, Yerushalmi, and Misrashic Literature* (New York: Judaica, 1992) represents a misconstrual of his definition s.v. גויה, 220b-221a.

31. E. Qimron, quoted in DJD 34:59.

Halakhic Elements in 4QInstruction

The editor of the passage in the *Zadokite Fragments*[32] has already called our attention to the fact that Josephus used similar imagery in his survey of the biblical legal system. According to *Ant.* 4.229, the purpose of the prohibition of the mixing of species is to make sure that "a disregard for the law of the breed not pass over even into the practices of humanity." If the purpose of the laws of the prohibition of mixed species is to prevent certain forms of human immorality, we can easily understand why the laws of mixed species would be cited to teach lessons regarding appropriate marriages. Yet we must note one essential difference. In our passage from the *Zadokite Fragments* we seem to deal more with a match between inappropriate marital partners, rather than with the issues of prohibited unions.[33]

The editor further points to rabbinic parallels to this same concept found in *Pereq 'Arayot* 11,[34] in a very late rabbinic compilation. This passage lists a variety of transgressions that one incurs should he have sexual relations with a handmaiden who is forbidden to him. Among these transgressions are listed: sowing a field with mixed species of seeds, plowing with a mixed team, and wearing clothes of mixed species. This example clearly reflects Deuteronomy 22 rather than Leviticus 19. What is particularly significant here is that prohibition of a sexual union regarded as forbidden is described in terms of violation of the laws of mixed species, in a way similar to what we encountered in the various Dead Sea Scrolls texts.

It emerges from this detailed discussion that while the imagery of mixed species denoting forbidden sexual unions is utilized by several Qumran texts, 4QInstruction shares the halakhic approach of the Pharisaic-rabbinic tradition. The other texts take the Saducean/Zadokite approach.

The Laws of the Firstborn

The final example of a halakhic issue dealt with in the Sapiential texts is that of firstborn animals. The passage (4Q423 3 4-5) is fragmentary and, therefore, can only be partially understood. Apparently, the blessing of having one's animals be fertile is being discussed as a reward for something. At this point the text turns to the bringing of firstborn animals as a sacrifice to God, in thankfulness for the plenty bestowed upon the flocks. Here the text states:[35]

---

32. Cf. Baumgarten, DJD 18:177.
33. Cf. Shemesh, "4Q271.3," 261-63, who sees this text as dealing with a prohibited union.
34. M. Higger, *Masekhtot Ze'irot* (Jerusalem: Makor, 1969/1970) 94, par. 19.
35. Strugnell and Harrington, DJD 34:514. Cf. also 1Q26 2 2-4 (reedited in DJD 34:538).

And you shall come before your God wi]th the firstfruits of your womb and the firstborn of all [your (domesticated) animals . . . and you shall come before]yo[ur God] saying: "And I have sanctified (set aside) every [firstborn of the womb to God."

The key halakhic detail in this passage is the requirement that there be a formal sanctification or consecration of the firstborn of pure, kosher animals that are without blemish. This requirement is clearly derived from Deut 15:19, which requires that תקדיש ליהוה אלהיך, "you must sanctify (it) to the Lord your God." This passage is understood to require a formal statement of sanctification.[36] This statement of consecration has essentially fixed the sanctity of the animal so that its use for any nonsacrificial purpose is considered to be an act of desacralization. The notion that there is a specific declaration to be made upon bringing the firstborn animals is itself based upon the analogous law of the bringing of firstfruits found in Deut 26:1-3. There, upon presenting his firstfruits in a special basket, the farmer is called upon to make a specific declaration.

This particular requirement is known from tannaitic law. According to *Sifre Deut* 124,[37] the rabbis required that a declaration of consecration be made when offering a firstborn animal. Various other texts such as the *Temple Scroll* (11QTemple 60:2-4) give specific details regarding firstborn offerings.[38] These texts do not testify to the specific requirement of a declaration or to any specific text to be recited for this purpose. In this case, therefore, we have direct evidence that our sapiential text agrees with the law later found in the Pharisaic-rabbinic tradition, but we cannot be sure at all that the sectarians of Qumran or those who shared their legal traditions would have disagreed with this ruling.

Conclusion

We have investigated several examples of halakhic excerpts that appear in the context of a sapiential composition. In studying these passages we have noted that they do not conform to sectarian halakhic rulings, but rather agree generally with the law as defined in what we later know as the Pharisaic-rabbinic tradition. In general terms, what we have observed accords well with the

---

36. Cf. other uses of root קדש in Exod 13:2 and Num 3:13.
37. L. Finkelstein, ed., *Sifre on Deuteronomy* (New York: Jewish Theological Seminary of America, 1969) 182-83.
38. Yadin, *Temple Scroll*, 2:271-72.

widespread view that the wisdom literature from Qumran is not sectarian in character. On the other hand, we must be extremely careful in reasoning from only three short examples. It appears that the halakhah of the sacrificial system in 4QWays of Righteousness^b (4Q421 12 1-5) is sectarian in nature. Therefore, these examples are valid only for 4QInstruction but not for other texts in the sapiential corpus.

At the same time, we have established an early dating, sometime in the second or first centuries B.C.E., for the laws in our text that accord with Pharisaic-rabbinic law. As we continue to study the legal material in the Qumran corpus, it becomes more and more certain that there is evidence here not only for the sectarian trend in Jewish law but also for the early dating of some aspects of what we later find in rabbinic texts. So while the results of our study have turned up a meager amount of halakhic material in 4QInstruction, the bits and pieces that we have uncovered have truly contributed to our study of the history of Jewish law in Second Temple times.

RELIGIOUS OUTLOOK
OF THE QUMRAN SECTARIANS

CHAPTER 13

The Early History of Jewish Liturgy and the Dead Sea Scrolls

One of the most serious problems confronting the student of the Dead Sea Scrolls is that of how to evaluate the significance of the scrolls for the reconstruction of the history of Judaism. The Qumran scrolls, emanating from the Hasmonean and Herodian periods, are the earliest postbiblical Hebrew texts that throw light on the nature of the varieties of Judaism of the Second Temple period. On the one hand, much of what is encountered in the Dead Sea Scrolls can be explained as the result of the peculiar ideology of the Qumran sect. On the other hand, much of the material may represent the common beliefs and practices of the Judaism of the time.

How can we determine if given practices are, in fact, typical for Jews of the period or if they belong only to the sectarians of Qumran? It would be easy to answer this question if we possessed documents from the Pharisees, Sadducees, or the large group later termed the ʿam ha-ʾareṣ that would allow us to make comparisons. However, for the period in which the Qumran scrolls were authored, we have only the account of Josephus and the scanty traditions of the Tannaim. In both cases, the material must be closely evaluated in terms of date and tendentiousness. Even more important, differences between religious groups constituted a subject of interest, whereas common beliefs and practices did not, so the latter naturally tended to be deemphasized while the former were often stressed.

It is in the methodological context just outlined that we approach the early history of Jewish liturgy as reflected in the Qumran scrolls. We shall attempt to evaluate the liturgical patterns in evidence at Qumran and to compare them with what is known of the early rabbinic traditions. When we have assembled a handsome list of parallels, we shall ask what their significance is and what conclusions may be drawn from them. The first part of this study will summarize the observations that emerge from the more well-known texts. The second will concentrate on the liturgical materials from Cave 4.

Temple and Synagogue

The sect that left us the Dead Sea Scrolls removed itself voluntarily from Hellenistic Jerusalem, most probably out of protest against the Hasmonean takeover of the high priesthood. Among its initial leaders were certainly members of the House of Zadok, the priestly family that had dominated the high priesthood during virtually all the years of the First and Second temples.[1] These priests, together with those who followed them to Qumran in the Judean Desert, forswore participation in the Jerusalem sacrificial service because of the manner in which it was conducted. They maintained that violations of the Law marred the temple and that its priests were illegitimate.[2] Presumably, the founders of the sect believed that the Jerusalem cult no longer served as a vehicle for contact between Israel and its God, and, therefore, they saw no value to their continued participation in it. Retiring to Qumran, they had to live a Judaism devoid of temple and sacrifice, a Judaism in which prayer, purity, study, and the sectarian life itself would serve as a replacement for the temple. Therefore, the sect viewed itself as a sanctuary that brought its members into the very same forms of contact with the Lord that they formerly experienced through cultic worship.[3] Despite some claims to the contrary, sacrifices were not performed at Qumran.[4]

The situation that faced the Tannaim in the early Yavnean period was very similar. Judaism had long been based on sacrificial worship in which Israel's relationship with God was secured through the proper and orderly conduct of the rites required by the Levitical Codes. Now, in the aftermath of the Great Revolt of 66-74 C.E., there was no longer any cult. The priest no longer sacrificed; the Levite no longer sang; Israel no longer made pilgrimages to the holy temple. Henceforth, only prayer and the life of rabbinic piety could en-

---

1. Cf. L. H. Schiffman, *The Halakhah at Qumran*. SJLA 16 (Leiden: Brill, 1975) 72-75.

2. F. M. Cross, "The Early History of the Qumran Community," in *New Directions in Biblical Archaeology*, ed. D. N. Freedman and J. C. Greenfield, 75-89 (Garden City: Doubleday, 1971).

3. B. Gärtner, *The Temple and the Community in Qumran and the New Testament* (Cambridge: Cambridge University Press, 1965).

4. L. H. Schiffman, *Sectarian Law in the Dead Sea Scrolls: Courts, Testimony and the Penal Code*. BJS 33 (Chico: Scholars, 1983) 201. Cf. J. M. Baumgarten, *Studies in Qumran Law*. SJLA 24 (Leiden: Brill, 1977) 39-56.

sure Israel's continued link to its Father in heaven. It is naive to assume that this eventuality came upon Pharisaic-rabbinic Judaism with no warning. Indeed, our historical hindsight allows us to see that throughout the Second Temple period, cult was on the wane and prayer and liturgy were on the rise. Gradually, prayer was making greater and greater inroads even in the temple. Those distant from the temple turned increasingly to prayer in the Second Commonwealth period. Pharisaism, in translating temple purity to the home and table, had helped to free the later sages from the inexorability of cult. But what seems most important to us here, in the context of this study, is that the Qumran sect had long ago demonstrated how to live a Jewish life without a temple. They had, as we shall see, developed both a liturgy and an ideology to accommodate their absence from the temple.[5]

Nevertheless, throughout its days, the sect yearned not for the restoration of the temple, since it still stood and still functioned (albeit improperly in their view), but for the return of their priestly leaders to dominance of the cult. This hegemony, to them, was tantamount to its restoration.[6] It would mean the establishment of the New Jerusalem[7] and of the ties that would then unite Israel and the God of Israel. The priests of the sect, in the end of days, would officiate at the temple, guaranteeing its practice and ensuring its utmost purity. Until that day, they would have to be satisfied with the efficacy of prayer and with the study of texts dealing with the worship and cult of the temple at which they would neither serve nor offer sacrifice.

The *Zadokite Fragments* (CD 11:21-22) make reference to some kind of place of worship: "And anyone who enters the house of prostration let him not come in a state of impurity requiring washing (טמא כבוס). . . ." The remainder of the passage is quite difficult. Nonetheless, this text seems to indicate that the sectarians living scattered in the towns and cities of Palestine established permanent places of sanctity for the conduct of sacred services. However, there is no evidence of the establishment of a synagogue or anything like it, in the sense of a fixed place of prayer, in the archaeological remains from Qumran. In fact, the Qumran settlement predates the earliest excavated synagogues in Palestine. It seems, therefore, that community prayers, certainly part of the life of the Qumran sectarians, were conducted in prem-

---

5. B. M. Bokser, *Philo's Description of Jewish Practices.* Protocol of the Thirtieth Colloquy (Berkeley: Center for Hermeneutical Studies in Hellenistic and Modern Culture, 1977); *The Origins of the Seder* (Berkeley: University of California Press, 1984) 4-13.

6. "The Concept of Restoration in the Dead Sea Scrolls," Chapter 17 below.

7. D. Barthélemy and J. T. Milik, *Qumran Cave I.* DJD 1 (Oxford: Clarendon, 1955) 134-35; M. Baillet, J. T. Milik, and R. de Vaux, *Les 'Petites Grottes' de Qumrân.* DJD 3 (Oxford: Clarendon, 1962) 84-89, 184-93.

ises used for other purposes, perhaps in the dining hall. A special building for worship would not be necessary at the sectarian center at Qumran since the entire settlement was dedicated to this purpose. Such a house of worship would be needed only by those who lived elsewhere in the land of Israel.

The Liturgical Texts

On the basis of a detailed study of the poem that concludes the *Rule of the Community*, Shemaryahu Talmon has suggested that there was a detailed series of prayer texts for the various times of prayer of the sect.[8] He maintained that the sect prayed three times each day and three times each evening, a matter to which we will return below. Talmon identified allusions to the reading of the Shemaʿ and a proto-ʿAmidah. He also found evidence for specific rituals for festivals, New Moons, Sabbaths, the Day of Atonement, and Sabbatical and Jubilee Years. While we will see that there is reason to question his conclusions regarding the six daily prayer times, liturgies for the various occasions he listed have now been identified in Cave 4.[9]

A text that may bear on the question of organized liturgy at Qumran is 11QPs^a.[10] This scroll contains canonical and noncanonical psalms, as well as numerous other interesting poetic texts. This text, when originally identified, was regarded as a scroll of Psalms.[11] It is, in fact, a liturgical collection.[12] Many of the canonical psalms in this text are exactly the same as those utilized in the later rabbinic liturgy. Even the organization of the psalms in the scroll seems to parallel the conceptual framework of the later rabbinic prayer book. Most important, many of the selections that figure in talmudic discussions as part of the prayer services appear here, and in one case liturgical re-

---

8. S. Talmon, "Maḥazor ha-Berakhot shel Kat Midbar Yehudah," *Tarbiz* 28 (1958/59) 1-20; "The 'Manual of Benedictions' of the Sect of the Judaean Desert," *RevQ* 2 (1959/1960) 475-500.

9. B. Nitzan, *Qumran Prayer and Religious Poetry*. STDJ 12 (Leiden: Brill, 1994) 47-63.

10. J. A. Sanders, *The Psalms Scroll of Qumran Cave 11 (11QPs^a)*. DJD 4 (Oxford: Clarendon, 1965); *The Dead Sea Psalms Scroll* (Ithaca: Cornell University Press, 1967).

11. J. A. Sanders, "Cave 11 Surprises and the Question of Canon," in Freedman and Greenfield, *New Directions in Biblical Archaeology*, 113-30; P. W. Flint, *The Dead Sea Psalms Scrolls and the Book of Psalms*. STDJ 17 (Leiden: Brill, 1997) 202-27.

12. Cf. S. Talmon, "Mizmorim Ḥisoniyim bi-Leshon ha-ʿIvrit mi-Qumran," *Tarbiz* 35 (1965/66) 215; P. Skehan, "A Liturgical Complex in 11QPs^a," *CBQ* 35 (1973) 195-205; "Jubilees and the Qumran Psalter (11QPs^a)," *CBQ* 37 (1975) 343-47; L. H. Schiffman, *Reclaiming the Dead Sea Scrolls: The History of Judaism, the Background of Christianity, the Lost Library of Qumran* (Philadelphia: Jewish Publication Society, 1994; repr. ABRL [New York: Doubleday, 1995]) 178-80.

sponses are included. Clearly, these very same psalms, most notably Psalm 145, were used in liturgical context by the Qumran sect.

It is tempting to see the *Hodayot Scroll*[13] as a series of hymns for public worship. In fact, there is no evidence for the liturgical nature of this material.[14] These poems are individual plaints, perhaps composed by a leader of the sect, maybe even the Teacher of Righteousness, and they concentrate on serious matters of theology and belief. These poems are certainly not part of a regular order of prayers.[15]

Numerous fragments found in the Qumran caves have been classified by scholars as liturgies. While many of these fragments are at best insubstantial, the material published in Discoveries in the Judaean Desert, vol. 7,[16] changes this picture radically. These texts show that numerous rituals and liturgies, similar in scope to those of tannaitic tradition, existed among the sectaries of Qumran. We must also note here the presence of fragments of Ben Sira at Qumran.[17] A poem substantially parallel to the conclusions of the blessings of the later tannaitic Eighteen Benedictions was appended in some Hebrew versions to the last chapter of Ben Sira (at 55:12).[18] We do not know if this passage was part of the Qumran recension of Ben Sira.

Finally, numerous phylacteries *(tefillin)* have been found at Qumran. The phylacteries are associated with liturgical practice in the rabbinic tradition. At Qumran, these ritual objects also bear witness to variations of custom, especially as regards the order and content of the biblical passages included in them.[19]

---

13. E. L. Sukenik, *'Oṣar ha-Megillot ha-Genuzot* (Jerusalem: Bialik Institute and Hebrew University, 1954/55); J. Licht, *Megillat ha-Hodayot mi-Megillot Midbar Yehudah* (Jerusalem: Bialik Institute, 1957); E. Schuller, "Hodayot," in E. G. Chazon et al., *Qumran Cave 4.XX: Poetical and Liturgical Texts, Part 2*. DJD 29 (Oxford: Clarendon, 1999) 70-71.

14. Nitzan, *Qumran Prayer and Religious Poetry*, 321-55.

15. Contrast S. Holm-Nielsen, "Thanksgiving Psalms," *EncJud* 5:1047.

16. M. Baillet, "Textes liturgiques," *Qumrân Grotte 4.III (4Q482-4Q520)*. DJD 7 (Oxford: Clarendon, 1982) 73-286.

17. Sir 51:13-20, 30 in Sanders, *Psalms Scroll*, 79-85, and the fragmentary 2Q18 in Baillet, Milik, and de Vaux, DJD 3:75-77.

18. M. Z. Segal, *Sefer Ben Sira ha-Shalem*, 2nd ed. (Jerusalem: Bialik Institute, 1971/72) 355-57; *Sefer Ben Sira: Ha-Maqor, Qanqordanṣiah, ve-Nittuaḥ ha-Millim* (Jerusalem: Academy of the Hebrew Language and Shrine of the Book, 1973) 55.

19. A. M. Habermann, "'Al ha-Tefillin bi-Yeme Qedem," *ErIsr* 3 (1953/54) 174-77; G. Vermes, "Pre-Mishnaic Jewish Worship and the Phylacteries from the Dead Sea," *VT* 9 (1959) 65-72; Y. Yadin, *Tefillin from Qumran (X Q Phyl 1-4)* (Jerusalem: Israel Exploration Society and Shrine of the Book, 1969); J. T. Milik, *Qumrân Grotte 4.II, Part 2: Tefillin, Mezuzot et Targums (4Q128-4Q157)*. DJD 6 (Oxford: Clarendon, 1977) 34-79. Cf. Schiffman, *Reclaiming the Dead Sea Scrolls*, 305-11; and "Phylacteries and Mezuzot," *EDSS* 2:675-77.

Common Liturgical Motifs

There are certain motifs found in later rabbinic traditions that have important parallels in the Qumran texts. Among the fragments from Caves 4 and 11 is the *Angelic Liturgy*[20] that describes the angelic praise of God. This composition is to be seen as a *merkavah* text,[21] and, indeed, this term itself appears in the work. It constitutes a description of the regular praise of God in the heavens by the angelic hosts. They are seen as praising him on a daily basis according to fixed rituals. This concept also appears in the rabbinic *qedushah* prayers[22] and is more fully developed in the early Hekhalot literature.[23]

Moshe Weinfeld has argued that elements of liturgical language found later in the rabbinic prayers are preserved already among the texts of the Qumran corpus.[24] Among the most prominent is the parallel with the rabbinic *qedushah* in the Hymn to the Creator found in 11QPs^a.[25] This poem is certainly similar to the Hekhalot hymn 'El 'Adon that found its way into the rabbinic liturgy.[26]

What is essential to our question is the methodological dilemma posed

---

20. J. Strugnell, "The Angelic Liturgy at Qumran — 4QSerek Šîrôt 'Ôlat Haššabbāt," *VTSup* 7 (1959) 318-45; A. S. van der Woude, "Fragmente einer Rolle der Lieder für das Sabbatoffer aus Hohle XI von Qumran (11Q SirSabb)," in *Vom Kanaan bis Kerala: Festschrift für J. P. M. van der Ploeg*, ed. W. C. Delsam et al., 311-35 (Kevelaer: Butzon and Bercker and Neukirchen-Vluyn: Neukirchener, 1982); Masada fragment in C. A. Newsom and Y. Yadin, "The Masada Fragment of the Qumran *Songs of the Sabbath Sacrifice*," *IEJ* 34 (1984) 77-88 and pl. 9; see Newsom in E. Eshel et al., *Qumran Cave 4.VI: Poetical and Liturgical Texts, Part 1*. DJD 11 (Oxford: Clarendon, 1998) 173-401.

21. L. H. Schiffman, "*Merkavah* Speculation at Qumran: The 4Q *Serekh Shirot 'Olat ha-Shabbat*," in *Mystics, Philosophers and Politicians: Essays in Jewish Intellectual History in Honor of Alexander Altmann*, ed. J. Reinharz and D. Swetchinski, with K. Bland, 15-47. Duke Monographs in Medieval and Renaissance Studies 5 (Durham: Duke University Press, 1982); J. M. Baumgarten, "The Qumran Sabbath Shirot and Rabbinic Merkabah Traditions," *RevQ* 13 (1988) 199-214.

22. I. Elbogen, *Ha-Tefillah be-Yiśra'el be-Hitpatḥutah ha-Historit* (Tel-Aviv: Dvir, 1972) 47-53.

23. A. Altmann, "Shire Qedushah be-Sifrut ha-Hekhalot ha-Qedumah," *Melila* 2 (1946) 8-10.

24. M. Weinfeld, "'Iqvot shel Qedushat Yoṣer u-Fesuqe de Zimra' be-Megillot Qumran u-ve-Sefer Ben Sira'," *Tarbiz* 45 (1975/76) 15-26; repr. in *Ha-Liturgiyah ha-Yehudit ha-Qedumah: Me-ha-Sifrut ha-Mizmorit ve-'ad li-Tefillot ba-Megillot Qumran u-ve-Sifrut Ḥazal* (Jerusalem: Hebrew University and Magnes, 2004) 167-78.

25. Sanders, DJD 4:89-91.

26. Amram Gaon, *Seder Rav 'Amram Ga'on*, ed. D. S. Goldschmidt (Jerusalem: Mosad Harav Kook, 1971) 71; Y. Baer, *Seder 'Avodat Yiśra'el* (Tel-Aviv: Or Torah, 1956/57) 211-12; Elbogen, *Ha-Tefillah be-Yiśra'el*, 87.

The Early History of Jewish Liturgy and the Dead Sea Scrolls

by these materials. How are we to account for the presence of these common motifs in the Qumran and rabbinic traditions? Are we to assume that the Qumran materials directly influenced the Hekhalot that, in turn, influenced the rabbinic liturgy? Or, perhaps, ought we even to assume direct influence? On the other hand, we might also be dealing with a simple case of parallel development. Perhaps, if we had Pharisaic texts from this period, we might discover that some of the Pharisaic sages were involved in the very same kinds of mystical speculation.

The Daily Prayers

Among the texts in Discoveries in the Judaean Desert, vol. 7, 4Q503 is one of extreme importance.[27] This manuscript, dated by the editor, Maurice Baillet,[28] to the Hasmonean period (100-75 B.C.E.), consists of a series of prayers to be recited on the various days of the month. Specific texts are designated for evening (ערב) and morning (צאת השמש), although no specific nighttime prayer appears to be included here. The material for each day of the month constitutes a literary unit, and the days are numbered according to lunar months. Each day's entry begins: "On the x of the month, in the evening (בערב), they shall bless, recite and say: Praised be the God of Israel who. . . . May peace be upon you, O Israel." Then the text takes up the morning prayer: "When the sun goes forth to illumine the earth they shall bless, recite and say: . . . Praised be the God of Israel. . . ." Most striking in its similarity to later Jewish liturgy is the benediction: "[Praised be the God of Israel w]ho cho[se] us from among all [the] nations."[29] Prominent phrases are אור היומם, "the light of day," in the morning prayer[30] and דגלי לילה,[31] "troops (i.e., stars) of the night," in the evening selections. Each day is described as having so many שערי אור, "gates of light,"[32] which seem to be equivalent to the number of the day in the lunar month.

The editor has observed that this text departs from the calendar of solar months and years that scholars previously identified as that of the Qumran

---

27. Cf. Nitzan, *Qumran Prayer and Religious Poetry*, 63-87; D. K. Falk, *Daily, Sabbath, and Festival Prayers in the Dead Sea Scrolls*. STDJ 27 (Leiden: Brill, 1998) 21-57.
28. Baillet, DJD 7:105.
29. Baillet, DJD 7:111.
30. 3:10, Baillet, DJD 7:106; 4:1, p. 108; 11:2, p. 116; frg. 15-16:6, p. 110.
31. 8:11, 19, Baillet, DJD 7:113; cf. frg. 39:3 [*dig*]*le 'erev* and *gorale ḥoshekh* (frg. 76, p. 127; frg. 215, p. 135).
32. 4:2, Baillet, DJD 7:108; 8:10, p. 113; frg. 19:2, p. 110.

sect.³³ Here we have a calendar of lunar months, probably synchronized by leap years, similar to those known from tannaitic tradition.³⁴ Baillet sees the text as starting with the month of Nissan, so that the festival described in frg. 24 (col. 7) as occurring on the fifteenth of the month seems to him to be Passover. The text describes this day as מנוח ותענוג [עד] מו,³⁵ "a time of rest and enjoyment." מנוח describes other days³⁶ that must have been Sabbaths or festivals.³⁷

The liturgical materials found here are too short to have constituted the entire liturgy. These appear to have represented a small section of the worship service that, in the ritual of the authors, changed on a daily basis throughout the month, and, perhaps, throughout the year. In view of the content of these prayers, it is most likely that the benedictions preserved here constituted an expansion upon a precursor of the first benediction before the Shemaʿ.³⁸ We do not mean to assert that this passage proves the recitation of the Shemaʿ at this date, although the Mishnah attributes it to temple times and it seems to be clearly alluded to in the *Rule of the Community*, 1QS 10:13-17.³⁹ This same passage in the Mishnah indicates that in the view of the Tannaim some benediction was already associated with the Shemaʿ in temple times.⁴⁰ Some early version of the blessing on the heavenly lights must have been in use.⁴¹ Although in rabbinic tradition this benediction was variable only for morning and evening, with later additions for Sabbaths and festivals, at Qumran it varied by the day. Further, the idea of "gates" or portals occurs in the rabbinic morning benediction.⁴² Much of the vocabulary of these prayers is found in the rabbinic liturgy as well.

Our text speaks of twice-daily prayer, morning and evening (late afternoon). Amoraic tradition saw prayer as a substitute for the temple sacrifices once the temple had been destroyed.⁴³ Nonetheless, some Tannaim argued that the very same services had already been conducted in the Second Temple

33. Baillet, DJD 7:105-6.
34. M. D. Herr, "The Calendar," in *The Jewish People in the First Century*, ed. S. Safrai and M. Stern (Philadelphia: Fortress, 1976) 2:843-57.
35. Frg. 24-5:5; Baillet, DJD 7:111.
36. 12:15, Baillet, DJD 7:118; frg. 41:3, p. 119.
37. Cf. 1QM 2:8-9; 1QpHab 11:6-7, 8.
38. Elbogen, *Ha-Tefillah be-Yiśraʾel*, 12-15.
39. *M. Tamid* 5:1.
40. Cf. *b. Ber.* 11b-12a; *y. Ber.* 1:5 (ed. Krot. 1:7, 3c).
41. Cf. J. Mann, "Genizah Fragments of the Palestinian Order of Service," *HUCA* 2 (1925) 273, 292, 323; Saʿadyah Gaon, *Siddur Rav Saʿadyah Gaʾon*, ed. I. Davidson, S. Assaf, and B. I. Joel (Jerusalem: Mass, 1970) 13, 26.
42. Amram Gaon, *Seder Rav ʿAmram Gaʾon*, 71.
43. *B. Ber.* 26a.

period, at which time the service could merely be said to have been instituted to correspond with the times of the daily sacrifices.[44] While still others argued that the prayers were instituted by the patriarchs,[45] the Amoraim explained that even this view admitted that the exact times for the services depended on the times for sacrificial worship.[46]

The link with sacrificial worship was apparently dominant. Otherwise, how can we explain the fact that the evening service was a matter of debate throughout the tannaitic period? Indeed, it was eventually decided that in halakhic terms, the evening service was optional.[47] The only reasonable explanation is that since there was no nighttime sacrifice, the evening prayer had an inferior status. Even the rabbinic explanation that the burning of limbs and fats throughout the night constituted the equivalent of the evening sacrifice was not sufficient to elevate the evening prayer to the status of a required daily service.

Our Qumran text mentions only the two required prayer times, testifying to a period in which, at least for some Jews, only twice-daily prayer was normative. In fact, our text supports the view of some Tannaim that originally prayer services were held only morning and evening. This system is in marked contrast to the six daily prayer times that Talmon[48] finds mentioned in the poem at the end of the *Manual of Discipline*. Several explanations are possible. First, it may be that Talmon's interpretation of the poetic material takes the imagery too literally, and that, as André Dupont-Sommer[49] has claimed, only two prayer times are in fact referred to in the poem. Second, it may be that the texts describe the ritual practices of different communities or different stages in the history of one community.

The Qumran Supplication Texts

4Q501 is entitled "Lamentation" by the editor. It is written in a Herodian hand, around 50-25 B.C.E. in the view of Baillet.[50] This text appeals to God to remember the downtrodden position and disgrace of Israel and not to hand

---

44. *T. Ber.* 3:1.
45. Daniel prayed thrice daily (Dan 6:11).
46. *B. Ber.* 26b; *y. Ber.* 4:1 (7b).
47. *B. Ber.* 27b; *y. Ber.* 4:1 (7c-d).
48. Talmon, *Tarbiz* 28 (1958/59) 1-20; *RevQ* 2 (1959/1960) 475-500.
49. A. Dupont-Sommer, "Contribution à l'exégèse du Manuel de Discipline X 1-8," *VT* 3 (1952) 232.
50. Baillet, DJD 7:79.

over the land (נחלה) to foreigners. God is asked to avenge the wrongs that the nations have perpetrated against his nation.[51]

While this text is extremely fragmentary, it contains parallels in theme and content to the rabbinic supplication, the Taḥanun for Mondays and Thursdays.[52] The Taḥanun, in its present form, has been dated to the Middle Ages. Most notable is the dependency of both texts on Joel 2:17.

A similar composition is the 4QDivre ha-Me'orot, preserved in three copies (4Q504-6).[53] The name of the text actually appears in the manuscript,[54] a rare phenomenon in the Qumran library. Jean Starcky, who first worked on these texts, considered it to be a "recueil d'hymnes liturgiques."[55] Baillet has suggested that this document provides material intended for use on specific days of the week. Indeed, Wednesday, which he terms "day of the covenant," and the Sabbath (Saturday), "the day of praise," are explicitly mentioned.[56] What precedes this Sabbath material he assumes to refer to Friday, "the day of confession of sins." He takes the absence of sectarian character as well as the date of the earliest exemplar, which is in his opinion around 150 B.C.E., to indicate that this text stems from the Hasidim of which, he says, the Essenes are the spiritual heirs.[57]

On the basis of the preliminary publication of this material,[58] M. R. Lehmann has taken issue with this analysis.[59] He points to the large number of parallels between the *Divre ha-Me'orot* and the Taḥanun. According to him, the earliest forms of the Taḥanun go back to the time of the Second Temple, and this prayer is termed *devarim* in tannaitic usage.[60] Lehmann raises

---

51. See Nitzan, *Qumran Prayer and Religious Poetry*, 89-116.

52. *Ve-Hu' Raḥum*. Amram Gaon, *Seder Rav 'Amram Ga'on*, 55- 58; Sa'adyah Gaon, *Siddur Rav Sa'adyah Ga'on*, 24-25; Baer, *Seder 'Avodat Yiśra'el*, 112-16; Elbogen, *Ha-Tefillah be-Yiśra'el*, 58-62.

53. Cf. E. G. Chazon, "Is *Divrei Ha-me'orot* a Sectarian Prayer?" in *The Dead Sea Scrolls: Forty Years of Research*, ed. D. Dimant and U. Rappaport, 3-17 (Leiden: Brill and Jerusalem: Magnes, Hebrew University, and Yad Izhak Ben-Zvi, 1992); "4QDibHam: Liturgy or Literature?" *RevQ* 15 (Mémorial Jean Starcky, 1992) 447-55; Falk, *Daily, Sabbath, and Festival Prayers*, 59-94.

54. 4Q504, Baillet, DJD 7:138.

55. J. Starcky, "Le travail d'édition des fragments manuscrits de Qumrân," *RB* 63 (1956) 66.

56. E. G. Chazon, "On the Special Character of Sabbath Prayer: New Data from Qumran," *Journal of Jewish Liturgy and Music* 15 (1992-93) 1-21.

57. Baillet, DJD 7:137.

58. M. Baillet, "Un recueil liturgique de Qumran, grotte 4: 'Les Paroles des Luminaires,'" *RB* 68 (1961) 195-250, pls. 24-28.

59. M. R. Lehmann, "A Re-interpretation of 4Q Dibrê Ham-Me'oroth," *RevQ* 5 (1964) 106-10; *Masot u-Masa'ot* (Jerusalem: Mosad Harav Kook, 1982) 169-73.

60. *T. Ber.* 3:6; cf. S. Lieberman, *Tosefta Ki-Fshuṭah*, vol. 1: *Seder Zera'im*, Part 1 (New York: Jewish Theological Seminary of America, 1955) 31.

some question about the reading *me'orot* while noting that this word is found in the first blessing before the Shemaʿ. An extensive and impressive list of linguistic parallels is then presented by him. He therefore classifies the *Divre ha-Me'orot* as the supplications of an individual to be recited after the priest has completed the service and goes even further to conclude that the length of this prayer requires us to see it as intended for Mondays and Thursdays. He states that the text is more appropriate to Monday and Thursday than to the days that Baillet has suggested. In his final, official publication, Baillet simply notes that he gives the same explanation he had given previously, despite the work of Lehmann.[61]

It is indeed surprising that Lehmann's explanation totally ignores the testimony of the text itself that mentions Wednesday and Saturday explicitly. Baillet's suggestion that there are preserved here prayers for each day of the week is quite convincing, despite the absence of the reference to the other days. On the one hand, the fragmentary nature of the text allows us to presume that the mention of the other days of the week would have appeared in the lacunae. On the other hand, the substantial list of parallels assembled by Lehmann seems to require attention.

We would therefore suggest that the text be identified as a series of daily supplications for liturgical use for each day of the week. That for the Sabbath apparently avoided topics judged improper for the Sabbath day.[62] *Divre ha-Me'orot* would have been recited as part of an organized ritual. It is not possible to tell if the particular text was written for temple service or for worship away from the temple. Nonetheless, if used at Qumran, our text would have been part of an organized liturgy.

Moreover, the texts we have examined show that although it cannot be claimed that rabbinic Taḥanun texts go back to temple times, it can be stated with assurance that some Jews, whose works are preserved at Qumran, were already reciting prayers with similar motifs as part of their prayer services in the first century B.C.E. Specific selections were in use for the various days of the week. Already by the time of the composition of 4QDivre ha-Me'orot, the uniqueness of the Sabbath and the inappropriateness of certain motifs on this holy day led to the inclusion of a special version for the Sabbath.

---

61. Baillet, DJD 7:137.
62. Cf. Schiffman, *The Halakhah at Qumran*, 87-90.

Festival Prayers

Prayers for festivals are preserved in three manuscripts from Cave 4 (4Q507-9) and, indeed, the very same text is found in 1Q34 and 34bis.[63] The Cave 4 manuscripts have been dated by Baillet to the beginning of the first century C.E.,[64] the early first century C.E.,[65] and to the end of the Hasmonean period, about 70-60 B.C.E.[66] The text specifically mentions the Day of Atonement and the Day of Firstfruits (Shavuot). Baillet has made a plausible reconstruction, according to which the text proceeds through the entire Jewish ritual calendar, beginning with the New Year on the first of Tishre, followed by the Day of Atonement, Tabernacles, Offering of the Omer or Barley Harvest, possibly the Second Passover, and Shavuot. The New Moon is also mentioned. (A reference to Passover has not been identified in the preserved portions of the text.)

The exact reconstruction of the ritual calendar of this text and of the prayers for each occasion is impossible, since the state of preservation of the manuscripts does not allow it. In addition, it cannot be determined whether the ritual calendar of this text is similar to that known from tannaitic Judaism or to the expanded calendar of the *Temple Scroll*.[67] One line that particularly stands out in this text reads: "And may you assemble our banished at the time of . . . and our dispersed [ones] may you soon gather."[68] The parallel to the Festival Musaf (additional service) of later rabbinic tradition is so clear as to suggest that the prayer recited on festivals[69] for the restoration of the Diaspora to the land of Israel may go back as early as the first century B.C.E.

It is not possible to determine the exact function of these prayers. They do not mention the sacrificial system so as to suggest that they were a substitute for it. Nor can we find any indication that they were intended to be recited along with sacrificial rites. Happiness and rejoicing are explicitly mentioned, so it is possible that they were meant to be recited as part of the celebration of these festivals at Qumran or elsewhere. The last three texts examined here contained prayers for each day of the month, to be recited

---

63. D. Barthélemy and J. T. Milik, "Recueil de prières liturgiques," in DJD 1:136, 152-55. Cf. Falk, *Daily, Sabbath, and Festival Prayers*, 155-87.

64. 4Q507, Baillet, DJD 7:175.

65. 4Q508, Baillet, DJD 7:177.

66. 4Q509, Baillet, DJD 7:184.

67. See Y. Yadin, *The Temple Scroll* (Jerusalem: Israel Exploration Society and Shrine of the Book, 1983) 1:89-142.

68. 4Q509 I 3 3-4; Baillet, DJD 7:186.

69. Amram Gaon, *Seder Rav 'Amram Ga'on*, 126; Sa'adyah Gaon, *Siddur Rav Sa'adyah Ga'on*, 151; Baer, *Seder 'Avodat Yiśra'el*, 352.

morning and evening, daily supplicatory prayers, and now, specific prayers for each festival. These constituted together a cycle of prayer texts that indicates a fairly developed liturgy. We cannot be sure if all three were recited by the same people, but it does seem likely that they constituted a unit, as part of the liturgy of the sect.

The Marriage Ritual

The next two texts to be treated here contain rituals for specific occasions. The first, 4Q502, is an extensive text that the editor has taken as a ritual for marriage.[70] Joseph M. Baumgarten[71] has disputed this interpretation. He sees the text as celebrating the place of honor accorded to elderly couples who joined the sect. Despite the claims of some that the sectarians of Qumran, identified as Essenes, were celibate, the Qumran texts speak of a society in which marriage is the norm.[72] Our text contains a direct parallel with the treatise of two spirits of the *Rule of the Community* that undoubtedly constituted part of the sectarian corpus.[73] Further, the clearly sectarian terms בני צדק[74] and תעודת[75] are used.

Baillet suggests that 4Q502 might have been part of a longer book of happy occasions, including marriage, circumcision, and bar mitzvah. This, however, is impossible. In the *Rule of the Congregation* we have a list of the ages of sectarian life.[76] While ten is the age of passage from the status of טף,[77] there is no mention of bar mitzvah in the sectarian corpus. Further, the list of stages does not mention circumcision,[78] even though the biblical command must have been fulfilled at eight days among the sectarians.

The text contains a series of prayers, apparently to be uttered by the principals in the ceremony. Each begins ... ברוך אל ישראל אשר.[79] The ap-

---

70. Baillet, DJD 7:81.

71. J. M. Baumgarten, "4Q502, Marriage or Golden Age Ritual?" *JJS* 35 (1983) 125-35.

72. Schiffman, *Sectarian Law*, 214-15; cf. F. M. Cross, *The Ancient Library of Qumran and Modern Biblical Studies*, rev. ed. (Grand Rapids: Baker, 1980) 97-100, 237-38.

73. Baillet, DJD 7:81; cf. frg. 16, p. 86, and 1QS 3:13-4:26.

74. Frg. 1:10, Baillet, DJD 7:82.

75. 8:9, Baillet, DJD 7:83; frg. 43:1, p. 91; 9:16, p. 83 [restored].

76. Cf. L. H. Schiffman, "The Eschatological Community of the Serekh ha-'Edah," *PAAJR* 51 (1984) 105-29.

77. 1QSa 1:8.

78. Gen 17:23-27; Lev 12:3; cf. L. H. Schiffman, *Who was a Jew? Rabbinic and Halakhic Perspectives on the Jewish Christian Schism* (New York: Ktav, 1985) 23-25.

79. Frg. 19:6, Baillet, DJD 7:86; frg. 24:2, p. 88.

pearance of such phrases as [בנ]ות ובנים], "sons and daugh[ters],"⁸⁰ רעייתו, "his wife,"⁸¹ פרי בטן, "the fruit of the womb,"⁸² לעשות זרע, "to reproduce,"⁸³ יחד שמחת, "mutual happiness,"⁸⁴ [א]בי הנערה, "the [fa]ther of the girl,"⁸⁵ and other such phrases would suggest that this is a marriage ritual. In addition, a fragmentary allusion indicates that it was a seven-day feast⁸⁶ as was the case also in biblical and talmudic traditions.

There are no perceptible parallels between this Qumran text and the marriage benedictions described in amoraic sources.⁸⁷ This text is totally unrelated to the liturgical traditions of the tannaitic period and, therefore, differs from the other liturgical materials from Qumran that we have examined.

The Purification Ritual

The final manuscript to be considered here, 4Q512, has been dated to the early first century B.C.E. Baillet has identified the following aspects discussed in this text: sexual impurities, purity of the cultic servitors, the laws of צרעת for both persons and houses, and contact with the dead.⁸⁸ In addition, there is explicit mention of the obligation to purify oneself for Sabbaths and festivals, for the equinoxes and solstices, and for the harvest festivals and the New Moon. This description seems to accord with the so-called sectarian calendar, based upon solar months and solar years.⁸⁹

Each person in association with his or her purification ritual would recite a prayer beginning with the clause: . . .ברוך אתה אל ישראל: "Blessed be you God of Israel who. . . ."⁹⁰ This series of recitations has a definite purpose intending to emphasize the spiritual dimension of the immersion ritual. One of the criticisms often leveled against the Jewish laws of ritual purity and impurity has been the apparent lack of concern with the ethical and religious dimension. The claim has been made that these rites are mechanical at best and

---

80. Frg. 14:6, Baillet, DJD 7:85.
81. Frg. 1:7, Baillet, DJD 7:82.
82. Partially restored in frg. 20:3, Baillet, DJD 7:87, and frg. 163:3, p. 99.
83. Frg. 1:4, Baillet, DJD 7:82.
84. Partially restored in frg. 4:3, Baillet, DJD 7:82, and frg. 105+106:2, p. 95.
85. Frg. 108:3, Baillet, DJD 7:95; cf. Judg 19:3.
86. Frg. 97:2, Baillet, DJD 7:94.
87. B. Ketub. 7b-8a.
88. Baillet, DJD 7:262.
89. See S. Talmon, "The Calendar Reckoning of the Sect from the Judean Desert," *Aspects of the Dead Sea Scrolls*, ed. C. Rabin and Y. Yadin, 162-99. ScrHier 4 (Jerusalem: Magnes, 1958).
90. Frg. 41:3, Baillet, DJD 7:274; frg. 42-4:3, p. 275.

that they represent taboos. This group of Jews, by at least the first century B.C.E., emphasized that these rituals have an important spiritual and religious meaning, that the purification from impurity must be preceded and accompanied by an inner turning, a dedication to the goals and aspirations that Judaism seeks. Indeed, this very idea is enshrined in the *Rule of the Community*,[91] which commands that only those who have done proper repentance may be permitted to enter the waters of purification. Purification is a deep spiritual process of self-improvement, not a mere cultic rite.[92]

Conclusion

If we may judge from the fragments found at Qumran, the sect practiced a regular order of prayer. Special texts were recited for each day of the month, morning and evening. Supplicatory prayers similar to the rabbinic Taḥanun were in use for the various days of the week. Special festival prayers were also recited. Liturgical materials accompanied the purificatory rituals, giving meaning and significance to these rites. Finally, there may have been a marriage ritual at Qumran.

By the Yavnean period (ca. 80-100 C.E.) the Shemaʿ and Eighteen Benedictions already formed the basis of the tannaitic liturgy, and the texts of some other important prayers must have been at least fairly fixed. Yet many disagreements existed, and much was left to be done. Clearly, the Yavnean sages were attempting to draw the community of Israel together around a common liturgy at a time when their traditions were diverse. An idea of the scope of this diversity can be gained by a look at the Qumran material, but much other temple and nontemple material must have existed as well. The task of the sages of Yavneh was to supplant this material and to crystallize a standardized Pharisaic-rabbinic liturgy that might serve as the basis of Jewish practice in future generations.

While many parallels exist in the area of liturgy between the practices of the Dead Sea sect and those of the early Tannaim, the differences are such as to require that we do not assume that Qumran materials typify Second Temple Judaism in all respects. After all, Judaism in this period was to a large extent a set of competing alternatives grappling with one another in what ultimately would turn out to be a test of the survival of the fittest. In that struggle, tannaitic Judaism would prevail. The Qumran sect came to an end

---

91. 1QS 2:26–3:12.
92. Cf. also E. Eshel, "4Q414, Ritual of Purification," in DJD 35:135-54.

in the early years of the revolt.[93] However, in those areas in which the parallels are clear, we are dealing most probably with elements common to the varieties of Judaism known from Second Temple times. These elements, represented at Qumran, constitute part of the heritage that tannaitic Judaism received from its spiritual forebears, the Pharisees. Some of the traditions in evidence at Qumran, common to most Second Temple Jews, therefore survived in the tannaitic tradition. Others might even have been bequeathed directly or through some intermediary to rabbinic Judaism. Many of the practices of the Qumran sect died out, and some went underground, only to emerge some seven centuries later in the Karaite movement.

The liturgy of rabbinic Judaism, then, has its roots in the traditions of the Second Temple period. Organized liturgical practices existed, at least among those Jews whose texts survived among the manuscripts of the Qumran library, already more than a century before the destruction of the temple. Prayer and the service of the heart were already becoming increasingly important. When the destruction of the temple brought to a close the age of sacrifice, the Tannaim, based on those inherited traditions, began to standardize and develop the system of prayer and ritual that later became embodied in the Jewish prayer book.

---

93. R. de Vaux, *Archaeology and the Dead Sea Scrolls*. Schweich Lectures 1959 (London: Oxford University Press, 1973) 38-41; J. Magness, *The Archaeology of Qumran and the Dead Sea Scrolls*. SDSSRL (Grand Rapids: Wm. B. Eerdmans, 2002) 61-62.

CHAPTER 14

The Concept of Covenant in the Qumran Scrolls and Rabbinic Literature

The Hebrew Scriptures speak of a series of covenants made by God with Israel or its forebears. These covenantal relationships are seen in the Bible to underlie Israel's relationship to God. Indeed, these covenants are axiomatic to Second Temple literature and talmudic texts and to their respective views of the place of Israel in the world and its unique place in history. This study will seek to compare the approaches taken to the concept of covenant and its role in Qumran texts[1] and rabbinic literature,[2] in the hope that we can make a modest contribution to the study of this idea and its role in the history of Judaism. The primary stress within the Qumran corpus will be on texts associated with the life and ideology of the Qumran sectarians.

It is certainly tempting to begin this paper with a lengthy discussion of the important conclusions of modern biblical studies regarding the notion of covenant in the ancient Near East, the literary form of suzerain treaties, and their relevance to the Bible.[3] Suffice it to say here, that the study of these materials has yielded the unanimous conclusion that the biblical covenantal formulations follow accepted ancient Near Eastern literary patterns and, therefore, that the biblical covenants are to be seen as statements of contractual relationship. The vassal binds himself to keep faith with the

---

1. See E. P. Sanders, *Paul and Palestinian Judaism* (Philadelphia: Fortress, 1997) 240-57; M. A. Elliott, *The Survivors of Israel: A Reconsideration of the Theology of Pre-Christian Judaism* (Grand Rapids: Wm. B. Eerdmans, 2000) 245-81; A. Deasley, *The Shape of Qumran Theology* (Carlisle: Paternoster, 2000) 138-64, dealing with the implications of covenant for the Qumran sect; and the thorough study of J. C. Volk, "Covenant," *EDSS* 1:151-55.

2. Sanders, *Paul and Palestinian Judaism*, 84-107.

3. D. R. Hillers, *Covenant: The History of a Biblical Idea* (Baltimore: Johns Hopkins, 1969).

suzerain. If the vassal keeps faith, so must the suzerain. If Israel keeps the Torah, God must keep his pledges. If Israel does not, it will suffer the consequences stipulated in the curse section of the contract. While such treaties or covenants were common in the ancient Near East, it was the unique contribution of Israel that such contracts could be made with God himself. Only in Israelite religion was the constancy of the covenant between God and humanity possible.[4]

We will define the corpus under study as those materials in which the term *berit*, "covenant," actually appears. We will let the ancient teachers speak for themselves. What did they consider to be the notion of covenant in the context of their specific approach to Judaism?

The Covenant of Noah

The *Genesis Apocryphon* originally contained an account of God's covenant with Noah (1QapGen 11:15–12:6),[5] even though the passage is fragmentary and the word for "covenant" does not occur. Column 14 may also be part of the account of this covenant. This covenant is also mentioned directly in 4Q370 *(Admonition Based on the Flood)* 1 7-8, which explicitly mentioned the rainbow as the symbol (ל[מען יזכור) of God's promise not to destroy the world again by a flood (Gen 9:8-17).[6] *Jub.* 6:1-14 describes God's covenant with Noah, which entails his promise not to bring another flood, and Noah and his sons' promise to abstain from eating blood. The text notes that this covenant was renewed at Sinai, where the obligation to sprinkle the blood of sacrifices was commanded. Here again, the rainbow is the sign of God's promise. These materials, we should note, are not part of the mainstream Qumranic sectarian compositions, but indicate that the Qumran sectarians were heir to a presectarian tradition regarding this venerable ancestor of Israel. The brief allusion to this covenant in the *Zadokite Fragments* (CD 3:1-4) reflects this presectarian tradition.

Rabbinic texts do not contain extensive discussion of a covenant with Noah. Yet this covenant gives rise to the benediction to be recited upon seeing

---

4. See the convenient summary of M. Weinfeld, "Covenant," *EncJud* 5:1012-22; "b^erîth," *TDOT* 2:253-79.

5. F. García Martínez and E. J. C. Tigchelaar, eds., *The Dead Sea Scrolls Study Edition* (Leiden: Brill and Grand Rapids: Wm. B. Eerdmans, 1997) 1:34-36.

6. C. A. Newsom, "4Q370: An Admonition Based on the Flood," *RevQ* 13 (1988) 23-43; in M. Broshi et al., *Qumran Cave 4.XIV: Parabiblical Texts, Part 2.* DJD 19 (Oxford: Clarendon, 1995) 85-97.

a rainbow. *T. Ber.* 6(7):5[7] provides that one who sees a rainbow recite: "Blessed [art Thou O Lord our God, King of the Universe] who is faithful to his covenant, who remembers the covenant" (נאמן בבריתו זכר הברית) *(ne'eman bivrito zokher ha-berit)*. This covenant with Noah extends God's promise to all humanity that he will not again destroy the world because of the transgressions of mankind (Gen 9:8-17).

Whereas the Qumran materials see Noah as occupying a central place in the chain of covenants leading to the formation of God's people of Israel,[8] the rabbis see him more as a transitional figure with whom a limited covenant was made. To the presectarian heritage, Noah was a great religious sage, but even to those rabbis who interpreted Gen 6:9 ("Noah was a righteous man, perfect in his generations") in a positive sense, he was not seen as an anachronistic tradent of the Jewish tradition in the pre-Abrahamic period. Such ideas are common in books like *Jubilees* and *Enoch*, but had only limited influence on rabbinic aggadah. No significant Noahide covenant was recognized by the rabbis.

Even the extensive Noahide laws, the rabbinic equivalent of natural law — the basic ethical and moral laws the observance of which was expected of all humanity — were actually understood to apply even from the time of Adam and Eve. Violation of these commandments led to the eradication of antediluvian society. Even where some of these laws were derived from verses connected with Adam, there was no sense of dependence on a two-sided covenant; rather, these natural laws were expressed as one-sided divine commands inherent in creation.[9]

The Covenant of Abraham

The *Genesis Apocryphon* contains an allusion to God's covenant with Abraham. In view of the fragmentary nature of this text, additional allusions originally may have stood in the text. In any case, 1Qap Gen[ar] 21:8-14 describes God's appearance to Abraham (still called Abram), his promise to him and his descendants of the land of Israel as an eternal inheritance, and his assur-

---

7. *Tosefta*, ed. S. Lieberman (New York: Jewish Theological Seminary of America, 1955-88) 1:34. Cf. Lieberman, *Tosefta Ki-Fshuṭah*, vol. 1: *Seder Zera'im* (New York: Jewish Theological Seminary of America, 1955) 108-9.

8. Cf. M. E. Stone, "Noah," *EDSS* 2:613-14.

9. See D. Novak, *The Image of the Non-Jew in Judaism*. Toronto Studies in Theology 14 (Lewiston: Mellen, 1983), esp. 3-35, 257-68; and A. Lichtenstein, *The Seven Laws of Noah* (Brooklyn: Berman, 1995).

ance that Abraham's descendants will be innumerable. This text represents an expanded version of Gen 13:14-17 that has been expanded harmonistically with details from other visions of Abraham, as is the method of the author of this text.

To be considered here as well is the concept of a covenant with the forefathers (ראשנים, lit., "first ones") mentioned in the *Zadokite Fragments* (CD 1:4-5; cf. 6:2) as the reason God chose to leave a remnant of Israel (the forerunners of the sectarians) when he brought destruction on the First Temple. This covenant is also mentioned in CD 3:1-4, which indicates that although Noah and his sons failed in this covenant, Abraham was able to pass it on to Isaac and Jacob. They fulfilled God's commandments, but Jacob's children did not keep the covenant and went into exile in Egypt. Because Israel did not follow the way of these forefathers, God brought upon them the punishments cataloged in the covenantal curses of the Bible (1:16-18; cf. 3:10-11;[10] see also 4Q463 *[Narrative D]* 1 1),[11] leading to the destruction of the temple (cf. CD 8:1). Among the transgressions of Israel was the causing of others to violate the covenant (1:20). Because of these transgressions, God transferred his covenant to those who held fast to the commandments (3:12-13). This remnant continued in the ways of the forefathers and their transgressions were forgiven (4:7-10). Since the covenant of God with Abraham and the Sinaitic covenant were both violated, God's covenant was then effectively transferred to the sect. An assumption of this text is that the laws of the Torah actually predated the Sinaitic revelation, a claim made consistently in *Jubilees* as well.

The Abrahamic covenant has one further ingredient, the practice of circumcision. This fact, which we will encounter so extensively in rabbinic literature, is attested rarely in the scrolls. However, CD 12:11 uses the phrase "covenant of Abraham" as a direct reference to circumcision, so closely associated with Abraham in Gen 17:10-15, 23-27. This covenant may be mentioned in 4Q378 (4QapocrJoshua^a) 22 i 4 (restoring הבר[ית),[12] or this passage may only be a general allusion to the covenant with Abraham.

M. B. Qam. 1:2-3 makes use of the phrase בני ברית, literally, "sons of the covenant," as a term for Israelites. Indeed, this usage is found throughout the entire rabbinic corpus. This incidental usage has behind it the entire notion of the Jews as a people who entered into a covenant with God. Most probably it refers to Abraham's covenant, the covenant of circumcision. This

---

10. Emending to *ḥavu*.
11. M. S. Smith, in Broshi et al., DJD 19:211-14.
12. C. A. Newsom, in G. J. Brooke et al., *Qumran Cave 4.XVII, Parabiblical Texts, Part 3.* DJD 22 (Oxford: Clarendon, 1996) 259.

interpretation is strengthened by the other references to this term in the Mishnah. *M. Ned.* 3:11, a beautiful lyrical passage extolling the importance of circumcision, says, "Great is circumcision, for thirteen covenants were made (lit., 'cut') for it." Here the Mishnah is referring to the occurrence of the word ברית thirteen times in the passage in which Abraham is commanded regarding circumcision (Genesis 17).

This term, *bene berit,* occurs in Qumran passages, also designating Israelites — male and female (1QM 17:8, 4Q284 *[Purification Liturgy]* frg. 4:2[13]). If we are correct in our analysis of the tannaitic usage, then the Qumran term may also be taken as based on the place of circumcision in the formation of Jewish identity, a role well attested in a variety of Greek and Latin texts from Late Antiquity.[14]

The evidence of the Mishnah points in only one direction. In the legal context of this text, and in its ideological underpinnings, the covenant is that of Abraham, symbolized by circumcision. The basis of Jewish obligation and relationship with God stems from this covenant. The term *berit,* "covenant," denoted circumcision in this legal context, not only as a ritual performed at a specific time in the life of the male Jew, but as a covenantal sign borne at all times, eternally binding the Jewish people to their God.

The Tosefta, the earliest commentary and supplement to the Mishnah, shows evidence of a somewhat wider usage of this term. Nonetheless, the covenant of circumcision is still quite prominent. In *t. Ber.* 6(7):12-13 there is a description of the benedictions to be recited upon performing a circumcision.[15] Before the ceremony the father is to intone: "Blessed art thou, O Lord our God, King of the Universe, who has commanded us to initiate him (the eight-day-old boy) into the covenant of Abraham our forefather." Those in attendance recite: "Just as he has been admitted to the covenant, thus may you admit him to observance of the Torah and to the marriage canopy." The benediction recited after the ritual refers to circumcision as "the sign of the holy covenant" and concludes: "Blessed art thou, O Lord, who made (lit., 'cut') the covenant."[16] The expression דם ברית, "the blood of the covenant," referring to the blood of the circumcision, appears twice in *t. Šabb.* 15(16):8-9.[17] This phrase continues to appear in all the later talmudic sources, often in quota-

---

13. J. M. Baumgarten, in J. M. Baumgarten et al., *Qumran Cave 4.XXV: Halakhic Texts.* DJD 35 (Oxford: Clarendon, 1999) 127.

14. L. H. Schiffman, *Who Was a Jew? Rabbinic and Halakhic Perspectives on the Jewish Christian Schism* (Hoboken: Ktav, 1985) 84, n. 35.

15. Cf. *Tosefta,* ed. Lieberman, 1:36-37.

16. Lieberman, *Tosefta Ki-Fshuṭah* 1:114-115.

17. *Tosefta,* ed. Lieberman, 2:70-72.

tions of this very text. Reference to those who perform epispasm as "effacing the covenant" occurs in *t. Sanh.* 12:9, where they are again said to lose their portion in the world to come.[18]

Mekhilta De-Rabbi Ishmael Be-Shallaḥ 3[19] contains the view that the covenant of circumcision, the covenant applying day and night, referred to in Jer 33:25, sustains the existence of heaven and earth. In other words, the text sees circumcision as the permanent sign of the Jew's connection to his Father in heaven.

The importance of the commandment of circumcision is implicit in the amoraic ruling of *y. Ber.* 1:5 (3d) to the effect that one who omits the mention of this commandment from the second benediction of the Grace after Meals must repeat the Grace. The Grace recounted all the gifts that God had bestowed upon his people, and the covenant of circumcision that God had "sealed in our flesh" had to be included.

A beautiful aggadah in *b. Men.* 53b pictures Abraham wandering in the temple on the eve of its destruction. God finds him and asks him what he is doing there. He says that he has come regarding his children and begins to entreat God on their behalf. When God answers by recounting their transgressions, Abraham, close to desperation, says to God: "You should have remembered their covenant of circumcision and saved them on this account." God retorts that even this sign of his covenant they have removed. Nonetheless, he assures Abraham that repentance will cause them eventually to be restored to their land and their temple. The covenant is eternal. Israel's repentance will always be accepted, and the land of Israel will be rebuilt.

While both the Qumran and rabbinic materials speak extensively about the covenant of Abraham, the emphases of these materials are completely different. For the Qumran and Second Temple texts, the covenant of Abraham is

---

18. *M. Abot* 3:11 lists several classes of individuals who have no portion in the world to come. This tradition is no doubt intended as a supplement to the better-known list in *m. Sanh.* 10:1. In any case, among these is listed "he who effaces the covenant of Abraham our father, may peace be upon him." This clearly refers to the practice of epispasm, the removal of the sign of circumcision, known to have been practiced by some extremely assimilating Jews in the Greco-Roman period. The numerous uses in the Palestinian Talmud of מפר ברית, to "efface the covenant," offer almost nothing that is not found in tannaitic sources. The only exception is the explicit identification in *y. Pe'ah* 1:1 (16b) and *y. Sanh.* 10:1 (27c) of such a person as the one who practices epispasm (זה שהוא מושך לו ערלה). Several passages in the Babylonian Talmud widen the meaning of מפר ברית from that of effacing the physical sign of circumcision to neglecting the Sinaitic covenant. Therefore, it is necessary for the Babylonian Talmud to refer to ברית בבשר to designate circumcision (*b. Šebu.* 13a; *b. Yoma* 85b; *b. Ker.* 7a; *b. Sanh.* 99a).

19. *Mekhilta de-Rabbi Ishmael*, ed. H. S. Horovitz and I. A. Rabin (Jerusalem: Bamberger and Wahrman, 1960) 98.

primarily tied up with the commitment of the patriarchs to follow God's teachings. For the rabbis, little else was symbolized by the Abrahamic covenant besides the centrality of circumcision.

Covenant of Jacob

Central to the *Temple Scroll* is a covenant of Jacob, which is mentioned at the end of the Sacrificial Festival Calendar source.[20] This passage, occupying virtually the whole of the preserved col. 29, is the conclusion, summing up the sacrifices, paralleling Num 29:39.[21] That text is expanded to refer not only to the various offerings but also to the temple in which God makes his name dwell (all stated in the first person, with God as the speaker) and promises that the offerings of the Jewish people will be accepted by God who will be their eternal God if they will be his people. The text then states that the temple it describes will be the seat of God's presence until the day of blessing (so Yigael Yadin; Elisha Qimron: "creation") — the dawn of the eschaton — when God himself will build a new one, "to establish it for myself for all times, according to the covenant which I have made with Jacob at Bethel" (29:10). This passage must have continued onto the top of col. 30 that is only minimally preserved.[22]

This notion of a covenant with Jacob at Bethel is based on the vision of Jacob's ladder, Gen 28:10-22 (cf. Lev 26:42).[23] The author of this section of the scroll understood Bethel, literally, "House of God," to be the location of God's temple in Jerusalem, for the text explicitly states in verses 17 and 22 that Jacob considered this place to be *Bet 'Elohim,* "the House of God." The covenant referred to in the *Temple Scroll,* therefore, is the establishment of the Temple Mount in Jerusalem as the permanent place of God's eternal temple.[24] This

20. See below, "Appendix: The Covenant of Jacob in the Temple Scroll" for more detailed treatment.

21. See the restorations of Y. Yadin, *The Temple Scroll* (Jerusalem: Israel Exploration Society and Shrine of the Book, 1983) 2:130; E. Qimron, *The Temple Scroll: A Critical Edition with Extensive Reconstructions* (Beersheva: Ben-Gurion University of the Negev and Jerusalem: Israel Exploration Society, 1996) 44, for 11QT^a 29:1-4. Cf. M. O. Wise, "The Covenant of Temple Scroll XXIX, 3-10," *RevQ* 14 (1989) 49-60; and H. A. Rapp, *Jakob in Bet-El: Gen 35,1-15 und die jüdische Literatur des 3. und 2. Jahrhunderts.* Herders biblische Studien 29 (Freiburg: Herder, 2001) 69-89.

22. Yadin, *Temple Scroll,* 2:130.

23. Rapp clearly sees Genesis 35 as the basis for this covenant. See *Jakob in Bet-El,* 25-63.

24. Cf. also the derivation of this same obligation from different biblical passages in 4QFlorilegium 1-2, col. i. Cf. G. J. Brooke, *Exegesis at Qumran: 4QFlorilegium in Its Jewish Context.* JSOTSup 29 (Sheffield: JSOT, 1985) 178-93; D. R. Schwartz, "The Three Temples of

promise was understood to have been made to Jacob at the time of his vision of the ladder.[25]

It is possible that this same covenant is alluded to in a sectarian manuscript, 5Q13 *(Sectarian Rule)* 2 6. As restored by Yadin, the passage reads, "]To Jacob you made known [your covenant] at Bethel."[26] The next lines (7-8) refer to the appointment of Levi to the priesthood, perhaps in accord with the passage in *Jubilees* to be discussed below.

The account of Gen 28:10-22 is repeated virtually verbatim in *Jub.* 27:19-27. But in *Jubilees* 32 Jacob returns to Bethel (paralleling Genesis 1–15, which appears at first glance to be a doublet of Genesis 28), this time with Levi, to sacrifice again. Here Levi had a dream that he was appointed to the eternal priesthood, and they sacrificed in order to fulfill the vow of Gen 28:20-22. Jacob, after these offerings, wanted to build a permanent temple there (v. 16) but God appeared and told him that it was not the correct place (v. 22). In other words, the covenant made with Jacob at Bethel in *Jubilees* (at his "second" visit) refers to the eternal priesthood of his son Levi, not to the location of the temple itself.[27]

Rabbinic sources do not speak of a covenant made with Jacob. But they do speak of the experience of the vision of the ladder as referring to the establishment of the Jerusalem temple. Effectively, two different views are expressed. One actually places the vision of "Bethel" on Mount Moriah — the Temple Mount. The other approach connects the Bethel vision with the Temple Mount by assuming that the ladder started in Bethel, extended such that its midpoint was over Jerusalem, and continued further to Haran in Assyria, the destination of Jacob.[28]

So on the one hand, one can say that there is effectively no covenant with Jacob in the rabbinic corpus. Yet, for the rabbis, the very same vision that lay at the core of the Jacob covenant of the *Temple Scroll* and *Jubilees* provided the patriarchal (or we might say pre-Israelite) basis for the same divine commitment to locate his eternal temple at Jerusalem.[29]

4Q*Florilegium*," *RevQ* 10 (1979) 83-92; M. O. Wise, "4QFlorilegium and the Temple of Man," *RevQ* 15 (1991) 103-32.

25. For this entire section, cf. Yadin, *Temple Scroll*, 2:182-7.

26. Yadin, *Temple Scroll*, 2:129; cf. M. Baillet, J. T. Milik, and R. de Vaux, *Les 'Petites Grottes' de Qumrân*. DJD 3 (Oxford: Clarendon, 1962) 182-83; L. H. Schiffman, "Sectarian Rule (5Q13)," in *The Dead Sea Scrolls: Hebrew, Aramaic, and Greek Texts with English Translations*, ed. J. H. Charlesworth, 1:134-35, and esp. n. 5 (Tübingen: Mohr [Siebeck] and Louisville: Westminster John Knox, 1994).

27. Cf. Rapp, *Jakob in Bet-El*, 171-202.

28. See *Gen. Rab.* 69:7, ed. J. Theodor and C. Albeck, 2:796 (Jerusalem: Wahrmann, 1965).

29. Some limited sense of a covenant with the sons of Jacob is found in rabbinic literature. In interpreting the priestly blessing, *Sifre Num.* 40 (*Sifre Be-Midbar*, ed. H. S. Horovitz [Je-

The Concept of Covenant in the Qumran Scrolls and Rabbinic Literature

The Covenant at Sinai

Mention of the covenant of Sinai occurs in 1Q Divre Mosheh (1Q22, *Words of Moses*), which is essentially a covenant renewal and summary text.[30] The text is a speech supposedly given by Moses forty years after the exodus, that is, in his last year. The people are to be assembled and told to remember the covenant of Sinai. The text relates, very much in a Deuteronomic manner, that they will sin and be punished. The Sabbath is referred to here as "the Sabbath of the covenant" (1:8). The Sabbath and the covenant are closely associated also in 4QapocrJer C^e (4Q390) 1 8.[31] Singled out for observance after Israel crossed the Jordan are the laws of the Sabbatical Year. This text appears to be some kind of a summary of the valedictory speech of Moses from Deuteronomy, rather than claiming to be an entirely different speech. But its main theme is the covenant of Sinai and the inevitable result of violation of its precepts.

Some sectarian texts use "covenant" to refer only to the Sinaitic covenant, as in the phrase עם קדושי ברית, "a nation sanctified through the covenant" (1QM 10:10). Similar is the mention of the covenant with "our forefathers" (1QM 13:7) that is understood to remain in force for their descendants (cf. 1QM 14:4, 8-9, 9-10). This covenant is probably referred to in 1Q34^{bis} 3 ii 6, "You renewed your covenant with them in vision(s) of glory."[32] "Visions of glory" refers to the vision of God at Sinai, and it is most unlikely, therefore, that this passage refers to the renewal of the covenant at the time of the establishment of the sect. 4QpsEzek^a (4Q385) 2 1 (= 4Q388 [psEzek^d] 7 2-3)[33] has God describing himself as having rescued his people, apparently from Egyptian bondage, "to give them the covenant," that is, the Torah that he gave them at Sinai.

---

rusalem: Wahrmann, 1966] 44) paraphrases, "God should preserve for you the covenant with your fathers." Indeed, the covenant was made even with the twelve sons of Jacob to the effect that their descendants would not be destroyed; *Sifra*, ed. I. H. Weiss (Vienna: Schlossberg, 1861/62; repr. New York: Om, 1946) p. 112c. The very same passage asserts that the covenant includes the right of possession of the land of Israel, an aspect of the Jacob covenant of 11QTemple 29.

30. D. Barthélemy and J. T. Milik, *Qumran Cave I*. DJD 1 (Oxford: Clarendon, 1955) 91-97.

31. D. Dimant, *Qumran Cave 4.XXI: Parabiblical Texts, Part 4: Pseudo-Prophetic Texts*. DJD 30 (Oxford: Clarendon, 2001) 237-44. Cf. also the list of sins, including Sabbath violation, connected with breaking the covenant in 4Q390 2 i 4-10 (DJD 30:244-49). Cf. Dimant, "New Light from Qumran on the Jewish Pseudepigrapha-4Q390," in *The Madrid Qumran Conference: Proceedings of the International Congress on the Dead Sea Scrolls, Madrid, 18-21 March 1991*, ed. J. Trebolle Barrera and L. Vegas Montaner, 2:405-48. STDJ 11/2 (Leiden: Brill and Madrid: Editorial Complutense, 1992).

32. Barthélemy and Milik, DJD 1:154.

33. Dimant, DJD 30:23-24, 83-84.

Numerous passages in the *Hodayot* seem to use the term ברית as equivalent to God's Torah and the covenant entered into at Sinai when it was given. The "laws of the covenant" (חוקי ברית) of CD 5:12 also refer simply to the laws of the Torah, although it is assumed that these laws existed already in the time of the Patriarchs. This Torah is to be observed even in the Babylonian exile, according to 4QapocrJerC[a] (4Q385a) 18 i a-b 7-11.[34] Similar use of "covenant" parallel to "Torah" occurs in Barkhi Nafshi[c] (4Q436) 1 i 4.[35]

The Jewish people seem to have been vouchsafed a "covenant of peace" (1QM 12:3).[36] An appeal to God's covenant is made in 1QM 18:7-8, reminiscent of biblical appeals to God's promises to Israel.

The covenant par excellence in rabbinic literature is certainly that of Sinai, where God and Israel were bound in an eternal relationship.[37] The expression הברית occurs in *t. Ḥal.* 1:6 as an oath formula in which a Tanna swears by the Torah. Certainly, here ברית is already a reference to the Sinaitic covenant, a usage that we will see appearing prominently in midrashic literature.

The picture of the concept of covenant that emerges from the Tosefta is considerably wider than that of the Mishnah. Here, in somewhat more aggadic context, we find a series of covenants of eternal validity. The covenant of circumcision made with Abraham remains the basis of Jewish identity. To this is added a Sinaitic covenant. Also, we hear of an eternal covenant made with the Aaronide priesthood providing them with the priestly dues. These covenants guarantee the natural order of creation that will never again be reversed, the relationship of Israel to its God, the special role of the priesthood, and the obligation of Israel to live according to the Torah given at Sinai.

Mekilta de-Rabbi Ishmael, Bo' 5[38] contains a fascinating expansion on the phrase *mefer berit* that in the Mishnah and Tosefta meant "efface the covenant." Here the expression is taken figuratively, in the sense of rejecting the Sinaitic covenant. This interpretation is accomplished through an exegesis of Deut 29:11 and 28:69. The net effect is that increasingly over time ברית is being

---

34. Dimant, DJD 30:159-62.

35. M. Weinfeld and D. Seely, in E. G. Chazon et al., *Qumran Cave 4.XX: Poetical and Liturgical Texts, Part 2.* DJD 29 (Oxford: Clarendon, 1999) 297-301.

36. Cf. 4Q491 *(War Scroll)* 11 ii 18 in M. Baillet, *Qumrân Grotte 4.III (4Q482-4Q520).* DJD 7 (Oxford: Clarendon, 1982) 31-34.

37. This study will not discuss the chosen people motif in the scrolls that has been discussed in L. H. Schiffman, "Non-Jews in the Dead Sea Scrolls," in *The Quest for Context and Meaning: Studies in Biblical Intertextuality in Honor of James A. Sanders,* ed. C. A. Evans and S. Talmon, 153-71 (Leiden: Brill: 1997).

38. Ed. Horovitz and Rabin, 15.

The Concept of Covenant in the Qumran Scrolls and Rabbinic Literature

taken in ways going far beyond the Mishnah's more limited usage to denote circumcision. The Sinaitic covenant is gradually upstaging the Abrahamic.

Sifra' Beḥukotai, *parashah* 2:3[39] draws a parallel between the notion of rejecting the covenant and rejecting God's sovereignty, כופר בעקר. Here the notion of covenant has been widened to the very existence of God himself that is so bound up with the idea of a covenantal relationship with Israel. After all, the essence of Israel's acceptance of the covenant with God is the recognition of God's power and authority over the world.[40]

One who worships idols is seen as negating the Sinaitic covenant in *Sifre Num.* 111.[41] The identity of the covenant with the Torah is explicitly stated, again indicating that this is the Sinaitic covenant, not the Abrahamic. Indeed, when *Sifre Num.* 112[42] wants to refer to the reversal of circumcision, it has to use the term ברית בשר, "the covenant of the flesh." By this time the use of ברית for the Sinaitic covenant had clearly become the most common.[43]

In *Sifra* Beḥukotai, *pereq* 6:1[44] the word ברית is used to refer to the covenant curses of Lev 26:14-46. Here we see the notion of the Tannaim that the entire Torah constituted the covenant made at Sinai, not just the Decalogue or some other portion of the Pentateuch.

---

39. Ed. Weiss, 111c.

40. That the *berit* is an oath, *shevu'ah*, that the Israelites have taken upon themselves is clear from *Mekhilta de-Rabbi Ishmael*, Shirah 9 (Horovitz and Rabin, 147; cf. Be-Shallaḥ 1, pp. 76-77). *Mekh.*, Yitro 5 (p. 219) goes a long way toward clarifying the nature of the Sinaitic covenant. Based on an exegesis of Deut 29:28 we are told that God promised Israel that he would enter into the covenant with them only concerning those commandments adherence to which is publicly known, but not regarding those kept hidden. By this he meant that Jews were to be held responsible for one another's actions only in regard to those that could be known. No Jew could be held responsible for the actions of another if they were done unbeknownst to him. This is an underlying concept of the rabbinic view of covenant. It is not simply that each Israelite at Sinai entered into a contract with the Deity; actually, the Jews banded together collectively to enter into this covenant to keep God's Torah. As such, they form a covenantal community. It is because of this aspect of the covenant that they must be responsible for each other's actions. Nonetheless, the Israelites stipulated at the outset that such responsibility could not be undertaken regarding violations of the covenant that were performed in private.

41. Ed. Horovitz, 116.

42. Ed. Horovitz, 121.

43. That the salt of the sacrifices is to be paid for with funds contributed by the community is derived in *Sifra Wa-Yiqra'*, *pereq* 12:6 (ed. Weiss, 12c) from the use of the phrase "salt of the covenant" (Lev 2:13). The significance of this passage is that the word ברית is taken automatically to indicate the communal nature of the obligation. After all, it flows from the covenantal community established at Sinai that collectively takes on the cultic obligations of the Levitical codes.

44. Ed. Weiss, 112a.

Rabbi Yonatan states in *Mekh.*, Yitro 10[45] that just as a covenant was made regarding the land of Israel, so was one made regarding chastisements. The people of Israel were promised eternally the land of Israel, yet the covenant included the provision that God would chastise Israel, but only temporarily and out of love.[46] Even if Israel is temporarily expelled from its land, it will eventually return.

A thrice repeated passage in *y. Pe'ah* 2:6 (17a); *y. Meg.* 4:1 (74d); and *y. Ḥag.* 1:8 (76d) makes the point that when God entered into the Sinaitic covenant with Israel, he told them that he was prepared to make the covenant with them only if they agreed to observe both the Oral Torah and the Written Torah. To the rabbis, the covenant was twofold. The validity of the Written Law was as interpreted in the Oral Law. Only the two together constituted the word of God.[47]

The Babylonian and Palestinian Talmuds really add only one significant idea to our understanding of the covenant in rabbinic literature. They emphasize the dual Torah concept. This notion was becoming more and more prominent in amoraic Judaism, both in Babylonia and Palestine, and it is only natural that the rabbis would have extended the covenant concept to include the oral law explicitly. Both Torahs provide the basis for the eternal covenant of the Jewish people and God. Both were given at Sinai.

In *b. Roš. Haš.* 17b a statement is quoted attributed to the Babylonian Amora Rav Judah regarding a covenant providing that the Thirteen Attributes (Exod 34:6-7) cannot go unanswered when recited in prayer. Again, this use of the term ברית is as a promise, not really a covenant. At the same time, this notion is linked with the Sinaitic covenant. The Thirteen Attributes are recited as part of the penitential prayers for forgiveness. God has promised Israel that their genuine repentance will indeed be accepted. Another figurative use of the term ברית is the notion that a covenant is made with the lips as found in *b. Mo'ed Qaṭ.* 18a and *Sanh.* 102a. This notion implies that whatever comes out of one's mouth will be fulfilled, even if it is not intended. Similarly eternal is the covenant of kingship promised to David in *Commen-*

---

45. Ed. Horovitz and Rabin, 240.

46. On chastisements and covenant, see *Sifre Deut.* 32 (ed. L. Finkelstein [New York: Jewish Theological Seminary of America, 1969], 57). We should note here the surprising paucity of material pertaining to the term ברית in *Sifre Deut.*

47. *B. Giṭ.* 60b states in the name of the Palestinian Amora Rabbi Yoḥanan that God entered into the Sinaitic covenant only for the sake of the Oral Law. This makes the point that it is the Oral Law, with its ability to adapt the Written Torah to new and varied circumstances, that makes the covenantal relationship of Israel and God permanent. He has given them a law that is truly eternal, not a stagnant system unfit for the vicissitudes of life and time.

tary on Genesis A (4Q252) col. 5[48] in accordance with this text's interpretation of Gen 49:10.

Both sectarian and rabbinic texts place the Sinai covenant squarely at the center of Jewish commitment and the authority of the Torah. For Qumran texts, the Sinai covenant is the central referent of the term ברית. For the rabbis, the covenant ("ברית") par excellence remains circumcision, and only in amoraic times does the Sinai covenant begin to rival circumcision as the essential and central covenant of God and Israel.

The Covenant with Levi and Aaron

Several Second Temple–period texts refer to a covenant with Levi, which essentially establishes the permanent priesthood of the descendants of this son of Jacob. This theme is prominent in the book of *Jubilees*. This covenant is repeated several times. As a result of the episode of Simeon and Levi and the people of Shechem (Genesis 34), it is emphasized (*Jub.* 30:17-19). It is again confirmed at length as part of the blessing of Levi by Isaac (*Jub.* 31:13-17). At Bethel (on which see above) this blessing is again confirmed (32:1-3).[49]

This same notion is found in the *Aramaic Levi Document*.[50] According to CTLevi Bodl. a[51] (=4Q213b[52]), apparently (in a lacuna) Isaac already designated Levi as priest and Jacob effected the actual appointment. This status was also consummated at Bethel according to Bodl. b. This text stresses the call to Levi (hence to the Aaronide priesthood) to maintain purity of behavior and family. Numerous laws of sacrifice, supposedly transmitted to Levi, then follow in the text.[53] We can be assured that somewhere in the unpreserved por-

---

48. Brooke, DJD 22:205-6.

49. None of these passages is preserved in the Qumran manuscripts. Cf. on these passages R. A. Kugler, *From Patriarch to Priest: The Levi-Priestly Tradition from* Aramaic Levi *to* Testament of Levi. SBLEJL 9 (Atlanta: Scholars, 1996) 161-67; and Rapp, *Jakob in Bet-El*, 202-27.

50. Cf. Kugler, *From Patriarch to Priest*, 146-55; and Rapp, *Jakob in Bet-El*, 91-109.

51. R. H. Charles, *The Greek Version of the Testaments of the Twelve Patriarchs*, 2nd ed. (Oxford: Clarendon, 1960) 246.

52. M. E. Stone and J. C. Greenfield, in Brooke, DJD 22:38-41. Cf. Kugler, *From Patriarch to Priest*, 77-93.

53. L. H. Schiffman, "Sacrificial Halakhah in the Fragments of the *Aramaic Levi Document* from Qumran, the Cairo Genizah, and Mt. Athos Monastery," in *Reworking the Bible: Apocryphal and Related Texts at Qumran, Proceedings of a Joint Symposium by the Orion Center for the Study of the Dead Sea Scrolls and Associated Literature and the Hebrew University Institute for Advanced Studies Research Group on Qumran, 15-17 January, 2002*, ed. E. G. Chazon, D. Dimant, and R. A. Clements. STDJ 58 (Leiden: Brill, 2005) 177-202.

tions of this text there is a mention of Aaron (his parents are mentioned), who was seen as a continuator of the priestly line of Levi as traced through Amram, whose name does appear in the text.

This priestly covenant is also echoed in the poem in 1QM 17:2-3 that refers to the eternal priestly covenant. The sons of Aaron as the maintainers of God's covenant, presumably of the priesthood, are mentioned in 4Q419 *(Instruction-like Composition A)* 1 1-3.[54] In *Rule of Benedictions* (1QSb) 3:22-30, there appears a blessing in honor of the Zadokite priesthood. This text asks God to renew "the covenant of [his] priest[hood]." This text indicates that the sectarians saw the priesthood as a covenant between God and specifically the Sons of Zadok, the only ones they (following the book of Ezekiel) regarded as legitimate priests.[55]

Rabbinic texts do not speak of a covenant with Levi, but rather mention extensively the covenant of Aaron, establishing the priesthood in his family. God's covenant with the descendants of Aaron to provide them the twenty-four priestly emoluments is the subject of *t. Ḥal.* 2:7.[56] Behind this lies the wider concept that there is a covenant with the sons of Aaron bestowing upon them eternal priesthood. This passage speaks of the twenty-four priestly gifts as having been given to Aaron and his sons through a "covenant of salt" (ברית מלח). The significance of the mention of salt is that it symbolizes the permanence of the covenant (cf. Num 18:19).[57]

That the priestly "covenant of salt," a biblical expression denoting a permanent covenant,[58] is to be eternal is stated in *Mekhilta de-Rabbi Ishmael, Pisḥa'* 1[59] based on citation of Num 18:19. Indeed, this covenant is singled out along with that of Sinai as being unconditional, as opposed to those pertaining to the land of Israel, the temple, and Davidic kingship (*Mekhilta de-Rabbi Ishmael,* ʿAmaleq 2).[60] While the land of Israel, the temple, and Davidic kingship can be taken away temporarily as a consequence of the transgressions of

---

54. S. Tanzer, in S. J. Pfann and P. S. Alexander et al., *Qumran Cave 4.XXVI: Cryptic Texts and Miscellanea, Part 1.* DJD 36 (Oxford: Clarendon, 2000) 322-24.

55. L. H. Schiffman, *The Halakhah at Qumran.* SJLA 16 (Leiden: Brill, 1975) 72-75.

56. Cf. Lieberman, *Tosefta Ki-Fshuṭah* 2:811-12.

57. The Temple Scroll (11QTemple[a] 20:13-14 [restored] and 11QTemple[b] 4 24) mentions the requirement of salting all offerings, in accordance with Lev 2:13; cf. Num 18:19. The covenant of salt refers, according to most commentators, to the permanence of God's covenantal sacrificial requirements.

58. H. Beinart, "Melaḥ," *EM* 4:1055-56.

59. Ed. Horovitz and Rabin, 2.

60. Ed. Horovitz and Rabin, 201. Cf. *Mekh. de-Rabbi Ishmael,* ʿAmaleq 2 (p. 200) on the covenant with Jonadab ben Rechab that was also unconditional. See also *Sifre Num.,* 118 (p. 142) on Aaron's "covenant of salt."

Israel, the Torah and the priestly status of the sons of Aaron can never be cancelled, not even temporarily.

Sifre Num. 117[61] repeatedly mentions the covenant God made with Aaron that his sons would be required to eat the holiest of offerings in the temple and that only male Aaronide priests who were ritually pure might eat of these sacrifices. In *Sifre Num.* 119[62] we hear of Aaron's joy at the covenant regarding the twenty-four priestly gifts. Aaron's covenant is greater than that of David. Whereas David can devolve his kingship only on those of his descendants who are righteous, the Aaronide pedigree of priesthood can be passed on even to those who are not righteous. This difference results from the nature of the priestly office, which is representative of Israel and not dependent on the character of the individual priest. Further, we learn that God also entered into a covenant promising the Levites that they would serve before him eternally.

It is apparent that a fundamental difference exists between the priestly covenants of the Second Temple materials, including the scrolls, and the rabbinic view. The earlier sources create a preexisting priesthood, starting with Levi, in consonance with their attribution of later biblical — even postbiblical — practices to the patriarchal family. While some tendencies of this kind are part of the rabbinic approach, they never gained prominence. So for the rabbis, the priestly covenant was with the first priest, Aaron, and not with any of his ancestors.

Covenant and the Qumran Sect

The use of the term "covenant" in reference to the sect itself is common, especially in the *Rule of the Community* (1QS). For example, in 1QS 1:8 ברית חסד appears as a descriptor for the sectarian group. To "enter (בוא) [the covenant of Go]d" (1QS 2:26-27) was tantamount to joining the sect (cf. CD 2:2).[63] To reject the covenant of the sect is to "despise" (מאס) it (cf. 4Q280 [Curses] 2 7 [restored]).[64] Those who attain the required state of purity are admitted to the covenant of the eternal community (ברית יחד עולמים; 1QS 3:11-12). God's covenant with the sect is eternal (1QS 4:22; 5:5-6). Further, the leadership of the sectarians is described as "the Sons of Zadok, the priests who

---

61. Ed. Horovitz, 134-36.
62. Ed. Horovitz, 143-45.
63. S. Lieberman, "The Discipline in the So-Called Dead Sea Manual of Discipline," in *Texts and Studies* (New York: Ktav, 1974) 203.
64. Nitzan, in Chazon et al., DJD 29:5-7.

guard his covenant, and . . . the majority of the men of the community who hold fast to the covenant" (1QS 5:2-3, 21-22; cf. 6:19). "A man from among the men of the community, the covenant of the community" can designate a sectarian (1QS 8:16-17).

The process in which the new sectarian swears allegiance when he begins the initiation process is termed "entering the covenant" and requires that he swear to return to the Torah of Moses, as well as to the sectarian interpretations derived by the Sons of Zadok and the sectarian assembly (1QS 5:8-10; cf. 5:20; 6:15; 1QSa 1:2-3). Those not in the sect will be punished with the covenant curses (1QS 5:10-13). They are described as outside of God's "covenant" (1QS 5:18-19) or as violators of the covenant (מרשיעי ברית, 1QM 1:2). This same phrase appears in 4Q387 (ApocrJer C^b) 3 6-8,[65] which describes, in an *ex eventu* prophecy, Hasmonean rule and the war that would erupt "over the Torah and over the covenant," apparently an allusion to the sectarian struggles of the Hasmonean age. Similar to the מרשיעי ברית are the עריצי הברית of *Pesher Psalms A* (4Q171 1-10 iii 12)[66] who oppose the sect. On the other hand, the sectarians are designated "[those] who observe (or maintain) the covenant, who turn aside from going [in the p]ath of the people" in 11QMelch (11Q13) 2:24.[67]

Apparently designating the sectarians are the expressions "the lot of his [co]venant" (1QM 17:6) and "sons of the covenant" (line 8). As noted above, rabbinic parallels indicate that the latter term often refers to the children of Israel and alludes to their observance of circumcision. In 1QSa 1:3, the eschatological *Rule of the Congregation*, we are told that the adherence of the sect to the covenant with God had atoned for the land. Had the sect not held fast to the correct interpretation of the law the land would have been destroyed.[68]

As has been amply noted, the procedures for joining the Qumran sect are very similar to those for joining the *ḥavurah* described in tannaitic sources.[69] Yet these groups are never termed a "covenant," and no connection

---

65. Dimant, DJD 30:191-4.
66. M. P. Horgan, *Pesharim: Qumran Interpretations of Biblical Books*. CBQMS 8 (Washington: Catholic Biblical Association of America, 1979) 97, translates "ruthless ones of the covenant." See her thorough discussion on p. 10.
67. F. García Martínez, E. J. C. Tigchelaar, and A. S. van der Woude, *Qumran Cave 11.II (11Q2-18, 11Q20-31)*. DJD 23 (Oxford: Clarendon, 1998) 226-33.
68. Cf. L. H. Schiffman, *The Eschatological Community of the Dead Sea Scrolls*. SBLMS 38 (Atlanta: Scholars, 1989) 11-13.
69. Lieberman, *Texts and Studies*, 200-7; C. Rabin, *Qumran Studies*. Scripta Judaica 2 (London: Oxford University Press, 1957) 1-21.

to "covenant" is made. It is because the Qumran sectarians considered themselves as the true biblical Israel that they believed they were vouchsafed a special covenantal status as a group.[70] Because the rabbis saw themselves as living in the postbiblical era, they saw their covenantal relationship as derivative from the Bible — but not from a direct, independent relationship with God. The Qumran sect, on the other hand, believed that it had an independent covenant with God.

Covenant Renewal Ceremony

A prominent part of the *Rule of the Community* (1QS 1:16–2:25)[71] is devoted to the description of the annual covenant renewal and mustering ceremony of the sectarians at Qumran.[72] The ceremony consists of blessings uttered by the priests and curses recited by the Levites,[73] based on the model of the biblical covenant ceremony of Deuteronomy 27–28 (cf. 11:29) that took place at Mounts Gerizim and Ebal. But the sectarian covenant renewal ceremony is rife with sectarian theological concepts, such as the division of light and darkness and predestination, as well as the isolationist worldview of the sect. Those who "pass" through the covenant, i.e., who are mustered, recited a confession based on biblical models and similar to that which became the norm in later Jewish penitential ritual. They also respond "amen" to the blessings and curses. The covenant renewal ceremony includes also a procession of priests, Levites and the rest of the sectarians, organized according to the military organization of the desert period.

It appears from 1QSa 1:5 that it was expected that there would be a covenant renewal at the onset of the end of days.[74] This covenant renewal cere-

---

70. S. Talmon, "The 'Desert Motif' in the Bible and in Qumran Literature," in *Biblical Motifs, Origins and Transformations*, ed. A. Altmann (Cambridge, MA: Harvard University Press, 1966) 55-63; repr. in Talmon, *Literary Studies in the Hebrew Bible: Form and Content: Collected Studies* (Leiden: Brill, 1993) 216-54.

71. Cf. also 4Q256 2; P. S. Alexander and G. Vermes, *Qumran Cave 4. XIX: Serekh ha-Yaḥad and Two Related Texts*. DJD 26 (Oxford: Clarendon, 1998) 47-52.

72. Cf. J. Licht, *Megillat ha-Serakhim mi-Megillot Midbar Yehudah* (Jerusalem: Bialik Institute, 1965) 63-65, 74-76; and R. Elior, *Miqdash u-Merkavah, Kohanim u-Mal'akhim, Hekhal ve-Hekhalot ba-Misṭiqah ha-Yehudit ha-Qedumah* (Jerusalem: Magnes, Hebrew University, 2002) 142-61.

73. Cf. also 4Q280 (Curses), ed. B. Nitzan, in Chazon et al., DJD 29:1-8; 4Q286 (Berakhot[a]) 7 ii, ed. Nitzan, in E. Eshel et al., *Qumran Cave 4.VI: Poetical and Liturgical Texts, Part 1*. DJD 11 (Oxford: Clarendon, 1998) 27-30.

74. Schiffman, *Eschatological Community*, 13.

mony is based on the sect's peculiar concept of covenant, as described above. Accordingly, we cannot expect any rabbinic parallels to the covenant renewal ceremony performed annually by the sect. Again, this ceremony was based on the self-conception of the sect as biblical Israel and would have been totally irrelevant to the rabbinic concept of covenant — a permanent relationship of God and Israel seared in the flesh by circumcision and consummated with the giving of the Torah at Sinai.

The Renewed Covenant

Much attention has been given to a passage in the *Zadokite Fragments* (CD 6:19) that refers to the sectarians not simply as those who have entered the covenant, but also as having entered "the new (or better, 'renewed') covenant,"[75] an allusion to Jer 31:31 that has resonated so deeply in the early Christian tradition (Luke 22:20; 1 Cor 11:25).[76] This same notion is paralleled in CD 8:21=19:33 and also in 20:12.

That the sect saw itself as a collective "renewed covenant" is clear from *Pesher Habakkuk* (1QpHab) 2:2-10. There, the "treacherous ones" and the Man of the Lie are castigated because they did not believe in the renewed covenant, apparently the sect that had been proclaimed by the Teacher of Righteousness, as had been revealed to him by divinely-inspired pesher exegesis of the biblical text. In rejecting the renewed covenant, apparently leaving the sect after initially being part of it, they profaned God's name. Early Christianity understood this passage in Jeremiah to refer to the replacement of God's covenant with the Jewish people by a "new covenant" with those who accepted the messiahship of Jesus. Needless to say, the Qumran view speaks of the renewal of God's ancient covenant with biblical Israel — with the sectarians who continue the role of ancient Israel — not of its replacement or displacement.

Sifra' Beḥukotai, *Pereq* 2:5[77] raises the notion of the "new covenant" of Jer 31:31-34. As opposed to the previous agreement that Israel cancelled by violating the Torah, Israel will be faithful to the renewed covenant. To the rab-

---

75. Deasley, *The Shape of Qumran Theology,* 140-50, deals with the renewed covenant.
76. For a thorough discussion of this motif, see J. R. Lundbom, "New Covenant," *ABD* 4:1088-94. Cf. S. Talmon, "The Community of the Renewed Covenant: Between Judaism and Christianity," in *The Community of the Renewed Covenant: The Notre Dame Symposium on the Dead Sea Scrolls,* ed. E. Ulrich and J. VanderKam, 12-15. CJAS 10 (Notre Dame: University of Notre Dame Press, 1994).
77. Ed. Weiss, 111a.

bis, this passage in Jeremiah referred not to a new covenant that would in some way replace the Torah, but to a renewal of commitment to the Torah of Sinai. It was to be not a new covenant, but a renewed covenant.[78]

There is agreement between the sectarian texts and the rabbis that the "new covenant" is in reality a "renewal covenant." At the same time, when we compare the sectarian and rabbinic views, there is a large discrepancy. For the rabbis the renewed covenant simply means a return by the entire Jewish people to the full observance of God's law that Israel had neglected. For the sectarians, the renewed covenant was the indication of their particular relationship with God — what made them the true Israel and disqualified the rest of the Jewish people. In this respect, some affinity does exist between the Qumran "new covenant" and that of the early Christians.

Conclusion

The results of our comparisons can be summed up in very simple terms. There is a large degree of incongruity between the concepts of covenant described in the sectarian and rabbinic corpora. While most of the basic elements are in some way shared, the differing ideological backgrounds and exegetical frameworks yielded basically disparate approaches to the details of the various covenants alluded to in our texts.

Despite these disagreements and the entirely different *Sitz-im-Leben* of each approach, all Jewish groups of Late Antiquity believed that Israel's covenant with God is an eternal covenant. It binds Israel to observe the commandments and to continue to live by the Torah. In return, God is to treasure Israel and to protect her. Israel is assured of the power of repentance. The sectarians and the rabbis agreed heartily with the words of Deut 5:2-3, "The Lord our God made a covenant with us at Horeb. It was not with our fathers that the Lord made this covenant, but with us, the living, every one of us who is here today."

Appendix: The Covenant of Jacob in the Temple Scroll

One cannot discuss the specifics of the covenant of Jacob without some detailed knowledge of the location of this motif in the *Temple Scroll* and its par-

---

78. Cf. the detailed discussion of this and related issues in W. D. Davies, *Torah in the Messianic Age and/or the Age to Come* (Philadelphia: SBL, 1952) 50-83.

ticular role. The allusion to this covenant comes at the end of the source known as the "Sacrificial Festival Calendar" that occupies cols. 13-29 of 11QTemple[a]. This section represents a reworking of Numbers 28–29 in light of other parallel sacrificial commands found elsewhere in the Torah, especially in Leviticus 23, also a sacrificial festival cycle. It is generally accepted today that the Festival Calendar was available to the author/redactor of the complete scroll when he did his work early in the Hasmonean period. This section demonstrates the technique of midrashically harmonizing the disparate biblical texts relating to a specific topic and creating out of them a newly redacted whole. This new whole comes to an end in col. 29. After concluding his discussion of the Eighth Day of Solemn Assembly *(Shemini Atseret)* (11QTemple 29:09-1), parallel to Num 29:35-38, the author of this section of the scroll turns to the summary section of Num 29:39–30:1 that was the conclusion of the Numbers Festival Calendar. Here the author mixes in language from the similar concluding passage from Lev 23:37-39.[79] At this point the scroll adds a section of original composition, either of the author of this source or the author/redactor of the scroll. In favor of the latter possibility is the presence of Deuteronomic name theology that plays so prominent a role throughout the *Temple Scroll* and may thus be attributed to the author/redactor of the complete scroll.[80]

In this passage (lines 4-10) we are told that offerings should be made "according to the law of this ordinance" (כתורת המשפט הזה) continuously, presumably on the festivals, besides the various freewill offerings and emoluments for priests and Levites, and that God promises to accept them. These rites are to continue in God's eternal dwelling place until the day of blessing (or [new] creation) when God will create a new temple. Here we must note that the temple of the *Temple Scroll* and its ritual law is therefore not eschatological, but rather intended by the text to be the correct (that is, reformist) law for the present, premessianic period. The text then, in its preserved state, ends with the key words, "according to the covenant which I have made (lit., 'cut') with Jacob at Bethel."

The top (the zero lines) of the following column, col. 30, may have contained further information on our topic. Yadin suggests that the text continued with details regarding the command to build the scroll's premessianic temple. This section would have ended in line 3 with some text similar to

---

79. See the differing restorations of Yadin, *Temple Scroll*, 2:127; and E. Qimron, *Temple Scroll*, 44.

80. L. H. Schiffman, "The Theology of the Temple Scroll," *JQR* 85 (Qumran Studies, 1994) 109-23.

The Concept of Covenant in the Qumran Scrolls and Rabbinic Literature

ושמרתה כל אשר צויתיכה ל[עשות, "and you shall be careful to do all which I have commanded you to do."[81]

The entire missing conclusion would therefore have contained 15 lines (contra Wise,[82] who suggests 12, the number of unpreserved lines at the top of the column). Basing himself on the mention of the covenant of Jacob in Lev 26:42, Michael O. Wise suggests that our text must have likewise mentioned all three forefathers. He accordingly restores, כברית אשר כרתי עם יעקב בבית אל ועם יצחק בגרר ועם אברהם בחרן, "according to the covenant which I made with Jacob at Bethel and Isaac at Gerar and with Abraham at Haran."[83] In this reading, the covenant of 11QTemple 29 is not to build the temple, but rather a broad covenant with the Patriarchs that God would be present in the land, and that they would worship and obey him. The breaking of this wider covenant, in this view, would cause the punishment described in Leviticus. Wise goes on to suggest that this view was shared by the author of the *Zadokite Fragments*.

We have noted already that the *Jubilees* material evinced by Yadin is not really parallel. But the rabbinic parallels certainly lead us to recognize the close link between the Jacob-Bethel experience and the Jerusalem temple. In fact, these parallels seem sufficiently clear to us to force rejection of Wise's reconstruction and maintenance of the basic idea of a Jacob covenant, partly similar and partly different from that of *Jubilees*.

---

81. Yadin, *Temple Scroll,* 2:130.
82. Wise, "The Covenant of Temple Scroll," 52.
83. Wise, "The Covenant of Temple Scroll," 57.

CHAPTER 15

Holiness and Sanctity in the Dead Sea Scrolls

Analysis of the concepts of holiness and sanctity in the Dead Sea Scrolls is at the same time simple and extremely complex. After all, these ideas are mentioned numerous times in the Dead Sea Scrolls, and these passages are easily flagged because of their use of the Hebrew root קדש.[1] Yet simply looking for the root קדש would only yield a collection of passages, easily categorized by subject according to the scheme proposed by Rudolph Otto.[2] Holiness and sanctity are multifaceted concepts, the definitions of which are much wider than the semantic fields bounded by the Hebrew word קדש.[3] Such an approach would not yield anything unique about the scrolls or the Dead Sea sectarians, and would not produce a study that could be helpful in contrasting Qumran materials with those of the Hebrew Bible, rabbinic literature, or early Christianity. Rather, the role of holiness and sanctity at Qumran must be investigated based on a wide appreciation of the literature and its religious aspects. Going way beyond the use of the term קדש in the texts, we will uncover the religious ideas of holiness and sanctity that were so crucial to the Dead Sea sect.

---

1. See W. Kornfeld and H. Ringgren, "קדש," *TDOT* 12:521-45. See esp. the section on Qumran by Ringgren, 544-45 and the bibliog. in 545, n. 100.

2. R. Otto, *The Idea of the Holy: An Inquiry into the Non-rational Factor in the Idea of the Divine and Its Relation to the Rational,* trans. J. W. Harvey. 2nd ed. (New York: Oxford University Press, 1950).

3. Cf. E. Berkovitz, *Man and God: Studies in Biblical Theology* (Detroit: Wayne State University Press, 1969) 141-223 for a wide-ranging study of holiness in biblical thought.

Holiness and Sanctity in the Dead Sea Scrolls

Sect as Temple

A long passage in col. 8 of the *Rule of the Community* (1QS) will be our starting point. The passage begins by setting out the nature of a community council (8:1-4) of twelve representatives, presumably one for each tribe, and three priests, presumably for the clans of Gershon, Kohath, and Merari. The text continues that when this council is formed, the community as a whole (עצת היחד) will be:

> Founded on truth, as an eternal plantation, a holy house for Israel, and the foundation of the holy of holies for Israel, . . . the most holy dwelling for Aaron, with all their knowledge of the covenant of justice (1QS 8:5-9=4Q259 ii 13-17[4]).

The text then tells us that after the council is organized for two years:

> They will be separated as a sanctuary in the midst of the council of the men of the community (1QS 8:11=4Q258 vi 5[5]).

Further, once this wider community is established, anyone who purposely violates a commandment "may not touch the pure food of the men of holiness (1QS 8:17=4Q258 vi 9)." In 8:20 (=4Q258 vi 11), a long section — termed the sectarian penal code — then starts off with, "these are the regulations by which the men of perfect holiness shall conduct themselves."[6]

These passages afford us a detailed sense of what holiness and sanctity meant to Qumran sectaries, in addition to what they had inherited from the traditions of the Hebrew Bible. The sect itself is seen as a holy house — this means that for all intents and purposes, the sect replaces the actual physical holy house, the Jerusalem temple, which the sectarians have shunned because in their view it is in violation of the Torah's laws.[7] Further, for the Aaronide priests who constituted the founders and earliest leaders of the sect, the group (or perhaps its council) constituted the true holy of holies. In fact, it is only

---

4. P. S. Alexander and G. Vermes, *Qumran Cave 4. XIX: Serekh ha-Yaḥad and Two Related Texts*. DJD 26 (Oxford: Clarendon, 1998) 139-44; cf. 4Q258 vi 1-3 (DJD 26:105-9) and 4Q265 (*Miscellaneous Rules*) in J. M. Baumgarten et al., *Qumran Cave 4.XXV: Halakhic Texts*. DJD 35 (Oxford: Clarendon, 1999) 69-72.

5. Alexander and Vermes, DJD 26:105-9.

6. Cf. L. H. Schiffman, *Sectarian Law in the Dead Sea Scrolls: Courts, Testimony and the Penal Code*. BJS 33 (Chico: Scholars, 1983) 155-59.

7. B. Gärtner, *The Temple and the Community in Qumran and the New Testament* (Cambridge: Cambridge University Press, 1965).

the sect that makes possible atonement (lines 6-7; not quoted above). It is in this substitute temple that the priests will offer the sacrifices.

We can already observe that the sectarians have transferred the sanctity of the temple, usually understood as spatial and as typifying holiness of place, to their group. Just as priests ministered in the temple, so they led the sect. Just as the sacrifices were supposed to bring atonement for the people and their land (line 6), so the life of the sect performed the same functions.

Another extremely important aspect of the life of the sect and its holiness is its separation from the rest of Israel, described in 1QS 8:12-13 (=4Q258 vi 6-7[8]=4Q259 ii 3-4[9]):

> When these have become a community in Israel, ... they are to separate (יבדלו) from the midst of the assembly of the men of iniquity to go to the desert. ...

This second aspect of sectarian holiness picks up on the root meaning of קדש — to separate, here translated with בדל. However, whereas in the Bible and rabbinic literature separation is from that which is impure or evil, here it is from the people of iniquity. However, this concept is closely linked with that of the sect as temple. Spatial sanctity of the temple is transferred to the group. What is inside is holy, as led by priests and others, but what is outside is not holy, and therefore to be separated from. The boundaries of a physical temple with its *temenos* and courtyards are here imitated in the life of the group. Its boundaries are understood to be those of the temple. The pure food of the sect (line 17) was equivalent to the sacrifices, and the sectarians were called holy men. Those who followed the way of the sect were termed "men of perfect holiness" and the sect is a "council of holiness" (lines 20-21).

Holiness and Purity

The Qumran sect also saw holiness as closely linked with ritual purity. From this point of view, like the members of the *havurah* discussed in rabbinic literature, the sectarians sought to observe the laws of temple purity in their regular daily lives. For the sectarians, the system of ritual purity was intimately connected with membership in the sect,[10] which, as we have seen, was tantamount to entry into the holy temple itself. Effectively, purity functioned

---

8. See esp. Alexander and Vermes, DJD 26:107 on the variant readings of the manuscripts.
9. Alexander and Vermes, DJD 26:144-48.
10. Schiffman, *Sectarian Law*, 161-65.

in the life of the sect in a way very similar to its role in the temple — as a sign of greater sanctity and closeness to the divine.

However, in addition, purity statutes served as a means of demarcation of levels of sanctity and, hence, sectarian status. This was the function of purity as a boundary marker in the temple — here transformed to the life of the sect.

The *Rule of the Community* describes the process of admission to the sect (1QS 6:13-23).[11] The first step was examination by the פקיד ברואש הרבים, the "official at the head of the community." If this official approved the candidate, the novice took his oath of admission and was then taught the sectarian regulations. Only then did the מושב הרבים, the sectarian assembly, render a decision regarding him, presumably based upon his performance to date. If he passed this examination, he attained a partial status. The novice was not permitted to touch the pure food of the community for one year until he was examined by the מושב הרבים once again. If he passed, he was elevated to a higher status whereby his property was temporarily admitted into communal use, but he still was not permitted to touch the liquid food of the community for another year. After the third examination by the מושב הרבים, he could be admitted as a full member of the sect with all privileges including entry into the sectarian assembly.

All these stages serve to link the instruction in sectarian teachings with the initiation into the sect through the medium of ritual purity. As the novice gained in knowledge of the sect's interpretations of biblical law and passed examinations, he was gradually admitted into greater confidence amongst the members, and he gradually rose in ritual purity until he was able to partake of all the pure food and drink of the sect.

Jacob Licht explains that the process of initiation accords well with tannaitic halakhah in which liquids are more prone to contract and pass on impurity than solids.[12] Thus, the touching of liquids is the last stage to which the novice was admitted.[13] Also, this theory explains why a member of the Qumran sect who sinned was removed from the pure food as a punishment. Since ritual purity was, to the sectarians, a symbol of inner, spiritual purity, he who transgressed slid back down the ranks through which he had risen.

---

11. Partially paralleled in 4Q256 11 11-13 (DJD 26:55-57); 4Q261 3 1 (DJD 26:177-78).

12. J. Licht, *Megillat ha-Serakhim mi-Megillot Midbar Yehudah* (Jerusalem: Bialik Institute, 1965) 294-303.

13. Cf. C. Rabin, *Qumran Studies*. Scripta Judaica 2 (London: Oxford University Press, 1957); S. Lieberman, "The Discipline in the So-Called Dead Sea Manual of Discipline," *JBL* 71 (1951) 199-206; repr. in *Texts and Studies* (New York: Ktav, 1974) 200-7.

He is once again forbidden from the food of the sectarians until he repents and regains his pure religious state.

Effectively, what has been created here by means of purity is a set of boundaries of increasing sanctity. Entering the sect is like entering the *temenos*, and proceeding through the levels of initiation is like entering further into the courts of the temple and then into the temple itself and the holy of holies. These purity rules and their connection with the initiation rites were what made the Qumran sect truly a "Holy House."

Holiness of Heaven on Earth

If holiness had been transferred "spatially" from the Temple Mount in Jerusalem to the sect and its life, which we may call a horizontal transference, we may also speak of a vertical transference, or better union, in which the holiness of the sect is the result of an angelic presence.[14] This concept is central to the *War Scroll* and its portrayal of the eschatological war to be conducted both in heaven and on earth. The *Rule of the Congregation* (1QSa 2:3-11) specifies that eschatological purity requires the absence of those with specific deformities, the impure, and the aged since the angels are regarded as being present in the assembly.[15] 1QM 7:6 gives the very same reason for the requirement that those impure from a seminal emission not participate in the eschatological battle: "For holy angels are together with their armies."[16] Baruch M. Bokser suggested that this is actually a reworking of Deut 23:15 that explains the requirement of ritual purity in the military camp as resulting from the presence of the Lord. Bokser maintains that the divine presence is represented here by the angels.[17]

A parallel to this very concept occurs in 1QM 12:7-8 where it is stated that the angels are fighting among the members of the sect: "A host of angels is mustered with us."[18] It was a cardinal belief of the sect that just as the world

---

14. For a somewhat different perspective on the priestly aspects of this notion, see R. Elior, *Miqdash u-Merkavah, Kohanim u-Mal'akhim, Hekhal ve-Hekhalot ba-Mistiqah ha-Yehudit ha-Qedumah* (Jerusalem: Magnes, Hebrew University, 2002) 174-202.

15. Cf. L. H. Schiffman, *The Eschatological Community of the Dead Sea Scrolls*. SBLMS 38 (Atlanta: Scholars, 1989) 37-52.

16. Y. Yadin, *The Scroll of the War of the Sons of Light against the Sons of Darkness* [hereafter *War Scroll*], trans. B. and C. Rabin, 290-91 (Oxford: Oxford University Press, 1962). Cf. 4Q491 1, 2+3 line 10; M. Baillet, *Qumrân Grotte 4.III (4Q482-4Q520)*. DJD 7 (Oxford: Clarendon, 1982) 13-18. On angels in the *War Scroll*, see Yadin, *War Scroll*, 229-42.

17. B. M. Bokser, "Approaching Sacred Space," *HTR* 78 (1985) 279-99.

18. Yadin, *War Scroll*, 316-17; cf. 4Q491 1, 2+3 line 10.

below is divided into the domain of the two spirits,[19] those of good and evil, so was the world of the angels. Just as the Teacher of Righteousness and the Wicked Priest represented the forces of good and evil to the sect in the present age,[20] so the Prince of Light (the angel Michael) and his enemy, Belial, represented the very same forces on high.[21] These forces would be arrayed against each other in the end of days, just as they are in the present, premessianic age.

The great eschatological battle would be fought, therefore, simultaneously both in heaven and on earth. In the actual battle angels and men would fight side by side. After the long series of engagements described in the *War Scroll*, the forces of good would be victorious. For this reason, the sect believed that in the end of days the angels would be present in the military camp described in the *War Scroll*. At the very same time, the eschatological council would also involve both the earthly and heavenly Sons of Light.[22] This angelic presence effectively merged the realms of heaven and earth for the sectarians. Living in the present in expectation of the messianic era meant living as though divine representatives were among them. The eschatological dream meant that somehow heaven and earth would meet and that heavenly sanctity would now be manifest on earth below.

Holiness and the Eschaton

A principle of the Qumran sect was its view that holiness would be perfected only in the end of days. In fact, the perfection of the end of days involved both the ultimate victory over and elimination of the forces of evil and also the perfect observance of Jewish law as interpreted by the sectarians. It was believed that when the messianic war began, the sect would be mustered to fight the battles against the evildoers and those who do not know the correct interpretation of the Torah that the sect expounds. As the sect finally overcame its ene-

---

19. 1QS 3:13-4:26. Cf. L. H. Schiffman, *Reclaiming the Dead Sea Scrolls: The History of Judaism, the Background of Christianity, the Lost Library of Qumran* (Philadelphia: Jewish Publication Society, 1994; repr. ABRL [New York: Doubleday, 1995]) 149-50; J. Duhaime, "Dualism," *EDSS* 1:215-20.

20. Schiffman, *Reclaiming the Dead Sea Scrolls*, 117-21, 231-35.

21. Yadin, *War Scroll*, 232-36.

22. In addition to those with deformities, the impure, and the aged, 1QM 7:3-4 states that women and children are also to be excluded from the military camp. It is most likely that the very same regulation was in force regarding the eschatological council. Although women and children would be part of the sect, as is evident from 1QSa 1:6-11, their presence among the angels in the council of the community would not be allowed, nor were they permitted in the military camp during the battle at the end of days.

mies and was victorious, the righteous of Israel who turn to God and adopt the sectarian way of life would also be included in the sect. Together with the original sectarians, they would constitute the eschatological community. This new community would gather together for the messianic banquet under the leadership of the Zadokite priestly messiah and the messiah of Israel.[23]

The messianic era was understood to constitute the ultimate utopia, a world in which perfection in purity and worship would surpass all of history. The sect of the future age — now really the only Jewish way — would fulfill all the aspirations of "the men of perfect holiness" (1QS 8:10). The end of days was to usher in unparalleled holiness and sanctity as the angels dwelled among the eschatological community.

The sect tried to actuate in the present, premessianic age the perfect holiness that they expected in the coming age.[24] For this reason, many of the prescriptions of the *War Scroll* and the *Rule of the Congregation* describing the eschatological congregation also parallel regulations found in other texts intended to legislate for the present age. In order to actualize its dreams for the future age, the sect referred to itself as the Sons of Zadok and held this group of priests in special esteem.[25] They expected these priests to constitute their leadership in the end of days. Likewise, the Levitical age limits of the Bible applied in the Dead Sea Scrolls to the present officials of the sect, the officers of the military units who would participate in the eschatological battle, and the leadership structure of the messianic community.[26]

Disqualifications from the eschatological assembly, as described in the *Rule of the Congregation* (1QSa), also followed Levitical legislation regarding those priests who were unfit for temple service. These were the impure, sufferers of physical deformities or old age (1QSa 2:3-11; cf. 1:19-22). After all, the sect saw itself as constituting a sanctuary through its dedication to a life of holiness and purity. At the brink of the dawn of the eschaton, during which they were living, the sect had to maintain the highest standard of purity. They preenacted the future messianic banquets in their communal meals by eating with a quorum of ten males, requiring ritual purity of the participants, and by performing the blessing of wine and bread presided over by the priest who then apportioned the food according to the status of the congregants (1QS 6:2-5).[27]

---

23. Cf. "Messianic Figures and Ideas in the Qumran Scrolls," Chapter 16 below.

24. Schiffman, *Eschatological Community*, 68-71.

25. L. H. Schiffman, *The Halakhah at Qumran*. SJLA 16 (Leiden: Brill, 1975) 70-75; Elior, *Miqdash u-Merkavah*, 202-11.

26. Schiffman, *Sectarian Law*, 32-5.

27. Cf. 1QSa 2:11-22 for the eschatological banquet; Schiffman, *Eschatological Community*, 53-67.

The messianic era is portrayed as a second redemption, the exodus from Egypt being the prototype. To this end, the sect used biblical terminology to describe the messianic era. The Dead Sea Scrolls speak of the encampments of Israel's wandering in the desert,[28] the restoration of the ancient monarchy, high priesthood, and tribal organization. The first redemption from Egypt represented the ultimate closeness to God and his direct intervention in history. At this stage, Israel was the most receptive to God's revelation and the most obedient to his law. The sectarians expected the renewal of this perfect condition in the soon-to-dawn eschaton. In addition, the world would attain a level of purity, sanctity, and observance of the law even more perfect than that experienced in the first redemption. The sectarians strove to live in perfect holiness so that they would experience the eschatological battles and tribulations of the dawning of the messianic era and the promised glory of the end of days.

Sacred Space: The Land of Israel in the Temple Scroll

The *Temple Scroll* presents an ideal vision of Israel as it should build its temple, worship its God, maintain ritual purity to the utmost degree, be governed by its king, and observe the laws of the Torah.[29] This ideal plan, according to the explicit statement of the scroll (11QTemple 29:2-10), was intended for the present age, not for the eschatological future. It was the intention of the author/redactor to put forward his scroll as an alternative to the "constitution" of Israel, religious and political, which was in place in the Hasmonean period. He called for a new temple building and for new settlement patterns as well. This polemic had a unique style.

In the area of temple building, settlement patterns, and his approach to the land of Israel, the author took a distinctly utopian view. Throughout, the author is informed by a notion of concentric spheres of holiness,[30] as well as by distinct concern for the sanctity of the entire land as sacred space.

---

28. Cf. S. Talmon, "The 'Desert Motif' in the Bible and in Qumran Literature," in *Biblical Motifs: Origins and Transformations*, ed. A. Altmann (Cambridge: Harvard University Press, 1966) 216-54; repr. in Talmon, *Literary Studies in the Hebrew Bible: Form and Content: Collected Studies* (Leiden: Brill, 1993) 55-63.

29. Y. Yadin, *The Temple Scroll*. 3 vols. (Jerusalem: Israel Exploration Society and Shrine of the Book, 1983).

30. W. O. McCready, "Temple and *Temple Scroll:* A Sectarian Alternative," *Proceedings of the Tenth World Congress of Jewish Studies, Division A: The Bible and Its World* (Jerusalem: World Union of Jewish Studies, 1990) 203.

The Temple City

For the *Temple Scroll*, the central point of the land of Israel and the source of its sanctity was the temple and the surrounding complex.[31] This new temple, of very different proportions from that which existed in First or Second Temple times, would be characterized by the enclosure of the temple building itself by three concentric courtyards.[32]

The Inner Court (11QTemple 36:3-7) was to measure some 280 cubits square, with four gates representing the four groups of the tribe of Levi: The Aaronide priests on the east, the Levites of Kohath on the south, Gershon on the west, and Merari on the north. This arrangement corresponds exactly to that of the desert camp as described in Num 3:14-39.

The Middle Court (38:12-15) was to be concentric with the Inner Court, 100 meters further out. The entirety was to be 480 cubits square, with three gates on each side. The gates (39:11-13) were to be distributed among the twelve tribes of Israel, each having its own gate.[33]

The Outer Court (40:5-11) was also concentric, with sides measuring some 1600 cubits. This wall would also have twelve gates (40:13–41:11), which

---

31. See Yadin, *Temple Scroll*, 1:177-276; L. H. Schiffman, "Architecture and Law: The Temple and Its Courtyards in the *Temple Scroll*," in *From Ancient Israel to Modern Judaism: Intellect in Quest of Understanding: Essays in Honor of Marvin Fox*, ed. J. Neusner, E. S. Frerichs, and N. M. Sarna, 1:267-84. BJS 159 (Atlanta: Scholars, 1989); J. Maier, "The Architectural History of the Temple in Jerusalem in the Light of the Temple Scroll," in *Temple Scroll Studies*, ed. G. J. Brooke, 23-62. JSPSup 7 (Sheffield: JSOT, 1989); "The *Temple Scroll* and Tendencies in the Cultic Architecture of the Second Commonwealth," in *Archaeology and History in the Dead Sea Scrolls: The New York University Conference in Memory of Yigael Yadin*, ed. L. H. Schiffman, 53-82. JSOTSup 8. JSOT/ASOR Monographs 2 (Sheffield: JSOT, 1990); *The Temple Scroll: An Introduction, Translation & Commentary*. JSOTSup 34 (Sheffield: JSOT, 1985); H. Stegemann, "The Institutions of Israel in the Temple Scroll," in *The Dead Sea Scrolls: Forty Years of Research*, ed. D. Dimant and U. Rappaport, 146-85 (Leiden: Brill; Jerusalem: Magnes, Hebrew University, and Yad Izhak Ben-Zvi, 1992).

32. Cf. J. Maier, "Die Hofanlagen im Tempel-Entwurf des Ezechiel im Licht der 'Tempelrolle' von Qumran," in *Prophecy: Essays Presented to Georg Fohrer on His Sixty-Fifth Birthday*, ed. J. A. Emerton, 55-67. BZAW 150 (Berlin: de Gruyter, 1980).

33. The apportionment of gates to the twelve tribes is found in regard to the city of Jerusalem in Ezek 48:31-34 and Rev 21:12-14. Fragments of virtually the same text are found in 4Q365a, published under the title "4QTemple?" by S. White (Crawford), in H. Attridge et al., *Qumran Cave 4.VIII, Parabiblical Texts, Part I*. DJD 13 (Oxford: Clarendon, 1994) 323-33. These are probably from the same manuscript as 4Q365 *(Reworked Pentateuch)*. The relation of this manuscript to the *Temple Scroll* was already noted by J. Starcky, "Jerusalem et les manuscrits de la Mer Morte," *MdB* 1 (1977) 38-40. On the relation of these texts to the *Temple Scroll*, see White, DJD 13:319-20.

are distributed such that they correspond exactly to those of the Middle Court.³⁴ The chambers in the outer wall which face inward (41:17–42:6) were to be apportioned (44:3–45:2) to the various tribes as well as to the priestly and Levitical groups we mentioned above. Aaron is assigned two groups of chambers as a member of the tribe of Levi as well as one of the Levitical priests and as a firstborn entitled to a double portion.

This unique temple plan represents the layout of the tabernacle and camp of Israel in the desert combined. The architect of this temple plan sought to place the camp of Israel within the expanded *temenos*. Hence, he called for a temple structure that made access to the tribes and even symbolic dwelling places for them a basic principle of design. Each tribe was assumed to enter the *temenos* through its prescribed gate and to proceed initially to its chambers. From there all members of the tribe or Levitical clan could circulate in the Outer Court. Those not disqualified by some impurity from entry into the Middle Court³⁵ could then proceed into that court, again through their respective gates. Only priests and Levites could proceed through their gates to the Inner Court wherein the temple and its furnishings were located.

This entire plan has behind it the assumption that the temple is the center of sanctity which can be reached by entering further and further into the concentric spheres of holiness of the *temenos*. The scroll makes clear repeatedly that it is the indwelling of the divine presence in the temple that imparts to it this level of sanctity.³⁶ The addition of the third court was intended to provide further protection for the sanctity of God's precincts. God is to dwell in the temple, among the children of Israel forever, according to many passages throughout the *Temple Scroll*.³⁷

---

34. We are unconvinced by M. Barker, "The Temple Measurements and the Solar Calendar," in Brooke, *Temple Scroll Studies*, 63-66, who sees the gates of the Outer Court as symbolizing the calendar and serving as a device for its calculation.

35. See L. H. Schiffman, "Exclusion from the Sanctuary and the City of the Sanctuary in the Temple Scroll," *HAR* 9 (1985) 303-6.

36. L. H. Schiffman, "The Theology of the Temple Scroll," *JQR* 85 (Qumran Studies, 1994) 118-21.

37. This theme appears in the conclusion of the festival calendar of the scroll (29:3-4, 7-8), the purity laws (45:12, 13-14, 46:11-12, 47:10-11), the commands for the construction of the temple (46:4 [partly restored]), the laws of forbidden food (51:7-8), the prohibition of nonsacral slaughter (52:19-20, 53:1 [restored]), the ban on the skins of such animals in the temple city (47:18), the laws of oaths and vows (53:9-10), and the authority of priests, Levites, and judges (56:5).

Installations Outside the Temple City

Beyond the *temenos* just described were a few installations designed to insure the sanctity of the holy place. Among them was the place for the latrines *(meqom yad)*, to be located northwest of "the city" (i.e., the temple city) at a distance of three thousand cubits (46:13-16),[38] probably derived from Num 35:4-5.

Further, the scroll requires (46:16–47:1) that outside the temple city, specific locations be assigned to the east for three groups that are impure: those with the skin disease צרעת, gonorrheacs, and those who had a seminal emission. Actually, the intention of the scroll is to locate the entire residence area outside of the temple city and to expand the *temenos* to include the entirety of what was Jerusalem in the author's time.[39] In this view, there would be no residents of the temple city, but those who came to the temple for their seven-day purification rites would stay in these areas during the rituals and then enter the temple to offer their sacrifices when their rites were completed and they had attained a state of purity. Clearly, the exclusion of these various groups was intended to guarantee the holiness of the temple precincts.

Beyond the temple city dwelled the tribes, each of whose territory was located directly opposite its respective gate. Indeed, it was through these gates that the tribal territory was to be tied to the sanctity of the central shrine and the divine presence that dwelled there. Each tribe was apportioned territory such that it would have direct access to the temple from which holiness emanated to the entire land.

The Cities of Israel

From the discovery of the *Zadokite Fragments* in the late nineteenth century on, and again after the publication of the *Temple Scroll*, there has been discussion about the meaning of the term עיר המקדש, literally, "city of the sanctu-

---

38. See Yadin, *Temple Scroll*, 1:294-304, and his earlier article, "The Gate of the Essenes and the Temple Scroll," in *Jerusalem Revealed: Archaeology in the Holy City 1968-1974*, 90-91 (Jerusalem: Israel Exploration Society, 1975). Cf. Schiffman, *Halakhah at Qumran*, 93-94, where 2000 (in relation to the 11QTemple) must be corrected to 3000.

39. Schiffman, *HAR* 9 (1985) 317; M. Broshi, "The Gigantic Dimensions of the Visionary Temple in the Temple Scroll," *BAR* 13/6 (1987) 36-7. McCready, "Temple and *Temple Scroll*," 203 suggests that this was essentially a protest against the nature of Second Temple period Jerusalem as a commercial and governmental center.

ary."⁴⁰ While some have taken this phrase as a reference to the city of Jerusalem as a whole, including the residential areas,⁴¹ we take it as referring only to the temple precincts.⁴² Accordingly, the restrictions on entry into the temple city of those with various disqualifications and impurities refer essentially to the *temenos*, the temple precincts.⁴³ It was the intention of the author of the scroll to expand the size of this *temenos* to cover almost the entirety of what was Jerusalem in his day.

Opposite the temple city were "their cities" (47:8) or "your cities" (47:14, 17) in which, if more than three days' journey from the temple, nonsacral slaughter was permitted. These cities are to be distinguished from God's city, referred to as "my city" or the temple city. Yet even these cities had to observe certain purity regulations. Areas were also set aside for those with impurities outside these cities: for those with various skin diseases (cf. 49:4), gonorrheacs, menstruants, or parturients. These locations were to be designated for each city (48:14-17). Likewise, burial in the cities was forbidden (48:11), and cemeteries were to be set aside, one for each four cities (48:11-13), equidistant from all of them.

The cities of Israel were apportioned by tribes. That is, each tribal area was expected to have cities in which the people (presumably of that tribe) dwelt. Not a single passage in the scroll describes anyone as living anywhere but in these cities. Within the cities the residents were all expected to live in stone houses. This is clear from the detailed discussion of the purification of the house in which a dead body had rested (49:5–50:16). The parts of the house and the equipment found in it are also listed in connection with the impurity of the dead.⁴⁴

What was the purpose of this complex geographic master plan? The *Temple Scroll* called for a total reconstruction of the temple and redistribution of the land around it, so as to grant to all the tribes of Israel direct access to the presence of God and an outflow of holiness to the entire land. Only in

---

40. Cf. L. H. Schiffman, "*Ir Ha-Miqdash* and Its Meaning in the Temple Scroll and Other Qumran Texts," in *Sanctity of Time and Space in Tradition and Modernity*, ed. A. Houtman, M. J. H. M. Poorthuis, and J. Schwartz. Jewish and Christian Perspectives Series 1 (Leiden: Brill, 1998) 95-109.

41. Yadin, *Temple Scroll*, 1:277-85.

42. B. A. Levine, "The Temple Scroll: Aspects of Its Historical Provenance and Literary Character," *BASOR* 232 (1978) 14-15; Schiffman, *HAR* 9 (1985) 301-20.

43. See the complete list in Schiffman, *HAR* 9 (1985) 314-15.

44. L. H. Schiffman, "The Impurity of the Dead in the *Temple Scroll*," in *Archaeology and History in the Dead Sea Scrolls: The New York University Conference in Memory of Yigael Yadin*, 135-56. JSOTSup 8. JSOT/ASOR Monographs 2 (Sheffield: Sheffield Academic, 1990).

this way, the author believed, would the future of Israel upon its land be guaranteed. Holiness and sanctity were the keys to living in the land.

The scroll's plan, as we have examined it here, bears little relationship to the teachings of the Qumran sect as they are known from the sectarian texts.[45] Further, there is no attempt in the architecture of the Qumran structures to follow any ideal blueprint. In this respect, this material supports our general conclusion that some of the sources of the *Temple Scroll* are pre-Qumranian and that the author/redactor, regardless of his own affiliation, does not reflect the ideas of the Qumran sect in his scroll. Neither did our author follow the vision of Ezekiel closely. Yet he and the prophet shared the desire to see the Jewish people, all twelve tribes, restored to their ancient glory in the sacred land of Israel. One component of this vision was to see the temple and its service conducted at an even greater level of sanctity than that required by the Torah.

Conclusion

The Qumran corpus as a whole seems to present two basic schemes of holiness and sanctity. According to the sectarian view, the locus of holiness and, therefore, the mode of access to it is the sect itself, a group of people devoted to representing in their individual lives the commitment to higher levels of purity and, accordingly, to the quest for higher levels of sanctity. This group aspired to the perfection of its holiness and to the fulfillment of its present-day quest in the soon-to-dawn eschaton. Only then would perfect holiness be achieved — not in the temple sancta, but in the life of the group and its victorious members.

The *Temple Scroll*, however, deriving from sources close to the Sadducean priesthood, hews more closely to the spatial aspect of holiness as known from the concepts of holy land, holy city, and holy temple in the Hebrew Bible. As a result, it maps out holiness and sanctity in geographical terms, rather than in human or group terms.

Both conceptual frameworks of sanctity do exist in the Hebrew Scriptures, and all Jews would have espoused them. What is significant here is the clearly differing emphases in the *Temple Scroll* and sectarian organizational texts.

This same distinction exists regarding the relationship of sanctity to the human being. Cultic, spatial sanctity maps out an area that a person enters to

---

45. Stegemann, "Institutions of Israel," 162-66.

access an already-existing, prepared, perhaps waiting, presence of God. Purity is required of those who seek to enter, as they must qualify to enter the sanctified realm.

Individual or group sanctity required that the individual or the aggregate group of individuals create in themselves a holiness and sanctity that is not externally defined. It comes about only through striving for spiritual and religious growth. Hence, purity — better purification — is a step toward that greater closeness to God. Together, the members of the group seek to raise themselves to approach a deity whom they effectively must bring down into their own daily, mundane lives. For them, the group and its religious life replace the temple and its *temenos*.

These two approaches existed in Qumran texts as in Judaism as a whole. God and his presence might occupy a holy place, but the ultimate shrine was the heart and soul of each individual who committed him or herself to seeking God's presence, both in this era and in the end of days.

CHAPTER 16

Messianic Figures and Ideas in the Qumran Scrolls

The opportunity to survey the "messianic" or "eschatological" materials in the Dead Sea Scrolls is both a source of satisfaction and of trepidation. The satisfaction stems from the central role that these finds must play in the reconstruction of the history of the messianic idea in Judaism and Christianity. The trepidation results from two concerns: First, there is little need for another in the long series of syntheses that attempt to present "the" messianism of the scrolls. Second, serious methodological problems — better, pitfalls — await anyone who seeks to investigate this area of Qumran studies.

Chief among these problems is the definition of the corpus to be studied. The Dead Sea Scrolls include a variety of materials. Central to our study will be the texts authored by the Qumran sect. Other materials, composed by earlier or related circles, including various apocryphal and pseudepigraphic works, some previously known and others not, constitute background for our work. Finally, biblical materials are important as they shed light on the state of the scriptural sources that underlie the messianic ideas of the Qumran sect.[1]

Moreover, the corpus, even as we have defined it, will provide us with a variety of messianic or eschatological approaches. This pluralism of ideas is susceptible to two possible explanations. It may result from the coexistence of different approaches within the group. Such is the case, for example, in regard to eschatological matters in the rabbinic tradition,[2] or it may also be in-

---

1. A detailed study of the eschatology of those materials not authored by the sect itself would also contribute greatly to our understanding of the background of the messianism of Judaism and Christianity, but unfortunately space does not permit it here.
2. See L. H. Schiffman, "The Concept of the Messiah in Second Temple and Rabbinic Lit-

Messianic Figures and Ideas in the Qumran Scrolls

dicative of historical development over time. Certain ideas may be earlier; others later.

More difficult to reckon with, and probably the case at Qumran, is the confluence of both these factors. The traditions of pre-Hasmonean Judaism, new ideas evolving both within the sect and in the general community outside, and the momentous historical forces at work in this period all joined together to produce a set of related but differing concepts distributed over both time and text, echoing certain common elements, yet testifying to diversity and pluralism, even within the Dead Sea sect.

These considerations make it virtually impossible to separate instances of historical development from those of coterminous variety, except in certain particular cases. For this reason, it will be advisable to analyze the major texts of the Qumran corpus individually, to determine the messianic and eschatological teachings of each. In this respect we will follow a method similar to that of Jacob Neusner's *Messiah in Context*, which deals similarly with rabbinic literature.[3] Like Neusner, we shall also be mindful of the absence of messianism in specific texts and, further, of the absence of certain motifs and ideas that we have come to identify with the end of days. We shall also attempt to pay careful attention to the terminology used in the various texts. Yet at the outset it must be admitted that there is little likelihood that we shall be able to sort out the complex history and variety of messianic figures and ideas in the Qumran scrolls in a definitive manner.[4]

The Zadokite Fragments (Damascus Document)

The *Zadokite Fragments* is certainly a composite work, consisting of an Admonition that serves as the preface to a number of short legal collections. Even within the Admonition, different documents may be discerned. Yet the final product presents a consistent approach to eschatology.[5] In CD 2:12, the phrase משיח[י] רוח קדשו, "those anointed with his holy spirit (of proph-

---

erature," *Review and Expositor* 84 (1987) 235-46; "Messianism and Apocalypticism in Rabbinic Texts," in *CHJ*, vol. 4: *The Late Roman-Rabbinic Period* (2006) 1053-72.

3. J. Neusner, *Messiah in Context: Israel's History and Destiny in Formative Judaism*, 2nd ed. (Philadelphia: Fortress, 1984). See also my review, "Neusner's *Messiah in Context*," *JQR* 77 (1987) 240-43.

4. J. J. Collins, *The Scepter and the Star: The Messiahs of the Dead Sea Scrolls and Other Ancient Literature*. ABRL (New York: Doubleday, 1995), esp. 49-135.

5. See L. H. Schiffman, *Sectarian Law in the Dead Sea Scrolls: Courts, Testimony, and the Penal Code*. BJS 33 (Chico: Scholars: 1983) 7-9.

ecy)," appears, parallel to הווה אמת, probably to be emended to חוזי אמת, "true prophets." CD 6:1 also uses משיחי הקודש (emended from משיחו), "holy anointed ones," to refer to the prophets. Clearly, the term משיח has not yet acquired its later, virtually unequivocal meaning of "messiah."

In CD 4:4 the author refers to the period of the life of the sect as אחרית הימים, "the end of days."[6] This usage betrays the text's concept of the periodization of history. The author sees the present age as being an intermediate step from the present into the future age. With the rise of the sect this intermediate stage began. It will end when the final age is ushered in. These stages are designated with the term קץ, meaning "period" in the terminology of Qumran. This term appears in CD 4:9-10, 5:20 and elsewhere. The present קץ (קץ הרשע, "the period [or age] of evil," CD 6:10, 14) requires that the sect separate itself from the house of Judah because of various violations of Jewish law (CD 6:11-7:4). Indeed, to the author of the *Zadokite Fragments,* the primary difference between this period and that of the future age is the correct observance of the law, both the revealed *(nigleh)* and hidden *(nistar).*[7] Indeed, the קץ הרשע will come to an end when "there shall arise the one who teaches righteousness (יורה הצדק) in the end of days (אחרית הימים)" (6:10-11). It is not yet clear, however, if this refers to the teacher of the sect himself, as the sect's own period is already the end of days, or if these terms have dual meanings, and this refers to an eschatological teacher who is yet to arise. Unfortunately, the syntax of this passage is exceedingly difficult.

Further evidence for the notion that the author saw the eschaton as having already partially dawned comes from 7:18-21. Here Num 24:17, a passage taken in later tradition as eschatological, is understood to refer to the sect and its leaders: "The Star is the searcher of the Law (דורש התורה). . . . the Sceptre is the prince of all the congregation (נשיא כל העדה)."[8] It has been suggested that the imagery of exile to Damascus used in 7:15-18 (immediately preceding) should also be taken as messianic. Evidence has been cited from various Jewish and Christian sources to confirm the widespread use of such a motif.[9] The clause משיח אהרן וישראל or בבוא משיחי, "with the coming of the messiah (or 'messiahs') of Aaron and of Israel," in 19:10-11 is certainly a reference to an eschatological era that is yet to arrive. Some seek to claim that this text expects one messianic figure, representative of the priesthood and the people of Israel. Others emend so that the text de-

---

6. A. Steudel, "אחרית הימים in the Texts from Qumran," *RevQ* 16 (1993-94) 225-46.
7. See L. H. Schiffman, *The Halakhah at Qumran.* SJLA 16 (Leiden: Brill, 1975) 23-60.
8. Translation from C. Rabin, *The Zadokite Documents* (Oxford: Clarendon, 1954) 30.
9. N. Wieder, *The Judean Scrolls and Karaism* (London: East and West Library, 1962) 1-51.

scribes two messiahs, the Aaronide, high-priestly messiah and the lay, temporal messiah. A further possibility is to eschew the emendation, yet to understand *mashiaḥ* as distributive over both modifiers, i.e., referring to two messiahs.

The problem is more acute in regard to 20:1, where the text has עד עמוד משיח מאהרן ומישראל, "until the rise of a messiah from Aaron and from Israel." Here there are only two possibilities. We can conclude that the text envisages only one messiah, or we can understand the word משיח as being modified by both prepositional phrases, yielding a two-messiah scheme. In 4QD^a (4Q266 10 i 12), the Qumran manuscript corresponding to the Genizah's CD 14:19, J. T. Milik reads עד עמוד משיח אהרן וישראל, showing that it is one messiah who was expected.[10] Whatever interpretation we follow, it is clear from the context of this passage that the present age is that between the death of the Righteous Teacher and the coming of the messianic era. According to CD 20:15, this period, like that of the desert wandering, is supposed to span forty years.

Attention must be called to David's appearance in 5:5. Yet David is in no way linked to the end of days or to a messianic role. The messiah of Israel, even if he is distinct in the *Zadokite Fragments*, is not singled out to be Davidic.

Megillat ha-Serakhim (The Rule Scroll)

The *Rule* is clearly a composite document. At the very least it is comprised of three distinct compositions, the *Rule of the Community (Manual of Discipline)*, *Rule of the Congregation*, and the *Rule of Benedictions*. These three components were joined by a redactor or at least by a scribe. We shall have to treat each component separately and then inquire about the unified scroll.

---

10. J. T. Milik, *Ten Years of Discovery in the Wilderness of Judaea*, trans. J. Strugnell. SBT 26 (London: SCM, 1959) 125-26. This text is now published in J. M. Baumgarten, *Qumran Cave 4.XIII: The Damascus Document (4Q266-273)*. DJD 18 (Oxford: Clarendon, 1996) 72-74. In fact, the text, as read in R. E. Brown et al., *Preliminary Concordance to the Hebrew and Aramaic Fragments from Qumrân Caves II-X, Including Especially the Unpublished Material from Cave IV*, (prepared and arranged by H.-P. Richter (Göttingen: Privately printed, 1988) 4:1545, is עד עמוד משיח אהרון וישראל. Baumgarten reads singly ממוד (line 12) and translates "until the rise . . . ," showing that he effectively emends to עמוד. The *mem* is clear on pl. XII. The passage is restored in CD: עד עמוד מש[י]ח אהרן וישראל. . . . We see the reading of 4Q266 as a case of a simple scribal error.

Rule of the Community

The Blessing and Curse ritual, 1QS 2:19 tells us, will continue only through the period of the reign of Belial, alluding to a notion that a new age will dawn at some future time. The appointed period (or end) of the rule of Belial is termed קץ in 3:23. The same notion appears in 4:16-17, where reference is made to קץ אחרון, "the final period" (age). Indeed a final destruction of all evil (פקודה, "visitation [for destruction]") is expected to take place after which the world will be perfected (4:18-20, 25-26). Here the text is speaking of a sort of Day of the Lord, although the term does not appear.

The most significant passage for our purposes is 9:11-12. Here it is stated that the prohibition on mingling property with those outside the sect is to remain in effect עד בוא נביא ומשיחי אהרון וישראל, "until the coming of a prophet and the messiahs (or anointed ones) of Aaron and Israel." In this text, as opposed to the *Zadokite Fragments,* there can be no question that we are speaking of two messiahs, as is the case in the *Rule of the Congregation.* This passage, however, is the conclusion of the section of 8:15b-9:11 that is missing in MS E, identified as the earliest copy of the *Rule of the Community.*[11] On the basis of this omission, it has been assumed by some that the original sources of the *Rule of the Community* made no mention of these messianic figures and that they were introduced either by the redactor of the *Rule of the Congregation* or even by the compiler of the entire *Megillat ha-Serakhim.*

It is difficult to accept this conclusion since the priestly role was strongest in the earliest stages in the history of the sect and gradually weakened as lay power increased. We would therefore expect to encounter the notion of priestly preeminence in the end of days early in the history of the sect, not later on. Also, the two-messiah concept is known from various other Second Temple sources,[12] and it could have entered the sect's thinking at any time.

Most important again is the omission of David from this scheme. The messiah of Israel is nowhere said to be Davidic. On the other hand, an eschatological prophet appears here alongside the messiahs. This prophet is to join the messiahs in deciding outstanding controversies in Jewish law.[13] In later rabbinic traditions this role was understood to belong to Elijah.

The communal meals of the sect are described in 1QS 6:2-5. At these repasts, the priest presided and received the first portions. Elsewhere we have

---

11. Milik, *Ten Years of Discovery,* 125.

12. See the sources cited in Schiffman, *Halakhah at Qumran,* 51, n. 202; and *Sectarian Law,* 208, n. 94.

13. See 1 Macc 14:41; 4:46.

shown that these meals were a reflection of the sect's eschatological banquets as described in the *Rule of the Congregation*. These eschatological banquets were to be presided over by the high priest and the messiah of Israel. The meals in the present age were led only by the priest, however.[14] The description in this same passage (6:6-7) of the איש דורש התורה, "the man who interprets the Torah," as "alternating, each with his fellow," shows that at least in the context of 6:6-7 this is not an official, and certainly not a messianic figure.

What emerges here is that there may or may not have been a two-messiah concept in the original text of the *Rule of the Community*. There was a notion of periods of history and the eventual destruction of the wicked on a day of visitation. Neither David nor Davidic descent plays any role whatsoever.

Rule of the Congregation

This text, also known as *Serekh ha-'Edah* (1QSa), is an appendix to the *Rule of the Community*, at least in the present manuscript.[15] Nonetheless, it may have originally been a separate composition. It begins by referring explicitly to itself as a סרך, a list of sectarian legal prescriptions for the life of the sect in the end of days (אחרית הימים). Foremost among these regulations is the series of stages of life that are described in detail, as well as the scroll's requirement of the absolute purity and purification of the members of the community, who are expected to fulfill the laws required for fitness for priestly service found in the Pentateuch.[16]

This text does not refer to the notion of historical ages since it concerns only the period after the dawn of the eschaton. The list of the stages of life does refer to subduing the nations (1:21) and to various military officers (1:24-25, 28-29). In these matters, the text stands roughly in agreement with the *War Scroll* (to which we will turn below). The *Rule of the Congregation* emphasizes the role of the Zadokite priests as leaders of the eschatological council (2:3).

---

14. Schiffman, *Sectarian Law*, 191-210.

15. See my detailed study of this text, *The Eschatological Community of the Dead Sea Scrolls*. SBLMS 38 (Atlanta: Scholars, 1989).

16. Those physically deformed are therefore to be excluded from the eschatological community. See L. H. Schiffman, "Purity and Perfection: Exclusion from the Council of the Community in the *Serekh Ha-'Edah*," in *Biblical Archaeology Today: Proceedings of the International Congress on Biblical Archaeology, Jerusalem, April 1984*, ed. J. Amitai, 373-89 (Jerusalem: Israel Exploration Society, Israel Academy of Sciences and Humanities, in cooperation with ASOR, 1985).

This scroll also describes the eschatological assembly, as well as the banquet presided over by the high priest and the messiah of Israel. We will not discuss the restoration of 2:11 except to note the possibility that it refers to the birth of the messiah. Line 12 refers to the messiah (המשיח) in the singular alongside the priest, הכוהן (restored). 1QSa 2:15 refers again to the messiah of Israel, and in 19-21 the priest and the messiah of Israel are again mentioned together. The priest is given prominence in both seating and in the recitation of the benediction over the bread and the wine. This dinner is an eschatological reflection of the almost identical pattern we observed in the *Rule of the Community* for the premessianic era. Indeed, the communal meals of the sect constituted an attempt to live in the present age in a way similar to that of the end of days. In the life of utmost purity and perfection, that goal was ultimately to be achieved.

It is important to emphasize a distinction between what appears here and what is the case in the *Rule of the Community* and, according to most readings, in the *Damascus Document*. Whereas in 1QS two messiahs, both termed משיח, are expected, in the *Rule of the Congregation* there are a priest and a משיח of Israel. The term משיח refers only to the lay messiah.

Again, David is not mentioned, only Israel. There are no details regarding the onset of the eschatological era or of the notion of periods in the history of the world. This is, indeed, a text describing the fulfillment of Jewish law and sanctity in the end of days.

Rule of Benedictions

The last item in this trilogy is the *Rule of Benedictions,* also called *Serekh ha-Berakhot*. Opinions differ on the exact reconstruction of this fragmentary series of blessings for various figures. 1QSb 4:22-28 appears to be a fragment of a benediction for the high priest. It follows a benediction for the Zadokite priests (1QSb 3:22-28). Neither of these is in any way eschatological in character. Yet, after the blessing of the high priest, in another fragmentary passage (4:18), there is mention of the קצי עד, "periods of eternity."

According to Jacob Licht's restoration, 5:20, the beginning of a benediction for the נשיא העדה, "the prince of the congregation," refers to an eschatological leader.[17] This restoration is supported by the fact that the benediction for the prince that follows is based on Isa 11:2-5, a passage referring to the

---

17. J. Licht, *Megillat ha-Serakhim mi-Megillot Midbar Yehudah* (Jerusalem: Bialik Institute, 1965).

Messianic Figures and Ideas in the Qumran Scrolls

Davidic messiah. If so, we have here another designation for the messiah of Israel, clearly based on the Ezekiel tradition (Ezek 34:24, 37:25). Ezekiel saw the eschatological community as led by a נשיא (chs. 44-48, passim). No idea of how the messianic era will come about is provided here.

The *Rule of Benedictions*, then, to the extent that it can be reconstructed, assumes a Davidic messiah to arise in the end of days. The author apparently has a notion of the periods of history. No explicit mention of a priestly messiah appears, but it is possible that the full text did make reference to such a figure.

War Scroll

The *Scroll of the War of the Sons of Light against the Sons of Darkness* is generally understood to describe the war that will usher in the end of days in the teaching of the Dead Sea sect. This scroll uses the key word קץ, "period, age" (cf. 1:8), and talks about the complete destruction of the wicked (1:5-7) that is predestined (1:10). This battle is to be fought not only on this earth, but by the heavenly beings above (1:15). The statement of 1QM 6:6 regarding victory, "And the kingdom will belong to the God of Israel . . . ," must refer to the eschaton.[18] This notion is so central to the scroll that it is repeated in 12:15 (partly restored) and 19:8.

Israel and Aaron appear on the banner of the entire congregation along with the names of the twelve tribes (1QM 3:12). According to 5:1-2, on the shield of the נשיא of the entire congregation are written his own name and the names Israel, Levi, and Aaron, as well as those of the twelve tribes. Again we see the same duality of Aaron and Israel that we have encountered elsewhere, but no mention is made here of two messiahs. Indeed, the term משיח in 11:7-8 refers to prophets in the phrase משיחיכה חוזי תעודות, "your anointed ones, the seers of things ordained."[19] Although 11:1-3 mentions David's defeat of Goliath, the passage has absolutely no messianic overtones. Num 24:17-19 is interpreted noneschatologically in 11:6-7,[20] in contrast to the interpretation of this passage in the *Damascus Document*.

The *War Scroll*, despite its clear description of an eschatological battle, does not mention the messianic figures, although the idea of stages of history

---

18. Cf. Y. Yadin, *The Scroll of the War of the Sons of Light against the Sons of Darkness* [hereafter: *War Scroll*], trans. B. and C. Rabin (Oxford: Oxford University Press, 1962) 286-87.
19. Yadin, *War Scroll*, 310.
20. Yadin, *War Scroll*, 310.

lies behind it. At the same time, the omission of messianic figures can be explained as the result of the text's describing only the events leading up to the messianic era, not that era itself. If, on the other hand, the prince of the congregation is identical with the lay messiah, we would look in vain in this text for a two-messiah concept.

The Thanksgiving Scroll

The *Thanksgiving Scroll (Hodayot)* contains a poem in 11:5-18[21] that seems to describe the birth of the messiah. He is designated by reference to the "wondrous counselor" of Isa 9:5. The poem as a whole recounts the initial spread of evil, followed by the rise of the messiah and then the destruction of all evil. In this sense it is apocalyptic in character. There is no mention of the word messiah, however, nor of David or Aaron. 1QH 11:35-6 seems to foretell the destruction of the wicked as does 15:19. It has been suggested by some that the נצר of 14:15; 15:19; and 16:6 is to be taken as a messianic figure, based on the prophetic background of this word (Isa 11:1).[22] However, there is little in the context of the Qumran hymn itself to support such a conclusion. It is more likely that this term is based on Isa 60:21 and refers to a plant.[23]

All in all, there is no real messianism to speak of in the *Thanksgiving Hymns*. There is no messiah, Davidic or otherwise, and only the echoes exist of the eventual dawning of an age in which the destruction of the wicked will take place.

Pesharim

The biblical commentaries from Qumran provide a form of contemporizing biblical exegesis that sees the words of the Scriptures as being fulfilled in the age of the author. These texts and related materials contain a significant amount of eschatological material.

---

21. Numbered col. 3 in E. L. Sukenik, 'Oṣar ha-Megillot ha-Genuzot. Jerusalem: Bialik Institute and Hebrew University, 1954/55.

22. See J. Carmignac, "Les Hymnes," in Carmignac et al., eds., *Les Textes de Qumran: traduits et annotés* (Paris: Letouzey et Ané, 1961-63) 1:222, who also rejects this view.

23. J. A. Fitzmyer, "The Aramaic 'Elect of God' Text from Qumran Cave 4," in *Essays on the Semitic Background of the New Testament* (Missoula: Scholars, 1974; repr. *The Semitic Background of the New Testament*. BRS [Grand Rapids: Wm. B. Eerdmans and Livonia: Dove, 1997]) 127-60.

Pesharim on Isaiah

4Q161 (pIsa^a) refers to אחרית הימים, "the end of days," in interpreting Isa 10:28-32 (frgs. 5-6). The Qumran passage speaks of the נשיא העדה, "the prince of the congregation," who will participate in an eschatological battle. The same text, in frgs. 8-10, lines 11-24, interprets Isa 11:1-5 as referring to a Davidic messiah who will arise in the end of days and rule over the nations (פשרו על צמח] דויד העומד באח[רית הימים]‏[24). The fragmentary material suggests that he will judge his people according to the rulings that the priests will teach him.

4Q162 (pIsa^b) speaks of the end of days in which there will be פקדת הארץ, "a visitation (of punishment) on the earth" (2:1-2), but the context is insufficient to determine what is being discussed. The passage may even refer to events of the author's own time period. In 4Q163 (pIsa^c), frgs. 4-7, 2:10-14, Isa 10:24 is taken to refer to the end of days in which, it appears, the evildoers will be taken into captivity.[25] Yet frg. 23, 2:10 shows how for the author the present Greco-Roman period can also be called the end of days. In this period there will arise the "seekers of smooth things" (דורשי החלקות), probably a designation for the Pharisees. 4Q164 (pIsa^d) frg. 1:7 refers to the heads of the twelve tribes in the end of days. This fragmentary passage appears to be messianic.

The author or authors of the *Pesharim on Isaiah* clearly expected the sect to be led in the end of days by the prince of the congregation and/or the Davidic messiah. These texts expect a final destruction yet do not speak of the periodization of history. No mention of a priestly eschatological figure appears in the preserved portions of the text.

Pesher Habakkuk

Pesher Habakkuk 7:7 and 12 allude to the קץ האחרון, "the final age," but it is not clear if in these passages the author speaks of the messianic future or of his own day. It is most likely that he sees his own times as the beginning of the future age, soon to lead to the eschatological fulfillment. This period, according to the author, is to be longer than the prophets had expected. The end of days mentioned in 9:6 must refer to the years preceding the dawn of the eschaton when the evildoers will be punished.

---

24. Restoring with J. M. Allegro, *Qumrân Cave 4.I (4Q158-4Q186)*. DJD 5 (Oxford: Clarendon, 1968) 14.

25. See frgs. 13 and 14, which also mention the end of days.

This text, then, seems to mention the periodization of history, believing the author's own day to be the very verge of the end of days. Yet no mention of any specific messianic figures occurs here.

Pesher Hosea and Pesher Nahum

4Q166 (pHos[a]) 1:9-10 refers to קץ, "period," and דור הפקודה, "the generation of the visitation [for punishment]," and line 12 mentions the קצי חרון, "periods of wrath." According to 4Q169 (pNah) 3:3, in the final period (באחרית הקץ), the evil deeds of the דורשי החלקות ("seekers after smooth things"), a term for the Pharisees, will be revealed to all Israel. In 4:3 the author tells us that in the final age (לקץ האחרון), Manasseh (probably a Hellenistic or Sadducean group) will cease to rule over Israel.[26]

While these texts have a sense that there will be a better future in the end of days, they exhibit nothing like the developed messianism of other texts. This is especially surprising in the case of *Pesher Nahum*, which is so extensively preserved.

Other Pesharim

1Q14 (pMic) frgs. 17-19:5 speaks of הדור ה[א]חרו[ן], "the final generation," but the fragmentary context does not allow any conclusions. 4Q171 (pPs[a]) 2:6-8 mentions a forty-year period after which all evil will be destroyed. This seems identical to the forty years of the eschatological war of the *War Scroll*. A fragmentary comment in 4Q173 (pPs[b]) 1:5 on Ps 127:2-3 talks about הכ[ו]הן לאחרית הק[ץ], "a priest for the final age." Needless to say, these brief references do not allow any conclusions about the messianic views of the authors of the respective texts.

4QFlorilegium

4QFlorilegium (4Q174) refers to an eschatological temple, . . . הבית אשר [ב]אחרית הימים ("the house which . . . [in] the end of days)." This temple will be of the highest purity and, accordingly, Ammonites, Moabites, the

---

26. S. L. Berrin, *The Pesher Nahum Scroll from Qumran: An Exegetical Study of 4Q169*. STDJ 53 (Leiden: Brill, 2004) 280-81.

mamzer, foreigners, and converts will be excluded from it (frgs. 1-2, 2:3-5). In addition, in the end of days there is to arise the shoot of David (צמח דויד), clearly a Davidic messiah, to save Israel. Along with the shoot of David, there will arise the דורש התורה, "the expounder of the Law" (frgs. 1-2, 2:10-13) whom some have seen as a priestly, messianic figure. The text interprets Ps 1:1 as foretelling the rise of the sect, which is constituted of those who have turned aside from the ways of the wicked (lines 14-19).

We have here the explicit notion that the rise of the sect constitutes the onset of the end of days (אחרית הימים) as well as explicit reference to a Davidic messiah.[27] The notion of an eschatological temple of perfect purity appears as well, but there is really no mention of the priestly messiah, unless we assume that the expounder of the law is to be so identified. Elsewhere, however, the function of the eschatological priest is envisaged as cultic, not educational or exegetical.

11QMelchizedek

11QMelchizedek is a text similar in literary character to 4QFlorilegium.[28] The text explicitly alludes to the end of days, interpreting the commandment of the Sabbatical Year (Lev 25:13; Deut 15:2) to refer to this period. At that time, Melchizedek will proclaim release for the captives. He and his lot (נחלה) will also be granted a special Sabbatical of atonement. He will then take vengeance on Belial and his lot with the help of the angels. The eschatological Isa 52:7 is then quoted, apparently to identify Melchizedek with the herald of the future age. There is a mention of the קצי [ח]רון, "the periods of wrath." But Melchizedek here is not himself a messianic figure. It seems best to see him as taking the very same role Michael takes in the *War Scroll,* leading the forces of good in the cosmic battle with Belial and his lot of evil. It is after this battle that the eschaton will be inaugurated.

This text mentions no messiah or messiahs and says nothing of a Davidic role (even though David is mentioned explicitly before a quotation from Psalms). The notion of stages of history, however, does appear.

---

27. See also frg. 14, which mentions the end of days.
28. See J. A. Fitzmyer, "Further Light on Melchizedek from Qumran Cave 11," in *Essays on the Semitic Background of the New Testament,* 245-67.

Other Texts

In this section we will survey a few texts that, because of size or state of preservation, yielded material too scant to allow useful conclusions, yet at the same time are worthy of notice. 4Q177 *(Catena A)* at the beginning mentions the end of days and *qiṣim*, "periods" (frgs. 1-4:10), but nothing can be gleaned from the context. The term *qeṣ* occurs as well (line 11). The mention of a second book of the Torah (line 14) has been taken by some to refer to an eschatological, new Torah, or even to the *Temple Scroll,* but lack of context makes it impossible to support any interpretation. Frg. 9:4 mentions the "seekers after smooth things" (partially restored) in an eschatological context (line 2, באחרי]ת הימים[; line 9, [בדור הא]חרון). Again, context is insufficiently preserved for any analysis. The same is the case with frgs. 12-13, 1:2 (cf. 2:3) and 4Q178 frgs. 2 and 3. 4Q182 *(Catena B)* frgs. 1 and 2 also contain eschatological references, but they are too fragmentary for consideration.

4QDivre ha-Me'orot 3:13-14 refers to אחרית הימים, "the end of days," but the passage is simply a reflex of Deut 31:29 and has no eschatological significance. In 4:6-8 the text refers to God's covenant with David as permanent king over Israel. 4QFestival Prayers (509) II 7:5 mentions the end of days, but the context is not understandable. The notion of periodization of history appears in 4QWisdom Canticles (511), frg. 35. 1QBook of Mysteries speaks of the disappearance of evil. The *David Apocryphon* (2Q22) supplies nothing messianic. The so-called *New Jerusalem* texts (1Q32, 2Q24, 5Q15, 11QJN) may describe a vision of the messianic Jerusalem, but they seem to be based on Ezekiel and make no explicit reference to messianism or the end of days. 4QTestimonia (4Q175) cites verses that may have had eschatological significance, but provides no interpretation. These minor references suffice to show that eschatological ideas must have originally been found in many other texts of the Qumran corpus, but that these are not sufficiently preserved.

Two texts are notable for their nonmessianic character. The so-called *Psalms Scroll* from Cave 11 is in actuality a liturgical compilation of Psalms, some in our biblical canon and some not. The section entitled David's Compositions (11QPs^a 27:2-11) makes absolutely no reference to messianism. The same is the case in the supernumerary Ps 151 A (11QPs^a 28:3-14) dealing with David's musical ability and his anointment.

Another text that should not be taken as eschatological is the *Temple Scroll.* This text describes a temple to be in use until the dawn of the eschaton, a notion explicitly stated in col. 29. At that time, the scroll expects, God will create his own eschatological sanctuary.

It has been maintained by some that the *Elect of God Text* (4QMess ar) speaks of the birth of the messiah. In actuality, this text mentions the בחיר אלהא, "the elect of God," and never uses the word משיח. There is no evidence from within the text that בחיר אלהא is indeed a messianic designation. Some have argued, however, based on one manuscript reading in John 1:34, ὁ ἐκλεκτὸς τοῦ θεοῦ, "the chosen one of God," referring to Jesus, that בחיר אלהא is a messianic title. Even if this were the correct reading, there is no indication that this designation in John is indeed a title.[29] Instead, the *Elect of God Text* seems to belong to one of the previously unknown pseudepigraphal compositions now attested at Qumran. Finally, the Aramaic literature from Qumran on the whole was not composed by the sect, but was imported. It is usually dated earlier than the sectarian compositions.

Conclusion

If anything is clear from the foregoing survey, it is that a variety of motifs and beliefs are distributed in almost random fashion through a variety of texts. Thus, either we are dealing with an example of the historical development of ideas, or of parallel approaches, or, most likely, of a combination of these factors.

Jean Starcky[30] sought to construct a history of the messianic idea at Qumran that went hand in hand with the stages in the archaeologically attested occupation of the site. In his view, the Teacher authored the *Thanksgiving Scroll* and the *Rule of the Community* in the Maccabean period. Messianic expectations do not appear in the hymns, and the earliest manuscript of the *Rule of the Community* does not contain a messianic allusion. Hence, Starcky concludes that messianic speculation was absent in this period. In the Hasmonean period, Pharisaic influence leads to the presence of messianism in the *Rule* (1QS), as well as in its appendices. Here we find the notion of two messiahs. Starcky identifies Pompeian-period references in the *Damascus Document*, where the two messiahs have become one priestly figure: the Teacher was the eschatological prophet, the interpreter of the Law. In the last period, the Herodian, the anti-Roman feeling exemplified in the *War Scroll* developed.

It seems to us, however, that there are numerous problems with this theory.[31] Chief among them is the presumption that the *Damascus Document*

---

29. Fitzmyer, "The Aramaic 'Elect of God,'" 157-60.
30. Starcky, "Les quatres étapes du messianisme à Qumran," *RB* 70 (1963) 481-505.
31. Fitzmyer, "The Aramaic 'Elect of God,'" 136-40.

should be dated much later than the *Rule of the Community* and that the omission of material found in 1QS from MS E of the *Rule*[32] can be taken as evidence for the history of the text. Furthermore, the claim that the messianic idea only entered through Pharisaic influence is a gross oversimplification. Finally, the theory in no way accounts for Davidic vs. non-Davidic lay messiahs.

We can augment the quest for a historical explanation by recognizing the various messianic trends that existed in Second Temple Judaism. Guided by the programmatic essay of Gershom Scholem,[33] we can discern the dominant trends in Jewish messianism and the tension between them. Scholem noted the poles of restorative vs. utopian messianism. The restorative seeks to bring back the ancient glories, whereas the utopian constructs a view of an even better future, one that surpasses all that ever came before.

The restorative can be described as a much more rational messianism, expecting only the improvement and perfection of the present world. It looks forward to the reestablishment of the Davidic empire, a process that can come about through natural developments.

The utopian is much more apocalyptic in character, looking forward to vast catastrophic changes in the world with the coming of the messianic age. Utopian messianism expects a world that never was, perfect and ideal. Such a world can only be built upon the ruins of this world, with its widespread evil and transgression. Whereas the prophecies of the reestablishment of Israel's power and prosperity inform the restorative trend, notions such as the Day of the Lord serve as the basis for the utopian approach.

It is not that either of these approaches can exist independently of the other. Rather, both are found in the messianic aspirations of the various Jewish groups. However, the balance or creative tension between these tendencies is what determines the character of the messianism in question.

With this background, we can return to the Qumran corpus. Those texts that espouse the Davidic messiah tend toward the restorative. They therefore emphasize much more the prophecies of peace and prosperity and do not expect the cataclysmic destruction of all evil. The more catastrophic, utopian, or even apocalyptic tendencies usually do not envisage a Davidic messiah. They seek instead to invest authority in a dominant priestly religious leader and a temporal prince who is to be subservient to the priestly figure. In this case,

---

32. G. Vermes and P. S. Alexander, *Qumran Cave 4. XIX: Serekh ha-Yaḥad and Two Related Texts*. DJD 26 (Oxford: Clarendon, 1998) 129-152.

33. G. Scholem, "Toward an Understanding of the Messianic Idea in Judaism," in *The Messianic Idea in Judaism and Other Essays on Jewish Spirituality* (New York: Schocken, 1971) 1-36; cf. S. Talmon, "Types of Messianic Expectation at the Turn of the Era," in *King, Cult and Calendar in Ancient Israel* (Jerusalem: Magnes, 1986) 202-24.

since there is no Davidic allegiance, the prominent role of the priesthood in the life of the sect is transposed onto the end of days. Some of the utopians sought to limit the leadership to one messianic figure. Sometimes we may encounter both trends side by side in the same text, influencing the author equally. This phenomenon testifies to the beginning of the long process by which these two trends ultimately fused into what later became the messianic ideal of rabbinic Judaism.

We will never be able to construct an exact historical sequence of the messianic ideas and texts found at Qumran. A matrix of history on the one axis and the restorative-utopian dichotomy on the other is the only framework within which to explain the rich and variegated eschatological ideas and approaches that are represented in the literature of the Dead Sea sect. This study should again caution us against seeing the materials found in the Qumran caves as a monolithic corpus, the elements of which may be harmonized with one another at will.

CHAPTER 17

The Concept of Restoration in the Dead Sea Scrolls

The subject of "restoration," when applied to the Dead Sea Scrolls, can be looked at through a narrow or a wide-angle lens. The narrower way of construing this topic would be to discuss only the restoration of Israel as a political entity in the aftermath of its destruction and exile under the Babylonians in 586 B.C.E. Such an approach would yield rather minimal results. A wider approach would instead include this return or restoration, as understood in the scrolls, but also the restoration that the sectarians expected in the aftermath of the Hasmonean period and the Roman domination that followed it. Further, the wider approach would speak of restoration on several planes: the restoration of the land of Israel, the Jewish people, Jerusalem and its temple, and the restoration of sacrificial worship and ritual purity and perfection.[1]

To make matters more complex, these various aspects of restoration may be looked at in various temporal planes. Sometimes we will find them expected in the present, premessianic age. At other times, that is, in other texts, they will be expected to occur in the end of days. But for some Qumran texts this distinction is hard to maintain, since, as has been argued by some, the sectarians who gathered the Qumran library and composed the sectarian texts saw themselves as living on the verge of the eschaton, with one foot in the present age and one foot in the future age.

The eschatological vision of the Qumran sectarians to a great extent

---

1. For a survey of restoration in the Qumran texts, see M. A. Elliot, *The Survivors of Israel: A Reconsideration of the Theology of Pre-Christian Judaism* (Grand Rapids: Wm. B. Eerdmans, 2000) 540-52.

merged the two trends of messianism, the restorative and utopian,[2] as did much of the other Second Temple literature. The visions that they express for the future, whether referring to the future in the present, premessianic era or in the eschatological era, tend to freely mix elements of both the restorative and utopian trends.[3] Accordingly, while this presentation is technically concerned only with the concept of restoration, we will see that to a great extent notions of restoration will have utopian aspects. This means that what is to be "restored" may in reality be a totally new, utopian creation.

The investigation of this complex of ideas — spatial, temporal, and spiritual — will be limited in this study to those Dead Sea Scrolls that give evidence of the ideas that molded and conditioned the life of the sectarians who lived at Qumran. We will not deal with the full corpus of texts collected by this group, omitting from our discussion the Qumran biblical texts as well as the apocryphal and pseudepigraphical compositions collected and even revered by the sect, but neither composed by them nor reflecting their particular approach. Even so, the decision of what to include among the uniquely sectarian texts remains a matter of debate among scholars.[4] We will, however, include texts that appear to have played a major role in the life of the sect or that illustrate ideas we can show the sectarians held, even if these texts may stem from related but different circles in the complex web of groups that characterized Second Temple Judaism.

Even so, the materials left by the Dead Sea sect, identified by most scholars with the Essenes described in Greek sources, are in no way uniform in their theory of restoration. We will encounter here a variety of ideas and approaches, and from them we have to try to draw some overall conclusions as to what unites them and in what ways they differ.

Further, we will see that Qumran sectarian understandings of restoration are often hard to distinguish from the related — indeed, overlapping — concepts of remnant, eschatology, and messianism. It is testimony to the rich-

---

2. G. Scholem, *The Messianic Idea in Judaism and Other Essays on Jewish Spirituality* (New York: Schocken, 1971) 37-48.

3. See "Messianic Figures and Ideas in the Qumran Scrolls," Chapter 16 above; L. H. Schiffman, *Reclaiming the Dead Sea Scrolls: The History of Judaism, the Background of Christianity, the Lost Library of Qumran* (Philadelphia: Jewish Publication Society, 1994; repr. ABRL [New York: Doubleday, 1995]) 317-50. For a full study of messianism in the Dead Sea Scrolls, see: J. J. Collins, *The Scepter and the Star: The Messiahs of the Dead Sea Scrolls and Other Ancient Literature*. ABRL (New York: Doubleday, 1995).

4. Cf. D. Dimant, "The Qumran Manuscripts: Contents and Significance," in *Time to Prepare the Way in the Wilderness: Papers on the Qumran Scrolls by Fellows of the Institute for Advanced Studies of the Hebrew University, Jerusalem, 1989-90*, ed. Dimant and L. H. Schiffman, 23-58. STDJ 16 (Leiden: Brill, 1994).

ness of Second Temple Jewish thought, as reflected in these texts, that the boundaries of concepts such as restoration can never be drawn exactly. The organic nature of Judaism in all its periods and manifestations implies an interlocking matrix of ideas that can never be totally disentangled from related concepts, especially under the systems of categorization of modern theological concepts.

One final introductory note: The various notions of restoration that we will see in the scrolls have one thing in common. They all are to take place in the physical universe of the land of Israel and the city of Jerusalem. Whether the events of the restoration expected are to take place in the present, nonmessianic here and now, or in the eschatological — even apocalyptic — future, the land and the city are real. There is no element of spiritualization in these sources. The restoration is to take place in the physical world and at a specific time.

Remnant and Restoration in the Zadokite Fragments

One of the most central texts for understanding the ideology of the Qumran sect is the manifesto, usually termed the Admonition, that precedes the long collection of laws in the *Zadokite Fragments (Damascus Document)*.[5] While aspects of this text clearly refer to those sectarians who lived in communities scattered throughout the land, its relevance to the sect as a whole, even to those at the sectarian center at Qumran, and its fundamental self-image are unquestionable. CD 1:1-8 makes reference to the remnant that God left to survive the destruction of Judah, its capital Jerusalem, and the First Temple by Nebuchadnezzer. According to this text, God caused to sprout forth a shoot (the nascent Qumran sect) to inherit the land, thereby effecting its restoration to the people of Israel. We should already note that this restoration of the land is not to the entire people of Israel, but only to those who have followed the teachings of the sectarians and their Teacher of Righteousness. Further, God predestined the period of destruction and the time of restoration in which this remnant (פליטה) would inherit the land (CD 2:7-12).

One of the features of the sectarian ideology of restoration in this and

---

5. E. Qimron, "The Text of CDC," in *The Damascus Document Reconsidered*, ed. M. Broshi, 9-49 (Jerusalem: Israel Exploration Society and Shrine of the Book, Israel Museum, 1992); J. M. Baumgarten, *Qumran Cave 4.XIII: The Damascus Document (4Q266-273)*. DJD 18 (Oxford: Clarendon, 1996).

other Qumran documents is the notion that the sectarians will share in the ultimate eschatological restoration, but not their opponents — always seen as evildoers. *Pesher Psalms*ᵃ (4Q171) 3:10-13 (on Ps 37:21-22)[6] may be restored to indicate that the sectarians will inherit the land and delight in it, while the evildoers will be destroyed forever. The passage may specifically refer to possession of Jerusalem, God's holy mountain, as well.

On the other hand, we should note that restoration of the people of Israel as a unity is clearly the message in 4Q385 *(Pseudo-Ezekielᵃ)* frg. 2,[7] which adapts the prophecy of the valley of the dry bones of Ezek 37:1-14,[8] and in 4Q386 *(Pseudo-Ezekielᵇ)* frg. 1 2:5-10.[9] 4QMMT, the "Halakhic Letter,"[10] also has a strong restorative element in the final section. There its authors speak of the repentance of their opponents, which is foretold in the Torah (C 15-16). The dawn of the end of days is said to lead to the repentance of all Israel (C 20-21) that will lead to joy in the end of days (C 30). Clearly, repentance is here part of an overall assumption that the unity of Israel and its following in the ways of God as interpreted by the writer will be part of the restoration at the end of days.

A related issue is that of the remnant (Hebrew שארית or פליטה). This concept, following the usage in the Hebrew Bible,[11] assumes that the sectarians represent the biblical remnant and that it is they who will therefore survive into the end of days. This notion appears in 4Q393 *(Communal Confession)* frg. 3:7,[12] where the author sees himself and his fellows (sectarians?) as the remnant of the patriarchs in accord with God's covenant with Abraham.

The *Zadokite Fragments (Damascus Document)* bring in another aspect of restoration by indicating that the offering of fat and blood on the sacrificial altar will be conducted by the Zadokite priests of the sectarian commu-

---

6. F. García Martínez and E. J. C. Tigchelaar, eds., *The Dead Sea Scrolls Study Edition* (Leiden: Brill and Grand Rapids: Wm. B. Eerdmans, 2000) 1:342-48; cf. Elliot, *Survivors of Israel*, 547-48 on the restoration of this fragmentary passage.

7. D. Dimant, *Qumran Cave 4.XXI: Parabiblical Texts, Part 4: Pseudo-prophetic Texts.* DJD 30 (Oxford: Clarendon, 2001) 23-29; J. Strugnell and Dimant, "4QSecond Ezekiel," *RevQ* 13 (1988) 45-58.

8. Cf. 4Q388 *(Pseudo-Ezekielᵈ)* frg. 7, line 6-7; Dimant, DJD 30:83-84.

9. Dimant, DJD 30:62-66.

10. E. Qimron and J. Strugnell, *Qumran Cave 4.V: Miqṣat Ma'aśe ha-Torah*. DJD 10 (Oxford: Clarendon, 1994) 44-63.

11. The pervasive nature of this motif in the Hebrew Scriptures is shown in L. V. Meyer, "Remnant," *ABD* 5:670-71. His survey of New Testament passages shows how Paul adopted a sectarian approach, seeing only those who accepted his teachings as being part of the remnant.

12. D. Falk, in E. Chazon et al., *Qumran Cave 4.XX: Poetical and Liturgical Texts, Part 2.* DJD 29 (Oxford: Clarendon, 1999) 53-58.

nity in the end of days (CD 3:21–4:4).[13] Apparently, the author expected that at that time Israel's sacrificial worship would be restored to its biblically mandated level of purity and conducted properly — by followers of the sect. Again, the sectarian approach to restoration assumes that only its followers, in this case the Zadokite priestly members of the group, will take the lead in the restored temple. Since the book of Ezekiel had long ago called for the limitation of priestly rights to officiate to Zadokites (44:6-16), our author is part of a tradition seeking to expand the purity of priestly lineage beyond that practiced in First Temple times. Yet here our author brings utopian elements into his vision of the future. That which is to be "restored," a totally Zadokite priesthood, had never existed before.

In CD 4:2 the priests of Ezek 44:15 are taken as symbolic of שבי ישראל, the "returnees" (or, according to an alternative vocalization and translation, the "captives") of Israel.[14] This term, however it is translated, might at first glance have been taken to refer to the exiles who had been taken away to Babylonia, but this is not its meaning in context. Here, the author, although he knows that historically there already was a return from exile, ignores it, since he sees the exilic period as continuing until the sectarians take control of the temple's ritual at the end of days. In other words, for the author, the restoration is not an event that had already taken place in the Persian period, but rather a part of the eschatological future being played out already in his own day.

Those same returnees — the Qumran sectarians — are understood to be hinted at in the description of the "diggers of the well" in Num 21:18 (CD 6:4-5 = 4QD[b] [4Q267] frg. 2:11) who ironically have not truly returned but are now in exile from Judea in "Damascus" — a code word for Qumran.[15] Their return will only take place at the end of days (cf. 2 11). Again, we see that restoration has become eschatological. Further, the sectarians are forbidden to worship in the temple until its rites are conducted in accord with their views (CD 6:11-14). Here we encounter another aspect of the restoration that is to take place at the end of time, that of religious life. The sectarians believed that the temple and its worship would be reestablished under their aegis in the end of days, after the defeat of their Jewish and non-Jewish enemies. Finally, the eschatological

---

13. On the Zadokite priesthood in Qumran texts, see L. H. Schiffman, *The Halakhah at Qumran*. SJLA 16 (Leiden: Brill, 1975) 70-75; J. Liver, "The 'Sons of Zadok the Priests' in the Dead Sea Sect," *RevQ* 6 (1967) 3-32.

14. Cf. Isa 1:27; 59:20. Cf. also the occurrence of שבי ישראל in the fragmentary 4QD[a] [4Q266] 5 i 15; and S. Iwry, "Was There a Migration to Damascus? The Problem of שבי ישראל," *ErIsr* 9 (W. F. Albright Volume, 1969) 80-88.

15. Cf. Schiffman, *Reclaiming the Dead Sea Scrolls*, 92-94.

restoration expected here includes, after a great war, the complete final victory of the righteous over the evildoers (CD 20:20-21, 32-33).

In this document, we find several central elements of the sectarian approach to restoration. Restoration is really reserved for the sectarians who are the true Israel, not for the entire Jewish people. It has been pushed off to the eschaton, which for the sectarians is in the process of dawning. Finally, it involves not only restorative, but also utopian elements, particularly as regards the destruction of all evildoers and the attainment of moral and religious perfection.

Eschatological Restoration in 11QMelchizedek

The *Melchizedek* text (11QMelch = 11Q13) is an eschatological text in which Melchizedek (cf. Gen 14:18; Ps 110:4) acts as heavenly high priest and as an eschatological figure, saving the righteous and condemning the wicked.[16] According to this text, the eschatological restoration is likened to the Sabbatical and Jubilee Years and takes place after the tenth Jubilee (11QMelch 2:6-7). The cancellation of debts is likened to the release of captives (2:2-4), here the captives of Israel (שבויים). Melchizedek will serve as God's agent in granting freedom to the captives as well as forgiveness for their transgressions (2:5-6). As in the *War Scroll* (on which see below), the good people who are to be redeemed are called the Sons of Light (2:8, restored). The forces of Belial and his evil hosts will be defeated. This victory will usher in the messianic era for the sectarians.

The question to be asked about this text is whether we can speak here of "restoration." The text explicitly refers to this motif in 2:5-6 that speaks of Melchizedek's returning (שוב in the *hifʿil*) their portion to them. Further, this text, because it is based on the model of the Sabbatical and Jubilee cycle, effectively asserts the cyclical nature of history, so that what is becoming is really what was, a fundamental definition of "restoration" as a religious phenomenon.[17] Yet this text expects a violent eschatological battle against the followers of Belial (2:13), similar to that described in the *War Scroll*. This era of destruction of the wicked is to be followed by the messianic era of peace (2:15-19), and it seems that this era of blessing is reserved for members of the sectarian brotherhood alone (2:24-25).

16. See A. Steudel, "Melchizedek," *EDSS* 1:535-37. For the text, see F. García Martínez, E. J. C. Tigchelaar, and A. S. van der Woude, *Qumran Cave 11.II (11Q2-18, 11Q20-31)*. DJD 23 (Oxford: Clarendon, 1998) 221-41; P. Kobelski, *Melchizedek and Melchirešaʿ*. CBQMS 10 (Washington: Catholic Biblical Association of America, 1981).

17. Cf. J. M. Robinson, "Restoration," *IDB* 4:38-39.

In this text we have a mixture of restorative and catastrophic, utopian elements. We will see that a similar form of messianism underlies the *War Scroll* and associated literature as well. Here again there is a concept of restoration of something that never was, a perfection longed for but never before achieved. What we have here is much more than purely restorative. Rather, the motif of "restoration" appears here to provide the underpinnings of the author's apocalyptic visions.

Restoration through Destruction in the War Scroll

The *Scroll of the War of the Sons of Light against the Sons of Darkness (War Scroll)*, in its complete form,[18] is an apocalyptic account of a war that the sectarians thought would take place to usher in the end of days. In its final form, nothing could be as utopian and catastrophic as this text. But the existence of various manuscripts, some of which may be evidence of a second recension of the text[19] and a variety of related "war" texts,[20] indicates that this was a complex and developing tradition, aspects of which may really have been based on the hope for restoration.

The *War Scroll*, if read in terms of its assumptions about its place in the transition from the present age to the final age, involves restoration that follows closely on destruction. A schematized set of battles are to take place between the sect, the nations of the world, and the rest of the people of Israel. In this worldview, again, we have the notion that restoration after the cataclysm is available only to those who are members of the sect. They are to inherit a restored land and city of Jerusalem that corresponds to nothing that ever existed, but that is imagined as the restoration of what was lost between the time of Nebuchadnezzar and the Roman period.

Much of the restoration ideology is found in the poetic sections that are

---

18. Y. Yadin, *The Scroll of the War of the Sons of Light against the Sons of Darkness*, trans. B. and C. Rabin (Oxford: Oxford University Press, 1962) 257-353.

19. 4Q491-496, M. Baillet, *Qumrân Grotte 4.III (4Q482-4Q520)*. DJD 7 (Oxford: Clarendon, 1982) 12-72. See J. Duhaime, "War Scroll," in *The Dead Sea Scrolls: Hebrew, Aramaic, and Greek Texts with English Translations*, ed. J. H. Charlesworth, 2:80-83 (Tübingen: Mohr [Siebeck] and Louisville: John Knox, 1994); and his complete edition of all *War Scroll* texts (1QM, 1Q33, 4QM1-6=4Q491-496, 4Q497) 2:96-203. See also Duhaime, *The War Texts: 1QM and Related Manuscripts* (London: T & T Clark, 2004) 45-61.

20. 4Q285, P. S. Alexander and G. Vermes, "4Q Sefer ha-Milḥamah," in Alexander et al., *Qumran Cave 4.XXVI: Miscellanea, Part 1*. DJD 36 (Oxford: Clarendon, 2000) 228-46 + pls. xii-xiii; 4Q497, M. Baillet, "Texte ayant quelque rapport avec la Règle de la Guerre (?)," DJD 7:69-72 + pl. xxvi; 4Q471, E. Eshel and H. Eshel, "4QWar Scroll-like Text B," DJD 36:439-45 + pl. xxx.

scattered throughout the scroll and that seem to have preexisted the scroll's final compilation from a number of sources.[21] The existence of such sources is clear from investigating the alternate recension and related materials mentioned above. In the various sources underlying this literature, we can discern a long and complex literary history that eventually produced 1QM, effectively a canonized *War Scroll*. In 1QM 1:8-9 (cf. 17:6-9), there is mention of the final peace and salvation that is to reign after the destruction of all the enemies of the sect, seen here as the true Israel. This text assumes that the entire set of twelve tribes will be represented in the eschatological battle and in the rituals attendant upon it (3:12-13; 5:1-2). The reconstitution of the organization and full scope of biblical Israel is central to the restorative approach, although judged from the historical vantage point of Greco-Roman times it is a utopian element. Indeed, the basic organization of the army as a whole harks back to that of biblical Israel, so that what is to be restored in the organization of Israel's eschatological army is that of the desert period.[22] In fact, in general it has been shown that the desert period was seen as an era of pristine perfection by the sect, and its various motifs have had substantial influence on Qumran texts.[23] In the aftermath of the set of ritualized wars described in the *War Scroll*, after the victory of the Sons of Light, the restoration of Zion, the city of Jerusalem, is to be achieved.[24] Indeed, the message of 1QM 12:12-15 (cf. 19:5-7 = 4Q492 frg. 1:5-6) is that at the end of days Jerusalem will again become a commercial center for the nations who will be subservient to Israel. To the scroll, this is to be understood as a restoration of the ancient glories of the Davidic and Solomonic periods.[25] According to a Cave 4 manuscript of the *War Scroll*, eternal peace will be the lot of the restored (sectarian) Israel (4Q491 11 ii 17-18; cf. 1QM 17:7-8).[26]

The *War Scroll*, like the *Melchizedek* text, has a strong catastrophic, utopian trend to its eschatology, but even so, there shines forth here a strong restorative element, particularly regarding the city of Jerusalem. In the battle

21. See P. R. Davies, *1QM, the War Scroll from Qumran: Its Structure and History*. BibOr 32 (Rome: Biblical Institute Press, 1977), esp. 71-73.

22. Cf. Yadin, *War Scroll*, 38-64.

23. Cf. S. Talmon, "The 'Desert Motif' in the Bible and in Qumran Literature," in *Biblical Motifs: Origins and Transformations*, ed. A. Altmann, 55-63 (Cambridge, MA: Harvard University Press, 1966); repr. in Talmon, *Literary Studies in the Hebrew Bible: Form and Content: Collected Studies* (Leiden: Brill, 1993) 216-54.

24. Cf. 4Q491 frg. 16, 4 for the ingathering of all Israel to Jerusalem.

25. A similar notion of the restoration of Jerusalem is found in the Apostrophe to Zion preserved in two "Psalms Scrolls." 4QTanḥumim (4Q176) collects verses from Isaiah that speak of the restoration of Jerusalem and its redemption (frgs. 1-2 i and ii and frgs. 8-11).

26. Baillet, DJD 7:31.

descriptions, the restored new Israel is that of the sectarians and those who join them, but in the poetry, it seems that the New Jerusalem will be for all Israel and the nations in the end of days. Nevertheless, in the *War Scroll* and related literature, the predominant notion is that the restoration achieved at the eschaton is reserved only for the sectarians, a notion very close to that found in the *Zadokite Fragments* and in the *Melchizedek* text.

The Temple Scroll — Restoration in the Present Age

The *Temple Scroll,* redacted from a variety of preexisting sources,[27] is a reformist document that calls for major changes in the architecture of the temple, the ritual calendar, the sacrificial ritual, and the political system as it was being practiced in Hasmonean Judea.[28] This scroll speaks of a very different kind of restoration from what we have encountered so far. Here restoration is not postponed to the messianic era, but it is expected to occur in the present, premessianic age.[29] The text expects a restoration of the people and the land, the temple and its ritual, and the political system of Israel that is at the same time a reformation and a quest for what we might term a sacral utopia. While this text speaks of preeschatological restoration, it shares with the messianic texts the notion that restoration is a concrete process that involves people, land, and temple.

It is not because this text in some way denies the future redemption that it places restoration in the present. In 11QTemple 29:9 it specifically refers to the eventual messianic era as the "day of blessing" (יום הברכה)[30] or (according to another reading) the "day of creation" (יום הבריה).[31] In either case, a

---

27. A. M. Wilson and L. Wills, "Literary Sources in the Temple Scroll," *HTR* 75 (1982) 275-88; M. O. Wise, *A Critical Study of the Temple Scroll from Qumran Cave 11.* SAOC 49 (Chicago: Oriental Institute, University of Chicago, 1990) 35-154.

28. On the dating of the scroll, see Yadin, *The Temple Scroll* (Jerusalem: Israel Exploration Society, Shrine of the Book, 1983) 2:386-90. Cf. also L. H. Schiffman, "The *Temple Scroll* and the Nature of Its Law: The Status of the Question," in *Community of the Renewed Covenant: The Notre Dame Symposium on the Dead Sea Scrolls,* ed. E. Ulrich and J. VanderKam, 37-55. CJAS 10 (Notre Dame: University of Notre Dame Press, 1994).

29. Contra B. Z. Wacholder, *The Dawn of Qumran: The Sectarian Torah and the Teacher of Righteousness* (Cincinnati: Hebrew Union College Press, 1983) 21-30; and M. O. Wise, "The Eschatological Vision of the *Temple Scroll,*" *JNES* 49 (1990) 155-72.

30. Yadin, *Temple Scroll,* 1:129.

31. E. Qimron, *The Temple Scroll: A Critical Edition with Extensive Reconstructions* (Beersheva: Ben-Gurion University of the Negev and Jerusalem: Israel Exploration Society, 1996) 44.

new, divinely-constructed temple is expected then, and no doubt a utopian order of affairs as well for all other aspects of Jewish life and society covered in the scroll.

The restoration of the temple in the end of days is also the theme of 4QFlorilegium 1 i 2-9, where we read of an eschatological temple.[32] However, this temple is to be distinguished from the imperfect "Temple of Man" that existed in Second Temple times.[33] The new temple will achieve a level of sanctity previously unknown and will be built in a time of peace for Israel. Yet this scheme differs from that of the *Temple Scroll*. For *Florilegium*, the earthly temple of the present is to give way to the eschatological temple. For the *Temple Scroll*, the new, perfect temple for the present will be built, only to be replaced in the eschaton with a divine temple.

We will, in turn, examine the nature of the restoration proposed by the *Temple Scroll* for various aspects of religious and political life. The notion of the Jewish people is perhaps the easiest to discuss. The *Temple Scroll* simply assumes that the ideal Jewish community in the land of Israel will consist of representatives of all the tribes of the desert period and First Temple times. Hence, accommodation is made for the participation of all the tribes in rituals required according to the scroll's expanded festival calendar, such as the ceremonies for firstfruits of wine (11QTemple 19:16; 21:2) and the wood offering (23:7). Rituals specifically require twelve animals, one for each tribe. The Law of the King also assumes the existence of all twelve tribes (57:6). Further, the gargantuan architectural plan for the temple includes twelve gates, each designated for a specific tribe, to allow entry into the temple precincts and into its middle court. Indeed, the assumption of the scroll was that its temple symbolized the desert sanctuary and camp of Israel, so it was natural that all the tribes would find their place in its ritual scheme.[34] Yet nowhere do we hear about the mechanism by which this restoration of an ancient utopia was supposed to happen. We have no indication how the author expected to reconstitute the tribal divisions and organization long lost among the Jewish people of his day.

Not only is it assured that all tribes would be in existence in the future

---

32. G. J. Brooke, *Exegesis at Qumran: 4QFlorilegium in Its Jewish Context*. JSOTSup 29 (Sheffield: JSOT, 1985) 86-87.

33. Cf. D. R. Schwartz, "The Three Temples of 4QFlorilegium," *RevQ* 10 (1979) 83-92; M. O. Wise, "4Q*Florilegium* and the Temple of Man," *RevQ* 15 (1991) 103-32.

34. L. H. Schiffman, "Architecture and Law: The Temple and Its Courtyards in the *Temple Scroll*," in *From Ancient Israel to Modern Judaism: Intellect in Quest of Understanding: Essays in Honor of Marvin Fox*, ed. J. Neusner, E. S. Frerichs, and N. M. Sarna, 1:267-84. BJS 159 (Atlanta: Scholars, 1989).

society, but it was also assumed in this text that each Jew would observe the high standards of ritual purity that the scroll, like the Dead Sea sectarians who cherished it, required.[35] Indeed, we do not know for sure that this text was even redacted by the Qumranites, but clearly its sources, which like 4QMMT follow the Sadducean halakhic traditions,[36] preexisted the sectarian settlement at Qumran. The sectarians apparently followed the author and looked forward to a realization of his extremely stringent purity measures in the real world of Second Temple times.

The restoration of the land of Israel as an independent Jewish polity is also expected by the scroll. No specific boundaries are given for the land, but it is clearly expected to have sufficient space for all twelve tribes grouped in areas surrounding the central sanctuary. Cities of stone houses are expected to be built with a cemetery for each four cities and an area in which to quarantine the ritually impure. The restoration of the land, then, requires that it be totally repopulated by the people of Israel and that the purity of its cities be maintained.

The spiritual center of this geographic universe is the city of Jerusalem, transformed into a "city of the sanctuary," or "temple city," in which secular life was impossible.[37] Essentially, the restored land of Israel, as envisaged in the *Temple Scroll*, was to be a living area surrounding the temple, the place of God's dwelling, the focal point of all existence. This scheme was itself, as was the temple plan we will discuss below, a reflection of the idealized picture that the scroll had of the desert camp of Israel as described in Numbers 2. There the tribes were arranged around the tabernacle and its sacral precincts that were the focal point of religious practice — the indwelling of God's presence. All twelve tribes surrounded God's sanctuary, and the *Temple Scroll* expected that this arrangement was to be restored, even in a not-yet-messianic context. Thus, the scroll's idealized view of the restored land was essentially a return to the pristine glory of Israel's earliest days as a people.[38]

The scroll's architectural plan for the restored temple was created in the same image, since it sought to create within the *temenos* of its ideal temple the

---

35. Yadin, *Temple Scroll*, 1:277-343.

36. See "The New Halakhic Letter (4QMMT) and the Origins of the Dead Sea Sect," Chapter 6 above.

37. See B. A. Levine, "The Temple Scroll: Aspects of Its Historical Provenance and Literary Character," *BASOR* 232 (1978) 13-17; and J. Milgrom, "Sabbath and Temple City in the Temple Scroll," *BASOR* 232 (1978) 25-27.

38. L. H. Schiffman, "Sacred Space: The Land of Israel in the *Temple Scroll*," in *Biblical Archaeology Today 1990: Proceedings of the Second International Congress on Biblical Archaeology*, ed. A. Biran and J. Aviram, 398-410 (Jerusalem: Israel Exploration Society, 1993).

image of the same desert camp. As a result, the temple was expanded greatly from a plan involving two courtyards, as was the case in the actual Jerusalem temple, to a design in which there were to be three courtyards arranged concentrically around the temple building. While the gates to the inner courtyard allowed only priests and Levites to enter, the middle courtyard and the outer courtyard were entered through gates apportioned also to the tribes of Israel. The middle court was entered only for the purpose of bringing an offering, but the outer court was a place of assembly.

Along with the restoration of the temple complex, there was to be an attendant restoration of the sacrificial system and the solar Jewish calendar. All sacrificial ritual was to be performed according to the scroll's interpretation of the Torah, and the Jewish holidays would fall on the same days of the week each year. The *Temple Scroll* shares this calendar of solar years and solar months with other Dead Sea Scrolls texts. The proponents of this calendar, both within and outside of the Qumran sect, claimed that it was Israel's original calendar. Yet the call for the "restoration" of this calendar was actually a call for reform, for the creation of a utopian calendar. Indeed, the renewed system of temple worship that the scroll required, actually new in its specific details — utopian and not restorative, would, in the view of the author/redactor of the *Temple Scroll,* achieve a level of purity and perfection that he saw as a restoration of the ideal era of worship in the desert tabernacle when the tabernacle drew the presence of God.

At the same time, the *Temple Scroll* expected the "restoration" of what was in reality a completely new form of government, as spelled out in the source known as the Law of the King (11QTemple 56:12–59:21), which was incorporated into the scroll.[39] Here a complete reformation of the Hasmonean polity was proposed, in which a hereditary monarchy would rule along with a council of thirty-six, consisting of twelve priests, twelve Levites, and twelve Israelites. However, this new constitution masquerades throughout, couched as it is in the language of the Torah, as a restoration of biblical law and tradition.

What we encounter in the *Temple Scroll,* therefore, is a mixture of restoration, reform, and utopia. Under the guise of a return to the perfection of the past, all kinds of specific changes, some indeed restorative, but many new and therefore utopian, are put forward. But this interesting combination of restoration and reform is placed in the here and now, and involves the entire Israel, with no sectarian indications anywhere in the document. For the author/redactor of the *Temple Scroll,* Israel is the entire people, who will partici-

---

39. Cf. L. H. Schiffman, "The King, His Guard, and the Royal Council in the *Temple Scroll,*" *PAAJR* 54 (1987) 237-59.

pate in his this-worldly vision, in the premessianic temple and society he wished to create.

The New Jerusalem

New Jerusalem is the name that has been given to a collection of Aramaic fragments that describe a renewed city of Jerusalem of massive proportions, as well as its temple and its sacrificial rites.[40] Despite the relatively large number of manuscripts of this composition that survive, it is only partially preserved.[41] Like the *Temple Scroll,* this text has been influenced by the techniques of architecture popular in the Hellenistic world.[42] Whereas the *Temple Scroll* clearly expected the restoration it describes to take place in the present age, there is no indication regarding this question in the preserved portions of the *New Jerusalem.* But it seems best to interpret this text as mixing the concepts of restoration with apocalypticism and, hence, referring to the end of days.

One of the central points about the futuristic city plan of the *New Jerusalem* is that it is intended to house all twelve tribes. This text expects a city of gargantuan size featuring a hippodamic city plan, such as that employed in the planning of ancient cities in the Hellenistic world, with huge blocks of insulae (apartment buildings) and a temple complex as well (1Q32; 2Q24; 4Q554-555; 5Q15; 11Q18).[43] The restoration of the city is assumed but not directly mentioned (4Q554 *[New Jerusalem*ᵃ*]* frg. 1:1). This text is certainly expecting the entire people of Israel to share in the restoration at the end of days. Accordingly, the *New Jerusalem* text seeks not to present a narrow sectarian vision of restoration but rather a broad one, intending to include the

---

40. Described more fully in "Jerusalem in the Dead Sea Scrolls," Chapter 18 below.

41. See the comprehensive study in F. García Martínez, "The 'New Jerusalem' and the Future Temple of the Manuscripts from Qumran," in *Qumran and Apocalyptic: Studies on the Aramaic Texts from Qumran,* 180-213. STDJ 9 (Leiden: Brill, 1992); "The Temple Scroll and the New Jerusalem," in *The Dead Sea Scrolls after Fifty Years: A Comprehensive Assessment,* ed. J. C. VanderKam and P. W. Flint, 2:431-60 (Leiden: Brill, 1999); M. Chyutin, "The New Jerusalem: Ideal City," *DSD* 1 (1994) 71-97; *The New Jerusalem Scroll from Qumran: A Comprehensive Reconstruction.* JSPSup 25 (Sheffield: Sheffield Academic, 1997).

42. M. Broshi, "Visionary Architecture and Town Planning in the Dead Sea Scrolls," in *Time to Prepare the Way in the Wilderness: Papers on the Qumran Scrolls by Fellows of the Institute for Advanced Studies of the Hebrew University, Jerusalem, 1989-1990,* ed. D. Dimant and L. H. Schiffman, 9-22. STDJ 16 (Leiden: Brill, 1995).

43. For text references, see García Martínez, *Qumran and Apocalyptic,* 180, n. 1. The official edition of 11Q18 appears in García Martínez, Tigchelaar, and van der Woude, DJD 23:305-55.

entire Jewish people. Such a conclusion is in consonance with the general principle that Aramaic texts found at Qumran predate the sectarians and form part of their heritage from the past.⁴⁴ If so, we should not be surprised to see here a case in which even a utopian view of the restoration of Jerusalem and the temple provides for the entire people of Israel to share in it. Again, the city to be built as part of the restoration of the ancient glories of Jerusalem is one that never existed before, but that constitutes the harnessing of Hellenistic architectural patterns to create a Jewish New Jerusalem.

Restoration in Prayers and Hymns

As is to be expected, issues of restoration enter into the various prayers and liturgical compositions collected in the Qumran library and perhaps recited by the sectarians. This material includes prayers for the restoration of Jerusalem and the ingathering of the exiles at a time when Jerusalem and its temple actually stood and when the bulk of the Jewish people remained in the Holy Land. Clearly, the concern for destruction and the attendant need for restoration results not only from physical conditions, but also from religious dissatisfaction with the state of the nation and its religious life.

Restoration is called for in this spirit in 4Q504 *(Words of the Luminaries)*⁴⁵ 1-2 recto iv 2-4, which speaks of Jerusalem as God's chosen city. The passage continues to call for recognition of the centrality of Jerusalem by the nations and for its peaceful existence (1-2 iv 8-13). God is asked to grant his blessings and his visitation for good to save Israel from the persecution of the nations. Further on, God is asked to save Israel from all the nations of their exile, near or far, as has been promised in Scripture (4Q504 1-2 recto vi:12-14). God is even asked to bring his people back on the wings of eagles (frg. 6:6-8). The ingathering of the exiles also features in the *Festival Prayers* (4Q509 frg. 3:3-5)⁴⁶ and also appears to be mentioned in 4Q528 *(Hymnic or Sapiential Work B)* 3.⁴⁷

A variety of Qumran hymnic or poetic texts also deal with aspects of

---

44. B. Z. Wacholder, "The Ancient Judeo-Aramaic Literature (500-165 BCE): A Classification of Pre-Qumranic Texts," in *Archaeology and History in the Dead Sea Scrolls: The New York University Conference in Memory of Yigael Yadin*, ed. L. H. Schiffman, 257-81. JSOTSup8. JSOT/ASOR Monographs 2 (Sheffield: JSOT, 1990).

45. Baillet, DJD 7:137-75.

46. Baillet, DJD 7:186.

47. É. Puech, *Qumrân Grotte 4.XVIII: Textes hébreux (4Q521-4Q528, 4Q576-4Q579)*. DJD 25 (Oxford: Clarendon, 1998) 188-89.

restoration. We cannot classify these as prayers because there is no evidence of liturgical recitation, despite the similarities in genre to the prayer texts. The Apostrophe to Zion (11QPs^a 22:1-15[48] and 4QPs^f 8 1-16[49]) speaks of a restored Jerusalem as the capital of Israel and economic and religious center for the nations. This is not only a restored Zion but an enlarged one. Zion is to be at peace and to fulfill the dreams of all the prophets.[50] This beautiful hymn bases itself on the restorative visions of the biblical prophets and seems to be devoid of any apocalyptic or utopian elements. Yet it is closely related to the similar poem that appears in the *War Scroll* (1QM 12:12-14).

On the other hand, the land of Israel is to be more than restored, but perfected totally in 4QPs^f 9.[51] Evil is to disappear, but the earth and its fruits are to provide for all who fear the Lord, apparently in the end of days. 4QPs^f 10, an Apostrophe to Judah,[52] refers also to the perfection of the land, the attendant joy for its inhabitants, and the elimination of evil. Some hints of a concept of restoration are also found in 1Q27 = 4Q299 Mysteries^a.[53] The text looks forward to the elimination of evil from the world and the full revelation of righteousness. Then knowledge of God and his mysteries will fill the earth.

The eventual perfection and peace of the earth after the destruction of the wicked is the subject of 4Q475 *(Renewed Earth),*[54] and a similar idea of eventual peace is mentioned in 4Q476 *(Liturgical Work B* frg. 1),[55] probably a Sabbath prayer. These texts certainly see peace and respite from the continuous onslaught of war as an end in and of itself for the messianic era. But it is difficult to see such goals as specifically an element of restoration.

In general, these liturgical and hymnic texts closely follow the biblical model, calling for restoration of Israel's ancient glories. It has long been realized that these texts do not betray sectarian terminology or animus, and may

---

48. J. A. Sanders, *The Psalms Scroll of Qumran Cave 11 (11QPs^a).* DJD 4 (Oxford: Clarendon, 1965) 85-89.

49. P. W. Skehan, E. Ulrich, and P. W. Flint, in Ulrich et al., *Qumran Cave 4.XI: Psalms to Chronicles.* DJD 16 (Oxford: Clarendon, 2000) 96-102.

50. See H. Eshel and J. Strugnell, "Alphabetical Acrostics in Pre-Tannaitic Hebrew," *CBQ* 62 (2000) 441-58.

51. Skehan, Ulrich, and Flint, DJD 16:102-4.

52. Skehan, Ulrich, and Flint, DJD 16:104-6.

53. D. Barthélemy and J. T. Milik, *Qumran Cave I.* DJD 1 (Oxford: Clarendon, 1955) 1:102-5; L. H. Schiffman, in T. Elgvin et al., *Qumran Cave 4.XV: Sapiential Texts, Part 1.* DJD 20 (Oxford: Clarendon, 1997) 33-38.

54. T. Elgvin, in S. J. Pfann, et al., *Qumran Cave 4.XXVI: Cryptic Texts and Miscellanea, Part 1.* DJD 6 (Oxford: Clarendon, 2000) 464-73.

55. T. Elgvin, in E. G. Chazon et al., *Qumran Cave 4.XX: Poetical and Liturgical Texts, Part 2.* DJD 29 (Oxford: Clarendon, 1999) 438-39.

in fact have already been in use before the sect came into being or may have been used by much wider circles of Second Temple–period Jews. If so, this theory would account for the absence of aspects limiting the scope of the Israel to be restored or expecting the catastrophic onset of the period of restoration.

Conclusions

We have seen that three major restorative themes emerge from the complex of texts that we call the Dead Sea Scrolls. Not only do these texts classify the ideology of the sectarians, but they also help us to identify more certainly the sources of their thought.

Present vs. eschaton. In most of these texts, there is a fundamental assumption that the restoration is not an event that took place in the Persian period. Rather, it is a still awaited event to take place as part of the unfolding of the eschaton and the ensuing escape from the limitations and imperfections of history. Effectively, the sectarian point of view saw the period of the Second Temple as a continuation of the period of exile, and so the restoration was still to come.

Israel vs. the sectarians. The sectarian texts tend to shift the focus of the restoration from the entire Jewish people to the sectarians, thus severely limiting the scope of those who can actually join in the restored Israel. The best example of this is the remnant ideology of the *Zadokite Fragments (Damascus Document)*. One further aspect of restoration needs stressing. It involves the vindication of the sectarians before all of Israel when only the "Sons of Light" or the elect are seen to be victorious. In some texts, the subsequent repentance of the rest of Israel is assumed, as in 4QMMT, while in others, like the *War Scroll,* their destruction is presumed. This vindication is always understood to be a public event. The main exception is the *Temple Scroll,* a text that cannot trace its fundamental ideology to the Qumran sectarians. This text and its sources actually lack the sectarian animus and mentality, so we should not be surprised to find that it does not limit its focus on restoration to the sectarian group. The same is the case with the liturgical and poetic fragments that seem to have been the heritage of a wider group in the Jewish community of the Second Temple period.

Restoration vs. utopia. In some of these texts, the idea of restoration has yielded a utopian vision that claims to be a return to the past, but is in actuality the creation of a new future. This is certainly the case for the *Temple Scroll,* writing for the present, premessianic age. It is also true of the *New Jerusalem* and of various fragmentary texts that speak about perfection or peace. What has actually happened is that the idea of restoration has served as a vehicle for putting forth various eschatological, even apocalyptic dreams. In these cases the entire notion of restoration has been subverted into a vehicle for utopian messianism, usually of a highly sectarian variety. In texts such as the *War Scroll* and related literature, this utopia can only be achieved by violent means. We have come full circle, therefore, from restoration to utopia.

CHAPTER 18

Jerusalem in the Dead Sea Scrolls

The literature gathered by the Dead Sea sect included biblical and apocryphal compositions, many of the latter previously unknown, and compositions that reflected the teachings of the Qumran sect itself.[1] This study will survey the references to Jerusalem and Zion in the latter two groups of Qumran texts, evaluating at the end the role of Jerusalem in the thought of the sect. Although many of the references will be to scattered sections of larger texts, we will deal at length with the concept of Jerusalem in the *New Jerusalem* texts and in the *Temple Scroll*.

Material for this study is of two types. There is a substantial body of materials that mention Jerusalem or Zion by name. Yet among the most prominent of our texts will be those that either for literary reasons or because of accident of preservation do not explicitly mention the city, while alluding to it extensively. In these materials we will find that Jerusalem plays three roles. We will encounter (1) the Jerusalem of history, that city actually experienced by the authors of our texts and reacted to by them, (2) the Jerusalem of the ideals of Jewish law, and (3) the Jerusalem of the age to come.

---

1. See D. Dimant, "The Qumran Manuscripts: Content and Significance," in *Time to Prepare the Way in the Wilderness: Papers on the Qumran Scrolls by Fellows of the Institute for Advanced Studies of the Hebrew University, Jerusalem, 1989-1990*, ed. Dimant and L. H. Schiffman, 23-58 (Leiden: Brill, 1995).

The Jerusalem of History

While most mentions of Jerusalem in the scrolls pertain to the Jerusalem of Hasmonean times, there is some allusion to the destruction of the First Temple for which Jews continued to mourn even after the construction of the Second Temple. 4QLamentations (4Q179) is such a text, adapting the biblical Lamentations with exegetical expansions.[2] We hear in this text of the destruction of Jerusalem and the cessation of its sacrifices (frg. 1, col. 1) as well as of the suffering of the "children of Zion," the inhabitants of the city (col. 2). Jerusalem is seen as mourning the destruction of its suburbs (col. 3). This text has no element in it peculiar to the Qumran sect and may represent the general sorrow of the Jewish people for the loss of the ancient glories of First Temple times. The pseudoprophetic texts mention Jews being taken into captivity by the Babylonians (4Q385b, formerly 4Q385 16 i 3-4)[3] and the worship by "priests of Jerusalem" of other gods (4Q387 3 iii 5-7).[4] The latter, however, may be a reflection of the author's views of the priests of his own time.

The destruction of Jerusalem is also the theme of 4QTanḥumim (4Q176),[5] which is essentially a series of biblical passages, mostly from Isaiah, that comforts the people of Israel and refers to the future rebuilding of Zion. In this text as well there are no sectarian elements, and we can take it as reflecting the typical sentiment of the committed Palestinian Jew of Second Temple times.[6] We should also call attention to the explicit mention of "the exile of Jerusalem" in the time of Zedekiah in 4QMMT (C 19).[7]

---

2. J. M. Allegro, *Qumrân Cave 4.I (4Q158-4Q186)*. DJD 5 (Oxford: Clarendon, 1968) 75-77. See also the corrections of J. Strugnell, "Notes en marge du volume V des 'Discoveries in the Judaean Desert of Jordan,'" *RevQ* 7 (1970) 250-52.

3. D. Dimant, "An Apocryphon of Jeremiah from Cave 4 (4Q385^B = 4Q385 16)," in *New Qumran Texts and Studies: Proceedings of the First Meeting of the International Organization for Qumran Studies, Paris 1992*, ed. G. J. Brooke, 14. STDJ 15 (Leiden: Brill, 1994), cf. p. 18; see *Qumran Cave 4.XXI: Parabiblical Texts, Part 4: Pseudo-Prophetic Texts*. DJD 30 (Oxford: Clarendon, 2001) 71-75.

4. Dimant, DJD 30:191.

5. Allegro, DJD 5:60-67; Strugnell, *RevQ* 7 (1970) 229-36.

6. Similar motifs appear in 4Q372 1 7-8. This text also refers to the temple as the "tent of Zion" (line 13). See E. M. Schuller, "4Q372 1: A Text about Joseph," *RevQ* 14 (The Texts of Qumran and the History of the Community: Proceedings of the Groningen Congress on the Dead Sea Scrolls 3, 1990) 349-76. Also relevant is 4Q434a 1+2 6, one of the so-called Barkhi Nafshi texts, which speaks of the comforting of Jerusalem, a well-known biblical motif. See M. Weinfeld, "Grace after Meals in Qumran," *JBL* 111 (1992) 427-40. We do not, however, agree with Weinfeld's thesis that this is a Grace after Meals, let alone that it is specific to the house of a mourner.

7. E. Qimron and J. Strugnell, *Qumran Cave 4.V: Miqsat Ma'aśe ha-Torah*. DJD 10 (Oxford: Clarendon, 1994) 60.

Jerusalem in the Dead Sea Scrolls

At the same time, it is apparent that the members of the Qumran sect stood apart from the Jerusalem of their own times, which they saw as the seat of an illegitimate priesthood. 1QpHab 9:4 speaks of:

> The recent (or last) priests of Jerusalem who will amass great property and wealth from the booty of the gentiles. But in the end of days their property will be delivered along with their booty into the hands of the army of the Kittim.[8]

The Kittim are the Romans, whose imminent attack on the land of Israel is expected by the pesher. The end of days is therefore about to dawn. Then, these priests will pay their just penalty, losing all the wealth they had gathered by attacking non-Jews. These same priests lead the people astray according to the fragmentary 1QpMic 11:1.[9] The punishment of these priests is probably described in the continuation of the fragment.[10]

It is likely that these priests are the same as the "men of scoffing who are in Jerusalem" described in 4QpIsa[b] 2:6-8 as "those who despised the Torah of the Lord and reviled the word of the Holy One of Israel" (Isa 5:24).[11] These are probably the allies of the wicked priest who may also be the "man of scoffing" described in the Qumran sectarian compositions.

Another group inimical to the sect's approach to Judaism was also centered in Jerusalem. 4QpIsa[c] 23 ii 10-11 locates the דורשי החלקות, the "seekers of smooth things," in Jerusalem.[12] This group is in actuality the Pharisees, and their sobriquet should be understood as "those who derive false laws through exegesis."[13]

4QpNah 3-4 i almost in its entirety refers to Jerusalem, which, according to this text, has become a place of dwelling for Gentiles.[14] The author re-

---

8. B. Nitzan, *Megillat Pesher Ḥabakkuk: mi-Megillot Midbar Yehudah (1Qp Hab)* (Jerusalem: Bialik Institute, 1986) 180. All translations in this article are mine except in a few cases where noted.

9. M. P. Horgan, *Pesharim: Qumran Interpretations of Biblical Books.* CBQMS 8 (Washington: Catholic Biblical Association of America, 1979) Part I: texts, 11; commentary, 61-62.

10. This seems to be the case in light of the citation from Mic 1:8-9 that the pesher could only have interpreted in that manner.

11. Horgan, *Pesharim*, texts, 19; commentary, 92-93.

12. Horgan, *Pesharim*, texts, 29; commentary, 120; S. L. Berrin, *The Pesher Nahum Scroll from Qumran: An Exegetical Study of 4Q169.* STDJ 53 (Leiden: Brill, 2004) 91-99.

13. Cf. L. H. Schiffman, *Reclaiming the Dead Sea Scrolls: The History of Judaism, the Background of Christianity, the Lost Library of Qumran* (Philadelphia: Jewish Publication Society, 1994; repr. ABRL [New York: Doubleday, 1995]) 250-51.

14. Horgan, *Pesharim*, texts, 47; commentary, 171-82; Berrin, *Pesher Nahum Scroll*, 130-92.

counts the alliance of the Pharisees (דורשי החלקות) with the Seleucids under Demetrius III Eukairos (96-88 B.C.E.) who together attempted to overthrow the Hasmonean Alexander Jannaeus (76-103 B.C.E.), termed "the lion of wrath," and his *gērousia* (council of elders). Specific reference is made to Jannaeus's garrison in Jerusalem as well as to the large amounts of money accumulated by the "priests of Jerusalem," no doubt a reference to the Sadducees who are elsewhere in this text described as wealthy.[15]

In 4QTestimonia (4Q175 21-30)[16] and 4QApocryphon of Joshua (4Q379 22 ii 7-14)[17] there appears an identical passage ascribed pseudepigraphically to Joshua.[18] In it he foretells, based on the canonical Josh 6:26, the rebuilding of Jericho and the attendant results. There we hear that some Hasmonean ruler, the identity of whom has been widely debated,

> will [spill bl]ood like water upon the barrier of the Daughter of Zion and in the precincts of Jerusalem (4QTest 29).

This reflection of the author's view would be in line with the sect's generally negative views on the Hasmoneans and their military exploits.

The city itself is spoken about in 1QpHab 12:7 as:

> the city in which the evil priest has undertaken abominable actions so as to render the temple impure.[19]

This passage clearly refers to Hasmonean Jerusalem and its temple, which were also regarded by the sect as impure. Its destruction at the hands of the Kittim seems to be foretold in 1QpPs 9:1-2.[20]

All in all, the sect continued to mourn the destruction of the First Temple as did other Jews in this period. It regarded the present city of Jerusalem, its priestly government, and its temple as totally unacceptable. Yet an exceptional passage mentions Jerusalem in a positive context. Jerusalem in Mic 1:5 is taken by 1QpMic 10:4-7 as referring to the Teacher of Righteousness and the

---

15. See "Second Temple Literature and the Cairo Genizah," chapter 24 below. Josephus (*Ant.* 13.298) states that the Sadducees were supported by the rich.

16. Allegro, DJD 5:58. Cf. Strugnell, *RevQ* 7 (1970) 226-27.

17. C. A. Newsom, "The 'Psalms of Joshua' from Qumran Cave 4," *JJS* 39 (1988) 56-73.

18. See the detailed study of H. Eshel, "The Historical Background of the Pesher Interpreting Joshua's Curse on the Rebuilder of Jericho," *RevQ* 15 (Mémorial Jean Starcky, 1992) 409-20; and Schiffman, *Reclaiming the Dead Sea Scrolls*, 235-36.

19. Nitzan, *Pesher Ḥabakkuk*, 194.

20. Horgan, *Pesharim*, texts, 14; commentary, 69. This may also be referred to in the difficult 4QpIsa[a] 2-6 ii 24-29. Cf. Horgan, commentary, 81.

sect that will be saved from the final destruction.[21] We will see that, despite the condemnation by the sect of virtually every feature of "present-day" Jerusalem of their times, the city remained at the center of the sect's halakhic and eschatological ideals.

The Jerusalem of Religious Law

For all groups of Jews in the Second Temple period, Jerusalem had special sanctity in Jewish law, as the temple located within it was the religious center of the Jewish people. Needless to say, those who left us the Dead Sea Scrolls had a particular view on this topic. At the outset it must be understood that despite the sect's condemnation of and abstention from the temple rituals of their own day, the Judaism they espoused in no way eschewed these rituals in principle. Rather, their position stemmed from specific objections to the conduct of affairs at the temple that they expected would change both in the present and in the eschatological future.

Jerusalem's centrality in Jewish ritual stemmed from the fact that it was understood to be God's chosen place that had been alluded to in Deuteronomy. Further, it was the place where God had directed that his ark of the covenant come to rest. Indeed, a passage in 4QDivre ha-Me'orot (4Q504) 1-2 iv 2-4[22] refers to the placement of the ark and temple in Jerusalem as follows:

> Its ta[ber]nacle [. . .] rest in Jerusa[lem, the city that] you [ch]ose from the entire land so that y[our name] would be there forever.

To this text, the placing of the ark and tabernacle in Jerusalem in the time of David secured the city's role as the spiritual center of the Jewish people. The passage goes on to recount the political and economic effects of the establishment of the religious capital in Jerusalem (1-2 iv 8-13):

> Then all the nations saw your glory in that you were sanctified among your people Israel, as well as your great name, and they brought their gift of silver and gold and precious stone(s) with all the treasure of their countrie(s) to honor your people and Zion your holy city, and your glori-

---

21. Horgan, *Pesharim*, texts, 10; commentary, 60-61.
22. M. Baillet, *Qumrân Grotte 4.III (4Q482-4Q520)*. DJD 7 (Oxford: Clarendon, 1982) 143; E. G. Chazon, "Te'udah Liturgit mi-Qumran ve-Hashlekhoteha: 'Divre ha-Me'orot'" (Ph.D. diss., Hebrew University, 1991) 226, 255-56. See also M. R. Lehmann, "A Re-interpretation of 4Q Dibrê Ham-Me'oroth," *RevQ* 5 (1964) 106-10; and Chazon, "4QDibHam: Liturgy or Literature?" *RevQ* 15 (Mémorial Jean Starcky, 1992) 447-55.

ous temple. And there was no adversary or misfortune, but rather peace and blessing. . . .²³

To this author the Davidic period was an ideal one in which Jerusalem, the city of Zion, was the religious, political and economic capital all in one.

The chosenness of Jerusalem is also the theme of a noncanonical psalm, part of which reads (4Q380 1 i 1-8):²⁴

> [Jeru]salem the city that the Lo]rd [chose] from eternity,
> [As a place of residence for²⁵] the holy ones.
> [For the na]me of the Lord has been invoked upon it,
> [And his glory] has appeared over Jerusalem [and] Zion.
>
> Who can declare the renown of the Lord,
> And announce all of [his] praise?

The fragment containing the prayer for Jonathan the King, probably to be identified with Alexander Jannaeus, also includes a section that is paralleled in "Psalm 154" from the *Psalms Scroll*²⁶ and that has been restored as follows:

> His habitation is in Zion,
> He ch[ooses Jerusalem forever.]²⁷

A very similar notion is found in the poem at the end of Ben Sira in the Hebrew version:

> Give thanks to the One who chooses Jerusalem,
> For his mercy endures forever.²⁸

---

23. Baillet, DJD 7:143-44; Chazon, "Teʿudah Liturgit," 227-28, 258-60.

24. E. M. Schuller, *Non-Canonical Psalms from Qumran: A Pseudepigraphic Collection.* HSS 28 (Atlanta: Scholars, 1986) 248. The translation is mine, however. Our line divisions are those of the poem, not of the MS. Cf. Schuller's commentary, 248-57.

25. This is not advanced as an exact restoration, but rather to convey the sense that the passage must have had in its entirety.

26. Cf. J. A. Sanders, *The Psalms Scroll of Qumrân Cave 11.* DJD 4 (Oxford: Clarendon, 1965) 64. The text is not preserved, but would have been found on col. 18:17 (below the last line on p. 39).

27. Adapted from E. Eshel, H. Eshel, A. Yardeni, "A Qumran Composition Containing Part of Ps. 154 and a Prayer for the Welfare of King Jonathan and His Kingdom," *IEJ* 42 (1992) 199-229. Their translation appears on p. 207.

28. *Sefer Ben Sira: Ha-Maqor, Qanqordanṣiah, ve-Nittuaḥ ha-Millim* (Jerusalem: Academy of the Hebrew Language and Shrine of the Book, 1973) 65. The poem appears in the medieval genizah MS B after Ben Sira 52:12, and is followed in MS B with 52:13. Because the poem is

Jerusalem in the Dead Sea Scrolls

Perhaps the most direct statement on the halakhic status of the city of Jerusalem comes from 4QMMT, the Halakhic Letter, that appears to be a foundation document for the Qumran sect.[29] This text must have been composed shortly after 152 B.C.E. when the Hasmoneans took over control of the temple and priesthood. At that time, as we can gather from this document, they put into effect many halakhic rulings that are known to us to be Pharisaic, against which the document polemicizes. In the course of this polemic, 4QMMT gives its own views on these halakhot that turn out to be those we know as Sadducean.[30]

The writers criticize their opponents in the Jerusalem establishment for "slaughtering [animals] outside the camp" (MMT B 27-28),[31] a reference to profane slaughter outside the temple yet in close proximity to Jerusalem. The text states that all slaughter is to take place "in the north of the camp." This law must refer to Lev 17:3-4. Yet the continuation of the text in B 28 is clearly dependent on Lev 1:11, where the sacrifice is to be offered "on the north side of the altar, before the Lord."[32] The authors of MMT apparently thought that even *shelamim* sacrifices offered in close proximity to the temple for eating purposes had to be sacrificed at the north. This ruling is in direct opposition to tannaitic law (*m. Zebaḥ.* 5:6-7) that permits these offerings to be offered anywhere in the inner court.[33] Thereupon the writers state (B 29-31):

---

an imitation of Psalm 136 and because it is missing in the Greek version, some have seen it as a medieval addition. But cf. M. Z. Segal, *Sefer Ben-Sira Ha-Shalem*, 2nd ed. (Jerusalem: Bialik Institute, 1971/72) 356, who takes it as authentic. Cf. also Sir 36:18; 47:11 (Jerusalem), and 36:19; 48:18, 24; 51:12 (Zion).

29. E. Qimron and J. Strugnell, "An Unpublished Halakhic Letter from Qumran," in *Biblical Archaeology Today: Proceedings of the International Congress on Biblical Archaeology, Jerusalem, April 1984*, ed. J. Amitai, 400-7 (Jerusalem: Israel Exploration Society, Israel Academy of Sciences and Humanities, in cooperation with ASOR, 1984); and (a different article by the same title) *IMJ* 4 (1985) 9-12. See also Qimron and Strugnell, DJD 10:113-21.

30. Schiffman, *Reclaiming the Dead Sea Scrolls*, 83-89; "The New Halakhic Letter (4QMMT) and the Origins of the Dead Sea Sect," Chapter 6 above; Y. Sussmann, "The History of the Halakha and the Dead Sea Scrolls: Preliminary Talmudic Observations on *Miqṣat Maʿaśe ha-Torah* (4QMMT)," in Qimron and Strugnell, DJD 10:179-200.

31. Cf. the halakhic commentary of Qimron in DJD 10:156-57; L. H. Schiffman, "Sacral and Non-Sacral Slaughter According to the Temple Scroll," in Dimant and Schiffman, *Time to Prepare the Way in the Wilderness*, 69-84; E. Eshel, "4QLev^d: A Possible Source for the Temple Scroll and *Miqṣat Maʿaśe ha-Torah*," *DSD* 2 (1995) 1-13.

32. So Qimron and Strugnell, DJD 10:157.

33. As opposed to sacrifices of the highest level of sanctity, termed by the Tannaim קדשי קדשים, which must be offered at the north of the temple court (*m. Zebaḥ.* 5:1-5). Cf. J. Milgrom, *Leviticus 1–16*. AB 3 (New York: Doubleday, 1991) 164-65.

> But we hold the view that the temple [is the (equivalent of) the tabernacle of the tent of meeting, and Je]rusalem is the camp, and outside of the camp [is (equivalent to) outside of Jerusalem]; it is the camp of their cities.[34]

The text then has a lacuna, followed by the complaint that the opponents of the sect do not slaughter in the temple, presumably directed at those who, despite proximity to Jerusalem, perform nonsacral slaughter.

This passage sets up a basic equivalency between the camp of Israel in the wilderness period and the sanctuary. It places the temple in the center as the equivalent of the tabernacle and the entire camp of the desert as equal to the city of Jerusalem. Since it was permitted to slaughter in the camp, and not outside, it is permitted to slaughter only in the city of Jerusalem. Those outside, presumably those living close by (cf. Deut 12:20-21), had to offer their animals as *shelamim* sacrifices in Jerusalem.

There is a second reference to this same matter in MMT B 59-62. After forbidding the bringing of dogs into the "camp of holiness," because they eat the bones and may therefore come to eat of sacrificial meat, the text states:

> For Jerusalem is the camp of holiness, and it is the place which he (God) chose from all the tribes of Israel, for Jerusalem is the chief of the camps of Israel.[35]

Here we find that it is only Jerusalem that has this exalted status since God chose it. Further, it is the equivalent for legal purposes to the wilderness camp. All offerings and restrictions that pertained to the entire camp here pertain to the entire city of Jerusalem.[36]

It is difficult to determine whether this is, in fact, the same view as that expressed in the *Temple Scroll*. The scroll also had to deal with the manifold laws of the Torah that referred to the "camp." To understand this issue, however, it is necessary first to discuss the more general question of the scroll's expectations for a rebuilt sanctuary.

The *Temple Scroll* presents a vision for reform of the religious and political life of Hasmonean Judea, calling, among other things, for a new temple of enormous proportions. The scroll is not messianic in character, but rather

---

34. Qimron and Strugnell, DJD 10:48, 50.

35. Qimron and Strugnell, DJD 10:52. Cf. the halakhic commentary by Qimron, DJD 10:143-45.

36. Cf. 4QTohorot A 1 i 6, as restored in J. Milgrom, "4QTohora[a]: An Unpublished Qumran Text on Purities," in Dimant and Schiffman, *Time to Prepare the Way in the Wilderness*, 59. The complete text appears in J. M. Baumgarten, *Qumran Cave 4.XXV: Halakhic Texts*. DJD 35 (Oxford: Clarendon, 1999) 99-109.

seeks to create an ideal society for the present premessianic age. Yet it puts itself forward as a Torah, with the author's views stated as the word of God. Because of this literary device, like the book of Deuteronomy, the scroll never mentions Jerusalem, speaking instead of the "place which I will choose to make my name dwell therein" (11QT^a 52:16; 56:5; 60:13-14; cf. 52:9 [restored]).[37] Yet we can confidently take this scroll as directly referring to Jerusalem because of the language reminiscent of Deuteronomy. Here the author/redactor hoped to see a new temple constructed in his own day.

If so, a description of that "Jerusalem" will be helpful for our study. But already at this point we find ourselves in the midst of a scholarly controversy. The scroll speaks of the temple as the central building not only of the city but of the nation as a whole. As opposed to the temple of his day, which had two courts arranged one within the other, our author expected a temple with three concentric courts. Like the author of Ezekiel 40–48, he intended the third court as a means of increasing the stringency of the purity regulations for the temple so as to further limit access to those who did not attain the necessary levels of purity.

Our detailed analysis of the architecture of this temple complex, and specifically of its gates and chambers, has shown that it was conceived by its planner as a replica of the desert camp.[38] Accordingly, the temple and the inner court were taken as equivalent to the tabernacle, the middle court to the area in which the Levites dwelled immediately around the tabernacle, and the outer court as the equivalent of the entire camp where the tribes of Israel dwelled.[39] We may add that for the scroll it was assumed in an idealistic manner that the tribes of Israel would dwell symmetrically around the central sanctuary in what must have been imagined as a square land of Israel.[40]

This temple complex is termed עיר המקדש, "the city of the sanctuary," in the scroll. There has been a debate since publication as to whether this term covers the entire city of Jerusalem or the temple complex only, what the

---

37. Cf. L. H. Schiffman, "The Theology of the Temple Scroll," *JQR* 85 (Qumran Studies, 1994) 118-21.

38. L. H. Schiffman, "Architecture and Law: The Temple and Its Courtyards in the Temple Scroll," in *From Ancient Israel to Modern Judaism: Intellect in Quest of Understanding: Essays in Honor of Marvin Fox*, ed. J. Neusner, E. S. Frerichs, and N. M. Sarna, 1:267-84. BJS 159 (Atlanta: Scholars, 1989).

39. L. H. Schiffman, "Exclusion from the Sanctuary and the City of the Sanctuary in the Temple Scroll," *HAR* 9 (1985) 301-20.

40. Cf. L. H. Schiffman, "Sacred Space: The Land of Israel in the Temple Scroll," in *Biblical Archaeology Today, 1990: Proceedings of the Second International Congress on Biblical Archaeology*, ed. A. Biran and J. Aviram, 398-410 (Jerusalem: Israel Exploration Society, 1993).

rabbis called the Temple Mount. Yigael Yadin, who first published this scroll, followed by Jacob Milgrom, took it as referring to the entire residence area of Jerusalem and, therefore, thought that the temple purity restrictions would be observed there.[41] Hence, we would have the earthly Jerusalem elevated to the status of a temple with the attendant rules and regulations.

Baruch Levine and I understand the עיר המקדש to refer to the *temenos* itself, in which case the residential area of Jerusalem was not part of the "city of the sanctuary."[42] That residential area would have surrounded the temple complex in the author/redactor's view but would not have been required to maintain the same high degree of purity as the temple itself. We should note here that if one looks at the dimensions of the enlarged *temenos* that the scroll calls for, it is to be close to the same size as Jerusalem was in his own day.[43] In our view, the author of that section of the scroll and the planner of the future temple expected the entire city of Jerusalem to be turned into the temple complex that was to be built so as to represent the wilderness camp of Israel.[44] This biblical ideal of the desert period in Israel's history[45] reflected the pristine era of Israel's uncompromising loyalty to God and his law.

We now return to the question of how the evidence of the *Temple Scroll* accords with the passages we cited from 4QMMT. Yadin was of the opinion

---

41. Y. Yadin, *The Temple Scroll* (Jerusalem: Israel Exploration Society, 1983) 1:277-85, 415-16; J. Milgrom, "'Sabbath' and 'Temple City' in the Temple Scroll," *BASOR* 232 (1978) 25-27.

42. B. A. Levine, "The Temple Scroll: Aspects of Its Historical Provenance and Literary Character," *BASOR* 232 (1978) 13-17; Schiffman, *HAR* 9 (1985) 317-18. See also L. R. Fisher, "The Temple Quarter," *JJS* 8 (1963) 34-41 on this usage of Hebrew עיר. The same issue was already debated after the discovery of the *Zadokite Fragments*, where this phrase appears in CD 12:1-2. Cf. L. Ginzberg, *An Unknown Jewish Sect* (New York: Jewish Theological Seminary of America, 1976) 73-74.

43. Cf. M. Broshi, "The Gigantic Dimensions of the Visionary Temple in the Temple Scroll," *BAR* 13/6 (1987) 36-37.

44. These three courtyards are quite similar to the way in which the Tannaim later understood the halakhic problem posed by the "camp" in biblical law. The Tannaim understood the various laws pertaining to the "camp" to refer to one of three concentric camps: the camp of the divine presence (i.e., the tabernacle), the camp of the Levites (the area of their encampment), and the camp of Israel (the rest of the desert camp). It is our view that the *Temple Scroll*, while holding different views on some of the particular regulations for the three camps, adopted the very same system as that held by the tannaitic sources.

45. S. Talmon, "The 'Desert Motif' in the Bible and in Qumran Literature," in *Biblical Motifs: Origins and Transformations*, ed. A. Altmann, 55-63 (Cambridge, MA: Harvard University Press, 1966); repr. in Talmon, *Literary Studies in the Hebrew Bible: Form and Content: Collected Studies* (Leiden: Brill, 1993) 216-54. Related issues are raised in D. R. Schwartz, "Temple and Desert: On Religion and State in Second Temple Period Judaea," in *Studies in the Jewish Background of Christianity* (Tübingen: Mohr [Siebeck], 1992) 29-43.

that the camp of MMT was the equivalent of the "city of the sanctuary" in the *Temple Scroll*.[46] Accordingly, MMT would prove that the scroll intends the entire city of Jerusalem to be bound by the laws of purity of the camp, even beyond the walls of the *temenos*. It is equally possible that these documents, despite their many points of agreement, do not correspond here. In this case the purity of the camp would be demanded by both documents only for the temple complex itself.

The authors of these documents certainly saw Jerusalem as the religious center of their universe, the place God had chosen to be his own. Accordingly, worship was to be conducted there according to their interpretation of the Torah. Even if this aspiration had not yet been achieved, it would take place even before the coming of the final age. It was to this end that the sectarians continued to study sacrificial laws and to dream of a new temple purer and more holy than that which they had abandoned.

The Eschatological Jerusalem

The Qumran sect expected that the end of days would be initiated by a great war in which they would be victorious both over the nations and over their Jewish opponents. This war is described in the *Scroll of the War of the Sons of Light against the Sons of Darkness,* a document that can be seen as a military manual for this expected struggle. The text includes sections that outline the tactics and rituals of the war as well as liturgical-poetic sections that constitute praises to be recited as part of the military campaign.

According to 1QM 1:3 the war is to start

> when the exiles of the Sons of Light return from the Wilderness of the Nations to encamp in the Wilderness of Jerusalem.[47]

Presumably this means that the first phase of the war will begin with deployment of the sectarians, now located at Qumran, to some position in the Judean wilderness in proximity to Jerusalem. This base of operations, or perhaps Jerusalem itself after its conquest, is alluded to in the scroll's description of the battle trumpets that serve to signal "the way of return from battle with the enemy so as to come unto the congregation to Jerusalem" (1QM 3:10-11).

---

46. "Discussion," in Amitai, *Biblical Archaeology Today,* 429.

47. The translation is from Y. Yadin, *The Scroll of the War of the Sons of Light Against the Sons of Darkness* [hereafter: *War Scroll*], trans. B. and C. Rabin, 256 (Oxford: Oxford University Press, 1962); cf. p. 7.

These trumpets were inscribed with the words "Rejoicings of God in peaceful return."[48]

A similar motif appears in 4QCatena (A) (4Q177), which is a "chain" of verses pertaining to the messianic era as interpreted by the sectarians. In a passage that seems to speak of the victory of the Sons of Light in the eschatological battle, the text states, "and they shall enter Zion with gladness and Jerusalem [with eternal joy]," paraphrasing Isa 35:10 and 51:11. There they will destroy Belial and the people of his lot and the Sons of Light will all be gathered, presumably to the Holy City (12-13 i 10-11).[49]

Further on in the *War Scroll*, in describing the purity rules for the military camp, we find that there is a prohibition to the effect that "no young boy and no woman shall enter their encampments when they go forth from Jerusalem to go to battle" (1QM 7:3-4). Again, the battle starts from Jerusalem.

A beautiful poetic passage, actually a pastiche of biblical phrases (much in the same style as the larger "Apostrophe to Zion"),[50] is found in 1QM 12:12-14:

> Zion, rejoice exceedingly,
> and shine forth in songs of joy, O Jerusalem,
> and be joyful, all (you) cities of Judah.
>
> Open [your] gates forever,
> to let enter into you the substance of the nations,
> and their kings shall serve you.
>
> All those who afflicted you shall bow down to you,
> And the dust [of your feet they shall lick.][51]

Then follows the notion that in the end of days Jerusalem will rejoice as its children are victorious over their enemies, and it will become an international trade emporium.[52]

---

48. Trans. from Yadin, *War Scroll*, 270.

49. Allegro, DJD 5:71; cf. Strugnell, *RevQ* 7 (1970) 246. A. Steudel, *Der Midrasch zur Eschatologie aus der Qumrangemeinde (4QMidrEschat^{a,b})*. STDJ 13 (Leiden: Brill, 1994), takes Catena A and Florilegium to be one text. Her reconstruction (p. 74) places our passage in col. 11:15-16.

50. There are additional Zion hymns in the scrolls as well, and a full study of this "genre" is needed. See Schuller, *Non-Canonical Psalms*, 257.

51. Trans. adapted from Yadin, *War Scroll*, 318. The same passage appears below in the scroll where the entire poem is repeated in col. 19. There the mention of Jerusalem (19:5) is omitted, leaving a more balanced line mentioning only Zion. Such duplications indicate that the poems were introduced into the *War Scroll* after being separately composed.

52. The reference to Jerusalem in 1QM 12:16 is too fragmentary to yield any data for this study.

But most important, Jerusalem is to be a spiritual center to the sect in the end of days. 4QFlorilegium (4Q174) describes the rebuilding of the temple by God himself and the increased severity of the purity standards for admission to it.[53] It is expected that the Shoot of David, certainly a messianic figure (in accord with Amos 9:11[54]), will (4QFlor 1:11-12)

> arise together with the Interpreter of the Law who [will rule] in Zi[on in the] end of days.[55]

A number of important Aramaic manuscripts, mostly very fragmentary, and one Hebrew fragment are designated the *New Jerusalem* texts because they describe an idealized version of the city, presumably that of the end of days.[56] The name of the city never appears in these texts, but the title of the text was given based on the New Testament parallel in Rev 21:1–22:5. The *New Jerusalem* texts are most probably part of the literary heritage that the sect had before it in its early years, but cannot have been composed before the Hellenistic period.[57]

This text, written in the form of a guided tour under the direction of a heavenly figure, seems to describe an ideal city plan for a rebuilt Jerusalem of gargantuan proportions.[58] All measurements are minutely recorded. The tour

---

53. G. J. Brooke, *Exegesis at Qumran: 4QFlorilegium in Its Jewish Context*. JSOTSup 29 (Sheffield: JSOT, 1985) 175-205; D. R. Schwartz, "The Three Temples of 4QFlorilegium," *RevQ* 10 (1979) 83-92; M. O. Wise, "4*QFlorilegium* and the Temple of Man," *RevQ* 15 (1991) 103-32. The same notion is found in *Jub.* 1:27-28 that is preserved in Jub^a 4:5-10 (J. VanderKam et al., *Qumran Cave 4.VIII, Parabiblical Texts, Part 1*. DJD 13 [Oxford: Clarendon, 1994] 11-120) and in 11QT^a 29:7-10. Cf. also Tob 14:5.

54. Cf. CD 7:16.

55. Brooke, *Exegesis at Qumran*, 87. According to the reconstruction of Steudel, *Der Midrasch zur Eschatologie*, 25, our passage is col. 3:11-12.

56. See the thorough discussion of F. García Martínez, "The 'New Jerusalem' and the Future Temple of the Manuscripts from Qumran," in *Qumran and Apocalyptic: Studies on the Aramaic Texts from Qumran*, 180-213. STDJ 9 (Leiden: Brill, 1992); "The Temple Scroll and the New Jerusalem," in *The Dead Sea Scrolls after Fifty Years: A Comprehensive Assessment*, ed. J. C. VanderKam and P. W. Flint, 2:431-60 (Leiden: Brill, 1998-99). For text references, see García Martínez, "The 'New Jerusalem,'" 180 n. 1. A new edition has since appeared for 11Q18 in García Martínez, E. J. C. Tigchelaar, and A. S. van der Woude, *Qumran Cave 11.II (11Q2-18, 11Q20-31)*. DJD 23 (Oxford: Clarendon, 1998) 305-55.

57. M. Broshi, "Visionary Architecture and Town Planning in the Dead Sea Scrolls," in Dimant and Schiffman, *Time to Prepare the Way in the Wilderness*, 9-22.

58. The description that follows is based on García Martínez, "The 'New Jerusalem,'" 193-202. Cf. J. Licht, "An Ideal Town Plan from Qumran — The Description of the New Jerusalem," *IEJ* 29 (1979) 45-59; B. Z. Wacholder, "The Ancient Judeo-Aramaic Literature (500-164 BCE): A Classification of Pre-Qumranic Texts," in *Archaeology and History in the Dead Sea Scrolls: The*

begins with the exterior walls that are fitted with gates bearing the names of the tribes of Israel, like the outer court of the *temenos* of the *Temple Scroll*. This Jerusalem is to be laid out in symmetrical manner, like the Hippodamic cities of Late Antiquity. The gates of the city are also described in detail. Major and minor cross streets are apportioned throughout, creating large blocks of houses in the style of insulae with smaller houses within them. The guide leads the visionary into one of these, beginning with a detailed account of the gate complex. Winding staircases of the type called מסיבה lead to the upper story of each house. While the city is of great proportions, the houses are of normal size. This description is followed by an account of the temple to be located within this ideal city. The visionary actually sees the sacrificial practices of the temple being performed in his vision.[59]

This text is clearly eschatological in nature, describing the city to be created in the end of days. It does not seem to reflect the ideals of the sect in a specific manner, yet it in no way contradicts their views.[60] What we have here is the aspiration that Jerusalem would fulfill the visions of the prophets and constitute a giant metropolis in the end of days. We can easily see that those who expected the defeat of all evil and the return of the temple into their hands after a great messianic battle would have longed for such a city in the future age.

Messianic Jerusalem was to be a place of sacrificial perfection and ritual purity. Its temple was to be built by God himself. The city of Jerusalem would spread out in enlarged proportions, having been designed with perfect architectural planning.

Conclusion

The city of Jerusalem was for the Dead Sea sect three things. It was a polluted society and sanctuary from which they chose to withdraw because of the transgressions of its leaders. It was the object of specific legal requirements

---

New York University Conference in Memory of Yigael Yadin, ed. L. H. Schiffman, 270-71. JSPSup 8. JSOT/ASOR Monographs 2 (Sheffield: JSOT, 1990). A further reference to a messianic Jerusalem is found in Tob 13:17-18, partly preserved in the Hebrew Tobit (4Q200 7 ii 1-2). See J. A. Fitzmyer, in M. Broshi et al., *Qumran Cave 4.XIV: Parabiblical Texts, Part 2*. DJD 19 (Oxford: Clarendon, 1995) 73.

59. See F. García Martínez, "The Last Surviving Columns of 11QNJ," in *The Scriptures and Scrolls: Studies in Honour of A. S. van der Woude on the Occasion of His 65th Birthday*, ed. García Martínez, A. Hilhorst, and C. J. Labuschagne, 178-92 and pls. 3-9. VTSup 49 (Leiden: Brill, 1992).

60. García Martínez, "The 'New Jerusalem,'" 211-13.

regarding the temple and its service, making it the place where the divine presence was supposed to dwell. Finally, it was the place to which the sectarians themselves would return in the end of days. There a perfect temple would be built by God, and a perfect city would stretch beyond that of the present day. We can be certain that the members of the sect would have shared, with all their fellow Jews in every age of Jewish history, in the prayer of the author of the "Apostrophe to Zion" included in the *Psalms Scroll* (11QPs^a) found at Qumran:[61]

> I will remember you for a blessing, O Zion,
> I have loved you with all my might.
> May your memory be blessed for ever!
>
> Great is your hope, O Zion,
> That peace and your longed-for salvation will come.
>
> Generation after generation will dwell in you,
> And generations of the pious will be your glory.
>
> Those who yearn for the day of your redemption,
> That they may rejoice in your great glory.
>
> They are nourished from the abundance of your glory,
> And in your beautiful squares they walk.
>
> You will remember the kindness of your prophets,
> And in the deeds of your pious ones you will glory.
>
> Purge violence from your midst,
> Falsehood and dishonesty should be eradicated from you.
>
> Your children will rejoice in your midst,
> And your friends will join together with you.
>
> How many have hoped for your redemption,
> And have mourned for you continuously.

---

61. The translation is mine and previously appeared in *Reclaiming the Dead Sea Scrolls*, 392-93; and "Apostrophe to Zion (11QPsalms Scroll 22:1-15)," in *Prayer from Alexander to Constantine*, ed. M. Kiley, 18-22 (London: Routledge, 1997). The translation of Sanders, DJD 4:87-88, who first published this psalm was of help in preparing this version. This translation is revised in light of H. Eshel and J. Strugnell, "Alphabetical Acrostics in Pre-Tannaitic Hebrew," *CBQ* 62 (2000) 441-58.

Your hope, O Zion, shall not perish,
Nor will your longing be forgotten.

Who is it who has ever perished in righteousness,
Or who is it that has ever escaped in his iniquity?

A person is tested according to his way(s),
One will be requited according to his deeds.

All around your enemies are cut off, O Zion,
And all those who hate you have scattered.

Praise of you is pleasing, O Zion,
Cherished throughout the world.

Many times will I remember you for a blessing,
With all my heart I will bless you.

May you attain everlasting justice,
And may you receive the blessings of magnates.
May you merit the fulfillment of the vision prophesied about you,
The dream of the prophets which was sought for you.

Be exalted and spread far and wide, O Zion,
Praise the Most High, your redeemer.
May my soul rejoice at (the revelation of) your glory!

QUMRAN SECTARIANS AND OTHERS

CHAPTER 19

The Pharisees and Their Legal Traditions according to the Dead Sea Scrolls

The revolution in our understanding of Judaism in Second Temple times being wrought by the discovery and now full publication of the Dead Sea Scrolls is still only in its infancy. Nevertheless, the scrolls are throwing light not only on the group of sectarians who gathered them in the caves of Qumran, but also on a variety of other groups of Second Temple Jews, most notably the Pharisees and Sadducees. To be sure, this evidence is often oblique, and its interpretation is beset with problems of method. But a general picture is certainly emerging. This picture, we will see, is in marked contrast to the skepticism of some scholars who deny, and therefore ignore, the accounts pertaining to the Pharisees preserved in the later rabbinic corpus. Indeed, we will see that elements of the picture of the Pharisees that emerges from Josephus, the New Testament, and rabbinic sources[1] are confirmed by evidence in the scrolls, and new information is being learned as well.

Before beginning, the principles of our method must be set forth. The textual material we will discuss is couched in sobriquets and symbolic designations. Further, most of our evidence consists of polemical materials in which the authors criticize or polemicize against the Pharisees, just as is the case in the New Testament. Here we must apply the usual caveats, testing the evidence and sifting it carefully. But when we find that it accords with later rabbinic evidence, we cannot just dismiss the latter as anachronistic in a knee-jerk manner. We have to give the scrolls a fair opportunity to revise

---

1. Collected and analyzed in J. Neusner, *From Politics to Piety: The Emergence of Pharisaic Judaism*, 2nd ed. (New York: Ktav, 1979) 45-141.

completely the general scholarly view that sees rabbinic evidence for the Pharisees as anachronistic and even false.[2]

The following presentation will treat the Qumran evidence for the Pharisees in the following sequence: (1) We will first discuss evidence for the history of the Pharisees and their involvement in Judean political affairs. (2) We will then treat the evidence regarding the nature of the Pharisees as a group. (3) We then turn to the basic conceptual principles and materials that underlie their approach, to the extent that it can be illuminated and contextualized. Finally, (4) we will discuss what can be learned from the scrolls about the state of Pharisaic halakhah in the Second Temple period.[3]

Political History

Josephus first mentions the Pharisees in his account of the time of Jonathan the Hasmonean (152-143 B.C.E.).[4] The earliest datable reference to them in the scrolls is oblique — in the MMT document.[5] This halakhic polemic, to which we will return below, includes a homiletical (or paranetic) section at the end (C 7-32) in which the author/authors of the text, who in the halakhic section above had addressed their fellow Aaronide priests, now turn to the ruler whom they compare to David and Solomon. This text is to be dated, most probably, to the beginning of the reign of Jonathan the Hasmonean in 152 B.C.E.[6] The halakhic section shows that the incipient sectarian group was in conflict with the application of Pharisaic halakhic norms in the temple. The ruler referred to at the end of the text must be taken as Jonathan the Hasmonean, who is being criticized for the adoption of Pharisaic rulings in the temple. Similarly, the priests are being criticized for giving in to and accommodating to this change.[7] The most likely scenario that would explain

---

2. For the history of the study of the Pharisees in modern scholarship, see R. Deines, *Die Pharisäer*. WUNT 101 (Tübingen: Mohr [Siebeck], 1997).

3. There is still much to learn from C. Rabin, *Qumran Studies*. Scripta Judaica 2 (London: Oxford University Press, 1957) 53-70, even though he reaches the incorrect conclusion that the sectarians of the scrolls are Pharisees.

4. Josephus, *Ant.* 13.171-73.

5. Cf. "The New Halakhic Letter (4QMMT) and the Origins of the Dead Sea Sect," Chapter 6 above.

6. E. Qimron and J. Strugnell, *Qumran Cave 4.V: Miqṣat Ma'aśe ha-Torah*. DJD 10 (Oxford: Clarendon, 1994) 117-21.

7. Cf. E. Qimron and J. Strugnell, "An Unpublished Halakhic Letter from Qumran," *Biblical Archaeology Today: Proceedings of the International Congress on Biblical Archaeology, Jerusalem, April 1984*, ed. J. Amitai, 400-7 (Jerusalem: Israel Exploration Society, Israel Academy of

this document is as follows: After the ascendance of Jonathan to control of Jerusalem and its temple in 152 B.C.E., he sought to rid the temple of the influence of the Hellenized Sadducees. The Hasmoneans blamed them for the entire course of events from the Hellenistic reform through the revolt and through the reassertion of Hellenistic Jewish control over the temple. Jonathan therefore made common cause with the Pharisees and conducted the priestly service in accord with their views. Thus, his early reign as high priest in Jerusalem marked the political and legal ascendance of the Pharisaic party to a role of authority such as that pictured in rabbinic sources and described by Josephus.

This position of leadership continued, apparently, up to the time of the banquet at which the Pharisees had their falling out with the Hasmoneans.[8] Josephus[9] tells this story pertaining to John Hyrcanus, and the Babylonian Talmud, in an early baraita,[10] ascribes it to the time of Alexander Jannaeus (103-76 B.C.E.). In either case, these bad relations were certainly remembered when the historical allusions to the Pharisees in *Pesher Nahum* were composed sometime soon after the Roman conquest of Judea in 63 B.C.E.[11] That text presents, as part of its contemporizing exegesis of the biblical book of Nahum, an account of the Pharisaic rebellion against Alexander Jannaeus that parallels that of Josephus.[12] By combining these two accounts, we can determine that in about 80 B.C.E. the Pharisees took the lead in inviting the Seleucid ruler Demetrius III Eukairos (95-88 B.C.E.) to invade Judea in an at-

---

Sciences and Humanities, in cooperation with ASOR, 1985); "An Unpublished Halakhic Letter from Qumran," *IMJ* 4 (1985) 9-12 (a different article with the same title).

8. E. Schürer, *The History of the Jewish People in the Age of Jesus Christ (175 B.C.-A.D. 135)*, rev. ed. by G. Vermes and F. Millar, with P. Vermes and M. Black, 1:213-14 (Edinburgh: T. & T. Clark, 1973).

9. *Ant.* 13.288-96.

10. *B. Qidd.* 66a. The early date of the baraita is established by its use of the *vav* consecutive.

11. Cf. "Pharisees and Sadducees in Pesher Nahum," Chapter 20 below.

12. *Ant.* 13.372-83. See the discussion of this episode in F. M. Cross, *The Ancient Library of Qumran and Modern Biblical Studies* (Garden City: Doubleday, 1958; repr. Grand Rapids: Baker, 1980) 122-27. The events are summarized in Schürer, 1:223-24; see esp. 224-25, n. 21 which refers to 4QpNah. See also J. D. Amoussine, "Éphraïm et Manassé dans le Péshèr de Nahum (4 Q p Nahum)," *RevQ* 4 (1963-64) 389-96; Amusin (Amoussine), "The Reflection of Historical Events of the First Century B.C. in Qumran Commentaries (4Q161; 4Q169; 4Q166)," *HUCA* 48 (1977) 134-46; D. Flusser, "Kat Midbar Yehudah ve-ha-Perushim," *Molad* 19 (1961) 456-58; "Perushim, Ṣeduqim, ve-'Issiyim be-Fesher Naḥum," *Essays in Jewish History and Philology, in Memory of Gedaliahu Alon*, ed. M. Dorman, S. Safrai, and M. Stern, 133-68 (Tel Aviv: Hakibbutz Hameuchad, 1970); S. L. Berrin, *The Pesher Nahum Scroll from Qumran: An Exegetical Study of 4Q169*. STDJ 53 (Leiden: Brill, 2004) 87-130.

tempt to dislodge Jannaeus, who was unpopular with the Pharisees and other elements of the population. Demetrius invaded as planned, but the cruelty of the war led the Jewish rebels to change sides in the middle, now supporting Jannaeus against the Syrians. When the war ended and he had regained his power and control over the nation, Jannaeus crucified eight hundred Pharisees, and others fled the country. While Josephus had related this story, it is only the Qumran text that allows us to be certain that Jannaeus was opposed primarily by Pharisees.

The Pharisees as a Group

The Pharisees are pictured in a number of texts, specifically the *Zadokite Fragments* (in the Admonition) and the pesharim. We learn of בוני החיץ, the "builders of the wall," a term for the Pharisees, who follow a teacher and in the view of the sectarians transgress regarding certain specific sins (CD 4:19–5:11).[13] Most prominent are allowing marriage to one's niece, a principle known from later rabbinic law, which the sect believed violated the Torah (by exegesis of Lev 18:13), and Pharisaic permission of polygamy (CD 4:20–5:11; 4Q269 4 i 3;[14] 6Q15 1:1-3[15]). They also claim that this group speaks against "the statutes of God's covenant," claiming they are not valid (CD 5:11-12). The Pharisees are seen as spinners of spiders' webs, that is, lies (CD 5:13-14; 4Q266 3 ii 1-2; 6Q15 2:1[16]).

The Pharisees are designated as "Ephraim" and seen as equivalent to despisers and renegades who have separated from the mainstream (CD 7:9-14; 4Q266 3 iii 1-3). God is portrayed as hating the builders of the wall, who are responsible for kindling his anger against all Israel (CD 8:18). We learn that they fail to understand the teachings of the sectarians because of false teachers. As a result, God is angry with and detests the Pharisees and their followers. They will eventually be smitten by the "last prince" (4QpHos[a] 2:3). It is apparently at this time that the sectarians expected the followers of the Pharisaic leaders to desert them (4QpNah 3-4 iii 4-6).

---

13. For the text of CD, see E. Qimron, "The Text of CDC," in *The Damascus Document Reconsidered*, ed. M. Broshi, 9-49 (Jerusalem: Israel Exploration Society and Shrine of the Book, Israel Museum, 1992). For the Qumran manuscripts from Cave 4, see J. M. Baumgarten, *Qumran Cave 4.XIII: The Damascus Document (4Q266-273)*. DJD 18 (Oxford: Clarendon, 1996).

14. Cf. also 4Q266 14 d 1.

15. M. Baillet, J. T. Milik, and R. de Vaux, eds., *Les 'Petites Grottes' de Qumrân*. DJD 3 (Oxford: Clarendon, 1962) 129.

16. Baillet, Milik, and de Vaux, DJD 3:129.

The Pharisees and Their Legal Traditions according to the Dead Sea Scrolls

It is probable that the Pharisees are described also (4Q266 3 ii 7-8; 4Q267 2 4-7; CD 5:20-21)[17] as those who removed the boundary (by teaching false laws), speaking rebelliously against God's commandments, prophesying deceit, and causing Israel to go astray. The problem of the Pharisees is that their leaders have led them astray (4QpNah 3-4 iii 5) to do evil (4QpPs[a] 1:24). It is this conception that lies behind the designation used for the Pharisees, דורשי חלכות, "expounders of false laws," punning on הלכות, "laws."[18] These false interpreters seek to destroy the sectarians (4Q177 Catena[a] ii:12-13).[19] In the same way it is said of them that בתלמוד שקרם, "their dishonesty (or falseness) is in their teaching" (4QpNah 3-4 ii 8),[20] referring to their method of deriving laws by logic, the strict sense of the term תלמוד in early rabbinic usage as well. It is likely that the איש הכזב ("man of lies") of the *Habakkuk Pesher* (1QpHab 2:1-2) is a Pharisaic teacher.[21] This individual had a public confrontation with the Teacher of Righteousness (1QpHab 5:10-11), apparently different from that of the Wicked Priest (1QpHab 11:4-9). The interpretations of the Man of Lies were regarded by the Qumran sectarians as absurdities (4QpPs[a] 1:26-27). He and his followers will be destroyed (4QpPs[a] 4:18-19).

In opposition to the Pharisees, besides the sect, is Manasseh, a term for the Sadducees (4QpIsa[c] 4-6 i 18-19). Both Ephraim and Manasseh will be arrayed against the sect, termed Judah. Manasseh is said to control Israel (4QpNah 3-4 iv 3) and is associated with nobility (line 4; 3-4 iii 9). Both the Pharisees and Sadducees are said to have attacked the sectarian priestly leader, the Teacher of Righteousness (4QpPs[a] 3:15-19), and his council (4QpPs[a] 2:18-19).

What concerns us in this lengthy survey of allusions to the Pharisees is the probable historical reality that lies behind the sectarian animus to the Pharisees. This material, though scanty in its direct historical allusions, provides important information about the Pharisees and their nature as a group.

First, the Pharisees were certainly opponents of the sect who, in turn, opposed them strongly. They had numerous halakhic disputes, and these

---

17. Cf. 4Q271 1 2.
18. Cf. Isa 30:10 and A. I. Baumgarten, "Seekers after Smooth Things," *EDSS* 2:857-9.
19. F. García Martínez and E. J. C. Tigchelaar, eds., *The Dead Sea Scrolls Study Edition* (Leiden: Brill and Grand Rapids: Wm. B. Eerdmans, 2000) 1:364-65.
20. Cf. B. Z. Wacholder, "A Qumran Attack on Oral Exegesis? The Phrase אשר בתלמוד שקרם in 4Q Pesher Nahum," *RevQ* 5 (1966) 351-69.
21. B. Nitzan, *Megillat Pesher Habakkuk: mi-Megillot Midbar Yehudah (1Qp Hab)* (Jerusalem: Bialik Institute, 1986) 136-38. Contrast W. H. Brownlee, *The Midrash Pesher of Habakkuk* (SBLMS 24; Missoula, Mont.: Scholars, 1979) 94-98; see also T. Lim, "Liar," *EDSS* 1:493-4.

were based on different philosophies and methodologies of law. The Pharisees were led by a teacher, probably the "Man of Lies," who had direct contact with the Teacher of Righteousness with whom he quarreled. This Pharisaic teacher, as well as his fellows, taught publicly and attracted a wide circle of followers. While the Pharisees were separate from the aristocratic Sadducees, they were allied against the sectarians. Apparently, the Pharisees, in certain periods, were dominated by the Sadducees. This is probably an indication of the gradual reentry of the Sadducees into political and religious dominance under Alexander Jannaeus (and again after the Roman conquest of 63 B.C.E.).

The Pharisaic Approach to Jewish Law

The scrolls say just enough about the general issues of the Pharisaic approach to Jewish law as to suggest that some discussion of this issue is in order. Admittedly this issue will take us a bit afield, but hopefully this digression will be worthwhile.

The fundamental question facing all systems of postbiblical Jewish law is how to justify the existence of so significant a presence of clearly nonbiblical laws. The Qumran sectarians considered biblical law to be the "revealed" law *(nigleh)* and the additional prescriptions as "hidden" *(nistar)*. This latter class of laws was revealed to the sect through inspired biblical exegesis in their regular study sessions. The claim of the sectarians was that tradition was not an authoritative guide to Jewish law. Nor did they accept the notion of any "extrabiblical" revelation at Sinai in addition to the written Torah.[22] The author of the *Temple Scroll* saw things differently, asserting by implication that his own interpretations were actually part of the written Torah. For this reason, he felt free to rewrite and re-redact the Torah to reflect his views and those of his sources. He apparently believed in a onetime revelation at Sinai, but saw that revelation as including laws and interpretations beyond those of the written law.[23]

Little is known about the Pharisaic view except for the reports of later sources. Josephus speaks of the traditions passed on by the elders,[24] as does the New Testament.[25] But this simply means that some teachings were passed on by the Pharisees that were not part of the written Torah. Later tannaitic sources

---

22. L. H. Schiffman, *The Halakhah at Qumran*. SJLA 16 (Leiden: Brill, 1975) 22-32.
23. Cf. Y. Yadin, *The Temple Scroll* (Jerusalem: Israel Exploration Society, 1983) 1:391-92.
24. *Ant.* 13.297. Cf. Philo, *Spec. Laws* 4.143-50.
25. Mark 7:1-8.

attribute to the Pharisees the dual Torah concept according to which God gave two Torahs to Israel at Sinai, the written text and its oral interpretation.[26] Josephus identifies the Pharisees as the leading experts in biblical interpretation,[27] but he nowhere claims divine inspiration for their teachings. We should note that the Sadducees rejected the extrabiblical traditions of the Pharisees while for the most part hewing closer to the literal text of the Bible.[28]

We may now return to the material from the scrolls that relates to the Pharisaic views on these issues. We have already surveyed these materials above, and will concentrate here on those aspects relevant to their general approach to the authority and derivation of law.

The designation "builders of the wall" (בוני החיץ)[29] recalls the statement attributed to the Men of the Great Assembly in *m. Avot* 1:1, "Make a fence around the Torah" (עשו סיג לתורה). The use of this term in the scrolls indicates that by ca. 120 B.C.E., when the *Zadokite Fragments (Damascus Document)* were composed (or redacted), this characteristic of the Pharisees was already in place — they added restrictions not required by biblical law in order to lessen the possibility of transgression of biblical commandments.[30] This practice was objected to by the sectarians, who followed the Sadducean/Zadokite approach, because it could not be justified by biblical exegesis, as their system required. They rejected all nonbiblical laws not based on (or justified by) scriptural interpretations. In fact, in the polemic against the Pharisaic practice of niece marriage found in the *Zadokite Fragments* (CD 5:7-8), the text makes very clear that the difference of opinion lay in the Pharisaic rejection of the sectarian exegesis that, in this case, was less literalistic than that of the Pharisees.[31]

The pun on הלכות in the phrase דורשי חלקות, "expounders of false laws," used for the Pharisees, refers specifically to their acceptance of laws not

---

26. *Sifre Deut* 351 (ed. L. Finkelstein [New York: Jewish Theological Seminary, 1969] 408); b. Šabb. 31a. Cf. L. H. Schiffman, *From Text to Tradition: A History of Second Temple and Rabbinic Judaism* (Hoboken: Ktav, 1991) 179-81; E. E. Urbach, *The Sages: Their Concepts and Beliefs,* trans. I. Abrahams (Jerusalem: Magnes, Hebrew University, 1987) 286-314.

27. *War* 2.162.

28. Contrary to some modern authors, there is no evidence that the Sadducees rejected the Prophets and Writings. The Samaritans, on the other hand, accepted only the Torah, as their separation from the people of Israel took place before the canonization of the Prophets and Writings.

29. See *DCH* 3.216.

30. See L. Finkelstein, "The Maxim of the Anshe Keneset ha-Gedolah," *JBL* 59 (1940) 455-69, for an opposing, idiosyncratic view of the original meaning of the rabbinic maxim, "make a fence around the Torah."

31. Cf. L. Ginzberg, *An Unknown Jewish Sect* (New York: Jewish Theological Seminary of America, 1976) 23-24.

derived from exegesis of Scripture as halakhah. Although we have documentation only for the later use of הלכות in rabbinic literature, it is clear that it had to be in use among the Pharisees, as otherwise the polemic in the scrolls would be inconceivable.[32] If so, we learn not only that the term was used, but that the tradition of the Pharisees included laws that were passed on with no scriptural justification or argumentation. This corroborates what is known of the Pharisaic teachings from Josephus and the New Testament.[33]

The term *talmud* is used to designate the Pharisaic teachings, the validity of which are denied by the sectarians. This usage concurs with early tannaitic usage of this term to indicate a specific method of logical deduction from one legal principle to another.[34] This form of deduction, again because of its being unconnected to scriptural proof texts, was rejected by the sectarians, but it was by this time certainly part of the Pharisaic approach.

The process of expounding and teaching this legal system is described by the verb *darash*, as used in the expression *dorshe ha-ḥalaqot*. The sectarians use this term and its nominal cognate, *midrash,* to refer to their own scriptural exegesis and the legal rulings derived from it, as well as to designate a compilation of such legal teachings.[35] It appears in reference to the Pharisees, however, with the more limited meaning "expound," in the sense of exposition of the law rather than scriptural interpretation.

The above terminology says quite a bit about the history of Pharisaic legal methods, even if the context is uniformly polemical. Pharisaic rulings were already known as halakhot in the Hasmonean period. These were taught by teachers who derived from them other laws by the logical method of *talmud*, an early form of logical deduction of laws one from the other. These unwritten laws were opposed by the Sadducees since they had no scriptural basis. These texts are in complete accord, therefore, with the description by Josephus, who is shown by the scrolls to have accurately portrayed the view of the Pharisees. Eventually, the Pharisees argued for the Sinaitic origin of what they would later term the oral law.[36]

---

32. For a possible Akkadian derivation of the term הלכה, see S. Lieberman, *Hellenism in Jewish Palestine* (New York: Jewish Theological Seminary, 1962) 83, n. 3.

33. Cf. J. M. Baumgarten, "The Unwritten Law in the Pre-Rabbinic Period," *JSJ* 3 (1972) 7-29; but contrast J. Neusner, "Rabbinic Traditions about the Pharisees before A.D. 70: The Problem of Oral Transmission," *JJS* 22 (1971) 1-18.

34. Cf. Rashi to *b. Sukkah* 28a. The uncensored text has *talmud* where the printed text has *gemara*.

35. Schiffman, *Halakhah at Qumran*, 54-59.

36. *M. Abot* 1:1, referring to the oral law and the term הלכה למשה מסיני; *m. Pe'ah* 2:6; *'Ed.* 8:7; *Yad.* 4:3.

The Pharisees and Their Legal Traditions according to the Dead Sea Scrolls

Pharisaic Halakhah

Perhaps the most central question of all in which the scrolls can contribute to our knowledge of the Pharisees is in the area of the history of Pharisaic halakhah. To be sure, this is not because the law of the scrolls sect is Pharisaic.[37] Rather, it is because the scrolls explicitly and implicitly polemicize against the law of the Pharisaic opponents of the sect, and in doing so, testify to the state of Pharisaic law in their time.

In the early days of the study of the history of halakhah, it was usual to assume that there was a linear development from a theoretical "old halakhah" to that of the Pharisaic-rabbinic tradition. We now know, and the material we will be examining certainly shows this, that there existed simultaneous and competing trends in halakhah in the Second Temple period, that of the priestly, Zadokite, or Sadducean trend and that of the Pharisees.[38] These competed in their exegetical system, basic principles, and specific rulings.[39]

We shall treat here a few different types of examples in order to illustrate how this material enlightens us about Pharisaic law. (a) We shall first survey a few cases in which the scrolls criticize the Pharisees for specific practices that we know of from later sources. (b) We shall then deal with cases in 4QMMT in which the scrolls testify to both sides of a controversy known from rabbinic literature to have occupied the Pharisees and the Sadducees. (c) We will then look at cases in which scrolls texts polemicize against views that we may presume to have been held by Pharisees, based on extrapolation from later tannaitic evidence. It is in this last area that much work is still to be done to determine the limits of the validity of using this material to recover early Pharisaic halakhah.

---

37. Such was the mistaken conclusion of Ginzberg, *An Unknown Jewish Sect,* 144, who was lulled by the many similarities in legal practice to conclude that the *Zadokite Fragments (Damascus Document)* represented a group of proto-Pharisees. Such a misjudgment was certainly understandable before the discovery of the rest of the Dead Sea Scrolls. He was also followed by Rabin, *Qumran Studies,* 69-70.

38. Y. Sussmann, "Ḥeqer Toldot ha-Halakhah u-Megillot Midbar Yehudah: Hirhurim Talmudiyim Rishonim le-'Or Megillat Miqṣat Ma'aśe ha-Torah," *Tarbiz* 59 (1989/1990) 11-76; "The History of the Halakha and the Dead Sea Scrolls: Preliminary Talmudic Observations on Miqṣat Ma'aśe ha-Torah (4QMMT)," DJD 10:179-200.

39. See "Halakhah and History: The Contribution of the Dead Sea Scrolls to Recent Scholarship," Chapter 3 above.

Direct Criticism of the Pharisees

Direct criticism of the halakhic practices of the Pharisees is limited to a few specific cases. In these cases, the code names we have encountered are used to designate those whose practices are unacceptable to the sectarians, and specific practices are condemned. The specific practices cited (CD 4:20-21) are marrying one's niece and taking two wives. We will briefly consider the Pharisaic views on these matters.

Later rabbinic texts inform us that the Pharisaic-rabbinic tradition considered it permitted — even praiseworthy — to marry one's niece.[40] Yet the *Zadokite Fragments* provide us with a lengthy biblical interpretation to prove that it is forbidden (CD 5:7-11). The *Temple Scroll* also forbids this, adding it to the scriptural list of consanguineous marriages (11QTemple 66:14).[41] In this case, the sectarian and rabbinic materials dovetail nicely, giving us both sides of the controversy.

The Pharisees are also said to violate the ban on polygamy (CD 4:21). But this is not all that is at stake in this example. Their offense is taking two wives "in their (fem.) lifetimes," that is, in the lifetimes of the wives. The most likely interpretation of this passage is that the sectarians prohibited polygamy and even considered it forbidden to take a second wife as long as the first lives, making the institution of divorce effectively what we call "legal separation." The *Temple Scroll*'s list of forbidden marriages (col. 66) does not contain such prohibitions, but this text is not complete as is clear from its ending in the middle of a sentence. But the king in the section of that text termed the Law of the King is prohibited from both polygamy and from remarriage after divorce (11QTemple 57:17-19).[42] The Pharisaic disagreement with and rejection of both these principles, in that they permitted (although barely practiced) polygamy and remarriage after divorce while both parties were still living, meant to the sectarians that the Pharisees were guilty of fornication. Here again, the later rabbinic reports exactly match the halakhic views that the sectarian documents have attributed to the Pharisees.

The briefer accusations of the sectarians to the effect that the Pharisees defile the temple and have relations with women who are menstrually impure (CD 5:6-7) also point to views held by the Pharisees, although here the specifics are not as clear. Defiling the temple alludes to following different purity

---

40. B. Yebam. 62b; see Ginzberg, *An Unknown Jewish Sect*, 23-24.
41. Yadin, *Temple Scroll*, 1:371-72. L. H. Schiffman, "Laws Pertaining to Women in the Temple Scroll," in *The Dead Sea Scrolls: Forty Years of Research*, ed. D. Dimant and U. Rappaport, 227 (Leiden: Brill and Jerusalem: Magnes, Hebrew University and Yad Izhak Ben-Zvi, 1992).
42. Yadin, *Temple Scroll*, 1:355-57; Schiffman, "Laws Pertaining to Women," 216-18.

laws, perhaps regarding two pillars of sectarian law: first-day ablutions and completing of the last purificatory day until sunset. The latter will be treated in the next section since both sides of the debate appear together in MMT. The case of the first-day ablutions we discuss here as exemplifying the controversies regarding ritual purity.

One of the fundamental differences between the sectarian purity laws and those of the Pharisees concerned a requirement that we know was held by the sectarians from the *Temple Scroll* (11QTemple 45:7-10; 49:16-17; 50:10-14),[43] 4QOrdinances[c] (4Q514) 1 3-8,[44] and 4QTohorot[a] 1 i.[45] When there was a seven-day purification period, with sprinkling on the third and seventh days according to the Torah, the Saducean/Zadokite legal system required purification on the first day in order to be permitted to eat anything.[46] This law is nowhere to be found in the rabbinic corpus and was no doubt rejected by the Pharisees. Such differences of opinion led the sectarians to see the Jerusalem temple worship as conducted in a state of ritual impurity and to withdraw from it at a time when Pharisaic law was being followed there.

Previously Known Pharisee-Sadducee Controversies

A number of controversies described in tannaitic literature as Pharisee-Sadducee debates are documented in 4QMMT. In this document, the founders of the Qumran sect take the view associated with the Sadducees and polemicize against that attributed to the Pharisees, or "sages of Israel" (חכמי ישראל) in the rabbinic version. In these cases, MMT proves that later tannaitic accounts accurately portray some disagreements regarding halakhic matters that took place in the early Hasmonean period. For our purposes, we will be able to collect additional information about the state of Pharisaic halakhah in this early period.

One such controversy concerns the ashes of the red heifer used to purify people who have contracted impurity of the dead, in accord with Numbers 19. MMT B13-17 criticizes the present procedure in the temple, asserting that it is required that those involved in the preparation of the ashes of the red heifer

---

43. J. Milgrom, "Studies in the Temple Scroll," *JBL* 97 (1978) 512-18.

44. See the edition of L. H. Schiffman, "Ordinances (4Q159 = 4QOrd[a])," in *The Dead Sea Scrolls: Hebrew, Aramaic, and Greek Texts with English Translations*, ed. J. H. Charlesworth, 1:151-58 (Tübingen: Mohr [Siebeck] and Louisville: Westminster John Knox, 1994).

45. J. M Baumgarten, *Qumran Cave 4.XXV: Halakhic Texts*. DJD 35 (Oxford: Clarendon, 1999) 100-3.

46. See Milgrom, *JBL* 97 (1978) 512-18.

must be fully pure, having experienced sunset on the last day of their ritual purification period.[47] This same view appears in 4QTohorot B[b] (4Q277 1 ii 2[48]) and in the *Zadokite Fragments* (4Q269 8 ii 4-6).[49] We know from tannaitic sources that this was a Sadducean position and that the Pharisees disagreed strongly.[50] To them, if the required sacrifices and ablutions had taken place on the last day, even if the sun had not set, purification was sufficient for preparation of the ashes. In this case, the Pharisaic acceptance of the almost complete purification of the *ṭevul yom,* the one who had immersed already on the final day of his purification period, is proven by MMT to be a view held by the Pharisees already in the mid-second century B.C.E.

The sectarian opposition to this view is expressed as well in connection with a wide variety of laws several times in the *Temple Scroll* and in the *Zadokite Fragments (Damascus Document).* It clearly represented a major controversy between the Pharisees and their Saducean/Zadokite opponents that had ramifications in many areas of Jewish law.[51]

MMT B 21-22 also argued against the making of handles for vessels for temple use out of animal hides and bones.[52] In the case of bones, this implies that the sectarians considered animal bones to be impure. This controversy is recorded in the Mishnah. The Sadducees argued that the bones of animals were impure but the Pharisees considered them pure.[53] Again, the historicity of the disagreement is confirmed and MMT allows us to date it to at least ca. 150 B.C.E.

The final example of this phenomenon to be considered here is that of flowing liquids. This controversy concerned the pouring of ritually pure liquids from a pure vessel into an impure vessel. MMT argues that the impurity flows up through the liquid stream (opposite to the direction of the flow) and renders the upper vessel impure.[54] This is a controversy known also from the Mishnah.[55] The Pharisees considered the upper vessel to remain pure, ruling

47. Cf. Qimron and Strugnell, DJD 10:152-54.
48. Baumgarten, DJD 35:116-17.
49. Cf. Baumgarten, DJD 18:131-32.
50. *M. Parah* 3:7; *t. Parah* 3:7-8; *Sifre Num* 124 in *Sifre Be-Midbar* (ed. H. S. Horovitz [Jerusalem: Wahrmann, 1966]) 167.
51. L. H. Schiffman, "Pharisaic and Sadducean Halakhah in Light of the Dead Sea Scrolls: The Case of Ṭevul Yom," *DSD* 1 (1994) 285-99.
52. Cf. Qimron and Strugnell, DJD 10:155.
53. *M. Yad.* 4:6.
54. Cf. Y. Elman, "Some Remarks on 4QMMT and the Rabbinic Tradition, or, When Is a Parallel Not a Parallel?" in *Reading 4QMMT: New Perspectives on Qumran Law and History,* ed. J. Kampen and M. J. Bernstein, 99-128. SBLSymS 2 (Atlanta: Scholars, 1996).
55. *M. Yad.* 4:7.

that impurity cannot flow against the direction of the stream while the Sadducees considered the upper vessel impure. Again, 4QMMT shows that the disagreement dates to early Hasmonean times and confirms its being rooted in the halakhic debates of the time.

Pharisaic Laws Based on Later Evidence and Qumran Polemics

A few more such passages could be cited, but those already discussed raise the possibility that other laws preserved in the scrolls corpus are also polemics against Pharisaic views. If so, then we would be able to recover a considerable number of additional Pharisaic laws that could be definitely dated to the Hasmonean period, primarily to the second half of the second century B.C.E. We shall confine ourselves here to a small number of examples that illustrate this approach. In these examples, Qumran texts present laws that oppose views, often by implication only, that are known from later tannaitic texts. In these cases, we are entitled to conclude that the tannaitic evidence reflects views developed by the Pharisees already in the Hasmonean period.

We begin with the example of nonsacral slaughter. The *Temple Scroll* required that all slaughter performed within three days' journey of the temple be done sacrificially. Nonsacral slaughter is permitted only beyond the three-day limit (11QTemple 52:13-16).[56] This same law is repeated in 4QMMT B 27-28.[57] The opposite view appears in tannaitic literature that rules that nonsacral slaughter is permitted even right outside the temple precincts.[58] At stake here is the interpretation of the words, "If the place is far from you" (כי־ירחק ממך המקום) in Deut 12:21. It seems reasonable to conclude that this Qumran regulation, which fits totally with the Sadducean/Zadokite view of the ultimate centrality of temple worship, is arguing against an already existing Pharisaic practice allowing nonsacral slaughter anywhere outside the sanctuary. If so, we have recovered another early Pharisaic law from the polemic against it.

A related example pertains to the slaughter of pregnant animals. The

---

56. Cf. Yadin, Temple Scroll, 1:312; L. H. Schiffman, "Sacral and Non-Sacral Slaughter according to the Temple Scroll," in *Time to Prepare the Way in the Wilderness: Papers on the Qumran Scrolls by Fellows of the Institute for Advanced Studies of the Hebrew University, Jerusalem, 1989-1990*, ed. D. Dimant and L. H. Schiffman, 69-84. STDJ 16 (Leiden: Brill, 1995). Cf. E. Eshel, "4QLev^d: A Possible Source for the Temple Scroll and Miqṣat Ma'aśe ha-Torah," DSD 2 (1995) 1-13.

57. Cf. Qimron and Strugnell, DJD 10:156-57.

58. *Sifre Deut* 75 (ed. Finkelstein, 140); Nahmanides to Deut 12:20; Yadin, Temple Scroll, 1:318-20.

Temple Scroll (11QTemple 52:5-7) forbids the slaughter of pregnant animals, quoting the prohibition on the slaughter of an animal and its young on the same day (Lev 22:28).[59] The very same law appears in 4QMMT (B 36-38)[60] in polemical context and in the Code of Punishments of the *Zadokite Fragments* (4Q270 2 ii 15).[61] Tannaitic sources indicate that the Pharisees permitted the slaughtering of pregnant animals, ruling that the fetus may be eaten without further slaughter.[62] The occurrence of this law in the polemical MMT, together with the appearance of the opposite point of view in tannaitic sources, allows us to conclude that the polemic was indeed against the Pharisees who held the view documented only later in the rabbinic material.

Another example reflected in both MMT (B62-63)[63] and the *Temple Scroll* (11QTemple 60:3-4)[64] is the case of fourth-year produce of fruit trees, termed by the rabbis נטע רבעי. The Torah (Lev 19:23-25) commanded that this crop be sanctified to God ("a holy offering of jubilation [קדש הלולים] to the Lord") and prohibited its nonsacral use. Both of these sectarian texts rule that this produce is to be given to the priests, but tannaitic sources require that it be brought to Jerusalem and eaten there by the owners, as the rabbis ruled also regarding the second tithe.[65] Here again, we can conclude that MMT and the *Temple Scroll* are arguing against an existing Pharisaic view, later reflected in tannaitic texts that interpreted the biblical text differently and reached different halakhic conclusions.

The final example we will present is a rule stated in the *Zadokite Fragments* (CD 12:17-18; cf. 4Q266 9 ii 4-5) to the effect that every "utensil," nail, or peg that is in a building in which there is a dead body becomes impure, "with the same impurity as tools for work."[66] This law is paralleled in the *Temple Scroll* (11QTemple 49:19-20) in a passage detailing the laws of purification from the impurity of the dead (cols. 49-50), but that text refers only to "utensils."[67]

---

59. Yadin, *Temple Scroll*, 1:312-14.

60. Cf. Qimron and Strugnell, DJD 10:157-58; L. H. Schiffman, "*Miqṣat Ma'aśeh ha-Torah* and the *Temple Scroll*," *RevQ* 14 (The Texts of Qumran and the History of the Community: Proceedings of the Groningen Congress on the Dead Sea Scrolls 3, 1990) 448-51.

61. See Baumgarten, DJD 18:146.

62. *M. Ḥul.* 4:5.

63. Cf. Qimron and Strugnell, DJD 10:164-65.

64. Yadin, *Temple Scroll*, 1:162-63; Schiffman, "*Miqṣat Ma'aśeh ha-Torah* and the *Temple Scroll*," 452-57.

65. *T. Ma'aś. Š.* 5:16; *m. Zebaḥ.* 5:8; cf. *t. Zebaḥ.* 6:18.

66. Cf. Ginzberg, *An Unknown Jewish Sect*, 82-84.

67. L. H. Schiffman, "The Impurity of the Dead in the *Temple Scroll*," in *Archaeology and History in the Dead Sea Scrolls: The New York University Conference in Memory of Yigael Yadin*, 146-48. JSOTSup 8. JSOT/ASOR Monographs 2 (Sheffield: Sheffield Academic, 1990).

Our text is probably a polemic against a Pharisaic law, known in tannaitic texts, to the effect that in order to incur impurity, an item must be considered to be a finished, complete vessel or tool.[68]

Our text goes out of its way to say that everything becomes impure, even nails or pegs that do not have a minimum size and are not containers, and that impurity is contracted even if these are not tools for work, that is, completed instruments, as required by Pharisaic-rabbinic law. Again we see that a law recorded only in tannaitic texts had to be in existence early in the Hasmonean period in order to have been the object of a polemical response, and we can accordingly date this Pharisaic principle at least to this period.

Many more such examples could be added to this section, but it is sufficient to have shown that there is a body of Pharisaic laws, known only from later rabbinic traditions, that can be shown through the evidence of the scrolls to date to as early as the years following the Maccabean Revolt (168-164 B.C.E.).

Conclusion

While it is certainly true that the Dead Sea Scrolls contain no Pharisaic text, the scrolls do reveal a considerable amount about this elusive group of Jews in the Hasmonean period. Some of this information comes from direct descriptions of them, but all of it appears in polemical context. Judicious use of the evidence allows us to establish the basic outline of the legal philosophy and rulings of the Pharisees, and to add to our store of data regarding their role in the political history of the nation. All in all, this evidence accords with what we know from Josephus and the rabbinic corpus.

As regards rabbinic literature, the conclusions are most significant. The Qumran evidence reveals that, contrary to widespread scholarly opinion, tannaitic literature preserves reliable information about the pre-70 C.E. Pharisees. These Pharisees, as they are illustrated by the Qumran material, are truly similar to what is described in the later rabbinic texts, especially as regards the specifics of their legal rulings. Talmudic sources, when used with adequate care and attention, can indeed play a significant role in the recovery of the history of Judaism in Second Temple times.

These scrolls truly contribute a new dimension in presenting us with a mass of data about the exegetical and halakhic approaches of the Saducean-Zadokite view that competed with that of the Pharisees in Hasmonean times.

---

68. Maimonides, *H. Kelim* 5:1.

This approach emerges in the legal teachings of the sectarian scrolls, as well as in works included in the Qumran library like *Jubilees,* as a well-developed and thought-out alternative, indeed a worthy competitor, to that of the Pharisees. The Pharisaic struggle for ascendancy in the spiritual and religious arena of Second Temple times can now be much better understood from the vantage point of our much more developed sense of the ideological and literary context, thanks to the discovery of the Qumran scrolls.

One thing is certain: the rabbinic system was not invented *de novo* after the destruction of the temple and the nation in the Great Revolt against Rome in 66-73 c.e. It was a continuation, albeit with numerous changes and innovations, that based itself on the long tradition of Pharisaic Judaism revealed more fully than ever before in the Dead Sea Scrolls.

CHAPTER 20

Pharisees and Sadducees in Pesher Nahum

Ever since the discovery of *Pesher Nahum* (4QpNah) in Qumran Cave 4 it has been realized that this text has significance that goes way beyond its value for understanding the Qumran sect and its ideology.[1] Indeed, it is the contemporizing form of biblical exegesis (better: eisegesis) called pesher[2] that makes these texts such important sources of historical information.

In the case of 4QpNah its significance is heightened because of the important information contained in this text regarding the history of the Pharisees and Sadducees, certainly the most important groups of Jews in Hasmonean times.[3] Clearly, a restudy of this document is necessary at this point in

---

1. For bibliog., see M. P. Horgan, *Pesharim: Qumran Interpretations of Biblical Books*. CBQMS 8 (Washington: Catholic Biblical Association of America, 1979) 158-59; and E. Schürer, *The History of the Jewish People in the Age of Jesus Christ (175 B.C.-A.D. 135)*, rev. ed. by G. Vermes and F. Millar, with P. Vermes and M. Black, 3/1:433 (Edinburgh: T. & T. Clark, 1986). On the language and the biblical text underlying 4QpNah, see J. Maier, "Weitere Stücke zum Nahumkommentar aus der Höhle 4 von Qumran," *Judaica* 18 (1962) 215-28. Recent exhaustive studies, appearing after this article was first published, are: S. L. Berrin, *The Pesher Nahum Scroll from Qumran: An Exegetical Study of 4Q169*. STDJ 53 (Leiden: Brill, 2004); and G. L. Doudna, *4Q Pesher Nahum: A Critical Edition*. JSPSup 35. Copenhagen International Series 8 (London: Sheffield Academic, 2001).

2. On this genre of biblical interpretation, see D. Dimant, "Qumran Sectarian Literature," in *Jewish Writings of the Second Temple Period*, ed. M. Stone, 505-8. CRINT II/2 (Philadelphia: Fortress, 1984); Berrin, *Pesher Nahum Scroll*, 9-19.

3. See J. D. Amoussine, "Éphraïm et Manassé dans le Péshèr de Nahum (4 Q p Nahum)," *RevQ* 4 (1963-64) 389-96; Amusin (Amoussine), "The Reflection of Historical Events of the First Century B.C. in Qumran Commentaries (4Q161; 4Q169; 4Q166)," *HUCA* 48 (1977) 134-46; D. Flusser, "Kat Midbar Yehudah ve-ha-Perushim," *Molad* 19 (1961) 456-58; "Perushim, Ṣeduqim, ve-'Issiyim be-Fesher Nahum," *Essays in Jewish History and Philology, in Memory of Gedaliahu*

the history of Dead Sea Scrolls research, in view of 4Q*Miqṣat Ma'aśe Ha-Torah* (4QMMT),[4] which has given us a wealth of information on the halakhic views of the Pharisees and the Sadducees in Hasmonean times[5] and in the years immediately preceding. It is now certain as well that the *Temple Scroll* (11QT) also contains numerous laws of Saducean origin and that it often polemicizes directly against Pharisaic views that were known beforehand in rabbinic literature, either as attributed to the Pharisees or to later Tannaim.[6] All this has given an impetus to the use of the scrolls to reconstruct the history of the Pharisees and the Sadducees in the Hasmonean period. It is to this effort that the present study seeks to contribute.

Date and Authorship

It is certain that 4QpNah is a "sectarian" text, one authored by a member or members of the Qumran community that transmits the teachings and ideology of that community. This is the case with all the pesharim found at Qumran. Indeed, the very nature of the exegesis found in this literature seems to be unique to the sect, although similar contemporizing interpretations exist in the New Testament.

The script of the manuscript of 4QpNah has been described as reflect-

---

Alon, ed. M. Dorman, S. Safrai, and M. Stern, 133-68 (Tel Aviv: Hakibbutz Hameuchad, 1970). While there are many allusions to these sects in other Qumran sectarian texts, this study will be limited to *Pesher Naḥum*. Further, the important issue of the relationship of the Essenes of Philo and Josephus to the Dead Sea sect will remain beyond the scope of this study. As is well known, most scholars see the tripartite array of groups in this text as equivalent to that of Josephus. Accordingly, they see this text as confirming the identity of the sect as Essenes. In our view, the term "Essene" must be seen as encompassing a variety of groups of which the Dead Sea Sect may be one.

4. E. Qimron and J. Strugnell, "An Unpublished Halakhic Letter from Qumran," in *Biblical Archaeology Today: Proceedings of the International Congress on Biblical Archaeology, Jerusalem, April 1984*, ed. J. Amitai, 400-7 (Jerusalem: Israel Exploration Society, Israel Academy of Sciences and Humanities, in cooperation with ASOR, 1985); and a different article with the same title, *IMJ* 4 (1985) 9-12 and pl. I.

5. See L. H. Schiffman, "The Temple Scroll and the Systems of Jewish Law of the Second Temple Period," in *Temple Scroll Studies*, ed. G. J. Brooke, 245-51 (Sheffield: JSOT, 1989); Y. Sussmann, "Ḥeqer Toldedot ha-Halakhah u-Megillot Midbar Yehudah: Hirhurim Talmudiyim Rishonim le-'Or Megillat Miqṣat Ma'aśe ha-Torah," *Tarbiz* 59 (1989-90) 11-76; and its English version, "The History of the Halakha and the Dead Sea Scrolls: Preliminary Talmudic Observations on Miqṣat Ma'aśe ha-Torah (4QMMT)," in *Qumran Cave 4.V: Miqṣat Ma'aśe ha-Torah*, ed. E. Qimron and J. Strugnell. DJD 10 (Oxford: Clarendon, 1994) 179-200.

6. See "The New Halakhic Letter (4QMMT) and the Origins of the Dead Sea Sect," Chapter 6 above.

ing a "formal" type, dating from the end of the Hasmonean period to the beginning of the Herodian.[7] This paleographic dating is extremely important because it is consistent with the *terminus a quo* required by the contents. Here we find a detailed description of the events surrounding the invasion of the Hasmonean kingdom by Demetrius III Eukairos (95-88 B.C.E.) as well as perhaps events during the rule of Salome Alexandra (76-67 B.C.E.).[8] These events bring us sufficiently close to the end of the Hasmonean dynasty (63 B.C.E.) to indicate that the text was composed at the latest shortly thereafter. Hence, the date of our preserved manuscript shortly before or after the Roman conquest would be most reasonable.[9]

We cannot rule out the possibility that parts of this text preexisted the invasion in question. We do know that some Qumran works circulated in varying recensions, which seem to testify to the growth of those compositions as a whole over time. Yet in this case, because we are dealing with a sustained interpretation of the biblical book of Nahum, it seems most reasonable to expect composition to have occurred at one time.[10]

The Pharisees

The text is unfortunately fragmentary at the beginning, so that it picks up with the interpretation of Nah 1:3 in col. 2 of the manuscript. After some references to the *kittiyim,* clearly an allusion to the Romans, the text continues in 4QpNah 1-2 ii 7-8 to comment on Nah 1:4:

> And the flower of Le[ba]non is[the congregation of the interpreters of smooth things[11] and the people of] their [coun]cil.[12] And they will be destroyed from before[the congregation of] the chosen one[s of God.[13]

---

7. J. Strugnell, "Notes en marge du volume V des 'Discoveries in the Judaean Desert of Jordan,'" *RevQ* 7 (1970) 205.

8. Horgan, *Pesharim,* 161-62.

9. Contrast the attempt to maintain a Roman period date for the events described in the pesher in G. R. Driver, *The Judaean Scrolls: The Problem and a Solution* (Oxford: Blackwell, 1965) 289-93.

10. For an estimate of the size of the entire scroll and the contents of the columns that were not preserved, see Horgan, *Pesharim,* 160.

11. The restoration is that of Horgan, *Pesharim,* 170 who suggests two alternatives: עצדת דורשי החלקות and ממשלת דורשי החלקות.

12. So Horgan, who added the initial ו to the restoration suggested by J. M. Allegro, *Qumrân Cave 4.I (4Q158-4Q186)*. DJD 5 (Oxford: Clarendon, 1968) 37. Strugnell, *RevQ* 7 (1970) 206, restores בני אשמ[תם. This reading seems too short, however.

13. Restoration of this line is with Horgan, *Pesharim,* 170.

Already here we see the basic motifs of the sectarian polemic against the Pharisees. They are identified by the pesher with the withered flower of Lebanon. The full citation from the end of Nah 1:4 is ופרח לבנון אמלל "and the flower of Lebanon withers."[14] Our text takes this clause to indicate that the Pharisees are to be destroyed (ואבדו). The difficult אמלל has been explained by the pesher as indicating destruction.

While it is true that crucial parts of these lines are restored, there is little question, as we will see below, that the Pharisees are intended. While it is tempting to address here, at the outset, the significance of the expression "interpreters of smooth things," methodological considerations make it appropriate to deal with it only in a context that is not restored. We should note that in this passage, even with its lacunae, it is certain that Nah 1:4 is seen as prophesying the destruction of a group of opponents of the "chosen one[s of God]," a term for the Qumran sect.

The Pharisees appear in a political context as 4QpNah relates the story of the invasion of Demetrius III Eukairos. In 4QpNah 3-4 i 2-3 there is an interpretation of Nah 2:12b:

> [Its interpretation concerns Deme]trius,[15] king of Greece,[16] who sought to enter Jerusalem on the advice of the interpreters of smooth things.[17]

This interpretation is based on the identification of Demetrius with the lion mentioned in Nahum. Whereas MT has אריה לביא, "lion and lion's breed,"[18] 4QpNah has a variant text in the lemma ארי לבוא, "the lion to come."[19] This reading was the basis for the interpretation that Demetrius (the lion) sought "to enter" Jerusalem, which is identified with the מעון אריות (MT to Nah 2:12), which, in turn, had already been explained by the pesher as מדור לרשעי גוים, "the dwelling place of the evil ones of the nations," in line 1.[20]

---

14. For MT לבנון the lemma in line 5 has לבנן, yet the pesher on line 7 agrees with MT.

15. Restored as דמי[טרוס with Allegro, DJD 5:38. It is also possible to read דמי[טריס, which is the view of Haberman and Yadin (Horgan, *Pesharim*, 173). On this passage, cf. Berrin, *Pesher Nahum Scroll*, 87-99.

16. For this phrase see Dan 8:21; cf. 10:20; 11:2.

17. For this expression, see עדת דורשי החלקות בירושלים "the congregation of the interpreters of smooth things in Jerusalem," mentioned in 4QpIsa^c 23, ii, 10; cf. 1QH 2:15, 32 (Horgan, *Pesharim*, 173).

18. So NJPS.

19. Many scholars read לביא in the lemma (Horgan, *Pesharim*, 172; Strugnell, *RevQ* 7 [1970] 207), in which case the pesher would have based its interpretation on the frequent confusion of ו and י in Qumran and other contemporary manuscripts.

20. Following A. Dupont-Sommer, "Le Commentaire de Nahum découvert près de la Mer Morte (4Q p Nah): Traduction et notes," *Sem* 13 (1963) 57; Horgan, *Pesharim*, 172.

Demetrius is termed here "king of Greece," but, of course, he was king of Seleucid Syria. As we know, his invasion of the Hasmonean state of Alexander Jannaeus (103-76 B.C.E.) was brought about by Jewish intervention.[21] We will return to this aspect below.[22] For now, it is important to examine the designation our text uses for the Pharisees. The Hebrew expression דורשי חלקות is actually a pun.[23] It begins with חלקות, literally, "smooth things" (i.e., "falsehoods"), which appears in Isa 30:10; Ps 12:3-4 and 73:18; and Dan 11:32. This word is intended here as a play on the word הלכות, a term attested otherwise only later that refers to the Pharisaic-rabbinic laws. While the noun חלקות appears in Isaiah with דבר, "to speak," it appears here, as well as in other sectarian documents, with דרש, which by this time meant "to interpret."[24] Accordingly, the expression דורשי החלקות is a designation for the Pharisees who, in the view of the sect, are false interpreters of the Torah who derive incorrect legal rulings from their exegesis. It is these false legalists who brought Demetrius to attack Jannaeus.

Despite all the information he provides, on the question of Alexander Jannaeus's relations with Pharisees and Sadducees, we have only a hint in Josephus that the enemies of Jannaeus who provoked Demetrius were Pharisees. Josephus discusses this episode,[25] and in both his descriptions he tells us only of opposition by the "Jews" who initiated the revolt against him and called in Demetrius. As a result, some of them were executed at the end. Thus, we have no direct claim in Josephus that the Pharisees played a leading role in these affairs.

But in both accounts we hear at the beginning that Jannaeus angered the populace at the Sukkot festival. This led to his initial slaughter of his own citizens. Whereas the account in *War*[26] is quite sketchy, *Antiquities*[27] gives us two reasons for the conflict. First, "as he stood beside the altar and was about to sacrifice, they pelted him with citrons." *Etrogim*, used to fulfill the biblical command of the four kinds,[28] were thrown at him for what in this account is an unknown reason. Second, his priestly legitimacy was challenged by those

---

21. See the discussion of this episode in F. M. Cross, *The Ancient Library of Qumran and Modern Biblical Studies* (Garden City: Doubleday, 1961; repr. Grand Rapids: Baker, 1980) 122-27.

22. The events are summarized in Schürer, *History of the Jewish People*, 1:223-24. See esp. 224-25, n. 21, which refers to 4QpNah.

23. See the analysis of Maier, *Judaica* 18 (1962) 234-37; Berrin, *Pesher Nahum Scroll*, 91-99.

24. See L. H. Schiffman, *The Halakhah at Qumran*. SJLA 16 (Leiden: Brill, 1975) 54-60.

25. *J.W.* 1.85-131 and *Ant.* 13.372-416.

26. *J.W.* 1.88-89.

27. *Ant.* 13.72-74.

28. Lev 23:40.

who said "that he was descended from captives and was unfit to hold (priestly) office."

Both of these aspects have parallels in tannaitic materials, and these will allow us to confirm the information in 4QpNah that the Pharisees were indeed the opponents of Jannaeus who, according to our text, took the lead in the revolt and in inviting Demetrius into the country. In the case of the pelting of Jannaeus with citrons, there is a parallel in *m. Sukkah* 4:9. There it is related that once a priest poured out the water libation on his feet and as a result was pelted by the people with their citrons (ורגמוהו כל העם באתרוגיהן). That this priest is to be identified with Alexander Jannaeus, about whom little factual detail was remembered in the tannaitic period, is certain in light of the parallel with Josephus.[29] The issue of the water-drawing ceremony was a longstanding debate between the Pharisees and the Sadducees.[30] His reason for pouring the water on his feet was to publicly indicate his disdain for the Pharisaic requirement of a special water libation during Sukkot. The revolt that began in the aftermath of this event would naturally have been led by Pharisees and, therefore, we can accept as historical this new detail that 4QpNah supplies in its account.

Josephus mentioned a second reason for popular objection to Jannaeus: there was a challenge to his priestly legitimacy. This very same challenge appears in two other places. In the well-known baraita describing Jannaeus's confrontation with the Pharisees in *b. Qidd.* 66a, the Pharisees say to him, "It is enough for you to have the crown of kingship. Leave the crown of priesthood to the descendents of Aaron," to which the comment is added, "for they were saying that his mother had been captured in Modiin." A captive woman is assumed to have been raped, and so she would be forbidden to her priestly husband and their sons would be rendered unfit for the priesthood. A parallel accusation appears in *Ant.* 13.291-92, where it is made by a certain Eleazar to John Hyrcanus (134-104 B.C.E.) in the context of his confrontation with the Pharisees.

Now there is little question that these two confrontations are one and the same, and critical scholarship has been unable to fix with certainty the date and the Hasmonean high priest to whom the story ought to refer. For our purposes it is important to note that the Pharisaic opposition to Jannaeus is again confirmed in this detail. Again, we have every reason to believe that

---

29. Cf. C. Albeck, *Shishah Sidre Mishnah* (Jerusalem: Bialik Institute and Tel Aviv: Dvir, 1954) *Seder Mo'ed*, 2:477.

30. L. Finkelstein, *The Pharisees: The Sociological Background of Their Faith*, 3rd ed. Morris Loeb Series (Philadelphia: Jewish Publication Society of America, 1966) 2:700-8.

Pharisees and Sadducees in Pesher Nahum

they are the opponents left unidentified in Josephus's account of the war with Demetrius.

Interpreting the end of Nah 2:13, the text explains in 4QpNah 3-4 i 6-8:

> Its interpretation concerns the Lion of Wrath [. . .] death to the interpreters of smooth things, for he hanged men alive [. . .] in Israel from of old, for one hanged alive on a tree shall [he] be called.

This passage indicates that as a result of their participation in the revolt, the Pharisees were crucified by Jannaeus. The exegesis already assumes the identification of Jannaeus as the Lion of Wrath who appears in line 5 (restored), interpreting Nah 2:13a.[31] He has literally fulfilled the words of this verse; he "filled his lair[32] with prey[33] and his den[34] with torn flesh." At the end of the passage, direct reference is made to Deut 21:22-23. It seems most likely that the language of this text is being used but that the explicit mention of hanging men "alive" is meant to distinguish Jannaeus's cruel crucifixion from the practice commanded in Deuteronomy.[35]

The account in this passage fits exactly with that of Josephus, who discusses eight hundred crucified by Jannaeus. *War* 1.97 simply terms them "captives," while *Ant.* 13.380 calls them "Jews." Our text, however, informs us that the victims of the reign of terror that Jannaeus engaged in after he forced Demetrius to withdraw were his erstwhile Pharisaic enemies.

We first encounter the designation "Ephraim" for the Pharisees in line 12 of the same column, but there is no real context preserved. A more complete sense of the use of this term, no doubt a pun on פרושים, "Pharisees," can be gleaned from the following column.[36] In an interpretation of Nah 3:1,

---

31. Cf. Horgan, *Pesharim*, 175.

32. The scroll has חורה for MT חריו.

33. The occurrence of this word above in line 4 is most probably a scribal error, not a double pesher.

34. The scroll has ומעונתו for MT ומענתיו.

35. We cannot accept the suggestion of Y. Yadin, "Pesher Nahum (4Q pNahum) Reconsidered," *IEJ* 21 (1971) 1-12; cf. *The Temple Scroll* (Jerusalem: Israel Exploration Society and Shrine of the Book, 1983) 1:373-79, that our text approves of crucifixion as a means of punishment. This would be the case even if 11QTemple 64:6-13 did allow this punishment for informers. For the vast literature on crucifixion in these two texts, see Horgan, *Pesharim*, 176-79. See esp. J. M. Baumgarten, *Studies in Qumran Law*, SJLA 24 (Leiden: Brill, 1977) 172-82. Note also M. J. Bernstein, "*Midrash Halakhah* at Qumran? 11Q Temple 64:6-13 and Deuteronomy 21:22-23," *Gesher* 7 (1979) 145-66; and "'Ki Qillat Elohim Talui' (Deut. 21:23): A Study in Early Jewish Exegesis," *JQR* 74 (1983) 21-45; Berrin, *Pesher Nahum Scroll*, 165-92.

36. Cf. Berrin, *Pesher Nahum Scroll*, 109-18.

הוי עיר דמים כלה כחש פרק מלאה, "Ah, city of crime,[37] utterly treacherous, full of violence," 4QpNah 3-4 ii 2 states:

> Its interpretation: it is the city of Ephraim, the interpreters of smooth things in the end of days, who live by falsehood and lie[s].

Here again the Pharisees appear as false interpreters of the law. It seems most likely that the "city" of Ephraim does not refer to some actual city, but rather to the Pharisaic community as a whole. Indeed, the word עיר is simply a reflection of the Hebrew of Nah 3:1. Further, in equating the verse with its interpretation, the sect took דמים, "crime" (lit., "blood"), to refer to the Pharisees, so that Ephraim replaces "violence." The difficult פרק מלאה is taken by the pesher to refer to the way of life of the Pharisees. It is possible that the choice of the verb יתהלכו may have been conditioned by its cognate הלכה, "religious law, way of life," which lies behind the pun חלקות.[38] The reference to the end of days refers to the sectarians' own view that they were living on the verge of the dawn of the eschaton, in the "last days."[39] It was this period of the end of days to which, in the view of the sect, the prophet Nahum had actually prophesied.

We have already encountered the use of חלקות, "smooth things," to indicate the teachings of the Pharisees that the sectarians considered false. Yet here there are added terms to make the same point, כחש and שקרים. The pesher, in fact, substitutes the hendiadys כחש ושקרים for the biblical כחש, no doubt for emphasis. Indeed, overall the claim of the sect against the Pharisees was that they falsely interpreted Scripture, a matter to which we will return below.

Turning to the exegesis of Nah 3:1b-3,[40] 4QpNah 3-4 ii 4-6 expounds:

> Its interpretation concerns the domain of the interpreters of smooth things from the midst of whose congregation there will not depart the

---

37. 4QpNah has הדמים for MT דמים.

38. The authors of our document seem to have regarded the unmentioned term הלכה as derived from the verb "to go," and understood it to mean "way of life." For the alternative derivation from the Aramaic הלך, a land tax (cognate to Akkadian *ilku*), see S. Lieberman, *Hellenism in Jewish Palestine* (New York: Jewish Theological Seminary, 1962) 83, n. 3.

39. I cannot agree with Horgan, *Pesharim*, 182, who explains that "the interpretation is shifting from a historical thrust to an eschatological focus." The sect saw its own history and its own times as eschatological. For this notion, see 4QMMT C 21-23. Cf. also Berrin, *Pesher Nahum Scroll*, 208-17.

40. The numerous differences with MT found in this citation are discussed in Horgan, *Pesharim*, 182-83.

sword of the nations, captivity, plunder and strife,[41] and exile because of fear of the enemy. For many guilty corpses will fall in their days, and there will be no end to the total of their slain. And they will even stumble over their decaying flesh because of their guilty council.

The description in Nahum of the city (Nineveh) is taken here to apply *in toto* to the Pharisees. Certain modifications of the language of the biblical material are especially significant. The text adds the idea of the עדה, "congregation" (i.e., community of the Pharisees), who in some way have banded together. This means that they are perceived as a party, not simply as isolated individuals who interpret the law. The "sword" of the verse has become the "sword of the nations," the non-Jews, with whom the Pharisees conspired to overthrow Alexander Jannaeus. Despite the sect's dislike for this ruler and disagreements with him, they still condemn the Pharisees for turning to the Seleucids.[42] The substitution of חלליהם for the biblical גויה is intended to avoid a term that can also be used for living bodies.

Extremely interesting is the manner in which the text deals with Nahum's וכשלו בגויתם (the *ketiv* is יכשלו).[43] This clause literally means "they will stumble over their (own) bodies," since the destruction will leave so many corpses. Our author interprets it to mean that the Pharisees will transgress in matters pertaining to their bodies, such as sexual prohibitions, as a result of their guilty council.

The use of ממשלת does not imply that the Pharisees were ruling.[44] Rather, it refers to their "domain," similar in meaning to the term גורל, "lot," in Qumran usage.[45] This passage clearly refers to the aftermath of the war with Demetrius, rather than to some period of Pharisaic rule such as probably took place in the days of Salome Alexandra, the wife of Alexander Jannaeus, and his successor.

The text notes that even after the war with Demetrius and his expulsion,

---

41. Following Horgan, *Pesharim*, 183, who notes this usage in postbiblical Hebrew, as opposed to Deut 28:22, "feverish heat." See E. Ben Yehuda, *Milon ha-Lashon ha-'Ivrit* (New York: Yoseloff, 1959) 3:1755, where all the examples cited are medieval.

42. Cf. the prohibition on informing to a foreign nation in 11QTemple 64:6-9.

43. The lemma's text, וגויתם, is certainly an error since the pesher has בגוית (Horgan, *Pesharim*, 183).

44. Alternatively, the text has been taken to refer to the period during the reign of Salome Alexandra when the Pharisees returned to power. See Amusin, *HUCA* 48 (1977) 143-45; A. Dupont-Sommer, "Lumières nouvelles sur l'arrière-plan historique des écrits de Qumran," *ErIsr* 8 (Sukenik Volume, 1967) 25*-36*.

45. Cf. J. Licht, "Ha-Munaḥ Goral be-Khetaveha shel Kat Midbar Yehudah," *Beth Mikra* 1 (1955/56) 90-99.

the Pharisees were still pursued by destruction and were forced to flee. Further, the text describes the slaying of large numbers of their comrades. All this the author blames on the plot hatched by the Pharisees to overthrow Jannaeus with the help of the Seleucids.

This picture corresponds closely with that of Josephus. *Ant.* 13.379-83[46] describes the manner in which Jannaeus dealt with his Jewish enemies who, in the course of later events, allied themselves with him to expel their erstwhile ally Demetrius. Jannaeus captured and killed the most powerful of them in what Josephus considers a cruel manner, crucifying them, as we have already seen. Then his remaining opponents fled the country and remained in exile for as long as he lived. There can be no question that these are the events described in our text, except that here the opponents of Jannaeus are correctly identified as the Pharisees.

The account continues as the text interprets Nah 3:4[47] in 4QpNah 3-4 ii 8-10:

> [Its] interpretation [con]cerns those who lead Ephraim astray, in whose teaching (תלמוד) is their falsehood, and whose lying tongue and dishonest lip(s) lead many astray, [their] kings, officers, priests, and people, with the proselyte who converts (lit., "joins"). They shall destroy cities and clans with their plot; nob[l]es and rul[ers] shall fall because of the [insol]ence of their speech.[48]

The text now centers on the leadership of the Pharisaic party. The verse being interpreted (Nah 3:4) speaks of the harlotry and magic with which the harlot (herself having already gone astray) led others to harlotry and magic. The author identifies the Pharisaic leadership as those who had, in the view of the sect, led others astray with false interpretations. Whatever the actual meaning of the verb found in MT as המכרת and in the lemma in 4QpNah as הממכרת, it is clear that the pesher took it in the sense of "ensnares," an explanation that seems to require emendation to הכמרת.[49]

According to the biblical text, "nations" and "families" are ensnared by the harlot. These terms are expanded considerably by the pesher, which takes גוים as referring to "nobles, eminences" (= גאים), who are the kings, officers,

---

46. Cf. *J.W.* 1.96-98.
47. For textual differences with MT in the lemma, see Horgan, *Pesharim*, 183-84.
48. Restored with Dupont-Sommer, *Sem* 13 (1963) 58, 77; cf. Strugnell, *RevQ* 7 (1970) 207.
49. Cf. Horgan, *Pesharim*, 183-84.

Pharisees and Sadducees in Pesher Naḥum

and priests.⁵⁰ The משפחות are taken to refer to the people, the proselytes and the various cities and clans of the Jewish people as well as their leaders. All of these are said to have been victimized by the insolent teachings of the Pharisees.

From this text it is certain that there is a distinction to be made between those who actually expounded the law themselves and their followers. The leaders are apparently able to influence even members of the aristocracy. We also hear that they influenced the common people, עם, as well as proselytes. This statement is significant in that it dovetails with Josephus's statement (*Ant*. 13.298) about the popularity of the Pharisees among the common people. This is probably a correct statement, although we cannot be certain if it applied at all times, nor can we gauge the extent and ramifications of this popularity.⁵¹

At this point we learn of the content of the lies described above. They refer specifically to the תלמוד of the Pharisees.⁵² We ought not to be surprised at this point to learn that such a *talmud* existed.⁵³ We have already seen that laws existed that were generally termed הלכות and that the use of the term דרש implied that the Pharisees used midrashic exegesis in analyzing biblical texts. Together with the method of logical deduction known as *talmud*,⁵⁴ these approaches were the mainstay of later tannaitic and amoraic learning, and our text indicates that these components existed already for the Pharisees. This *talmud* was the method of logical analysis that must have already been part of the intellectual equipment of Pharisaic endeavor, and it was regarded as false by the Qumran sectarians, as were also the exegesis and the laws of the Pharisaic tradition.

The author of our text continues his polemic against the Pharisees and tells us that in the end of days the evil of their ways will become manifest and those whom they have led astray (the "simple ones of Ephraim") will leave those who have led them astray. These Pharisaic followers are then expected, in the sectarian understanding of the prophecies of Nah 3:5, to rejoin the true

---

50. For this list, but including also the prophets, see Jer 2:26 and 32:32, where they appear with third person plural possessive suffixes, as in our text.

51. Amusin, *HUCA* 48 (1977) 145. On the Pharisees in Josephus, see J. Neusner, *From Politics to Piety: The Emergence of Pharisaic Judaism*, 2nd ed. (Englewood Cliffs: Prentice Hall, 1973) 45-66.

52. The extensive bibliog. on this term is reviewed in Horgan, *Pesharim*, 184. See Berrin, *Pesher Nahum Scroll*, 201-5.

53. See B. Z. Wacholder, "A Qumran Attack on the Oral Exegesis? The Phrase אשר בתלמוד שקרם in 4Q Pesher Nahum," *RevQ* 5 (1964-6) 575-78.

54. See Rashi to *b. Sukkah* 28a, s.v. תלמוד in the uncensored Venice edition. Later editions, as a result of Christian censorship, substitute גמרא in this passage.

House of Israel, thought by the sect to be itself (4QpNah 3-4 iii 1-8). These dreams of the sect, of course, were never realized.

Sadducees

Pesher Nahum also provides some information about the Sadducees. It appears that had the text survived in its entirety, there would have been more information since the preserved text effectively breaks off in the middle of discussing this group. We will first gather this data and analyze it and then discuss its connection to the Sadducean background of the founders of the Qumran sect and their halakhic traditions.

Towards the end of the preserved portion of the scroll, the author turns to the Sadducees, who are designated by him as "Manasseh."[55] He most probably chose this term in opposition to Ephraim, which was recommended as a term for the Pharisees by its similar consonants. Interpreting Nah 3:8a, 4QpNah 3-4 iii 9-10 describes them and their aristocratic leaders:

> Its interpretation is (that) Amon,[56] they are Manasseh, and the rivers are the magnates of Manasseh, the honored ones of the [city who suppo]rt[57] Manasseh.

To understand this point, careful attention must be paid to the biblical text being interpreted. The text in Nah 3:7 regarding Nineveh and its destruction was interpreted by the pesher to refer to the prophesied devastation of the Pharisees. It is then that the biblical prophet turns to Jerusalem and asks her whether she is really better than No-Amon (Thebes), which had been destroyed only shortly before by the Assyrians (in 663 B.C.E.). In context, therefore, the pesher is arguing that we can be certain that the Pharisees (= Nineveh) will be destroyed because of the destruction of the Sadducees that had taken place previously.

This interpretation presumes that the Sadducees had met their match and been weakened before the Pharisees.[58] Indeed, to a great extent Hasmonean priestly power came at the expense of their Sadducean predecessors. Yet

---

55. Cf. Berrin, *Pesher Nahum Scroll*, 268-71.
56. Although MT has מנא אמון, the lemma in 4QpNah has מני, "from," here meaning "than" (reading with Allegro, DJD 5:39; and Horgan, *Pesharim*, 188). That this is the correct reading (rather than מנו=phonetic spelling of מנא) is most likely in view of the omission of נא from the pesher.
57. Restoring with Horgan, *Pesharim*, 188.
58. Cf. Amusin, *HUCA* 48 (1977) 144.

in our text we learn additional facts about the Sadducees in the author's day or earlier. The magnates of the Sadducees were the honored ones of the city, that is, the aristocracy, religious and economic. The very same claim was made by Josephus based on his experience of later Judean society (*Ant.* 13.298),[59] and this claim seems to be borne out by our text as well. These aristocrats were "supporters" of Manasseh. This indicates that, besides the Sadducees themselves, various others connected with the upper classes supported this group even while not being full-fledged members. Indeed, this same situation seems to be described above for the Pharisees.

Interpreting Nah 3:9,[60] 4QpNah 3-4 iv 1 explains:

> Its interpretation is that it is the evil [ones of Manass]eh,[61] the House of Peleg, who have joined Manasseh.

Here we again hear about the followers of the Sadducees, termed the House of Peleg (lit., "division"), who have joined the Sadducees.[62] From the designation we can already see that they are regarded as a group of evildoers within the Sadducean camp. The interpretation is probably based on the end of the verse, "Put and the Libyans, they were your helpers." Presumably, the pesher understands the House of Peleg, equivalent to Put and Libya, as the helpers (i.e., associates) of Manasseh who are the Sadducees. These again are supporters, what are usually termed "retainers." Apparently, large groups of Jews had allegiance to the teachings of these groups without full membership.

To a great extent our understanding of this passage is dependent on the identity of the House of Peleg. This term also occurs in the *Zadokite Fragments* (CD 20:22). The passage is only preserved in the medieval manuscript B. There it refers to: מבית פלג אשר יצאו מעיר הקדש וישענו על אל בקץ מעל ישראל ויטמאו את המקדש ושבו עד אל, "from the House of Peleg who left the holy city (Jerusalem) and were dependent on God, during the period of the transgression of Israel when they defiled the temple; but they (i.e., the House of Peleg) returned to God." This parallel gives the distinct impression that the House of Peleg is the sect. After all, they are the ones who, when transgression set in as the temple was taken over by Hasmoneans, left and formed a sect dedicated to returning to God.

---

59. For parallels, see Schürer, *History of the Jewish People*, 2:404-5.
60. According to Carmignac's placement of the fragments; J. Carmignac, in Carmignac et al., eds., *Les Textes de Qumran: traduits et annotés* (Paris: Letouzey et Ané, 1963) 2:92; cf. Strugnell, *RevQ* 7 (1970) 210.
61. Restored with Horgan, *Pesharim*, 189.
62. See Berrin, *Pesher Nahum Scroll*, 271-75.

But if we were to restore differently, and accept the reading רשע[י יהוד]ה, "the evil [ones of Jud]ah," it would allow us to see this as a reference to evil members of the sect who attached themselves to the Sadducees.[63] In any case, this difficult phrase is likely to remain a matter of debate.

In the interpretation of Nah 3:10,[64] 4QpNah 3-4 iv 3 states:

> Its interpretation concerns Manasseh in the final period (end of days) when his kingdom will be brought low in Is[rael. . . .] Its women, children, and infants will go into captivity. Its mighty ones and honored ones [will perish][65] at the sword.

Nah 3:10 speaks of the destruction of No-Amon. It tells us that the city went into captivity, that her children were slaughtered, that its honored men were distributed by lot as spoils of war, and that her nobles were led off in chains. This fate, according to the pesher, refers to the overturning of the power of the Sadducees, they who are indeed "honored men" and "nobles" of Israel. The text specifically mentions Israel so as to apply the prophecies directed at No-Amon to the Jewish people.

This text effectively sees the Sadducees as a kingdom, or dominion, that will be destroyed. The text continues to describe the exile of the women and children of the Sadducees and the slaughter of their elite at the sword.

The final preserved material relevant to our study appears in 4QpNah 3-4 iv 5-6, commenting on Nah 3:11:[66]

> Its interpretation concerns the evil ones of E[phraim] whose cup (of destruction) will come after that of Manasseh.

This excerpt is important only in that it understands the destruction of the Sadducees to precede that of the Pharisees, a notion we already saw above. The author interprets Nah 3:11 as saying to the Pharisees: you too will be overcome and have to flee the enemy, now that the Sadducees have been devastated. To be sure, the author(s) of this document had distinctively and consistently worked out ideas on the fate that the Sadducees and then the Pharisees would experience. Unfortunately for this study, little else is preserved of 4QpNah, so that we hear no more about the text's views on the two major sects of Jews of the Second Temple period.

---

63. J. Licht, "Dapim Nosafim li-Fesher Naḥum," *Molad* 19 (1961) 455.

64. For textual differences with MT, see Horgan, *Pesharim*, 190.

65. Restored with Horgan, *Pesharim*, 190. Strugnell, *RevQ* 7 (1970) 208; and, apparently, Carmignac in *Les Textes de Qumran*, 2:92, יפולו.

66. For textual differences with MT, see Horgan, *Pesharim*, 190.

Although the sins of the Sadducees are not specifically detailed here, it is certain that a catalog of misdeeds, like those of the Pharisees, led the Qumran sect to expect the utter destruction of the Sadducees in the now dawning eschaton. In short, the Sadducees are here seen as villains.

It is difficult at first glance to reconcile this image with our conclusions relating to the Sadducean character of the founders of the sect and the halakhic traditions of the group. Why does 4QpNah condemn so roundly the very group from which the sect seems to have emerged?

The answer to this question lies in the complex historical processes that affected both the sect and the Sadducees in the years between the founding of the group, ca. 152 B.C.E., and the writing of this text, some time after 63 B.C.E. In the case of the Qumran sect, the evidence of the initial section of the *Zadokite Fragments (Damascus Document)* indicates that the Teacher of Righteousness who developed the basic sectarian stance of the group only entered the picture after the initial break had already taken place (CD 1:10-12).[67] Over time, the sect became increasingly radicalized and isolated and adopted the apocalyptic messianism and ethical dualism that became its hallmarks. For this reason, it began to look at the Sadducean way from which it had emerged as improper, while still retaining the substratum of Sadducean law that it had brought into the sect in the early years.

In the case of the Sadducees, the processes of change also help to explain the problem. The sect was formed by Sadducees who represented the "lower clergy" and who, therefore, were not hellenized to a great extent. More-hellenized Sadducees played an increasing role in the Hasmonean dynasty over time. Both Josephus and the baraita recorded in the Babylonian Talmud testify to a sharp break with the Pharisees that took place, as we have mentioned, either under John Hyrcanus or Alexander Jannaeus. By the time of this break, the Sadducees in Jerusalem, as well as their Maccabean colleagues, had traversed a great distance from the days when Jonathan the Hasmonean had instituted adherence to Pharisaic law in the temple and its service. Now the Sadducees had gained control. It is these hellenized Sadducees against which our text foments. Opposition to them comes not from the legal traditions they espouse, but rather from their having strayed from the strict adherence to the Torah required by the sectarians.

---

67. This picture is not changed by the additional lines that in the Qumran manuscripts precede the text preserved on p. 1 of the medieval copy. See J. M. Baumgarten, *Qumran Cave 4.XIII: The Damascus Document (4Q266-273)*. DJD 18 (Oxford: Clarendon, 1996) 1 (4QD^a 1 1-17), 4 (4QD^b 2 i 1-14), 31 (4Q266 1 a-b), and 96 (4Q267 1).

Conclusion

4QpNah testifies to the nature of the Pharisees and Sadducees in the period of Alexander Jannaeus. During his tenure he was seriously challenged by the Pharisees while the Sadducees drew closer to him. From the examination of this document we have been able to confirm the general outlines of the picture of these groups presented in Josephus as well as to gain new details about the episode of Demetrius III Eukairos's invasion of Judea.

Although little of the text's critique of the Sadducees survives, we can at least observe their aristocratic character. Yet of the Pharisees so much more can be said. We learn here of the role of halakhic midrash in their method of deriving law, as well as of a system of logical deduction termed *talmud*. We hear much about the manner in which the leadership of this group allegedly led the people astray, indicating that they did indeed have a considerable following among the people. For both the Pharisees and Sadducees we hear of the "retainers," those followers who were at the outer fringes of the power elite but who were themselves part of the Pharisaic or Sadducean group in one way or another. In general, we realize that no group of Jews in this period automatically commanded the allegiance of large numbers of people. Rather, they functioned by teaching and influencing, a process in which the Pharisees indeed excelled.

Taking 4QpNah together with 4QMMT and other texts, we can sketch a history of the fortunes of these two groups in the Hasmonean period. In the early days of the dynasty, the Pharisees were allied with the Hasmoneans and their views were dominant. At some point, a break in relations took place, and this led to the reentry of the Sadducees, who then were associated with the much more hellenized Hasmoneans. The Pharisees tried the ultimate power play, perhaps driven by genuine religious motives, but it backfired, leading to execution and exile for many of them. Presumably, the aristocratic Sadducees described in our text then retained power, and their rulings came to be observed in the temple in place of the Pharisaic views put into effect in the early Hasmonean period. Finally, and after the period of our text, we hear of a rapprochement between Salome Alexandra (76-67 B.C.E.) and the Pharisees.

The picture we have painted admittedly differs only in details from that of Josephus and rabbinic sources. For a generation now scholars have complained that we have no contemporary accounts of the Pharisees and Sadducees from the Hasmonean period. In the Dead Sea Scrolls, it turns out, we do have these sources, and they verify the essential historicity of the later accounts. Both for the ideological and religious issues and for those of political history the information of our later sources is confirmed by *Pesher Nahum*.

CHAPTER 21

Inter- or Intra-Jewish Conflict? The Judaism of the Dead Sea Scrolls Community and Its Opponents

In investigating the limits of the religious community or communities of Second Temple–period Jews, and in particular the question of whether there existed a unifying core or not, we may consider the relationship of the Qumran sect to its opponents — the remainder of the Jewish people, as a fitting test case, perhaps a "worst-case scenario." Here we investigate the group most noted, at least among modern scholars, for its sectarian invective and polemic, in terms of its attitudes regarding and relations to other Second Temple–period Jews. Surely, if we can justify the claim that this highly separatist, elitist, and even disdainful group of people could see themselves as part of a larger whole, then it will be the case, *a fortiori,* for groups that represent more irenic approaches to their own self-definition. But, if there really were different Judaisms, then our friends on the shore of the Dead Sea would be an easy group to define within this fractured Jewish religious *oikumene*.

To my mind, a "Judaism" must be not simply a variety of Judaism expressed in a pluralistic, tolerant, or even intolerant wider Jewish community. Such are in my definition either groups, "sects," or approaches.[1] In this case, the group may even delegitimize the others, but in a halakhic sense accepts the Jewish status of the others and shares both a common, basic core of faith and practice (or an agenda that it opposes) as well as a common view of the "national" mission and destiny. Such groups are distinguished from "Judaisms,"

---

1. Cf. S. Talmon, "The Community of the Renewed Covenant: Between Judaism and Christianity," in *The Community of the Renewed Covenant: The Notre Dame Symposium on the Dead Sea Scrolls,* ed. E. Ulrich and J. VanderKam, 7-8. CJAS 10 (Notre Dame: University of Notre Dame Press, 1994); A. I. Baumgarten, *The Flourishing of Jewish Sects in the Maccabean Era: An Interpretation.* JSJSup 55 (Leiden: Brill, 1997) 1-18; A. J. Saldarini, "Sectarianism," *EDSS* 2:853-57.

competing groups that deny the Jewish status of the other (more than just claiming to be the true Israel), do not share a common past and future, and whose fundamental beliefs do not overlap sufficiently as to furnish a common basis for their disputes and disagreements.[2]

Further, the status of groups of "Jews" in this regard may be fluid, not static. In the course of Jewish history, some specific ideologies have placed particular groups — Samaritans, Christians, and Karaites — outside of the *consensus ha-le'umi,* the "national Jewish (informal) consensus," so that these groups are regarded as totally separated from the Jewish people or sufficiently marginalized that they are hovering close to full separation.

In this model, Jews and Judaism — that is, identity, nationalism (an admittedly anachronistic term), and religion — are so closely intertwined that in our view there cannot be different "Judaisms" if there is only one group of Jews. For this reason, despite the tremendous disparity experienced within and among Jewish groups today, this model will not label them "Judaisms," while recognizing that breakdowns in areas of consensus could lead to change over time.

It is with this set of definitions that this study will investigate the question regarding Qumran sectarians and other Jews, generally regarded as the sect's opponents, picking up on the title of a chapter in Chaim Rabin's *Qumran Studies* ("The Sect and Its Opponents").[3] We will see that common beliefs, common practices, a common agenda, and common terms of discourse show that even the Dead Sea sectarians did not merit the distinction of constituting a separate "Judaism."

A brief supplement to these general considerations is in order. If one postulates a system in which debate, polemic, even sectarian political struggle are part of the system, actually a "religious act," then it will be futile to claim that disagreements and strife indicate multiple "Judaisms." In such a case, indications of Judaisms to some will be evidence of the vitality of an ongoing tradition — albeit one of dispute. Such a model, in accord with our previous discussion, will mean that only by crossing certain red lines could one create an alternative Judaism.

Behind this approach is a view of Judaism in its many manifestations that postulates an essential theological and historical unity expressed by core

---

2. Cf. L. H. Schiffman, *From Text to Tradition: A History of Second Temple and Rabbinic Judaism* (Hoboken: Ktav, 1991) 4-5. Contrast J. Neusner, "Preface," in *Judaisms and Their Messiahs at the Turn of the Christian Era,* ed. Neusner, W. S. Green, and E. Frerichs, ix-xii (New York: Cambridge University Press, 1987).

3. C. Rabin, *Qumran Studies.* Scripta Judaica 2 (Oxford: Oxford University Press, 1957) 53-70.

beliefs and commitments. These seem to us to have defined the collective term "Judaism." Our definitions assume such a concept, and it is in this spirit that we will evaluate the attitudes of the Dead Sea sectarians.

Several issues need to be explored to test our hypothesis that according to our definitions of the problem, the sectarians at Qumran, understood by most scholars to be the Essenes described by Philo and Josephus, retain a Judaism fundamentally common with that of their neighbors. We will look in turn at the following issues: (1) purity and other sectarian markers, (2) polemic and invective, (3) consensus and disagreement in matters of Jewish law, (4) shared canon of Scripture, (5) shared national aspirations and exclusivist eschatology.

Purity and Other Sectarian Markers

There can be no question that the Qumran sectarians intentionally erected barriers between themselves and much of the rest of the Jewish community. Certainly, the most prominent was that of ritual purity. This aspect of their approach is so opposite to that of early Christianity, as portrayed in the Gospels,[4] that it is hard to grasp the facile links between these two groups so often suggested.

The Qumran sect had complex admissions procedures.[5] These procedures, like those of the ḥavurah described in tannaitic sources,[6] depended on progression through stages of learning and commitment, reflected in the progressive ritual purity of the candidates until they became full members and were permitted to come in contact with both the solid and liquid foods of the sect. In this way, candidates for admission — novices — were distinguished from those in process and, in turn, from full members. All of them as a collective were to separate themselves from nonsectarians to avoid ritual impurity. Behind this concept is a close linkage between repentance and purifications, since purity was clearly seen by the Qumran sect as a sign of inner repentance that was, in turn, a *sine qua non* for ritual purity.[7]

---

4. S. Westerholm, "Clean and Unclean," *DJG* 125-32.

5. J. Licht, *Megillat ha-Serakhim mi-Megillot Midbar Yehudah* (Jerusalem: Bialik Institute, 1965) 145-48; L. H. Schiffman, *Sectarian Law in the Dead Sea Scrolls: Courts, Testimony and the Penal Code*. BJS 33 (Chico: Scholars, 1983) 161-65.

6. S. Lieberman, "The Discipline in the So-Called Dead Sea Manual of Discipline," *JBL* 71 (1951) 199-206; repr. *Texts and Studies* (New York: Ktav, 1974) 200-7; Rabin, *Qumran Studies*, 1-21.

7. Cf. L. H. Schiffman, *Reclaiming the Dead Sea Scrolls: The History of Judaism, the Back-*

Members of the sect did, however, live among ordinary Israelites outside the sectarian settlement at Qumran, in what are termed "camps" in the Qumran texts. Here there were also miniversions of the sectarian assembly, so that sectarians in "camps" practiced many things presumed to have been practiced also at Qumran. But scholars have noticed that only the first two of the four initiatory stages can be traversed in these camps, and we assume that it was necessary to come to the sectarian center to complete the last two stages. If so, then we see that there was a kind of concentric set of purity barriers for sectarians. It was not just "are you in or out?" but "how in or out?" By definition, this progressive initiation process meant that the walls of the sect were subject to entry and exit over time, the latter clear from the role of expulsion in sectarian life.[8] But on the periphery, sectarians lived in wider Jewish communities and must have interacted with fellow Jews. The purity aspect has an intrinsic assumption to it that is central for our argument. Ritual defilement, assumed always to characterize those outside the group, is also possible for insiders, and those outside the group can enter if they fulfill the initiatory rites and pass the various tests. This is because the system of ritual purity and, most importantly, the possibility of purification are only attainable by fellow Israelites.[9] Incidentally, contrary to some false claims, terms referring to proselytism are not used for joining the sect, and terms referring to non-Jews are not used for those Jews outside the sect. In fact, the sectarian purity rites are common with priests in the temple and the ḥavurah. The point is that use of such boundaries of impurity only makes sense within the Jewish community.

A further boundary of interest here is commercial. It is clear that sectarians throughout the country, but even at Qumran, engaged in commercial activity with others. In this context we find a restriction requiring that all transactions with nonmembers of the group be for cash.[10] This might be to avoid

---

ground of Christianity, the Lost Library of Qumran (Philadelphia: Jewish Publication Society, 1994; repr. ABRL [New York: Doubleday, 1995]) 97-103.

8. Schiffman, *Sectarian Law*, 168-73; G. Forkman, *The Limits of the Religious Community* (Lund: Gleerup, 1972) 39-78.

9. S. Stern, *Jewish Identity in Early Rabbinic Writings*. AGJU 23 (Leiden: Brill, 1994) 52-63; J. Klawans, *Impurity and Sin in Ancient Judaism* (Oxford: Oxford University Press, 2000) 43-62; C. Hayes, *Gentile Impurities and Jewish Identities: Intermarriage and Conversion from the Bible to the Talmud* (Oxford: Oxford University Press, 2002) 45-67.

10. 1QS 5:16-17; cf. 4Q256 ix 10-12 (P. S. Alexander and G. Vermes, *Qumran Cave 4. XIX: Serekh ha-Yaḥad and Two Related Texts*. DJD 26 [Oxford: Clarendon, 1998] 53-54) and 4Q258 ii 9-10 (DJD 26:94-5), both of which are a different recension from 1QS; CD 13:14-15; cf. 4Q267 9 iv 11 for the beginning of this law (J. M. Baumgarten, *Qumran Cave 4.XIII: The Damascus Document (4Q266-273)*. DJD 18 [Oxford: Clarendon, 1996] 108-9).

problems regarding specific regulations pertaining to interest, but in any case, commercial behavior constitutes another type of boundary. Apparently, a series of such regulations provided social boundaries together with the ritual ones — separating sectarians from others in varying degrees in accord with levels of membership. Yet all this separation and differentiation seems to take place on the assumption that outsiders share the same Judaism but do not observe it properly.

Polemic and Invective

There is nothing more particular to the sectarian scrolls than the strong invective against other Jews that fills the texts.[11] One can easily see, when examining all these expressions and the objectives behind them, that it might seem to some that the sect must see itself as believing in a Judaism separate from that (or those) of other Jews. After all, a list of negative expressions taken from the *Rule of the Community* alone includes "guilt, eyes of fornication" (1:16), "your evil, guilt-ridden deeds" (2:5), "the zeal of God's punishments will burn him for eternal destruction" (2:15), and this brief selection is without most of the familiar terms discussed in surveys of this issue. Outsiders are people of darkness who follow evil ways. It is not just their behavior that is illegitimate, but their spiritual makeup is predestined to this violation of God's law. So, one might say that if these transgressors take refuge behind the claim of following the Torah of God, they must truly constitute an alternative Judaism in the eyes of the sect.

But here the *Heilsgeschichte* of the sect, as set out in the first pages of the *Zadokite Fragments* (CD 1-3), argues otherwise. Here we find a pseudohistorical account, according to which the rest of Judean Jewish society turned aside from the true path of God's revelation while the sectarians stayed faithful. The sectarians assert their view that only they are the legitimate continuators of ancient Israel, the real survivors.[12] But here also, in their view, other Jews remain errant members of the same divine covenantal community — albeit violators of that covenant.[13]

From our discussion so far, regarding the use of boundary markers such as ritual purity and the sect's virulently negative language in describing its

11. Cf. Rabin, *Qumran Studies*, 53-70.

12. M. A. Elliott, *The Survivors of Israel: A Reconsideration of the Theology of Pre-Christian Judaism* (Grand Rapids: Wm. B. Eerdmans, 2000) 48-72.

13. See "The Concept of Covenant in the Qumran Scrolls and Rabbinic Literature," Chapter 14 above.

opponents, one might have concluded that even if they saw themselves as part of the same Judaism as their errant neighbors, we should not. This is because, so far in our discussion, we have ignored the commonalities and shared features. As we turn now to several other aspects, we will see why not only the ancient sectarians, but even we should see them and their opponents as sharing the same Judaism.

Consensus and Disagreement in Matters of Jewish Law

The case of Jewish law (halakhah in rabbinic terminology) affords the best example of shared but diverse patterns that unify the approaches to ancient Judaism. This aspect begins with the common recognition of the divine origin of the laws revealed in the Torah and also includes the differing approaches used by ancient Jewish groups to legitimate nonbiblical, or better, extrabiblical, law. It also includes techniques of biblical halakhic exegesis and finally relates to the specific laws under discussion.

We will refer below to the shared biblical canon. Suffice it to say here that this shared set of authoritative Scriptures served as the basis for an understanding that the Written Torah, indeed the entire Hebrew Bible, constituted God's revelation and was therefore obligatory.[14] The Qumran sectarians, like the Pharisees, saw the need to supplement this law, in their case the *nigleh*, "revealed," by positing a second stream of revelation, the *nistar*, "hidden," that was constituted of laws only revealed through what the sect saw as divinely-inspired biblical interpretation.[15] In this manner, they claimed divine authority for many of their legal and exegetical views and postulated a hidden Torah that paralleled some of the functions of the Pharisaic traditions of the fathers and the later full-blown rabbinic oral law. This supplementing of the law also included the closer-to-literal forms of biblical exegesis, a sort of midrash halakhah, that the sectarians had inherited from the Saducean trend in Jewish law. Such exegesis is in evidence in the *Temple Scroll*'s sources and in some other sectarian works. Functionally, this phenomenon is similar to the combined role of oral law and halakhic midrash in the later rabbinic tradition and, it seems, not as distant from Pharisaic traditions and early tannaitic or pre-tannaitic midrash as some would have it.[16] The fact that the Qumran law even-

---

14. This Torah existed in more or less the same form we know it, but with some textual variation, as observed in the Qumran biblical manuscripts.

15. L. H. Schiffman, *The Halakhah at Qumran*. SJLA 16 (Leiden: Brill, 1975) 22-32.

16. Cf. J. M. Baumgarten, "The Unwritten Law in the Pre-Rabbinic Period," *JSJ* 3 (1972) 7-29; repr. in *Studies in Qumran Law*. SJLA 24 (Leiden: Brill, 1977) 13-35.

tually comes in both Bible-like texts such as the *Temple Scroll* and apodictic laws as in the *Zadokite Fragments,* for example, seems to also bind these sectaries to other Jews in legal methodology, even while we admit fully the differences. The pesharim and the *Zadokite Fragments* testify to sectarian disagreement with Pharisaic exegetical approaches, and, of course, other groups did not accept the revealed nature of the *nistar*. But this idea does parallel in some ways the rabbinic idea of a second Torah revealed by God at Sinai.[17]

When we come to the content of the exegesis and law, it is hard to fail to see the combination of commonality and disagreement, which in our view always marks subgroups in the context of Judaism.[18] To understand the complexity of this issue, we are best served by addressing some temple-related examples at the outset. The *Zadokite Fragments* prohibit sectarian participation in the temple because of its illegitimate practices, whereas the *Temple Scroll* and related materials legislate for an ideal temple. (The Essenes of Josephus, we will remember, had a separate area for preparing their temple offerings according to their stricter purity laws.[19])

The *Temple Scroll* and MMT apparently share with the later rabbinic tradition the notion of the three camps of the desert period and their transference of purity regulations from the desert tabernacle to the Jerusalem temple context.[20] By placing all three camps in the temple precincts, these documents, like the minicode at the end of Ezekiel (chs. 40–48), raise the level of purity laws. But, in fact, these texts and what we assume to be the rest of the Jewish people, the Pharisees and the priesthood in Jerusalem, must share these basic exegetical and legal assumptions, which in the Qumran scrolls seem to derive from pre-Hasmonean Saducean/Zadokite sources. But at the same time, this trend in sectarian law clearly forbids nonsacral slaughter within three-days' journey of the temple (11QTemple[a] 52:13-16), in marked contrast to the Pharisaic/rabbinic assumption that maximizes the interpretation of the permissibility of nonsacral slaughter described in Deut 12:20-25.[21]

---

17. B. Z. Wacholder, *The Dawn of Qumran: The Sectarian Torah and the Teacher of Righteousness* (Cincinnati: Hebrew Union College Press, 1983) 1-32.

18. Schiffman, *From Text to Tradition*, 4-5.

19. Josephus, *Ant.* 18.19.

20. L. H. Schiffman, "Exclusion from the Sanctuary and the City of the Sanctuary in the Temple Scroll," *HAR* 9 (1985) 301-20.

21. L. H. Schiffman, "Sacral and Non-Sacral Slaughter according to the Temple Scroll," in *Time to Prepare the Way in the Wilderness: Papers on the Qumran Scrolls by Fellows of the Institute for Advanced Studies of the Hebrew University, Jerusalem, 1989-1990,* ed. D. Dimant and Schiffman, 69-84. STDJ 16 (Leiden: Brill, 1995); E. Tov, "Deut. 12 and 11QTemple LII-LIII: A Contrastive Analysis," *RevQ* 15 (1991) 169-73; E. Eshel, "4QLev[d]: A Possible Source for the Temple Scroll and Miqṣat Maʿaśe ha-Torah," *DSD* 2 (1995) 1-13.

It must be emphasized that the same passages in the Hebrew Bible are being debated, and the only question is the interpretation of Scripture — strict or loose constructionist for the most part.

Another well known example is the case of *ṭevul yom,* one who had immersed but awaited sunset on the last day of his/her purification period.[22] According to the Zadokite/Sadducean approach, such a person was completely impure, whereas to the Pharisees, he/she was pure for certain purposes. Here we see that, distributed over a list of issues, about which the groups generally agreed, they disputed considerably regarding the *ṭevul yom,* and the sectarians took the more literalist — indeed, the direct — meaning of ובא השמש וטהר, "and when the sun sets he shall become pure" (Lev 22:7). Indeed, this is an example of the notion of a shared, but disputed, Judaism.

A few Sabbath laws may also illustrate the same point. Both the scrolls and later rabbinic tradition derive from the same verse (Deut 5:12) the notion that Sabbath observance begins a short time before actual sunset, תוספת מלאכה, in rabbinic terms. Like some later rabbis, the *Zadokite Fragments* see this as a Torah law.[23] Indeed, the scrolls, like *Jubilees,* see all Sabbath laws as Torah laws and have no concept of rabbinic ordinances. But when one compares, for example, the rabbinic laws derived from Isa 58:13 (*b. Šabb.* 150a-b) with those of the Qumran texts (CD 10:17-21),[24] they are almost the same. This is the case even though the *Zadokite Fragments* are generally stricter than tannaitic law.

These are intended only as illustrations, to which many more can be added. The interwoven agreed-upon principles and interpretations combine in an organic way with the disputed aspects in ways that do not allow us to separate these Judaisms. It seems as though they are truly fated to be interlocked. Indeed, in the area of halakhah the disputes among the groups were often no wider than those within the Pharisaic/rabbinic tradition and its extensive literature.

Shared Canon of Scripture

In regard to the issue of the biblical canon of the Qumran sectarians, there has been much dispute.[25] Early scrolls scholars maintained that the scrolls

---

22. L. H. Schiffman, "Pharisaic and Sadducean Halakhah in Light of the Dead Sea Scrolls: The Case of Ṭevul Yom," *DSD* 1 (1994) 285-99.

23. Schiffman, *Halakhah at Qumran,* 84-87.

24. Schiffman, *Halakhah at Qumran,* 87-91.

25. E. Ulrich, "Canon," *EDSS* 1:117-20; "The Notion and Definition of Canon," in *The Canon Debate,* ed. L. M. McDonald and J. A. Sanders, 21-35 (Peabody: Hendrickson, 2002).

sect had a still open canon and that the large number of what are noncanonical books, or "excluded books," in the rabbinic view, were considered authoritative at Qumran.[26] This complex issue can only be summarized here.[27] To be "canonized," that is, authoritative, a book must be used to generate other, later books or must be cited directly as an authority.[28] No book comes close to this status at Qumran except the books in the traditional canon, plus perhaps *Jubilees* and the *Aramaic Levi Document,* apparently a source for the Greek *Testament of Levi.* We must remember that while Esther was not found among the Qumran biblical manuscripts, it was used secondarily in other texts and so was probably part of their canon.[29]

Related to this is the division of the canon. The tripartite canon, known from the later rabbinic Bible and talmudic literature, is evidenced at Qumran.[30] A number of references exist to the authority of the books of Moses and the prophets.[31] Beyond this, 4QMMT refers to Torah, prophets, and books of David and history, what we call "Writings."[32] This part of the canon was apparently not totally closed as appears also from the New Testament's reference to the Torah, prophets, and Psalms (Luke 24:44) and from tannaitic debates about canonicity.[33] The existence of this same tripartite division in the scrolls, however, again points to common conceptions of authority, divine inspiration, and holiness among a wide spectrum of Second Temple–period Jews.

---

26. See J. C. VanderKam and P. Flint, *The Meaning of the Dead Sea Scrolls: Their Significance for Understanding the Bible, Judaism, Jesus, and Christianity* (San Francisco: HarperSanFrancisco, 2002) 154-81.

27. Cf. Schiffman, *Reclaiming the Dead Sea Scrolls,* 162-69.

28. C. A. Newsom, "'Sectually Explicit' Literature from Qumran," in *The Hebrew Bible and Its Interpreters,* ed. W. H. Propp, B. Halpern, and D. N. Freedman (Winona Lake, Ind.: Eisenbrauns, 1990) 167-87.

29. S. Talmon, "Was the Book of Esther Known at Qumran?" *DSD* 2 (1995) 249-67; S. W. (White) Crawford, "Has *Esther* Been Found at Qumran? *4QProto-Esther* and the *Esther* Corpus," *RevQ* 17 (Hommage à József T. Milik, 1996) 307-25.

30. Cf. J. C. Trebolle Barrera, "Origins of a Tripartite Old Testament Canon," in McDonald and Sanders, *The Canon Debate,* 128-45.

31. 1QS 1:3; 8:15-16; 4Q504 1-2 iii 12-13.

32. E. Qimron and J. Strugnell, *Qumran Cave 4. V: Miqṣat Ma'aśe ha-Torah.* DJD 10 (Oxford: Clarendon, 1994) 58-61; Schiffman, *Reclaiming the Dead Sea Scrolls,* 165-66. Contrast E. Ulrich, "The Non-attestation of a Tripartite Canon in 4QMMT," *CBQ* 65 (2003) 202-14.

33. N. M. Sarna, "Bible, the Tripartite Canon," *EncJud* 4:821-25.

QUMRAN SECTARIANS AND OTHERS

Shared National Aspirations and Exclusivist Eschatology

The Qumran sectarians, no doubt like most Hasmonean and Herodian-period Jews, were aware of the processes by which independence had been gained and then lost by the Hasmoneans and of the threats that Roman rule (or perhaps Jewish reaction to Roman rule, depending on one's place on the ancient political spectrum) posed for the Jewish future. The ideals and aspirations of the Qumran sectarians were such that they opposed and roundly condemned the Hasmonean polity both in theoretical and practical terms. They virulently opposed the Romans and expected to participate in a great eschatological war that would begin in the Jewish struggle against the Kittim, a sobriquet for the Romans.[34] The sectarians opposed the Hasmoneans because they had usurped the high priesthood from the Zadokite priests[35] and saw the Romans as the embodiment of evil and idolatry.[36]

Our detailed knowledge of Judean political affairs in the Greco-Roman period is such that it is not difficult to place these views in the context of the variety of political and ideological trends of the period. But what interests us presently is the bifurcated realization of these political ideas in the sect's ideology and eschatology.

On the one hand, numerous passages speak of the Jewish people as a whole and its chosen status, and its hopes for future redemption. Reading some of these passages would give one the impression that the sect was truly open to love of its fellow Jews regardless of their sectarian affiliation. Such passages pray for rebuilding of the temple and regaining the independence of the people and land and mourn the destruction of the first temple and the Davidic empire. Yet along with this trend, there is a plethora of material indicating that only the Qumran sectarians and their associates elsewhere in the

---

34. T. H. Lim, "Kittim," *EDSS* 1:469-71; B. Nitzan, *Megillat Pesher Ḥabakkuk: mi-Megillot Midbar Yehudah (1Qp Hab)* (Jerusalem: Bialik Institute, 1986) 123-32; S. L. Berrin, *The Pesher Nahum Scroll from Qumran: An Exegetical Study of 4Q169*. STDJ 103 (Leiden: Brill, 2004) 101-4; J. H. Charlesworth, *The Pesharim and Qumran History: Chaos or Consensus?* (Grand Rapids: Wm. B. Eerdmans, 2002) 109-12; J. Duhaime, *The War Texts: 1QM and Related Manuscripts* (London: T & T Clark, 2004) 77-81; H. Eshel, "The Kittim in the War Scroll and in the Pesharim," in *Historical Perspectives: From the Hasmoneans to Bar Kokhba in Light of the Dead Sea Scrolls. Proceedings of the Fourth International Symposium of the Orion Center for the Study of the Dead Sea Scrolls and Associated Literature, 27-31 January, 1999*, ed. D. Goodblatt, A. Pinnick, and D. R. Schwartz, 29-44. STDJ 37 (Leiden: Brill, 2001).

35. F. M. Cross, *The Ancient Library of Qumran*, 3rd ed. (Sheffield: Sheffield Academic, 1995), 109.

36. Cf. Y. Yadin, *The Scroll of the War of the Sons of Light against the Sons of Darkness*, trans. B. and C. Rabin (Oxford: Oxford University Press, 1962) 22-26.

country are the true remnant of Israel and that the messianic wars of the *War Scroll* and similar texts will lead to utter destruction of all Israelites who do not join the sect. They will be destroyed with the rest of the nations. But at the same time, curiously, this vision is not carried through in the *War Scroll* and related literature consistently. Instead, alternatively, all humanity can be pictured as sharing in the end of days (1QM 12:12-14).

But for our purposes here, in trying to see if we should speak of Judaisms, it should be noted that there are no discussions in this context of groups or sects of Jews, only of individuals. The sect seems to have expected massive support from the Jewish people in the end of days. The significance of this for us is that even though the sect had an exclusivist view of the eschaton, such that accepting its beliefs and practices was a prerequisite for participation and survival in it,[37] the assumption was that other Jews would see that the sectarian views were correct. So it seems that the sect, again, did not see the other views as Judaisms, creating an unbreachable gulf, but simply as violations of the one, true Judaism of which they were the true representatives.

Conclusion

Despite the exclusiveness of the sectarians' views, they seem to have believed that there was only one Judaism, which some followed and most violated. But the real question is: what do we think? That is, the theme we have set asks whether we ought to be sufficiently affected by the differences, and so little impressed by the overlaps and commonalities, as to see each Judaism as an independent religious system. In our view, the overlaps and interactions, as well as the complex system of isoglosses that links the various groups of Jews and their approaches to Judaism, are so extensive and overlapping as to require that we treat the groups as holding a common Judaism at the core and disagreeing with one another extensively at the same time. To some extent, this is the nature of the complex organism we call Judaism — it is not just a religion, or a nation without boundaries or within territory. It is not just one simply defined set of beliefs and aspirations. But somehow, in every generation, the isoglosses have outnumbered and outweighed the centripetal forces, or the Jewish people would not still be here today. And in regard to today — as modern religious movements came to the fore in modern Europe and Jews had to decide if they would formally challenge the official, governmentally recognized unity of "Judaism," very few voices called for such a formal

---

37. See "The Concept of Restoration in the Dead Sea Scrolls," Chapter 17 above.

breach. Basically, at the risk of being anachronistic, the lesson of today is that the Jewish "body religious" is attracted in the end to the unifying core and so sees itself as one religion, even with its manifold competing, even delegitimizing, approaches. One Judaism, but one characterized by dispute and disagreement, is the model that despite all attempts to paint it otherwise, has typified Judaism throughout the ages.

CHAPTER 22

Non-Jews in the Dead Sea Scrolls

The Dead Sea Scrolls contain a wide variety of texts composed in the latter part of the Second Temple period, mostly from the second century B.C.E. through the first century C.E. Attempts to refute this dating can easily be discounted in light of archaeological, paleographic, and textual data, and now by the recently completed carbon 14 dating.[1]

This library consisted of biblical scrolls, apocryphal compositions, and the documents that describe the beliefs, history, and law of a sectarian group. In this study we will concentrate on the sectarian corpus — those documents that were authored by the sect and that testify to its particular approach.[2] We will want to know, in particular, how the sect who gathered the scrolls in the Qumran collection looked at their non-Jewish neighbors.

Most Jews throughout the ages defined themselves over and against non-Jewish majorities. More often than not, these majorities were hostile to the Jews and helped in the erection of the very barriers that the Jews employed to define themselves. In the case of Qumran, the sect defined itself primarily over and against other Jews. It took a particularly dim view — indeed, an intolerant one — of the Pharisees and Sadducees and clearly had little use for the approaches to Judaism of the Hasmoneans and, to say the least, of the hellenized Jews. Here we will examine the sectarian outlook on the nations surrounding them. Attitudes to non-Jewish religious groups focus on the pagans who populated the land of Israel in the Greco-Roman period.

---

1. See G. Bonani et al., "Radiocarbon Dating of the Dead Sea Scrolls," ʿAtiqot 20 (1991) 27-32; A. J. T. Jull et al., "Radiocarbon Dating of Scrolls and Linen Fragments from the Judean Desert," ʿAtiqot 28 (1996) 85-61.

2. We have also omitted *Jubilees, 1 Enoch, Genesis Apocryphon,* and *Aramaic Levi Document.*

The scrolls contain no references to Christianity because the sectarian documents were authored before the careers of Jesus and John the Baptist. They are in no way mentioned or alluded to in the scrolls — all fallacious claims to the contrary notwithstanding.[3] Christianity does not appear in any of the scrolls, even though the sectarian settlement at Qumran continued to be occupied until 68 C.E., and even though some of the manuscripts may have been copied in the first century C.E.

There are numerous references to non-Jews in the scrolls. Quite prominent are texts dealing with the halakhic status of non-Jews regarding Sabbath law, purity regulations, and commerce. Other passages deal with the application of the biblical laws banning idolatrous practices. Another major theme is the role of the Gentiles in the expected eschatological battle in which they are to be defeated by the sectarians. In this case, the "nations" play a central role in the unfolding of God's plan of history. A number of texts base themselves on biblical precedent and refer to the demonstration of God's might in the presence of the nations. Others speak of the chosen people. We can also discern the attitude to proselytes in the Qumran texts. These aspects will clarify the general picture in order to sketch the overall history of the relations of Jews and non-Jews.

Non-Jews in the Sectarian Law of the Zadokite Fragments

While the Qumran corpus contains no specific information about what constitutes Jewish identity and, hence, how to define a non-Jew, it does give us quite a number of laws relating to non-Jews.[4] At the outset, we should turn to a series of laws regarding gentiles in the *Zadokite Fragments (Damascus Document)* that directly addresses this issue.[5] While the *Zadokite Fragments* legislate for members of the sect who lived throughout the land of Israel, it is clear that the legal sections of this document were also in force for members of the sect at the Qumran center.[6]

---

3. See G. Vermes, "The Oxford Forum for Qumran Research: Seminar on the Rule of War from Cave 4 (4Q285)," *JJS* 43 (1992) 85-90, excerpted in "The 'Pierced Messiah' Text — An Interpretation Evaporates," *BAR* 18/6 (1992) 80-82.

4. It seems most likely that there was already a consensus on the definitions of a Jew and, for that reason, we encounter no argument on this question. See L. H. Schiffman, *Who Was a Jew? Rabbinic and Halakhic Perspectives on the Jewish Christian Schism* (Hoboken: Ktav, 1985) 1-39.

5. For a detailed study of these laws, see L. H. Schiffman, "Legislation Concerning Relations with Non-Jews in the *Zadokite Fragments* and in Tannaitic Literature," *RevQ* 11 (1983) 379-89.

6. While this text was first uncovered in medieval manuscripts in the Cairo Genizah, some ten manuscripts were found in the Qumran caves. See J. M. Baumgarten, *Qumran Cave*

The regulations of this text begin by indicating that it is forbidden to "shed the blood of anyone from among the non-Jews for the sake of wealth and profit" (CD 12:6-7).[7] Our text makes no reference to any penalty. Solomon Schechter is probably correct in noting that killing for self-defense would have been permitted.[8] We see this law as a polemic against the Hasmonean rulers, intended to prohibit the undertaking of campaigns designed only to add territory to their country or to accumulate spoils of war.[9] A similar view is expressed in *Pesher Habakkuk* that condemns "the last priests of Jerusalem who gather wealth and property from the spoil of the nations" (1QpHab 9:4-6).

In accord with this same purpose, the text goes on to prohibit carrying off the property of non-Jews "so that they not blaspheme, except if it be done in accord with the decision of the Community of Israel" (CD 12:7-8). This is certainly a prohibition on robbing non-Jews, in this context prohibiting military action to take their property. Most interesting is the explanation given: lest they blaspheme God. This idea is the same as the tannaitic ruling (*t. B. Qam.* 10:15) that stealing from non-Jews is prohibited because it leads to profanation of God's name. Such actions reflect badly on the Jewish people and, hence, on their God. Finally, this prescription also makes clear that war might only be undertaken with the permission of the council. Under such conditions, the war could be considered just and certainly not undertaken solely in order to plunder the enemy.[10]

The series of laws then turns to the prohibition of selling pure (kosher) animals and fowl to non-Jews lest they sacrifice them (CD 12:8-9). Such laws also existed in tannaitic tradition and were intended to make certain that Jews did not support, even indirectly, idolatrous worship.[11]

Also prohibited here is the sale to non-Jews of the produce "from his threshing floor and from his winepress" (CD 12:9-10). This law prohibits the sale of the produce directly from these installations, i.e., before it is tithed. Sale to non-Jews does not exempt Jewish produce from tithing.[12]

The final law in this series prohibits selling male or female servants to

---

4.XIII: The Damascus Document (4Q266-273). DJD 18 (Oxford: Clarendon, 1996). There is no question, therefore, that this text reflects the law and ideology of the Qumran sect.

7. The beginning of this law is preserved in 4QD^f 5 i 21, in Baumgarten, DJD 18:181.

8. S. Schechter, *Documents of Jewish Sectaries*, Vol. 1: *Fragments of a Zadokite Work* (Cambridge: Cambridge University Press, 1910; repr. Library of Biblical Studies. New York: Ktav, 1970) 82, n. 13.

9. Schiffman, *RevQ* 11 (1983) 380-82.

10. Schiffman, *RevQ* 11 (1983) 382-85.

11. Schiffman, *RevQ* 11 (1983) 385-87.

12. Schiffman, *RevQ* 11 (1983) 387-88.

non-Jews "since they (the servants) have entered into the covenant of Abraham" (CD 12:10-11). This law clearly concerns those servants who, like the tannaitic classification עבד כנעני (lit., "Canaanite slave") have begun a process of conversion to Judaism.[13] The same regulation exists in tannaitic law under which such slaves automatically gained their freedom if sold to non-Jews (*m. Git.* 4:6). This law was intended to allow such slaves to continue to fulfill the commandments that they had undertaken.[14] In this context, we should note that 4QOrdinances prohibits a Jew from being a servant to a non-Jew (4Q159 2-4 2).[15]

In the area of Jewish/non-Jewish relations, the *Zadokite Fragments* present a sort of summary of what later rabbinic tradition would enshrine in the Mishnah tractate *'Abodah Zarah*. From the point of view of the laws of the sect, we can conclude that in this area, their laws are simply a reflection of those followed by a number of Jewish groups, including the Pharisees. The sectarians, like other nonhellenized Jews of the Second Temple era, eschewed the killing or robbing of Gentiles, as was to be expected, but also in accord with the sectarian understanding of the Torah's legislation, they made sure to avoid supporting or encouraging idolatrous worship in any way.

Another area of law in the *Zadokite Fragments* where non-Jews are discussed is that of the Sabbath.[16] The text, again exactly like tannaitic law, prohibits the sending of non-Jews to do labor prohibited on the Sabbath on behalf of Jews (CD 11:2). The non-Jew would then become an agent of the Jew who would be violating the Sabbath law indirectly.[17] Indeed, a similar prohibition exists regarding male and female servants (CD 11:12). This law certainly refers to the "Canaanite slaves" in the process of conversion.[18]

A strange prescription, most likely with no parallel in tannaitic law but perhaps parallel to some later Karaite views, prohibits spending the Sabbath "[in] a place close to the Gentiles" (CD 11:14-15). This law is most probably aimed to ensure ritual purity on the Sabbath, a matter important in sectarian circles. On the other hand, it might indicate that a technical residency for carrying or traveling on the Sabbath may not be made in partnership with non-

---

13. See Schiffman, *Who Was a Jew?* 36-37.
14. Schiffman, *RevQ* 11 (1983) 388.
15. See my edition, translation, and commentary to 4QOrdinances, in *The Dead Sea Scrolls: Hebrew, Aramaic, and Greek Texts with English Translations*, ed. J. H. Charlesworth, 1:145-57 (Tübingen: Mohr [Siebeck] and Louisville: Westminster John Knox, 1994).
16. For detailed discussion of Qumran Sabbath law, see L. H. Schiffman, *The Halakhah at Qumran*. SJLA 16 (Leiden: Brill, 1975) 84-131.
17. Schiffman, *Halakhah at Qumran*, 104-6.
18. Schiffman, *Halakhah at Qumran*, 120-21.

Jews (*b. 'Erub.* 62a), as they do not have Sabbath obligations in Jewish law. This interpretation would accord fully with later rabbinic tradition.[19]

Here we see that although non-Jews are not obligated to observe the Jewish Sabbath, it is forbidden for Jews to employ them to do prohibited labor, whether they are free or "Canaanite slaves." Again we observe that the sect's views on this topic are sufficiently close to those of the Pharisaic-rabbinic tradition as to suggest that these were the views of many observant Jews in this period. A passing reference in CD 14:15 (also in 4QD^b 10 i 8) recognizes the need to redeem captives who may be "captured by a foreign nation."[20] Priests once captured by non-Jews were, in the view of the sect, rendered unfit for priestly service.

A fragmentary law preserved in three Qumran manuscripts of the *Zadokite Fragments* seems to outlaw the bringing (perhaps to the temple or to the sectarian communal meals) of meat slaughtered by non-Jews. Further, metals — gold, silver, brass, tin, and lead — that have been used by non-Jews to make an idol were prohibited in the same manner (4Q269 8 ii 2-3=4Q270 3 iii 20-21=4Q271 9-10).[21] It was considered permitted, in line with Deut 15:3, to take interest from non-Jews, but not from Jews, according to 1QWords of Moses (3:6).[22] The *Zadokite Fragments* similarly castigate anyone who takes interest from a fellow Jew (4Q267 4 9-10).[23]

Extremely important, especially in light of the material to be cited below from the *Temple Scroll*, is an enigmatic passage providing that "Any man who shall dedicate (or destroy) any man according to the laws of the nations (בחוקי הגוים) is to be put to death" (CD 9:1).[24] This passage, certainly based on Lev 27:29 and Gen 9:6, has been debated by scholars, and a number of views have been put forth. It is most probable that we are dealing here with a law stating that one who has recourse to non-Jewish courts to accuse a fellow Jew of a crime is himself to be put to death (in the view of the sect) because he has informed against his fellow Jew.[25] Clearly, informing was a problem at

---

19. Schiffman, *Halakhah at Qumran*, 123-24.
20. Baumgarten, DJD 18:72-74.
21. Baumgarten, DJD 18:130-31, 151, 173-74.
22. D. Barthélemy and J. T. Milik, *Qumran Cave I.* DJD 1 (Oxford: Clarendon, 1955) 94-95.
23. Baumgarten, DJD 18:99-100.
24. That this passage is textually reliable is shown from comparison with 4QD^a 8 ii 8-9 (see Baumgarten, DJD 18:65). Further, it is written immediately after a *vacat* (paragraph marker), indicating that no preceding text provides a fuller context for understanding this law.
25. The opposite view, namely that Jews are to be handed over to the non-Jewish authorities for execution (C. Rabin, *The Zadokite Documents* [Oxford: Clarendon, 1954] 44), is impossible in light of comparison with the *Temple Scroll* and all other systems of Jewish law.

this time, as we know also from somewhat later rabbinic texts,[26] and strong measures to prevent it were necessary.

Informing also is prohibited in a passage that is in agreement with what we will see in the *Temple Scroll*. The *Zadokite Fragments*, in a passage preserved only in a Qumran copy (4QD^e 2 ii 13-15)[27] that appears to be a list of offenses, include "the person who reveals the secret of his people to the nations, or one who curses o[r speaks] slanderously" regarding the sect's leaders[28] or "leads [his people astray]."

Prohibitions of Idolatry

We have already seen that the *Zadokite Fragments* deal with the need to avoid supporting idolatrous practices in any way. 1QWords of Moses places into the mouth of Moses the assertion that Jews would go astray after the abominations of the nations (1:6-8, partly restored).[29] The issue of idolatry is dealt with in the *Temple Scroll* in its recapitulation of the biblical legislation on this topic. The *Temple Scroll* and its connection to the life of the Qumran sect are themselves a matter of controversy. Our view is that the scroll was edited in Hasmonean times by someone belonging to the sect or a related group and that it includes Saducean sources that the founders of the sect brought with them when they left the temple service after the Hasmonean revolt. It is for this reason that the scroll has many important parallels with the laws of 4QMMT.[30] The *Temple Scroll* assembles biblical laws and then, by a combination of exegesis, modification, and addition, sets forth its views on how Jewish ritual, law, and society should be structured in the Hasmonean period.[31] It takes up the biblical laws of idolatry as part of the Deuteronomic paraphrase, the section at the end of the scroll that was composed to round out the sources the author had in front of him and to give the impression that the scroll was a complete Torah.[32]

---

26. Cf. Schiffman, *Who Was a Jew?* 46-47.
27. Baumgarten, DJD 18:144-45.
28. Or perhaps its prophets; cf. CD 5:21–6:1 (משחי רוח הקודש).
29. Barthélemy and Milik, DJD 1:92.
30. L. H. Schiffman, "*Miqsat Ma'aseh Ha-Torah* and the *Temple Scroll*," *RevQ* 14 (The Texts of Qumran and the History of the Community: Proceedings of the Groningen Congress on the Dead Sea Scrolls 3, 1990) 435-57.
31. That it is not a messianic text is clear from an explicit statement in 11QTemple 29:1-10.
32. See L. H. Schiffman, "Laws Concerning Idolatry in the Temple Scroll," in *Uncovering Ancient Stones: Essays in Memory of H. Neil Richardson*, ed. L. M. Hopfe, 159-75 (Winona Lake:

Indeed, in the introduction to the scroll the author, basing himself on Exod 34:10-17, incorporates the obligation to destroy idolatrous cult objects and to avoid idolatrous worship (11QTemple 2:6-12). His extensive treatment begins with the prohibition of idolatrous practice (11QTemple 51:19–52:3). This passage is based on Deut 16:21-22 (cf. Lev 26:1) and outlaws sacrificing throughout the land, the planting of *asherot*, and the erecting of cultic pillars and figured stones. This law, however, adds nothing to biblical law, except as regards its formulation.

The scroll next paraphrases the law of the idolatrous prophet of Deut 13:2-6 (11QTemple 54:8-18). Although there are minor variations in the textual traditions behind this passage, as well as a few changes to eliminate ambiguities, the text simply repeats the biblical law requiring the death penalty for a "prophet" who advocates worship of other gods. Similar is the manner in which the scroll reviews the law of the enticer to idolatry of Deut 13:7-12 (11QTemple 54:19–55:1). In accord with Deuteronomy such a person is to be put to death. No significant innovations in the laws involved are introduced by the scroll.

More significant variants appear in the paraphrase of the law of the idolatrous city of Deut 13:13-19 (11QTemple 55:2-14). The biblical legislation requires that a city that has gone astray and worshipped idols is to be totally destroyed, its inhabitants killed, and its spoils burned. The scroll introduces a number of requirements: All the inhabitants must have worshipped idols for the city to be entirely destroyed, as opposed to the notion that only the majority must have transgressed as known from tannaitic halakhah (*m. Sanh.* 4:1). That all the inhabitants are to be killed, in the view of the scroll, contrasts with the tannaitic view that the children are to be spared (*t. Sanh.* 14:3). The *Temple Scroll* mandates that all the animals are to be destroyed, in contrast to the tannaitic interpretation according to which those dedicated for certain sacrificial offerings are to be spared (*t. Sanh.* 14:5; *Sifre Deut* 94).[33]

The final law on idolatry in the *Temple Scroll* is the law of the idolatrous individual in Deut 12:2-7 (11QTemple 55:15–56:04). While some ambiguities are eliminated, the text is essentially a recapitulation of the Deuteronomic prescription that an idolater be put to death if he can be convicted of his transgression in court under the applicable rules of testimony.

In all these laws we have seen that the text simply adhered to the biblical

---

Eisenbrauns, 1994). Philological commentary is available in Y. Yadin, *The Temple Scroll* (Jerusalem: Israel Exploration Society and Shrine of the Book, 1983) 2:244-49.

33. Cf. L. H. Schiffman, "The Septuagint and the Temple Scroll: Shared 'Halakhic Variants'," in *Septuagint, Scrolls and Cognate Writings*, ed. G. J. Brooke and B. Lindars, 283-84. SBLSCS 33 (Atlanta: Scholars, 1992).

prohibitions with little addition or modification. In the case of the changes made in the law of the idolatrous city, it is possible that they resulted from the Hasmonean attempts to eradicate idolatry from the country, which led at times to the destruction, without the necessary investigation and trial, of entire cities.[34] Our author may have wanted to clarify that Hellenistic Jews, no matter how extreme, could not be destroyed in this manner if, as he argued, the entire city had not participated in idolatrous worship.

What emerges is that the author/redactor of the *Temple Scroll* had little if anything to add to the Torah's legislation on idolatry. Further, he says nothing about non-Jews who worship idols except that their cultic objects and cult places are to be destroyed. Following Deuteronomy, he is almost entirely concerned with eliminating idolatrous worship from amongst the Jews, an agenda that fit both the author of Deuteronomy and the author/redactor of our scroll.

Other Laws in the Temple Scroll

At the beginning of the preserved portion of the *Temple Scroll* (11QTemple 2:1-15), in the same context as the requirement to destroy pagan cult objects, we find a recapitulation of the biblical prohibition on making covenants with the nations of Canaan who are to be destroyed (Exod 34:10-16). Both the Bible and our scroll state explicitly that this restriction is intended to prevent intermarriage with these nations. This passage adheres so closely to the biblical source that we cannot tell from it if the prohibition of intermarriage was widened to include all nations, as took place already in the biblical period (1 Kgs 11:1-2; Ezra 9:1-2; Neh 10:31). But from elsewhere in the scroll it seems that all marriage between Jews and Gentiles was prohibited (11QTemple 57:15-17).

The scroll no doubt would have prohibited non-Jews from entering the temple since even proselytes were restricted from entering into the middle court until the fourth generation (11QTemple 39:5-7). Indeed, non-Jews as well as proselytes are excluded from the sanctuary, apparently in the end of days, according to 4QFlorilegium (4Q174 1-2 i 4).[35]

In connection with the impurity of the dead we learn that the nations bury their dead everywhere, but Israel, in the view of the scroll, is to bury in

---

34. On the destruction or Judaization of pagan cities by the Hasmoneans, see E. Schurer, *The History of the Jewish People in the Age of Jesus Christ (175 B.C.-A.D. 135)*, rev. ed. by G. Vermes and F. Millar, with P. Vermes and M. Black, 1:191-92, 207, 228 (Edinburgh: T. & T. Clark, 1973).

35. See L. H. Schiffman, "Exclusion from the Sanctuary and the City of the Sanctuary in the Temple Scroll," *HAR* 9 (1985) 303-5 and the bibliography cited there.

specially set-out cemeteries, one for every four cities (11QTemple 48:11-14). The purpose of this regulation is to maintain the ritual purity of the land of Israel. While the phraseology of this legislation has roots in biblical language,[36] the contents here are unique to the scroll.[37] This law is to be compared with the scroll's condemnation of the practice of the nations to offer sacrifice and erect cult places everywhere (11QTemple 15:19-21), thus defiling the land of Israel. The unstated (or perhaps unpreserved) implication is that Israel is to perform sacrificial worship only at its central temple complex in Jerusalem.

The abominations of the "nations" are listed as well: passing children through fire as part of Molekh worship, divination, augury and sorcery of different types, and necromancy.[38] Israel is told that because of these abominations the Canaanite nations have been expelled[39] from the land (11QTemple 60:16–61:02). But this passage is no more than a verbatim quotation of Deut 18:9-14 with minor textual variation.

The nations appear several times in the Law of the King, a separate source that the author/redactor of the scroll incorporated into his scroll.[40] Although Israel is to have a king "like all the (other) nations," that king must be Jewish (11QTemple 56:13-15), an exact echo of Deut 17:14-15.[41] He may only marry a Jewish woman (11QTemple 57:15-16).[42] Lest he be kidnapped by "the nations" or "a foreign nation," he must be protected by a guard of twelve thousand chosen men (11QTemple 57:5-11). This was a central concern if we can judge from the repetition within the passage, undoubtedly intended for emphasis. The scroll also expects that foreign nations will attack the land of Israel to take booty and specifies the necessary defensive military action (11QTemple 58:3-10).[43] Indeed, such action is conceived as a fundamental duty of the king.

---

36. Yadin, *Temple Scroll*, 2:209.

37. See L. H. Schiffman, "The Impurity of the Dead in the Temple Scroll," in *Archaeology and History in the Dead Sea Scrolls: The New York University Conference in Memory of Yigael Yadin*, 137-38. JSOTSup 8. JSOT/ASOR Monographs 2 (Sheffield: Sheffield Academic, 1990).

38. Cf. the prohibition of 'ov and yid'oni alluded to in CD 12:2-3.

39. The text uses the present tense, reflecting the language of the Bible. But in the context of the *Temple Scroll* the message is certainly that of the recounting of past events.

40. L. H. Schiffman, "The King, His Guard, and the Royal Council in the *Temple Scroll*," *PAAJR* 54 (1987) 237-59.

41. The prohibition on returning the people to Egypt is here interpreted to refer to making war (11QTemple 56:16).

42. Cf. the requirement that the high priest marry a "virgin from his people" (NJPS "kin") in Lev 21:14.

43. Cf. L. H. Schiffman, "The Laws of War in the Temple Scroll," *RevQ* 13 (Mémorial Jean Carmignac, 1988) 302-4.

After the conclusion of the Law of the King there is again a recapitulation of the Deuteronomic laws of war according to which it is obligatory to kill all the Canaanites lest Israel learn from their abominable ways (11QTemple 62:11-16). Yet again we deal with a text of Deut 20:15-18,[44] rather than with independent Second Temple–period material.

Two final examples from the *Temple Scroll* concern those to be punished by "hanging."[45] The first prescribes that one who informs against his people or delivers them to "a foreign nation" shall be executed, apparently by crucifixion (11QTemple 64:6-9). The second is a law regarding one subject to the death penalty who flees "to the midst of the nations" and curses his people, the Israelites. He is to be put to death, apparently by crucifixion as well (11QTemple 64:9-13). Like the Targumim and the rabbis, the *Temple Scroll* saw informing to the non-Jews as a particularly heinous crime, and, indeed, it has always been taken this way in Jewish tradition. This law is based on an exegesis of Lev 19:16, "Do not go about slandering your people." The prohibition of execration of the Jewish people and the punishment of this offense by "hanging," most probably crucifixion, are based on an interpretation of Deut 21:22-23.[46]

In general, most of the mentions of the non-Jews ("the nations") in the *Temple Scroll* are in material taken almost verbatim from Scripture. Particularly significant are those passages that the author created on his own. In this respect we saw the need to reject non-Jewish burial practices to ensure the purity of the land, the requirement that the king marry only a Jewish bride, fear of enemy attack by the non-Jews, fear that the king might be kidnapped, and the problem of informers and execrators against the Jewish people. In these areas, the concerns of the author/redactor or his sources, writing in the Second Temple period, can be observed. Indeed, intermarriage, treason, and the complex web of Hasmonean vs. pagan military activity were major concerns in this period.

Non-Jews in 4QMMT

4QMMT, known as the *Halakhic Letter,* is a foundation document for the Qumran sect. It specifies the reasons for the schism in which a group of Sadducean priests left the temple service after the Hasmoneans took over the temple ca. 152 B.C.E. and began to conduct the rituals in accord with Pharisaic

---

44. Schiffman, *RevQ* 13 (1988) 304.
45. See Yadin, *Temple Scroll*, 1:373-9.
46. Yadin, *Temple Scroll*, 2:291.

views.⁴⁷ This document contains two laws (of a total of twenty-two) relating to non-Jews.

The founders of the sect write to their erstwhile priestly colleagues in Jerusalem and criticize them for accepting grain offerings *(terumah)* from the produce of non-Jews. In their view, such produce is not to enter the temple lest it defile the offerings collected from Jews. In fact, say the sectarians, it is forbidden to eat of such produce. No such law is known from the Pharisaic-rabbinic tradition. The authors of MMT also oppose accepting sacrificial offerings *(zevaḥ)* from non-Jews that was the practice in the temple.

These two cultic matters were certainly among those important to the founders of the sect. The ritually exclusivistic view of the authors fits well with the eschatological views that the sect developed. They expected the nations ultimately to disappear from the face of the earth. The alternative approach of the Pharisaic-rabbinic tradition envisioned the nations as coming to Jerusalem to recognize God's sovereignty and participate in the worship of the Lord.

Non-Jews in Sectarian Teaching

The long admonition at the beginning of the *Zadokite Fragments* (pp. 1-9 and 19-20 in the Genizah version) is almost entirely directed to intra-Jewish issues, especially to the sect's self-image and polemic with the Pharisees.⁴⁸ The only time that non-Jews appear is in a pesherlike exegesis of Deut 32:33 that mentions the "kings of the peoples," their evil ways, and the "king of Greece" (i.e., Rome) who will take vengeance, most probably on the other kings (CD 8:9-12 = 19:21-25). This passage certainly looks like a reflection of the affairs of the Hasmonean period in which the Romans were slowly gobbling up the various local kings of the Mediterranean Basin and the Near East. The very same assumption is made in *Pesher Habakkuk* (3:2-13; 3:17–4:9).⁴⁹

A seemingly strange passage appears as part of a ritual for expelling miscreants from the sect in the *Zadokite Fragments,* preserved only in the Qumran manuscripts (4QDᵃ 11 5-14).⁵⁰ There we read that God created the

---

47. See "The New Halakhic Letter (4QMMT) and the Origins of the Dead Sea Sect," Chapter 6 above.

48. See L. H. Schiffman, "New Light on the Pharisees: Insights from the Dead Sea Scrolls," *BR* 8 (1992) 30-33, 54.

49. This text specifically identifies the Romans as worshipping idols (4QpHab 12:10–13:4).

50. Baumgarten, DJD 18:76-77.

various peoples of the earth "and you led them astray in confusion, and with no path, but you chose our forefathers..." (lines 10-11). We will encounter the chosen people motif in other texts as well. But here we are told that God caused the other nations to go astray. In other words, they were predestined to go astray, a view that fits well with the sect's predestinarian outlook and with the extreme ethical dualism in which they believed.[51]

The punishment of the Jews for their transgressions is to take place in the presence of the nations according to *Pesher Hosea* (4QpHos^a 2:12-13). The same text lists as a primary transgression the scheduling of feasts "according to the appointed times of the nations" (lines 15-16), i.e., following the wrong calendar. This is most probably a reference to the sect's adoption of a calendar based on solar months and solar years that it believed to be correct, as opposed to the calendar of lunar months adjusted to solar years that was followed by most of the Jewish community.[52]

The Destruction of the "Nations"

The Dead Sea sect expected that the end of days would soon dawn. Their apocalyptic, messianic tendencies led them to develop a body of literature outlining the eschatological battle that would usher in the final age. From the study of the manuscripts of the *Scroll of the War of the Sons of Light against the Sons of Darkness* from Caves 1 and 4 it is clear that varying recensions of these texts existed. This view is further supported by the existence of other related texts on this topic (including one that has been incorrectly and irresponsibly interpreted as describing the execution of a messiah[53]). In fact, it is most likely that the *War Scroll* as a whole was assembled from preexistent sources by a redactor. We can state with certainty that the *War Scroll* was in existence before the Roman conquest of 63 B.C.E.

A very schematized view of the battles that will take place is presented in the *War Scroll* (1QM). The "Sons of Light" are the sectarians who are to emerge victorious in the end of days. The nations are grouped with the "Sons of Dark-

---

51. J. Licht, "An Analysis of the Treatise of the Two Spirits in DSD," in *Aspects of the Dead Sea Scrolls*, ed. C. Rabin and Y. Yadin, 88-100. ScrHier 4 (Jerusalem: Magnes, Hebrew University, 1958).

52. See S. Talmon, "The Calendar Reckoning of the Sect from the Judaean Desert," in Rabin and Yadin, *Aspects of the Dead Sea Scrolls*, 162-99, which must be corrected in light of recent evidence that the prayer texts preserved by the sect presumed lunar months and that the solar and lunar systems were coordinated in some sectarian texts.

53. See Vermes, *JJS* 43 (1992) 85-90; and *BAR* 18/6 (1992) 80-82.

ness," including also those Jews who do not indicate by their behavior that they are predestined to be among the Sons of Light. They are also assigned to the lot of Belial. The place of exile of the sect before this battle is termed "the desert of the peoples (*'amim*)." No remnant of these evil nations is to survive in the end of days (1QM 1:1-7; 14:5, 4QM^a 8-9 3; cf. 4QpHab 4:3-5).

In the author's scheme the peoples are designated by names from the table of nations in Genesis 10 (cf. 1QM 2:10-14). Most prominent of these are Assyria (Seleucid Syria) and the Kittim (Rome), the destruction of which is high on the author's agenda (1QM 1:4-6; 2:9-12; 11:11; 4QM^a 11 ii). The battles are assumed to take place in "all the lands of the nations" (1QM 2:7; cf. 11:12-13). Indeed, as one of their banners testified, the sect expected the "annihilation by God of all nations of vanity" (1QM 4:12).[54] The final battle would exact retribution on these nations for their wickedness (1QM 6:6; cf. 9:8-9) and they would all be killed (1QM 19:10-11).

The text echoes the chosen people motif of the Bible (Deut 7:6; 14:2; 1 Chr 17:21) when it declares, "Who is like unto your people Israel whom you have chosen for yourself from all the nations of the lands, a people of those holy through the covenant?" (1QM 10:9-10; 4QM^e 1). The passage continues to describe this chosenness as indicated by Israel's willingness to receive its revelation and openness to probe the depths of God's commands (lines 10-11). This passage, like other poetic and liturgical sections of the scroll, probably predated its final authorship. Further on, the sectarians themselves are designated "the chosen ones of the holy nation" (12:1).

One particular poem included twice in the scroll seems to be at variance with the assumption of the complete document that all the nations are to be destroyed in the end of days (1QM 12:9-15; 19:2-8; also in 4QM^b 1 2-8). Addressed primarily to God who is asked to crush the nations, his adversaries, the poem turns to the city of Jerusalem and calls on it to "open your gates forever, so that there will be brought in to you the wealth of the nations, and their kings shall serve you . . . and rule over the king[dom of the Kittim]." Certainly, this passage, based almost entirely on Isa 60:10-14, expects the nations, including the Romans, to survive into the messianic era when they will be subservient to Israel. That the nations will continue to exist but under the rule of the Davidic Messiah is expected in *Pesher Isaiah* (4QpIsa^a 7 25).

This idea may also lie behind the expression "to subdue the nations" in the messianic *Rule of the Congregation* (1QSa 1:21). While this expression might

---

54. Translation following Y. Yadin, *The Scroll of the War of the Sons of Light against the Sons of Darkness*, trans. B. and C. Rabin, 277 (Oxford: Oxford University Press, 1962). War Scroll translations below are mine.

mean that the nations will be subservient to Israel, some scholars argue that it is a reference to their destruction. The same idea has been restored in the *Rule of Benedictions* (1QSb 3:18).[55] This approach may be in evidence again in the same text where we are told in a blessing for the Prince of the Congregation that "be[fore you will bow all peoples, and all the nat]ions will serve you" (1QSb 5:28-29).[56]

Certainly, however, the dominant theme of the *War Scroll* is that the nations are predestined to be destroyed in the great war that will usher in the end of days. The sectarians, aided by angelic forces, will defeat and kill all the non-Jews, and even those Jews who do not join the group will be destroyed. In the end of days, the world will be populated only by the members of the sect.

Israel and the Nations in Liturgical Texts

A "Lamentation" asks God "not to give our inheritance to strangers nor our property (or possessions) to foreigners" (4Q501 1). This text betokens an understanding of the coming conquest and destruction by Rome.

The chosen people motif appears again in a fragmentary prayer, most probably for the Festival of Passover, in which God "[w]ho cho[se] us from among [the] nations" (4Q503 24-25 vii 4) is praised.[57] The same is asserted in the noncanonical Psalms (4Q381 76-77 15).[58]

4QDivre ha-Me'orot *(Words of the Luminaries)* is a propitionary-type prayer very much like the Rabbinic *taḥanun* ("supplication") prayers. It appeals to God to remember "your wonders that you did before *(le-'ene)* the nations" (4Q504 1-2 ii 12), appealing to the miracles of biblical times and recalling "that (God) took us out (of Egypt) before all the nations" (4Q504 1-2 v 10). Yet the very same nations are regarded as "[no]thing before you" (4Q504 1-2 iii 3). God has created the Jewish people, made them his children, and called them "My son, My first born" before the nations (lines 4-6).

The chosen people motif is also prominent in this text: "You have loved Israel more than the (other) peoples" (4Q504 1-2 iv 4-5).[59] As a result, "all the

---

55. Barthélemy, DJD 1:124.
56. As restored by J. Licht, *Megillat ha-Serakhim mi-Megillot Midbar Yehudah* (Jerusalem: Bialik Institute, 1965) 289.
57. M. Baillet, *Qumran Grotte 4.III (4Q482-4Q520)*. DJD 7 (Oxford: Clarendon, 1982) 111.
58. E. M. Schuller, *Non-Canonical Psalms from Qumran: A Pseudepigraphic Collection*. HSS 28 (Atlanta: Scholars, 1986) 215.
59. Cf. 4Q504 5 ii 1-2 and the parallels in 4Q505 124 6 and 4Q506 124 1-2.

nations saw your glory in that you were sanctified among your people Israel" (lines 8-9).[60]

This motif also occurs in 4QPrayers for Festivals (4Q508 4 2). In one prayer we hear that "You chose a people . . . You set them aside for yourself as holy (or for sanctity) from all the peoples" by vouchsafing to them visions of the divine and revelation of God's word (1Q34^{bis} 3 ii 5-7 = 4Q509 97-98 7-10).

Proselytes in the Dead Sea Scrolls

Despite the sect's notions of predestination and their view that the nations, the non-Jews, would be destroyed in the end of days, it recognized the institution of proselytism, or religious conversion to Judaism, that apparently existed by this time. Proselytes appear in the *Zadokite Fragments* (CD 14:3-6) in lists of the classes that made up the sect — priests, Levites, Israelites, and proselytes. During the sectarian occupation of Qumran, sectarian officials maintained actual written documents that the sect used for the purposes of its mustering ceremony, and these mentioned proselytes.[61] The *Zadokite Fragments* expect that the proselyte may be in need of economic help (6:21).

The sectarians saw the proselytes as constituting a class within their society of a status different from that of full Israelites. In this respect, they agreed with an approach known to have been held by a minority of Tannaim (*t. Qidd.* 5:1). Accordingly, as mentioned already above, the *Temple Scroll* expected that proselytes would be permitted to enter the temple only in the fourth generation. The author of 4QFlorilegium wanted converts to be excluded from his messianic sanctuary.

We have seen that, in the Qumran documents, slaves who had entered the status that the Tannaim called "the Canaanite slave" were considered involved in a conversion process and, hence, might not be sold to non-Jews. Therefore, there can be no question that there were converts and conversion in the worldview of the sect and probably actually in its ranks.

---

60. A similar idea occurs in 4QVision of Samuel where it states, "that all the peoples of your lands will know [. . .] many [will] understand that your people is [. . . ho]ly that you sanctified (4Q160 3-4 ii 5-7). Cf. the alternate restoration of this column in J. Strugnell, "Notes en marge du volume V des 'Discoveries in the Judaean Desert of Jordan,'" *RevQ* 7 (1970) 180-82.

61. Schiffman, *Halakhah at Qumran*, 66-67.

Conclusion

Although there is a certain animosity to other Jews who did not follow their laws, the distinction between Jews and non-Jews is never blurred in the Dead Sea Scrolls, and the sect's Jewish opponents are never accused of non-Jewish status. The material studied here presents a paradox. On the one hand, we have encountered non-Jews in what may be considered the classic position assigned to them by the Jewish legal system. They are not obligated to observe the laws of, for example, the Sabbath, or other Jewish commandments, yet they are forbidden to worship idols or to blaspheme God. Hence, our texts go out of their way to set forth the laws pertaining to idolaters and idolatry. Some of these laws deal, in reality, with the problems of the impact of pagan religious behavior on Jews. Nonetheless, non-Jews, even if idolaters, are to be protected from depredation and pillage from Jewish armies intent solely on enriching Jewish rulers or their subjects.

On the other hand, we find in some of the sectarian documents an eschatological view that, for the most part, expects that in the end of days the non-Jews, along with Jews who do not accept (or who are predestined not to accept) the way of the sect, will all be destroyed. For the Qumran sect, the eschaton was not to be the universal experience that was expected by the prophet Isaiah; it was to be theirs and theirs alone.

Ultimately, Judaism accepted many aspects of the common Jewish law of the Second Temple period as well as Pharisaic teachings, and these served as the basis for tannaitic halakhah. Many aspects of the Qumran legal tradition share the same presuppositions and rulings that we find in the Pharisaic-rabbinic tradition. Yet at the same time, the Pharisaic-rabbinic worldview accorded much more fully with the words of the prophets of Israel, who saw the coming of the nations to the worship of God, under the leadership of Israel and at its holy mountain, as the true fulfillment of the ideals and aspirations of the messianic future.

LANGUAGE AND LITERATURE

CHAPTER 23

Pseudepigrapha in the Pseudepigrapha: Mythical Books in Second Temple Literature

The purpose of this study is to investigate a phenomenon observable in a variety of Second Temple–period texts, namely reference to, or even quotation of, texts that do not exist. Such references appear in various documents preserved in the Dead Sea Scrolls and the corpus usually termed the Pseudepigrapha.[1] In the study that follows we hope to call attention to and analyze this phenomenon.

We need to say at the outset that such references may theoretically be of two types. There may be references to books that once existed but are lost. The phenomenon of "lost apocrypha" has long been known, and such texts are often quoted in the church fathers. In fact, this assumption underlies the method for giving names to some Qumran texts that are designated by the term "apocryphon." The original editorial team named these texts as if they were in fact dealing with works once known and now recovered.[2] The second possibility, which will constitute the bulk of our discussion, concerns the quotation of pseudepigraphic texts that never existed. Nonetheless, they were mentioned or even quoted as if they were real in preserved apocryphal or pseudepigraphic texts. We might go so far as to term this phenomenon "fictitious pseudepigrapha."[3]

---

1. On the problematics of this term, see J. H. Charlesworth, *OTP,* 1:xxiv-xxv.

2. Often they were guided by M. R. James, *The Lost Apocrypha of the Old Testament: Their Titles and Fragments* (London: Society for Promoting Christian Knowledge and New York: Macmillan, 1936).

3. Cf. L. Jacobs, "Are There Fictitious Baraitot in the Babylonian Talmud?" *HUCA* 42 (1971) 185-96; "How Much of the Babylonian Talmud Is Pseudepigraphic?" *JJS* 28 (1977) 46-59; M. Bregman, "Pseudepigraphy in Rabbinic Literature," in *Pseudepigraphic Perspectives: The*

The phenomenon we are describing is found as well in the biblical corpus. Numerous books that are not extant today are referred to in the Bible.[4] It is certainly true that some of these books may be actual books that were lost in antiquity. They might have been lost for a variety of reasons, most likely because they were overpowered by those books eventually canonized in the Hebrew Bible but also because of the change in the script.[5] This is most likely the case for books like the Chronicles of the Kings of Judah and Israel.[6] It is probable that those books once actually existed since all ancient Near Eastern monarchs kept such chronicles.[7] But other books referred to in the Bible may simply be literary devices, books that never existed, the quotation of which served the needs of the author who cited them. An example may be the Book of the Wars of the Lord.[8] The rabbis saw the Book of Jashar as referring to an existing book of the Bible, as they thought that no separate book with this title had ever really existed.[9]

Finally, a brief word about two subjects not to be included in this paper. The first is that of the heavenly tablets.[10] This motif involves the notion of a preexistent divine revelation not found in the canonical Bible but claimed by the author who mentions it to have been vouchsafed to him, often through the intermediacy of an angel. This subject has been studied by others and will be omitted here. The other subject is that of heavenly books of life and death.[11] These do not relate at all to our subject. This concept, which is also found in rabbinic literature,[12] refers to the fate or destiny of a person in sys-

---

Apocrypha and Pseudepigrapha in Light of the Dead Sea Scrolls: Proceedings of the International Symposium of the Orion Center for the Study of the Dead Sea Scrolls and Associated Literature, 12-14 January, 1997, ed. E. G. Chazon, M. Stone, and A. Pinnick, 27-41. STDJ 31 (Leiden: Brill, 1999).

4. For a listing, see C. F. Craft, "Books Referred to," *IDB* 1:453-54.

5. E. Würthwein, *The Text of the Old Testament*, trans. E. F. Rhodes. 2nd ed. (Grand Rapids: Wm. B. Eerdmans, 1995) 1-4; E. Tov, *Textual Criticism of the Hebrew Bible* (Minneapolis: Fortress, 1992) 217-20.

6. D. L. Christensen, "Chronicles of the Kings (Israel/Judah), Book of the," *ABD* 1:991-92.

7. Many are collected in W. W. Hallo, ed., *The Context of Scripture*, vol. 2: *Monumental Inscriptions from the Biblical World* (Leiden: Brill, 2000).

8. D. L. Christensen, "Wars of the Lord, Book of the," *ABD* 6:880, takes it to be an actual book.

9. B. ʿAbod. Zar. 25a, where Genesis, Deuteronomy, and Judges were suggested. Contrast D. L. Christensen, "Jashar, Book of," *ABD* 3:646-67, who sees it as a real book.

10. See L. Ravid, "The Heavenly Tablets and the Concept of Impurity in the Book of Jubilees" (M.A. thesis, Bar-Ilan University, 1997) [Hebrew]; H. Najman, *Seconding Sinai: The Development of Mosaic Discourse in Second Temple Judaism*. JSJSup 77 (Leiden: Brill, 2003) 60-68 and the bibliography cited in 62-63 n. 55.

11. S. M. Paul, "Book of Life," *EncJud* 4:1217-18.

12. L. I. Rabinowitz, "Book of Life," *EncJud* 4:1218.

tems assuming predestination,[13] or to God's verdict regarding that person's future assuming free will, as is the case in rabbinic Judaism.[14] In any case, such books do not intend to pass down either divine revelation or human ancestral teaching and so are irrelevant to this discussion.

The Textual Tradition

A number of cases of "pseudepigraphal pseudepigrapha" involve the claim that biblical figures passed on their traditions from generation to generation in written form. In some of these examples, the Bible does not even indicate that there existed any tradition, let alone that it was passed down. But to fill gaps in the chain of biblical tradition, and to endow ancestors, especially of the priests, with primeval authority, it is claimed that actual books were passed down. While there is certainly no historical evidence that such books existed in patriarchal or First Temple times, literature claiming to constitute the teachings or testaments of these figures did indeed circulate in the form of pseudepigraphic books in Second Temple times.

The most famous biblical character in this regard is Enoch. *1 Enoch* 13:7, preserved in 4QEn^c 1 vi 2-3,[15] refers to Enoch in the land of Dan, reading a book of the account (probably correctly restored as *sefer dikhron*) of the Watchers' requests — a sort of petition. This takes place soon after the Watchers were expelled from heaven as a result of their sins in having relations with human women and bringing evil into the world. Enoch writes out a petition for forgiveness on their behalf. *1 Enoch* 14:1, partially preserved in 4QEn^c 1 vi 9, refers to the "Book of the Words of Truth and Reprimand" that Enoch apparently sent to the Watchers. The book itself represents a vision that Enoch had received indicating the banishment of the Watchers from heaven.[16]

The Book of Giants (4QEnGiants^a 8 1) begins by alluding to a book

---

13. J. Duhaime, "Determinism," *EDSS* 1:194-98.

14. E. E. Urbach, *The Sages: Their Opinions and Beliefs*, trans. I. Abrahams (Jerusalem: Magnes, Hebrew University, 1987) 255-85.

15. J. T. Milik, *The Books of Enoch: Aramaic Fragments from Qumrân Cave 4* (Oxford: Clarendon, 1976) 193-95.

16. See Milik, *Books of Enoch*, 261-62, on Enoch as a scribe. Cf. *1 En.* 14:7: *min ketava de-'ana katvet* (4QEn^c 1 vi 19; Milik, *Books of Enoch*, 194-95; L. T. Stuckenbruck, *The Book of Giants from Qumran* [Tübingen: Mohr (Siebeck), 1997] 87-93). Here the *ketav* seems to refer to the petition on behalf of the Watchers that, incidentally, was not accepted. It is not a reference to a specific pseudobook.

(sefer). Apparently this is the beginning of a section of the text that describes fictitious writings of Enoch. Indeed, line 3 continues by mentioning a copy *(parshegen)* of the second tablet of the epistle *('igarta')* written by Enoch's own hand *(bi-khetav yad)*. This epistle seems to have been written to Shemiḥazah and his companions.[17] Here Enoch does not petition on behalf of the Watchers but functions only as a scribe so that he does not take the side of the Watchers.

In *1 Enoch* 82, a chapter that is the conclusion of the Book of the Heavenly Luminaries (chs. 72–82), Enoch refers to the books he has written for Methuselah and other writings he is passing down to him (82:1-2). Methuselah is commanded to preserve them and deliver them to posterity. *1 Enoch* 92:1 reflects this same motif in referring to the Epistle of Enoch (92–105) as written by "Enoch the Scribe of distinction and the wisest of men." The text is partly preserved in 4QEn^g 1 ii 22, which refers to "that which Enoch wrote *(ktb)* and gave to Methuselah," his son, and to all his brothers to pass on to future generations.[18] This clearly refers to a book or epistle that was imagined to have been written by Enoch for the purpose of passing down primeval Israelite tradition.

1 Enoch 104:10, in the Epistle of Enoch, tells us that there will be sinners who will write books of evil and deceit. But the words of Enoch will be written down in various languages correctly and accurately. The books will be given to the righteous and the wise, and these books will be a source of joy, goodness, and wisdom. Since this passage occurs near the end of the Epistle of Enoch, it is obviously a reference to this literary unit, not some imagined literary texts. In this way, the Epistle is understood to be the means for passing on Enoch's teachings to future generations.

2 Enoch represents an adaptation of Enoch traditions found in the *1 Enoch* corpus as well as others not included there. Chapter 2 deals specifically with books attributed to Enoch. In *2 En.* 33:9-10, God instructs Enoch to take the books that he has written and to go down to earth. He is told to give the people manuscripts of his works so that mankind will recognize the uniqueness of the God of Israel. These books are supposed to be passed down in manuscript from generation to generation. Version B refers also to writings of Adam and Seth, in which God is shown to be especially concerned that these texts not perish in the upcoming flood.[19]

---

17. See Milik, *Books of Enoch*, 314-15.
18. Milik, *Books of Enoch*, 260-63.
19. See N. Forbes and R. H. Charles, "2 Enoch, or the Book of the Secrets of Enoch," in *The Apocrypha and Pseudepigrapha of the Old Testament in English*, ed. Charles, 2:452, n. to v. 9 (1913; repr. Oxford: Oxford University Press, 1968).

In *2 Enoch* 47, Enoch gives his children his writings, and tells them to read them and follow their wisdom (vv. 1-3). In 48:7-9 he commands them to make them known among their children for all generations. Those who reject these books will incur great punishment. In ch. 54, they are commanded not to keep these books secret.

Jubilees 45:16 speaks of the books of Jacob as well as the books of his forefathers that he gave to Levi to preserve and renew for his children. A very similar idea is found in the *Aramaic Levi Document* (Cairo Genizah MS Cambridge) col. e. Here Levi refers to a *sefer musar ḥokhmah*, "a book of instruction in wisdom," which he commands his family to teach to their posterity (lines 17-18, 23^{20}=4Q213 1 i 9, 12).[21] Apparently this is meant as a book that had been passed down to him, most probably from his father Jacob, bearing the proto-Israelite tradition, which he was now, soon before his death, passing on to his sons.

In *Jub.* 10:14 the same is asserted about Noah, who is said to have given his writings to Shem. Indeed, 1QApGen 5:29 mentions a "book *(ketav)* of the words of Noah."[22] This seems to be an introductory title to a section of the work that purported to be a Book of Noah.[23] Essentially, then, we have a mention here, in a pseudepigraphal book, of an "earlier" imaginary pseudepigraphal book. According to *Jub.* 12:24-26, God taught Abraham Hebrew since it had been forgotten in the aftermath of the flood. Then Abraham took the books of his forefathers, which were in Hebrew, copied them, and started to study them. These works apparently motivated him to leave Haran and to set out for the land of Canaan.

4Q542 *(Testament of Qehat)* frg. 1 col. 2 includes a passage that sets forth a chain of tradition.[24] The narrator is giving a testament-type speech and asking his children to observe the religion of Israel. The narrator is Qehat, the father of Amram, who is mentioned explicitly. He seems to refer to books that have been passed on from him to Amram, whom he addresses, to be passed

---

20. R. H. Charles, *The Greek Versions of the Testaments of the Twelve Patriarchs*, 2nd ed. (Oxford: Clarendon, 1960) 255.

21. M. E. Stone and J. C. Greenfield in G. Brooke et al., *Qumran Cave 4.XVII: Parabiblical Texts, Part 3*. DJD 22 (Oxford: Clarendon, 1996) 9-13. There the text has *sefer u-musar ve-ḥokhmah*.

22. F. García Martínez and E. J. C. Tigchelaar, eds., *The Dead Sea Scrolls Study Edition* (Leiden: Brill and Grand Rapids: Wm. B. Eerdmans, 1997-98) 1:29.

23. F. García Martínez, *Qumran and Apocalyptic: Studies on the Aramaic Texts from Qumran*. STDJ 9 (Leiden: Brill, 1992) 24-44; C. Werman, "Qumran and the Book of Noah," in Chazon, Stone, and Pinnick, *Pseudepigraphic Perspectives*, 171-81.

24. García Martínez and Tigchelaar, *Dead Sea Scrolls Study Edition*, 2:1082-83; É. Puech, "Le Testament de Qahat en araméen de la grotte 4 *(4QTQah)*," *RevQ* 15 (1991) 23-54.

on to his progeny, and these writings *(ketave)* are explicitly stated to have been given by Levi to Qehat. Amram is commanded to take care of them and to pass them on. Frg. 2 refers to reading, apparently referring to the same books.

A close counterpart to this narrative appears in 4Q543 *(Visions of Amram^a)*, the beginning of which is apparently preserved. The text begins by referring to itself as "A copy of the writing of the words of the vision of Amram that he revealed to his sons."[25] Here the term is *parshegen ketav*, "a copy of the text." 4Q545 *(Visions of Amram^c)* starts out with the exact same introduction as does *Amram^a* in frg. 1 col. 1,[26] and they clearly represent the exact same text. In frg. 4 of *Amram^e* (4Q547 9 8) he refers to the fact that he wrote *(ketavet)* the vision,[27] so that we are clearly dealing with a pseudepigraphic writing.

The narrator of 4Q541 *(Apoc of Levi^{b?})* frgs. 1+2 says that someone else will utter words and then, in conformity with God's will, keep something (perhaps a book) and then write another book and a second.[28] This enigmatic passage refers clearly to some biblical figure, perhaps Levi, who will pass on at least two books. Here the term is *ketav*, meaning "text." Frg. 7 of this text mentions a text *(ketav)* and then books of wisdom *(sifre hokhme[ta)* that will be opened containing the words of this figure or of God. The author of these texts seems to be distinct from the narrator, and, if frg. 9 col. 1 is relevant, then this figure appears to be an eschatological one, probably messianic, or may be foretelling the messianic future.[29]

4Q536 *(Book of Noah)* 1 ii 12-13 discusses a figure who will reveal mysteries, presumably in the end of days. The narrative voice then says, "Who will write these, my words, in a book that does not wear out? And my sayings [. . .]?"[30] This speaker is obviously a biblical hero who expects that his words will be written in some pseudepigraphic work and passed down so that, unlike all normal books, this one will not wear out. In this case, the purpose of the books seems to be to provide apocalyptic revelation at the end of days.

An interesting example of levels of pseudepigraphic writing is found in 4Q529 *(Words of Michael)* frg 1.[31] The text purports to be a writing *(ketava)* by

---

25. É. Puech, *Qumrân Grotte 4.XXII: Textes araméens, première partie, 4Q529-549*. DJD 31 (Oxford: Clarendon, 2001) 292-93.
26. Puech, DJD 31:333-35.
27. Puech, DJD 31:388-89.
28. Puech, DJD 31:231-33.
29. Puech, DJD 31:241-45.
30. Puech, DJD 31:167-70.
31. Puech, DJD 31:4-7.

the angel Michael, and it describes how the writer saw Gabriel, in some kind of cosmic journey, and Gabriel himself, in a vision, described to Michael the books of the Great One, the Eternal Master (line 6). The text as a whole is some kind of *ex eventu* prophecy in which events of the end of days are foretold.

Various sources mention assumed historical books, similar in some ways to those referred to in the Bible. 1 Esd 1:33 refers to Books of the Histories of the Kings of Judea where the acts of Josiah can be found. But in fact this is simply a reference to the unknown book mentioned in the Bible, the Books of the Chronicles of the Kings of Judah. The entire passage is parallel to 2 Chr 35:27. The same verse in Esdras refers to the Book of the Kings of Israel and Judah, an exact quotation of the same biblical passage.

In the so-called *Proto-Esther*^{a} text (4Q550 lines 3-5)[32] there is reference to the books of his father *(sifre avohi)*, Darius, being read before the Persian king. This is a reflection of the biblical reference in Esth 6:1 *(sefer ha-zikhronot)* and refers to books of chronicles of his father's reign. These were apparently routinely and officially kept court chronicles. But of course the books quoted in *Proto-Esther*^{a} were not real. We read in *Proto-Esther*^{a} that a scroll *(megillah)*, presumably the court chronicles, was opened and read before the king, and the text, in turn, quotes a passage supposedly found in this fake pseudepigraphon. In 4Q550c *(Proto-Esther*^{d}*)* 3:3-5, in a difficult fragmentary passage, there is reference to the command of the king to Bagasro to write apparently historical data; then some plural group is commanded to read from this text *(ketava)*.[33]

Orality, Books, and the Transmission of Tradition

The presence of so many pseudepigraphal allusions to fictitious books in a relatively limited corpus of early Jewish literature needs to be explained. Before going further, we should call attention to the fact that the examples that we have discussed here are primarily concentrated in a group of texts composed in Aramaic during a specific period of Jewish history, in the fourth through second centuries B.C.E., when Aramaic was dominant. Aramaic literature flourished until the onset of the Maccabean era, when Jewish writers again returned to Hebrew as a sign of incipient nationalist feeling. For this reason, virtually the entire rest of the literature found at Qumran was com-

---

32. García Martínez and Tigchelaar, *Dead Sea Scrolls Study Edition*, 2:1090-97.
33. García Martínez and Tigchelaar, *Dead Sea Scrolls Study Edition*, 2:1100-1.

posed in Hebrew. Several studies have already noted that the Aramaic literature we are discussing, most of it pseudepigraphal works regarding specific heroes of the book of Genesis, constitutes a distinctive stage in the evolution of Jewish literature and a distinctive genre within the so-called apocrypha and pseudepigrapha.[34]

In all the texts we have discussed, the function of the books in question has been to provide accurate transmission of the traditions of ancient Israel through the generations of the pre-Sinaitic period. According to all these works, pre-Sinaitic traditions were passed on in the form of such books from generation to generation until they finally reached the entire Jewish people even before the giving of the Torah at Sinai. In order to properly understand the significance of this notion, we have to consider what the alternative would have been. The only alternative form of transmission of tradition known to the Jewish people in antiquity was, of course, oral transmission. Indeed, it was the view of the later Pharisaic-rabbinic sages that oral tradition did, in fact, exist this early. This explanation, in the view of the sages, accounted for the patriarchal observance of many prescriptions of the still-to-be-given Written Torah even before the revelation at Sinai. The rabbis even assumed that many aspects of the Oral Torah, understood by them to have also been revealed at Sinai, were already known to the patriarchs.[35] Some rabbinic traditions even attributed observance of the Written or Oral Torah to biblical figures who lived before Abraham.

The Pharisaic-rabbinic system, as can readily be seen, is dependent on the assumption that oral tradition has a central role in the historical development of Judaism. Yet it is clear from the study of the legal materials preserved in the Dead Sea corpus that, alongside the notion of oral transmission of the Pharisaic-rabbinic tradition, there was a second trend. This trend, the Saducean/Zadokite one, rejected oral tradition and the dual Torah concept of tannaitic literature.[36]

---

34. Cf. B. Z. Wacholder, "The Ancient Judeo-Aramaic Literature (500-165 BCE): A Classification of Pre-Qumranic Texts," in *Archaeology and History in the Dead Sea Scrolls: The New York University Conference in Memory of Yigael Yadin*, ed. L. H. Schiffman, 257-81. JSOTSup 8. JSOT/ASOR Monographs 2 (Sheffield: JSOT, 1990); D. Dimant, "Apocalyptic Texts at Qumran," in *The Community of the Renewed Covenant: The Notre Dame Symposium on the Dead Sea Scrolls*, ed. E. Ulrich and J. VanderKam, 175-91. CJAS 10 (Notre Dame: University of Notre Dame Press, 1994).

35. *M. Qidd.* 4:14 (end). Cf. C. Albeck, *Shishah Sidre Mishnah* (Jerusalem: Bialik Institute and Tel Aviv: Dvir, 1954) *Seder Nashim*, 3:416.

36. Cf. L. H. Schiffman, *Reclaiming the Dead Sea Scrolls: The History of Judaism, the Background of Christianity, the Lost Library of Qumran* (Philadelphia: Jewish Publication Society, 1994; repr. ABRL [New York: Doubleday, 1995]) 245-55.

Pseudepigrapha in the Pseudepigrapha

Moreover, this distinction regarding the role of oral tradition applies not only to matters of halakhah, but also to what the rabbis termed aggadah, the legends and teachings that make up much of midrashic literature. Just as the Pharisaic/rabbinic and the Sadducean/Zadokite approaches diverge regarding legal materials and their origins and source of authority, they also diverge regarding so-called aggadic materials. Such a distinction helps to explain the phenomenon that we have observed. The pseudepigraphal texts that we have examined allow no role for oral tradition or transmission. Hence, in order to place the later biblical tradition, from the patriarchs and Sinai on, squarely within the context of a tradition reaching all the way back to the beginning of Genesis, the only possible mechanism was to understand the tradition as having been passed down in a series of books described in the works we have studied but that, in fact, never existed in ancient times.[37]

This does not mean that none of the books ever existed. Although some of the books referred to, even cited or quoted in our texts, were a result of the interpretive imagination of the authors or their sources, some of the books mentioned, or at least books by the same names, in fact existed in Second Temple times. This is the case, for example, with literary allusions to books of Enoch and Noah referred to in our texts. But, of course, those texts preserved for us are not the ones alluded to in Second Temple literature. It was the fertile imagination of our authors that furnished those books that are alluded to or quoted in the Aramaic pseudepigrapha we have been studying. They attempted to pass off their own works as the words of ancient biblical heroes and had no hesitation in describing the contents of a work supposedly written by those heroes and passed on by them to posterity.[38]

The invention of pseudepigrapha within pseudepigraphal works did not actually die out in Second Temple times. It somehow reemerged in the great Jewish mystical work the Zohar. This work, and various other medieval mystical tracts, assumed the existence of ancient Jewish pseudepigraphal works that were no longer available. Accordingly, several such books, as well as quotations from them and allusions to them, are invented by the author in order to invest some of his teachings with the hoary antiquity and authority that these biblical figures had held for the authors of our Second Temple pseudepigraphal works. The Zohar alludes to the books of Adam[39] and

---

37. A similar notion traces a series of covenants with these early figures in Qumran literature. Cf. "The Concept of Covenant in the Qumran Scrolls and Rabbinic Literature," Chapter 14 above, and M. E. Stone, "The Axis of History at Qumran," in Chazon, Stone, and Pinnick, *Pseudepigraphic Perspectives*, 133-49.

38. Cf. Najman, *Seconding Sinai*, 4-6.

39. Zohar I, 37b; II, 70a.

Enoch[40] that are understood to teach ancient esoteric traditions. Yet the Zohar, at least in those parts that are attributed to the Tanna Simeon bar Yohai, is itself pseudepigraphal. After studying the material discussed here, we should not be surprised at all to see a pseudepigraphal work quoting other pseudepigraphic works that in fact had never existed.[41]

Both pseudepigraphal tradition and the later rabbinic aggadah attributed great antiquity to traditions only later revealed. In the case of the Pharisaic-rabbinic tradition, it was held that such traditions had been passed down orally in the patriarchal period, until they were eventually made part and parcel of the heritage of the biblical people of Israel and the later Jewish tradition. For those who composed the pseudepigraphal books that we have been discussing, an alternative system that typified the Sadducean/Zadokite approach to Judaism was used, based on the tradition of written composition and transmission of all extrabiblical traditions. A long list of putative books of biblical wisdom, which of course had never existed, was created to fill a gap that could only be bridged for the authors with the transmission of authoritative written tradition.

Had these books ever, in fact, existed we should hope that they would have been preserved according to the instructions given in the *Assumption of Moses* (*As. Mos.* 1:15-18). At the end of ch. 1, Moses, referring to the Torah, instructs Joshua as follows: "And now I warn you that . . . I am about to pass on to sleep with my fathers. . . . So study this writing carefully, so that you may know how to preserve the books that I entrust with you. Set them in order and anoint them with cedar-oil and store them away in jars of earthenware in the place the Lord intended. . . ."[42] We should not be surprised that these pseudepigrapha in the pseudepigrapha never made it into the earthenware jars. After all, this rich pseudolibrary, unlike the collection that was preserved at Qumran, never existed.

---

40. Zohar I, 13a, 37b, 55b; II, 277a; Tiqqune Zohar 70, 136a.

41. Cf. the use of chains of tradition patterned on *m. Abot* 1:1 in early Jewish mystical and magical literature as described in M. D. Swartz, *Scholastic Magic: Ritual and Revelation in Early Jewish Mysticism* (Princeton: Princeton University Press, 1996) 178-99.

42. R. H. Charles, trans., rev. by J. P. M. Sweet, "The Assumption of Moses," *AOT,* 607.

CHAPTER 24

Second Temple Literature and the Cairo Genizah

It is usual to see the discovery of the Cairo Genizah in the context of the history of Judaic Studies in the nineteenth century. Such an approach places the Genizah within the history of the *Wissenschaft des Judentums,* showing how the Genizah materials provided a treasure trove of manuscripts upon which the new, recently-developed methods of academic study could be put to thorough use.[1] This approach is certainly valid for providing an understanding of the historical significance of most of the materials found in the Genizah. Yet a different approach must be taken to the medieval copies of Second Temple texts found among the manuscripts of the Genizah. In this case, we are dealing with the recovery of texts from Jewish and Christian Late Antiquity, a process that has been going on from the Renaissance up to our own day. There can be no question that much of the agenda of this recovery lay, not in issues pertaining to the history of the Jews and Judaism, but, rather, in the long-standing quest for the recovery of what was termed Christian origins. Nonetheless, the significance of the Genizah for the study of the history of Judaism in Late Antiquity has been immense.

Much of Second Temple literature was lost to the Jewish people and its traditional scholars already in antiquity. For example, the books of the Apocrypha and Pseudepigrapha, that is, a large number of books that originated in the Second Temple period, were known at best only obliquely to Jews in Late Antiquity and the Middle Ages. The work of Philo can be said to have been al-

---

1. See S. C. Reif, *A Jewish Archive from Old Cairo: The History of Cambridge University's Genizah Collection* (Richmond, Surrey: Curzon, 2000), which provides a detailed history of the field from the vantage point of the role of Cambridge.

most completely lost,[2] but that of Josephus, in the form of Yossipon, an abbreviated but reworked version of a Latin translation, did reenter the Jewish tradition in medieval times although it had limited effect on Jewish historical consciousness.[3] While some apocryphal traditions certainly influenced medieval Jewish texts, Jews did not have direct access to this literature in the talmudic period and the Middle Ages.[4]

It was the Renaissance that brought these texts back to the Jewish people, albeit to a small number of dedicated scholars who sought to use this material to understand properly that little understood period that formed the bridge between the Hebrew Bible and the Mishnah.[5] At the same time, Christian scholars, as a result of the general attraction of the study of antiquity stimulated by the Renaissance, turned simultaneously to the study of Hebrew and Jewish texts and to the historical background of Christianity. Indeed, for Christian Europe one might say that the very notion of antiquity, let alone its study, was a creation of Renaissance Italy.

For the study of Judaism, the Renaissance greatly widened the available corpus of literature so that it now included the Greek and Latin texts of the Apocrypha and the works of Philo and Josephus. Even the New Testament began to play a role in the reconstruction of Jewish history.

For Christian students of Jewish Late Antiquity, who sought to understand the background of Christianity in Second Temple Judaism, the next significant developments took place after the Reformation, to a great extent in an England then virtually devoid of Jews. Here Hebraism was married to the search for Christian origins, and the result was an investigation of rabbinic literature intended to shed light on the Jewish practices and beliefs that lay behind the documents of the New Testament. It was an activity and interest that created the background for the gathering in England of the great collections of Hebrew manuscripts that play so significant a part in our research to-

2. For a possible reflection of Philo in the guise of "Judah the Alexandrian," cf. Y. Yadin, *The Temple Scroll* (Jerusalem: Israel Exploration Society and Shrine of the Book, 1983) 1:119-22.

3. D. Flusser, *Sefer Yosifon* (Jerusalem: Bialik Institute, 1980) 2:3-120.

4. Christians also had but indirect access to many of these texts. See M. R. James, *The Lost Apocrypha of the Old Testament: Their Titles and Fragments* (London: Society for Promoting Christian Knowledge and New York: Macmillan, 1936), which was used by the early Qumran editors to indicate what lost books might be found among the scrolls. The problem of the indirect survival of this heritage into the medieval period is addressed in a collection of essays: J. C. Reeves, ed., *Tracing the Threads: Studies in the Vitality of Jewish Pseudepigrapha*. SBLEJL 6 (Atlanta: Scholars, 1994). This volume indicates that the effects of this literature were considerable, even if the texts themselves did not circulate.

5. Cf. C. Roth, *The Jews in the Renaissance* (Philadelphia: Jewish Publication Society of America, 1959) 310-11.

day.⁶ Much later, long after the return of Jews to Britain, this interest would lie at the basis of the appointment of Solomon Schechter to the faculty of Cambridge University.⁷

In the interim, other developments would further widen the corpus of known Second Temple literature, even before the discovery of the Genizah. In the seventeenth and eighteenth centuries, Christian scholars scoured the literature — indeed, the unpublished manuscripts — of a variety of Eastern Christian churches that were in possession of various Second Temple–era documents. These were sometimes preserved in secondary translations of their original languages in far-flung places. For example, from Ethiopic came *Jubilees* and *1 Enoch*, two works also known in partial Greek translations that must lie at the base of the Ethiopic. As a result of these developments, when in the latter part of the nineteenth century the Hebrew manuscripts of the Cairo Genizah began to make their way to various European collectors and libraries,⁸ the discovery in them of remnants of some Second Temple texts was part of the continuing process of the recovery of the literature of this period. This process would reach its climax with the discovery of the Dead Sea Scrolls and other Judean Desert texts from 1947 on.⁹ It should be no surprise, therefore, that just as the Qumran scrolls would later be seen from the point of view of their significance to the history of Christianity,¹⁰ the same would be the case with the Second Temple texts discovered in the Cairo Genizah. However, for scholars of Second Temple Judaism, the discovery of these important Genizah texts, some of which parallel the Dead Sea Scrolls, opened up a valuable window on Judaism in the Hellenistic age. Let us now turn to those texts that were recovered in the Genizah and are known to date to Second Temple times, Ben Sira, the *Zadokite Fragments (Damascus Document)*, and the *Testament of Levi* (now called *Aramaic Levi Document*).

---

6. Reif, *Jewish Archive*, 27-31.

7. On Schechter, see Reif, *Jewish Archive*, 47-54.

8. S. D. Goitein, *A Mediterranean Society* (Berkeley: University of California Press, 1967) 1:1-28; S. C. Reif, *A Guide to the Taylor-Schechter Genizah Collection* (Cambridge: Cambridge University Library, 1973); idem, *Jewish Archive*, 70-72.

9. L. H. Schiffman, *Reclaiming the Dead Sea Scrolls: The History of Judaism, the Background of Christianity, the Lost Library of Qumran* (Philadelphia: Jewish Publication Society, 1994; repr. ABRL [New York: Doubleday, 1995]) 3-16.

10. L. H. Schiffman, "Confessionalism and the Study of the Dead Sea Scrolls," *JS* 31 (1991) 3-14.

Ben Sira

Of all the works of Second Temple literature, Ben Sira, also known as Ecclesiasticus, is unique in its transmission history. This is the only noncanonical work of the Greco-Roman period to be quoted in rabbinic literature.[11] Parts of Ben Sira, both in the original Hebrew and in an Aramaic translation, are cited in the Babylonian and Palestinian Talmuds as well as in a variety of midrashic texts. (The rabbis also quoted other aphorisms in the name of Ben Sira that are not found in the book.[12]) The dissemination of the book of Ben Sira in the Middle Ages, or at least knowledge about its having existed, was sufficiently widespread as to create an entire secondary apocryphal literature based on this apocryphal text, a sort of apocryphal apocrypha.[13]

This text was preserved in Greek as part of the Alexandrian Jewish canon of Scripture translated under the general title of Septuagint. In addition, a Syriac text exists that all scholars see as translated directly from the Hebrew, although based on a somewhat corrupt textual version of the Hebrew. Nonetheless, it is valuable for exegetical purposes and even, to some extent, for textual criticism.[14] Ben Sira was composed ca. 180 B.C.E. in Hebrew and was translated into Greek by the grandson of the author in about 130 B.C.E. In essence, Ben Sira is a wisdom book that continues the biblical wisdom tradition in pre-Maccabean times.[15]

Previous to the discovery of the Cairo Genizah, it was known that Ben Sira had originally been composed in Hebrew for it was stated directly by his grandson in the prologue to his Greek translation. Further, the Hebrew text of this book was known to Jerome (342-420 C.E.).[16] Beginning in 1896, Schechter began to analyze fragments from the Genizah. He identified part of the Hebrew text of Ben Sira, but immediately there ensued a debate about whether the Genizah fragments of this book were retranslations from the Greek or other ancient versions or texts of the original Hebrew.[17] The

---

11. M. Z. Segal, *Sefer Ben Sira ha-Shalem,* 2nd ed. (Jerusalem: Bialik Institute, 1971/2) 37-40.

12. Segal, *Sefer Ben Sira ha-Shalem,* 40-41.

13. E. Yasif, *Sippure Ben Sira bi-Yeme ha-Benayim* (Jerusalem: Magnes, Hebrew University, 1984).

14. E. Schürer, *The History of the Jewish People in the Age of Jesus Christ (175 B.C.-A.D. 135),* rev. ed. by G. Vermes, F. Millar, with P. Vermes and M. Black (Edinburgh: T. & T. Clark, 1987) 3/1:205-6; Segal, *Sefer Ben Sira ha-Shalem,* 53-63.

15. Schürer, *History of the Jewish People,* 3/1:198-202.

16. Schürer, *History of the Jewish People,* 3/1:202-3.

17. Reif, *Jewish Archive,* 72-78.

discoveries in the Judean Desert settled this question once and for all, but some fifty years later.

Even before 1947, several manuscripts of the Hebrew Ben Sira had been recovered from the Genizah. Schechter's original fragments were followed by various others between 1897 and 1931. Additional material continued to come to light even after the discovery of the scrolls. Parts of five Genizah manuscripts have been recovered, and these manuscripts do indeed cover much of the book.[18]

Those scholars who argued for the originality, or better, authenticity, of the Genizah texts were indeed vindicated by the presence of this text at Qumran and Masada. The Academy for the Hebrew Language edition of Ben Sira lists three Judean Desert manuscripts: 2Q18, *Psalms Scroll* from Cave 11, and Ben Sira from Masada.

2Q18 is an extremely fragmentary text, dating to the second half of the first century B.C.E., that has been ingeniously restored by Maurice Baillet.[19] Baillet based his restoration on Genizah MS B, and, indeed, his fragment seems to have fit that text well, providing a Hebrew text from the pre-Christian era for Sir 6:14-15, 20-31. With publication of this fragment in 1962 there could no longer be any question of the authenticity of the Hebrew manuscripts of Ben Sira from the Genizah.[20]

Further evidence for Ben Sira from the Qumran scrolls came within a larger scroll known as the Cave 11 *Psalms Scroll* (11QPs^a). Before turning to the Ben Sira material within this scroll, we must explain the controversy that surrounded this document since its publication by James A. Sanders in 1965.[21] The text has been dated to the first half of the first century C.E.[22] Because this manuscript contains, sometimes in different order, Psalms from the end of the book, certain previously-known apocryphal Psalms, and some additional hymns,[23] it has been characterized as a prayer collection for liturgical purposes.[24] Sanders,

---

18. On the rediscovery of the Hebrew manuscripts and for a basic description, see Segal, *Sefer Ben Sira ha-Shalem*, 47-53. Segal provides editions of these manuscripts along with his own translations throughout his book. For the text of these fragments, see *Sefer Ben Sira: Ha-Maqor, Qanqordansiah, ve-Nittuah ha-Millim* (Jerusalem: Academy of the Hebrew Language and Shrine of the Book, 1973); Schürer, *History of the Jewish People*, 3/1:203, n. 14, 209.

19. M. Baillet, "Ecclésiastique (Texte hébreu; Fl. XV)," in *Les 'Petites Grottes' de Qumrân*, ed. Baillet, J. T. Milik, R. de Vaux. DJD 3 (Oxford: Clarendon, 1962) 75-77.

20. Schürer, *History of the Jewish People*, 3/1:203-5.

21. J. A. Sanders, *The Psalms Scroll of Qumran Cave 11 (11QPs^a)*. DJD 4 (Oxford: Clarendon, 1965). Cf. *The Dead Sea Psalms Scroll* (Ithaca: Cornell University Press, 1967).

22. Sanders, DJD 4:9.

23. Sanders, DJD 4:53-93; *Psalms Scroll*, 93-138.

24. S. Talmon, "Mizmorim Hisoniyim bi-Leshon ha-'Ivrit mi-Qumran," *Tarbiz* 35 (1965/

followed by other scholars, has seen this text as evidence that the canonical book of Psalms had not yet been closed when this manuscript was written. Other Qumran Psalms manuscripts show evidence of both expanded collections of this type as well as collections containing only masoretic Psalms.²⁵ Within this expanded *Psalms Scroll*, whatever its purpose, there is found an excerpt from Ben Sira.²⁶

Columns 21 and 22 of the scroll contain a Hebrew text of Sir 51:13-19, 30. In its complete form in antiquity, the manuscript must have included this entire passage, 51:13-30. The missing text is the result of the decomposition of the bottom of the scroll. The most significant results of the publication of this Ben Sira text relate not to the Hebrew text recovered but rather to what it teaches us about the Greek translation. This passage is clearly erotic in its imagery, describing the acquisition of wisdom in sexual terms. The translator has provided us a sanitized version, however, from which no one would ever know the literal meaning of the expressions used by the author of the Hebrew text. Here again parallels were found with Genizah MS B. Since the Qumran text is sufficiently extensive, detailed comparison is possible and, in fact, reveals considerable variation.

Before leaving the discussion of the *Psalms Scroll*, we should note that immediately before the Ben Sira passage, Genizah MS B includes a passage not known from any of the ancient versions nor from the few ancient manuscripts in our possession. In the Genizah version, immediately before our passage, there appears a poem structured on a pattern similar to that of Psalm 136, each verse of which ends, כי לעולם חסדו "for his mercy endures forever." This poem is not found in the Greek or Syriac versions. A few phrases in this poem parallel some of the ends of the benedictions of the weekday Amidah. Some have therefore seen this poem as an early liturgical text dating to Second Temple times. It has been suggested that because this text fell into disuse as part of the liturgy, it was deleted from both the Greek and Syriac versions.²⁷ This explanation seems far-fetched, especially in light of its being an imitation of the biblical Psalm 136 that found its way into the rabbinic liturgy. Accordingly, it is best to see this poem, preserved only in the medieval Genizah manuscript, as a late addition, not part of the ancient text.

The crowning glory of the recovery of the original Hebrew of Ben Sira

---

66) 214-34; M. Goshen-Gottstein, "The *Psalms Scroll* (11QPsᵃ): A Problem of Canon and Text," *Textus* 5 (1966) 22-33.

25. P. W. Flint, *The Dead Sea Psalms Scrolls and the Book of Psalms*. STDJ 17 (Leiden: Brill, 1997) 31-49, 155-71, 204-27.

26. Sir 51:13-30; 11QPsᵃ 21:11–22:1.

27. Segal, *Sefer Ben Sira ha-Shalem*, 355-56.

was the finding at Masada of the *Ben Sira Scroll*.[28] In this case, the complete scroll in antiquity would have contained the entire book of Ben Sira. As presently preserved, the scroll includes Sir 39:27–43:30. At last, with the publication of this text in 1965 (on the occasion of the opening of the Shrine of the Book of the Israel Museum), a sustained exemplar of the ancient text of Ben Sira is now available. This manuscript dates to the first half of the first century B.C.E., most probably between 100 and 75 B.C.E.

For most of the Masada manuscript, parallel text has been preserved also in MS B from the Genizah. Here we are truly able to compare the readings of the two texts in order to determine the relationship between the ancient and medieval manuscripts. Despite some simplistic portrayals claiming complete agreement, which may represent modern Hebrew triumphalism as much as scholarly judgment, there are considerable differences between the readings preserved in the Masada text and those of both the main text and marginal glosses in MS B. Nonetheless, the similarities are great enough to allow us to conclude that the medieval manuscript is ultimately derived from the same text as preserved in the Masada scroll. Nevertheless, the medieval manuscripts do indeed show evidence of considerable later textual development. This should not surprise us since the existence of this text in several Genizah manuscripts, as well as its function as the basis for a variety of "apocryphal" medieval texts, indicate that it was in use among medieval Jews. For this reason, the suggestion that this text came into medieval Jewish hands as a result of the finding of biblical manuscripts near Jericho[29] must be rejected. Further, use of this text in rabbinic literature leads us to expect its circulation and transmission among Jews in Late Antiquity and the early Middle Ages.

MS B includes extensive marginal notes. It can be determined that the text and margin of this manuscript represent two separate recensions of the Hebrew Ben Sira that diverged from one another at some date before the copying of the various Genizah manuscripts. This picture fits with our view of the continued transmission of the Hebrew Ben Sira in the Middle Ages. We should also note that the Masada scroll of Ben Sira often agrees with the marginal readings of MS B, the readings of which tend to agree with the Hebrew text used by the Greek translator.

The finding of manuscripts of Ben Sira in the Cairo Genizah was the

---

28. Y. Yadin, *The Ben Sira Scroll from Masada* (Jerusalem: Israel Exploration Society and Shrine of the Book, 1965). The text has been reprinted in *Masada VI, Yigael Yadin Excavations 1963-1965, Final Reports*, ed. S. Talmon, with C. Newsom and Y. Yadin (Jerusalem: Israel Exploration Society, 1999) 151-252; see E. Qimron, "Notes on the Reading," in *Masada VI*, 227-31. A bibliography compiled by F. García Martínez has also been included.

29. Schürer, *History of the Jewish People*, 3/1:205-6.

beginning of the recovery of the original Hebrew of this text, a process that culminated with the discovery of the Ben Sira manuscripts from Qumran and Masada. However, comparison of these manuscripts indicates that Ben Sira had a complex textual history in rabbinic and medieval times that has yet to be fully analyzed or appreciated. This complex history itself is evidence of the continuing lure of the wisdom of this great teacher whose words had been prohibited — at least for public reading — by the very same sages who quoted them[30] and admiringly used them to support their teachings.

The Zadokite Fragments

Of the Second Temple texts found in the Cairo Genizah, there can be no question that the most significant document for the history of Judaism is that known as the *Zadokite Fragments* or *Damascus Document*.[31] This text was found in two manuscripts, each partially preserved, among the texts brought to Cambridge from Cairo by Solomon Schechter.[32] Schechter dated the manuscripts to the tenth and eleventh-twelfth centuries respectively,[33] but did not notice that MS B must be seen as an expanded version or recension of MS A for those sections of the text preserved in both manuscripts.[34] It was this text that, in the hands of Schechter,[35] and later Louis Ginzberg,[36] made possible the understanding of much of the life and teachings of the Dead Sea sect.[37]

This document, as preserved in the two partial medieval copies, was understood to contain two sections. The first is an admonition, setting forth the basic self-image, history, and ideology of what appeared to be a previously

---

30. Segal, *Sefer Ben Sira*, 45-46.

31. S. Schechter, *Documents of Jewish Sectaries*, vol. 1: *Fragments of a Zadokite Work* (1910; repr. Library of Biblical Studies. New York: Ktav, 1970).

32. See S. C. Reif, "The Damascus Document from the Cairo Genizah: Its Discovery, Early Study and Historical Significance," in *The Damascus Document: A Centennial of Discovery: Proceedings of the Third International Symposium of the Orion Center for the Study of the Dead Sea Scrolls and Associated Literature, 4-8 February 1998*, ed. J. M. Baumgarten, E. G. Chazon, and A. Pinnick, 109-31. STDJ 34 (Leiden: Brill, 2000); *Jewish Archive*, 113-15.

33. Schechter, *Documents of Jewish Sectaries*, 1:ix-x.

34. Schechter, *Documents of Jewish Sectaries*, 1:x; S. A. White (Crawford), "A Comparison of the 'A' and 'B' Manuscripts of the Damascus Document," *RevQ* 12 (1987) 537-53.

35. Schechter, *Documents of Jewish Sectaries*, 1:xii-xxix.

36. L. Ginzberg, *Eine unbekannte jüdische Sekte* (New York: L. Ginzberg, 1922); *An Unknown Jewish Sect* (New York: Jewish Theological Seminary of America, 1976).

37. J. A. Fitzmyer, "Prolegomenon," in Schechter, *Documents of Jewish Sectaries*, 1:9-20.

"unknown Jewish sect," to borrow a term from Ginzberg. The second section is a series of laws on topics known from biblical and later Jewish law, for example, laws of the Sabbath, civil law, purity and impurity. These laws in many cases agreed with those of later rabbinic law, but in cases of disagreement they were often more stringent.

The discovery of this document immediately raised two major issues. First, and we may say foremost as well, was the fundamental question usually expressed by the phrase, "Who wrote the scrolls?" Indeed, the discovery of these manuscripts led to suggested provenance of every possible kind: Pharisees, Sadducees, Essenes, Samaritans, Christians, and Karaites.[38] Each of these views was later to be put forward again after the discovery of the Dead Sea Scrolls. Schechter saw the authors as members of the Dosithean sect of Samaritans, a small group known through later Samaritan literature.[39] Ginzberg, however, argued for Pharisaic identification because of shared halakhic rulings.[40]

The second debate concerned the question of how, if Schechter and Ginzberg were right that the text was ancient, these manuscripts describing a Second Temple–period Jewish sect could have found their way into the medieval treasure trove we call the Cairo Genizah. Reading various sources referring to the predecessors of the Karaite movement, some saw this material as the result of a living tradition that extended from ancient sectarian circles to medieval Karaism and thence to the Cairo Genizah.[41] Others pointed to reports of premodern discoveries of Hebrew manuscripts in the Judean Desert and suggested that such texts as the *Zadokite Fragments* and Ben Sira were among those discovered.[42] These references, and certain parallels in content and terminology, had led some scholars, mistakenly as we now know as a result of the carbon 14 dating of the Dead Sea Scrolls, to identify the authors of these texts as Karaites.[43]

The discovery of the Dead Sea Scrolls changed this situation in various ways. When the initial discovery of the scrolls became known to Eleazar Sukenik,[44] he immediately suggested that the new documents were to be re-

---

38. L. H. Schiffman, *The Halakhah at Qumran* (Leiden: Brill, 1975) 1-2.
39. Schechter, *Documents of Jewish Sectaries*, 1:xxi-xxv.
40. Ginzberg, *An Unknown Jewish Sect*, 124-30.
41. N. Wieder, *The Judean Scrolls and Karaism* (London: East and West Library, 1962) 254-55.
42. P. E. Kahle, *The Cairo Geniza*, 2nd ed. (Oxford: Blackwell, 1959) 13-28.
43. Cf. e.g., S. Zeitlin, "History, Historians and the Dead Sea Scrolls," *JQR* n.s. 55 (1964/65) 97-116.
44. On Sukenik and the scrolls, see N. A. Silberman, *A Prophet from Amongst You: The*

lated to the *Zadokite Fragments*.[45] This meant that future analysis of the newly-found scrolls, because of common features of language and content, would be based on the assumption that these texts all belonged to the same sect. Since we now see CD as referring to the scattered sectaries who lived throughout the land and some other texts, like 1QS, as referring to life in the sectarian center at Qumran, this point of view has been refined only to some extent. Still it remains a pillar of scholarship on the Dead Sea Scrolls.

The second proposal, also put forward by Sukenik, was that the sectarian group featured in both the Genizah texts of the *Zadokite Fragments* and the new Dead Sea Scrolls should be identified with the Essenes described by the classical authors.[46] This remained the dominant theory of sectarian identification in present-day scholarship, despite a variety of challenges.[47]

Our understanding of this document, however, changed appreciably with the discovery of fragmentary manuscripts of this text in the caves of Qumran in the early 1950s. Yet it would be a long time until the contents of these manuscripts would be in the hands of wide circles of scholars. Evidence for this text now available to us comes from several caves. Two manuscripts, 5Q12 and 6Q15, were published in 1962.[48] The remaining manuscripts, all from Cave 4, appeared only in 1996 after the complete reorganization of the Dead Sea Scrolls publication program.[49] Cave 4 yielded eight fragmentary manuscripts, bringing the total of Qumran copies of this work to ten, certainly enough to lead us to believe that this was a popular work among the sectarians.

Even before the publication of these texts, progress had taken place in interpreting the Genizah material, specifically regarding its halakhah.[50] Fur-

---

Life of Yigael Yadin, Soldier, Scholar and Mythmaker of Modern Israel (Reading, MA: Addison-Wesley, 1993) 89-100.

45. E. L. Sukenik, *Megillot Genuzot mi-tokh Genizah Qedumah she-Nimṣe'ah be-Midbar Yehudah* (Jerusalem: Bialik Institute, 1948-1950) 2:21.

46. Sukenik, *Megillot Genuzot*, 1:16.

47. F. M. Cross, *The Ancient Library of Qumran*, 3rd ed. (Sheffield: Sheffield Academic, 1995) 54-87; J. C. VanderKam, *The Dead Sea Scrolls Today* (Grand Rapids: Wm. B. Eerdmans, 1994) 71-98.

48. DJD 3:128-31, 181; J. H. Charlesworth, ed., *The Dead Sea Scrolls: Hebrew, Aramaic, and Greek Texts with English Translations* (Tübingen: Mohr [Siebeck] and Louisville: Westminster John Knox, 1995) 2:59-79.

49. J. M. Baumgarten, *Qumran Cave 4.XIII: The Damascus Document (4Q266-273)*. DJD 18 (Oxford: Clarendon, 1996).

50. Ginzberg, *An Unknown Jewish Sect*, 105-54; C. Rabin, *Qumran Studies*. Scripta Judaica 2 (Oxford: Oxford University Press, 1957) 82-111; L. H. Schiffman, *Halakhah at Qumran*. SJLA 16 (Leiden: Brill, 1975); *Sectarian Law in the Dead Sea Scrolls: Courts, Testimony and the Penal Code*. BJS 33 (Chico: Scholars, 1983).

ther, the suggestion had been widely accepted that whereas the *Rule of the Community,* found in an almost complete manuscript[51] and in several fragmentary copies in the Qumran scrolls,[52] set down rules for the central sectarian community, the *Zadokite Fragments* legislated for the so-called camps, the far-flung settlements of sectarians throughout the land of Israel.

The true scope of the work as a whole became known only with the publication, first in bootleg form and later in the official edition, of the fragments from Cave 4. Already in 1954 Chaim Rabin had written to Yigael Yadin of the importance of these fragments. J. T. Milik had given some description of these texts and of the nature of the document as a whole.[53] When the documents were finally published by Joseph M. Baumgarten in 1996, what we found out was that this was truly a book of laws on a variety of topics of general Jewish law and sectarian procedure, and that the admonition constituted only some 25 percent of the surviving parts of the work as a whole — apparently intended as an introduction.[54] Even before the publication of these materials Milik had presented a reconstruction of the entire document including the rearrangement of the order of some pages in MS A that had been incorrectly placed by Schechter.[55] Study of all the Cave 4 manuscripts is simply not advanced enough to allow us to suggest a new table of contents that would represent the order of the original text. Further, we cannot be entirely certain that all fragments have been properly grouped, since classification of manuscripts generally assumes that all fragments in the hand of one scribe belong to the same text. Nevertheless, it remains possible that some scribe had copied more than one halakhic text, and that some fragments do not belong with the *Zadokite Fragments.*

Before proceeding to discuss what we have learned from the new fragments in light of other recently published texts, something must be said about the name of the document. Between Schechter's *editio princeps* and the now standard Rabin edition, published in 1954,[56] the name of the text

---

51. M. Burrows, *Plates and Transcription of the Manual of Discipline,* in *The Dead Sea Scrolls of St. Mark's Monastery,* ed. Burrows, J. C. Trever, and W. H. Brownlee, vol. 2, fasc. 2 (New Haven: ASOR, 1950-51).

52. P. S. Alexander and G. Vermes, *Qumran Cave 4. XIX: Serekh ha-Yaḥad and Two Related Texts.* DJD 26 (Oxford: Clarendon, 1998) 102-206.

53. J. T. Milik, *Ten Years of Discovery in the Wilderness of Judaea,* trans. J. Strugnell. SBT 26 (London: SCM, 1959) 38-39.

54. Baumgarten, DJD 18:6-7. An important study using all the Cave 4 materials is C. Hempel, *The Laws of the Damascus Document: Sources, Tradition and Redaction.* STDJ 29 (Leiden: Brill, 1998).

55. See the outline in Fitzmyer, "Prolegomenon," 18-19; cf. that of Baumgarten in DJD 18:4-5.

56. C. Rabin, *The Zadokite Documents* (Oxford: Clarendon, 1954).

changed, first to *Damascus Covenant* (based on Hebrew ברית דמשק) and then, in common usage today, to *Damascus Document*. The name change based itself upon references to Damascus at several points in the admonition.[57] Some scholars took these references as referring literally to this place,[58] even suggesting that it be excavated, or that these references bespoke a Babylonian origin for the Dead Sea sect.[59] Yet our view remains that the use of Damascus here is symbolic, in accord with the imagery of Amos 5:27.[60] For this reason, we see little reason to call this document by a name that attributes its origins to a Syrian city. In light of the repeated references to the sect's leaders as Sons of Zadok in this text and in other sectarian documents, we would have preferred to retain Schechter's nomenclature.

On the basis of the Genizah manuscripts alone, in a previous study, we suggested that the various legal compilations in the *Zadokite Fragments* originated in the study sessions of the community. We argued that laws derived from scriptural interpretation at these sessions were collected into lists of regulations known as *serakhim*.[61] The existence of additional collections of this type in the newly published fragments from Qumran,[62] as well as the presence there of headings of the kind also found in the Genizah texts (e.g., "Regarding the Sabbath to observe it according to its regulation" [CD 10:14]),[63] confirm this assumption. At the same time we see evidence for subject organization of Jewish legal traditions even before the Mishnah began to be edited. Further, the assertion that the laws in this text stemmed from biblical interpretation is likewise confirmed by investigation of those laws that we encounter for the first time in the Qumran manuscripts of the *Zadokite Fragments*.

The availability of a much wider selection of halakhic documents of the Dead Sea Scrolls has made it possible to better understand the context of the halakhic materials in the *Zadokite Fragments*. Especially important here are the *Temple Scroll*, recovered during the 1967 War,[64] and the *Halakhic Letter*

---

57. CD 6:5, 19; 7:15, 19; 8:21; 19:34; 20:12.

58. Milik, *Ten Years of Discovery*, 87-93; Fitzmyer, "Prolegomenon," 16; and most cautiously, Baumgarten, DJD 18:9-10. Cf. P. R. Davies, *The Damascus Covenant: An Interpretation of the "Damascus Document."* JSOTSup 25 (Sheffield: JSOT, 1983) 16-17.

59. E.g., J. Murphy-O'Connor, "The Essenes and Their History," *RB* 81 (1974) 215-44; cf. Davies, *Damascus Covenant*, 41-7.

60. Schiffman, *Reclaiming the Dead Sea Scrolls*, 92-94.

61. Schiffman, *Halakhah at Qumran*, 60-68; *Sectarian Law in the Dead Sea Scrolls*, 9.

62. See, e.g., E. Larson, M. R. Lehmann, and L. H. Schiffman, "4QHalakha A," in *Qumran Cave 4.XXV: Halakhic Texts*, ed. J. M. Baumgarten et al. DJD 35 (Oxford: Clarendon, 1999) 25-51, pls. III-IV.

63. Cf. על העריות in 4QHalakha A, frg. 17 line 1 (p. 45).

64. Yadin, *Temple Scroll*; cf. 1:1-5 for Yadin's account of the acquisition of the scroll.

(4QMMT), announced only in 1984.⁶⁵ Both of these texts have direct legal parallels, and in some cases exegetical parallels, to the laws of the *Zadokite Fragments*.⁶⁶ Further, some texts in the *Zadokite Fragments* are formulated quite closely to parallels in the *Temple Scroll*. At the same time, some laws in the *Zadokite Fragments*, specifically the penal code, are shared with the corresponding penal code in the *Rule of the Community*,⁶⁷ although they exhibit recensional variations. Other parallels, or perhaps we should say common use of exactly the same material, exist between the *Zadokite Fragments* and a text called SD *(Serekh-Damascus* or *Miscellaneous Rules)*, which is a compilation of materials from the *Zadokite Fragments* and the *Rule of the Community*.⁶⁸

Several conclusions emerge now from the picture we have just outlined, a picture that could not have been sketched previous to the release of the entire Qumran corpus in 1991. To start with, it is now clear that the *Zadokite Fragments*, the *Temple Scroll*, and 4QMMT share a halakhic substratum that we may identify with the Sadducean trend in Jewish law known from rabbinic sources.⁶⁹ The *Zadokite Fragments* embody many older halakhic traditions and interpretations that stem from this common priestly tradition that was inherited by the Dead Sea sectarians.

The existence of material held in common between the *Zadokite Fragments* and the *Rule of the Community* makes clear that the initial association of these documents, immediately after the discovery of the first Qumran scrolls,

---

65. E. Qimron and J. Strugnell, "An Unpublished Halakhic Letter from Qumran," in *Biblical Archaeology Today: Proceedings of the International Congress on Biblical Archaeology, Jerusalem, April 1984*, ed. J. Amitai, 400-7 (Jerusalem: Israel Exploration Society, Israel Academy of Sciences and Humanities, in cooperation with ASOR, 1985).

66. Cf. "The Place of 4QMMT in the Corpus of Qumran Manuscripts," Chapter 7 above; C. Hempel, "The Laws of the Damascus Document and 4QMMT," in Baumgarten, Chazon, and Pinnick, *The Damascus Document: A Centennial of Discovery*, 69-84; and L. H. Schiffman, "The Relationship of the Zadokite Fragments to the Temple Scroll," in *The Damascus Document: A Centennial of Discovery*, 133-45.

67. J. M. Baumgarten, "The Cave 4 Versions of the Qumran Penal Code," *JJS* 43 (1992) 268-76; cf. Schiffman, *Sectarian Law*, 155-73.

68. J. M. Baumgarten, "4QMiscellaneous Rules," DJD 35:57-78; cf. L. H. Schiffman, "Serekh-Damascus," *EDSS* 2:868-69.

69. Y. Sussmann, "Ḥeqer Toldot ha-Halakhah u-Megillot Midbar Yehudah: Hirhurim Talmudiyim Rishonim le-'Or Megillat Miqṣat Maʿase ha-Torah," *Tarbiz* 59 (1989/1990) 11-77; English version: "The History of the Halakha and the Dead Sea Scrolls: Preliminary Talmudic Observations on *Miqṣat Maʿase ha-Torah* (4QMMT)," in *Qumran Cave 4.V: Miqṣat Maʿase ha-Torah*, ed. E. Qimron and J. Strugnell. DJD 10 (Oxford: Clarendon, 1994) 179-200. Various historical conclusions have been suggested based on this halakhic characterization, but these will not be our concern here. See "The New Halakhic Letter (4QMMT) and the Origins of the Dead Sea Sect," Chapter 6 above.

was correct.[70] In particular, the inclusion of sectarian regulations among the Jewish legal rulings in this text certainly argues for its character as a Qumran sectarian document. Yet it remains probable, in view of the truncated nature of the admission process to sectarian membership described here, that this text does indeed refer to communities throughout the land of Israel. Full status at the highest level, however, could only be attained in the more intense sectarian center, the communal life of which is described in the *Rule of the Community*.

Aramaic Levi Document

The final major text to be discussed is that usually called *Testament of Levi*. For a variety of reasons, this text has come most recently to be termed the *Aramaic Levi Document*. To understand the significance of this text and the problems posed by it, we must first discuss the general problem of the *Testaments of the Twelve Patriarchs*.

The *Testaments of the Twelve Patriarchs* is generally considered to be part of the Pseudepigrapha, a loose collection of Second Temple–period Jewish texts.[71] This text includes exhortations supposedly delivered by each of the twelve sons of Jacob soon before their deaths. It was first published in Greek in the late seventeenth century, although in the early sixteenth century a thirteenth-century Latin translation was also available. Among other themes, we should mention that this text emphasizes Levitical priesthood and precedence of the tribe of Levi even over that of Judah. While the text contains many clearly Jewish elements, it was immediately realized that some passages had to have been written by Christians. Scholars have accordingly debated as to whether we are dealing here with a Jewish work to which Christian additions have been made, a Jewish-Christian text, or an entirely Christian work. Further, it was generally assumed that the Twelve Testaments constitute one unified text, although there is now good reason to believe that it represents a collection of individual compositions, or perhaps that a few compositions have been subsumed into a larger work.

This debate was greatly enriched by the finding of a version of the *Testament of Levi* in Aramaic in the Cairo Genizah.[72] Essentially the same text

---

70. Cf. H. H. Rowley, *The Zadokite Fragments and the Dead Sea Scrolls* (Oxford: Blackwell, 1952).

71. R. A. Kugler, *The Testaments of the Twelve Patriarchs*. Guides to Apocrypha and Pseudepigrapha (Sheffield: Sheffield Academic, 2001) 11-40.

72. R. H. Charles, *The Greek Versions of the Testaments of the Twelve Patriarchs*, 2nd ed. (Oxford: Clarendon, 1960) liii-lvii, 245-56.

would be found in the Qumran caves as well. Further, some medieval versions (not found in the Geniza) of a *Testament of Naphtali* would also find parallels in the Qumran texts.[73]

Fragments of the Aramaic *Testament of Levi* were first identified in Genizah manuscripts now located at Cambridge and Oxford.[74] These manuscripts may be dated to the eleventh or perhaps tenth century C.E. and roughly parallel *Testament of Levi* 9–13. This text however, does not correspond exactly to the *Testament of Levi* known in the Greek *Testaments of the Twelve Patriarchs*. Rather, from the Genizah copy alone, it is apparent that the Aramaic *Testament of Levi* was a related text or source for that larger composition. The existence of a Greek manuscript from the monastery at Mount Athos, which parallels parts of the Genizah fragments, also indicates that these fragments are only part of a larger composition that existed in antiquity.

Already with the publication of Cave 1 texts in 1955,[75] it was clear that this *Aramaic Levi Document* (as it is now called to distinguish it from the *Testament of Levi* in the Greek *Testaments*) was an ancient composition that somehow had survived into the Genizah period. 1Q21 was in some way related to *Testament of Levi* 8 and to the Oxford Genizah fragments. Yet it soon became clear that in the Aramaic text we do not deal with copies of the same material preserved in the Greek texts of the *Testament of Levi*. Rather, these are sources or alternative recensions of similar material. This explains why 4QTest Levi ar[a] corresponds also partly to the Oxford fragments and partly to the aforementioned Greek manuscript. Another section of this Qumran manuscript parallels *Testament of Levi* 14 as well as parts of both the Oxford and Cambridge Genizah manuscripts.[76] The attempt to relate additional Aramaic texts from Cave 4 to the *Aramaic Levi Document*[77] has not been successful. We should, however, take note of the fact that the *Zadokite Fragments* 4:14-18 may contain a quotation from the *Testament of Levi* or *Levi Document* in Hebrew.[78]

Before proceeding to draw general conclusions, the data regarding the

---

73. Cf. Schürer, *History of the Jewish People*, 3/2:767-68.

74. M. E. Stone and J. C. Greenfield, "Remarks on the Aramaic Testament of Levi from the Geniza," *RB* 86 (1979) 214-30; M. E. Stone, "Levi, Aramaic," *EDSS* 1:486-88.

75. D. Barthélemy and J. T. Milik, *Qumran Cave I*. DJD 1 (Oxford: Clarendon, 1955) 87-91.

76. See M. E. Stone and J. C. Greenfield, in *Qumran Cave 4.XVII: Parabiblical Texts, Part 3*, ed. G. J. Brooke et al. DJD 22 (Oxford: Clarendon, 1996) 1-72.

77. É. Puech, "Fragment d'un apocryphe de Lévi et le personnage eschatologique: 4QtestLévi[c-d](?) et 4QAJa," in *The Madrid Qumran Conference: Proceedings of the International Congress on the Dead Sea Scrolls, Madrid, 18-21 March, 1991*, ed. J. Trebolle Barrera and L. Vegas Montaner, 2:449-501. STDJ 11/2 (Leiden: Brill, 1992).

78. J. C. Greenfield, "The Words of Levi Son of Jacob in *Damascus Document* IV, 15-19 (CD)," *RevQ* 13 (1988) 319-22; Schürer, *History of the Jewish People*, 3/2:776-77.

related *Testament of Naphtali* must be briefly sketched.[79] Here there are no Genizah fragments to be discussed, but some version of this text survived into the Middle Ages in midrashic texts. Previous to the discovery of the Qumran material, it had been assumed that the medieval version derived from the Greek *Testament of Naphtali* found in the full *Testaments*. An Oxford manuscript of the Chronicles of Yerahmeel includes a version of this *Testament*.[80] Material related to the *Testament of Judah* survives also in medieval texts, but the fragments identified as a *Testament of Judah* from Qumran[81] exhibit no real parallels, and the identification of this material is highly speculative. Cave 4 did preserve fragments of a Hebrew *Testament of Naphtali* that contains a longer version of *T. Naph.* 1:6-12.[82]

In any case, of all the *Testaments* collected in the Greek *Testaments of the Twelve Patriarchs*, only versions of *Levi* and *Naphtali* were found among the Qumran documents. This has led to the proposal that, in fact, only these texts, and perhaps some passages still unidentified, were available to the author of the Greek *Testaments of the Twelve Patriarchs*. In this case we would conclude that the *Testaments* as a whole, with their Christian references, should be seen as a Christian work that made use of those Jewish *Testaments*, *Levi* and *Naphtali*, that were available to the author. The rest of the *Testaments*, providing texts for each of the twelve sons of Jacob, were essentially original compositions, whereas those of *Levi* and *Naphtali* were based on preexisting Jewish documents that must have created the pattern for the composition as a whole.[83]

It is precisely the fact that *Levi* is preserved in Aramaic and *Naphtali* in Hebrew that leads to the conclusion that these are separate works, rather than parts of some Second Temple–period prototype of the later Greek text. However, it must be admitted that *Naphtali* could, in fact, be a translation from an Aramaic original that was not preserved. Such a possibility is supported by the existence of one Hebrew manuscript at Qumran of a translation of Tobit from its original Aramaic.[84]

Focusing again on the Genizah manuscripts of the *Testament of Levi*, we

---

79. Kugler, *Testaments of the Twelve Patriarchs*, 71-74.

80. M. Gaster, "The Hebrew Text of One of the Testaments of the Twelve Patriarchs," *Society of Biblical Archaeology: Proceedings* 16-17 (1894) 33-49.

81. Cf. R. Good, "Judah," *EDSS* 1:438, for possible Judah texts from Qumran.

82. É. Puech, *Qumrân Grotte 4.XVIII, Textes hébreux (4Q521-4Q528, 4Q576-4Q579)*. DJD 25 (Oxford: Clarendon, 1998) 73-82.

83. Schürer, *History of the Jewish People*, 3/2:772-75.

84. J. Fitzmyer in *Qumran Cave 4.XIV, Parabiblical Texts: Part 2*, ed. M. Broshi et al. DJD 19 (Oxford: Clarendon, 1995) 63-76.

can now say that they represent exactly the same text as was later found in ancient manuscripts at Qumran and that is found in the Greek manuscript from Mount Athos. These texts are substantially different from the Greek *Testament of Levi*, for which reason they are termed the *Aramaic Levi Document*.[85] Finally, examination of this text as well as the Hebrew *Testament of Naphtali* from Qumran favors the likelihood that the entire *Testaments of the Twelve Patriarchs*, as known in Greek, is a Christian work that made use of the *Levi* and *Naphtali* material represented at Qumran and perhaps of some other similar sources.[86]

Conclusion

A few conclusions emerge from the study of the very few works from the Second Temple period that survived in the Cairo Genizah. First, we should note that in view of the very large number of manuscripts in the Genizah collections, it is likely that very little more of Second Temple literature than what has been identified so far survived among Jews in the early medieval period.[87] It is possible that some fragments may still be discovered in the collections in Russia, but the picture is not likely to change substantially. The discovery of a few Second Temple–period texts in the Genizah in no way contradicts our general impression that the literature of Second Temple Judaism was for the most part lost to the Jews of the talmudic and medieval periods. That this is the case for literature written in Greek is self-evident, but it was certainly the case also for the vast Aramaic and Hebrew literature of Second Temple times — much of which was found at Qumran. This literature was virtually extinct in talmudic circles, even though its influence is sometimes apparent, especially in the aggadic sphere.

We must, therefore, provide some explanation for the survival of these particular texts and their presence in the Genizah. After the discovery of the Dead Sea Scrolls, scholars turned to several accounts of the discovery of scrolls near Jericho in Late Antiquity and the early Middle Ages, but these accounts generally describe the finding of biblical scrolls. In the case of Ben Sira, it is clear that this book was being used in rabbinic circles and in the general Jewish community and, therefore, must have circulated widely.

85. R. A. Kugler, "Testaments," *EDSS* 2:933-36, esp. 934; *Testaments of the Twelve Patriarchs*, 47-56.
86. Cf. Kugler, *Testaments of the Twelve Patriarchs*, 31-39.
87. One small fragment from the Genizah concerning the Sons of Zadok may originate from the Second Temple period. See Fitzmyer, "Prolegomenon," 14 and bibliography in 36, n. 9.

We cannot ascertain the origin of the *Zadokite Fragments* in the Genizah. Some have sought to explain the presence of ancient sectarian ideas in Karaism as resulting from the discovery of ancient texts in the early Middle Ages.[88] Nevertheless, it seems more logical to postulate that these texts survived in a continuing sectarian tradition that persisted throughout talmudic times and that emerged anew into the light of day after lying dormant for some time. In such a case, the Genizah copies of the *Zadokite Fragments* would have originated, not in an earlier discovery of the Dead Sea Scrolls, but in this continuing sectarian tradition.

The *Aramaic Levi Document,* however, is even more difficult to pin down. Like Ben Sira, this is not a text peculiar to the Qumran sect. Rather, it was part of the common literary heritage of the Jews of the Second Temple period. It seems to have had no influence in the rabbinic period, and the emergence of the Aramaic original in the Genizah could be explained equally well by an early "archaeological" discovery as by textual transmission. The existence of a translation of this document in an eleventh-century Greek manuscript indicates circulation beyond the Jewish community.

The contribution of the Cairo Genizah to reclaiming the literature of Second Temple Judaism is a pivotal one. In many ways, it was the discovery of the Genizah that spurred on the search for original Hebrew texts from Second Temple times, a search that would literally hit pay dirt at Qumran. The Cairo Genizah and the ancient library of Qumran are in some ways inseparable. After more than a century of research on the Genizah, and more than a half century of study of the Dead Sea Scrolls, we can only stand in awe of the precious legacy that has been returned to us.

---

88. S. Lieberman, "Light on the Cave Scrolls from Rabbinic Sources," *PAAJR* 20 (1951) 402-4; cf. P. Kahle, *The Cairo Geniza,* 2nd ed. (Oxford: Blackwell, 1959) 17-28.

CHAPTER 25

Inverting Reality:
The Dead Sea Scrolls in the Popular Media

The second "battle of the scrolls," which took place in the late 1980s and early 1990s,[1] culminated in the successful publication of all the scrolls and in the tremendous advances in the field of Dead Sea Scrolls studies that we all take for granted within the walls of Academe. Yet we are aware that there still remains a large gap between the realities of scrolls research and public perception. It is virtually impossible to give a lecture on the scrolls without being asked the usual questions: Is it true that the Vatican is hiding (or was hiding) the Dead Sea Scrolls?[2] or: Isn't it true that Jesus and/or John the Baptist are mentioned (or referred to) in the scrolls?[3] It is the contention in this chapter that these misconceptions, as well as a host of related false information, result from the nature of the press coverage given, from the very beginning of the story until today, of the scrolls, their discovery, contents, and publication history. In general, the media have tended to invert reality and to portray the scrolls as relevant to Christianity but not Judaism, as remaining

---

1. Cf. "The Many 'Battles of the Scrolls,'" Chapter 1 above; L. H. Schiffman, *Reclaiming the Dead Sea Scrolls: The History of Judaism, the Background of Christianity, the Lost Library of Qumran* (Philadelphia: Jewish Publication Society, 1994; repr. ABRL [New York: Doubleday, 1995]) 3-31; P. R. Davies, G. J. Brooke, and P. R. Callaway, *The Complete World of the Dead Sea Scrolls* (London: Thames and Hudson, 2002) 22-27.

2. This claim is featured in M. Baigent and R. Leigh, *The Dead Sea Scrolls Deception* (New York: Summit, 1991), and is systematically refuted in O. Betz and R. Riesner, *Jesus, Qumran and the Vatican* (New York: Crossroad, 1994).

3. Such views have been propounded recently by R. H. Eisenman, *The Dead Sea Scrolls and the First Christians: Essays and Translations* (Rockport, MA: Element, 1996); B. E. Thiering, *Jesus & the Riddle of the Dead Sea Scrolls* (San Francisco: HarperCollins, 1992).

unpublished (or hidden) due to alleged threats to Christian (or even Jewish) faith, and as still under the control (although they never were) of the Vatican. This inversion of reality is of course to be expected in sensationalist or lowbrow articles or videos. More surprising is the fact that supposedly responsible journalists often use these misconceptions as a come-on, allow responsible scholars to counter them, and then leave readers with the impression that there are varying views. Even such articles or videos will give equal time to impossible one-person theories on the false assumption that "all Dead Sea Scrolls theories are created equal."[4] Thus, the inversion of reality in the public mind results from its inversion in media coverage. In this respect, like so many other aspects of our modern culture, the media do not simply report "the facts and all the facts" or "all the news that's fit to print," but they in fact shape the public perception.[5] We will see as well that, besides being simply a shaper of the public image of the scrolls, the media have been a player in the history of scrolls research, leading to a sort of conflict of interest that here again is not atypical of trends in our general culture, as, for example, in the area of domestic politics.

The early publicity surrounding the scrolls pointed to a desire by legitimate scholars to carry their point of view to the public by using the media. In fact, in this respect, Dead Sea Scrolls scholars, like some archaeologists, have had privileged access to media exposure when compared to their academic colleagues in other fields. From the earliest days of scrolls research, we have to admit that, realizing the public fascination with the scrolls and their almost magical attention for media coverage, scholars have sought and cultivated the media spotlight. This has been a double-edged sword: interest in the scrolls has been greatly encouraged, but room has been made for the presentation of skewed pictures and even irresponsible scholarship.

Original Controversies

From the beginning, the popular media played "an important role in arousing worldwide public interest in and even fascination with" the Dead Sea Scrolls. Nevertheless, as noted by Neil Asher Silberman, "on more than a

---

4. For a survey of Dead Sea Scrolls theories, see M. Broshi, *Bread, Wine, Walls and Scrolls*. JSPSup 36 (London: Sheffield Academic, 2001) 269-73.

5. See M. Silk, *Unsecular Media: Making News of Religion in America* (Urbana: University of Illinois Press, 1998) (mentions the Dead Sea Scrolls on p. 120); S. M. Hoover, "Religion, Media and the Cultural Center of Gravity," http://www.colorado.edu/Journalism/MEDIALYF/analysis/umcom.html.

few occasions, media coverage of the scrolls has transcended strictly scientific reporting to become deeply intertwined with wider modern political and religious controversies."[6] This was already the case with the very early announcements of the finds in the New York Times of 25 April 1948, by Millar Burrows on behalf of the American School (now Schools) of Oriental Research. Immediately, Eleazar Sukenik of the Hebrew University responded with his own press conference, determined to prove his right of scholarly primogeniture as the first to have correctly dated and identified the scrolls, as well as to advance the claim of the new State of Israel to the scrolls. In August 1949, Professor Godfrey Driver criticized the Americans in the London Times for encouraging Archbishop Athanasius Samuel to bring the scrolls in his possession to the U.S. and for not sharing their information adequately with other scholars. Likewise, through 1949, as a result of the genuine excitement caused by the announcements of the discovery of the scrolls, questions of their antiquity and authenticity were often discussed in the press.

The early years saw an ongoing, sub rosa, cat-and-mouse game between the American Christian scholars and Israelis to gain possession of the scrolls in the hands of Athanasius Samuel.[7] When the American scholars could not find a buyer for the scrolls, Mar Samuel eventually hawked the scrolls through an ad in the Wall Street Journal, resulting in their being bought by Yigael Yadin and their return to Israel in 1954.[8] Here it was the use of the press's advertising power that facilitated the acquisition of this group of scrolls by Israel.

The first discoveries in the caves of Qumran took place amidst the events surrounding the Israeli War of Independence in 1948. The caves themselves are located in territory that was first British Mandate Palestine, then Jordan, then territory conquered by Israel in 1967. Hence, their political value as a source of national pride and contested legal status. After Yadin's purchase, the reclamation of the scrolls for Israel was announced in a 1955 press conference by the prime minister of Israel, Moshe Sharett. The theme of the announcement was the great pride Israelis could feel as a result of the discovery of the scrolls and the connection they fostered between the ancient Jewish state and the modern state of Israel. Yadin himself often stressed this connec-

---

6. N. A. Silberman, "Media," *EDSS* 1:532. For what follows, see Silberman, 532-35.

7. J. C. Trever, *The Dead Sea Scrolls: A Personal Account*, rev. ed. (Grand Rapids: Wm. B. Eerdmans, 1977) 15-147; N. A. Silberman, *The Hidden Scrolls: Christianity, Judaism, & the War for the Dead Sea Scrolls* (New York: Putnam's, 1994) 28-53.

8. Y. Yadin, *The Message of the Scrolls* (New York: Simon & Schuster, 1969) 39-52; N. A. Silberman, *A Prophet from Amongst You: The Life of Yigael Yadin, Soldier, Scholar, and Mythmaker of Modern Israel* (Reading, MA: Addison-Wesley, 1993) 202-23.

tion in his various publications as well.⁹ Yet curiously, this motif was lost to the Israeli press as the scrolls began increasingly to be interpreted as relevant primarily to the study of Christianity.

Scrolls and Christianity

The almost instantaneous attention the scrolls got, dependent in part on the naïve popular notion that the scrolls might present some kind of *deus ex machina* revelation for a world still reeling from World War II and the Holocaust, was no doubt a major factor in contributing to the immense popularity of the now famous *New Yorker* article by Edmund Wilson,[10] which was soon issued in an expanded version as a book.[11] This article/book brought to the public not only the mystery of the scrolls and a summary of their story and significance, but also popularized the views put forward in scholarly circles by André Dupont-Sommer,[12] many of which were later picked up by John Allegro,[13] a member of the International Team set up in Jordan to publish the scrolls discovered there after the 1948 war. The marketing of these views by Wilson, because of his substantial reputation, influenced the whole later development of how the scrolls have been seen in the popular media. Wilson and Allegro argued that many of the key theological beliefs of Christianity had originated in the obscure sect of the Dead Sea Scrolls which they identified with the Essenes. Qumran was then the true cradle of Christianity. The purpose of Allegro's work[14] was to undermine Christianity by claiming that Christianity was not the result of a unique revelation but a logical develop-

---

9. This was especially the case with the Masada excavations. See Silberman, *A Prophet from Amongst You*, 288-93.

10. E. Wilson, "A Reporter at Large," *New Yorker* 31/13 (14 May 1955) 45-121.

11. E. Wilson, *The Scrolls from the Dead Sea* (New York: Oxford University Press, 1955), and in an expanded edition, *Israel and the Dead Sea Scrolls* (New York: Farrar, Straus, and Giroux, 1978).

12. A. Dupont-Sommer, *The Dead Sea Scrolls: A Preliminary Survey*, trans. E. M. Rowley (Oxford: Blackwell, 1952); *The Jewish Sect of Qumran and the Essenes*, trans. R. D. Barnett (London: Vallentine, Mitchell, 1954).

13. J. M. Allegro, *The Dead Sea Scrolls* (Harmondsworth: Penguin, 1956); *The People of the Dead Sea Scrolls* (London: Routledge and Kegan Paul, 1959); *The Mystery of the Dead Sea Scrolls Revealed* (New York: Gramercy, 1981). Allegro was later revealed to be a racist and anti-Semite. Cf. E. M. Cook, *Solving the Mysteries of the Dead Sea Scrolls: New Light on the Bible* (Grand Rapids: Zondervan, 1994) 150 n. 14.

14. J. M. Allegro, *The Dead Sea Scrolls and the Christian Myth* (1979; 2nd rev. ed. Amherst, NY: Prometheus, 1992).

ment out of Jewish circles.[15] Wilson's presentation had, in fact, been supported by the iconoclastic — indeed contrarian — Israeli scholar David Flusser, who because of his access to the Israeli press and public opinion (and later television) would eventually convince most Israelis that the scrolls were of interest only for the history of Christianity.[16]

The press reported on the theories of Dupont-Sommer, and Allegro defended his conclusions on BBC. The other members of the International Team rebutted Allegro in the London *Times* and elsewhere, pointing to his many excesses and incorrect interpretations. But all of this was to no avail. It is our view that the Wilson article permanently shaped the entire thrust of Dead Sea Scrolls reporting as it has continued up until now. In light of this article and its formative influence, it has been extremely difficult to achieve a hearing for scrolls research in the media that is not integrally — indeed directly — connected to issues of Christian origins.

Already in the debate over Christian origins we can see the inversion of reality in which the real scholars have to defend themselves and their work against unlikely, illogical, or unfounded theories. These theories, often sensational, spark debate in the press because the media often focus on the sensational and then pit the legitimate scholars against the proponent of the latest theory. This continues into the present and is heightened by the false claim that the scrolls are "hidden" and authoritative scholars must be involved in a fraud or cover-up while the others are telling the truth. To be sure, the initial secrecy of the International Team has always helped to foster such conspiracy theories regarding the Dead Sea Scrolls.

This inversion is the case with the theories of Barbara Thiering and Robert Eisenman, who see Christian figures as having lived or visited Qumran, and Norman Golb,[17] who claims that the scrolls are the remnants of the Jerusalem library of the temple, brought to Qumran for safekeeping during the revolt of 66-73 C.E., and not the library of a sectarian group who lived at Qumran. These theories are actually impossible, from an objective, that is, scientific, point of view. But the media continue to give these views equal play, as if they have the same claim to column inches and attention — even a greater claim — than the more prosaic conclusions of everyone else in the academic world. This trend of reversing reality was most prominent in coverage of the "discovery" of the falsely labeled "Pierced Messiah" text by

---

15. See M. G. Hall, "Foreword," in Allegro, *The Dead Sea Scrolls and the Christian Myth*, ix.

16. Cf. D. Flusser, *Judaism and the Origins of Christianity* (Jerusalem: Magnes, 1988); *The Spiritual History of the Dead Sea Scrolls* (Tel Aviv: MOD, 1989).

17. N. Golb, *Who Wrote the Dead Sea Scrolls? The Search for the Secret of Qumran* (New York: Scribner, 1995).

Eisenman and Michael Wise[18] and the supposed mention of Jesus (Yeshua — actually the biblical Joshua) in 4QTestimonia "identified" by two Orthodox rabbis and featured in an article in the *Los Angeles Times*. These were portrayed in the press as serious, and true and responsible scholars were left to defend the so-called "consensus" or "cabal" against the most ridiculous of claims.[19]

This is not to say that throughout the history of newspaper journalism connected with the scrolls there has not been any totally balanced reporting. But usually balanced reporting will still use the come-on of the issues of Christian origins as a means of exciting readers, so that the message somehow still comes through to many readers that the scrolls are, as it were, "Christian."

The Scrolls and the Irrational

But of course, nothing discussed so far ranks with media reports of the appearance of Elvis in the Dead Sea Scrolls, the cure for AIDS, proof of life after death, and the prediction of the end of the world, all found in the scrolls according to various supermarket tabloids. Such statements, as ridiculous as they are, were mocked in a cartoon which shows scholars eating chocolate brownies and declaring that this great recipe was discovered in the Dead Sea Scrolls. This cartoon nevertheless points up the fascination for the scrolls and the public interest in what research will discover next.[20]

Beyond this, such reports also relate to a cultural aspect that may underlie some of the almost irrational fascination with the scrolls in the media and popular culture. One often gets the feeling, especially in some of the videos and TV programs, that the scrolls are perceived as some kind of potential new revelation, a secret gospel waiting to be revealed and, hence, kept secret by its custodians. This new revelation may be understood in one of two ways. It may be taken as the solution to the problem of Christian origins, assuming that the scrolls tell some alternative story of Jesus and the earliest Christians,

---

18. R. H. Eisenman and M. O. Wise, eds., *The Dead Sea Scrolls Uncovered: The First Complete Translation and Interpretation of 50 Key Documents Withheld for over 35 Years* (Shaftesbury, Dorset: Element, 1992). Cf. also Eisenman and G. Vermes, "More on the Pierced Messiah Text from Eisenman and Vermes," *BAR* 19/1 (1993) 66-67.

19. Cf. the systematic response to these views in Betz and Riesner, *Jesus, Qumran and the Vatican*, 50-160; see also R. Price, *Secrets of the Dead Sea Scrolls* (Eugene: Harvest House, 1996), 165-90, 311-98.

20. This aspect of American popular culture awaits a serious study.

Inverting Reality

a sort of apocryphal gospel;[21] or it can relate to some assumed guidance for the present, our own trying times, an irrational pipe dream that we of course know neither the scrolls nor any other archaeological discovery can fulfill.[22]

Publication Controversy

Perhaps one of the most active areas of press activity in relation to the Dead Sea Scrolls was in the publication controversy that raged in the late 1980s and early 1990s. Here the media became an active participant in the calls for reform and, in fact, may be considered the arena in which the campaign to "liberate" the scrolls was defined, conducted, and won.

John Allegro had long ago accused the International Team of hiding the scrolls because of the problems they supposedly posed to traditional Christian beliefs.[23] He had sought to protest the ongoing failure of the members of the team to do their share, as he had, in publishing the scrolls assigned to them. The International Team worked on assembling the fragments and sorting the manuscripts until 1960, when they lost interest or their funding dried up. In the aftermath of the 1967 Arab-Israeli War, the Palestine Archaeological Museum (now Rockefeller Museum) in East Jerusalem found itself in Israeli territory. Soon scholars all over the world began to realize that not only were the scrolls not being published, but many of the early scholars on the International Team claimed "rights" to be the first to publish them and denied access to anyone else but their select group. It was then that the struggle over the publication (or better nonpublication) of the scrolls began. This battle was fought largely in the press.

Already in the late 1970s, Geza Vermes at Oxford and Morton Smith of Columbia University protested that the scrolls were unavailable to scholars. In 1984, Hershel Shanks, editor of the *Biblical Archaeology Review,* joined ranks with them to launch a media campaign in the pages of his journal to

---

21. This is the case with the immensely popular novel by D. Brown, *The Da Vinci Code* (New York: Doubleday, 2003), itself based on M. Baigent, R. Leigh, and H. Lincoln, *Holy Blood, Holy Grail* (New York: Dell, 1983), which includes a patently false history of Christianity. Such books are part of a conspiracy theory/pseudohistorical literature that influences many American readers. Such studies often invert the real dating of the canonical and apocryphal gospels to provide support for their theories.

22. Silk, *Unsecular Media,* 49-56, proposed that certain *topoi* underlie media coverage of religion in America. A full study of the place of the scrolls would, I am sure, bear this out and lead to a widening of the list of *topoi.*

23. Allegro, *The Dead Sea Scrolls and the Christian Myth,* xxi-xxvi.

"liberate" the scrolls.[24] This campaign started as a result of the 1985 Dead Sea Scrolls Conference held at New York University.[25]

A few words should be said about the particular role of Shanks and *BAR* in the scrolls publication controversy. Shanks and his periodical are, on the one hand, part of the "media" in terms of archaeology and Dead Sea Scrolls. On the other hand, their links with certain scholars and other players in the controversy, as well as their role as a purveyor of scholarship, even to scholars, have made them a special case. But most importantly, Shanks and his magazine have gained a kind of de facto control over the news media in the U.S. when it comes to biblical archaeology. They have effectively become a gatekeeper for most major newspapers, the *New York Times* being the best example. This is also the result of a peculiar fact about the *Times,* the newspaper of record for the Dead Sea Scrolls controversy, and many other newspapers in the U.S., namely, that archaeology, including the scrolls, is considered the responsibility of the science desk of the paper. This means that those who write about these issues know little about religion or its history, and less about the scrolls and their contents. The availability of a source for significant and authoritative information, as well as ready-made stories, makes *BAR* their best friend. It was this fact that resulted in the role of the *Times* as an echo of *BAR,* both editorially and in news articles (for the most part in the science section). Effectively, and for good reason, Shanks had an ally in John Noble Wilford, then science editor at the *Times,* as he sought to bring about the release of the scrolls and their publication. Further, as a result of his status and position at *BAR,* Shanks found it easy to get op-eds accepted in the *Times* and *Washington Post,* and these articles contributed greatly to public awareness of the scrolls and what was at that time their plight.

As a result of the *BAR*-led campaign, it was not long before the media not only was reporting on the controversy but becoming a major participant. The PBS Nova film "Secrets of the Dead Sea Scrolls" was released early in October 1991, and it in fact was a major stimulus for the timing of the release of the Huntington Library's microfilm copies of the photographs of the Dead

---

24. H. S. Shanks, "Failure to Publish Dead Sea Scrolls Is Leitmotif of New York University Scroll Conference," *BAR* 11/5 (1985) 4.

25. L. H. Schiffman, ed., *Archaeology and History in the Dead Sea Scrolls: The New York University Conference in Memory of Yigael Yadin.* JSOTSup 8. JSOT/ASOR Monographs 2 (Sheffield: Sheffield Academic, 1990). Smith's paper in this volume (181-88) was actually not delivered at the conference. Instead, Smith set it aside to speak eloquently in protest of the "scandal" of the failure of the International Team to publish the scrolls and demanded that photographs of them be released. Ben Zion Wacholder, at the same conference, said that he thought he would never live to work with the full scrolls corpus but, happily, he did!

Sea Scrolls. The availability of the microfilms, reported in major American newspapers,[26] as well as the publication of the Eisenman-Robinson photographs[27] and the Wacholder-Abegg reconstructions,[28] all in quick succession, led to mounting press coverage that, in turn, created what was virtually a media assault on the Israel Antiquities Authority (IAA). This caused its director, Amir Drori, to formally grant access to the manuscripts for research by qualified scholars.[29]

A further role of the press concerns the replacement of John Strugnell as editor-in-chief of the International Team as a result of an antisemitic interview published in the prestigious Israeli Hebrew daily *Ha'aretz*.[30] The interview, later excerpted in translation in the *Times* and *BAR*, was conducted by Avi Katzman, a pugnacious journalist, who sees reporters as involved activists. This interview, and the storm it precipitated, convinced both the International Team and the Israel Antiquities Authority that Strugnell was no longer appropriate to serve as editor-in-chief, and the IAA appointed Emanuel Tov of the Hebrew University to the position, a decision that was the key to achieving the goal of full scholarly publication of the scrolls.

The press, therefore, played a significant role in bringing about major changes regarding access to the scrolls, the leadership and composition of the International Team, and the pace of the official publication in the Oxford University Press series Discoveries in the Judean Desert (DJD). The media accomplished far more than the individual scholars who petitioned to see particular manuscripts and far more than the decision of the IAA to set, but never meet, official deadlines for the publication of the texts.

Video Review

To illustrate these trends and others there follows a brief survey of a number of documentaries for television (usually cable) and scrolls videos. Considering

---

26. E.g., W. Safire, "Breaking the Cartel," *New York Times*, 24 September 1991.

27. R. H. Eisenman and J. M. Robinson, *A Facsimile Edition of the Dead Sea Scrolls, Prepared with an Introduction and Index*, 2 vols. (Washington: Biblical Archaeology Society, 1991); Publisher's Foreword by H. Shanks. Vol. 1:xxiii-xlv also contains some documents and press articles relating to the struggle to "liberate" the scrolls, as well as the infamous purloined edition of 4QMMT.

28. B. Z. Wacholder and M. G. Abegg, eds., *A Preliminary Edition of the Unpublished Dead Sea Scrolls: The Hebrew and Aramaic Texts from Cave Four*. 4 fasc. (Washington: Biblical Archaeology Society, 1991-96).

29. Cf. Silberman, *Hidden Scrolls*, 213-45.

30. A. Katzman, "Cave Men," *Ha'aretz Supplement*, 9 November 1990 (Hebrew).

the overarching, maybe dominant, role of television in shaping American popular culture, these examples (in almost all of which I had the opportunity to appear, often in a hopeless attempt to provide balance) should be helpful in understanding the issues. Of course, this survey is not exhaustive.

The Nova documentary "Secrets of the Dead Sea Scrolls"[31] was for many of us our first experience with the medium and also with its power as a force for shaping events. This program, aired right after the congressional vote on U. S. Supreme Court Justice Clarence Thomas, truly pictured in as close to an objective way as possible the issues and debates regarding the scrolls, as well as the publication problem. If only it had truly set a pattern for all to follow.

Another excellent documentary was produced for *Compass,* Australian Broadcasting Company's religion program. Rachael Kohn, working along with the Art Museum of New South Wales in Sydney and in preparation of their scrolls exhibit, produced an excellent program in which all theories were aired, fairly and reasonably. One-person views got their due (maybe more than their due) but were in proper context, and the debate was engaged by a series of excellent and appropriate scholars. Viewers truly got a fair picture. Similarly responsible is the program "Revelations of the Dead Sea Scrolls" from the Arts and Entertainment series Mysteries of the Bible,[32] which always tried to bring to bear a fair representation of scholars and views on all the issues it tackled. (While we are not dealing here with educational entries, not aired on television, we should make special mention of the lectures on the scrolls available on video from the Biblical Archaeology Society.[33] These are fair and balanced and represent scholarly lectures by first-rate academics.)

BBC Horizon's entry, "Resurrecting the Dead Sea Scrolls,"[34] as its title indicates, uses the Christianity issue as a come-on. This program essentially sets the issues in the story of the controversy over the Eisenman-Wise book[35] and the claim of Eisenman regarding the scrolls as the real account of Christianity. It has many worthwhile interviews, but the introduction of footage of monks and monastic buildings and other such techniques makes clear that it is truly aimed at the assumption that the scrolls are most important for Christianity. Here the Eisenman theories are set out as if they are the equivalent of other views, to the extent that even the so-called Pierced Messiah text is portrayed as if the question of its meaning is a legitimate case of scholarly

---

31. Produced by WGBH, Boston. The program aired for the first time on 15 October 1991.
32. Pts. I and 2; Multimedia Entertainment and A & E Network, 1993.
33. "The Dead Sea Scrolls." 6 pts. (Washington: Biblical Archaeology Society, 1993).
34. Aired 22 March 1993.
35. Eisenman and Wise, *Dead Sea Scrolls Uncovered.*

debate.[36] The scrolls supposedly call into question the uniqueness of Jesus and the Gospels and will shake up Christians. Jesus is at the beginning and the end, good marketing since there are actually more Christians than Jews in the target audience.

In the same way, the Learning Channel's entry, "History's Mysteries: The Dead Sea Scrolls,"[37] begins with a fair and balanced picture of the controversy over the release of the scrolls and their contents and of the archaeology of Qumran (I can be seen in Cave 4), but then dedicates the rest of the program to a survey of the Eisenman views. Even though I and others are allowed to rebut him, the agenda of the program clearly makes it out as if his lone voice were that of truth (or light) against the other voices of cover-up (or darkness).

A fair and straightforward argument against programs skewed to misleading pictures of the relation of the scrolls to Christianity is "Secrets of the Sea" from the Everyman series on BBC.[38] Here viewers get a truly objective sense of scrolls scholarship and of the real significance of the scrolls for the background of Christianity. Other views are fairly and clearly debunked. There is no pandering here. Another excellent program, from the Discovery Channel, is "The Dead Sea Scrolls: Voices of the Desert," produced by Brigham Young University.[39] This, like the video on the scrolls and Masada made for their campus exhibit,[40] is well balanced and properly discusses the Jewishness of the material and its use for understanding the background of Christianity. There is an overemphasis on science and technology and their contribution to scrolls research that is partly institutionally encouraged because of the role of BYU in these areas, and partly the result of the program's placement with Discovery. But this does not interfere with the straightforwardness of the reporting.

The Dead Sea Scrolls segment of "Doomsday"[41] is an example of how a scrolls segment, not in itself poorly done, could be modified to make it fit into a particular type of pseudo-technoscience series, Discover Magazine on the Discovery Channel. It sets the scrolls as "a doomsday cult" "that may have written the Bible" and also emphasizes the use of scientific techniques in scrolls research, a strange combination of motifs. But doomsday and technol-

---

36. Cf. Schiffman, *Reclaiming the Dead Sea Scrolls*, 344-47.
37. Aired 11 April 1994.
38. Produced by Michael Waterhouse. BBC, 1994.
39. KBYU/Scandinature Films, 1998.
40. "Masada and the Dead Sea Scrolls" (Provo: Foundation for Ancient and Mormon Studies, 1997).
41. Providence Pictures (December, 1997).

ogy — and the images of Waco burning, only present at the beginning and end — created an unbalanced presentation. Although the information about the relevance of the scrolls to Christianity, explained by Hershel Shanks, properly complemented the Jewish data that I had presented, all in all the framework so skewed the program that it was not unnatural for it to conclude by saying that "the scrolls may reveal the secrets of the end of days."

"Traders of the Lost Scrolls," also broadcast on BBC in 1997,[42] tells the story of James Charlesworth as a scrolls discoverer and features a variety of scholars and others, always in automobiles (yours truly in a Manhattan yellow cab). There is some interesting information, but it is all set in the story of discovery that never materializes.

Probably most problematical of all the programs that we will survey here is "The Pharaoh's Holy Treasure,"[43] another BBC entry. It presents the unsupportable theory of Robert Feather that the Copper Scroll describes treasures — for the most part brought by the Jews from Egypt — which originated with Akhenaton and his followers.[44] While I had ample time to rebut this impossible view, one has to question the wisdom of BBC in portraying Feather's views at all, given their clear and obvious impossibility.

All things considered, this survey shows that television programs are of several kinds: the really balanced material that can popularize while staying true to reality; the kind that uses Christianity as a come-on, but that can, in any case, present a fair and accurate picture; the kind of program that basically falls into the trap of seeing the scrolls as if they directly describe the beginnings of Christianity; and finally, the absolutely imaginary, parallel to the journalism of the tabloids. When skewed pictures of the scrolls are presented, essentially following the tradition of Wilson and Allegro, now greatly expanded by Eisenman, Thiering, etc., it is still the norm that others are allowed to rebut them, a task that may appear successful, and which we must continue to undertake, but which for many viewers somehow remains irrelevant.

Conclusion

Several lessons are apparent from the difficulties that scholars of the Dead Sea scrolls have had in representing this discovery to the media.

42. BBC/CTVC. J. Drury, Executive Producer; G. Judd, Producer. Aired in Great Britain 2 November 1997; in the U.S. 9 November 1997.

43. Focus Productions, Bristol UK; first aired on 31 March 2002.

44. R. Feather, *The Copper Scroll Decoded: One Man's Search for the Fabulous Treasures of Ancient Egypt* (London: Thorsons, 1999).

Inverting Reality

First, we have to understand that those who seek to use the press, either for publicity, informing the public, or gaining prestige, will have to deal with the reality that the press and media take on a life of their own, beyond scholarly control. Their need to sell their product to the public, as well as the fact that they themselves may look askance at mainstream scholarship may cause them to invert reality.

Second, in the case of the scrolls, certain formative concepts began a process of scroll imaging in the media that will not so easily be reversed. The scrolls discovery and story have spawned a host of notions that conflict with reality but which go back to the early writings of Wilson and Allegro. These were fostered by secrecy and have never been overcome. The media and public have had consistent problems in distinguishing the often subtle differences between use of the scrolls to illumine the background of Christianity — a legitimate and necessary academic enterprise — and the confused reading of the scrolls as Christian texts.

Finally, no matter what scholars do or say, the inevitable desire for a solution to the problem of Christian origins and the hope for a new, secret gospel are so strong that they have and will continue to dog the Dead Sea Scrolls and to determine much of the media's perspective and the character of its portrayal of the residents of Qumran and the texts they left us.

The debates over the scrolls in some ways mirror the ancient reality in which they were composed and gathered. The public culture of the Dead Sea Scrolls in our own day is one of conflict, invective, secrecy, and of the inversion of reality. The life of the sectarians in antiquity was one of conflict with other Jewish groups and severe condemnation of them, secret teachings, and hope for the inversion of this world into a sectarian utopia in the end of days. I leave you with one final thought: Did the culture of the ancient sectarians, as expressed in their scrolls, affect the public culture that now surrounds them? Is there some unbreakable link between the ancient message of the scrolls and their portrayal in the media today? Has the sectarian urge to invert reality and the often-skewed ways in which the Qumranites saw the world around them led to the same skewing and the attendant inversion of reality on the part of the modern media? Is it the fault of the media, or is it inherent in the scrolls themselves and in the modern scholars who study them? Whatever the case, the intimate relationship of scrolls scholarship and the media is a permanent and complex part of the world of contemporary scholarship, showing how important the relics of the past can be in the formation of modern culture.

Bibliography

Abegg, M. G. "The Hebrew of the Dead Sea Scrolls." In *The Dead Sea Scrolls after Fifty Years: A Comprehensive Assessment*, ed. P. W. Flint and J. C. VanderKam, 1:325-58. Leiden: Brill, 1998.

———. "Messianic Hope in 4Q285: A Reassessment." *JBL* 113 (1994) 81-91.

Albeck, C. *Das Buch der Jubiläen und die Halacha*. Siebenundvierzigster Bericht der Hochschule für die Wissenschaft des Judentums in Berlin, 1930.

———. *Mavo' la-Mishnah*. Jerusalem: Bialik Institute and Tel-Aviv: Dvir, 1959.

———. *Shishah Sidre Mishnah*. 6 vols. Jerusalem: Bialik Institute and Tel Aviv: Dvir, 1954.

Albright, W. F. "New Light on Early Recensions of the Hebrew Bible." *BASOR* 140 (1955) 27-33.

Alexander, P. S. "The Redaction-History of Serekh ha-Yaḥad: A Proposal." *RevQ* 17 (Hommage à Józef T. Milik, 1996) 437-47.

———, and G. Vermes. *Qumran Cave 4. XIX: Serekh ha-Yaḥad and Two Related Texts*. DJD 26. Oxford: Clarendon, 1998.

Allegro, J. M. *The Dead Sea Scrolls*. Harmondsworth: Penguin, 1956.

———. *The Dead Sea Scrolls and the Christian Myth*. 1979; 2nd rev. ed. Amherst, NY: Prometheus, 1992.

———. *The Mystery of the Dead Sea Scrolls Revealed*. New York: Gramercy, 1981.

———. *The People of the Dead Sea Scrolls*. London: Routledge and Kegan Paul, 1959.

———. *Qumrân Cave 4.I (4Q158-4Q186)*. DJD 5. Oxford: Clarendon, 1968.

———. *The Treasure of the Copper Scroll*. Garden City: Doubleday, 1960.

Alon, G. "The Bounds of the Laws of Levitical Cleanness." In *Jews, Judaism and the Classical World,* trans. I. Abrahams, 190-234. Jerusalem: Magnes, Hebrew University, 1977.

Alt, A. "The Origins of Israelite Law." In *Essays on Old Testament History and Religion*, trans. R. A. Wilson, 103-71. Garden City: Doubleday, 1968.

Altmann, A. "Shire Qedushah be-Sifrut ha-Hekhalot ha-Qedumah." *Melila* 2 (1946) 8-10.

Amoussine, J. D. "Éphraïm et Manassé dans le Péshèr de Nahum (4 Q p Nahum)." *RevQ* 4 (1963-64) 389-96.

Bibliography

———. (Amusin). "The Reflection of Historical Events of the First Century B.C. in Qumran Commentaries (4Q161; 4Q169; 4Q166)." *HUCA* 48 (1977) 134-46.
Amram Gaon. *Seder Rav 'Amram Ga'on.* Ed. D. S. Goldschmidt. Jerusalem: Mosad Harav Kook, 1971.
Attridge, H., et al. *Qumran Cave 4.VIII: Parabiblical Texts, Part I.* DJD 13. Oxford: Clarendon, 1994.
Avigad, N., and Y. Yadin, eds. *A Genesis Apocryphon: A Scroll from the Wilderness of Judaea.* Jerusalem: Magnes, Hebrew University, and Shrine of the Book, 1956.
Babad, J. "Minḥat Ḥinukh." In *Sefer ha-Ḥinukh*. 3 vols. Jerusalem: Mekhon Yerushalayim, 1989/1990.
Baer, Y. *Seder 'Avodat Yiśra'el.* Tel-Aviv: Or Torah, 1956/57.
Baigent, M., and R. Leigh. *The Dead Sea Scrolls Deception.* New York: Summit, 1991.
———, R. Leigh, and H. Lincoln. *Holy Blood, Holy Grail.* New York: Dell, 1983.
Baillet, M. "Un livret magique en christo-palestinen à l'Université de Louvain." *Mus* 76 (1963) 375-401.
———. *Qumrân Grotte 4.III (4Q482-4Q520).* DJD 7. Oxford: Clarendon, 1982.
———. "Un recueil liturgique de Qumran, grotte 4: 'Les Paroles des Luminaires.'" *RB* 68 (1961) 195-250, pls. 24-28.
———, J. T. Milik, and R. de Vaux, eds. *Les 'Petites Grottes' de Qumrân.* DJD 3. Oxford: Clarendon, 1962.
Barker, M. "The Temple Measurements and the Solar Calendar." In *Temple Scroll Studies,* ed. G. J. Brooke, 63-66. JSPSup 7. Sheffield: JSOT, 1989.
Baron, S. W. *A Social and Religious History of the Jews.* Vol. 5: *Religious Controls and Dissensions.* New York: Columbia University Press and Philadelphia: Jewish Publication Society of America, 1957.
Barr, J. "Hebrew, Aramaic and Greek in the Hellenistic Age." In *CHJ,* vol. 2: *The Hellenistic Age,* 79-114. 1989.
Barthélemy, D., and J. T. Milik. *Qumran Cave I.* DJD 1. Oxford: Clarendon, 1955.
Baumgarten, A. I. *The Flourishing of Jewish Sects in the Maccabean Era: An Interpretation.* JSJSup 55. Leiden: Brill, 1997.
Baumgarten, J. M. "The Cave 4 Versions of the Qumran Penal Code." *JJS* 43 (1992) 268-76.
———. "The Disqualifications of Priests in 4Q Fragments of the 'Damascus Document': A Specimen of the Recovery of pre-Rabbinic Halakha." In *The Madrid Qumran Congress,* ed. J. Trebolle-Barrera and L. Vegas Montaner, 2:503-4. STDJ 11/2. Leiden: Brill, 1992.
———. "4Q502, Marriage or Golden Age Ritual?" *JJS* 35 (1983) 125-35.
———. "4Q503 (Daily Prayers) and the Lunar Calendar." *RevQ* 12 (1986) 388-407.
———. "The Laws of the *Damascus Document* in Current Research." In *The Damascus Document Reconsidered,* ed. M. Broshi, 51-62. Jerusalem: Israel Exploration Society, 1992.
———. "The Pharisaic-Sadducean Controversies about Purity and the Qumran Texts." *JJS* 31 (1980) 157-70.
———. *Qumran Cave 4.XIII: Damascus Document (4Q266-273).* DJD 18. Oxford: Clarendon, 1996.
———. "The Qumran Sabbath Shirot and Rabbinic Merkabah Traditions." *RevQ* 13 (1988) 199-214.

———. "Sadducean Elements in Qumran Law." In *The Community of the Renewed Covenant: The Notre Dame Symposium on the Dead Sea Scrolls*, ed. E. Ulrich and J. VanderKam, 27-36. CJAS 10. Notre Dame: University of Notre Dame Press, 1994.
———. *Studies in Qumran Law*. SJLA 24. Leiden: Brill, 1977.
———. "The Unwritten Law in the Pre-Rabbinic Period." *JSJ* 3 (1972) 7-29. Repr. in *Studies in Qumran Law*, 13-35. SJLA 24. Leiden: Brill, 1977.
——— et al., eds. *Qumran Cave 4.XXV: Halakhic Texts*. DJD 35. Oxford: Clarendon, 1999.
Beal, T. S. *Josephus' Description of the Essenes Illustrated by the Dead Sea Scrolls*. SNTSMS 58. New York: Cambridge University Press, 1988.
Belkin, S. *Philo and the Oral Law: The Philonic Interpretation of Biblical Law in Relation to the Palestinian Halaka*. Cambridge, MA: Harvard University Press, 1940.
Ben-Hayyim, Z. "Traditions in the Hebrew Language with Special Reference to the Dead Sea Scrolls." In *Aspects of the Dead Sea Scrolls*, ed. C. Rabin and Y. Yadin, 200-14. ScrHier 4. Jerusalem: Magnes, Hebrew University, 1958.
Ben Yehuda, E. *Milon ha-Lashon ha-'Ivrit*. 8 vols. New York: Yoseloff, 1959.
Ben-Yehuda, N., J. Zias, and Z. Meshel. "Questioning Masada." *BAR* 24/6 (1998) 30-53, 64-68.
Benoit, P., J. T. Milik, and R. de Vaux. *Les Grottes de Murabba'at*. DJD 2. Oxford: Clarendon, 1960.
Berger, K. *The Truth under Lock and Key? Jesus and the Dead Sea Scrolls*. Trans. J. S. Currie. Louisville: Westminster John Knox, 1995.
Bergmeier, R. *Die Essener-Berichte des Flavius Josephus: Quellenstudien zu den Essenertexten im Werk des jüdischen Historiographen*. Kampen: Kok Pharos, 1993.
Berkovitz, E. *Man and God: Studies in Biblical Theology*. Detroit: Wayne State University Press, 1969.
Bernstein, M. J. "The Employment and Interpretation of Scripture in 4QMMT: Preliminary Observations." In *Reading 4QMMT: New Perspectives on Qumran Law and History*, ed. Bernstein and J. Kampen, 29-51. SBLSymS 2. Atlanta: Scholars, 1996.
———. "4Q252: From Re-written Bible to Biblical Commentary." *JJS* 45 (1994) 1-27.
———. "4Q252: Method and Context, Genre and Sources." *JQR* 85 (1994-1995) 61-79.
———. "4Q252 as Early Jewish Commentary." *RevQ* 17 (1996) 385-401.
———. "The Genre of 4Q252: From Poetry to Pesher." *DSD* 1 (1994) 160-79.
———. "Introductory Formulas for Citation and Re-citation of Biblical Verses in the Qumran Pesharim." *DSD* 1 (1994) 30-70.
———. "Ki Qillat Elohim Talui" (Deut. 21:23): A Study in Early Jewish Exegesis." *JQR* 74 (1983) 21-45.
———. "*Midrash Halakhah* at Qumran? 11Q Temple 64:6-13 and Deuteronomy 21:22-23." *Gesher* 7 (1979) 145-66.
———. "Pseudepigraphy in the Qumran Scrolls: Categories and Functions." In *Pseudepigraphic Perspectives: The Apocrypha and Pseudepigrapha in Light of the Dead Sea Scrolls: Proceedings of the International Symposium of the Orion Center for the Study of the Dead Sea Scrolls and Associated Literature, 12-14 January, 1997*, ed. E. G. Chazon, M. Stone, and A. Pinnick, 1-26. STDJ 31. Leiden: Brill, 1999.
Berrin, S. L. *The Pesher Nahum Scroll from Qumran: An Exegetical Study of 4Q169*. STDJ 53. Leiden: Brill, 2004.
Betz, O., and R. Riesner. *Jesus, Qumran and the Vatican*. New York: Crossroad, 1994.

Bibliography

Biblical Archaeology Society. "The Dead Sea Scrolls." 6 pts. Washington: Biblical Archaeology Society, 1993. (video)

Bickerman, E. *The God of the Maccabees.* Leiden: Brill, 1979.

Black, M., ed. *The Scrolls and Christianity: Historical and Theological Significance.* Theological Collections 11. London: SPCK, 1969.

Bokser, B. M. "Approaching Sacred Space." *HTR* 78 (1985) 279-99.

———. *The Origins of the Seder.* Berkeley: University of California Press, 1984.

———. *Philo's Description of Jewish Practices.* Protocol of the Thirtieth Colloquy. Berkeley: Center for Hermeneutical Studies in Hellenistic and Modern Culture, 1977.

Bonani, G., et al. "Radiocarbon Dating of the Dead Sea Scrolls." *'Atiqot* 20 (1991) 27-32.

Botterweck, G. J., H. Ringgren, and H. J. Fabry, eds. *Theological Dictionary of the Old Testament.* Trans. J. T. Willis et al. 17 vols. Grand Rapids: Wm. B. Eerdmans, 1974-.

Bowersock, G. W. *Roman Arabia.* Cambridge, MA: Harvard University Press, 1983.

Braun, H. *Qumran und das Neue Testament.* 2 vols. Tübingen: Mohr (Siebeck), 1966.

Bregman, M. "Pseudepigraphy in Rabbinic Literature." In *Pseudepigraphic Perspectives: The Apocrypha and Pseudepigrapha in Light of the Dead Sea Scrolls: Proceedings of the International Symposium of the Orion Center for the Study of the Dead Sea Scrolls and Associated Literature, 12-14 January, 1997,* ed. E. G. Chazon, M. Stone, and A. Pinnick, 27-41. STDJ 31. Leiden: Brill, 1999.

Brin, G. "Ha-Miqra bi-Megillat ha-Miqdash." *Shnaton* 4 (1979/1980) 182-225.

Brooke, G. J. "4Q252 as Early Jewish Commentary." *RevQ* 17 (1996) 385-401.

———. *Exegesis at Qumran: 4QFlorilegium in Its Jewish Context.* JSOTSup 29. Sheffield: JSOT, 1985.

———. "The Genre of 4Q252: From Poetry to Pesher." *DSD* 1 (1994) 160-79.

———. "Messiah of Aaron in the Damascus Document." *RevQ* 15 (1991) 215-31.

———. "Qumran Pesher: Toward the Redefinition of a Genre." *RevQ* 10 (1979-1980) 483-503.

———. "The Thematic Content of 4Q252." *JQR* 85 (1994-95) 33-59.

———, et al., eds. *Qumran Cave 4.XVII: Parabiblical Texts, Part 3.* DJD 22. Oxford: Clarendon, 1996.

Broshi, M. *Bread, Wine, Walls and Scrolls.* JSPSup 36. London: Sheffield Academic, 2001.

———. "The Gigantic Dimensions of the Visionary Temple in the Temple Scroll." *BAR* 13/6 (1987) 36-37.

———. "Religion, Ideology and Politics and Their Impact on Palestinian Archaeology." *Israel Museum Journal* 6 (1987) 17-32.

———. "Visionary Architecture and Town Planning in the Dead Sea Scrolls." In *Time to Prepare the Way in the Wilderness: Papers on the Qumran Scrolls by Fellows of the Institute for Advanced Studies of the Hebrew University, Jerusalem, 1989-1990,* ed. D. Dimant and L. H. Schiffman, 9-22. STDJ 16. Leiden: Brill, 1995.

———, ed. *The Damascus Document Reconsidered.* Jerusalem: Israel Exploration Society, Shrine of the Book, Israel Museum, 1992.

———, and Z. Sternhell. *The Shrine of the Book.* Jerusalem: Israel Museum, 1991.

———, et al. *Qumran Cave 4.XIV: Parabiblical Texts, Part 2.* DJD 19. Oxford: Clarendon, 1995.

Brown, D. *The Da Vinci Code.* New York: Doubleday, 2003.

Brown, R. E., et al. *Preliminary Concordance to the Hebrew and Aramaic Fragments from*

Qumrân Caves II-X: Including Especially the Unpublished Material from Cave IV. Prepared and arranged by H.-P. Richter. 5 vols. Göttingen: Privately printed, 1988.

Brownlee, W. H. *The Midrash Pesher of Habakkuk.* SBLMS 24. Missoula: Scholars, 1979.

Bruce, F. F. *Second Thoughts on the Dead Sea Scrolls.* Grand Rapids: Wm. B. Eerdmans, 1977.

Buchanan, G. W. "The Office of Teacher of Righteousness." *RevQ* 9 (1977) 237-40.

Burgmann, H. "11QT: The Sadducean 'Torah.'" In *Temple Scroll Studies,* ed. G. J. Brooke, 257-63. JSPSup 7. Sheffield: JSOT, 1989.

Burrows, M. *The Dead Sea Scrolls.* New York: Viking, 1955.

———. *More Light on the Dead Sea Scrolls.* New York: Viking, 1958.

———, J. C. Trever, and W. H. Brownlee, eds. *The Dead Sea Scrolls of St. Mark's Monastery.* Vol. 1 and vol. 2, fasc. 2. New Haven: ASOR, 1950-51.

Buttrick, G. A., ed. *Interpreter's Dictionary of the Bible.* 4 vols. + sup. Nashville: Abingdon, 1962.

Carmignac, J., et al., eds. *Les Textes de Qumran: traduits et annotés.* 2 vols. Paris: Letouzey et Ané, 1961-63.

Charles, R. H. *The Book of Jubilees, or, the Little Genesis.* 1917; repr. Jerusalem: Makor, 1971/72.

———. *The Greek Versions of the Testaments of the Twelve Patriarchs.* 1908. 2nd ed. Oxford: Clarendon, 1960.

———, ed. *The Apocrypha and Pseudepigrapha of the Old Testament in English.* Vol. 1: *Apocrypha.* Vol. 2: *Pseudepigrapha.* 1913. Repr. Oxford: Oxford University Press, 1963.

———, ed. *The Book of Enoch or 1 Enoch.* 1912; repr. Jerusalem: Makor, 1972/73.

Charlesworth, J. H. *The Pesharim and Qumran History: Chaos or Consensus?* Grand Rapids: Wm. B. Eerdmans, 2002.

———, ed. *The Dead Sea Scrolls: Hebrew, Aramaic, and Greek Texts with English Translations.* 6 vols. to date. Tübingen: Mohr (Siebeck) and Louisville: Westminster John Knox, 1994-.

———, ed. *The Messiah: Developments in Earliest Judaism and Christianity.* The First Princeton Symposium on Judaism and Christian Origins. Minneapolis: Fortress, 1992.

———, ed. *The Old Testament Pseudepigrapha.* 2 vols. Garden City: Doubleday, 1983-85.

———, and W. P. Weaver, eds. *The Dead Sea Scrolls and the Christian Faith.* Harrisburg: Trinity Press International, 1998.

———, et al. *Miscellaneous Texts from the Judaean Desert.* DJD 38. Oxford: Clarendon, 2000.

Chazon, E. G. "4QDibHam: Liturgy or Literature?" *RevQ* 15 (Mémorial Jean Starcky, 1992) 447-55.

———. "Hymns and Prayers in the Dead Sea Scrolls." In *The Dead Sea Scrolls after Fifty Years,* ed. P. Flint and J. C. VanderKam, 244-70. Leiden: Brill, 1998.

———. "Is *Divrei Ha-me'orot* a Sectarian Prayer?" In *The Dead Sea Scrolls: Forty Years of Research,* ed. D. Dimant and U. Rappaport, 3-17. Leiden: Brill and Jerusalem: Magnes, Hebrew University, and Yad Izhak Ben-Zvi, 1992.

———. "On the Special Character of Sabbath Prayer: New Data from Qumran." *Journal of Jewish Liturgy and Music* 15 (1992-93) 1-21.

———. "Prayers from Qumran and Their Historical Implications." *DSD* 1 (1994) 265-84.

---. "*Te'udah Liturgit Mi-Qumran Ve-Hashlekhoteha: 'Divre Ha-Me'orot.'*" Ph.D. diss., Hebrew University, 1991.

---, et al. *Qumran Cave 4.XX: Poetical and Liturgical Texts, Part 2*. DJD 29. Oxford: Clarendon, 1999.

Chyutin, M. "The New Jerusalem: Ideal City." *DSD* 1 (1994) 71-97.

---. *The New Jerusalem Scroll from Qumran: A Comprehensive Reconstruction*. JSPSup 25. Sheffield: Sheffield Academic, 1997.

Cohen, G. D. *Sefer Ha-Qabbalah: The Book of Tradition by Abraham ibn Daud*. Philadelphia: Jewish Publication Society, 1967.

Cohen, S. J. D. *The Beginnings of Jewishness: Boundaries, Varieties, Uncertainties*. Berkeley: University of California Press, 1999.

Collins, J. J. "Apocalyptic and the Discourse of the Qumran Community." *JNES* 49 (1990) 135-44.

---. *The Apocalyptic Imagination*. New York: Crossroad, 1984. 2nd ed. BRS. Grand Rapids: Wm.. B. Eerdmans and Livonia: Dove, 1998.

---. *Apocalypticism in the Dead Sea Scrolls*. London: Routledge, 1997.

---. *The Scepter and the Star: The Messiahs of the Dead Sea Scrolls and Other Ancient Literature*. ABRL. New York: Doubleday, 1995.

---. "Was the Dead Sea Sect an Apocalyptic Movement?" In *Archaeology and History in the Dead Sea Scrolls: The New York University Conference in Memory of Yigael Yadin*, ed. L. H. Schiffman, 25-51. JSPSup 8. JSOT/ASOR Monographs 2. Sheffield: Sheffield Academic, 1990.

Cook, E. M. *Solving the Mysteries of the Dead Sea Scrolls*. Grand Rapids: Zondervan, 1994.

Cotton, H. M., and A. Yardeni. *Aramaic, Hebrew and Greek Documentary Texts from Naḥal Ḥever and Other Sites: With an Appendix Containing Alleged Qumran Texts (The Seiyâl Collection II)*. DJD 27. Oxford: Clarendon, 1997.

---, and J. Geiger. *Masada II: The Latin and Greek Documents*. Jerusalem: Israel Exploration Society, 1989.

Crawford, S. White. "A Comparison of the 'A' and 'B' Manuscripts of the Damascus Document." *RevQ* 12 (1987) 537-53.

---. "Has *Esther* Been Found at Qumran? *4QProto-Esther* and the *Esther* Corpus." *RevQ* 17 (Hommage à Józef T. Milik, 1996) 307-25.

Cross, F. M. *The Ancient Library of Qumran*. 3rd ed. Sheffield: Sheffield Academic, 1995.

---. *The Ancient Library of Qumran and Modern Biblical Studies*. Garden City: Doubleday, 1961. Repr. Grand Rapids: Baker, 1980.

---. "The Contribution of the Qumran Discoveries to the Study of the Biblical Text." *IEJ* 16 (1966) 81-95.

---. "The Development of the Jewish Scripts." In *The Bible and the Ancient Near East: Essays in Honor of William Foxwell Albright*, ed. G. E. Wright, 133-202. Garden City: Doubleday, 1961.

---. "The Early History of the Qumran Community." In *New Directions in Biblical Archaeology*, ed. D. N. Freedman and J. C. Greenfield, 70-89. Garden City: Doubleday, 1971.

---. "The Evolution of a Theory of Local Texts." In *Qumran and the History of the Bib-*

lical Text, ed. Cross and S. Talmon, 306-20. Cambridge, MA: Harvard University Press, 1975.

———. "Samaria Papyrus 1: An Aramaic Slave Conveyance of 335 BCE Found in the Wâdi ed-Dâliyeh." *ErIsr* 18 (N. Avigad Festschrift, 1985) 7-17.

Davies, P. R. *1QM, the War Scroll from Qumran: Its Structure and History.* BibOr 32. Rome: Biblical Institute Press, 1977.

———. *The Damascus Covenant: An Interpretation of the "Damascus Document."* JSOTSup 25. Sheffield: JSOT, 1983.

———. "Qumran and Apocalyptic or Obscurum per Obscurius." *JNES* 49 (1990) 127-34.

———, G. J. Brooke, and P. R. Callaway. *The Complete World of the Dead Sea Scrolls.* London: Thames and Hudson, 2002.

Davies, W. D. *Torah in the Messianic Age and/or the Age to Come.* Philadelphia: SBL, 1952.

Davis, M. "Jewish Religious Life and Institutions in America (A Historical Study)." In *The Jews: Their Religion and Culture,* ed. L. Finkelstein, 274-379. 4th ed. New York: Schocken, 1971.

"The Dead Sea Scrolls: Voices of the Desert." Discovery Channel. Produced by Brigham Young University, KBYU/Scandinature Films, 1998. (video)

Deasley, A. *The Shape of Qumran Theology.* Carlisle: Paternoster, 2000.

Deines, R. *Die Pharisäer.* WUNT 101. Tübingen: Mohr (Siebeck), 1997.

Dimant, D. "Apocalyptic Texts at Qumran." In *The Community of the Renewed Covenant: The Notre Dame Symposium on the Dead Sea Scrolls,* ed. E. Ulrich and J. VanderKam, 175-91. CJAS 10. Notre Dame: University of Notre Dame Press, 1994.

———. "An Apocryphon of Jeremiah from Cave 4 ($4Q385^B$ = 4Q385 16)." In *New Qumran Texts and Studies: Proceedings of the First Meeting of the International Organization for Qumran Studies, Paris 1992,* ed. G. J. Brooke, 11-31. STDJ 15. Leiden: Brill, 1994.

———. "Ben Miqra' la-Megillot: Siṭaṭot min ha-Torah bi-Megillat Berit Dameseq." In *"Sha'arei Talmon": Studies in the Bible, Qumran, and the Ancient Near East Presented to Shemaryahu Talmon,* ed. M. Fishbane and E. Tov, with W. W. Fields, 113*-22*. Winona Lake: Eisenbrauns, 1992.

———. "New Light from Qumran on the Jewish Pseudepigrapha-4Q390." In *The Madrid Qumran Conference: Proceedings of the International Congress on the Dead Sea Scrolls, Madrid, 18-21 March 1991,* ed. J. Trebolle Barrera and L. Vegas Montaner, 2:405-48. STDJ 11/2. Leiden: Brill and Madrid: Editorial Complutense, 1992.

———. *Qumran Cave 4.XXI: Parabiblical Texts, Part 4: Pseudo-Prophetic Texts.* DJD 30. Oxford: Clarendon, 2001.

———. "The Qumran Manuscripts: Contents and Significance." In *Time to Prepare the Way in the Wilderness: Papers on the Qumran Scrolls by Fellows of the Institute for Advanced Studies of the Hebrew University, Jerusalem, 1989-90,* ed. Dimant and L. H. Schiffman, 23-58. STDJ 16. Leiden: Brill, 1995.

———. "Qumran Sectarian Literature." In *Jewish Writings of the Second Temple Period,* ed. M. Stone, 483-550. CRINT II/2. Philadelphia: Fortress, 1984.

Donner, H., and W. Röllig. *Kanaanäische und aramäische Inschriften.* 3 parts. Wiesbaden: Harrassowitz, 1966.

"Doomsday." Discover Magazine (Discovery Channel). Providence Pictures. December, 1997. (video)

Doudna, G. L. *4Q Pesher Nahum: A Critical Edition*. JSPSup 35. Copenhagen International Series 8. London: Sheffield Academic, 2001.

Drawnel, H. *An Aramaic Wisdom Text from Qumran: A New Interpretation of the Levi Document*. JSJSup 86. Leiden: Brill, 2004.

Driver, G. R. *The Judaean Scrolls: The Problem and a Solution*. Oxford: Blackwell, 1965.

Dubnov, S. *Toledot ha-Ḥasidut bi-Tequfat Ṣemiḥatah ve-Giddulah*. Tel Aviv: Dvir, 1932.

Duhaime, J. "War Scroll (1QM; 1Q33; 4Q491-496=4QM1-6; 4Q497)." In *The Dead Sea Scrolls*, vol. 2: *Damascus Document, War Scroll, and Related Documents*, ed. J. H. Charlesworth, 80-141. Tübingen: Mohr (Siebeck) and Louisville: Westminster John Knox, 1995.

———. *The War Texts: 1QM and Related Manuscripts*. London: T & T Clark, 2004.

Dupont-Sommer, A. "Le Commentaire de Nahum découvert près de la Mer Morte (4Q p Nah): Traduction et notes." *Sem* 13 (1963) 55-88.

———. "Contribution à l'exégèse du Manuel de Discipline X 1-8." *VT* 3 (1952) 229-43.

———. *The Dead Sea Scrolls: A Preliminary Survey*. Trans. E. M. Rowley. Oxford: Blackwell, 1952.

———. *Les écrits ésseniens découverts près de la Mer Morte*. Paris: Payot, 1959.

———. "Exorcismes et guérisons dans les manuscrits de Qoumrân." *VTSup* 7 (1959) 246-61.

———. *The Jewish Sect of Qumran and the Essenes: New Studies on the Dead Sea Scrolls*. Trans. R. D. Barnett. London: Vallentine, Mitchell, 1954.

———. "Lumières nouvelles sur l'arrière-plan historique des écrits de Qumran." *ErIsr* 8 (Sukenik Volume, 1967) 25*-36*.

Eisenman, R. H. *The Dead Sea Scrolls and the First Christians: Essays and Translations*. Rockport, MA: Element, 1996.

———. *James the Brother of Jesus*. New York: Penguin, 1998.

———, and J. M. Robinson. *A Facsimile Edition of the Dead Sea Scrolls: Prepared with an Introduction and Index*. 2 vols. Washington: Biblical Archaeology Society, 1991. Publisher's Foreword by H. Shanks.

———, and G. Vermes. "More on the Pierced Messiah Text from Eisenman and Vermes." *BAR* 19/1 (1993) 66-67.

———, and M. O. Wise, eds. *The Dead Sea Scrolls Uncovered: The First Complete Translation and Interpretation of 50 Key Documents Withheld for over 35 Years*. Shaftesbury, Dorset: Element, 1992.

Elbogen, I. *Ha-Tefillah be-Yiśra'el be-Hitpatḥutah ha-Historit*. Tel-Aviv: Dvir, 1972.

Elgvin, T., et al. *Qumran Cave 4.XV: Sapiential Texts, Part 1*. DJD 20. Oxford: Clarendon, 1997.

Eliade, M., ed. *Encyclopedia of Religion*. 16 vols. New York: Macmillan and Free Press, 1987.

Elior, R. *Miqdash u-Merkavah, Kohanim u-Mal'akhim, Hekhal ve-Hekhalot ba-Mistiqah ha-Yehudit ha-Qedumah*. Jerusalem: Magnes, Hebrew University, 2002.

Elledge, C. D. *The Statutes of the King: The Temple Scroll's Legislation on Kingship (11Q19 LVI 12–LIX 21)*. Paris: Gabalda, 2004.

Elliott, M. A. *The Survivors of Israel: A Reconsideration of the Theology of Pre-Christian Judaism*. Grand Rapids: Wm. B. Eerdmans, 2000.

Ellis, E. E. "Biblical Interpretation in the New Testament Church." In *Mikra: Text, Transla-*

tion, Reading and Interpretation of the Hebrew Bible in Ancient Judaism and Early Christianity, ed. M. J. Mulder, 691-725. CRINT 1. Minneapolis: Fortress, 1990.

Elman, Y. "Some Remarks on 4QMMT and the Rabbinic Tradition, or, When Is a Parallel Not a Parallel?" In *Reading 4QMMT: New Perspectives on Qumran Law and History,* ed. J. Kampen and M. J. Bernstein, 99-128. SBLSymS 2. Atlanta: Scholars, 1996.

Elon, M. *Ha-Mishpaṭ ha-ʿIvri.* Jerusalem: Magnes, Hebrew University, 1973.

Elwolde, J. F. "Developments in Hebrew Vocabulary between Bible and Mishnah." In *The Hebrew of the Dead Sea Scrolls and Ben Sira: Proceedings of a Symposium Held at Leiden University, 11-14 December 1995,* 17-55. STDJ 26. Leiden: Brill, 1997.

Eshel, E. "4QLev^d: A Possible Source for the Temple Scroll and *Miqṣat Maʿaśe ha-Torah*." *DSD* 2 (1995) 1-13.

———. "4Q477: The Rebukes by the Overseer." *JJS* 45 (1994) 111-22.

———, H. Eshel, and A. Yardeni. "A Qumran Composition Containing Part of Ps. 154 and a Prayer for the Welfare of King Jonathan and His Kingdom." *IEJ* 42 (1992) 199-229.

———, et al. *Qumran Cave 4. VI: Poetical and Liturgical Texts, Part 1.* DJD 11. Oxford: Clarendon, 1998.

Eshel, H. "The Historical Background of the Pesher Interpreting Joshua's Curse on the Rebuilder of Jericho." *RevQ* 15 (Mémorial Jean Starcky, 1992) 409-20.

———. "The Kittim in the War Scroll and in the Pesharim." In *Historical Perspectives: From the Hasmoneans to Bar Kokhba in Light of the Dead Sea Scrolls. Proceedings of the Fourth International Symposium of the Orion Center for the Study of the Dead Sea Scrolls and Associated Literature, 27-31 January, 1999,* ed. D. Goodblatt, A. Pinnick, and D. R. Schwartz, 29-44. STDJ 37. Leiden: Brill, 2001.

———, and D. Amit. *Meʿarot ha-Miflaṭ mi-Tekufat Mered Bar-Kokhva (Refuge Caves of the Bar Kokhba Revolt).* "Eretz," Geographic Research and Publications Project for the Advancement of Knowledge of Eretz Israel, Tel-Aviv University. Tel-Aviv: Israel Exploration Society, College of Judea and Samaria, and C. G. Foundation Jerusalem, 1998.

———, and J. Strugnell. "Alphabetical Acrostics in Pre-Tannaitic Hebrew." *CBQ* 62 (2000) 441-58.

Evans, C. A., and S. E. Porter, eds. *Dictionary of New Testament Background.* Downers Grove: InterVarsity, 2000.

Ewing, U. C. *The Prophet of the Dead Sea Scrolls: The Essenes and the Early Christians — One and the Same People, Their Seven Devout Practices.* 3rd ed. Joshua Tree, CA: Tree of Life, 1994.

Falk, D. K. *Daily, Sabbath, and Festival Prayers in the Dead Sea Scrolls.* STDJ 27. Leiden: Brill, 1998.

Feather, R. *The Copper Scroll Decoded: One Man's Search for the Fabulous Treasures of Ancient Egypt.* London: Thorsons, 1999.

Finkelstein, L. "The Maxim of the Anshe Keneset ha-Gedolah." *JBL* 59 (1940) 455-69.

———. *Ha-Perushim ve-Anshe Keneset ha-Gedolah (The Pharisees and the Men of the Great Synagogue).* Texts and Studies of the Jewish Theological Seminary of America 15. New York: Jewish Theological Seminary of America, 1950.

———. *The Pharisees: The Sociological Background of Their Faith.* 2 vols. 3rd ed. Morris Loeb Series. Philadelphia: Jewish Publication Society of America, 1966.

———, ed. *Sifre on Deuteronomy*. New York: Jewish Theological Seminary of America, 1969.
Fisdel, S. A. *The Dead Sea Scrolls: Understanding Their Spiritual Message*. Northvale, NJ: Aronson, 1997.
Fisher, L. R. "The Temple Quarter." *JJS* 8 (1963) 34-41.
Fitzmyer, J. A. *Essays on the Semitic Background of the New Testament*. Missoula: Scholars, 1974. Repr. *The Semitic Background of the New Testament*. BRS. Grand Rapids: Wm. B. Eerdmans and Livonia: Dove, 1997.
———. "Further Light on Melchizedek from Qumran Cave 11." In *Essays on the Semitic Background of the New Testament*, 245-67.
———. *The Genesis Apocryphon of Qumran Cave 1: A Commentary*. BibOr 18A. Rome: Biblical Institute Press, 1971.
———. "Prolegomenon." In S. Schechter, *Documents of Jewish Sectaries*. Vol. 1: *Fragments of a Zadokite Work*, 9-37. Library of Biblical Studies. New York: Ktav, 1970.
———. *A Wandering Aramean: Collected Aramaic Essays*. SBLMS 25. Missoula: Scholars, 1979. Repr. *The Semitic Background of the New Testament*. BRS. Grand Rapids: Wm. B. Eerdmans and Livonia: Dove, 1997.
———, and D. J. Harrington. *A Manual of Palestinian Aramaic Texts*. BibOr 34. Rome: Biblical Institute Press, 1978.
Fleischer, E. "Le-Qadmoniot Tefillot ha-Ḥovah be-Yisra'el." *Tarbiz* 59 (1990) 397-441.
Flint, P. W. *The Dead Sea Psalms Scrolls and the Book of Psalms*. STDJ 17. Leiden: Brill, 1997.
Flusser, D. *Judaism and the Origins of Christianity*. Jerusalem: Magnes, 1988.
———. "Kat Midbar Yehudah ve-ha-Perushim." *Molad* 19 (1961) 456-58.
———. "Perushim, Ṣeduqim, ve-'Issiyim be-Fesher Naḥum." In *Essays in Jewish History and Philology, in Memory of Gedaliahu Alon*, ed. M. Dorman, S. Safrai, and M. Stern, 133-68. Tel Aviv: Hakibbutz Hameuchad, 1970.
———. *Sefer Yosifon*. 2 vols. Jerusalem: Bialik Institute, 1980.
———. *The Spiritual History of the Dead Sea Scrolls*. Tel Aviv: MOD, 1989.
———. *Yahadut u-Meqorot ha-Naṣrut: Meḥqarim u-Masot*. Sifre Daʿat Zemanenu. Israel: Sifriyat Poʿalim, Ha-Kibuṣ Ha-ʿArṣi Ha-Shomer Ha-Ṣaʿir, 1979.
Forbes N., and R. H. Charles. "2 Enoch, or the Book of the Secrets of Enoch." In *The Apocrypha and Pseudepigrapha of the Old Testament in English*, vol. 2: *Pseudepigrapha*, ed. Charles, 425-69. 1913; repr. Oxford: Oxford University Press, 1968.
Forkman, G. *The Limits of the Religious Community*. Lund: Gleerup, 1972.
Frankel, Z. *Ueber den Einfluss der palaestinischen Exegese auf die alexandrinische Hermeneutik*. Leipzig: Barth, 1851.
———. *Vorstudien zu der Septuaginta*. Leipzig: Vogel, 1841.
Freedman, D. N., ed. *Anchor Bible Dictionary*. 6 vols. New York: Doubleday, 1992.
García Martínez, F. *The Dead Sea Scrolls Translated*. Trans. W. G. E. Watson. 2nd ed. Leiden: Brill and Grand Rapids: Wm. B. Eerdmans, 1996.
———. "The Last Surviving Columns of 11QNJ." In *The Scriptures and Scrolls: Studies in Honour of A. S. van der Woude on the Occasion of His 65th Birthday*, ed. García Martínez, A. Hilhorst, and C. J. Labuschagne, 178-92 and pls. 3-9. VTSup 49. Leiden: Brill, 1992.
———. "Messianische Erwartungen in den Qumranschriften." *JBTh* 8 (1993) 171-208.

———. "The 'New Jerusalem' and the Future Temple of the Manuscripts from Qumran." In *Qumran and Apocalyptic: Studies on the Aramaic Texts from Qumran*, 180-213. STDJ 9. Leiden: Brill, 1992.

———. "Notas al margen de *The Dead Sea Scrolls Uncovered.*" *RevQ* 16 (1993) 123-50.

———. *Qumran and Apocalyptic: Studies on the Aramaic Texts from Qumran*. STDJ 9. Leiden: Brill, 1992.

———. "El Rollo del Templo (11QTemple): Bibliografia sistematici." *RevQ* 12 (1985-87) 425-40.

———. "Significado de los Manuscritos de Qumran para el Conocimiento de Jesucristo y del Cristianismo." *Communio* 22 (1989) 338-42.

———. "Sources et rédaction du *Rouleau du Temple.*" *Hen* 13 (1991) 219-32.

———. "The Temple Scroll and the New Jerusalem." In *The Dead Sea Scrolls after Fifty Years: A Comprehensive Assessment*, ed. J. C. VanderKam and P. W. Flint, 2:431-60. Leiden: Brill, 1998-99.

———, and D. W. Parry. *A Bibliography of the Finds in the Desert of Judah, 1970-95*. STDJ 19. Leiden: Brill, 1996.

———, and E. J. C. Tigchelaar, eds. *The Dead Sea Scrolls Study Edition*. 2 vols. Leiden: Brill and Grand Rapids: Wm. B. Eerdmans, 2000.

———, E. J. C. Tigchelaar, and A. S. van der Woude. *Qumran Cave 11.II (11Q2-18, 11Q20-31)*. DJD 23. Oxford: Clarendon, 1998.

———, and A. S. van der Woude. "A 'Groningen' Hypothesis of Qumran Origins and Early History." *RevQ* 14 (The Texts of Qumran and the History of the Community: Proceedings of the Groningen Congress on the Dead Sea Scrolls 3, 1990) 521-41.

Gärtner, B. *The Temple and the Community in Qumran and the New Testament*. Cambridge: Cambridge University Press, 1965.

Gaster, M. "The Hebrew Text of One of the Testaments of the Twelve Patriarchs." *Society of Biblical Archaeology: Proceedings* 16-17 (1894) 33-49.

Geiger, A. *Urschrift und Übersetzungen der Bibel in ihrer Abhängigkeit von der innern Entwicklung des Judentums*. Breslau: Hainauer, 1857. Hebrew trans. Y. L. Baruch, *Ha-Miqra ve-Targumav be-Ziqatam le-Hitpathutah ha-Penimit shel ha-Yahadut*. Jerusalem: Bialik Foundation, 1948/49.

Gevaryahu, M. "Tefillat Nabonid mi-Megillot Midbar Yehudah." In *'Iyyunim bi-Megillot Midbar Yehudah*, ed. J. Liver. 12-23. Jerusalem: Kiryat Sepher, 1957.

Ginzberg, L. *Eine unbekannte jüdische Sekte*. New York: L. Ginzberg, 1922. Repr. from *MGWJ* 55 (1911)–58 (1914).

———. *An Unknown Jewish Sect*. New York: Jewish Theological Seminary of America, 1976.

Glassman, S. *Megiles fun Yam Hamelach (Scrolls of the Dead Sea)*. New York: Yiddish Kultur Farband, 1965.

Goitein, S. D. *A Mediterranean Society*. 6 vols. Berkeley: University of California Press, 1967.

Golb, N. "The Dead Sea Scrolls: A New Perspective." *American Scholar* 58 (1989) 177-207.

———. *Who Wrote the Dead Sea Scrolls? The Search for the Secret of Qumran*. New York: Scribner, 1995.

Goshen-Gottstein, M. H. "Linguistic Structure and Tradition in the Qumran Documents."

In *Aspects of the Dead Sea Scrolls,* ed. C. Rabin and Y. Yadin, 101-37. ScrHier 4. Jerusalem: Magnes, Hebrew University, 1958.

———. "The *Psalms Scroll* (11QPsª): A Problem of Canon and Text." *Textus* 5 (1966) 22-33.

Greenfield, J. C. "The Words of Levi Son of Jacob in *Damascus Document* IV, 15-19 (CD)." *RevQ* 13 (1988) 319-22.

———. "The Languages of Palestine, 200 BCE-200 CE." In *Jewish Languages: Theme and Variations,* ed. H. H. Paper. 143-54. Cambridge, MA: Association for Jewish Studies, 1978.

———, and S. Shaked. "Three Iranian Words in the Targum of Job from Qumran." *ZDMG* 122 (1972) 37-45.

———, and M. Sokoloff. "Astrological and Related Omen Texts in Jewish Palestinian Aramaic." *JNES* 48 (1989) 202.

———, and M. Sokoloff. "The Names of the Zodiac in Aramaic and Hebrew." In *Au carrefour des religions: Mélanges offerts à Phillipe Gignoux,* ed. R. Gyselen, 95-101. Res orientales 7. Bures-sur-Yvette: Groupe pour l'étude de la civilisation du Moyen-Orient, 1995.

———, M. E. Stone, and E. Eshel, eds. *The Aramaic Levi Documents: Edition, Translation, Commentary.* SVTP 19. Leiden: Brill, 2004.

Grohmann, A. *Arabic Papyri from Ḥirbet el-Mird.* Bibliothèque du Muséon 52. Louvain: Publications universitaires, 1963.

Gropp, D. M. "The Samaria Papyri from the Wâdi ed-Dâliyeh: The Slave Sales." Ph.D. diss., Harvard, 1986.

———. *Wadi Daliyeh II: The Samaria Papyri from Wadi Daliyeh;* M. Bernstein et al., with J. VanderKam and M. Brady. *Qumran Cave 4.XXVIII: Miscellanea, Part 2.* DJD 28. Oxford: Clarendon, 2001.

Gulak, A. *Ha-Sheṭarot ba-Talmud: Le-'Or ha-Papirusim ha-Yevaniyim mi-Miṣrayim ule-'Or ha-Mishpaṭ ha-Yevani veha-Romi.* Ed. and suppl. R. Katzoff. Jerusalem: Magnes, Hebrew University, 1994.

Habermann, A. M. "'Al ha-Tefillin bi-Yeme Qedem." *ErIsr* 3 (1953/54) 174-77.

Hayes, J. *Gentile Impurities and Jewish Identities: Intermarriage and Conversion from the Bible to the Talmud.* Oxford: Oxford University Press, 2002.

Halivni, D. See, Weiss Halivni, D.

Hallo, W., ed. *The Context of Scripture.* Vol. 2: *Monumental Inscriptions from the Biblical World.* Leiden: Brill, 2000.

Hanson, K. *The Dead Sea Scrolls: The Untold Story.* Tulsa: Council Oak, 1997.

Harrington, D. J. *Wisdom Texts from Qumran.* London: Routledge, 1996.

Heisey, T. M. "Paradigm Agreement and Literature Obsolescence: A Comparative Study in the Literature of the Dead Sea Scrolls." *JD* 44 (1988) 285-301.

Hempel, C. "The Laws of the Damascus Document and 4QMMT." In *The Damascus Document: A Centennial of Discovery: Proceedings of the Third International Symposium of the Orion Center for the Study of the Dead Sea Scrolls and Associated Literature, 4-8 February, 1998,* ed. J. M. Baumgarten, E. G. Chazon, and A. Pinnick, 69-84. STDJ 34. Leiden: Brill, 2000.

———. *The Laws of the Damascus Document: Sources, Tradition and Redaction.* STDJ 29. Leiden: Brill, 1998.

———. "Who Rebukes in 4Q477?" *RevQ* 16 (1995) 655-56.
Hengel, M., J. H. Charlesworth, and D. Mendels. "The Polemical Character of 'On Kingship' in the Temple Scroll: An Attempt at Dating 11QTemple." *JJS* 37 (1986) 28-38.
Herr, M. D. "The Calendar." In *The Jewish People in the First Century*, ed. S. Safrai and M. Stern, 2:834-64. CRINT 1. Philadelphia: Fortress, 1976.
———. "Hashpaʿot Helenisṭiyot ba-ʿIr ha-Yehudit be-Ereṣ Yiśraʾel ba-Meʾot ha-Reviʿit veha-Shishit la-Sefirat ha-Noṣrim." *Cathedra* 8 (1977/78) 90-94.
———. "Hashpaʿot Ḥiṣṣoniyot be-ʿOlamam shel Ḥakhamim be-Ereṣ Yiśraʾel — Qeliṭah u-Deḥiyah." In *Hitbolelut u-Ṭemiʿah*, ed. Y. Kaplan and M. Stern, 83-106. Jerusalem: Merkaz Zalman Shazar le-Toldot Yiśraʾel, 1988/89.
Heschel, S. *Abraham Geiger and the Jewish Jesus*. CSJH. Chicago: University of Chicago Press, 1998.
Higger, M. *Masekhtot Zeʿirot*. Jerusalem: Makor, 1969/1970.
Hillers, D. R. *Covenant: The History of a Biblical Idea*. Baltimore: Johns Hopkins, 1969.
"History's Mysteries: The Dead Sea Scrolls." Learning Channel. Aired April 11, 1994.
Holdheim, S. "Maʾamar ha-ʾIshut ʿal Tekhunat ha-Rabbanim ve-ha-Qaraʾim." Berlin: Bevet ʾAlmanat ha-Rav ha-Manoaḥ, 1861.
Hoover, S. M. "Religion, Media and the Cultural Center of Gravity." http://www.colorado.edu/Journalism/MEDIALYF/analysis/umcom.html.
Horgan, M. P. *Pesharim: Qumran Interpretations of Biblical Books*. CBQMS 8. Washington: Catholic Biblical Association of America, 1979.
Horovitz, H. S., ed. *Sifre Be-Midbar*. Jerusalem: Wahrmann, 1966.
———, ed. *Sifre Zuṭaʾ*. In *Sifre Be-Midbar*, 227-336. Jerusalem: Wahrmann, 1966.
———, and I. A. Rabin, eds. *Mekhilta de-Rabbi Ishmael*. Jerusalem: Bamberger and Wahrmann, 1960.
Humbert, J.-B. "L'espace sacré à Qumrân." *RB* 101-2 (1994) 199-201.
Idel, M. *Hasidism: Between Ecstasy and Magic*. Albany: SUNY Press, 1995.
Iwry, S. "Was There a Migration to Damascus? The Problem of שבי ישראל." *ErIsr* 9 (W. F. Albright Volume, 1969) 80-88.
Jacobs, L. "Are There Fictitious Baraitot in the Babylonian Talmud?" *HUCA* 42 (1971) 185-96.
———. *Hasidic Prayer*. Littman Library of Jewish Civilization. New York: Jewish Publication Society of America and Schocken, 1975.
———. "How Much of the Babylonian Talmud Is Pseudepigraphic?" *JJS* 28 (1977) 46-59.
James, M. R. *The Lost Apocrypha of the Old Testament: Their Titles and Fragments*. London: Society for Promoting Christian Knowledge and New York: Macmillan, 1920.
Jastrow, M. *Dictionary of the Targumim, Talmud Babli, Yerushalmi, and Midrashic Literature*. New York: Judaica, 1992.
Jeremias, J. *Der Lehrer der Gerechtigkeit*. Göttingen: Vandenhoeck & Ruprecht, 1963.
Jongeling, B., C. J. Labuschagne, and A. S. van der Woude. *Aramaic Texts from Qumran: With Translations and Annotations*. SSS N.S. 4. Leiden: Brill, 1976.
Josephus. Trans. H. St. J. Thackeray et al. 10 vols. LCL. Cambridge: Harvard University Press, 1926-1965.
Jull, A. J. T., et al. "Radiocarbon Dating of Scrolls and Linen Fragments from the Judean Desert." *ʿAtiqot* 28 (1996) 85-61.

Bibliography

Kahle, P. E. *The Cairo Geniza*. 2nd ed. Oxford: Blackwell, 1959.

Kampen, J. I. "The Diverse Aspects of Wisdom in the Qumran Texts." In *The Dead Sea Scrolls after Fifty Years: A Comprehensive Assessment,* ed. P. W. Flint and J. C. VanderKam, 1:211-43. Leiden: Brill, 1998.

———. *The Hasideans and the Origin of Pharisaism: A Study in 1 and 2 Maccabees.* SBLSCS 24. Atlanta: Scholars, 1988.

Katz, J. *Halakhah ve-Qabbalah: Mehqarim be-Toldot Dat Yiśra'el 'al Medurehah ve-Ziqatah ha-Ḥevratit.* Jerusalem: Magnes, Hebrew University, 1984.

———. *Tradition and Crisis: Jewish Society at the End of the Middle Ages.* Trans. B. D. Cooperman. New York: New York University Press, 1993.

Katzman, A. "Cave Men." *Haaretz Supplement,* 9 November 1990. (Hebrew)

———. "Chief Dead Sea Scrolls Editor Denounces Judaism, Israel." *BAR* 17/1 (1991) 64-65, 70, 72. Originally appeared in Hebrew in *Haaretz,* 9 November 1990.

Kaufman, S. A. "The Temple Scroll and Higher Criticism." *HUCA* 53 (1982) 29-43.

Kaufman, Y. *The History of the Religion of Israel.* Vol. 4: *From the Babylonian Captivity to the End of Prophecy.* New York: Ktav, 1977.

Khan, G. "The Pre-Islamic Background of Muslim Legal Formularies." *Aram* 6 (1994) 193-224.

Klawans, J. *Impurity and Sin in Ancient Judaism.* Oxford: Oxford University Press, 2000.

Knohl, I. "Qabbalat Qorbanot min Ha-Nokhrim." *Tarbiz* 48 (1969/1970) 341-45.

Kobelski, P. J. *Melchizedek and Melchireša'.* CBQMS 10. Washington: Catholic Biblical Association of America, 1981.

Koffmahn, E. *Die Doppelurkunden aus der Wüste Juda.* STDJ 5. Leiden: Brill, 1968.

Kosmala, H. "Maskil." *JANESCU* 5 (1973) 235-41.

———. "The Three Nets of Belial (A Study in the Terminology of Qumran and the New Testament)." *ASTI* 4 (1965) 91-113.

Kugler, R. A. *From Patriarch to Priest: The Levi-Priestly Tradition from* Aramaic Levi *to* Testament of Levi. SBLEJL 9. Atlanta: Scholars, 1996.

———. "Rewriting Rubrics: Sacrifice and the Religion of Qumran." In *Religion in the Dead Sea Scrolls,* ed. J. J. Collins and Kugler, 90-112. SDSSRL. Grand Rapids: Wm. B. Eerdmans, 2000.

———. *The Testaments of the Twelve Patriarchs.* Guides to Apocrypha and Pseudepigrapha. Sheffield: Sheffield Academic, 2001.

Kuhn, K. G. "The Two Messiahs of Aaron and Israel." In *The Scrolls and the New Testament,* ed. K. Stendahl and J. H. Charlesworth, 54-64. New York: Crossroad, 1992.

Kutscher, E. Y. *Ha-Lashon veha-Reqa' ha-Leshoni shel Megillat Yesha'yahu ha-Shelemah mi-Megillot Yam ha-Melaḥ.* Jerusalem: Magnes, 1959.

———. "Leshonan shel ha-'Iggerot ha-'Ivriyot veha-'Aramiyot shel Bar Kosiba u-Vene Doro: Ma'amar Sheni: Ha-'Iggerot ha-'Ivriyot." *Leshonenu* 26 (1961/62) 7-21.

Lambert, G. *Le Maître de justice et la communauté de l'alliance.* ALBO 2/28. Louvain: Publications universitaires, 1952.

Lange, A. *Weisheit und Prädestination: Weisheitliche Urordnung und Prädestination in den Textfunden von Qumran.* STDJ 18. Leiden: Brill, 1995.

LaSor, W. S. *The Dead Sea Scrolls and the New Testament.* Grand Rapids: Wm. B. Eerdmans, 1972.

———. "The Messiah of Aaron and Israel." *VT* 6 (1956) 425-29.
Laurin, R. B. "The Problem of the Two Messiahs in the Qumran Scrolls." *RevQ* 4 (1963) 39-52.
Lauterbach, J. Z. "Midrash and Mishnah." *JQR* N.S. 5 (1914/15) 503-27; 6 (1915/16) 23-95, 303-23.
Lefkovits, J. K. *The Copper Scroll (3Q15): A Reevaluation, a New Reading, Translation, and Commentary*. STDJ 25. Leiden: Brill, 2000.
Lehmann, M. R. *Masot u-Masa'ot*. Jerusalem: Mosad Harav Kook, 1982.
———. "Megillat ha-Miqdash ke-Maqor le-Halakhah Kitatit." *Beth Mikra* 25 (1980) 302-8.
———. "A Re-interpretation of 4Q Dibrê Ham-Me'oroth." *RevQ* 5 (1964) 106-10.
———. "The *Temple Scroll* as a Source of Sectarian Halakhah." *RevQ* 9 (1978) 579-88.
Levine, B. A. "A Further Look at the Mo'adim of the Temple Scroll." In *Archaeology and History in the Dead Sea Scrolls: The New York University Conference in Memory of Yigael Yadin*, ed. L. H. Schiffman, 53-66. JSPSup 8. JSOT/ASOR Monographs 2. Sheffield: Sheffield Academic, 1990.
———. "The Temple Scroll: Aspects of Its Historical Provenance and Literary Character." *BASOR* 232 (1978) 5-23.
Lewis, N., ed. *The Documents from the Bar Kokhba Period in the Cave of Letters: Greek Papyri*. Jerusalem: Israel Exploration Society, Hebrew University, Shrine of the Book, 1989.
Licht, J. "An Analysis of the Treatise of the Two Spirits in DSD." In *Aspects of the Dead Sea Scrolls*, ed. C. Rabin and Y. Yadin, 88-100. ScrHier 4. Jerusalem: Magnes, Hebrew University, 1958.
———. "Dapim Nosafim li-Fesher Naḥum." *Molad* 19 (1961) 454-56.
———. "The Doctrine of the Thanksgiving Scroll." *IEJ* 6 (1956) 1-13, 89-101.
———. "An Ideal Town Plan from Qumran — The Description of the New Jerusalem." *IEJ* 29 (1979) 45-59.
———. *Megillat ha-Hodayot mi-Megillot Midbar Yehudah*. Jerusalem: Bialik Institute, 1957.
———. *Megillat ha-Serakhim mi-Megillot Midbar Yehudah*. Jerusalem: Bialik Institute, 1965.
———. "Ha-Munaḥ Goral be-Khetaveha shel Kat Midbar Yehudah." *Beth Mikra* 1 (1955/56) 90-99.
Lichtenstein, A. *The Seven Laws of Noah*. Brooklyn: Berman, 1995.
Lichtenstein, H. "Die Fastenrolle: Eine Untersuchung zur jüdisch-hellenistischen Gerichte." *HUCA* 8-9 (1931-32) 257-351.
Liddell, H. G., and R. Scott. *A Greek-English Lexicon*. Rev. by H. S. Jones with R. McKenzie. Oxford: Clarendon, 1968.
Lieberman, S. "The Discipline in the So-Called Dead Sea Manual of Discipline." *JBL* 71 (1951) 199-206. Repr. in *Texts and Studies*, 200-7. New York: Ktav, 1974.
———. *Hellenism in Jewish Palestine*. New York: Jewish Theological Seminary, 1962.
———. "Light on the Cave Scrolls from Rabbinic Sources." *PAAJR* 20 (1951) 395-404. Repr. in *Texts and Studies*, 190-99. New York: Ktav, 1974.
———. *Tosefta Ki-Fshuṭah*. 10 vols. New York: Jewish Theological Seminary of America, 1955.

———, ed. *Tosefta*. 5 vols. New York: Jewish Theological Seminary of America, 1955-1988.
Lim, T. H., H. L. MacQueen, and C. M. Carmichael, eds. *On Scrolls, Artefacts, and Intellectual Property*. JSPSup 38. Sheffield: Sheffield Academic, 2001.
Liver, J. "Bene Ṣadoq shebe-Khat Midbar Yehudah." *ErIsr* 8 (1966/67) 71-81.
———. "The Doctrine of the Two Messiahs in Sectarian Literature in the Time of the Second Commonwealth." *HTR* 52 (1959) 149-85.
———. "The 'Sons of Zadok the Priests' in the Dead Sea Sect." *RevQ* 6 (1967) 3-32.
Magness, J. *The Archaeology of Qumran and the Dead Sea Scrolls*. SDSSRL. Grand Rapids: Wm. B. Eerdmans, 2002.
Maier, J. "The Architectural History of the Temple in Jerusalem in Light of the Temple Scroll." In *Temple Scroll Studies*, ed. G. J. Brooke, 23-62. JSPSup 7. Sheffield: JSOT, 1989.
———. "Die Hofanlagen im Tempel-Entwurf des Ezechiel im Licht der 'Tempelrolle' von Qumran." In *Prophecy: Essays Presented to Georg Fohrer on His Sixty-Fifth Birthday*, ed. J. A. Emerton, 55-67. BZAW 150. Berlin: de Gruyter, 1980.
———. *The Temple Scroll: An Introduction, Translation & Commentary*. JSOTSup 34. Sheffield: JSOT, 1985.
———. "The *Temple Scroll* and Tendencies in the Cultic Architecture of the Second Commonwealth." In *Archaeology and History in the Dead Sea Scrolls: The New York University Conference in Memory of Yigael Yadin*, ed. L. H. Schiffman, 53-82. JSPSup 8. JSOT/ASOR Monographs 2. Sheffield: Sheffield Academic, 1990.
———. "Weitere Stücke zum Nahumkommentar aus der Höhle 4 von Qumran." *Judaica* 18 (1962) 215-28.
Mann, J. "Genizah Fragments of the Palestinian Order of Service." *HUCA* 2 (1925) 269-338.
Marcus, R. "*Mebaqqer* and *Rabbim* in the *Manual of Discipline* VI, 11-13." *JBL* 75 (1956) 398-402.
"Masada and the Dead Sea Scrolls." Provo: Foundation for Ancient and Mormon Studies, 1997. (video)
McCready, W. O. "Temple and *Temple Scroll*: A Sectarian Alternative." In *Proceedings of the Tenth World Congress of Jewish Studies, Division A: The Bible and Its World*, 199-204. Jerusalem: World Union of Jewish Studies, 1990.
Metso, S. "The Redaction of the Community Rule." In *The Dead Sea Scrolls: Fifty Years after Their Discovery: Proceedings of the Jerusalem Congress, July 20-25, 1997*, ed. L. H. Schiffman, E. Tov, and J. C. VanderKam, 377-84. Jerusalem: Israel Exploration Society, Shrine of the Book, Israel Museum, 2000.
———. *The Textual Development of the Qumran Community Rule*. STDJ 21. Leiden: Brill, 1997.
Meyer, M. A. *Response to Modernity: A History of the Reform Movement in Judaism*. New York: Oxford University Press, 1988.
Milgrom, J. "4QTohora^a: An Unpublished Qumran Text on Purities." In *Time to Prepare the Way in the Wilderness: Papers on the Qumran Scrolls by Fellows of the Institute for Advanced Studies of the Hebrew University, Jerusalem, 1989-1990*, ed. D. Dimant and L. H. Schiffman, 59-68. STDJ 16. Leiden: Brill, 1995.
———. *Leviticus 1–16*. AB 3. New York: Doubleday, 1991.

———. "The Qumran Cult: Its Exegetical Principles." In *Temple Scroll Studies*, ed. G. J. Brooke, 165-80. JSPSup 7. Sheffield: JSOT, 1989.
———. "'Sabbath' and 'Temple City' in the Temple Scroll." *BASOR* 232 (1978) 25-27.
———. "The Scriptural Foundations and Deviations in the Laws of Purity of the Temple Scroll." In *Archaeology and History in the Dead Sea Scrolls: The New York University Conference in Memory of Yigael Yadin*, ed. L. H. Schiffman, 83-99. JSPSup 8. JSOT/ASOR Monographs 2. Sheffield: Sheffield Academic, 1990.
———. "Studies in the Temple Scroll." *JBL* 97 (1978) 501-23.
Milik, J. T. *The Books of Enoch: Aramaic Fragments from Qumrân Cave 4*. Oxford: Clarendon, 1976.
———. "Une inscription et une lettre en araméen christo-palestinien." *RB* 60 (1953) 526-39, pl. XIX. Update with photo in G. R. H. Wright, "Archaeological Remains at el Mird in the Wilderness of Judea, with an appendix by J. T. Milik." *Bib* 42 (1961) 21-27.
———. "*Megillat milḥemet bene 'or bivene ḥoshek* by Y. Yadin (review)." *RB* 64 (1957) 585-93.
———. "'Prière de Nabonide' et autres écrits d'un cycle de Daniel: fragments araméens de Qumrân 4." *RB* 63 (1956) 407-15.
———. "Le rouleau de cuivre de Qumrân (3Q15): traduction et commentaire topographique." *RB* 66 (1959) 321-57.
———. *Ten Years of Discovery in the Wilderness of Judaea*. Trans. J. Strugnell. SBT 26. London: SCM, 1959.
———, and R. de Vaux. *Qumrân Grotte 4.II*, Part 1: *Archéologie*; Part 2: *Tefillin, Mezuzot et Targums (4Q128-4Q157)*. DJD 6. Oxford: Clarendon, 1977.
Millar, F. *The Roman Near East, 31 BC -AD 337*. Cambridge, MA: Harvard University Press, 1993.
Moore, G. F. *Judaism in the First Centuries of the Christian Era: The Age of the Tannaim*. 2 vols. Cambridge, MA: Harvard University Press, 1927.
Müller-Kessler, C., and M. Sokoloff, eds. *A Corpus of Christian Palestinian Aramaic*. Vol. 1: *The Christian Palestinian Aramaic Old Testament and Apocrypha Version from the Early Period*. Groningen: Styx, 1997. Vols. 2A and 2B: *The Christian Palestinian Aramaic New Testament Version from the Early Period*. Groningen: Styx, 1998.
Muro, E. "The Greek Fragments of Enoch from Qumran Cave 7 (7Q4, 7Q8, & 7Q12= 7QEn gr= Enoch 103: 3-4, 7-8)." *RevQ* 70 (1998) 307-12.
Murphy-O'Connor, J. "The Essenes and Their History." *RB* 81 (1974) 215-44.
———. "La genèse littéraire de la Règle de la Communauté." *RB* 76 (1969) 528-49.
———. "A Literary Analysis of Damascus Document XIX, 33-XX, 34." *RB* 79 (1972) 544-64.
Mussies, G. "Greek in Palestine and the Diaspora." In *The Jewish People in the First Century*, ed. S. Safrai and M. Stern, 2:1040-64. CRINT 1. Philadelphia: Fortress, 1976.
Najman, H. *Seconding Sinai: The Development of Mosaic Discourse in Second Temple Judaism*. JSJSup 77. Leiden: Brill, 2003.
Naveh, J. *Masada I: The Aramaic and Hebrew Ostraca and Jar Inscriptions*. Jerusalem: Israel Exploration Society, 1989.
Nebe, G. W. "Die hebräische Sprache der Naḥal Ḥever Dokumente 5/6Hev 44-46." In *The Hebrew of the Dead Sea Scrolls and Ben Sira: Proceedings of a Symposium Held at*

Leiden University, 11-14 December 1995, ed. T. Muraoka and J. F. Elwolde, 150-57. STDJ 26. Leiden: Brill, 1997.

Nemoy, L. *Karaite Anthology.* Yale Judaica Series 7. New Haven: Yale University Press, 1952.

Netzer, E. *Masada III: The Yigael Yadin Excavations 1963-1965: Final Reports, the Buildings: Stratigraphy and Architecture.* Jerusalem: Israel Exploration Society, Hebrew University, 1991.

Neusner, J. *Fellowship in Judaism.* London: Vallentine, Mitchell, 1963.

———. *From Politics to Piety: The Emergence of Pharisaic Judaism.* 2nd ed. New York: Ktav, 1979.

———. *Messiah in Context.* 2nd ed. Philadelphia: Fortress, 1984.

———. "Rabbinic Traditions about the Pharisees before A.D. 70: The Problem of Oral Transmission." *JJS* 22 (1971) 1-18.

———. *The Rabbinic Traditions about the Pharisees before 70.* 3 vols. Leiden: Brill, 1971.

———, W. S. Green, and E. Frerichs, eds. *Judaisms and Their Messiahs at the Turn of the Christian Era.* New York: Cambridge University Press, 1987.

Newsom, C. A. "Apocalyptic and the Discourse of the Qumran Community." *JNES* 49 (1990) 135-44.

———. "4QSerek Šîrôt 'Ôlat Haššabbāt (The Qumran Angelic Liturgy)." Diss. abstract. *HTR* 75 (1982) 132.

———. "4Q370: An Admonition Based on the Flood." *RevQ* 13 (1988) 23-43.

———. "The 'Psalms of Joshua' from Qumran Cave 4." *JJS* 39 (1988) 56-73.

———. "'Sectually Explicit' Literature from Qumran." In *The Hebrew Bible and Its Interpreters,* ed. W. H. Propp, B. Halpern, and D. N. Freedman, 167-87. Winona Lake: Eisenbrauns, 1990.

———, and Y. Yadin. "The Masada Fragment of the Qumran *Songs of the Sabbath Sacrifice.*" *IEJ* 34 (1984) 77-88 and pl. 9.

Newton, M. *The Concept of Purity at Qumran and in the Letters of Paul.* Cambridge: Cambridge University Press, 1985.

Nimmer, D. "Copyright in the Dead Sea Scrolls: Authorship and Originality." *Houston Law Review* 38/1 (2001) 5-217.

Nitzan, B. "Harmonic and Mystical Characteristics in Poetic and Liturgical Writings from Qumran." *JQR* 85 (1994) 163-83.

———. *Megillat Pesher Ḥabakkuk: mi-Megillot Midbar Yehudah (1Qp Hab).* Jerusalem: Bialik Institute, 1986.

———. *Qumran Prayer and Religious Poetry.* STDJ 12. Leiden: Brill, 1994.

Noam, V. *Megillat Ta'anit: ha-Nusaḥim, Pishram, Toledotehem, be-Ṣeruf Mahadurah Biqortit.* Jerusalem: Yad Ben-Zvi, 2003.

North, R. "The Damascus of Qumran Geography." *PEQ* 87 (1955) 34-38.

Novak, D. *The Image of the Non-Jew in Judaism.* Toronto Studies in Theology 14. Lewiston: Mellen, 1983.

Oppenheimer, A. *The 'Am ha-Aretz: A Study in the Social History of the Jewish People in the Hellenistic-Roman Period.* Trans. I. H. Levine. ALGHJ 8. Leiden: Brill, 1977.

Otto, R. *The Idea of the Holy: An Inquiry into the Non-rational Factor in the Idea of the Divine and Its Relation to the Rational.* Trans. J. W. Harvey. 2nd ed. New York: Oxford University Press, 1950.

Parry, D. W., and E. Tov, eds. *The Dead Sea Scrolls Reader*. 6 vols. Leiden: Brill, 2004.

Penny, D. L., and M. O. Wise. "By the Power of Beelzebub: An Aramaic Incantation Formula from Qumran (4Q560)." *JBL* 113 (1994) 627-50.

Perrot, C. "Un fragment christo-palestinien découverte à Khirbet Mird (Actes des apôtres, X, 28-29; 32-41)." *RB* 70 (1963) 506-55 and pls. XVIII, XIX.

Pfann, S. J. "History of the Judean Desert Discoveries." In *The Dead Sea Scrolls on Microfiche: A Comprehensive Facsimile Edition of the Texts from the Judean Desert: Companion Volume*, ed. E. Tov with Pfann, 97-108. 2nd ed. Leiden: Brill and IDC, 1995.

———, and P. S. Alexander et al. *Qumran Cave 4.XXVI: Cryptic Texts and Miscellanea, Part 1*. DJD 36. Oxford: Clarendon, 2000.

"The Pharaoh's Holy Treasure." Focus Productions, Bristol UK. First aired on BBC, 31 March 2002.

Philo. Trans. F. H. Colson, G. H. Whitaker, and R. Marcus. 10 vols + 2 sup. LCL. Cambridge: Harvard University Press, 1929-1953.

Pike, D. "Is the Plan of Salvation Attested in the Dead Sea Scrolls?" In *LDS Perspectives on the Dead Sea Scrolls*, ed. D. W. Parry and Pike, 73-94. Provo: Foundation for Ancient Research and Mormon Studies, 1997.

Pliny the Elder. *Natural History*. Trans. D. E. Eichholz. LCL. Cambridge, MA: Harvard University Press, 1962.

Pouilly, J. *La Règle de la Communauté de Qumrân: son évolution littéraire*. CahRB 17. Paris: Gabalda, 1976.

Price, R. *Secrets of the Dead Sea Scrolls*. Eugene: Harvest House, 1996.

Priest, J. "*Mebaqqer, Paqqid* and the Messiah." *JBL* 81 (1962) 55-61.

Puech, É. "Les deux derniers psaumes Davidiques du ritual d'exorcisme, 11QPsAp^a IV4–V 14." In *The Dead Sea Scrolls: Forty Years of Research*, ed. D. Dimant and U. Rappaport, 64-89. Leiden: Brill and Jerusalem: Magnes, Hebrew University, and Yad Izhak Ben-Zvi, 1992.

———. "11QPsAp^a: Un rituel d'exorcismes: Essai de reconstruction." *RevQ* 14 (1989) 377-408.

———. "Fragment d'un apocryphe de Lévi et le personnage eschatologique: 4QtestLévi^{c-d}(?) et 4QAJa." In *The Madrid Qumran Conference: Proceedings of the International Congress on the Dead Sea Scrolls, Madrid, 18-21 March, 1991*, ed. J. Trebolle Barrera and L. Vegas Montaner, 2:449-501. STDJ 11/2. Leiden: Brill, 1992.

———. *Qumrân Grotte 4.XVIII: Textes hébreux (4Q521-4Q528, 4Q576-4Q579)*. DJD 25. Oxford: Clarendon, 1998.

———. *Qumrân Grotte 4.XXII: Textes araméens, première partie, 4Q529-549*. DJD 31. Oxford: Clarendon, 2001.

———. "Review of M. Weinfeld, *The Organizational Pattern*." *RevQ* 14 (1989) 147-48.

———. "Le Testament de Qahat en araméen de la grotte 4 *(4QTQah)*." *RevQ* 15 (1991) 23-54.

Qimron, E. *The Hebrew of the Dead Sea Scrolls*. HSS 29. Atlanta: Scholars, 1986.

———. "Le-Nusḥah shel Megillat ha-Miqdash." *Leš* 42 (1978) 136-45.

———. "Observations on the History of Early Hebrew (1000 BCE-200 CE) in the Light of the Dead Sea Documents." In *The Dead Sea Scrolls: Forty Years of Research*, ed.

D. Dimant and U. Rappaport, 349-61. Leiden: Brill and Jerusalem: Magnes, Hebrew University, and Yad Izhak Ben-Zvi, 1992.

———. *The Temple Scroll: A Critical Edition with Extensive Reconstructions.* Beersheva: Ben-Gurion University of the Negev and Jerusalem: Israel Exploration Society, 1996.

———. "The Text of CDC." In *The Damascus Document Reconsidered,* ed. M. Broshi, 9-49. Jerusalem: Israel Exploration Society and Shrine of the Book, Israel Museum, 1992.

———, and J. Strugnell. *Qumran Cave 4.V: Miqṣat Ma'aśe ha-Torah.* DJD 10. Oxford: Clarendon, 1994.

———, and J. Strugnell. "An Unpublished Halakhic Letter from Qumran." In *Biblical Archaeology Today: Proceedings of the International Congress on Biblical Archaeology, Jerusalem, April 1984,* ed. J. Amitai, 400-7. Jerusalem: Israel Exploration Society, Israel Academy of Sciences and Humanities, in cooperation with ASOR, 1985.

———. "An Unpublished Halakhic Letter from Qumran." *IMJ* 4 (1985) 9-12.

Rabin, C. "Hebrew and Aramaic in the First Century." In *The Jewish People in the First Century,* ed. S. Safrai and M. Stern, 2:1007-39. CRINT 1. Philadelphia: Fortress, 1976.

———. "The Historical Background of Qumran Hebrew." In *Aspects of the Dead Sea Scrolls,* ed. C. Rabin and Y. Yadin, 144-61. ScrHier 4. Jerusalem: Magnes, Hebrew University, 1958.

———. *Qumran Studies.* Scripta Judaica 2. Oxford: Oxford University Press, 1957.

———. *The Zadokite Documents.* Oxford: Clarendon, 1954.

Rabinowitz, J. J. *Jewish Law: Its Influence on the Development of Legal Institutions.* New York: Bloch, 1956.

Rapp, H. A. *Jakob in Bet-El: Gen 35,1-15 und die jüdische Literatur des 3. und 2. Jahrhunderts.* Herders biblische Studien 29. Freiburg: Herder, 2001.

Ravid, L. "The Heavenly Tablets and the Concept of Impurity in the Book of Jubilees." M.A. thesis, Bar-Ilan University, 1997. (Hebrew)

Reed, S. A., comp., with M. J. Lundberg and M. B. Phelps. *The Dead Sea Scrolls Catalogue: Documents, Photographs and Museum Inventory Numbers.* SBLRBS 32. Atlanta: Scholars, 1994.

Reeves, J. C., ed. *Tracing the Threads: Studies in the Vitality of Jewish Pseudepigrapha.* SBLEJL 6. Atlanta: Scholars, 1994.

Regev, E. *Ha-Ṣeduqim ve-Hilkhatam: 'Al Dat ve-Ḥevrah bi-Yeme Bayit Sheni.* Jerusalem: Yad Izhak Ben-Zvi, 2005.

Reif, S. C. "The Damascus Document from the Cairo Genizah: Its Discovery, Early Study and Historical Significance." In *The Damascus Document: A Centennial of Discovery, Proceedings of the Third International Symposium of the Orion Center for the Study of the Dead Sea Scrolls and Associated Literature, 4-8 February 1998,* ed. J. M. Baumgarten, E. G. Chazon and A. Pinnick, 109-31. STDJ 34. Leiden: Brill, 2000.

———. *A Guide to the Taylor-Schechter Genizah Collection.* Cambridge: Cambridge University Library, 1973.

———. *A Jewish Archive from Old Cairo: The History of Cambridge University's Genizah Collection.* Richmond, Surrey: Curzon, 2000.

Rendsburg, G. A. *Diglossia in Ancient Hebrew.* AOS 72. New Haven: American Oriental Society, 1990.

"Resurrecting the Dead Sea Scrolls." BBC Horizon. Aired 22 March 1993.

Revel, B. *The Karaite Halaka*. Philadelphia: Dropsie College, 1913.
"Revelations of the Dead Sea Scrolls." Mysteries of the Bible, parts 1 & 2. Multimedia Entertainment and A & E Network, 1993.
Rhoads, D. M. *Israel in Revolution 6-74 CE: A Political History Based on the Writings of Josephus*. Philadelphia: Fortress, 1976.
Ricks, S. D. "The Book of Mormon and the Dead Sea Scrolls." In *LDS Perspectives on the Dead Sea Scrolls*, ed. D. W. Parry and D. M. Pike, 177-89. Provo: Foundation for Ancient Research and Mormon Studies, 1997.
Ritter, B. *Philo und die Halacha*. Leipzig: Hinrichs, 1879.
Rodrigues Pereira, A. S. *Studies in Aramaic Poetry (c. 100 BCE-c. 600 CE): Selected Jewish, Christian and Samaritan Poems*. SSN 34. Assen: Van Gorcum, 1997.
Rofé A. "The Nomistic Correction in Biblical Manuscripts and Its Occurrence in 4QSam[a]." *RevQ* 14 (1989) 247-54.
Roth, C. *The Historical Background of the Dead Sea Scrolls*. Oxford: Blackwell, 1958.
———. *The Jews in the Renaissance*. Philadelphia: Jewish Publication Society of America, 1959.
———, ed. *Encyclopaedia Judaica*. 16 vols. Jerusalem: Keter, 1971.
Rowley, H. H. *The Zadokite Fragments and the Dead Sea Scrolls*. Oxford: Blackwell, 1952.
Rubinstein, A. "Urban Halakhah and Camp Rules in the 'Cairo Fragments of a Damascus Covenant.'" *Sefarad* 12 (1952) 283-96.
Rubenstein, J. L. *The History of Sukkot in the Second Temple and Rabbinic Periods*. BJS 302. Atlanta, Ga.: Scholars, 1995.
Saʿadyah Gaon. *Siddur Rav Saʿadyah Gaʾon*. Ed. I. Davidson, S. Assaf, and B. I. Joel. Jerusalem: Mass, 1970.
Safire, W. "Breaking the Cartel." *New York Times*, 24 September 1991.
Safrai, Z. *The Economy of Roman Palestine*. London: Routledge, 1994.
Saldarini, A. J. *Pharisees, Scribes and Sadducees in Palestinian Society: A Sociological Approach*. Wilmington: Michael Glazier, 1988. Repr. BRS. Grand Rapids: Wm. B. Eerdmans and Livonia: Dove, 2001.
Sanders, E. P. *Jewish Law from Jesus to the Mishnah*. London: SCM and Philadelphia: Trinity Press International, 1990.
———. *Judaism: Practice and Belief, 63 BCE–66 CE*. London: SCM and Philadelphia: Trinity Press International, 1992.
———. *Paul and Palestinian Judaism*. Philadelphia: Fortress, 1997.
Sanders, J. A. "Cave 11 Surprises and the Question of Canon." In *New Directions in Biblical Archaeology*, ed. D. N. Freedman and J. C. Greenfield, 113-30. Garden City: Doubleday, 1971.
———. *The Dead Sea Psalms Scroll*. Ithaca: Cornell University Press, 1967.
———. *The Psalms Scroll of Qumran Cave 11 (11QPs[a])*. DJD 4. Oxford: Clarendon, 1965.
Sarna, N. M. *Songs of the Heart: An Introduction to the Book of Psalms*. New York: Schocken, 1993.
Schechter, S. *Aspects of Rabbinic Theology*. New York: Macmillan, 1909.
———. *Documents of Jewish Sectaries*. Vol. 1: *Fragments of a Zadokite Work*. Cambridge: Cambridge University Press, 1910. Repr. Library of Biblical Studies. New York: Ktav, 1970.

Bibliography

Schiffman, L. H. "An Apostrophe to Zion." *Long Island Jewish World*, 29 May-4 June 1992, 4.

———. "Apostrophe to Zion (11QPsalms Scroll 22:1-15)." In *Prayer from Alexander to Constantine*, ed. M. Kiley, 18-22. London: Routledge, 1997.

———. "The Architectural Vocabulary of the Copper Scroll and the Temple Scroll." In *Copper Scroll Studies*, ed. G. J. Brooke and P. R. Davies, 180-95. JSPSup 40. London: Sheffield Academic, 2002.

———. "Architecture and Law: The Temple and Its Courtyards in the *Temple Scroll*." In *From Ancient Israel to Modern Judaism: Intellect in Quest of Understanding: Essays in Honor of Marvin Fox*, ed. J. Neusner, E. S. Frerichs, and N. M. Sarna, 1:267-84. BJS 159. Atlanta: Scholars, 1989.

———. "The Concept of the Messiah in Second Temple and Rabbinic Literature." *Review and Expositor* 84 (1987) 235-46.

———. "Confessionalism and the Study of the Dead Sea Scrolls." *JS* 31 (1991) 3-14.

———. "The Construction of the Temple according to the *Temple Scroll*." *RevQ* 17 (Hommage à Józef T. Milik, 1996) 555-71.

———. "The Deuteronomic Paraphrase of the *Temple Scroll*." *RevQ* 15 (1992) 543-68.

———. "The Early History of the Public Reading of the Torah." In *Jews, Christians, and Polytheists in the Ancient Synagogue: Cultural Interaction during the Greco-Roman Period*, ed. S. Fine, 44-56. London: Routledge, 1999.

———. *The Eschatological Community of the Dead Sea Scrolls: A Study of the Rule of the Congregation*. SBLMS 38. Atlanta: Scholars, 1989.

———. "The Eschatological Community of the Serekh ha-'Edah." *PAAJR* 51 (1984) 105-29.

———. "Exclusion from the Sanctuary and the City of the Sanctuary in the *Temple Scroll*." *HAR* 9 (1985) 301-20.

———. *From Text to Tradition: A History of Second Temple and Rabbinic Judaism*. Hoboken: Ktav, 1991.

———. "The Halakhah at Qumran." Ph.D. diss., Brandeis: 1974.

———. *The Halakhah at Qumran*. SJLA 16. Leiden: Brill, 1975.

———. *Halakhah, Halikhah u-Meshiḥiyut be-Khat Midbar Yehudah*. Jerusalem: Merkaz Shazar, 1993.

———. "The Impurity of the Dead in the *Temple Scroll*." In *Archaeology and History in the Dead Sea Scrolls: The New York University Conference in Memory of Yigael Yadin*, ed. Schiffman, 135-56. JSPSup 8. JSOT/ASOR Monographs 2. Sheffield: Sheffield Academic, 1990.

———. "'*Ir Ha-Miqdash* and Its Meaning in the Temple Scroll and Other Qumran Texts." In *Sanctity of Time and Space in Tradition and Modernity*, ed. A. Houtman, M. J. H. M. Poorthuis, and J. Schwartz, 95-109. Jewish and Christian Perspectives Series 1. Leiden: Brill, 1998.

———. "The King, His Guard, and the Royal Council in the *Temple Scroll*." *PAAJR* 54 (1987) 237-59.

———. "The Law of the Temple Scroll and Its Provenance." *FO* 25 (1988) 85-98.

———. "The Law of Vows and Oaths (Num. 30,3-16) in the *Zadokite Fragments* and the *Temple Scroll*." *RevQ* 15 (Mémorial Jean Starcky, 1991) 199-214.

———. "Laws Concerning Idolatry in the Temple Scroll." In *Uncovering Ancient Stones:*

Essays in Memory of H. Neil Richardson, ed. L. M. Hopfe, 159-75. Winona Lake: Eisenbrauns, 1994.

———. "The Laws of War in the Temple Scroll." *RevQ* 13 (Mémorial Jean Carmignac, 1998) 299-311.

———. "Laws Pertaining to Women in the *Temple Scroll.*" In *The Dead Sea Scrolls: Forty Years of Research,* ed. D. Dimant and U. Rappaport, 210-28. Leiden: Brill and Jerusalem: Magnes, Hebrew University, and Yad Izhak Ben-Zvi, 1992.

———. "Legislation Concerning Relations with Non-Jews in the *Zadokite Fragments* and in Tannaitic Literature." *RevQ* 11 (1983) 379-89.

———. "*Merkavah* Speculation at Qumran: The 4Q *Serekh Shirot 'Olat ha-Shabbat.*" In *Mystics, Philosophers and Politicians: Essays in Jewish Intellectual History in Honor of Alexander Altmann,* ed. J. Reinharz and D. Swetchinski, with K. Bland, 15-47. Duke Monographs in Medieval and Renaissance Studies 5. Durham: Duke University Press, 1982.

———. "Messianism and Apocalypticism in Rabbinic Texts." In *CHJ,* vol. 4: *The Late Roman-Rabbinic Period,* 1053-72. 2006.

———. "Milḥemet ha-Megillot: Hitpatḥuyot be-Ḥeqer ha-Megillot ha-Genuzot." *Cathedra* 61 (1991) 3-23.

———. "*Miqṣat Ma'aseh ha-Torah* and the *Temple Scroll.*" *RevQ* 14 (The Texts of Qumran and the History of the Community: Proceedings of the Groningen Congress on the Dead Sea Scrolls 3, 1990) 435-57.

———. "Neusner's *Messiah in Context.*" *JQR* 77 (1987) 240-43.

———. "New Halakhic Texts from Qumran." *HS* 34 (1993) 21-33.

———. "New Light on the Pharisees: Insights from the Dead Sea Scrolls." *BRev* 8 (1992) 30-33, 54. Repr. in *Understanding the Dead Sea Scrolls,* ed. H. Shanks, 217-24. New York: Random House, 1992.

———. "Pharisaic and Sadducean Halakhah in Light of the Dead Sea Scrolls: The Case of Ṭevul Yom." *DSD* 1 (1994) 285-99.

———. "The Prohibition of Judicial Corruption in the Dead Sea Scrolls, Philo, Josephus and Talmudic Law." In *Hesed ve-Emet: Studies in Honor of Ernest S. Frerichs,* ed. J. Magness and S. Gitin, 155-78. BJS 320. Atlanta: Scholars, 1998.

———. "The Prohibition of the Skins of Animals in the Temple Scroll and Miqsat Ma'ase ha-Torah." In *Proceedings of the Tenth World Congress of Jewish Studies, Division A,* 191-98. Jerusalem: World Union of Jewish Studies, 1990.

———. "Purity and Perfection: Exclusion from the Council of the Community in the *Serekh Ha-'Edah.*" In *Biblical Archaeology Today: Proceedings of the International Congress on Biblical Archaeology, Jerusalem, April 1984,* ed. J. Amitai, 373-89. Jerusalem: Israel Exploration Society, Israel Academy of Sciences and Humanities, in cooperation with ASOR, 1985.

———. *Reclaiming the Dead Sea Scrolls: The History of Judaism, the Background of Christianity, the Lost Library of Qumran.* Philadelphia: Jewish Publication Society, 1994. Repr. ABRL. New York: Doubleday, 1995.

———. "Reflections on the Deeds of Sale from the Judean Desert in Light of Rabbinic Literature." In *Law in the Documents of the Judaean Desert,* ed. R. Katzoff and D. Schaps, 185-203. JSJSup 96. Leiden: Brill, 2005.

Bibliography

———. "The Relationship of the Zadokite Fragments to the Temple Scroll." In *The Damascus Document: A Centennial of Discovery: Proceedings of the Third International Symposium of the Orion Center for the Study of the Dead Sea Scrolls and Associated Literature, 4-8 February, 1998*, ed. J. M. Baumgarten, E. G. Chazon, and A. Pinnick, 133-45. STDJ 34. Leiden: Brill, 2000.

———. "Reproof as a Requisite for Punishment in the Law of the Dead Sea Scrolls." In *Jewish Law Studies II, the Jerusalem Conference Volume*, ed. B. S. Jackson, 59-74. Atlanta: Scholars, 1986.

———. Review of Y. Yadin, "The Temple Scroll." *BA* 48 (1985) 122-25.

———. "Sacral and Non-Sacral Slaughter According to the Temple Scroll." In *Time to Prepare the Way in the Wilderness: Papers on the Qumran Scrolls by Fellows of the Institute for Advanced Studies of the Hebrew University, Jerusalem, 1989-1990*, ed. D. Dimant and Schiffman, 69-84. STDJ 16. Leiden: Brill, 1995.

———. "Sacred Space: The Land of Israel in the *Temple Scroll*." In *Biblical Archaeology Today 1990: Proceedings of the Second International Congress on Biblical Archaeology*, ed. A. Biran and J. Aviram, 398-410. Jerusalem: Israel Exploration Society, 1993.

———. "Sacrificial Halakhah in the Fragments of the *Aramaic Levi Document* from Qumran, the Cairo Genizah, and Mt. Athos Monastery." In *Reworking the Bible: Apocryphal and Related Texts at Qumran, Proceedings of a Joint Symposium by the Orion Center for the Study of the Dead Sea Scrolls and Associated Literature and the Hebrew University Institute for Advanced Studies Research Group on Qumran, 15-17 January, 2002*, ed. E. G. Chazon, D. Dimant, and R. A. Clements. 177-202. STDJ 58. Leiden: Brill, 2005.

———. "The Sacrificial System of the *Temple Scroll* and the *Book of Jubilees*." In *SBLSP 1985*, ed. K. H. Richards, 217-33. Atlanta: Scholars, 1985.

———. "Sadducean Halakhah in the Dead Sea Scrolls: The Case of the *Tevul Yom*." *DSD* 1 (1994) 285-99.

———. *Sectarian Law in the Dead Sea Scrolls: Courts, Testimony and the Penal Code*. BJS 33. Chico: Scholars, 1983.

———. "The Septuagint and the Temple Scroll: Shared 'Halakhic Variants.'" In *Septuagint, Scrolls and Cognate Writings*, ed. G. J. Brooke and B. Lindars, 277-97. SBLSCS 33. Atlanta: Scholars, 1992.

———. "The Significance of the Scrolls." *BRev* 6 (1990) 18-27, 52.

———. "Some Laws Pertaining to Animals in *Temple Scroll*, Column 52." In *Legal Texts and Legal Issues: Proceedings of the Second Meeting of the International Organization for Qumran Studies, Cambridge, 1995*, ed. M. Bernstein, F. García Martínez, and J. Kampen, 167-78. STDJ 23. Leiden: Brill, 1997.

———. "The Temple Scroll and the Halakhic Pseudepigrapha of the Second Temple Period." In *Pseudepigraphic Perspectives: The Apocrypha and Pseudepigrapha in Light of the Dead Sea Scrolls: Proceedings of the International Symposium of the Orion Center for the Study of the Dead Sea Scrolls and Associated Literature, 12-14 January, 1997*, ed. E. G. Chazon, M. Stone, and A. Pinnick, 121-32. STDJ 31. Leiden: Brill, 1999.

———. "The *Temple Scroll* and the Nature of Its Law: The Status of the Question." In *The Community of the Renewed Covenant: The Notre Dame Symposium on the Dead Sea*

Scrolls, ed. E. Ulrich and J. VanderKam, 37-55. CJAS 10. Notre Dame: University of Notre Dame Press, 1994.

————. "The Temple Scroll and the Systems of Jewish Law in the Second Temple Period." In *Temple Scroll Studies*, ed. G. J. Brooke, 239-55. JSPSup 7. Sheffield: JSOT, 1989.

————. "*The Temple Scroll* in Literary and Philological Perspective." In *Approaches to Ancient Judaism*, ed. W. S. Green, 2:143-58. BJS 9. Chico: Scholars, 1980.

————. *Texts and Traditions: A Source Reader for the Study of Second Temple and Rabbinic Judaism*. Hoboken: Ktav, 1998.

————. "The Theology of the Temple Scroll." *JQR* 85 (Qumran Studies, 1994) 109-23.

————. "*An Unknown Jewish Sect* by L. Ginzberg." *JAOS* 99 (1979) 113-14.

————. *Who Was a Jew? Rabbinic and Halakhic Perspectives on the Jewish Christian Schism*. Hoboken: Ktav, 1985.

————, ed. *Archaeology and History in the Dead Sea Scrolls: The New York University Conference in Memory of Yigael Yadin*. JSPSup 8. JSOT/ASOR Monographs 2. Sheffield: Sheffield Academic, 1990.

————, and M. D. Swartz. *Hebrew and Aramaic Incantation Texts from the Cairo Genizah: Selected Texts from Taylor-Schechter Box K1*. Sheffield: JSOT, 1992.

————, and J. C. VanderKam, eds. *Encyclopedia of the Dead Sea Scrolls*. 2 vols. New York: Oxford University Press, 2002.

Schniedewind, W. M. "Qumran Hebrew as an Antilanguage." *JBL* 118 (1999) 235-52.

Schochet, E. J. *The Hasidic Movement and the Gaon of Vilna*. Northvale, NJ: Aaronson, 1994.

Scholem, G. G. *Major Trends in Jewish Mysticism*. New York: Schocken, 1965.

————. *The Messianic Idea in Judaism and Other Essays on Jewish Spirituality*. New York: Schocken, 1971.

Schorsch, I. *From Text to Context: The Turn to History in Modern Judaism*. Waltham, MA: Brandeis University Press and Hanover, NH: University Press of New England, 1994.

Schuller, E. M. "4Q372 1: A Text about Joseph." *RevQ* 14 (The Texts of Qumran and the History of the Community: Proceedings of the Groningen Congress on the Dead Sea Scrolls 3, 1990) 349-76.

————. *Non-Canonical Psalms from Qumran: A Pseudepigraphic Collection*. HSS 28. Atlanta: Scholars, 1986.

————. "Prayer, Hymnic, and Liturgical Texts from Qumran." In *The Community of the Renewed Covenant: The Notre Dame Symposium on the Dead Sea Scrolls*, ed. E. Ulrich and J. VanderKam, 153-71. CJAS 10. Notre Dame: University of Notre Dame Press, 1994.

Schürer, E. *The History of the Jewish People in the Time of Jesus Christ*. Trans. by S. Taylor and P. Christie. 5 vols. + index. New York: Scribner's, 1890-91.

————. *The History of the Jewish People in the Age of Jesus Christ (175 B.C.-A.D. 135)*. Rev. ed. by G. Vermes, F. Millar, with P. Vermes and M. Black. 3 vols. in 4. Edinburgh: T. & T. Clark, 1973-1987.

Schwartz, D. R. "On Two Aspects of a Priestly View of Descent at Qumran." In *Archaeology and History in the Dead Sea Scrolls: The New York University Conference in Memory of Yigael Yadin*, ed. L. H. Schiffman, 157-79. JSPSup 8. JSOT/ASOR Monographs 2. Sheffield: Sheffield Academic, 1990.

———. *Studies in the Jewish Background of Christianity.* Tübingen: Mohr (Siebeck), 1992.
———. "Temple and Desert: On Religion and State in Second Temple Period Judaea." In *Studies in the Jewish Background of Christianity*, 29-43. Tübingen: Mohr (Siebeck), 1992.
———. "The Three Temples of 4QFlorilegium." *RevQ* 10 (1979) 83-92.
"Secrets of the Dead Sea Scrolls." Nova Documentary. Produced by WGBH, Boston. First aired 15 October 1991.
"Secrets of the Sea." Everyman. Produced by Michael Waterhouse. BBC, 1994.
Segal, L. A. *Historical Consciousness and Religious Tradition in Azariah de' Rossi's* Me'or 'Einayim. Philadelphia: Jewish Publication Society, 1989.
Segal, M. Z. *Sefer Ben Sira: Ha-Maqor, Qanqordansiah, ve-Nittuaḥ ha-Millim.* Jerusalem: Academy of the Hebrew Language and Shrine of the Book, 1973.
———. *Sefer Ben Sira ha-Shalem.* 2nd ed. Jerusalem: Bialik Institute, 1971/72.
Shanks, H. "Dead Sea Scrolls: Dead Sea Scroll Variation on 'Show and Tell' — It's Called 'Tell, But No Show,'" *BAR* 16/2 (1990) 18-21.
———. "Dead Sea Scrolls Scandal — Israel's Department of Antiquities Joins Conspiracy to Keep Scrolls Secret." *BAR* 15/4 (1989) 18-21, 55.
———. "Failure to Publish Dead Sea Scrolls Is Leitmotif of New York University Scroll Conference." *BAR* 11/5 (1985) 4-6, 66-70.
———. "Intrigue and the Scroll." In *Understanding the Dead Sea Scrolls*, 116-25. New York: Random House, 1992.
———. *The Mystery and Meaning of the Dead Sea Scrolls.* New York: Random House, 1998.
Shemesh, A. "4Q271.3: A Key to Sectarian Matrimonial Law." *JJS* 49 (1998) 244-63.
Sheres, I., and A. Kohn Blau. *The Truth about the Virgin: Sex and Ritual in the Dead Sea Scrolls.* New York: Continuum, 1995.
Silberman, L. "Two Messiahs of the Manual of Discipline." *VT* 5 (1955) 77-82.
Silberman, N. A. *The Hidden Scrolls: Christianity, Judaism & the War for the Dead Sea Scrolls.* New York: Putnam's, 1994.
———. *A Prophet from Amongst You: The Life of Yigael Yadin, Soldier, Scholar and Mythmaker of Modern Israel.* Reading, MA: Addison-Wesley, 1993.
Silk, M. *Unsecular Media: Making News of Religion in America.* Urbana: University of Illinois Press, 1998.
Skehan, P. W. "Jubilees and the Qumran Psalter (11QPs[a])." *CBQ* 37 (1975) 343-47.
———. "A Liturgical Complex in 11QPs[a]." *CBQ* 35 (1973) 195-205.
———, E. Ulrich, and J. E. Sanderson. *Qumran Cave 4.IV: Palaeo-Hebrew and Greek Biblical Manuscripts.* DJD 9. Oxford: Clarendon, 1992.
Smith, M. "Palestinian Judaism in the First Century." In *Israel: Its Role in Civilization*, ed. M. Davis, 73-78. New York: Harper & Row, 1956.
Sokoloff, M. *The Targum to Job from Qumran Cave XI.* Bar-Ilan Studies in Near Eastern Languages and Culture. Ramat-Gan: Bar-Ilan University, 1974.
Solomon, A. "The Prohibition against Ṭevul Yom and Defilement of the Daily Whole Offering in the Jerusalem Temple in CD 11:21-12:1: A New Understanding." *DSD* 4 (1997) 1-20.
Sparks, H. F. D., ed. *The Apocryphal Old Testament.* Oxford: Clarendon, 1984.
Starcky, J. "Jerusalem et les manuscrits de la Mer Morte." *MdB* 1 (1977) 38-40.

———. "Les quatre étapes du messianisme à Qumran." *RB* 70 (1963) 481-505.
———. "Le travail d'édition des fragments manuscrits de Qumrân." *RB* 63 (1956) 66.
Stegemann, H. "Die Bedeutung der Qumranfunde für die Erforschung der Apokalyptik." In *Apocalypticism in the Mediterranean World and the Near East: Proceedings of the International Colloquium on Apocalypticism,* ed. D. Hellholm, 495-530. Tübingen: Mohr (Siebeck), 1983.
———. "The Institutions of Israel in the Temple Scroll." In *The Dead Sea Scrolls: Forty Years of Research,* ed. D. Dimant and U. Rappaport, 146-85. Leiden: Brill and Jerusalem: Magnes, Hebrew University, and Yad Izhak Ben-Zvi, 1992.
———. "Is the Temple Scroll a Sixth Book of the Torah Lost for 2,500 Years?" *BAR* 13/6 (1987) 28-35. Repr. in *Understanding the Dead Sea Scrolls,* 126-36. New York: Random House, 1992.
———. "Methods for the Reconstruction of Scrolls from Scattered Fragments." In *Archaeology and History in the Dead Sea Scrolls: The New York University Conference in Memory of Yigael Yadin,* ed. L. H. Schiffman, 189-220. JSPSup 8. JSOT/ASOR Monographs 2. Sheffield: Sheffield Academic, 1990.
———. "The Origins of the Temple Scroll." In *Congress Volume: Jerusalem 1986,* ed. J. A. Emerton, 235-56. VTSup 40 (1988).
Steiner, R. C. "The *MBQR* at Qumran, the *Episkopos* in the Athenian Empire, and the Meaning of *LBQR'* in Ezra 7:14: On the Relation of Ezra's Mission to the Persian Legal Project," *JBL* 120 (2001) 623-46.
Stendahl, K., and J. H. Charlesworth. *The Scrolls and the New Testament.* 1957; repr. New York: Crossroad, 1992.
Stern, E. "The Persian Empire and the Political and Social History of Palestine in the Persian Period." In *CHJ,* vol. 1: *Introduction; The Persian Period,* 70-87. 1984.
Stern, M. "Zealots." In *Encyclopaedia Judaica Yearbook,* 135-40. Jerusalem: Keter, 1973.
Stern, S. *Jewish Identity in Early Rabbinic Writings.* AGJU 23. Leiden: Brill, 1994.
Steudel, A. "אחרית הימים in the Texts from Qumran." *RevQ* 16 (1993-94) 225-46.
———. *Der Midrasch zur Eschatologie aus der Qumrangemeinde (4QMidrEschat$^{a.b}$).* STDJ 13. Leiden: Brill, 1994.
Stone, M. E. "The Axis of History at Qumran." In *Pseudepigraphic Perspectives: The Apocrypha and Pseudepigrapha in Light of the Dead Sea Scrolls: Proceedings of the International Symposium of the Orion Center for the Study of the Dead Sea Scrolls and Associated Literature, 12-14 January, 1997,* ed. E. G. Chazon, Stone, and A. Pinnick, 133-49. STDJ 31. Leiden: Brill, 1999.
———, and J. C. Greenfield. "Remarks on the Aramaic Testament of Levi from the Geniza." *RB* 86 (1979) 214-30.
Strack, H., and P. Billerbeck. *Kommentar zum Neuen Testament aus Talmud und Midrasch.* 6 vols. Munich: Beck, 1974-78.
Strugnell, J. "The Angelic Liturgy at Qumran — 4QSerek Šîrôt 'Ôlat Haššabbāt." *VTSup* 7 (1959) 318-45.
———. "MMT: Second Thoughts on a Forthcoming Edition." In *The Community of the Renewed Covenant: The Notre Dame Symposium on the Dead Sea Scrolls,* ed. E. Ulrich and J. VanderKam, 57-73. CJAS 10. Notre Dame: University of Notre Dame Press, 1994.

———. "Notes en marge du volume V des 'Discoveries in the Judaean Desert of Jordan.'" *RevQ* 7 (1970) 163-276.
———, and D. Dimant. "4QSecond Ezekiel." *RevQ* 13 (1988) 45-58.
———, D. J. Harrington, and T. Elgvin. *Qumran Cave 4.XXIV: Sapiential Texts, Part 2.* DJD 34. Oxford: Clarendon, 1999.
Stuckenbruck, L. T. *The Book of Giants from Qumran.* Tübingen: Mohr (Siebeck), 1997.
Sukenik, E. L. *Megillot Genuzot mi-tokh Genizah Qedumah She-Nimṣe'ah be-Midbar Yehudah.* 2 vols. Jerusalem: Bialik Institute, 1948-1950.
———. *Naḥamu, Naḥamu 'Ami.* Jerusalem: Mosad Bialik, 1948.
———. *'Oṣar ha-Megillot ha-Genuzot.* Jerusalem: Bialik Institute and Hebrew University, 1954/55 = *The Dead Sea Scrolls of the Hebrew University.* Jerusalem: Magnes, 1955.
———, U. M. D. Cassuto et al. *'Enṣiqlopedyah Miqra'it.* 9 vols. Jerusalem: Bialik Institute, 1950-1988.
Sussmann, Y. "Ḥeqer Toldot ha-Halakhah u-Megillot Midbar Yehudah: Hirhurim Talmudiyim Rishonim le-'Or Megillat Miqṣat Ma'aśe ha-Torah." *Tarbiz* 59 (1989/1990) 11-76.
———. "The History of the Halakha and the Dead Sea Scrolls: Preliminary Talmudic Observations on *Miqṣat Ma'aśe ha-Torah* (4QMMT)." In *Qumran Cave 4.V: Miqṣat Ma'aśe ha-Torah,* ed. E. Qimron and J. Strugnell, 179-200. DJD 10. Oxford: Clarendon, 1994.
Swanson, D. D. *The Temple Scroll and the Bible: The Methodology of 11QT.* STDJ 14. Leiden: Brill, 1995.
Swartz, M. D. *Scholastic Magic: Ritual and Revelation in Early Jewish Mysticism.* Princeton: Princeton University Press, 1996.
Talmon, S. "The Calendar Reckoning of the Sect from the Judean Desert." In *Aspects of the Dead Sea Scrolls,* ed. C. Rabin and Y. Yadin, 162-99. ScrHier 4. Jerusalem: Magnes, Hebrew University, 1958.
———. "The Community of the Renewed Covenant: Between Judaism and Christianity." In *The Community of the Renewed Covenant: The Notre Dame Symposium on the Dead Sea Scrolls,* ed. E. Ulrich and J. VanderKam, 3-24. CJAS 10. Notre Dame: University of Notre Dame Press, 1994.
———. "The 'Desert Motif' in the Bible and in Qumran Literature." In *Biblical Motifs: Origins and Transformations,* ed. A. Altmann, 31-63. Cambridge, MA: Harvard University Press, 1966. Repr. in Talmon, *Literary Studies in the Hebrew Bible: Form and Content: Collected Studies,* 216-54. Leiden: Brill, 1993.
———. "Fragments of a Psalms Scroll from Masada, MPs[b] (Masada 1103-1742)." In *Minḥah le-Naḥum: Biblical and Other Studies Presented to Nahum M. Sarna in Honour of His 70th Birthday,* ed. M. Brettler and M. Fishbane, 318-27. JSOTSup 154. Sheffield: JSOT, 1993.
———. "Fragments of Two Scrolls of the Book of Leviticus from Masada." *ErIsr* 24 (1993) 99-110.
———. "Hebrew Fragments from Masada." In *Masada VI: Yigael Yadin Excavations 1963-1965: Final Reports,* ed. Talmon, with C. Newsom and Y. Yadin, 31-149. Jerusalem: Israel Exploration Society, Hebrew University of Jerusalem, 1999.
———. "Hebrew Written Fragments from Masada." *DSD* 3 (1996) 168-77.

———. *King, Cult and Calendar in Ancient Israel.* Jerusalem: Magnes, 1986.
———. "Maḥazor ha-Berakhot shel Kat Midbar Yehudah." *Tarbiz* 28 (1958/59) 1-20.
———. "The 'Manual of Benedictions' of the Sect of the Judaean Desert." *RevQ* 2 (1959/1960) 475-500.
———. "Mizmorim Ḥisoniyim bi-Leshon ha-ʿIvrit mi-Qumran." *Tarbiz* 35 (1965/66) 214-34.
———. "Qetʿa mi-Megillah Ḥiṣṣonit le-Sefer Yehoshuaʿ mi-Meṣadah." In *Shai le-Ḥayim Rabin: ʾAsuppat Meḥqere Lashon li-Khevodo bi-Melʾot Lo Shivʿim ve-Ḥamesh,* ed. M. Goshen-Gottstein, S. Morag, and S. Kogut, 147-57. Jerusalem: Akademon, 1990.
———. "Qitʿe Ketavim Ketuvim ʿIvrit mi-Meṣadah." *ErIsr* 20 (Yadin Volume, 1989) 278-86.
———. "The Sectarian yḥd — a Biblical Noun." *VT* 3 (1953) 133-40.
———. "Types of Messianic Expectation at the Turn of the Era." In *King, Cult and Calendar in Ancient Israel,* 202-24. Jerusalem: Magnes, 1986.
———. "Was the Book of Esther Known at Qumran?" *DSD* 2 (1995) 249-67.
———. *The World of Qumran from Within.* Jerusalem: Magnes and Leiden: Brill, 1989.
———, J. Ben-Dov, and U. Glessmer. *Qumran Cave 4.XVI: Calendrical Texts.* DJD 21. Oxford: Clarendon, 2001.
———, with C. Newsom and Y. Yadin. *Masada VI: The Yigael Yadin Excavations 1963-1965: Final Reports.* Jerusalem: Israel Exploration Society and Hebrew University of Jerusalem, 1999.
Tcherikover, V. *Hellenistic Civilization and the Jews.* Trans. S. Applebaum. Philadelphia: Jewish Publication Society of America, 1966.
Theodor, J., and C. Albeck, eds. *Genesis Rabbah.* Jerusalem: Wahrmann, 1965.
Thiede, C. P. *The Earliest Gospel Manuscripts? The Qumran Papyrus 7Q5 and Its Significance for New Testament Studies.* Exeter: Paternoster, 1992.
Thiering, B. *Jesus & the Riddle of the Dead Sea Scrolls.* San Francisco: HarperCollins, 1992.
Tigay, J. H. *Deuteronomy.* Jewish Publication Society Torah Commentary. Philadelphia: Jewish Publication Society, 1996.
Tigchelaar, E. J. C. *To Increase Learning for the Understanding Ones: Reading and Reconstructing the Fragmentary Early Jewish Sapiential Text 4QInstruction.* STDJ 44. Leiden: Brill, 2001.
Tov, E. "ʿAl Maṣav ha-Meḥqar bi-Megillot Qumran le-ʾor ha-Meḥqar he-Ḥadash." *Madaʿe ha-Yahadut* 34 (1994) 37-67.
———. "Excerpted and Abbreviated Biblical Texts from Qumran." *RevQ* 16 (1995) 581-600.
———. "Deut. 12 and 11QTemple LII-LIII: A Contrastive Analysis." *RevQ* 15 (1991) 169-73.
———. *The Greek Minor Prophets Scroll from Naḥal Ḥever (8ḤevXIIgr) (The Seiyâl Collection I).* DJD 8. Oxford: Clarendon, 1990.
———. "Groups of Biblical Texts Found at Qumran." In *Time to Prepare the Way in the Wilderness: Papers on the Qumran Scrolls by Fellows of the Institute for Advanced Studies of the Hebrew University, Jerusalem, 1989-1990,* ed. D. Dimant and L. H. Schiffman, 85-102. STDJ 16. Leiden: Brill, 1995.
———. "Hebrew Biblical Manuscripts from the Judaean Desert: Their Contribution to Textual Criticism." *JJS* (1988) 5-37.
———. "Megillot Qumran le-ʾor ha-Meḥqar he-Ḥadash." *JS* 34 (1994) 37-67.

———. "A Modern Textual Outlook Based on the Qumran Scrolls." *HUCA* 53 (1982) 11-27.
———. "The Nature and Background of Harmonizations in Biblical Manuscripts." *JSOT* 31 (1985) 3-29.
———. "The Orthography and Language of the Hebrew Scrolls Found at Qumran and the Origin of These Scrolls." *Textus* 13 (1986) 32-57.
———. "Scribal Practices and Physical Aspects of the Dead Sea Scrolls." In *The Bible as Book — The Manuscript Tradition,* ed. J. L. Sharpe and K. Van Kampen, 9-33. London: British Museum and New Castle, DE: Oak Knoll, 1998.
———. "Scribal Practices Reflected in the Documents from the Judean Desert and in the Rabbinic Literature: A Comparative Study." In *Texts, Temples, and Traditions: A Tribute to Menahem Haran,* ed. M. V. Fox et al., 383-403. Winona Lake: Eisenbrauns, 1996.
———. "*Tefillin* of Different Origin from Qumran?" In *A Light for Jacob: Studies in the Bible and the Dead Sea Scrolls in Memory of Jacob Shalom Licht,* ed. Y. Hoffman and F. H. Polak, 44*-54*. Jerusalem: Bialik Institute and Tel Aviv: Chaim Rosenberg School of Jewish Studies, Tel Aviv University, 1997.
———. *Textual Criticism of the Hebrew Bible.* Minneapolis: Fortress, 1992.
———, ed. *The Texts from the Judaean Desert: Indices and an Introduction to the Discoveries in the Judaean Desert Series.* DJD 39. Oxford: Clarendon, 2002.
———, with S. J. Pfann. *The Dead Sea Scrolls on Microfiche: Companion Volume.* Leiden: Brill, 1993.
"Traders of the Lost Scrolls." BBC/CTVC. J. Drury, Executive Producer; G. Judd, Producer. Aired in Great Britain 2 November 1997; in the U.S. 9 November 1997.
Trebolle Barrera, J. C. "Origins of a Tripartite Old Testament Canon." In *The Canon Debate,* ed. L. M. McDonald and J. A. Sanders, 128-45. Peabody: Hendrickson, 2002.
Trever, J. C. *The Dead Sea Scrolls: A Personal Account.* Rev. ed. Grand Rapids: Wm. B. Eerdmans, 1977.
Twersky, I. *Introduction to the Code of Maimonides (Mishneh Torah).* Yale Judaica Series 22. New Haven: Yale University Press, 1980.
———. "The *Shulḥan Aruk:* Enduring Code of Jewish Law." In *The Jewish Expression,* ed. J. Goldin, 322-43. New York: Bantam, 1970.
Ulrich, E. "The Non-attestation of a Tripartite Canon in 4QMMT." *CBQ* 65 (2003) 202-14.
———. "The Notion and Definition of Canon." In *The Canon Debate,* ed. L. M. McDonald and J. A. Sanders, 21-35. Peabody: Hendrickson, 2002.
———, et al. *Qumran Cave 4.XI: Psalms to Chronicles.* DJD 16. Oxford: Clarendon, 2000.
Urbach, E. E. "Ha-Derashah ke-Yesod ha-Halakhah u-Veʻayat ha-Soferim." *Tarbiz* 27 (1957/58) 166-82.
———. *The Sages: Their Concepts and Beliefs.* Trans. I. Abrahams. Jerusalem: Magnes, Hebrew University, 1987.
VanderKam, J. C. *Calendars in the Dead Sea Scrolls: Measuring Time.* London: Routledge, 1998.
———. *The Dead Sea Scrolls Today.* Grand Rapids: Wm. B. Eerdmans, 1994.
———. "The Poetry of 1QApGen XX, 2-8a." *RevQ* 10 (1979) 57-66.
———. "The Putative Author of the Book of Jubilees." *JSS* 26 (1981) 209-17.
———, and P. Flint. *The Meaning of the Dead Sea Scrolls: Their Significance for Under-

standing the Bible, Judaism, Jesus, and Christianity. San Francisco: HarperSanFrancisco, 2002.

Vaux, R. de. *Archaeology and the Dead Sea Scrolls.* Schweich Lectures 1959. London: Oxford University Press, 1973.

———. *Die Ausgrabungen von Qumran und En Feschcha. Deutsche Übersetzung und Informationsaufbereitung durch F. Rohrhirsch und B. Hofmeir.* NTOA.SA 1A. Freiburg: Universitätsverlag and Göttingen: Vandenhoeck & Ruprecht, 1996.

———. "Fouille au Khirbet Qumran: Rapport préliminaire." *RB* 60 (1953) 83-106.

———. "Fouilles de Khirbet Qumran: Rapport préliminaire sur la deuxième campagne." *RB* 61 (1954) 206-36.

———. "Fouilles de Khirbet Qumran: Rapport préliminaire sur les 3a, 4e, et 5e campagnes." *RB* 63 (1956) 533-77.

———. *Fouilles de Khirbet Qumrân et de Ain Feshka: Album de photographies, répertoire du fonds photographique, synthèse des notes de chantier du Père Roland de Vaux.* Presented by J.-B. Humbert et A. Chambon. NTOA.SA 1. Fribourg: Éditions universitaires and Göttingen: Vandenhoeck & Ruprecht, 1994.

Vermes, G. *The Complete Dead Sea Scrolls in English.* 1997. Rev. ed. London: Penguin, 2004.

———. "The Oxford Forum for Qumran Research: Seminar on the Rule of War from Cave 4 (4Q285)." *JJS* 43 (1992) 85-90.

———. "The 'Pierced Messiah' Text — An Interpretation Evaporates." *BAR* 18/6 (1992) 80-82.

———. "Pre-Mishnaic Jewish Worship and the Phylacteries from the Dead Sea." *VT* 9 (1959) 65-72.

Wacholder, B. Z. "The Ancient Judeo-Aramaic Literature (500-165 BCE): A Classification of Pre-Qumranic Texts." In *Archaeology and History in the Dead Sea Scrolls: The New York University Conference in Memory of Yigael Yadin,* ed. L. H. Schiffman, 257-81. JSPSup 8. JSOT/ASOR Monographs 2. Sheffield: Sheffield Academic, 1990.

———. *The Dawn of Qumran: The Sectarian Torah and the Teacher of Righteousness.* Cincinnati: Hebrew Union College Press, 1983.

———. "A Qumran Attack on Oral Exegesis? The Phrase אשר בתלמוד שקרם in 4Q Pesher Nahum." *RevQ* 5 (1966) 351-69.

———, and M. G. Abegg, eds. *A Preliminary Edition of the Unpublished Dead Sea Scrolls: The Hebrew and Aramaic Texts from Cave Four.* 4 fasc. Washington: Biblical Archaeology Society, 1991-96.

Weinfeld, M. "Grace after Meals in Qumran." *JBL* 111 (1992) 427-40.

———. "'Iqvot shel Qedushat Yoṣer u-Fesuqe de Zimra' be-Megillot Qumran u-ve-Sefer Ben Sira'." *Tarbiz* 45 (1975/76) 15-26.

———. *Ha-Liturgiyah ha-Yehudit ha-Qedumah: Me-ha-Sifrut ha-Mizmorit ve-'ad li-Tefillot ba-Megillot Qumran u-ve-Sifrut Ḥazal.* Jerusalem: Hebrew University and Magnes, 2004.

———. "'Megillat Miqdash' 'o 'Torah la-Melekh,'" *Shnaton* 3 (1978/79) 214-37.

———. *The Organizational Pattern and the Penal Code of the Qumran Sect.* NTOA 2. Fribourg: Éditions Universitaires and Göttingen: Vandenhoeck & Ruprecht, 1986.

———. "The Temple Scroll or 'The Law of the King.'" In *Normative and Sectarian Judaism in the Second Temple Period,* 158-85. London: T. & T. Clark, 2005.

Bibliography

Weiss, I. H., ed. *Sifra*. Vienna: Schlossberg, 1861/62. Repr. New York: Om, 1946.
Weiss Halivni, D. *Midrash, Mishnah, and Gemara: The Jewish Predilection for Justified Law*. Cambridge, MA: Harvard University Press, 1986.
Weitzman, S. "Why Did the Qumran Community Write in Hebrew?" *JAOS* 119 (1999) 35-45.
Werman, C. "Qumran and the Book of Noah." In *Pseudepigraphic Perspectives: The Apocrypha and Pseudepigrapha in Light of the Dead Sea Scrolls: Proceedings of the International Symposium of the Orion Center for the Study of the Dead Sea Scrolls and Associated Literature, 12-14 January, 1997*, ed. E. G. Chazon, M. Stone, and A. Pinnick, 171-81. STDJ 31. Leiden: Brill, 1999.
White, S. A. See, Crawford, S. White.
Wieder, N. *The Judean Scrolls and Karaism*. London: East and West Library, 1962.
Wilson, A. M., and L. Wills, "Literary Sources of the Temple Scroll." *HTR* 75 (1982) 275-88.
Wilson, E. *Israel and the Dead Sea Scrolls*. New York: Farrar, Straus, and Giroux, 1978.
―――. "A Reporter at Large." *New Yorker* 31/13 (14 May 1955) 45-121.
―――. *The Scrolls from the Dead Sea*. New York: Oxford University Press, 1955.
Wise, M. O. "The Covenant of Temple Scroll XXIX, 3-10." *RevQ* 14 (1989) 49-60.
―――. *A Critical Study of the Temple Scroll from Qumran Cave 11*. SAOC 49. Chicago: Oriental Institute, University of Chicago, 1990.
―――. "The Eschatological Vision of the *Temple Scroll*." *JNES* 49 (1990) 155-72.
―――. "4QFlorilegium and the Temple of Man." *RevQ* 15 (1991) 103-32.
―――. *Thunder in Gemini and Other Essays on the History, Language and Literature of Second Temple Palestine*. JSPSup 15. Sheffield: JSOT, 1994.
―――, M. Abegg, and E. Cook. *The Dead Sea Scrolls: A New Translation*. San Francisco: HarperSanFrancisco, 1996.
―――, et al., eds. *Methods of Investigation of the Dead Sea Scrolls and the Khirbet Qumran Site: Present Realities and Future Prospects*. Annals of the New York Academy of Sciences 722. New York: New York Academy of Sciences, 1994.
Wolfson, E. R. "Mysticism and the Poetic-Liturgical Compositions from Qumran." *JQR* 85 (1994) 185-202.
Woude, A. S. van der. "Fragmente einer Rolle der Lieder für das Sabbatoffer aus Hohle XI von Qumran (11Q SirSabb)." In *Vom Kanaan bis Kerala: Festschrift für J. P. M. van der Ploeg*, ed. W. C. Delsam et al., 311-35. Kevelaer: Butzon and Bercker and Neukirchen-Vluyn: Neukirchener, 1982.
Wright, G. R. H. "Archaeological Remains at el Mird in the Wilderness of Judea, with an appendix by J. T. Milik." *Bib* 42 (1961) 1-27.
Würthwein, E. *The Text of the Old Testament*. Trans. E. F. Rhodes. 2nd ed. Grand Rapids: Wm. B. Eerdmans, 1995.
Yadin, Y. *Bar Kokhba: The Rediscovery of the Legendary Hero of the Second Jewish Revolt against Rome*. New York: Random House, 1971.
―――. *The Ben Sira Scroll from Masada*. Jerusalem: Israel Exploration Society and Shrine of the Book, 1965. Repr. in *Masada VI, Yigael Yadin Excavations 1963-1965, Final Reports*, ed. S. Talmon, with C. Newsom and Y. Yadin, 135-40. Jerusalem: Israel Exploration Society, Hebrew University, 1999.
―――. "The Gate of the Essenes and the Temple Scroll." In *Jerusalem Revealed: Archaeol-

ogy in the Holy City 1968-1974, ed. Yadin, 90-91. Jerusalem: Israel Exploration Society, 1975.

———. "Is the Temple Scroll a Sectarian Document?" In *Humanizing America's Iconic Book,* ed. G. M. Tucker and G. A. Knight, 153-69. SBLBSNA. Chico: Scholars, 1980.

———. *Masada: Herod's Fortress and the Zealots' Last Stand.* New York: Random House, 1966.

———. *Megillat ha-Miqdash.* 3 vols. Jerusalem: Israel Exploration Society and Shrine of the Book, 1977.

———. *Megillat Milḥemet Bene 'Or bi-Vene Ḥoshekh mi-Megillot Midbar Yehudah.* Jerusalem: Bialik Institute, 1955.

———. *The Message of the Scrolls.* New York: Simon & Schuster, 1957.

———. "Pesher Nahum (4Q pNahum) Reconsidered." *IEJ* 21 (1971) 1-12.

———. *The Scroll of the War of the Sons of Light against the Sons of Darkness.* Trans. B. and C. Rabin. Oxford: Oxford University Press, 1962.

———. *Tefillin from Qumran (X Q Phyl 1-4).* Jerusalem: Israel Exploration Society and Shrine of the Book, 1969.

———. "The Temple Scroll." *BA* 30 (1967) 135-39.

———. "The Temple Scroll." In *New Directions in Biblical Archaeology,* ed. D. N. Freedman and J. C. Greenfield, 156-66. Garden City: Doubleday, 1971.

———. *The Temple Scroll.* 3 vols. Jerusalem: Israel Exploration Society and Shrine of the Book, 1983.

———. *The Temple Scroll: The Hidden Law of the Dead Sea Sect.* New York: Random House, 1985.

———, et al. *The Documents from the Bar Kokhba Period in the Cave of Letters: Hebrew, Aramaic, and Nabatean-Aramaic Papyri.* 2 vols. Jerusalem: Israel Exploration Society, Institute of Archaeology, Hebrew University, Shrine of the Book, Israel Museum, 2002.

Yardeni, A. *Textbook of Aramaic, Hebrew and Nabataean Documentary Texts from the Judaean Desert and Related Material.* 2 vols. Jerusalem: Hebrew University, Ben-Zion Dinur Center for Research in Jewish History, 2000.

Yaron, R. *Introduction to the Law of the Aramaic Papyri.* Oxford: Clarendon, 1961.

Yasif, E. *Sippure Ben Sira bi-Yeme ha-Benayim.* Jerusalem: Magnes, Hebrew University, 1984.

Zeitlin, S. "History, Historians and the Dead Sea Scrolls." *JQR* N.S. 55 (1964/65) 97-116.

Index of Modern Authors

Abegg, M., 16n., 19, 23, 36n., 131-32n., 419
Albeck, C., 66n., 90n., 181n., 189n., 242n., 342n., 390n.
Albright, W. F., 38
Alexander, P. S., 36n., 40n., 153n., 168n., 169n., 248n., 251n., 257n., 258n., 284n., 292n., 356n., 403n.
Allegro, J. M., 19-20, 25, 118n., 119n., 152n., 279n., 304n., 306n., 314n., 339n., 340n., 348n., 414, 415, 417, 422, 423
Alt, A., 170n.
Altmann, A., 224n.
Amit, D., 55n.
Amoussine, J. D., 323n., 337n.
Applebaum, S., 54n., 81n., 185n.
Avigad, N., 19

Babad, J., 211
Baer, Y., 224n., 228n., 230n.
Baigent, M., 411n., 417n.
Baillet, M., 2n., 17n., 21, 53n., 54n., 56n., 60n., 61n., 144n., 153n., 188n., 221n., 223n., 225-32, 242n., 244n., 260n., 292n., 293n., 299n., 307n., 308n., 324n., 378n., 397
Barker, M., 265n.
Barr, J., 56n.

Barthélemy, D., 60n., 221n., 230n., 243n., 300n., 369n., 370n., 378n., 407n.
Baumgarten, A. I., 4n., 325n., 353n.
Baumgarten, J. M., 2n., 3n., 4n., 16n., 40, 60n., 62n., 69n., 74, 75n., 86, 87n., 89n., 104n., 105n., 114n., 127n., 129n., 132n., 133n., 143n., 144n., 145n., 146n., 163n., 164n., 167n., 168n., 178n., 180n., 201n., 206n., 211, 212n., 213n., 220n., 224n., 231n., 239n., 257n., 273n., 288n., 310n., 324n., 328n., 331n., 332n., 334n., 343n., 351n., 356n., 358n., 366n., 367n., 369n., 370n., 375n., 402n., 403, 404n., 405n.
Beal, T. S., 174n.
Beinart, H., 248n.
Belkin, S., 66
Ben-Dov, J., 41n., 126n., 189n.
Benoit, P., 22, 50n.
Ben Yehuda, E., 345n.
Ben-Yehuda, N., 48n.
Bergmeier, R., 174n.
Berkovitz, E., 256n.
Bernstein, M. J., 40n., 43n., 52n., 59n., 135n., 200n., 343n.
Berrin, S. L., 34n., 77n., 280n., 305n., 323n., 337n., 340n., 341n., 343n., 344n., 347n., 348n., 349n., 362n.

457

INDEX OF MODERN AUTHORS

Betz, O., 411n., 416n.
Bickerman, E., 81n.
Bokser, B. M., 221n., 260
Bonani, G., 24n., 45n., 365n.
Bowersock, G. W., 56n.
Brady, M., 43n., 52n.
Bregman, M., 383n.
Brooke, G. J., 37n., 40n., 59n., 92n., 96n., 109n., 135n., 152n., 172n., 241n., 247n., 295n., 315n.
Broshi, M., 20n., 93n., 143n., 191n., 266n., 298n., 312n., 315n., 412n.
Brown, D., 417n.
Brown, R. E., 19, 273n.
Brownlee, W. H., 18n., 197n., 325n.
Bruce, F. F., 106n.
Buchanan, G. W., 106n.
Burgman, H., 121n.
Burrows, M., 18n., 26, 403n., 413

Carmichael, C. M., 25n.
Carmignac, J., 278n., 349n., 350n.
Charles, R. H., 57n., 247n., 386n., 387n., 392n., 406n.
Charlesworth, J., 51n., 57n., 137n., 153n., 156n., 162n., 190n., 362n., 383n., 402n., 422
Chazon, E. G., 59n., 89n., 228n., 307n., 308n.
Christensen, D. L., 384n.
Chyutin, M., 93n., 298n.
Cohen, G. D., 63n.
Cohen, S. J. D., 186n.
Collins, J. J., 42n., 60n., 95n., 108n., 109n., 271n., 287n.
Cook, E. M., 16n., 414n.
Cotton, H. M., 18n., 51n., 55n.
Craft, C. F., 384n.
Crawford, S. A. White 40, 46n., 91n., 144n., 159n., 177n., 264n., 361n., 400n.
Cross, F. M., 26, 38, 43n., 45n., 82n., 102n., 113n., 120n., 220n., 231n., 323n., 341n., 362n., 402n.

Davies, P. R., 22, 61n., 69n., 109n., 146n., 293n., 404n., 411n.

Davies, W. D., 253n.
Davis, M., 5n.
Deasley, A., 235n., 252n.
Deines, R., 322n.
De Vaux, R., 2n., 17n., 21, 22, 26, 45n., 50n., 53n., 87n., 102n., 144n., 153n., 188n., 221n., 223n., 234n., 242n., 324n.
Dimant, D., 22, 29n., 42n., 45n., 46n., 47n., 52n., 59n., 61n., 98n., 243n., 244n., 250n., 287n., 289n., 303n., 304n., 337n., 390n.
Doudna, G. L., 337n.
Drawnel, H., 91n., 187n.
Duhaime, J., 4n., 61n., 261n., 292n., 362n., 385n.
Dupont-Sommer, A., 227, 340n., 345n., 346n., 414-15

Eisenman, R. H., 22, 24, 25, 123n., 411n., 415-16, 419, 420, 422
Elbogen, I., 224n., 226n., 228n.
Elgvin, T., 42n., 60n., 204n., 205, 300n.
Elior, R., 251n., 260n., 262n.
Elledge, C. D., 176n.
Elliott, M. A., 235n., 357n.
Elman, Y., 332n.
Elon, M., 4n.
Eshel, E., 91n., 124n., 169n., 187n., 233n., 292n., 308n., 309n., 333n., 359n.
Eshel, H., 55n., 124n., 292n., 300n., 306n., 308n., 317n., 362n.

Falk, D. K., 60n., 225n., 228n., 230n., 289n.
Feather, R., 422n.
Finkelstein, L., 104n., 193n., 194n., 214n., 246n., 327n., 333n., 342n.
Fitzmyer, J. A., 3n., 19, 41n., 54n., 67n., 146n., 278n., 281n., 283n., 316n., 400n., 403n., 404n., 408n., 409n.
Flint, P., 42n., 222n., 300n., 361n., 398n.
Flusser, D., 323n., 337n., 394n., 415
Forbes, N., 386n.
Frankel, Z., 64, 66

García Martínez, F., 16n., 36n., 52n.,

74n., 93n., 108n., 121n., 123n., 159n.,
188n., 189n., 236n., 250n., 289n., 291n.,
298n., 315n., 316n., 325n., 387n., 389n.,
399n.
Gärtner, B., 88n., 220n., 257n.
Geiger, A., 64, 65, 67, 68, 75
Geiger, J., 18n.
Ginzberg, L., 3n., 17, 27, 67, 69, 87n.,
143n., 147, 207n., 312n., 327n., 329n.,
330n., 334n., 400-401, 402
Glessmer, U., 41n., 189n.
Goitein, S. D., 395n.
Golb, N., 121n., 415
Good, R., 408n.
Goshen-Gottstein, M., 398n.
Greenberg, M., 9n.
Greenfield, J. C., 41n., 51n., 52n., 90n.,
91n., 187n., 247n., 387n., 407n.
Grohmann, A., 57n.
Gropp, D. M., 42n., 52n.
Gulak, A., 58n.

Habermann, A. M., 9n., 223n.
Hallo, W. W., 384n.
Harrington, D. J., 42n., 60n., 204n.,
205n., 209n., 212n., 213n.
Harvey, J. W., 256n.
Hayes, C., 356n.
Heisey, T. M., 28n.
Hempel, C., 145n., 146n., 164n., 169n.,
178n., 180n., 403n., 405n.
Hengel, M., 137n., 162n., 190n.
Herr, M. D., 226n.
Heschel, S., 2n.
Higger, M., 213n.
Hillers, D. R., 235n.
Holm-Nielsen, S., 223n.
Hoover, S. M., 412n.
Horgan, M. P., 59n., 197n., 250n., 305n.,
306n., 307n., 337n., 339n., 340n., 343-
50nn.
Humbert, J.-B., 87n.

Iwry, S., 290n.

James, M. R., 383n., 394n.

Jeremias, G., 106n.
Jull, A. J. T., 24n., 45n., 365n.

Kahle, P. E., 401n., 410n.
Kampen, J., 121n., 204n.
Katz, J., 71
Katzman, A., 23n., 419
Kaufman, S. A., 176n.
Kaufman, Y., 186n.
Khan, G., 55n.
Knibb, M. A., 153n., 154n.
Kobelski, P., 291n.
Kornfeld, W., 256n.
Kosmala, H., 86n., 107n.
Kugler, R. A., 90n., 187n., 247n., 406n.,
408n., 409n.
Kuhn, K. G., 109n.
Kutscher, E. Y., 51n., 53n., 56n.

Lambert, G., 106n.
Lange, A., 60n.
Larson, E., 40n., 166n., 174n., 177n.,
181n., 202n., 210n , 404n.
LaSor, W. S., 108-9n.
Laurin, R. B., 109n.
Lauterbach, J. Z., 170n., 194n.
Lefkovits, J. K., 53n.
Lehmann, M. R., 40n., 75n., 127n., 166n.,
177n., 181n., 202n., 228, 229, 307n.,
404n.
Leigh, R., 411n., 417n.
Levine, B. A., 94n., 99n., 127n., 148n.,
162n., 267n., 296n., 312
Levine, I. H., 6n., 174n.
Lewis, N., 18n., 55n.
Licht, J., 7n., 59n., 70, 87n., 165n., 179n.,
223n., 251n., 259, 276, 315n., 345n.,
350n., 355n., 376n., 378n.
Lichtenstein, A., 237n.
Lichtenstein, H., 182n.
Lieberman, S., 3n., 7n., 69, 103n., 174n.,
228n., 237n., 239n., 248n., 249n., 250n.,
259n., 328n., 344n., 355n., 410n.
Lim, T. H., 25n., 325n., 362n.
Lincoln, H., 417n.
Liver, J., 102n., 109n., 290n.

Lundberg, M. J., 23n., 56n.
Lundbom, J. R., 252n.

MacQueen, H. L., 25n.
Magness, J., 26n., 45n., 87n., 146n., 234n.
Maier, J., 93n., 191n., 264n., 337n., 341n.
Mann, J., 226n.
Marcus, R., 107n.
McCready, W. O., 263n., 266n.
Mendels, D., 137n., 162n., 190n.
Meshel, Z., 48n.
Metso, S., 41n., 153n., 164n., 178n.
Meyer, L. V., 289n.
Meyer, M. A., 5n., 64n.
Milgrom, J., 96n., 162n., 167n., 176n., 191n., 199n., 296n., 309n., 310n., 312, 331n.
Milik, J. T., 2n., 9n., 17n., 19, 20n., 21n., 28, 29n., 41, 50n., 52n., 53n., 56n., 60n., 69, 75n., 104n., 131n., 144n., 145n., 146n., 153n., 188n., 221n., 223n., 230n., 242n., 243n., 273, 274n., 300n., 324n., 369n., 370n., 385n., 386n., 403, 404n., 407n.
Millar, F., 2n., 56n., 72n., 109n., 185n., 323n., 337n., 372n., 396n.
Müller-Kessler, C., 56n.
Muro, E., 36n.
Murphy, R. E., 204n.
Murphy-O'Connor, J., 178n., 404n.
Mussies, G., 51n.

Najman, H., 176n., 199n., 384n., 391n.
Naveh, J., 18n.
Netzer, E., 48n.
Neusner, J., 33n., 72-73, 271, 321n., 328n., 347n., 354n.
Newsom, C. A., 31n., 42n., 49n., 59n., 61n., 62n., 109n., 224n., 236n., 238n., 306n., 361n., 399n.
Nimmer, D., 25n.
Nitzan, B., 59n., 60n., 62n., 89n., 222n., 223n., 225n., 228n., 249n., 251n., 305n., 306n., 325n., 362n.
Noam, V., 182n.
North, R., 145n.

Novak, D., 237n.

Oppenheimer, A., 6n., 8n., 174n.
Otto, R., 256n.
Oxtoby, W., 19

Parry, D. W., 16n., 74n.
Paul, S. M., 384n.
Perrot, C., 56n.
Pfann, S. J., 36n., 56n., 132n.
Phelps, M. B., 23n., 56n.
Pouilly, J., 178n.
Price, R., 416n.
Priest, J., 107n.
Puech, E., 6n., 23, 41, 42n., 61n., 159n., 202n., 299n., 387n., 388n., 407n., 408n.

Qimron, E., 2n., 3n., 22, 24, 25, 31n., 52n., 53n., 54n., 75n., 84n., 86n., 91n., 96n., 101n., 112n., 114n., 115n., 116n., 117n., 118n., 123, 124n., 125, 126n., 127n., 128n., 129n., 130n., 131, 132n., 133n., 134n., 135n., 149n., 150n., 151n., 153n., 191n., 192n., 198n., 201n., 205n., 210n., 211, 212n., 241, 254n., 288n., 289n., 294n., 304n., 309n., 310n., 322n., 324n., 332n., 333n., 334n., 338n., 361n., 399n., 405n.

Rabin, B., 70n., 92n., 260n., 292n., 313n., 362n., 377n.
Rabin, C., 7n., 51n., 52n., 69, 70n., 76n., 89n., 92n., 103n., 145n., 165n., 174n., 178n., 202n., 260n., 272n., 277n., 292n., 313n., 329n., 354n., 355n., 357n., 362n., 369n., 377n., 402n., 403
Rabin, I. A., 240n., 244n., 245n., 246n., 248n., 250n., 259n.
Rabinowitz, L. I., 384n.
Rapp, H. A., 241n., 242n., 247n.
Ravid, L., 384n.
Reed, S., 23, 56n., 57n.
Reeves, J. C., 394n.
Regev, E., 127n.
Reif, S. C., 16n., 57n., 66n., 143n., 393n., 395n., 396n., 400n.

Rendsburg, G., 54n.
Riesner, R., 411n., 416n.
Ringgren, H., 256n.
Ritter, B., 66
Robinson, J. M., 24, 25, 291n., 419
Rodrigues Pereira, A. S., 59n.
Roth, C., 394n.
Rowley, E. M., 414n.
Rowley, H. H., 3n., 406n.
Rubenstein, J. L., 186n.
Rubinstein, A., 147n.

Safire, W., 419n.
Safrai, Z., 210n.
Saldarini, A. J., 4n., 353n.
Sanders, E. P., 8, 60, 222n., 223n., 224n., 235n., 317n.
Sanders, J. A., 300n., 308n., 397
Sanderson, J. E., 54n.
Sarna, N. M., 136n., 361n.
Schechter, S., 2n., 4, 16, 17, 25n., 66, 67, 69, 131n., 143n., 144, 367, 396, 400, 401n., 403, 404
Schiffman, L. H., 3n., 6n., 7n., 9n., 10n., 16n., 26n., 29n., 32n., 34n., 35n., 36n., 39n., 40n., 42n., 45n., 48n., 53n., 54n., 56n., 58n., 59n., 60n., 67n., 68n., 73n., 78n., 81n., 83n., 85n., 86n., 87n., 89n., 90n., 92n., 94n., 95n., 96n., 99n., 101n., 102n., 103n., 104n., 105n., 106n., 108n., 109n., 110n., 111n., 112n., 116n., 117n., 118n., 121n., 124n., 125n., 126n., 127n., 128n., 129n., 130n., 132n., 133n., 134n., 135n., 136n., 137n., 138n., 143n., 144n., 145n., 146n., 147n., 149n., 153n., 156n., 157n., 158n., 159n., 161n., 162n., 163n., 164n., 165n., 166n., 168n., 169n., 171n., 173n., 174n., 175n., 176n., 177n., 178n., 180n., 181n., 185n., 186n., 187n., 189n., 190n., 191n., 192n., 197n., 198n., 199n., 200n., 201n., 202n., 203n., 204n., 206n., 208n., 210n., 220n., 222n., 223n., 224n., 229n., 231n., 239n., 242n., 244n., 247n., 248n., 250n., 251n., 254n., 257n., 258n., 260n., 261n., 262n., 264n., 265n., 266n., 267n., 270n., 271n., 274n., 275n., 287n., 290n., 294n., 295n., 296n., 297n., 300n., 305n., 306n., 309n., 311n., 312n., 326n., 327n., 328n., 330n., 331n., 332n., 333n., 334n., 338n., 341n., 354n., 355n., 356n., 358n., 359n., 360n., 361n., 366n., 367n., 368n., 369n., 370n., 371n., 372n., 373n., 374n., 375n., 379n., 390n., 395n., 401n., 402n., 404n., 405n., 411n., 418n., 421n.
Schniedewind, W. M., 53n.
Scholem, G., 284, 287n.
Schorsch, I., 2n., 64n., 75n.
Schuller, E., 41n., 59n., 223n., 304n., 308n., 314n., 378n.
Schürer, E., 1n., 72n., 109n., 185n., 323n., 337n., 341n., 349n., 372n., 396n., 397n., 399n., 407n., 408n.
Schwartz, D. R., 96n., 101n., 120n., 241n., 295n., 312n., 315n.
Seely, D., 244n.
Segal, L. A., 65n.
Segal, M. Z., 61n., 223n., 309n., 396n., 397n., 398n., 400n.
Shaked, S., 52n.
Shanks, H., 21n., 22-25, 417-19, 422
Shemesh, A., 210n., 213n.
Silberman, L., 109n.
Silberman, N. A., 21n., 68n., 401n., 412, 413n., 414n., 419n.
Silk, M., 412n., 417n.
Skehan, P. W., 54n., 222n., 300n.
Smith, M., 22, 42n., 238n., 417, 418n.
Sokoloff, M., 56n.
Starcky, J., 109n., 228, 264n., 283
Stegemann, H., 30, 41, 99n., 109n., 148n., 161n., 162n., 264n., 268
Steiner, R. C., 107n.
Stern, E., 52n.
Stern, M., 48n.
Stern, S., 356n.
Sternhell, Z., 2on.
Steudel, A., 272n., 291n., 314n., 315n.
Stone, M. E., 41n., 90n., 91n., 187n., 237n., 247n., 387n., 391n., 407n.

INDEX OF MODERN AUTHORS

Strugnell, J., 3n., 22-23, 25, 29, 31n., 40, 42n., 53n., 60n., 75n., 84n., 91n., 101n., 112n., 113n., 114n., 115n., 117n., 118n., 119n., 123, 124n., 125, 126n., 127n., 128n., 129n., 130n., 131, 132n., 133n., 134n., 135n., 138n., 145n., 149n., 150n., 151n., 152n., 179n., 191n., 192n., 204n., 205n., 209n., 210n., 211n., 212n., 213n., 224n., 273n., 289n., 300n., 304n., 306n., 309n., 310n., 314n., 317n., 322n., 332n., 333n., 334n., 338n., 339n., 340n., 346n., 349n., 350n., 361n., 379n., 403n., 405n., 419
Stuckenbruck, L. T., 385n.
Sukenik, E. L., 18n., 26, 41, 68, 71, 144n., 223n., 278n., 401-2, 413
Sussmann, Y., 66n., 75n., 95n., 127n., 128n., 150n., 192n., 200n., 309n., 329n., 338n., 405n.
Swanson, D. D., 176n.
Swartz, M. D., 392n.

Talmon, S., 18n., 19n., 30, 31n., 38n., 41n., 46n., 48n., 54n., 55n., 85n., 102n., 108n., 113-14n., 125n., 126n., 150n., 154n., 173n., 189n., 190n., 201n., 222, 227, 232n., 251n., 252n., 263n., 284n., 293n., 312n., 353n., 361n., 376n., 397n., 399n.
Tanzer, S., 248n.
Tcherikover, V., 54n., 81n., 82n., 185n.
Thiede, C. P., 36n.
Thiering, B. E., 411n.
Tigchelaar, E. J. C., 60n., 159n., 236n., 250n., 289n., 291n., 298n., 315n., 325n., 387n., 389n.
Tov, E., 9n., 16n., 22, 23, 30n., 39n., 40n., 46n., 47n., 50n., 53n., 54n., 56n., 57n., 78n., 81n., 132n., 163n., 359n., 384n., 419
Trever, J. C., 18, 413n.
Twersky, I., 171n.

Uhrig, J., 20
Ulrich, E., 23, 54n., 102, 115n., 136n., 300n., 360n., 361n.

Urbach, E. E., 194n., 327n., 385n.

VanderKam, J. C., 41n., 43n., 49n., 52n., 59n., 150n., 185n., 189n., 190n., 315n., 361n., 402n.
Vermes, G., 2n., 16n., 36n., 40n., 72n., 88n., 109n., 153n., 168n., 185n., 223n., 251n., 257n., 258n., 284n., 292n., 323n., 337n., 356n., 366n., 372n., 376n., 396n., 403n., 416n., 417
Volk, J. C., 235n.

Wacholder, B., 19n., 23, 52n., 77n., 91n., 95n., 131-32n., 294n., 299n., 315n., 325n., 347n., 359n., 390n., 418-19
Weinfeld, M., 6n., 100n., 174n., 175n., 199n., 224, 236n., 244n., 304n.
Weiss Halivni, D., 10n., 171n., 184n.
Weitzman, S., 53n.
Westerholm, S., 355n.
White, S. *See* Crawford, S.
Wieder, N., 8n., 272n., 401n.
Wills, L., 58n., 91n., 99n., 127n., 161n., 175n., 190n., 294n.
Wilson, A. M., 58n., 91n., 99n., 127n., 161n., 175n., 190n., 294n.
Wilson, E., 70, 414, 422-23
Wilson, R. A., 170n.
Wise, M. O., 16n., 58n., 91n., 95n., 96n., 99n., 123n., 127n., 161n., 175n., 190n., 241n., 242n., 255, 294n., 295n., 315n., 416n., 420
Wolfson, E. R., 60n.
Woude, A. S. van der, 121n., 159n., 224n., 250n., 315n.
Wright, G. R. H., 56n.
Würthwein, E., 384n.

Yadin, Y., 3n., 9n., 10n., 18, 19, 21, 22, 28, 29n., 40, 47n., 48, 49n., 50, 51n., 52n., 58n., 61n., 62n., 68n., 69, 70n., 71n., 73, 75, 85n., 92n., 93n., 96n., 99n., 116n., 118, 119, 125n., 127n., 129n., 130n., 131n., 133n., 137n., 148, 150n., 159n., 162, 175n., 176n., 186n., 189n., 190n., 191n., 198n., 199n., 207n., 208n., 214n., 223n.,

224n., 230n., 241, 242, 254, 255, 260n., 261n., 263n., 264n., 266n., 267n., 277n., 292n., 293n., 294n., 296n., 312, 313n., 314n., 326n., 330n., 333n., 334n., 343n., 362n., 371n., 373n., 374n., 377n., 394n., 399n., 403, 404n., 413

Yardeni, A., 18-19n., 51n., 55n., 113n., 124n., 308n.
Yasif, E., 396n.

Zeitlin, S., 25, 401n.
Zias, J., 48n.

Index of Subjects

Aaron, 247-49
Abraham, 237-41, 387
Academy for the Hebrew Language, 392
Achaemenid. *See* Persian Empire (Achaemenid)
Adam, 386, 391
Admonition (MMT), 145-47, 201, 271
Alcimus (Hellenistic high priest), 82
Alexander Balas. *See* Balas, Alexander
Alexander Jannaeus. *See* Jannaeus, Alexander
Alexander the Great, 43, 52
'Am ha-areṣ, 8
American School of Oriental Research, 18, 413
Amida Prayer, 222-23, 233
Amram, 387
Ancient Biblical Manuscripts Center, 23
Angelic Liturgy, 61-62, 224
Angels, 260
Apocalyptic groups, 35
Apocalypticism: Jewish, 42; literature, 60-61
Apocrypha, 29, 57, 65, 383, 393-94, 396
Apostrophe to Zion, 293n., 300, 314, 317
Aramaic, 44, 46, 48, 50-52, 54, 55, 58, 389, 408

Aramaic Levi Document, 41, 65-66, 90, 97, 187-88, 194, 361, 387, 395, 406-10
Architecture of Temple. *See* Temple, Architecture

Babatha, 50
Balas, Alexander, 82
Bar Kokhva: caves, 18, 42, 45, 49, 55, 78; collection, 55-56, 58; revolt, 2, 18, 49, 55, 109; Simeon, 50; texts, 49-51
Bar Kosiba, 50-51, 55
Bar Yohai, Simeon, 392
Battle of the Scrolls, 15-43, 411
BBC, 421-22
Belial, 261, 274, 281, 377
Belkin, Samuel, 66
Bene Ṣadok. *See* Sons of Zadok
Benoit, Pierre, 22
Ben Sira (Ecclesiasticus), 16, 49, 52-53, 55, 60-61, 66, 395, 400, 410
Berit. *See* Covenant
Bethel, 241-42, 247, 254-55
Bible Translation, 39
Biblical Archaeology Review (BAR), 22, 417-19
Biblical Archaeology Society, 23
Biblical Text: Masoretic, 38, 47; Samari-

tan, 38, 39, 47; Septuagint, 38-39, 47, 208
Blessing and Curse Ritual, 274
Book of Giants, 385
Book of Mysteries, 282
Book of Noah, 35, 387, 391
Book of the Heavenly Luminaries, 385
Book of the Words of Truth and Reprimand, 385
Brigham Young University, 421
Brill, Dutch Publishing House, 25
Brown, Raymond, 19
"Builders of the Wall," 86

Cairo Geniza, 2, 3, 16, 40, 49, 57, 66, 86, 104, 131, 143-144, 393-410
Calendar, 85, 91, 94, 97, 124-28, 149, 150, 161, 175, 189, 191, 192, 223-26
California State University, 24
Cambridge University, 395, 400
Canaanite Slave, 368-70
Canonized Books, 360-61, 384, 398
Carbon 14 Dating, 26, 45
Catholic Church, 57
Cave 1 texts, 20, 41, 46, 68, 407
Cave 4 texts, 19, 20, 30, 45, 46, 51, 68, 71, 143, 145, 147, 212, 222, 224, 230, 337, 402-3
Cave 7, 46
Cave 11, 71, 159, 224, 282
Charity, 7
Christianity, 2, 394-95, 406, 411, 414-16, 423, 420-21
Christians, Early, 17, 27, 32, 35-37, 42, 51, 70, 74, 144, 148, 202, 253, 416
City of the Sanctuary, 266, 296, 312, 317
Code of Punishments, 334
Codes, 171-79
Columbia University, 417
Community Council, 257
Compass, Australian Broadcasting Company's Religion Program, 420
Concordance, 19
Copper Scroll, 19, 20, 53, 422
Council of Elders (*Gērousia*), 305
Council of the Community, 155, 157, 180

Courts of the Sect, 104, 105
Covenant, 235-55; at Sinai, 243-47; of Abraham, 237-41; of Jacob, 241-43, 253-55; of Levi and Aaron, 247-49; renewal ceremony, 252-53

Damascus Covenant, 404
Damascus Document. See *Zadokite Fragments*
David Apocryphon, 282
David, King, 273-77, 281-84, 307, 315
David's Compositions, 282
Day of Atonement, 230
Day of Firstfruits. See Shavuot
Day of Remembrance, 125n.
"Dead Sea Scrolls: Voices from the Desert," 421
Dead Sea Sect, 3, 82
Demetrius III Eukairos. See Eukairos, Demetrius
Department of Antiquities. See Israel Antiquities Authority
Deuteronomic Paraphrase, 161, 175, 176, 379
Discoveries in the Judean Desert (DJD), 22, 23, 81, 124, 419
Discovery Channel, 421
Doctrine of the Two Spirits, 155
Dositheanite Sect of the Samaritans, 17, 401
Drori, Amir, 22, 419

Ecclesiasticus. See Ben Sira
École Biblique, 18, 23, 26
Ein Gedi, 50
Elect of God Text, 282
End of Days, 261, 272, 276-77, 279, 282, 286, 289-90, 293, 376, 380
Enoch, 21, 28, 36, 41, 85, 113, 385-87, 391-92, 395; Epistle of, 386
"Ephraim" (code word for Pharisees), 33, 343-44, 338
Eschatological Jerusalem, 313-17
Eschatological Priest, 95
Eschatological Temple, 295
Essene hypothesis, 29, 31, 32

465

INDEX OF SUBJECTS

Essenes, 7, 26, 27, 29, 69, 76, 87, 98, 121, 143, 154, 162, 174, 231, 287, 338n, 355, 359, 402, 414
Eukairos, Demetrius III (Seleucid ruler, 95-88 B.C.E.), 323-24, 339-43, 345-46, 352
Exegesis, 197-203
Ezekiel, 42, 49, 93, 268, 267, 282, 290, 359

Festival Calendar, 127, 189
Festivals: firstfruits, 161; wine, 150; wood offering, 150
Firstborn Animals, Rules of, 204, 213-14
Fourth-year produce, 91, 130, 334
Fragments of a Zadokite Work, 4, 16
Frankel, Zacharias, 64, 66
French Catholic Biblical Archaeological School, 18

Gabriel, Angel, 389
Geiger, Abraham, 64, 65, 67, 68, 75
Genesis Commentary, 40
Gērousia. *See* Council of Elders
Gottesman family, 20
Grain Offerings, 84
Great Revolt (66-73 C.E.), 26, 35, 37, 45, 48, 61, 84, 134n, 220, 416
Greco-Roman Period, 365

Ha'aretz (Israeli Hebrew Daily), 419
Hagop Kevorkian Center for Near Eastern Studies at NYU, 29
Halakhah, 3-10, 63; messianic, 180; pre-Maccabean, 184-96
Halakhic Letter. See MMT
Hasmonean Kingship, 100, 101
Hasmonean Period, 5, 10-11, 26, 31-34, 37-38, 45, 48, 53, 62, 76-77, 82-83, 85, 91, 99, 100-101, 106, 113n, 117, 120, 121n, 137, 139, 145, 149, 151-52, 156, 159, 161-63, 190, 192n, 195, 219, 225, 230, 245, 254, 263, 283, 294, 304, 306, 309-10, 323, 331,333, 335, 337-39, 352, 362, 370, 374, 378
Harvesting (*Leqeṭ*), 168
Ḥavurah, 6, 7n.

Hebrew Language, 389-90
Hebrew University, 413, 319
Hellenistic era, 5, 36-37, 43, 54, 81, 100, 101, 146, 185, 190, 194, 198, 315, 395
Herod the Great, 93, 94
Herodian Period, 26, 45, 48, 53, 83, 113n, 149, 159, 163, 189, 219, 227, 362
"History's Mysteries: The Dead Sea Scrolls," 421
Hodayot (Thanksgiving) Scroll, 41, 59, 220, 244, 278, 283
House of Peleg, 349
Huntington Library, 24, 25, 418
Hymn of Praise, 156
Hymn to the Creator, 224
Hyrcanus, John, 99, 101, 137, 146, 162, 323, 342, 351

Idolatry, 370-72
Impurity of the Dead, 84
Independence, National, 362-62
Institute for Antiquity and Christianity at Claremont, 24
Intermarriage, 186, 190, 193
International Conference on Biblical Archeology, 22
International Team, 19-22, 28, 70, 415, 417, 419
Israel: government of, 20; land of, 263; Supreme Court, 25
Israel Antiquities Authority, 22, 23, 24, 25, 44, 419
Israel Department of Antiquities. *See* Israel Antiquities Authority
Israel Museum, 17, 399

Jacob, 241-43, 253-55, 387, 406, 408
Jannaeus, Alexander (103-76 B.C.E.), 99, 101, 146, 162, 305, 308, 323-24, 341-42, 345-46, 351-52
Jericho, 44, 409
Jerusalem, 81, 82, 93, 131, 133n., 200-201, 266-67, 293, 296, 298-99, 303-18, 377
Jesus, 36-37, 51, 52, 73, 197, 252, 283, 416, 421
John Hyrcanus. *See* Hyrcanus, John

466

Index of Subjects

Jonathan, the Hasmonean, 82, 103, 106, 117n., 137, 162, 351
Jordan, 17, 20, 50, 71
Josephus, 1, 9, 26-27, 33, 39, 48, 52, 65, 75, 83-84, 87, 98, 101, 117n., 119n., 139, 147, 151, 160, 162, 174, 213, 321-23, 326-28, 338, 343, 355
Joshua Apocrypha, 55
Jubilees, 39, 41, 49, 52, 53, 65, 68, 72, 85, 90, 97, 113, 146, 181, 185, 189, 190, 242, 247, 255, 360-61, 387, 395
Judaism: Dead Sea Scroll community, 353-64; Greco-Roman period, 36, 43, 44; late antiquity, 1-3, 72; medieval, 399; Persian period, 43, 44; rabbinic, 1-11, 32, 37, 38; Second Temple, 1-5, 15, 28, 32, 35, 36, 42, 44, 72, 103, 146-47, 158, 160, 169, 184, 202, 232-34, 284, 287, 301, 304, 321, 335, 353, 361, 395; Talmudic period, 1

Kando. *See* Shahin, Khalil Iskander
Karaites, 17, 25, 75, 234
Ketef Jericho, 51
Khirbet Mird, 56
Kittim. *See* Romans
Kohn, Rachel, 420

Lamentation, 227, 304
Law, Jewish. *See* Halakhah
"Law of the King," 99-100, 136, 199, 295, 297, 330, 373-74
Laws (MMT), 145, 147
Leadership, Sectarian, 106-8
Learning Channel, The, 421
Legal Texts, 143-69
Leprosy, 167
Leqet. See Harvesting
Levi, 242, 247-49, 387-88, 406
Levites, 251
Library, the Ancient, 29-31, 416
Linguistics: Judean scrolls, 51-57; Second Temple period, 51, 55, 62
Literary Genres of the Scrolls, 57-62
Literature: Greco-Roman period, 58; late

Second Temple period, 49, 57, 61-62, 383-92, 393-410
Liturgy, Jewish, 219-34; texts, 222-25
Los Angeles Times, 416
Lost Apocrypha, 383
LXX. *See* Biblical Text, Septuagint

Maccabean Revolt, 31, 54, 76, 81, 82, 101, 119, 151, 185, 195
Man of Lies, 325-26
Manasseh (term for Sadducees), 34, 348-50
Manasseh, House of. *See* Manasseh
Manual of Discipline. See Rule of the Community
Marriage Laws, 202, 210-12
Marriage Ritual, 231-32
Married Woman, Oaths. *See* Vows of a Married Woman
Masada, 18, 19, 30, 42, 45, 47-49, 54, 55, 60-62, 190, 397, 399
Maskilim (lay leaders), 107
Masoretic Text. *See* Biblical Text, Masoretic
Media, Role of, 24, 411-23
Megillat ha-Miqdash. See Temple Scroll
Megillat ha-Serakhim. See Rule Scroll
Melchizedek, 281, 291-94
Men of the Great Assembly, 193
Merkavah Mysticism, 62
Messiah, 95, 108-10, 157, 158
Messiah in Context, 271
Messianic: assembly, 110; banquet, 8, 180, 262, 275; council, 275-76; era, 108, 109, 110, 261-63, 273, 291-92, 300; figures, 270-86, 388
Messianic Rule. See Rule of the Congregation
Messianism: Christian, 35, 252, 270; Jewish, 36, 270
Methuselah, 386
Mevaqqer (sectarian overseer or examiner), 7, 103, 107, 108, 169
Mezuzah, 29, 52
Michael, The Angel, 261, 389
Midrash Halakhah, 187

467

INDEX OF SUBJECTS

Minor Prophets, 59
Miqṣat Ma'aśe ha-Torah. See MMT
Miscellaneous Rules, 163-66
Mishmarot (Priestly Courses), 41, 125
Mixed Species, Rules of *(Kil'ayim),* 204, 209-13
Mysteries Text, 42, 60
Mythical Books, 383-92

Naḥal Ḥever Texts, 18, 50
Naḥal Ḥever/Seiyal, 51
Naḥal Mishmar, 51
Naḥal Sdeir, 51
Naḥal Ṣe'elim Texts, 50, 51
Nash Papyrus, 9
Neo-Babylonian Empire, 52
New Jerusalem, 93, 187-89, 282, 298-99, 303, 315
New Testament, 2, 9, 27, 33, 35-36, 51, 54, 60, 70, 72, 197, 321, 361
New York Times, 413
New York University, 418
Nigleh (revealed law), 7, 173, 202-3, 272, 326, 358-59
Nistar (hidden law), 7, 106, 173, 178, 202-3, 272, 326, 358
Non-Jews, relations with, 365ff.
Nova, TV documentary, 23
Nuzi Documents, 70
NYU Conference on the Dead Sea Scrolls, 22

Oil Festival, 150
Omer: count, 95; festival, 161
Operation Scroll, 44

Paleography, 26, 45
Palestine, British Mandatory, 71, 413
Palestine Archaeological Museum. *See* Rockefeller Museum
Paqid, 107, 108
Passover, 96, 181, 188, 378
Payṭanim (Jewish liturgical poets of the Byzantine period), 59
Penal Code, 155, 164, 180
Persian Empire (Achaemenid), 51-52

Pesharim, 278-80
Pesher Literature, 59, 76, 77, 197, 203, 280, 337-52, 367, 375-76
"Pharaoh's Holy Treasures," 422
Pharisaism, 37
Pharisees, 6, 10, 31-34, 72, 75-78, 82-86, 90, 101-3, 119, 121, 128, 139, 145, 150-52, 163, 169, 192, 194, 200-201, 211, 213-15, 221, 223, 321-36, 337-52, 358-59, 368, 375, 380, 390-91
Philo, 7, 26, 65-66, 98, 147, 174, 338n., 355, 393-94
Phylacteries. *See Tefillin*
"Pierced Messiah," 36, 416, 420
Pliny the Elder, 26-27
Poetry, 59-61
Polygamy, 330
Prayer, 89, 97; daily, 225-27; festival, 230-31, 282; Sabbath, 228-29
Prayer of Nabonidus, 42
Priestly Gifts, 149
Priests, 88, 99-104, 110, 134, 184, 186, 188, 249, 322
Prince of Light. *See* Michael, the Angel
Prince of the Congregation, 107, 110, 378
Proselytes, 379
Psalms Scroll, 282, 308, 317, 397-98
Pseudepigrapha, 29, 42, 57, 65, 383-92, 393, 406
Pseudo-Daniel, 42
Pseudo-Jubilees, 41, 49
Purification Periods, 85, 96, 167
Purification Ritual, 232-33
Purity Laws, 88-92, 128-29, 132, 133, 146, 149, 150, 152, 168, 175, 180, 191, 192, 258-59, 355-57, 359

Qehat, 387-88
Qumran: halakhah, 5, 7, 143; Hebrew, 53-54
Qumran Studies, 69, 354

Rabbinic Oral Law, concept, 6
Rebukes by the Overseer, 169
Red Heifer, 129, 168
Remnant, 288-91

Index of Subjects

Restoration, 286-318; eschatological, 291-92
"Resurrecting the Dead Sea Scrolls," 420
Revelation, 190
"Revelations of the Dead Sea Scrolls," 420
Rewritten Pentateuch, 39, 177n.
Rockefeller Family, 20
Rockefeller Museum, 18-20, 22, 71, 417
Roman era, 104
Romans, 305, 339, 362, 375, 377-78
Rule of Benedictions, 107, 153, 156, 178, 248, 273, 276-77, 378
Rule of the Community, 87, 90, 103, 107, 110, 126, 139, 145, 147, 152, 153-56, 158, 163-65, 173, 178-79, 226, 231, 233, 249, 251, 257, 259, 273-76, 283-84, 357, 403, 405-6
Rule of the Congregation, 8, 88, 109-10, 133, 153, 156-59, 178, 180, 260, 262, 273-75, 377
Rule Scroll, 70, 273-74

Sabbath, 165, 166, 180, 181, 186, 242, 360
Sacrifices, 84, 86-97, 112, 130, 134, 149, 187, 188, 192, 220, 226-27, 258; *Shelamim*, 128, 309-10
Sadducees, 10, 17, 31-35, 39, 65, 67, 75-78, 82-86, 91, 95-96, 99-102, 119, 121-22, 127-28, 131-32, 136, 138-39, 150-52, 169, 175, 179, 182, 187, 189, 191-94, 200, 211, 213, 268, 323, 325, 327, 337-52, 370, 374, 390-92
Salome Alexandra (76-67 B.C.E.), 339, 345, 352
Samaria Papyri, 18, 42
Samaritan: schism, 193; society, 52, 67, 401. *See also* Biblical Text, Samaritan
Samuel, Athanasius (Archbishop), 413
Sanctity. *See* Holiness
Sapiential texts, 60
"Secrets of the Dead Sea Scrolls," 23, 418, 420
"Secrets of the Sea," 421
Sectarian: calendar, 41, 124, 128; halakhah, 5; leadership, 106

Sectarianism: Jewish, 4; purity regulations, 7; rules of entry, 6
Seleucids, 345-46, 377
Septuagint, 38-39, 47, 57, 64, 66, 396
Serakhim (Lists of Laws), 58, 178
Serekh Damascus. *See Miscellaneous Rules*
Serekh ha-Berakhot. *See Rule of Benedictions*
Serekh ha-'Edah. *See Rule of the Congregation*
Serekh ha-Yaḥad. *See Rule of the Community*
Shahin, Khalil Iskander, 19, 21
Shavuot, 96, 230
Shelamim. *See* Sacrifices, *Shelamim*
Shema, 222, 233
Shrine of the Book, 17, 20, 69, 159, 399
Shulḥan 'Arukh, 171
Sicarii, 48
Simon, the Maccabee, 106, 117n.
Sinai, covenant at, 243-47
Six Day War (Israel), 20, 71, 143, 417
Slaughter, Nonsacral, 333-34, 359
Solomon (biblical king), 94
Songs of the Sabbath Sacrifice, 49, 59, 61
Sons of Light and the Sons of Darkness, 154, 292, 376
Sons of Zadok, 102, 119n., 120, 151, 157, 250, 261, 404
Sukkot, 186, 341-42
Synagogue, 220-22
Syrian Metropolitan, 71

Tabernacle, 199-201, 307
Tabernacles. *See* Sukkot
Tablets, Heavenly, 384
Taḥanun, 228-29
Tannaim, 11, 151, 201, 208
Teacher of Righteousness, 41, 106-7, 110, 117n., 118-20, 138, 145, 154, 197, 223, 252, 261, 306, 325-26
Tefillin (phylacteries), 9, 29, 52, 78, 223
Temenos (Temple precincts), 201, 260, 265-67, 296, 312-13, 316
Temple: architecture of, 93-95, 160, 191,

469

198-200, 265, 296-97, 311; destruction of, 11, 89, 97, 304, 306; Herod's, 94; in Jerusalem, 81, 82, 85-94, 97, 138-39, 257, 326, 330-31, 333; messianic, 94-97; Solomon's, 94; withdrawal from, 81-97
Temple City, 133n., 160, 256-57, 296, 312; inner court, 264; middle court, 264-65; outer court, 264-65
Temple Scroll, 3, 10, 20-22, 28, 34, 35, 39-40, 53, 58, 71-76, 85, 91-101, 105, 110, 112, 117, 118, 121, 125, 127-33, 135, 139, 147, 150, 152, 159-63, 173, 175, 176, 177, 186, 189, 190-92, 198-200, 208-9, 214, 230, 241-42, 253, 263, 265-68, 294-98, 310, 313, 316, 326, 330-31, 333, 338, 358-59, 369-72, 374, 379
Testament of Levi, 146, 361
Testament of Naphtali, 41, 66
Testament of Qahat, 41, 387
Ṭevul Yom, 128, 129, 131, 134, 191, 332, 360
Thanksgiving Hymns. See Hodayot
Tithes, 130, 186
Torah Study, 90, 92, 97
"Traders of the Lost Scrolls," 420
"Traditions of the Elders," 6
Treatise of the Two Spirits, 179
Twelve Prophets, 50

Uhrig, Joseph, 20

Visions of Amram, 42
Vows of a Married Woman, 204-9

Wadi Daliyeh, 18, 42, 52, 55, 78

Wadi Murabbaʿat, 50, 69, 71
Wadi Qumran, 17
Wall Street Journal, 413
War of Independence (Israel), 71, 413-14
Watchers, 385
Wicked Priest, 106, 118, 261, 325
Wilford, John Noble, 418
Wine Festival. *See* Festivals, wine
Wisdom Canticles, 282
Wisdom Literature, 60, 204, 396
Wissenschaft des Judentums, 2, 64-65, 75, 393
Witnesses, 105, 146
Wood Offering, 161
Words of Michael, 388

Yadin, Yigael, 18, 19, 21-22, 28, 40-41, 47n., 48-50, 69, 70-73, 75, 119, 133n., 147, 159, 162, 242, 254, 311, 403, 413
Yavnean Period, 11
Yossipon, 394

Zadokite: *Document*, 58; *Fragments*, 2, 3, 7, 22, 25, 27, 40, 66-67, 69, 76-77, 85-87, 89, 91, 92, 95, 97, 104, 110, 114, 118, 129, 131-35, 138-39, 143, 144, 177, 182, 187, 191, 201-2, 206-7, 209-10, 212-13, 221, 236-37, 252, 255-56, 266, 271-74, 288-91, 294, 327, 330, 332, 334, 357, 359-60, 366-68, 369, 375, 379, 395, 400-407, 410; priests, 82, 83, 92, 98, 103, 104, 107, 119, 120, 131, 151, 155, 157, 176, 289-90, 362
Zohar, 391-92

Index of Ancient Sources

HEBREW BIBLE

Genesis
2:24	205
6:9	237
8:8-17	236, 237
9:6	369
13:14-17	238
14:18	291
17:10-15	238
17:23-27	231n., 238
28:10-22	241, 242
49:10	247

Exodus
12:3-4	164
12:8	193
13:2	214n.
15:17	96
23:2	103
34:6-7	246
34:10-16	372
34:10-17	371
34:15-16	186

Leviticus
1:11	309
2:13	245n., 248n.
12:1-6	166
12:3	231n.
14:33-57	199
15:4-15	168
15:25-30	132
17:3-4	309
18:13	324
19:9-10	168
19:16	374
19:19	210, 212
19:23-25	334
19:24	91
21:14	373n.
21:16-24	88
22:7	360
22:17-25	88
22:27	166
22:28	129-30, 334
23:9-22	95
23:22	168
23:37-39	254
23:39-42	186
23:40	186, 341n.
25:13	281
25:14-17	166
26:1	371
26:14-46	245
26:15	137
26:31-32	137
26:42	241, 255
27:29	369

Numbers
3:13	214n.
3:14-39	264
18:19	248
21:18	290
24:17	272
24:17-19	277
29:35-38	254
29:39	241
29:39–30:1	254
30:3-16	205
30:7-9	205, 206
30:7-15	208
30:16	208
35:4-5	266

Deuteronomy
5:2-3	253
5:11	360
7:3	186
7:6	377
9:12, 16	116n.
11:28	116n.
11:29	251
12:2-7	371
12:20-21	310
12:20-25	359

12:21	333	**Isaiah**		2:12	340
13:2-6	371	1:27	290n.	2:13	343
13:7-12	371	5:24	305	3:1	344
13:13-19	371	7:14	158	3:4	346
14:2	377	9:5	158, 278	3:5	347
15:2	281	10:24	279	3:7	348
15:3	369	10:28-32	279	3:8	348
15:19	214	11:1	278	3:9	349
16:7	193	11:1-5	279	3:10	350
16:13-17	186	11:2-5	276	3:11	350
16:21-22	371	30:10	325n., 341		
17:14-15	373	35:10	314	**Psalms**	
17:14-20	100	51:11	314	1:1	281
18:9-14	373	54:1-2	163	12:3-4	341
19:14	205	54:11-12	164	37:21-22	289
20:15-18	374	58:13	187, 360	73:18	341
21:22-23	343, 374	59:20	290n.	110:4	291
22:6-7	129	60:21	278	127:2-3	280
22:9-11	210, 212			136	309n.
22:10-11	133	**Jeremiah**			
23:2-9	135	2:3	210	**Proverbs**	
23:15	260	2:26	347n.	14:28	115n.
23:22-24	205	17:21-22, 24, 27	187		
26:1-3	214	25:9	137	**Daniel**	
27:17	205	31:31-34	252	6:11	227n.
28:22	345n.	32:32	347n.	8:21	340n.
28:36-37	137	33:25	240	10:20	340n.
28:48	137			11:2	340n.
28:64	137	**Ezekiel**		11:32	341
28:69	244	34:24	277		
29:11	244	37:25	277	**Ezra**	
29:28	245n.	44:6-16	290	9:1-2	186, 372
30:1-2	116-18	48:31-34	264n.	10:3	186
30:1-3	136				
30:1-10	118n.	**Joel**		**Nehemiah**	
31:16-18	137	2:17	228	8:13-18	186
31:29	116-17, 136, 282			10:31	186, 372
		Amos			
Joshua		5:27	145n., 404	**1 Chronicles**	
6:26	306	9:11	305	17:21	377
23:7	186				
23:12-13	186	**Micah**		**2 Chronicles**	
		1:5	306	35:13	193
1 Kings				35:27	389
11:1-2	372	**Nahum**			
		1:3-4	339		
		1:4	340		

Index of Ancient Sources

APOCRYPHA AND PSEUDEPIGRAPHA

1 Maccabees
4:46	274n.
13:24	162
14:41	274n.

Ecclesiasticus (Ben Sira)
6:14-15	397
6:20-31	397
36:18-19	309n.
39:27–43:30	399
47:11	309n.
48:18, 24	309n.
51:12	309n.
51:13-20, 30	223n., 397
52:12-13	308n.
55:12	223

Jubilees
1:27-28	305n.
2:17-33	181
3:9-14	166
6:1-14	236
6:23-29	125n.
6:30	125n.
10:14	387
12:24-26	387
13:25-26	135n.
27:19-27	242
30:17-19	247
31:13-17	247
32:1-3	247
45:16	387
49:17	164
50:6-13	181

Tobit
1:6	135n.
13:17-18	306n.
14:5	305n.

1 Enoch
13:7	385
14:1	385
14:7	385n.
82:1-2	386
92:1	386
104:10	386

2 Enoch
33:9-10	386
47:1-3	387
48:7-9	387

Assumption of Moses
1:15-18	392

SEPTUAGINT

1 Samuel
1:23	208n.

1 Esdras
1:33	389

DEAD SEA SCROLLS

1Q14 (Pesher Micah)
10:4-7	306
11:1	305
17-19:5	280

1Q21 (Aramaic Levi) 407

1Q22 (Words of Moses)
1:6-8	370
1:8	243
3:6	369

1Q27 (Mysteries) 282, 300

1Q28a (Rule of the Congregation)
1:2-3	250
1:5	251
1:6-11	261n.
1:8	231n.
1:19-22	262
1:21	275, 377
1:24-25	275
1:25-27	110
1:28-29	275
2:3	275
2:3-11	88, 133, 260, 262
2:11-12	158, 276
2:11-22	110n., 262n.
2:15	276
2:22-23	158

1Q28b (Rule of Benedictions)
1:1	107n.
3:18	378
3:22-28	107n., 276
3:22-30	248
4:18	276
4:22-28	276
5:20	276
5:20-29	107n.
5:28-29	378

2Q18 (Ben Sira) 397

2Q22 (David Apocryphon) 282

2Q24 (New Jerusalem) 282

4Q159 (Ordinances)
2-4 2	368

1Q32 (New Jerusalem) 282

1Q34^{bis} (Liturgical Prayers)
3 ii 5-7	379
3 ii 6	243

1QapGen (Genesis Apocryphon)
5:29	387
11:15–12:6	236

INDEX OF ANCIENT SOURCES

21:8-14	237	12:15	277	1:16	357
		12:16	304n.	1:16–2:25	251
1QH (Hodayot)		13:7	243	1:16–3:12	154
2:15	340n.	14:4	243	2:5	357
2:32	340n.	14:5	377	2:15	357
10:15, 32	76n.	14:8-10	243	2:19	274
11:5-18	278	17:2-3	248	2:26-27	249
11:35-36	278	17:6	250	2:26–3:12	233n.
14:15	278	17:6-9	293	3:11-12	249
15:19	278	17:7-8	293	3:13	107n.
16:6	278	17:8	239	3:13–4:1	179
		18:7-8	244	3:13–4:26	155, 231n., 261n.
1QM (War Scroll)		19:2-8	377	3:23	274
1:1-7	377	19:5-7	293	4:16-17	274
1:2	250	19:8	277	4:18-20	274
1:3	313	19:10-11	377	4:22	249
1:4-6	377			4:25-26	274
1:5-7	277	**1QpHab (Pesher Habakkuk)**		5:1–7:25	155
1:8	277			5:2-3	103n., 250
1:8-9	293	2:1	324	5:5-6	249
1:10	277	2:2	76n.	5:8-10	250
1:15	277	2:2-10	252	5:9-10	103n.
2:7	377	2:5-10	197n.	5:10-13	250
2:8-9	226n.	2:8	106n.	5:16-17	356n.
2:9-12	377	3:2-13	375	5:18-19	250
3:10-11	313	3:17–4:9	375	5:20	250
3:12	277	5:10-11	325	5:21-22	250
3:12-13	293	5:11	76n.	6:2-5	262, 274
4:12	377	7:1-5	197n.	6:3	159
5:1-2	277, 293	7:7, 12	279	6:3-4	165
6:6	277, 377	9:4	305	6:3-5	158
7:3-4	261n., 314	9:4-6	367	6:6	159
7:6	260	9:6	279	6:6-7	275
9:8-9	377	11:4-9	325	6:13-23	259
10:9-10	377	11:6-8	226n.	6:14-23	164
10:10	243	12:7	306	6:15	250
11:1-3	277	12:10–13:4	375n.	6:19	103n., 250
11:6-7	277			6:24–7:27	164
11:7-8	277	**1QpPs (Pesher Psalms)**		7:1-2	168n.
11:11	377			7:18-19	168n.
11:12-13	377	9:1-2	306	7:22-25	168n.
12:1	377			8:1-2	165
12:3	244	**1QS (Rule of the Community)**		8:1-4	257
12:7-8	260			8:1-16	87n.
12:9-15	377	1:1-15	154	8:1–9:26a	155
12:12-14	300, 304, 363	1:3	361n.	8:5-6	88
12:12-15	293	1:8	249	8:5-9	257

474

8:8-10	88	4Q166 (Pesher Hoseaª)		9:4	282	
8:9	165	1:9-10	280	12-13 i 10-11	314	
8:10	262	2:3	324	12-13 1:2	282	
8:11	257	2:12-13	376	ii 12-13	325	
8:12-13	258					
8:15-16	361n.	4Q169 (Pesher Nahum)		4Q178 (Unclassified Fragments)		
8:15b–9:11	274	3:3	280	2-3	282	
8:16-17	250	3:4 i	305			
8:17	257	3-4 ii 8	325	4Q179 (Lamentation A)	304	
8:20	257	3-4 iii 4-6	324			
8:21–9:2	168n.	3-4 iii 5	325	4Q182 (Catenaᵇ)		
9:3-5	88	3-4 iii 9	325	1-2	282	
9:11-12	274	3-4 iv 3	325			
9:12-26	107n.	4:3	280	4Q213 (Aramaic Leviª)		
9:13	203			1 i 9, 12	387	
9:26–11:22	156	4Q171 (Pesher Psalmsª)	118			
10:9-17	156	1-10 iii 12	250	4Q251 (Halakha A)	166	
10:13-17	226	1:24	325	12 1	181	
		1:26-27	325	17 2-3	202	
4Q160 (Vision of Samuel)		2:6-8	280			
3-4 ii 5-7	379n.	2:18-19	325	4Q252 (Commentary on Genesis A)	40, 247	
		3:10-13	289			
4Q161 (Pesher Isaiahª)		3:15-19	325	4Q256 (Rule of the Communityᵇ)		
2-6 ii 24-29	306n.	4:18-19	325	2	251n.	
5-6	279			11 11-13	259n.	
7 25	377	4Q173 (Pesher Psalmsᵇ)		ix 10-12	356n.	
8-10	279	1:5	280			
				4Q258 (Rule of the Communityᵈ)		
4Q162 (Pesher Isaiahᵇ)		4Q174 (Florilegium)		ii 9-10	356n.	
2:1-2	279	1-2 i 4	372	vi 1-3	257n.	
2:6-8	305	1-2 2:3-5	280-81	vi 5	257	
		1-2 2:10-13	281	vi 6-7	258	
4Q163 (Pesher Isaiahᶜ)		1:11-12	305	vi 9	257	
4-6 i 18-19	325			vi 11	257	
4-7 2:10-24	279	4Q175 (Ordinances)	282			
23 2:10	279	21-30	306	4Q259 (Rule of the Communityᵉ)		
23 ii 10	340n.					
23 ii 10-11	305	4Q176 (Tanhumim)	304			
		1-2 i-ii	293n.			
4Q164 (Pesher Isaiahᵈ)		8-11	293n.	ii 3-4	258	
1:7	164 279	4Q177 (Catenaª) 1-4:10	282	ii 13-17	257	

4Q261 (Rule of the Community[g])	4Q269 (Damascus Document[d])	4Q277 (Tohorot B[b]) 129n., 168
3 1 259n.	4 i 3 324	1 ii 2 332
	8 ii 2-3 369	
4Q265 (Miscellaneous Rules)	8 ii 4-6 332	4Q278 (Tohorot C) 168n.
	9:2-3 133, 212n.	
	10:3-6 134	4Q280 (Curses) 251n.
3.3-6 163		
4 i-ii.2 164	4Q270 (Damascus Document[e])	4Q284 (Purification Liturgy)
4 ii.3-9 164		
5 164	2 ii 13-15 370	Frg. 4:2 239
6-7.5 164	2 ii 15 334	
7.6-10 164	3 iii 20-21 369	4Q284a (Harvesting [Leqet]) 168
7.11-17 164	5:15-16 133	
	5:15-17 212n.	4Q286 (Berakhot[a])
4Q266 (Damascus Document[a])	7 i 1-14 164	7 ii 251n.
	7:20-21 134	
3 ii 1-2 325	9 ii 7-9 134	4Q299 (Mysteries[a]) 300
3 ii 7-8 324	9 ii 14-15 135	
3 iii 1-3 324	10 ii 7-9 132	4Q320 (Calendrical Document/ Mishmarot A 126
5 i 15 290n.		
5 ii 1-3 146n.	4Q271 (Damascus Document[f])	
5 ii 1-14 89n.		4Q364-67 (Reworked Pentateuch) 177n.
7 i-ii 5-15 168n.	1 i 9-11 133	
8 ii 8-9 369n.	1 ii 8-11 134	
9 ii 1-4 132	1 2 325n.	4Q365a (Reworked Pentateuch[c], Temple Scroll?) 159, 177n.
9 ii 4-5 334	3 9-10 212	
10 i 11-ii 15 164	4 ii 10-12 206	
10 i 12 273	9-10 369	
11 5-14 375		4Q370 (Admonition Based on the Flood)
13 4-5 132	4Q273 (Damascus Document[h])	
14 d 1 324n.		1 7-8 236
17 i 6-9 132	2 1 146n.	
		4Q378 (Apocryphon of Joshua[a])
4Q267 (Damascus Document[b])	4Q274 (Tohorot A, 4QPurification Rules A) 167	
		22 i 4 238
2:11 290	1 i 331	
2 4-7 325	1 i 6 310n.	4Q379 (Apocryphon of Joshua[b])
4 9-10 369		
5 iii 89n.	4Q275 (Tohorot B, 4QCommunal Liturgy) 168n.	22 ii 7-14 305
5 iii 3-5 146n.		
9 iv 11 356n.		4Q380 (Non-Canonical Psalms A)
10 i 8 369	4Q276 (Tohorot B[a]) 129n., 168	
11 ii 10-13 107n.		1 i 1-8 308

476

Index of Ancient Sources

4Q381 (Non-Canonical Psalms B)
76-77 15 — 378

4Q385 (Pseudo-Ezekiel[a])
2 1 — 243, 289

4Q385a (Apocryphon of Jeremiah C[a])
18 i a-b 7-11 — 244

4Q385b (Pseudo-Ezekiel[c]) — 304

4Q386 (Pseudo-Ezekiel[b])
1 2:5-10 — 289

4Q387 (Apocryphon of Jeremiah C[b])
3 iii 5-7 — 304
3 6-8 — 250

4Q388 (Pseudo-Ezekiel[d])
7 2-3 — 243
7 6-7 — 289n.

4Q390 (Apocryphon of Jeremiah C[e])
1 8 — 243
2 i 4-10 — 243n.

4Q393 (Communal Confession)
3:7 — 289

4Q394. See also 4QMMT
1-2 i-v (MMT) — 124-25
3-7 i (MMT) — 124-25

4Q415 (Instruction[a])
11 6-7 — 212

4Q416 (Instruction[b])
2 iv 8-10 — 205

4Q418 (Instruction[d])
10 8-10 — 205
103 ii 6-9 — 209
167a+b 6-7 — 212

4Q419 (Instruction-like Composition A)
1 1-3 — 248

4Q421 (Ways of Righteousness[b])
12 1-5 — 215

4Q423 (Instruction[g])
3 4-5 — 213

4Q434a (Barkhi Nafshi)
1+2 6 — 304n.

4Q436 (Barkhi Nafshi[c])
1 i 4 — 244

4Q448 (Apocryphal Psalm and Prayer)
124n.

4Q463 (Narrative D)
1 1 — 238

4Q475 (Renewed Earth) — 300

4Q476 (Liturgical Work B)
1 — 300

4Q477 (Rebukes by the Overseer) — 169

4Q481 (Text Mentioning Mixed Kinds)
1 2 — 210

4Q491 (War Scroll[a])
1, 2+3 l. 10 — 260n.
8-9 3 — 377
11 ii — 377
11 ii 17-18 — 293
11 ii 18 — 244n.
16 4 — 293n.

4Q492 (War Scroll[b])
1 2-8 — 377
1:5-6 — 293

4Q495 (War Scroll[e])
1 — 377

4Q501 (Lamentation)
1 — 378

4Q503 (Daily Prayers[a])
3:10 — 225n.
4:1 — 225n.
4:2 — 225n.
11:2 — 225n.
8:10 — 225n.
8:11, 19 — 225n.
12:15 — 226n.
24-25 vii 4 — 378

4Q504 (Divre ha-Me'orot, Words of the Luminaries)
1-2 recto iv 2-4 — 299, 307
1-2 iv 8-13 — 299, 307
1-2 recto vi 12-14 — 299
1-2 ii 12 — 378
1-2 iii 3 — 378
1-2 iii 12-13 — 361n.
1-2 iv 4-5 — 378
1-2 v 10 — 378
3:13-14 — 282

477

4:6-8	282	4Q536 (Book of Noah)		4QFlorilegium	
5 ii 1-2	378			1:3-4	135
6:6-8	299	1 ii 12-13	388	1 i 2-9	295

4Q505 (Divre ha-Me'orot^b)

4Q541 (Apocryphon of Levi^{b?})

4QHalakha A

124 6	378	1+2	388	17:1	404n.

4Q506 (Divre ha-Me'orot^c)

4Q542 (Testament of Qehat)

4QMess ar. *See* 4Q534

124 1-2	378	1 col. 2	387	

4QMMT *(Miqṣat Ma'aśe ha-Torah)*

4Q508 (Festival Prayers^b)

4Q543 (Visions of Amram^a)

See also 4Q394   31-34

				B 8-9	134
4 2	379		388	B 9-13	128
				B 13-17	129, 151, 168, 331

4Q509 (Festival Prayers^c)

4Q545 (Visions of Amram^c)

				B 18-20	134
I 3 3-4	230n.		388	B 18-23	129
II 7:5	282			B 21-22	332
3:3-5	299	4Q547 (Visions of Amram^e)		B 27-28	309, 333
97-98 7-10	379			B 29-31	131, 309
		9 8	388	B 36	135, 166
				B 36-38	129, 334

4Q511 (Wisdom Canticles)

4Q550 (Proto-Esther^a)

				B 39-49	135
35	282	3:3-5	389	B 57-59	130
				B 59-62	310

4Q514 (Ordinances^c)

4Q550c (Proto-Esther^d)

				B 60-62	131
1 3-8	331	3:3-5	389	B 62-63	132, 166, 334
				B 63-64	134

4Q524 (Temple Scroll)

4Q554 (New Jerusalem^a)

				B 75-82	133, 210
	159	1:1	298	C 7-32	322
15-22 4	202			C 10-11	136
				C 15-16	289

4Q528 (Hymnic or Sapiential Work B)

4QEn^c (Enoch^c)

				C 19	304
		1 vi 2-3	385	C 20-21	289
2	299	1 vi 9	385	C 21-23	344n.
		1 vi 19	385n.	C 23-26	138
				C 30	289

4Q529 (Words of Michael)

4QEn^g (Enoch^g)

4QSam^a (Samuel^a)

1	388	1 ii 22	386	1 Sam 1:23	208n.

4QEnGiants^a (Book of Giants)

4QpNah (Pesher Nahum)

4Q534 (Elect of God, Birth of Noah^a)

				1-2 ii 7-8	339
	282-83	8 1	385	3-4 i 2, 7	76n.
				3-4 i 2-3	340

Index of Ancient Sources

3-4 i 2-8	83n.	22:1-15	300
3-4 i 6-8	343	27:2-11	282
3-4 ii 2	344	28:3-14	282
3-4 ii 4-6	344		
3-4 ii 8	77n.	**11QTemple (11Q19)**	
3-4 ii 8-10	346	2:1-15	372
3-4 iii 1-8	348	2:1–47:18	161
3-4 iii 9-10	348	13:9–29:1	161
3-4 iv 1	349	13:9–30:2	175
3-4 iv 3	350	15:19-21	373
3-4 iv 5-6	350	17:8-9	164
		18–23	166
4QPs^f (Psalms^f)		19:16	295
8 1-16	300	20:11-13	128
9	300	20:13-14	248n.
10	300	21:2	295
		23:7	295
4QSe (Rule of the Community^e)	126	29:09-1	254
		29:1-10	370n.
5Q13 (Sectarian Rule)		29:2-10	160, 263
2 6	242	29:3-4, 7-8	265n.
		29:8-10	95n., 96n.
5Q15 (New Jerusalem)	282	29:9	116n., 294
		29:10	241
6Q15 (Damascus Document)		36:3-7	264
1:1-3	324	38:12-15	264
2:1	324	39:5-7	372
		39:11-13	264
11Q13 (Melchizedek)	281	40:5-11	264
2:2-4	291	41:17–42:6	265
2:5-6	291	42:3-17	186
2:6-7	291	44:3–45:2	265
2:13	291	44:6-10	186
2:15-19	291	45:7-10	167, 331
2:24	250	45:9-10	129
2:24-25	291	45:12-14	132, 265n.
		46:4	265n.
11QJN (New Jerusalem)	282	46:11-12	265n.
		46:13-16	266
11QPs^a (Psalms Scroll)		46:16–47:1	266
21:11–22:1	398n.	47:7-15	129
		47:8	267
		47:10-11	265n.
		47:14	267
		47:17	267
		47:18	265n.
		48:1–51:10	161

48:10–51:10	175		
48:11-13	267		
48:11-14	373		
48:14-15	167		
48:14-17	267		
49:4	267		
49:5–50:16	267		
49:16-17	331		
49:19-20	334		
49:19-29	129		
50:10-14	331		
50:12	199		
51:2-5	129		
51:7-8	265n.		
51:11-18	105		
51:11–56:21	161, 176		
52:5	166		
52:5-7	129, 334		
52:9	311		
52:13-16	333, 359		
52:16	311		
52:18-19	165		
52:19-20	265n.		
53:1	265n.		
53:9-10	265n.		
53:9–54:7	206		
53:16-19	207		
54:2-3	207		
54:8-18	371		
54:19–55:1	371		
55:2-14	371		
55:15–56:04	371		
56:5	265n., 311		
56:12–59:21	161, 297		
56:13-15	373		
56:16	373n.		
57–59	175		
57:5-11	373		
57:6	295		
57:9-11	137		
57:15-16	373		
57:15-17	372		
57:17-19	330		
57:19-21	106		
58:3-10	373		
58:21	137		
59	136		

479

INDEX OF ANCIENT SOURCES

59:2-21	137	4:19–5:11	324	11:14-15	368
59:16-21	118	4:20-21	330	11:16-17	165
60:1–66:17	161	5:1	202	11:21-22	221
60:2-4	130, 214	5:1-6	116n.	12:1-2	312
60:2-5	134	5:5	273	12:2-3	373n.
60:3-4	166, 334	5:6-7	330	12:6-7	367
60:12–66:12	176	5:6-8	86	12:7-8	367
60:13-14	311	5:7-8	327	12:8-9	367
60:16–61:02	373	5:7-11	330	12:9-10	367
62:11-16	374	5:8	202	12:10-11	368
64:6-9	345n., 374	5:9-10	202	12:11	238
64:6-13	343n.	5:11-12	324	12:17-18	334
64:9-13	374	5:12	244	12:20-22	107n.
66:11-17	167	5:13-14	324	12:21	203
66:14	330	5:20	272	13:2-3	165
66:16-17	202	5:20-21	325	13:14-15	356n.
		5:21–6:1	370n.	13:22	107n.
CD (Damascus Document)		6:1	271	14:3-6	379
		6:2	238	14:6-8	107n.
1:1-8	288	6:4-5	290	14:12-16	7n.
1:4-5	238	6:5	404n.	14:15	369
1:9-10	118	6:7-8	95	14:18-22	164
1:10-12	351	6:10	272	14:19	273
1:16-18	238	6:10-11	272	15:15-17	132
1:18	76n.	6:11-12	86	16:3	146
1:20	238	6:11-14	290	16:6-13	205
2:2	249	6:11–7:4	272	16:10-12	206
2:7-12	288	6:14	272	19:10-11	272
2:12	271	6:17-18	86	19:21-25	375
2:16–3:14	120n.	6:19	252, 404n.	19:25, 31	76n.
3:1-4	236, 238	6:21	379	19:33	252
3:10-11	238	7:9-14	324	19:34	404n.
3:12-13	238	7:15	404n.	20:1	273
3:20–4:4	120n.	7:16	305n.	20:1-8	168n.
3:21–4:4	290	7:18-21	272	20:12	252, 404n.
4:2	290	7:19	145, 404n.	20:15	76n., 273
4:4	272	8:1	238	20:20-21	291
4:7-10	238	8:9-12	375	20:22	349
4:7–5:11	201	8:12, 18	76n.	20:32-33	291
4:9-10	272	8:18	324		
4:12-17	201	8:21	252, 404n.	**Temple Scroll[b] (11Q20)**	159
4:12-19	86n.	9:1	369		
4:12–5:14	114n.	9:8	181	4 24	248n.
4:14-18	407	10:14	181, 404		
4:15	146	10:17-21	360	**Temple Scroll[c] (11Q21)**	159
4:17-18	86	11:2	368		
4:19	76n.	11:12	368		

Index of Ancient Sources

HELLENISTIC JEWISH AUTHORS

Philo
Good Person
87   7n.

Special Laws
4.143-50   326n.

Josephus
Antiquities
4.229	213
12.186	202n.
13.72-74	341n.
13.171-73	322n.
13.238-96	83n.
13.288-96	323n.
13.291-92	342
13.297	1n., 182n., 326n.
13.298	349
13.301	117n.
13.372-83	323n.
13.372-416	341n.
13.379-83	346
13.380	343
18.12	1n.
18.17	182n.
18.19	87n., 359n.
18.288-96	101n.

Jewish War
1.85-131	341n.
1.88-89	341n.
1.96-98	346
1.97	343
2.162	327n.
2.409-17	84n.
2.409-21	134n.
6.426	164

NEW TESTAMENT

Mark
7:1-8	326
7:3	1n.

Matthew
12:11	165
15:2	1n.

John
1:34   283

Luke
22:20	252
24:44	361

1 Corinthians
11:25   252

Revelation
21:1–22:5	305
21:12-14	264n.

RABBINIC SOURCES

Mishnah
'Abot
1:1	77n., 327, 328n., 392n.
3:11	240n.

Bava Qamma
1:2-3   238

Berakhot
1:1   128n.

'Eduyyot
8:7   328n.

Gittin
4:6   368

Ḥagigah
2:2   194

Ḥullin
4:5   130n., 334n.

Menaḥot
10:3   189

Nedarim
11:1	206n.
2:2	207n.
3:11	239

Nega'im
14:3   128n.

Parah
3:1	191n.
3:7	129n., 151, 332n.

Pe'ah
2:6   328n.

Pesaḥim
8:1   164

Qiddushin
4:4	189
4:14	390n.

Sanhedrin
4:1   371

Sukkah
3:1-8	186n.
4:9	342

Tamid
5:1   226n.

Yadayim
4	10
4:3	328n.
4:6	332n.
4:7	332n.

Zebaḥim
5:1-5	309n.
5:6-7	309
5:8	135n., 334n.
6:1	128n.

Tosefta
Bava Qamma
10:15   367

Berakhot
3:1	227n.
3:6	228n.
6(7):5	237
6(7):12-13	239

Ḥagigah
2:2   194

Ḥalah
1:6	244
2:7	248

Kelim Bava Qamma
1:12	130n., 200n.

Ma'aśer Sheni
5:16	334n.

Parah
3:7-8	151, 332n.

Qiddushin
5:1	379

Sanhedrin
12:9	239
14:5	371

Shabbat
15(16):8-9	239

Zebaḥim
6:18	135n., 334n.

Palestinian ("Jerusalem") Talmud

Berakhot
1:5 (3c)	226n.
1:5 (3d)	240
4:1 (7b, c-d)	227n.

Gittin
83a	202n.

Ḥagigah
1:8 (76d)	246

Megillah
4:1 (74d)	246

Pe'ah
1:1 (16b)	240
2:6 (17a)	246

Sanhedrin
10:1 (27c)	240n.

Yebamot
13:2 (13c)	202n.

Babylonian Talmud

'Abodah Zarah
25a	384n.

Berakhot
11b-12a	226n.
26a	226n.
26b	227n.
27b	227n.

'Erubin
62a	369

Gittin
56a	134n.
60b	246n.

Ḥullin
5a	134n.

Keritot
7a	240n.

Ketubbot
7b-8a	232n.

Menaḥot
53b	240

Mo'ed Qatan
18a	246

Nedarim
79b	206n.

Pesaḥim
37a	135n.
56a	135n.
64b	135n.

Qiddushin
66a	83n., 101n., 323n., 342

Rosh HaShanah
17b	246

Shabbat
31a	327n.
150a-b	360

Sanhedrin
76b	202n.
99a	240n.
102a	246

Shebu'ot
13a	240n.

Yebamot
62b	202n., 330n.

Yoma
28b	189n.
85b	240n.

Zebaḥim
116b	200n.

Halakhic Midrash

Mekhilta de-Rabbi Ishmael (Exodus)
Bo 5	244
Be-Shallaḥ 3	240
Shirah 9	245n.
Amaleq 2	248
Yitro 5	245n.
Yitro 10	246

Sifra (Leviticus)
Wa-Yiqra 12:6	245n.
Qedoshim 3:8	132n.
Qedoshim 4:15 (89b)	211n.
Emor 4:8	128n.
Beḥukotai 2:3	245
Beḥukotai 2:5	252
Beḥukotai 6:1	245

Sifre Numbers
1	130n., 200n.
4	132n.
40	242n.
111-12	245
117	249
118	135n., 248n.
119	249
124	332n.
153	206n.
155	206n., 208n.

Sifre Zuta
Num 30:6	206n.

Sifrei Deuteronomy
32	246n.
75	333n.

78	135n.	Onqelos	118n., 209n.	**NACHMANIDES**	
94	371	Pseudo-Jonathan	118n.		
124	214			Deut 12:20	333n.
153	104n.				
246-49	135n.	**RASHI**			
351	327n.			**ZOHAR**	
		Deut 22:9	209n.		
Aggadic Midrash		bSukk 28a	328n., 347n.	I:13a	392n.
Genesis Rabbah				I:37b	391n., 392n.
69:7	242n.			I:55b	392n.
		MAIMONIDES		II:70a	391n.
Numbers Rabbah				II:277a	392n.
7:8	200n.	**Hilkhot Bet ha-Beḥirah**		Tiqqune Zohar	
Pereq ʿArayot				70, 136a	392n.
11	213	7:14	200n.		
Targum		**Hilkhot Kelim**			
Neophyti	118n.	5:1	335n.		